D0031204

Footprint story

It was 1921
Ireland had just been partitioned, the British miners were striking for more pay and the federation of British industry had an idea. Exports were booming in South America – how about a handbook for businessmen trading in that far away continent? The Anglo-South American Handbook was born that year, written by W Koebel, the most prolific writer on Latin America of his day.

1924
Two editions later, the book was 'privatized' and in 1924, in the hands of Royal Mail, the steamship company for South America, it became The South American Handbook, subtitled 'South America in a nutshell'. This annual publication became the 'bible' for generations of travellers to South America and remains so to this day. In the early days travel was by sea and the Handbook gave all the details needed for the long voyage from Europe. What to wear for dinner; how to arrange a cricket match with the Cable & Wireless staff on the Cape Verde Islands and a full account of the journey from Liverpool up the Amazon to Manaus: 5898 miles without changing cabin!

1939
As the continent opened up, the South American Handbook reported the new Pan Am flying boat services, and the fortnightly airship service from Rio to Europe on the Graf Zeppelin. For reasons still unclear but with extraordinary determination, the annual editions continued through the Second World War.

1970s
Many more people discovered South America and the backpacking trail started to develop. All the while the Handbook was gathering fans, including literary vagabonds such as Paul Theroux and Graham Greene (who once sent some updates addressed to "The publishers of the best travel guide in the world, Bath, England").

1990s
During the 1990s the company set about developing a new travel guide series using this legendary title as the flagship. By 1997 there were over a dozen guides in the series and the Footprint imprint was launched.

2000s
The series grew quickly and there were soon Footprint travel guides covering more than 150 countries. In 2004, Footprint launched its first thematic guide: *Surfing Europe*, packed with colour photographs, maps and charts. This was followed by further thematic guides such as *Diving the World, Snowboarding the World, Body and Soul escapes, Travel with Kids* and *European City Breaks*.

2010
Today we continue the traditions of the last 89 years that have served legions of travellers so well. We believe that these help to make Footprint guides different. Our policy is to use authors who are genuine experts who write for independent travellers; people possessing a spirit of adventure, looking to get off the beaten track.

East Coast Australia Handbook

Darroch Donald

It's easy to see why they call Australia the 'Lucky Country'. You only have to look at its East Coast. Here, on the edge of the world's largest and driest island, a remarkable biodiversity and range of habitats combines to form one of the most exceptional environments on earth. Where else would you find two completely different and accessible World Heritage parks – Daintree and the Great Barrier Reef – separated only by the tide? And these are just two examples of Australia's embarrassing wealth of natural assets. There are over 580 national parks and nature reserves in New South Wales alone.

Of course, all these natural assets create their own wealth of attraction and beauty, not to mention a vast array of amazing wildlife, from the cuddly koala to the duckbilled platypus, an utterly bizarre creature that looks like it was designed by committee. Then there is the Great Barrier Reef where you can actually find Nemo, come face to face with an 'old wife', or glide clumsily past a mighty big 'bucket mouth'.

But for many travellers 'doing the coast' the urban scene is of equal importance. Here too, you have the size and the diversity so typical of the country as a whole. Sydney, Melbourne and Brisbane are equally absorbing but significantly different. There are the resorts with their pure tourist appeal: Byron Bay, well known for its artistic, alternative community; the high-rises and hyperbole of Surfers Paradise; and the picture-postcard milieu of Noosa and the Whitsunday Islands.

In a way, Australia's East Coast is a microcosm of all that the vast continent of Australia has to offer. It is big and beautiful, weird and wonderful: a wholesale bombardment of the senses. Surely you can't find a more varied and visually appealing stretch of coastline anywhere?

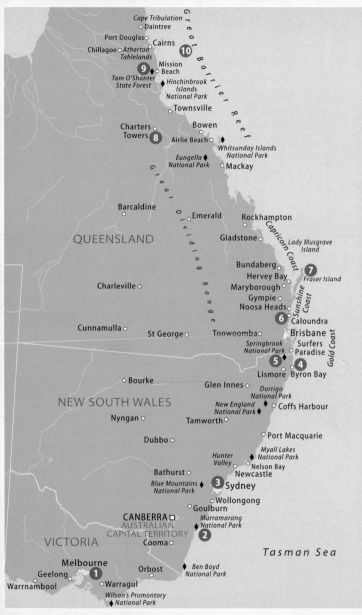

East Coast Australi[a] highlights

See colour maps at end of book

South Pacific Ocean

200 km
200 miles

Perth
CANBERRA

1 So which will be your favourite? Cultured, cosmopolitan and self-assured Melbourne. Or brash, celebrity Sydney. ▶▶ page 46.

2 Protect your picnic from some friendly natives at Pebble Beach in the Murramarang National Park. ▶▶ page 149.

3 When it comes to the man-made and city views, can there be one more iconic than the Sydney Opera House and Harbour Bridge? ▶▶ page 92.

4 Don't miss Byron Bay, the most popular town on the East Coast. Despite the hype, it has an undeniable appeal. ▶▶ page 187.

5 Explore Lamington and Springbrook national parks near the Gold Coast. ▶▶ pages 213 and 214.

6 Make up yo[ur mind] about the comm[emoration of the] late Steve Irwin [at] Australia Zoo. ▶▶

7 Take a dip i[n the] clear waters of L[ake McKenzie] on Fraser Island, [the world's] largest sand islan[d].

8 Get a taste [of the outback] at one of its bett[er known] 'gatekeepers', the [historic] mining town of [Charters Towers.] ▶▶ page 282.

9 Try to spot a[n elusive] cassowary amid [the rainforest] palms of the Tam[borine] State Forest, Mis[sion Beach.] ▶▶ page 285.

10 Visit a tropi[cal island in] the Great Barrie[r Reef like] Dunk Island. ▶▶

Top Sydney Harbour.
Mid-left Murramarang National Park.
Mid-right Lamington and Springbrook
national parks.
Above Melbourne.
Right Byron Bay.

Title page Blue Mountains.
Pages 2-3 Beach huts.

Left Mission Beach.
Below left Charters Towers.
Below right Australia Zoo.
Bottom Fraser Island.
Next page Barrier Reef Islands.

Contents

CENTRAL &
FAR NORTH
QUEENSLAND

BRISBANE &
SOUTH COAST
QUEENSLAND

CENTRAL & NORTH
COAST NEW
SOUTH WALES

SYDNEY & SOUTH COAST
NEW SOUTH WALES

MELBOURNE &
SOUTH EAST
VICTORIA

Contents

Footprint features

Essentials

Planning your trip

Where to go

With a combined landmass of over 2.7 million sq km, Victoria, New South Wales and Queensland form an area 11 times the size of the UK. Although the interior does not possess the same diverse scenery as the UK and is certainly far less populated (14% of the UK's population and 7% of the USA's), it is obvious that if you have no more than one or two weeks for a visit, you can dismiss the idea of trying to see too much of all three states and certainly of attempting to see very much of the outback – unless you intend to fly.

This is why the route from Sydney to Cairns in particular is so popular: a 2685-km journey along some of the world's favourite coastline. The entire journey covered in this guide, from Melbourne to Cairns via the coast (approximately 3725 km), stopping only to sleep, takes six days by car (Sydney to Cairns, four). To give US residents some idea of scale, the distance between Seattle and San Diego (essentially the entire western seaboard of the USA) is just over 2000 km.

Where you choose to visit will primarily be determined by the time of year. Broadly speaking, the far north from October to April is extremely hot, humid and monsoonal. Cairns still gets visitors who want to see the Great Barrier Reef, but most people will want to enjoy the glorious summer weather in the southern regions and avoid the humidity up north. A visit during May to September not only opens up the north, but also allows an itinerary to range almost anywhere within the two states. See also Climate, page 16. ▶ *See Getting around, page 21.*

One- to two-week trip

A trip of one or two weeks could only ever sample a specific area between Sydney and Cairns with perhaps a flying visit (literally) to Melbourne. The following tips suggest making the most out of Sydney, Brisbane, the Gold Coast and Cairns with your own transport. Other specific recommended destinations en route include the **Myall Lakes National Park**, **Byron Bay**, **Fraser Island**, **Magnetic Island** (off Townsville) and the **Whitsunday Islands**.

If you visit **Sydney**, allow at least three days to do it justice. Add to that a three-day trip to the **Blue Mountains**, a two-day trip to the **Hunter Valley** vineyards or, alternatively, the Myall Lakes National Park. **Brisbane** will require at least two days and the **Gold Coast** at least three days, with added exploration of Coolangatta, the Gold Coast hinterland national parks and (from Brisbane) Moreton or North Stradbroke Islands or Noosa also being recommended. **Cairns and the Barrier Reef** could occupy anyone for months, never mind a week or two. However, the 'must see and do's' include a reef island trip with snorkelling or a dive (you can do an introductory dive even if you are not certified), **Kuranda** and the rainforest gondola, **Daintree**, **Cape Tribulation** and the perfect retreat from the coastal heat, the **Atherton Tablelands**.

Three- to four-week trip

Ideally, this is the minimum amount of time a visitor from Europe or the USA should spend in the region. A three to four week trip could comfortably involve a few days in Sydney, then a trip north to Byron Bay, or the less visited Port Macquarie, or alternatively a visit to Brisbane and the Gold Coast then a rather hurried drive to Cairns. The route south of

Packing for Australia

Anything you will need, from pharmaceuticals to camping gear, is readily available in the main centres throughout the country. Given the dollar rate if you are coming from Europe, it might be better to travel light and buy as you go. The major cities can supply just about all your needs including quality maps and travel books. Backpackers are advised to bring a good sleeping bag and a bed sheet. These are not always provided in hostels. A good pair of boots and a large rucksack are a good idea if you are intending to hike. Memory cards for digital cameras are readily available but best bought in duty free. Also remember to bring an electrical adaptor plug. Binoculars are recommended as are a sun hat, sunscreen and sunglasses.

Sydney to Melbourne has lots to offer but, if you are pushed for time, the New South Wales and Queensland coasts undoubtedly take precedence. That said, a flight to Melbourne is recommended to explore Australia's 'second city'. The one-way 2685-km trip between Sydney and Cairns by car is possible in four weeks, but pushing it, so you may like to consider doing one of the sections below, then flying from Brisbane to Sydney or Brisbane to Cairns and perhaps from there to Melbourne. Although there is not much in it, of the two coastal sections the Queensland trip (Brisbane to Cairns) is the best. Added to the city-based suggestions in the one-to-two week section above, you should consider the following itineraries:

Sydney to Brisbane Between Sydney (five days) and Brisbane you can visit Port Stephens (two days), Myall Lakes National Park (three days), Hunter Valley (two days), Port Macquarie (three days), South West Rocks (two days), Bellingen including the Dorrigo and New England National Parks (two to three days), Coffs Harbour (two days), Iluka and Woody Head (two days) and Byron Bay (four days). All are recommended.

Brisbane to Cairns Between Brisbane (three days) and Cairns, the Sunshine Coast and Noosa (three days) are excellent locations for a short break along with an additional day trip along the hinterland Blackall Range. Fraser Island (three days) is, of course, a major highlight, while Bundaberg (especially the turtle rookery) and the twin towns of 1770 and Agnes Waters are both great venues off the beaten track (two days each). Around Rockhampton (one day) try to take in Yeppoon and Great Keppel Island (two to three days) and around Mackay the Eungella National Park (one to two days). In and around Townsville don't miss Magnetic Island (three days) and Charters Towers (one day). Airlie Beach (two days) and the Whitsunday Islands (two to three days) are almost obligatory while just south of Cairns, Mission Beach (two days) and Dunk Island (one to two days) are also well worth visiting. With all that to consider, make sure you leave at least five days in and around Cairns and the Great Barrier Reef.

Over one month

To make the trip by car or campervan between Melbourne and Cairns, taking in the cities, the prime destinations mentioned above and other recommended side trips comfortably will require 10-15 weeks one way. You can then fly back to Sydney or Melbourne, or, if you own a vehicle, endure the four to six day drive. Of course, provided you have the time you should aim to arrive in Melbourne as opposed to Sydney, then do the entire trip from Melbourne to Cairns, using Sydney and Brisbane as the two main city stops along the way. As well as the locations mentioned above other recommended short-stay destinations (with an emphasis on ecology and camping) include:

Melbourne to Sydney Ben Boyd National Park, Batemans Bay (Murramarang National Park), Jervis Bay (Booderee National Park).

Sydney to Brisbane Barrington Tops National Park, Yuraygir National Park and Byron Bay Hinterland national parks.

Brisbane to Cairns Cooloola Coast (Great Sandy National Park), Lady Musgrave Island (from Town of 1770), Heron Island (from Gladstone), Hinchinbrook Island (from Cardwell), Lizard Island (Great Barrier Reef from Cairns or Cooktown), Undara Lava Tubes (from Cairns), Cooktown and a 4WD tour to Cape York.

When to go

One of the joys of the East Coast is that at any time of year there is always some section where the weather is just right. The converse, of course, is that those particular about their destination need good timing. Due to its southerly position Victoria is the coldest and wettest state, especially in winter. However, that said, inland areas of the state (including Melbourne) can get very hot in summer (hotter than Sydney) with much of the interior currently sharing the protracted drought issues of New South Wales and Queensland. The heightened variance in Victoria's climate is due to the influence of northerly winds from the interior and the ocean-borne influences from the south and west. The former, known as the 'southerly change', is essentially Victorian for 'put the fire on and find the umbrella'. Melbourne is famous for its 'four seasons in one day' with a southerly change from a northerly influence seeing the temperature drop dramatically by over 20°C, often with lively thunderstorms.

In 2009 Victoria's extremes were highlighted when, in February, temperatures reached 46°C in and around Melbourne. This was a pivotal factor that led to Australia's worst natural disaster, 'Black Saturday', when fires raged around the state with the loss of over 173 lives and 2000 properties. See also box, opposite

Broadly speaking, the peak season between Sydney and Brisbane is from mid-December to the end of January. Conversely autumn to spring (March to October) is considered the peak season north of Rockhampton (Tropic of Capricorn), when dry, warm weather is the norm. The 'stinger season' between October and May also presents its own dangers (see box, page 37). Generally, accommodation and tourist sites in all three states stay open year round, the main exceptions being in the far north in midsummer (December to March).

Watch out for school holidays and peak seasons, when some areas get completely booked out months in advance (particularly between Sydney and Brisbane). School holidays tend to take place from mid-December to late January, a week or two around Easter, a couple of weeks in June and July and another couple during September and October. If planning a long trip, say three months or more, try to make spring or autumn the core of your time. Also note that during big sporting events such as cricket (summer) and rugby tests (winter) as well as the Aussie Rules football finals (again in spring, especially in Victoria), you are strongly advised to book transport tickets and accommodation as far ahead as possible. ▸▸ *See Public holidays, page 40.*

The bushfire phenomenon

Bushfires have always been an integral part of the Australian environment and its complex ecosystem. Indeed, many native plants and trees have evolved to be almost dependent on fire to seed and, despite the loss of all their foliage, can regrow and even flourish as a result. The Aboriginals used fire for many centuries prior to the arrival of the Europeans to hunt native wildlife, but Aboriginals aside, ignition came from only one purely natural source: lightning.

But for modern human beings it's a very different matter. For us, bushfires represent a major threat to life and property and the fact that it's primarily a natural phenomenon is forgotten. Also, through our own activities, fires start for many more reasons. Lightning remains the main source, but faulty electricity pylons, discarded cigarette butts and, remarkably, arson have become major factors. Also, with much of the country suffering some of the worst droughts on record in summer, given the right conditions it becomes a disaster just waiting to happen.

Many fatalities occur due to 'firestorm' conditions caused by a sudden and violent wind change, which can rapidly change the direction and size of the fire front. The sheer speed and ferocity of the flames, aided by abundant fuels and a landscape immersed in smoke, often make fire suppression and containment impossible. In many cases, residents have to fend for themselves as the fires break communications, cut off escape routes and sever electricity and water supplies.

Many fires have ravaged the land, and lives and properties have been lost. Prior to 2009, the best known of these events was Ash Wednesday in February 1983. Within the space of 24 hours, almost 200 fires raged across Victoria and South Australia, fanned by 100-kph northerly winds. Despite the evacuation of 8000 people, 75 people lost their lives, including 17 firefighters.

But by far the worst event so far was 'Black Saturday' in Victoria, in February 2009. On that day a combination of high temperatures (up to 46°C) and strong northerly winds reaching over 100 kph created potentially catastrophic conditions. Some small fires created by fallen electricity pylons and, in some cases, deliberate starting of fire, combined to create several massive firestorms that raged unabated and were completely unstoppable. By dawn the following morning 173 lives had been lost and over 2000 homes had been destroyed. Entire villages had been wiped out, including Kinglake and Marysville, with many residents who had chosen to stay and defend their homes simply not having time to get out, or not having enough warning. The scene was like something from an apocalyptic Hollywood movie. Australia was stunned. Over 450,000 ha of bush was also destroyed and native wildlife was devastated.

Black Saturday (as it became known) remains the country's worst natural disaster to date and has led to a major overhaul in the policies towards bushfires and community preparedness. Tragically, however, no doubt it won't be the last bushfire, and for many people in Victoria their lives will never be the same.

Climate

As a general rule of thumb, the further north you travel, and the further in time from July, the hotter it gets. And hot means very hot: days over 40°C regularly occur in summer in the arid regions and even cities as far south as Melbourne average around 25°C. In the north of the country summer (November to April) is synonymous with 'the wet', a period characterized by high humidity, heat, tremendous monsoonal rainfall and occasional, powerful cyclones. Periods of prolonged showers, particularly late in the wet season, are also common. Australia is the driest inhabited continent and most areas are currently suffering the longest and most protracted drought on record. Drought or no drought, virtually nowhere further than 250 km inland gets more than an average of 600 mm of rain a year. About half the continent, in a band across the south and west, gets less than 300 mm and much of it is desert. Naturally, the East Coast and elevated areas along the Great Divide see much higher rainfall. For comprehensive weather forecasts, see www.bom.gov.au.

What to do

Australia is one of the world's great adventure countries and the East Coast can offer a tremendous range of activities. Many of the best experiences are offered by specialist tour and hire operators along the coast and if you have some specific goals it is essential to check out your options carefully in advance, as the time of year and availability of spaces can make a big difference to what is possible.

Aboriginal tours
For local and authentic aboriginal tours, see www.aboriginalaustralia.com.au.

Canoeing, kayaking, rafting
Australia may be the driest continent but there are a few opportunities for river rafting. Tropical Queensland rivers can generate quite a bit of white water in winter, and the Snowy Mountains of New South Wales are another top destination for those seeking a rough and exciting ride. Sea kayaking is obviously huge and there are numerous operators in almost every major coastal town along the coast. Good spots include the Great Barrier Reef (QLD), page 304, Kosciusko National Park (NSW), page 152, and the Whitsunday Islands (QLD), page 276.

The Australian canoeing website, www.canoe.org.au, concentrates on competitive canoeing, but some of the state links have good river descriptions and links to commercial operators. Whitewater rafting companies are mentioned in the text and predominate in Cairns, Mission Beach and Airlie Beach (QLD).

Climbing and abseiling
Although much of Australia is flat as a tack there are a few fabulous climbing spots. Most of the recognized routes are in the eastern half of the country in the Great Dividing Range. If you want to find out more get hold of *Climbing Australia: The Essential Guide* by Greg Pritchard, or see www.climbing.com.au, which picks out abseiling operators.

Canyoning is a sport almost exclusively restricted to the Great Dividing Range of New South Wales and involves a combination of climbing, abseiling, wading and swimming through the canyons and gorges of the Blue Mountains and Manning Valley.

Cycling and mountain biking

Bicycles are commonly available for hire in cities and major towns but facilities are scarce otherwise. Huge as the country is, cycling around it is a popular pastime and some states, notably Victoria with its Rail Trails, are actively promoting the activity. Brisbane is also noted for its inner city cycling paths and in Melbourne, given the protracted problems with public transport, cycling is hugely popular and not just for recreation. If you plan to do most of your touring on a bike you will need to either bring your own or buy in Australia, as long-term hire facilities are virtually non-existent. One alternative is to join a cycle-based tour. For more information, see www.cycling.org.au. Sydney-based companies are an excellent source of information. See page 131.

Diving

From the very tip of Queensland to the very bottom of Australia's East Coast, there are unlimited scuba diving possibilities. What makes this coast so interesting for divers is that the huge expanse covers several different climatic zones. The far north is tropical, then as you head south it becomes subtropical and eventually temperate, and the sheer variety of marine species is vast. The undoubted highlight is the Great Barrier Reef, the planet's longest coral reef system, page 304. Stretching for 2000 km, it has 3000 individual reefs, 1500 species of fish, 400 corals and 4000 molluscs. A major attraction across all regions is the shark, closely followed by marine mammals. Other top destinations include Byron Bay (NSW), page 187, Great Keppel, page 262, Jervis Bay (NSW), page 149, Lady Musgrave Island (QLD), page 257, Sydney (NSW), page 128 and the Whitsunday Islands (QLD), page 276.

Australia's oceans are known for as many rare and indigenous species as its land. The websites www.diveoz.com.au, www.scubaaustralia.com.au and www.reefteach.com.au have some useful general information as well as fairly comprehensive, though not qualitative, state-by-state directories including sites, dive centres and charter boats. Details of several multi-day diving trips can be found on www.divedirectory.net.

Fishing

One of Australia's favourite hobbies, fishing is pursued with an almost religious obsession. As you head north, surfboards begin to disappear from vehicle roof racks, only to be replaced by the 'tinnies', short aluminium boats that allow the fishing family to go where they please. Inland fishing, mostly for barramundi in the north and the feral trout in the south, requires a licence in some states, though beach and sea fishing do not. Good spots for fishing include Cairns (QLD), page 299, Kosciusko National Park (NSW), page 152, Port Macquarie to Byron Bay coast (NSW), page 178 and Sydney and around (NSW), page 90.

Whatever your requirements, tour operators and hire companies will usually organize it for you. Excellent offshore sports fishing is widely available as a day tour, usually for around $150-250. There are several excellent websites on recreational fishing in Eastern Australia, including www.fishingaustralia.com.au and www.sportsfish australia.com.au.

Gliding and hang-gliding

Gliding is particularly popular in inland towns, often bordering the wheatbelts, where there is a rich harvest of sunny days and strong thermals, and most commonly out on the plains of inland New South Wales. For a comprehensive list of gliding clubs, see www.gfa.org.au.

Hang-gliding, while still requiring thermals for extended flights, makes use of elevated areas for take-off and so is most popular in upland and coastal cliff areas.

Flying in microlights, also known as 'trikes', and ultralights, similar but more airplane-like, is a fast-growing activity in Australia, where weather and space make it an ideal sport or simply a way of getting around.

A few operators offer hang-gliding and paragliding lessons and some one-off flights. You'll find a listing of top sites at www.hgfa.asn.au, the website of the Hang Gliding Federation of Australia, T03-9379 2177.

A few operators around the country offer scenic flights in two-seater microlights but if you're interested in getting more involved, contact one of the local clubs listed on www.auf.asn.au.

Horse riding

Australia has a great number of horse riding schools and station stays, both offering recreational rides, and you can't travel far in the more populated regions without finding one. Rides can be from 30 minutes to several days' duration.

The high country, between Mansfield, in Victoria, and Canberra, is where the most awesome Australian horse riding can be experienced, but there are many places along the East Coast that offer fine scenic trails or multi-day treks and these are listed under the relevant destination.

Parachuting and bungee jumping

Many of the several dozen skydiving clubs in Australia offer short, usually one-day, courses in parachuting (also known as skydiving), including a jump or two. Some cut out much of the training by organizing tandem jumps where you're strapped, facing forward, to the chest of the instructor. If a quick thrill is all you're after then the latter is the better option as it usually involves 30-60 seconds of freefall, by far the most exhilarating part of the experience, and costs around $300-400.

A list of skydiving clubs affiliated to the Australian Parachute Federation, T02-6281 6830, can be found at www.apf.asn.au, and there are numerous opportunities to make the big leap all along the East Coast and around Sydney.

If you fancy jumping out into thin air without a parachute then bungee jumping is just about the safest option going and available from a site just north of Cairns, see page 321. For a list of bungee operators, see www.bungee-experience.com.

Skiing and snowboarding

Australia boasts some world-class resorts, though these are mostly confined to the Snowy Mountains in NSW, with some notable slopes also in the Victorian Alps. The peak season is from June to September. Of course Australia is not a country one associates with snow or the Alberto Tombas of this world, but in the 2010 Winter Games in Vancouver two Australians took gold: Torah Bright in the women's snowboard halfpipe and Lydia Lassila in the freestyle skiing aerials.

Surfing and waterskiing

If an Aussie lives near the beach there's a fair bet they'll be a surfer; if they're inland and anywhere near water then it'll be waterskiing. This makes for a great many local clubs, tuition and equipment hire. Surfing is generally best in the southern half of the country, from Sydney north to the QLD border. There are quite a few websites dedicated to surfing, including www.surfinfo.com.au and www.surfingaustralia.com, which link to a great many surfie retail and travel businesses, and www.real surf.com, which has condition

How big is your footprint?

One of Australia's main attractions is the natural environment and its wildlife and there are many opportunities for ecotourism. CALM (the Department of Conservation and Land Management) promotes a minimal impact bushwalking code that is aimed at protecting the environment, which is also a useful guide for minimizing your footprint in other natural environments. Fire is a critical issue in Australia's hot, dry environments where only a spark is needed to create a fire that can get out of control and destroy an area the size of a small European country in a day or two, perhaps threatening lives and property. The national parks around Sydney have been especially badly hit in the last decade. For this reason, in some areas there are total fire bans, either for a seasonal period or on days when a high risk of fire is predicted. In extreme circumstances a national park, scenic attraction or walking trail may be closed because the risk of fire is so high. Fire bans or restrictions usually apply in summer (November to March) in the south and during the late dry season in the north (July to November). Check fire restrictions before travel with the nearest parks, shire, police or tourist office as they may affect your preparations; on days of total fire ban you will have to take food that doesn't need cooking.

If you want to know more about environmental issues or get involved in conservation, contact the Australian Conservation Foundation, T02-8270 9900, www.acfonline.org.au, or the Wilderness Society, T02-6249 6491, www.wilderness.org.au. Other organizations include: Parks Victoria, T03-8627 4699 (T131963 within Australia), www.parkweb.vic.gov.au; NSW National Parks and Wildlife Service, T02-9995 5000 (T131555), www.nationalparks.nsw.gov.au; Queensland Parks and Wildlife Service, T07-3227 8185, www.epa.qld.gov.au; National Trust Queensland, T07-3229 1788, www.nationaltrustqld.org. The quarterly wilderness adventure magazine *Wild* is a good source of information on environmental issues and campaigns.

→ Campers should always carry a fuel stove for cooking as many national parks or public reserves forbid campfires or the collection of wood or both. It is also good practice to clean your walking or camping gear before moving to a different environment.

→ Travellers in Australia will also come across 'sacred sites', areas of religious importance to indigenous people, and naturally it is important to respect any restrictions that may apply to these areas. Permission is usually required to enter an Aboriginal community, and you may be asked to comply with restrictions such as a ban on alcohol. If you visit a community, or travel through Aboriginal land, respect the privacy of Aboriginal people and never take photographs without asking first.

reports from all the major spots around the country. You can make surfing the core activity on your travels with a number of companies offering specialist surf tours up and down the East Coast. A four-night trip between Sydney and Byron Bay will cost around $600, www.surfaris.com.au.

Windsurfing and kitesurfing (or kiteboarding) are also widespread, with Noosa (Queensland) and Melbourne both being good places to learn the art of kitesurfing. See www.windsurfing.org, with windsurfing club, holiday and tuition details on the state pages. For information on kitesurfing schools, see www.kitesurfingschool.org.

Walking and trekking

Australia boasts a great range of short, day and overnight walks, mostly in the many national parks, and even a few multi-day treks that rank alongside the world's best.

Many of Australia's natural ecologies are particularly sensitive to human activity and you should take care to disturb as little as possible. All the state conservation authorities have a minimal impact bushwalking code, published on their websites and printed on the park notes for all the national parks; see also box, page 19. Most of the longer walks, and some even as short as two hours, have a walker registration system in place, ensuring that if you get lost or injured someone will come looking for you. If there is no such system in place make sure someone (the local park ranger or the police) knows where you are going and how long you plan to be. The indefatigable Tyrone T Thomas has penned the best series of books on walking in Australia. Bushwalking clubs are a good source of local advice and often welcome visitors on their regular expeditions. For a comprehensive list of clubs, see www.bushwalking.org.au.

Top walking destinations include the Blue Mountains (NSW), page 135, Kosciusko National Park (NSW), page 152, Thorsborne Trail on Hinchinbrook Island (QLD), page 284 and the Great Ocean Walk (VIC), page 62.

Getting there

Air

There are international flights direct to Melbourne, Sydney, Brisbane and Cairns and it is quite possible to have different points of arrival and departure that complement your intended itinerary. If there is not a direct flight to your primary choice there will usually be a same-day connection from Sydney or Melbourne. It is usually possible to book internal Australian flights when booking your international ticket, at lower prices than on arrival. Some do not even require a stated departure and arrival point. If you have any plans to fly within New South Wales or Queensland check this out prior to booking.

Fares depend on the season, with prices higher during December and January unless booked well in advance. Mid-year sees the cheapest fares. **Qantas**, www.qantas.com.au, is Australia's main international and domestic airline and flies from most international capitals and major cities. That said, with the advent of the global financial crisis, competition is fiercer than ever, and Qantas is struggling in international and domestic markets against other airlines like Emirates, V Australia and Tiger Airways. Most other international major airlines have flights to Australia from their home countries.

Airport information

Melbourne, Sydney, Brisbane and Cairns are the main airports and all have excellent services. All the main airlines fly to these airports with regular connections from international and national destinations. Facilities are good and include banks, ATMs and tourist offices where help is on hand with booking accommodation and organizing tours and transport. All the airports offer regular and efficient connections with the city centres either by coach or rail. See the respective sections for further details or refer to www.melbourneairport.com.au; www.sydneyairport.com.au and www.bne.com.au.

From Europe

With the advent of the global financial crisis it is now considerably cheaper to fly to Australia than it was three years ago. The main route, and the cheapest, is via Asia, though fares will also be quoted via North America or Africa. The Asia route usually takes 20-30 hours including stops. There are no non-stop routes so it's worth checking out which stopovers are on offer. Stopovers of a few nights do not usually increase the cost of the ticket appreciably. The cheapest return flights, off season, will be around £700 (€774), with prices rising to at least £1000 (€1100) around Christmas.

From North and South America

There are direct **Qantas** flights from Los Angeles to Brisbane and Sydney, and from Vancouver and New York to Sydney. Connections to Melbourne and Cairns are available from Auckland. The cost of a standard return in the high season from Vancouver starts at around US$1800, from New York at US$1900 and from Los Angeles at US$1500. Flights take around 11 hours. There are also direct flights from Buenos Aires to Sydney.

Departure tax

There are currently a number of departure taxes levied by individual airports (such as noise tax) and the government. All taxes are included in the cost of a ticket.

Discount flight agents

Ebookers, www.ebookers.com. Comprehensive travel ticket booking website.
Expedia, www.expedia.com. Another travel site based only on the internet, with lots of background information.
Webjet, www.webjet.com.au. Popular Australian flight portal
STA Travel, T0871-230 0040, www.statravel .co.uk. Specialists in student discount fares, IDs and other travel services. Branches in most major cities. In Australia: **STA**, T134782, www.statravel.com.au.
Trailfinders, 194 Kensington High St, London W8 6FT, T0845-058 5858 / T020-7938 3939, www.trailfinders.com. Particularly good on personalized itineraries and adventure travel.
Flight Centre, T133133, www.flightcentre.com.au.
Harvey World Travel, T1300 855492, www.harveyworld.com.au.

Getting around

Public transport is generally good and efficient and often easier than driving. Most cities have good metropolitan bus services, though some are curiously unaware of tourist traffic and there is many an important outlying attraction poorly served by public transport, or even missed off the bus routes completely. Some cities are compact enough for this to be a minor irritation, others are so spread out that the visitor must invest in an expensive tourist bus service or taxis. In such places staying at a hostel or B&B with free or low-cost bike hire can save a lot of money. Bear in mind that when it comes to public transport in the major centres, Australia is hardly comparable to Japan or to a lesser extent Europe or North America. In cities like Melbourne, if you ask a local to comment on their public transport system, the reply will be a few choice words and a considerable degree of frustration and anger.

By far the best way of seeing the East Coast is under your own steam, or with a tour operator with an in-depth itinerary. See Tours operators, page 41, and individual town and city sections for details. The further from the cities you go, the more patchy and irregular public transport becomes. All the states have networks based on a combination of air, bus and train. Some of these services connect up at border towns but check first. If you are short on time and long on funds, flying can save a lot of time, money and effort, both interstate and within New South Wales and Queensland. In some cases it is the only real option. Most other interstate options involve long-distance buses, and on a few routes, trains. Train fares and domestic air travel can be considerably cheaper if booked in advance and on the net. For flights within Australia, try www.webjet.com.au.

Air

Qantas, T131313, www.qantas.com.au, **Tiger Airways**, T03-9335 3033, www.tigerairways.com, **Jetstar**, T131538, www.jetstar.com.au, and **Virgin Blue**, T136789, www.virginblue.com.au, link most state capitals to each other and to many of the larger towns and main tourist destinations. There are also several regional airways operating smaller planes on specialist routes including **Regional Express (REX)**, T131713, www.regionalexpress.com.au. Domestic fares have dropped dramatically in recent years. In 2009 a one-way ticket between Melbourne and Sydney was available for as little as $40 and for Sydney to Cairns for $175. But bear in mind with budget airlines this does not take into account cargo baggage, for which you will pay significantly more. For up-to-date information on whether a destination is served by scheduled or charter flights, contact your destination's tourist office or each airline direct.

Bear in mind that many provincial airports may not be staffed when you arrive. Check with the local tourist office regarding transport from the airport to the town.

Rail

Train travel up and down the East Coast is a viable mode of transport and can be a delightful way to get from A to B, especially if you are short of time. Given the distances between the main centres, Australia lends itself to rail travel and you may find routes with such evocative names as **Sunlander** and **Spirit of the Outback** irresistible. That said, a car or coach is a better option if you wish to explore or get off the beaten track. The East Coast offers endless beaches and numerous national parks that are well away from any railway stations. Also bear in mind that track gauges differ in NSW and Queensland, so the crossing between the two takes in an intriguing transition by road. Also, note that overnight travel by rail is possible, though often expensive, if you wish to have the comfort of your own compartment and to do it in style. Well worth considering is a jaunt into the outback from Brisbane to Longreach on board the **Spirit of the Outback**.

In New South Wales, **Countrylink**, T132232 (within Australia), www.countrylink .nsw.gov.au, offers rail and rail/coach services state-wide and to Brisbane. There are several Countrylink travel centres at principal stations in Sydney including the Sydney Central Railway Station, T02-99379 3800. A useful website for travel throughout New South Wales is www.webwombat.com.au/transport/nsw.htm.

In Queensland, **Queensland Rail**, T131617, www.qr.com.au, offers a range of rail services up and down the coast and into the outback. Brisbane (Roma Street) Transit Centre in Brisbane, T07-3236 2528, hosts offices for most major coach and rail service providers and is a fine source of general travel information. Outback Queensland is also well served by all of the above but stopovers and less frequent travel schedules are obviously the norm.

In Victoria state, **V-Line**, T136196, www.vline.com.au, is the principal service provider.

Road

Bus

State and interstate bus services offer the most cost-effective way of constructing an itinerary for a single traveller. A large selection of bus services can be found at www.buslines.com.au. Always check the journey duration and time of arrival, as some routes can take days, with just a couple of short meal stops. Many coaches are equipped with videos but you may also want something to read. It's also a good idea to take warm clothing, socks, a pillow, toothbrush and earplugs. There's a good chance you'll arrive in the late evening or the early hours of the morning. If so, book accommodation ahead and, if possible, transfer transportation.

The main operator throughout New South Wales and Queensland is **Greyhound Pioneer**, T1300 473946, www.greyhound.com.au (referred to simply as Greyhound throughout this guide), while in Victoria the principal service provider is **V-Line**, T136196, www.vline.com.au. Their networks follow all the main interstate highways up and down the coast with offshoots including the Blue Mountains, New England (Hunter Valley), Armidale, Charters Towers, the Atherton Tablelands and so on. As well as scheduled routes, they offer a range of passes. There are also many other smaller regional companies. Most are listed under the relevant destinations. **Countrylink**, T132232, www.countrylink.info, also offers coach services to some centres in conjunction with rail schedules between New South Wales and Queensland.

Greyhound offer a wide variety of passes with several jump-on, jump-off options. The **Day Passes** system has three options: the **Standard Day Pass** allows you to travel anywhere on the Greyhound network for the number of consecutive days you choose with a pre-set kilometre limit. You can buy a pass for three days (1000 km limit, $154), five days (1500 km limit, $223), seven days (2000 km limit, $286), 10 days (3000 km limit, $398), 20 days (6000 km limit, $755), 30 days (10,000 km, $1030). The **Flexi Day Pass** gives you total flexibility without a kilometre restriction. Customers purchase the number of days' travel required (10, 15 or 21) and have up to 60 days to use the travelling days purchased, while The **Fixed Day Pass** gives you freedom to travel for a consecutive number of days (10, 15 and 21) without a kilometre restriction.

The **Explorer Pass** commits you to a set one-way or circular route and is valid for between 30 and 365 days. There are a couple of dozen options including **Best of the East**, which takes in Cairns to Melbourne and the Red Centre at around $1451, and an **All Australian** at $2988.

Other passes include the **Mini Traveller**, which provides travel between two popular destinations; in between you can hop on and hop off as much as you like in the one direction, over 45 days. From Cairns to Sydney will cost around $408.

Backpacker buses There are now several operators who make the assumption that the most important part of your trip is the journey. These companies combine the roles of travel operator and tour guide, taking from two to five times longer than scheduled services (a good indicator of just how much they get off the highway). They are worth considering, especially if you are travelling alone. In terms of style, price ($95-175 per day) and what is included, they vary greatly and it is important to clarify this prior to booking. Some offer transport and commentary only, others include accommodation and some meals, a few specialize in 4WD and bush camping. A few, including **Oz Experience** (see below) offer jump-on, jump-off packages and are priced more on distance. The popular option of flying Sydney to Cairns independently and then returning by bus (or vice versa) is also worth considering and would cost about $675. The main backpacker bus company in NSW and Queensland is **Oz Experience**, T1300 300028, www.ozexperience.com.

Buying a vehicle

Buying a vehicle in Australia is a relatively simple process, provided you have somewhere you can give as an address. Bona fide cars and vans can be picked up for as little as $2500, or $8000 for a 4WD. Paying more increases peace of mind but obviously increases possible losses when you sell it. If you're negotiating with a second-hand car dealer you may be able to agree a 'buy-back' price, saving considerable hassle, and usually you will be offered some sort of warranty. Alternatively, you can acquire a vehicle from fellow travellers, or through hostel notice boards and the classifieds. Buying privately is usually cheaper and real bargains can be had from travellers in a hurry to close a deal before returning home. But there are no guarantees: without a warranty it is, legally, a simple case of 'buyer beware' regardless of what transpires once you pass over the cash. So get a car checked out before parting with your cash, even twice to make sure, and scrutinize service records. If in doubt DON'T. State motoring organizations offer vehicle checks for around $175, but don't rely on these 100%; many are simply lazy with their checks or not at all thorough. An older vehicle may need a little TLC. The availability of spares is a consideration; Toyota is seen as the safest bet for parts and in Australia, especially in rural areas, the flatbeds and 4WDs are everywhere. Avoid all Japanese imports like Mitsubishi Delica vans, as many mechanics will not even go near them.

Every car is registered within the state where it is first purchased and the registration papers must be transferred at each sale. If a car is to be resold in a different state it has first to be re-registered in that state. It must also have an Australian Compliance Plate. You will need to formally complete the transfer of registration with the transport department, presenting them with the papers, a receipt (there is a stamp duty tax of about 5%), plus in some states a certificate of roadworthiness. The seller may provide the latter or you may have to get a suitable garage to check the vehicle. Registration must be renewed, in the state the vehicle was last sold, every six or 12 months. Victoria is a good state in which to buy and register a vehicle, while NSW is considered the most complex – and expensive. Do not, if you can possibly avoid it, let your vehicle registration run out in New South Wales. The best option is to make sure the car you purchase has a registration covering the entire period of your stay and preferably longer to make a resale more viable. Third-party personal injury insurance may be included in the registration. You are advised, however, to invest in third-party vehicle and property insurance, or even comprehensive cover if you cannot afford to lose the value of your vehicle.

Car

If you live in a small and populous country, travelling by car in Australia will be an enlightening experience, as well as an enervating one. Distances are huge and travelling times between the major cities, towns and sights can seem endless, so put on some tunes and make driving part of the whole holiday experience.

You should consider buying a car if you are travelling for more than three months. Consider a campervan if hiring or buying. Traffic congestion is rarely an issue on the East Coast route – only Sydney has anything like the traffic of many other countries, so driving itineraries can be based on covering a planned distance each day, up to, say, 100 km for

Driving safely

→ If you stray from the coast and 'go outback', watch out for large animals such as kangaroos and emus. Hitting a kangaroo, emu or sheep can write off the vehicle and cause injury. Dawn and dusk are the worst times so try to avoid travelling then. Do not expect any animal to get out of your way. Many, through sheer angst, will head towards the vehicle or run into its path at the last second.

→ On country and outback roads you will also meet road trains (trucks up to four times the size you are most probably used to). Overtake them with great care.

→ If you're on a single-track bitumen road or an unsealed road pull right over when a road train comes the other way. Not only can dust cause zero visibility but you will also minimize the possibility of stones pinging up and damaging your windows.

→ If travelling in the outback always carry extra water and food. If you do break down and are out of mobile coverage DO NOT leave your vehicle. Stay with it and on the road until help arrives.

→ Drive only in full daylight if possible.

→ Always check with the hire company where you can and cannot take your 4WD vehicle (some will not allow them off graded roads or on sand, like Fraser Island) and also what your liability will be in the case of an accident.

→ To minimize costs on long journeys: ensure correct tyre pressures, avoid using air conditioning if possible, pack luggage in the car rather than on the roof, check the oil regularly and stick to 90-100 kph.

→ Some hire companies offer one-way hire on certain models and under certain conditions.

→ The general breakdown number for all associations is T131111.

→ For excellent travel route planning along the East Coast consult the Travel Planner section on the RACQ website, www.racq.com.au.

each solid hour's driving. The key factor in planning is distance. It is pretty stress-free and as the distances can be huge, drivers can get bored and sleepy. There are a lot of single-vehicle accidents in Australia, many the result of driver fatigue.

The other major factor when planning is the type of roads you may need to use. Almost all the main interstate highways between Sydney and Cairns are 'sealed', though there are a few exceptions. Many country roads are unsealed, usually meaning a stony or sand surface. When recently graded (levelled and compacted) they can be almost as pleasant to drive on as sealed roads, but even then there are reduced levels of handling. After grading, unsealed roads deteriorate over time. Potholes form, they can become impassable when wet and corrugations usually develop, especially on national park roads, with heavy usage. These are regular ripples in the road surface, at right angles to the road direction, that can go on for tens of kilometres. Small ones simply cause an irritating judder, large ones can reduce tolerable driving speeds to 10-20 kph. Generally, the bigger the wheel size and the longer the wheel base, the more comfortable the journey over corrugations will be. Many unsealed roads can be negotiated with a two wheel-drive (2WD) low-clearance vehicle but the ride will be a lot more comfortable, and safer, in a 4WD high-clearance one. Most 2WD hire cars are uninsured if driven on unsealed roads. Some unsealed roads (especially in the outback) are designated as 4WD-only or tracks, though individual definitions can differ according to the map or authority you consult. If in doubt, stick to the roads you are certain are safe for your vehicle and you are sufficiently prepared for. With careful preparation, however, and the right vehicles (convoys are recommended), traversing the major outback tracks is an awesome experience.

If you stray far from the coast, and certainly anywhere outback, prepare carefully. Carry essential spares and tools such as fan belts, hoses, gaffer tape, a tyre repair kit, extra car jack, extra spare wheel and tyre, spade, decent tool kit, oil and coolant and a fuel can. Membership of the NRMA (NSW) or the RACQ (QLD) is recommended (see below), as is informing someone of your intended itinerary. Above all carry plenty of spare water, at least 10 litres per person, 20 if possible. As far as the best make of vehicle for the outback, in Australia it is the iconic Toyota Landcruiser every time. Break down in a cruiser and the chances are spare parts can be sourced quite easily, without waiting days for foreign hard-to-come-by items. Break down in a Mitsubishi Delica and you may as well look for a job and get married to a local.

Rules and regulations To drive in Australia you must have a current driving licence. Foreign nationals also need an international driving licence, available from your national motoring organization. In Australia you drive on the left. Speed limits vary between states, with maximum urban limits of 50-60 kph and maximum country limits of 100-120 kph. Speeding penalties include a fine and police allow little leeway. Seatbelts are compulsory for drivers and passengers. Driving under the influence of alcohol is illegal over certain (very small) limits and penalties are severe.

Petrol costs Fuel costs are approximately half that in Britain and twice that in the US, but due to the recent increase in the price of crude are following the global trend and rising rapidly. In mid-2010 they were fluctuating between $1.20 and $1.30 a litre in city centres and marginally more in the outback. Diesel was traditionally more expensive than unleaded at about $1.35, but it's less prone to price fluctuations and in recent times can actually beat unleaded at a more consistent $1.20. When budgeting, allow at least $15 for every estimated 100 km. A trip around the eastern circuit can easily involve driving 20,000 km. Picking an economical vehicle and conserving fuel can save hundreds of dollars.

Motoring organizations Every state has a breakdown service that is affiliated to the **Australian Automobile Association (AAA)**, www.aaa.asn.au, with which your home country organization may have a reciprocal link. You need to join one of the state associations: in New South Wales **NRMA**, T132132, www.nrma.com.au, in Victoria **RACV**, T131329, www.racv.com.au, and in Queensland **RACQ**, T131905, www.racq.com.au. Note also that you may be covered for only about 100 km (depending on the scheme) of towing distance and that without cover towing services are very expensive. Given the sheer distances you are likely to cover by car, joining an automobile organization is highly recommended but read the fine print with regard to levels of membership in relation to coverage outside metropolitan areas and in the outback.

Vehicle hire Car rental costs vary considerably according to where you hire from (it's cheaper in the big cities, though small local companies can have good deals), what you hire and the mileage/insurance terms. You may be better off making arrangements in your own country for a fly/drive deal. Watch out for kilometre caps: some can be as low as

100 km per day. The minimum you can expect to pay in Australia is around $250 a week for a small car. Drivers need to be over 21. At peak times it can be impossible to get a car at short notice and some companies may dispose of a booked car within as little as half an hour of you not showing up for an agreed pick-up time. If you've booked a car but are going to be late, ensure that you let them know before the pick-up time.

Cycling

Long-term bicycle hire is rarely available and touring cyclists should plan to bring their own bike or buy in Australia. Bicycle hire is available in most towns and cities and companies are listed in the relevant sections of this book. See page 17. If you do plan on touring the coast by bicycle, the website www.cycling.org.au is recommended.

Hitchhiking

Hitchhiking, while not strictly illegal in New South Wales and Queensland, is not advised by anyone. The tragic events near Barrow Creek in 2001 demonstrate that there will always be twisted souls who will assault or abduct people for their own evil ends. This is not to say that hitching is more dangerous in Australia than elsewhere else.

Maps

Several publishers produce hard-copy countrywide and state maps. Regional maps are also available and the most useful for general travel. The best and cheapest of these are generally published by each state's motoring organization, see page 26. Road and street maps for all the major Australian regions, cities and towns can be found at www.ltl.com.au/sydneymapshop.htm.

AUSLIG, the national mapping agency, publishes 54 x 54 km topographical maps, at 1:100,000 scale, of every area in Australia, recommended for any long-distance trekking or riding. Most areas are now in print, but if not black and white copies can be obtained. For a map index, place name search, details of distributors or mail order, contact T1800 800173, www.auslig.gov.au. AUSLIG also publishes a 1:250,000 series, covering the whole country, useful for those heading outback on 4WD trips. If you're thinking of tackling one of the major outback tracks, such as the Great Central Road, Tanami, Birdsville or Strzelecki, then get hold of the appropriate map published by Westprint, T03-5391 1466, www.westprint.com.au, which is the acknowledged expert in this field.

In the cities it is worth getting hold of a mini version of the street map tomes. In Sydney it is Sydway, Melbourne Melway and Brisbane, yes you got it, Brisway. Sadly, being so small, there is no 'TittyBongWay', or indeed 'WaggaWaggaWay'. Shame.

Recommended outlets are given throughout the book, listed in the Shopping sections for the larger towns and cities. Specialist map shops to contact or visit before your trip include the following outlets (who also offer online shopping): Stanfords, 12-14 Longacre, London, WC2E 9LP, T020-7836 1321, www.stanfords. co.uk; and Rand McNally, 150E 52nd Street, Midtown East, New York, T212-758 7488, www.randmcnally.com.

And of course, to really whet your appetite, it's worth a muse online with Google Earth, especially for Sydney, Melbourne and places like the Blue Mountains, Fraser Island and the Great Barrier Reef.

Sleeping

East Coast Australia presents a diverse and attractive range of accommodation options, from cheap national park campsites to luxurious Great Barrier Reef island retreats. The real beauty here, given the weather and the environment, is that travelling on a budget does not detract from the enjoyment of the trip. On the contrary, this is a place where a night under canvas in any of the national parks is an absolute delight.

Booking accommodation in advance is highly recommended, especially in peak seasons. Booking online will usually secure the best rates. Especially beyond the Queensland border, check if your accommodation has air conditioning (a/c) when booking. Rooms without air conditioning are almost impossible to sleep in during hot weather. Note that single rooms are relatively scarce. Twin or double rooms let to a single occupant are rarely half the price and you may even be charged the full cost for two people.

Hotels, lodges, motels and resorts

At the top end of the scale, especially in the state capitals, the Gold Coast, Moreton Bay Islands, Fraser Island, Whitsunday Islands, Cairns and the Great Barrier Reef Islands there are some impressive international-standard hotels, lodges and resorts, with luxurious surroundings and facilities, attentive service and often outstanding locations. For examples refer to the Kingfisher Bay Resort, www.kingfisherbay.com; the Daintree Eco-lodge and Spa, www.daintree-ecolodge.com.au; or the Park Hyatt in Sydney, www.hyatt.com.au.

Rooms in hotels and lodges will typically start in our **L** range. In the main cities are a few less expensive hotels in the **A-B** range. Most 'hotels' outside of the major towns are pubs with upstairs or external accommodation. If upstairs, a room is likely to have access to shared bathroom facilities, while external rooms are usually standard en suite motel units. The quality of pub-hotel accommodation varies considerably but is usually a budget option (**C-D**). Linen is almost always supplied.

Motels in Australia are usually depressingly anonymous but dependably clean and safe and offer the cheapest en suite rooms. Most have dining facilities and free, secure parking. Some fall into our **D** range, most will be a **B-C**. Linen is always supplied.

B&Bs and self-catering

Bed and breakfast (B&B) is in some ways quite different from the British model. Not expensive, but rarely a budget option, most fall into our **B-C** ranges. They offer very comfortable accommodation in usually upmarket, sometimes historic houses. Rooms are usually en suite or have access to a private bathroom. Most hosts are friendly and informative. Some B&Bs are actually semi or fully self-contained cottages or cabins with breakfast provisions supplied. Larger ones may have full kitchens. As well as private houses, caravan parks and hostels and some resorts and motels provide self-contained, self-catering options with apartment-style units. Linen may not be supplied in self-catering accommodation.

A couple of good websites are www.bedandbreakfast.com.au, www.bbbook.com.au and www.bedandbreakfastnsw.com (NSW).

National parks, farms and stations

Some national parks and rural cattle and sheep stations have old settlers' or workers' homes that have been converted into tourist accommodation, which is usually

Sleeping price codes

LL	$300 and over	B	$110-149	E	$31-49
L	$200-299	C	$80-109	F	$30 and under
A	$150-199	D	$50-79		

Price codes refer to the cost of two people sharing a double or a twin room in the high season, with breakfast where included. Many places offer discounts during low season or for long stays.

All prices are for a double or a twin, except F, which is for a single or a dorm or a powered/non-powered site in a motor park.

self-contained. They are often magical places to stay and include many old lighthouse keepers' cottages and shearers' quarters. Stations may also invite guests to watch, or even get involved in, the day's activities. Transport to them can be difficult if you don't have your own vehicle. Linen is often not supplied in this sort of accommodation. For a few examples in Queensland, see page 282.

Hostels
For those travelling on a tight budget there is a large network of hostels offering cheap accommodation (D-F). These are also popular centres for backpackers and provide great opportunities for meeting fellow travellers. All hostels have kitchen and common room facilities, almost all now have internet and some have considerably more. A few, particularly in cities, will offer freebies including breakfast and pick-ups. Many are now open 24 hours, even if the front desk is closed at night. Standards vary considerably and it's well worth asking the opinions of other travellers. Most are effectively independent – even most YHAs are simply affiliates – but the best tend to be those that are owner-managed. Of several hostel associations, YHA, www.yha.org.au, and NOMADS, T02-9299 7710, www.nomadsworld.com, no membership fee, seem to keep the closest eye on their hostels, ensuring a consistency of quality. The YMCA, T03-9699 7655, www.ymca.org.au, and YWCA, T02-6230 5150, www.ywca.org.au, are usually a clean and quiet choice in the major cities. International visitors can obtain a Hostelling International Card (HIC) from any YHA hostel or travel centre: it's valid for one year and costs $32. For this you get a handbook of YHA hostels nationwide and around $3 off every night's accommodation. Some transport and tourist establishments also offer discounts to HIC holders. For more information, see www.hihostels.com.

Caravan and tourist parks
Almost every town will have at least one caravan park, with unpowered and powered sites varying from $25-40 (for two) for campers, caravans and campervans, an ablutions block and usually a camp kitchen or barbecues. Some will have permanently sited caravans (onsite vans) and cabins. Onsite vans are usually the cheapest option (E-F) for families or small groups wanting to self-cater. Cabins are usually more expensive (C-D). Some will have televisions, en suite bathrooms, separate bedrooms with linen and well-equipped kitchens. Power is rated at the domestic level (240/250v AC), which is very

10 of the best caravan and tourist parks

- Tidal River, Wilsons Promontory National Park (VIC).
- Port Stephens (NSW).
- Sandbar Caravan Park, Myall Lakes (NSW).
- Seal Rocks Camping Reserve, Myall Lakes (NSW).
- Horseshoe Bay Beach Park, SW Rocks (NSW).
- Emerald Beach Holiday Park, Emerald Beach, Coffs Harbour (NSW).
- Broken Head Caravan Park, Broken Head, Byron Bay (NSW).
- Noosa River Caravan Park, Noosa (QLD).
- Beachcomber Caravan Village, Mission Beach South (QLD).
- Happy Wanderer Village, Hervey Bay (QLD).

convenient for budget travellers. Some useful organizations are: **Big 4**, T0300-738044 / T03-9811 9300, www.big4.com.au; **Family Parks of Australia**, T02-6021 0977, www.familyparks.com.au; and **Top Tourist Parks**, T08-8363 1901, www.toptourist.contact.com.au. Joining a park association will get you a discount in all parks that are association members.

If you intend to use motor parks, get hold of the latest editions of the tourist park guides published by the NMRA, RACV and RACQ. They are an essential resource.

Camping
Bush camping is the best way to experience the natural environment. Some national parks allow camping, mostly in designated areas only, with a few allowing limited bush camping. Facilities are usually minimal, with basic toilets, fireplaces and perhaps tank water; a few have barbecues and shower blocks. Payment is often by self-registration (around $6-15 per person) and barbecues often require $0.20, $0.50 or $1 coins, so have small notes and change ready. In many parks you will need a gas stove. If there are fireplaces you must bring your own wood as collecting wood within parks is prohibited. No fires may be lit, even stoves, during a total fire ban (see box, page 15). Even if water is supposedly available it is not guaranteed so take a supply, as well as your own toilet paper. Camping in the national parks is strictly regulated. For details of the various rules, contact the National Parks Wildlife Service (NPWS) and Queensland Parks and Wildlife Service (QPWS) or Parks Victoria. See box, page 339, for details and for park fees.

Campervans
A popular choice for many visitors is to hire or buy a vehicle that can be slept in, combining the costs of accommodation and transport (although you will still need to book into caravan parks for power and ablutions). Ranging from the popular VW Kombi to enormous vans with integral bathrooms, they can be hired from as little as $60 per day to a de luxe 4WD model for as much as $800. A van for two people at around $130 per day compares well with hiring a car and staying in hostels and allows greater freedom. High-clearance, 4WD campervans are also available and increase travel possibilities yet further. Kombis can usually be bought from about $2500. An even cheaper, though less comfortable, alternative is to buy a van or station wagon (estate car) from around $2000 that is big enough to lay out a sleeping mat and bag in.

10 great national park and island campsites

- Tidal River, Wilsons Promontory NP (VIC)
- Booderee National Park, near Jervis Bay (NSW).
- Arakoon State Recreation Area, Hat Head NP (NSW).
- Woody Head Campsite, Iluka NP (NSW).
- Green Mountains, Lamington NP (QLD).
- Lady Musgrave Island (Bundaberg, QLD).
- Masthead and North West Islands (Gladstone, QLD).
- Heron Island (Gladstone, QLD).
- Frankland Island (Cairns, QLD).
- Hinchinbrook Island (Cardwell, QLD).

Sales outlets **Apollo**, T+800 3260 5466, www.apollocarrentals.com.au; **Backpacker**, T03-8379 8893, www.backpackercampervans.com; **Britz**, T03-8379 8890, www.britz.com.au; **Getabout**, T02-9380 5536, www.getaboutoz.com; **Maui**, T03-8379 8891 (T800 2008 0801), www.maui.com.au; **Wicked**, T07-3634 9000, www.wickedcampers.com.au. The latter are proving immensely popular with the backpacker set and you will see their vivid, arty vans everywhere. However, they may not suit everybody (you'll see what we mean).

Eating

The quintessential image of Australian cooking may be of throwing some meat on the barbie but Australia actually has a dynamic and vibrant cuisine all its own. Freed from the bland English 'meat and two veg' straitjacket in the 1980s by the skills and cuisines of Chinese, Thai, Vietnamese, Italian, Greek, Lebanese and other immigrants, Australia has developed a fusion cuisine that takes elements from their cultures and mixes them into something new and original.

Asian ingredients are easily found in major cities because of the country's large Asian population. Australia makes its own dairy products so cheese or cream may come from Tasmania's King Island, Western Australia's Margaret River or the Atherton Tablelands in Far North Queensland. There is plenty of seafood, including some unfamiliar creatures such as the delicious Moreton bugs (crabs), yabbies and crayfish. Mussels, oysters and abalone are all also harvested locally. Fish is a treat too: snapper, dhufish, coral trout and red emperor or the dense, flavoursome flesh of freshwater fish such as barramundi and Murray cod. Freshness is a major feature of modern Australian cuisine, using local produce and cooking it simply to preserve the intrinsic flavour. Native animals are used, such as kangaroo, emu and crocodile, and native plants that Aboriginal people have been eating for thousands of years such as quandong, wattle seed or lemon myrtle leaf. A word of warning, however: this gourmet experience is mostly restricted to cities and large towns. There are pockets of foodie heaven in the country but these are usually associated with wine regions and are the exception rather than the rule.

Eating price codes

♀♀♀ Expensive (over $35)
♀♀ Mid-range ($25-35)
♀ Cheap ($18-24)

Prices refer to the average cost of a two-course meal for one person, excluding drinks.

Eating out

Eating habits in Australia are essentially the same as in most Western countries and are of course affected by the climate. The barbecue on the beach or in the back garden is an Aussie classic but you will find that most eating out during daylight hours takes place outdoors. Weekend brunch is hugely popular, especially in the cities, and often takes up the whole morning. Sydney and Melbourne are the undisputed gourmet capitals, where you will find the very best of modern Australian cuisine as well as everything from Mexican to Mongolian, Jamaican to Japanese. Brisbane also boasts some fine eateries. Restaurants are common even in the smallest towns, but the smaller the town the lower the quality, though not usually the price. Chinese and Thai restaurants are very common, with most other cuisines appearing only in the larger towns and cities. Corporate hotels and motels almost all have attached restaurants, as do traditional pubs, which also serve counter meals. Some may have a more imaginative menu or better quality fare than the local restaurants. Most restaurants are licensed, others BYO only, in which case you provide wine or beer and the restaurant provides glasses. Despite the corkage fee this still makes for a better deal than paying the huge mark-up on alcohol. Sadly, Australians have taken to fast food as enthusiastically as anywhere else in the world. Alongside these are food courts, found in the shopping malls of cities and larger towns. Also in the budget bracket are the delis and milk bars, serving hot takeaways together with sandwiches, cakes and snacks.

Drinks

Australian **wine** will need no introduction to most readers. Many of the best-known labels, including **Penfolds** and **Jacob's Creek**, are produced in South Australia but there are dozens of recognized wine regions right across the southern third of Australia, where the climate is favourable for grape growing and the soil sufficient to produce high-standard grapes. The industry has a creditable history in such a young country, with several wineries boasting a tradition of a century or more, but it is only in the last 25 years that Australia has become one of the major players on the international scene, due in part to its variety and quality. There are no restrictions, as there are in parts of Europe, on what grape varieties are grown where, when they are harvested and how they are blended.

Visiting a winery is an essential part of any visit to the country, and a day or two's tasting expedition is a scenic and cultural as well as an epicurean delight. Cellar doors range from modern marble and glass temples to venerable, century-old former barns of stone and wood, often boasting some of the best restaurants in the country. In New South Wales the Hunter Valley provides one of the best vineyard experiences in the world with more than a 100 wineries, world-class B&Bs and tours ranging from cycling to horse-drawn carriage.

Australians themselves drink more and more wine and less beer. The average rate of consumption is now 20 litres per person per year, compared to eight litres in 1970. Beer has dropped from an annual 135 litres per person in 1980 to 95 litres now. The price of wine, however, is unexpectedly high given the relatively low cost of food and beer. Visitors from Britain will find Australian wines hardly any cheaper at the cellar door than back home in the supermarket.

The vast majority of **beer** drunk by Australians is lager, despite often being called 'ale' or 'bitter'. The big brands such as **VB** (Victoria), **Tooheys** (NSW) and **Castlemaine XXXX** (QLD) are fairly homogenous but refreshing on a hot day. If your palate is just a touch more refined, hunt out some of the imported beers on tap that are predominantly found in the pseudo-Irish pubs in almost all the main coastal towns. Beer tends to be around 4-5% alcohol, with the popular and surprisingly pleasant-tasting 'mid' varieties about 3.5%, and 'light' beers about 2-2.5%. Drink driving laws are strict and the best bet is to not drink alcohol at all if you are driving. As well as being available on draught in pubs, beer can also be bought from bottleshops (bottle-o's) in cases (slabs) of 24-36 cans (tinnies or tubes) or bottles (stubbies) of 375 ml each. This is by far the cheapest way of buying beer (often under $4 per can or bottle).

Shopping

Most tourist merchandise seems to consist of soft toy kangaroos and koalas or brightly coloured clothing featuring the same creatures. Another typical item, which perpetuates the Australian stereotypes, is the hat strung with corks. Don't even think about it.

Corkless hats, however, are popular and practical souvenirs, particularly the distinctive Akubras, made from felt in muddy colours. Along the same lines, stockman's clothing made by **RM Williams** is also popular and very good quality. Two of the company's bestsellers are elastic-sided boots and moleskins. The Driza-bone long oilskin raincoat is another Aussie classic. Australian surfwear is sought after worldwide and is a good buy while in the country. Look for labels such as **Ripcurl**, **Quiksilver**, **Mambo** and **Billabong**.

Australia is also a good place to buy **jewellery**. Sydney in particular offers plenty of choice for precious gems such as opal, pearl and diamonds. The widest range will be available in the cities but, as in most countries, products are often cheapest at the source and a wonderful memento of a particular place.

Aboriginal designs are as ubiquitous as cuddly toys and printed on everything from T-shirts to tea towels. Some of these designs can be beautiful but be aware that many have no link to Aboriginal people and do not benefit them directly – check the label. **Desert Designs** is a successful label printing the stunning designs of the Great Sandy Desert artist Jimmy Pike on silk scarves and sarongs. It is possible to buy genuine Aboriginal arts and crafts but pieces are more commonly available in country areas close to Aboriginal communities or from Aboriginal-owned or -operated enterprises. Buying arts and crafts from reputable sources ensures that the money ends up in the artist's pocket and supports Aboriginal culture, skills and self-reliance.

Many people are keen to buy an Aboriginal **dot painting**, usually acrylic on canvas, and there are different styles, depending on the region the artist comes from. The best paintings sell for many thousands of dollars but simple works on canvas can be as little as $100. A good painting will cost at least $800-1500. Take your time and have a good look around. Visit public and private galleries where you can see work of the highest quality – you may not be able to afford it but you'll learn something of what makes a good piece of Aboriginal art. Sydney has a number of excellent commercial galleries selling Aboriginal arts and crafts, see page 125.

Essentials A-Z

Accident & emergency

Dial 000 for the emergency services. The 3 main professional emergency services are supported by several others, including the **State Emergency Service (SES)**, **Country Fire Service (CFS)**, Surf Life Saving Australia (SLSA), **Sea-search and Rescue** and **St John's Ambulance**. The SES is prominent in coordinating search and rescue operations. The CFS provides invaluable support in fighting and controlling bush fires. These services, though professionally trained, are mostly provided by volunteers.

Children

Australia is a wonderful place to take children. Far-fetched stories and rumours about poisonous snakes and insects, man-eating sharks and crocs can put parents off but they shouldn't. If children are aware and sufficiently supervised, Australia will provide a memorable holiday experience for all the right reasons.

The vast majority of establishments welcome kids and offer reasonable financial concessions. Tourist-based attractions and activities, many of which are directed at the children's market, usually offer reduced rates for children and family concessions. When it comes to eating out, some places welcome children while others don't. In general you are advised to stick to eateries that are obviously child friendly or ask before making a booking.

Customs and duty free

The limits for duty-free goods brought into the country include: 2.25 litres of alcoholic beverages for each passenger aged 18 years or over and 250 cigarettes, or 250 g of cigars

or tobacco. There are various import restrictions, many to help protect Australia's fragile ecology. These primarily involve live plants and animals, plant and animal materials (including all items made from wood) and foodstuffs. If in doubt, bring processed food only, though even this may be confiscated. Even muddy walking boots may attract attention. Declare any such items for inspection on arrival if you are unsure.

There are strict prohibitions when exiting Australia. Plant and animal life, including derivative articles and seeds, cannot be taken from the country. Australia's cultural heritage is also protected and though a dot painting or didgeridoo are fine to take home, some artworks and archaeological items are definitely not.

Almost all goods in Australia are subject to a Goods and Services Tax (GST) of 10%. Visitors from outside Australia will find certain shops can deduct the GST if you have a valid departure ticket. See www.customs.gov.au for more details.

Disabled travellers

Facilities for disabled travellers are spread quite thinly, especially outside the major cities, but high-profile sights and attractions and even parks generally have good access. **Qantas**, T1800 652660 (TTY), has considerable experience with disabled passengers and offers passengers with a nominated carer a 50% discount. The interstate railways generally have facilities for the disabled but public transport is not always well designed for disabled travel without assistance. The major car hire companies have adapted vehicles available. A good resource for travel related businesses is **Disabilities On-line**,www.disability-online.com/Travel. For more information, the following organizations are helpful: **Access**

Foundation, Suite 33, 61 Marlborough St, Surry Hills, NSW, T1300 797025, www.accessibility.com.au, provides information, resource contacts and links; National Disability Services, 33 Thesiger Ct, Deakin, ACT 2600, T02- 6283 3200, www.nds.org.au, is the industry association for disability services; and NICAN, Unit 5, 48 Brookes St, Mitchell, ACT 2911, T1800 806769, www.nican.com.au, has accommodation and service directories relating to tourism. In Sydney the free leaflet 'CBD Access Map Sydney', available from the VICs or information booths, is a very useful map and guide for the disabled. For more detailed information contact Disability Services Australia, T02-9791 6599, www.dsa.org.au.

Electricity

The current in Australia is 240/250v AC. Plugs have 2- or 3-blade pins and adaptors are widely available.

Embassies and high commissions

For a list of Australian embassies and high commissions worldwide, see www.embassy.gov.au.

Gay and lesbian travellers

The gay community in Australia is vibrant, vocal and visible. Sydney is the undoubted capital of gay and lesbian Australia, hosting in February the annual Gay and Lesbian Mardi Gras (see page 123), www.mardigras.org.au, the biggest event of its kind in the world and, incidentally, one of the biggest and most watched events in the country. Melbourne also has a very active gay and lesbian scene. Outside of the major cities, however, discrimination is not unknown and the locals may not enthusiastically receive public displays of affection. The International Gay &

Lesbian Travel Association (IGLTA), T02-9818 6669, www.iglta.org, has several members in Australia happy to help with travel and accommodation advice. There are several national magazines keeping lesbians and gays in touch with what's going on, including Lesbians on the Loose, T02-8347 1033, www.lotl.com.au, DNA www,dnamagazine.com.au, and The Sydney Star Observer, www.ssonet.com.au. Dedicated to lesbian- and gay-friendly accommodation is www.qbeds.com. See also www.gayaustralia.com. For counselling and support services contact the Gay and Lesbian Counselling Service, T1800 184527, www.glccs.org.au.

Health

Before you go
Ideally, you should see your GP or travel clinic at least 6 weeks before your departure for general advice on travel risks, malaria and vaccinations. No vaccinations are required or recommended for travel to Australia unless travelling from a yellow fever-infected country in Africa or South America. Check with your local Australian Embassy for further advice. A tetanus booster is advisable, however, if you have one due. Make sure you have travel insurance, get a dental check (especially if you are going to be away for more than a month), know your own blood group and, if you suffer a long-term condition such as diabetes or epilepsy, make sure someone knows or that you have a Medic Alert bracelet/necklace with this information on it.

A-Z of health risks
There are three main threats to health in Australia: the powerful sun, dengue fever and poisonous snakes and spiders.

For sun protection, a decent wide-brimmed hat and factor 30 suncream (cheap in Australian supermarkets) are essential. Follow the Australians with their

Keeping safe in the bush

→ The main dangers while bushwalking are dehydration, heatstroke and getting lost. Before setting out seek advice about how to access the start and finish of the track, the terrain you are planning to traverse, how long it will take given your party's minimum fitness level and the likely weather conditions – and prepare accordingly. Park rangers and the police are good sources of information.

→ Take a decent map of the area, a compass and a first-aid kit. Take full precautions for the sun, but also be prepared for wet or cold weather. Take plenty of water; in hot weather, you'll need at least one litre for every hour you plan to walk (a frozen plastic bottle will ensure cold water for hours). On long-distance walks take something to purify stream and standing water as giardia is present in some areas.

→ Wear stout walking shoes and socks. Tell someone where you are going and when you plan to get back. Plan, if possible, to walk in the early morning or late afternoon when the sun is at its least powerful. These are also the best times for viewing wildlife.

→ Learn about the various local poisonous snakes, their seasonal habits, tell-tale wound marks and symptoms and the correct procedure for treatment.

→ Avoid striding through long grass and try to keep to tracks. If the path is obscured, make plenty of noise as you walk.

→ If you do see a snake, give it a wide berth. If you need to squat to go to the toilet, or are collecting firewood, bash the undergrowth around your position.

→ If you do get bitten by either a spider or snake stay calm and still, apply pressure to the bite area and wind a compression bandage around it (except for redback bites). Remain as still as possible and keep the limb immobile. Seek urgent medical attention. A description of the creature and residual venom on the victim's skin will help with swift identification and therefore treatment. Anti-venom is available for most spider and snake bites.

Slip, Slap, Slop campaign: slip on a shirt, slap on a hat and slop on the sunscreen.

Dengue can be contracted throughout Australia. In travellers this can cause a severe flu-like illness, which includes symptoms of fever, lethargy, enlarged lymph glands and muscle pains. It starts suddenly, lasts for 2-3 days, seems to get better for 2-3 days and then kicks in again for another 2-3 days. It is usually all over in an unpleasant week. The mosquitoes that carry the dengue virus bite during the day, unlike the malaria mosquitoes, which sadly means that repellent application and covered limbs are a 24-hr issue. Check your accommodation for flower pots and shallow pools of water since these are where the dengue-carrying mosquitoes breed.

In the case of **snakes and spiders**, check loo seats, boots and the area around you if you're visiting the bush. A bite itself does not mean that anything has been injected into you. However, a commonsense approach is to clean the area of the bite (never have it sutured early on) and get someone to take you to a medical facility fast. The most common poisonous spider is the tiny, shy redback, which has a shiny black body with distinct red markings. It regularly hides under rocks or in garden sheds and garages. Outside toilets are also a favourite. Far more dangerous, though restricted to the Sydney area only, is the Sydney funnel-web, a larger and more aggressive customer, often found in outdoor loos. There are dozens of venomous snake species in Australia. Few are

Keeping safe in the water

→ When swimming in the sea, keep between the patrolled flags and beware of the rip, a strong, offshore undertow that can sweep even waders off their feet, submerge them and drown them astonishingly quickly. Always look out for signs indicating common rip areas, and ask locals if at all unsure. See the Surf Life Saving Australia website, www.slsa.asn.au, for more information.

→ While snorkelling or diving, do not touch either creatures or coral. Even minor coral scratches can lead to infections and it doesn't do the coral any good either. Wear a wetsuit or t-shirt and shorts even if the water is warm. This will lessen the effect of any sting and help protect against the sun.

→ If you are bitten or stung, get out of the water, carefully remove and keep any spine or tissue, seek advice as to appropriate immediate treatment and apply it and quickly seek medical help.

→ The biggest danger in the water is from Estuarine crocodiles (salties) in northern Queensland. Always check whether a waterhole or river is likely to be a home for a crocodile and if in doubt assume it is.

→ Beware the box jellyfish, whose highly poisonous tentacles trail several metres behind it. *Chironex fleckeri*, *Carukia barnesi* and *Malo kingi* are among the most venomous creatures in the world. They pose a significant threat between October and May. If you are stung, your blood pressure triples, CPR must be administered and an ambulance duly called to the scene. An antivenin is widely available at hospitals. Take these simple precautions: do not swim in the sea (outside the stinger nets provided at most major beaches) during the stinger season (October to May); do not swim alone during the stinger season; be aware of the effectiveness of vinegar for immediate treatment and call the emergency services as soon as possible; seek local knowledge as to the best locations to swim.

→ Other jellyfish also sting but with less effect and can swarm in certain areas in summer and at anytime depending on currents and conditions. The Portuguese Man o' War (*Physalia physalis*) is a common danger. Again the tentacles can separate from the creature's body and still sting. If stung, do not panic, find hot water (not vinegar) to bathe the wounds and take strong painkillers. If in doubt, seek advice from any surf lifesavers that are present.

actively aggressive and even those only during certain key times of year, such as mating seasons, but all are easily provoked and for many an untreated bite can be fatal (see box opposite).

Australia has reciprocal arrangements with a few countries allowing citizens of those countries to receive free emergency treatment under the **Medicare** scheme. Citizens of New Zealand and the Republic of Ireland are entitled to free care as public patients in public hospitals and to subsidized medicines under the Pharmaceutical Benefits Scheme. Visitors from Finland, Italy, Malta, the Netherlands, Sweden and the UK also enjoy subsidized out-of-hospital treatment (ie visiting a doctor). If you qualify, contact your own national health scheme to check what documents you will require in Australia to claim **Medicare**. All visitors are, however, strongly advised to take out medical insurance for the duration of their visit.

For safety tips in the water, see box above.

Insurance

It is essential to take out some form of travel insurance, wherever you're travelling from. This should cover you for theft or loss of possessions and money, the cost of medical and dental treatment, cancellation of flights, delays in travel arrangements, accidents, missed departures, lost baggage, lost passport, and personal liability and legal expenses. Also check on inclusion of 'dangerous activities' such as climbing, diving, skiing, horse riding, even trekking, if you plan on doing any. Always read the small print carefully. Not all policies cover ambulance, helicopter rescue or emergency flights home. Find out if your policy pays medical expenses direct to the hospital or doctor, or if you have to pay and then claim the money back later. If the latter applies, make sure you keep all records. If you have something stolen, get a copy of the police report – you will need this to substantiate your claim. There are a variety of policies to choose from, so it's best to shop around. Your travel agent can advise on the best deals.

Internet

Landline internet access, and thus email, is widely available in hostels, hotels and cafés. Expect to pay about $4-8 for 30 mins.

Wireless access is widely available and improving rapidly, but do not expect to have strong connections and fast speeds outside the main centres. Thoroughly check the coverage of your service provider and do not believe all they say about speed. As a rule of thumb many suggest you should halve that quoted in the sales pitch, at least.

State governments are keen for their citizens to have access to the internet and some have set up schemes to allow cheap or even free access. Based either in libraries or dedicated centres, they are usually also accessible to visitors.

Media

The Australian (www.theaustralian.com.au) is the only national paper and has the biggest readership of them all (453,000). It is generally popular, politically middle-of-the-road and publishes a good glossy magazine with the weekend edition. *Sydney Morning Herald* (www.smh.com.au) is considered by many to be the unofficial national tabloid voice. *Courier Mail* (www.couriermail.com.au) is the main newspaper in Brisbane and southern Queensland. *The Age* (www.theage.com.au) and *Herald Sun* (www.heraldsun.com.au) are the main newspapers in Melbourne and Victoria.

Foreign newspapers and magazines are widely available in the main urban centres. It is also possible to buy special weekly editions of British papers such as *The Guardian*. There are Asian editions of *Time* and *The Economist*.

There are 5 main television channels in New South Wales and Queensland: the publicly funded *ABC* and *SBS*, and the independent, commercial stations, *Channel 7*, *Channel 9* and *Channel 10*. *ABC* aims for Australian high-quality content including many BBC programmes. *SBS* focuses on multinational culture, current affairs, sport and film. It has the best world news, shown daily at 1830.

Money

All dollars quoted in this guide are Australian unless specified otherwise. The Australian dollar ($) is divided into 100 cents (c). Coins come in denominations of 5c, 10c, 20c, 50c, $1 and $2. Banknotes come in denominations of $5, $10, $20, $50 and $100. The Australian dollar is currently at a record high – almost a dollar for a dollar US and, sadly for Britons, at a 25-year high against the pound. **Exchange rates** as of June 2010 were as follows: US$1 = A$1.18; £1 = A$1.73; €1 = A$1.43.

Banks, ATMs, credit and cash cards

The four major banks, the **ANZ**, **Challenge/Westpac**, **Commonwealth** and **NAB (National Australia Bank)** are usually the best places to change money and traveller's cheques, though bureaux de change tend to have slightly longer opening hours and often open at weekends. You can withdraw cash from ATMs with a cash card or credit card issued by most international banks and they can also be used at banks, post offices and bureaux de change. Most hotels, shops, tourist operators and restaurants in Australia accept the major credit cards, though some places may charge for using them. When booking always check if an operator accepts them. EFTPOS (the equivalent of Switch in the UK) is a way of paying for goods and services with a cash card. Unfortunately EFTPOS only works with cards linked directly to an Australian bank account. Bank opening hours are Mon-Fri, from around 0930 to 1630.

Traveller's cheques

The safest way to carry money is in traveller's cheques, though they are fast becoming superseded by the prevalence of credit cards and ATMs. **American Express**, **Thomas Cook** and **Visa** are the cheques most commonly accepted. Remember to keep a record of the cheque numbers and the cheques you've cashed separate from the cheques themselves. Traveller's cheques are accepted for exchange in banks, large hotels, post offices and large gift shops. Some insist that at least a portion of the amount be in exchange for goods or services. Commission when cashing traveller's cheques is usually 1% or a flat rate. Avoid changing money or cheques in hotels as rates are often poor.

Money transfers

If you need money urgently, the quickest way to have it sent is to have it wired to the nearest bank via **Western Union**, T1800 337377, www.travelex.com.au. Charges apply but on a sliding scale. Money can also be wired by **Amex** or **Thomas Cook**, though this may take a day or two, or transferred direct from bank to bank, but this again can take several days. Within Australia use money orders to send money. See www.auspost.com.au.

Cost of travelling

By European, North American and Japanese standards Australia is an inexpensive place to visit. Accommodation, particularly outside the main centres, is good value, though prices can rise uncomfortably in peak seasons. Transport varies considerably in price and can be a major factor in your travelling budget. Eating out can be indecently cheap. There are some restaurants in Sydney comparable with the world's best where $175 is enough to cover dinner for 2 people. The bill at many excellent establishments can be half that. Australian beer is about $4-8 and imported about $6-8 in most pubs and bars, as is a neat spirit or glass of wine. Wine will generally be around 1½ times to double the price in restaurants than it would be from a bottleshop. The minimum budget required, if staying in hostels or campsites, cooking for yourself, not drinking much and travelling relatively slowly, is about $80 per person per day, but this isn't going to be a lot of fun. Going on the odd tour, travelling faster and eating out occasionally will raise this to a more realistic $100-130. Those staying in modest B&Bs, hotels and motels as couples, eating out most nights and taking a few tours will need to reckon on about $220 per person per day. Costs in the major cities will be 20-50% higher. Non-hostelling single travellers should budget on spending around 60-70% of what a couple would spend.

Opening hours

Generally Mon-Fri 0830-1700. Many convenience stores and supermarkets are open daily. Late night shopping is generally either Thu or Fri. For banks, see above.

Post

Most post offices are open Mon-Fri 0900-1700, and Sat 0900-1230. Airmail for postcards and greetings cards is $1.40 anywhere in the world, small letters (under 50 g) are $1.45 to southeast Asia and the Pacific, $2.10 beyond. Parcels can be sent either by sea, economy air or air. Most of the principal or main offices in regional centres or cities offer poste restante for those peripatetic souls with no fixed address, open Mon-Fri 0900-1700. For more information contact **Australia Post** on T131318, www.auspost.com.au.

Public holidays

New Years Day; **Australia Day** (26 Jan 2011); **Good Friday** (22 April 2011); **Easter Monday** (25 April 2011); **Anzac Day** (25 Apr 2011); **Queen's Birthday** (13 Jun 2011); **Labour Day** (3 Oct 2011 in NSW, 2 May 2011 in QLD); **Christmas Day** (25 Dec); **Boxing (Proclamation) Day** (26 Dec).

Safety

Australia certainly has its dangers, but with a little common sense and basic precautions they are relatively easy to minimize. The most basic but important are the effects of the **sun**, see Health, page 35. In **urban areas**, as in almost any city in the world, there is always the possibility of muggings, alcohol-induced harassment or worse. The usual simple precautions apply, like keeping a careful eye and hand on belongings, not venturing out alone at night and avoiding dark, lonely areas. For information on road safety see page 26, or contact one of the AAA associations, see page 26.

Smoking

This is not permitted in restaurants, cafés or pubs where eating is a primary activity, or on any public transport.

Student travellers

There are various official youth/student ID cards available, including the widely recognized **International Student ID Card (ISIC)**, www.isic.org/www.isiccard.com. This conveys benefits from simply getting discounts to emergency medical coverage and 24-hr hotlines. Student travel agencies and hostelling organizations issue the cards. Backpackers will find a YHA or VIP membership card just as useful. Students are also eligible for discounts on many forms of transport and most tourist sites and tours.

Taxes

Most goods are subject to a **Goods and Services Tax** (GST) of 10%. Some shops can deduct the GST if you have a valid departure ticket. GST on goods over $300 purchased (per store) within 30 days before you leave are refundable on presentation of receipts and purchases at the GST refund booth at Sydney International Airport (boarding pass and passport are also required). For more information, T1300 363263.

Telephone

Most public payphones are operated by nationally owned **Telstra**, www.telstra.com. au. Some take phonecards, available from newsagents and post offices, and credit cards. A payphone call within Australia requires $0.40 or $0.50. If you are calling locally (within approximately 50 km) this lasts indefinitely but only a few seconds , outside the local area. Well worth considering if you are in Australia for any length of time is a pre-paid mobile phone. Telstra and **Vodafone** give the best coverage and their phones are widely available from as little as $150, including some call time. There are also some smaller companies like '3' and **Optus** offering attractive deals. By far the cheapest way of calling overseas is to use an international pre-paid phone card (though they cannot be used from a mobile phone, or some of the blue and orange public phones). Available from city post offices and newsagents, every call made with them may initially cost about $1 (a local call plus connection) but subsequent per-minute costs are a fraction of Telstra or mobile phone charges.

There are no area phone codes. Use a state code if calling outside the state you are in. These are: 02 for ACT/ NSW (08 for Broken Hill), 03 for VIC and 07 for QLD. To call Eastern Australia from overseas, dial the international prefix followed by 61, then the state phone code minus the first 0, then the 8-digit number. To call overseas from Australia dial 0011 followed by the country code. Country codes include: Republic of Ireland 353; New Zealand 64; South Africa 27; the USA and Canada 1; the UK 44. Directory enquiries: 1223. International directory enquiries: 1225.

Telephones numbers starting with 1300 or 1800 are toll free within Australia. Where 2 telephone numbers are listed in this guide, this toll-free number appears in brackets.

Time

Australia covers 3 time zones: Queensland and New South Wales are in Eastern Standard GMT+10 hrs. NSW and Victoria operate daylight saving, which means that clocks go forward 1 hr from Oct and Mar.

Tipping

Tipping is not the norm in Australia, but a discretionary 5-10% tip for particularly good service will be appreciated.

Tour operators

There are a host of companies offering general or special interest tours. Most are district, state or multi-centre based. See individual town and city sections for details. There are several companies offering 1- to 10-day trips along parts of the coast and many others venturing inland from the main centres. Most involve coach travel or some degree of 4WD manoeuvring and adventure activities.

In UK and Ireland

Australia Travel Centre, 43-45 Middle Abbey St, Dublin, Ireland, T01-804 7100, australi@ abbeytravel.ie. Good source of advice for those travelling from Ireland.
Contiki Wells House, 15 Elmfield Rd, Bromley, Kent BR1 1LS, T0845-075 0990, www.contiki.com. One of the world's largest travel companies catering primarily for the 18-35s market, with affordable options.
Travelbag, T0871-703 4698, www.travel bag.co.uk. Reputable UK-based firm offering a good range of general and tailor-made trips to Eastern Australia at reasonable prices.
Wildlife Worldwide , T0845-130 6982, www.wildlifeworldwide.com. One of the best wildlife-oriented global operators offering tailor-made, mainly small group trips to Australia including Queensland's Lamington National Park and the Great Barrier Reef.

In North America

Abercrombie and Kent, 1520 Kensington Rd, Suite 212, Oak Brook, Illinois, 60523-2156, T800-554 7016, www.abercrombiekent.com. Well-established US company offering a diverse range of luxury, locally guided global trips to Australia.

Earthwatch Research and Exploration, PO Box 75, Maynard, MA, 01754, T978-461 0081 (Melbourne T61-3968 26828), www.earthwatch.org. Excellent ecotourism trips to Eastern Australia in combination with conservation research on Australian wildlife. Offices in USA, UK and Australia.

Wilderness Travel, 1102 Ninth St, Berkeley, CA, 94710, T1800 368 2794, www.wilderness travel.com. 10 or 12-day cultural, wildlife and hiking trips to Australia from US$5000.

Tourist information

Tourist offices, or Visitor Information Centres (VICs), can be found in all but the smallest Australian towns. Generally speaking you are advised to stick with accredited VICs for the best, non-biased advice. Their locations, phone numbers, website or email addresses and opening hours are listed in the relevant sections of this guide. In larger towns they have met certain criteria to be officially accredited. This usually means that they have some paid staff and should be open daily 0900-1700. Smaller offices may close at weekends. All offices will provide information on accommodation, local sights and tours. Many will also have information on eating out, local history and the environment, and will sell souvenirs, guides and maps. Most provide a free town map. Some in high-density tourist destinations like Airlie Beach and Cairns in Queensland also double as privately run booking agencies, but may simply promote those that pay them a booking commission.

The Australian Tourism Commission website, www.australia.com, is a good place to start, but almost all regions have excellent, informative websites and these are listed in the relevant areas in the text.

Both the national and regional tourist boards and VICs are generally good at replying to specific enquiries, especially by email, and are usually willing to send heaps of useful information by snail mail.

Visas and immigration

Visas are subject to change, so check with your local Australian Embassy or High Commission. For a list of these, see www.embassy.gov.au. All travellers to Australia, except New Zealand citizens, must have a valid visa to enter Australia. These must be arranged prior to travel (allow 2 months) and cannot be organized at Australian airports. Tourist visas are free and are available from your local Australian Embassy or High Commission, or in some countries, in electronic format (an Electronic Travel Authority or ETA) from their websites and from selected travel agents and airlines. Passport holders eligible to apply for an ETA include those from Austria, Belgium, Canada, Denmark, France, Germany, the Irish Republic, Italy, Japan, Netherlands, Norway, Spain, Sweden, Switzerland, the UK and the USA. Tourist visas allow visits of up to 3 months within the year after the visa is issued. Multiple-entry 6-month tourist visas are also available to visitors from certain countries. Application forms can be downloaded from the embassy website or from www.immi.gov.au. Tourist visas do not allow the holder to work in Australia. See also www.immi.gov.au/visitors.

Weights and measures

The metric system is universally used.

Contents

Footprint features

Melbourne & Southeast Australia

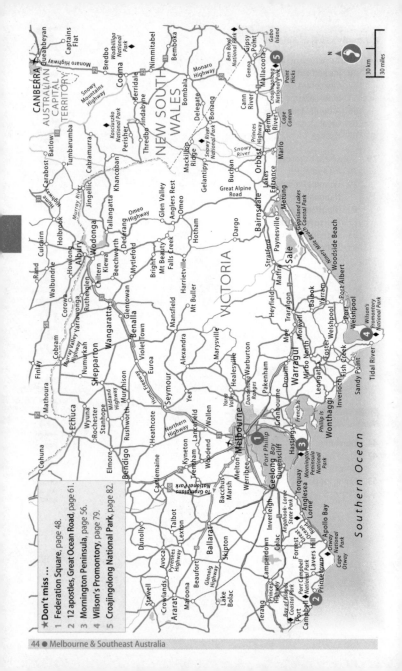

Don't miss ...

★ Federation Square, page 48.
1 12 apostles, Great Ocean Road, page 61.
2 Mornington Peninsula, page 56.
3 Wilson's Promontory, page 79.
4 Croajingolong National Park, page 82.

Victoria is Australia's smallest and most populous mainland state. By Australian standards, you could almost say it is crowded. Despite its size, however, it is incredibly diverse: mountains, deserts, rainforest, beaches and plains make up the landscape. The state also has a rich historical heritage, multicultural people and a large sophisticated city.

The state revolves around Melbourne, a city that combines the gracious character of its Victorian past with style, innovation and energy. Not only is Melbourne pretty to look at, with its beautiful parks and gardens and its serpentine Yarra River, but it is the most cosmopolitan of all Australian cities, with a huge cultural mix.

Within just an hour or two of Australia's second largest city, you can swim with dolphins or try local wines in the Yarra Valley. To the west are the popular coastal towns of the Great Ocean Road. Inland is one of the state's best national parks, the magnificent Grampians, where craggy sandstone rockfaces tower above swathes of forest. Towards the coast the foothills run down to the moist green fields of Gippsland and come to an end in the perfect sandy coves of Wilson's Promontory and the series of tranquil lakes, lagoons and inlets further east.

Melbourne and around → Colour map 1, B2/3

Melbourne has always been impressive, right from its earliest days when it was the largest, wealthiest and most refined city in the country. This former wealth, reflected in the ornate 19th-century architecture and spacious public gardens, has also bred an innate confidence and serious sophistication that gets right up the noses of Sydneysiders. By the same token, Melbournians see their New South Wales cousins as insufferably brash and hedonistic.

The Victorian capital is the most European of Australia's cities. Its theatres, bookshops and galleries all vibrate with the chatter of cosmopolitan urbanites, and its famously damp, grey weather lends the city an air of introspection lacking in other state capitals. Melbourne is also known as the events capital of Australia, with such high-profile annual extravaganzas as the Melbourne Cup (Spring Carnival) and Grand Prix, together with recent major showcases like the Commonwealth Games in 2006, all raising the international profile of the city – and sending Sydney quietly green with envy. ▶▶ *For listings, see pages 62-78.*

Ins and outs

Getting there

Melbourne's **Tullamarine airport** ① *20 km northwest of the city, www.melair.com.au*, has both domestic and international flights. Terminal facilities include car hire, bank ATMs, currency exchange and a **Travellers' Information Desk** ① *T9297 1805, open almost 24 hrs*, which provides accommodation and tour bookings as well as general information. From the airport, the **Skybus** ① *T9335 2811, www.skybus.com.au*, runs every 10 or 15 minutes 0355-2355 and half hourly or hourly 0025-0325 between the International terminal and the Spencer Street Coach Station (one way $16, return $26) in the city centre, also stopping near the YHAs in Abbotsford Street, North Melbourne and Courtney Street, Carlton. Tickets can be bought on board or from the information desk. A taxi between the airport and the city costs around $50.

The Bus Transit Centre, Franklin Street, is the terminal and ticket office for interstate operators **Greyhound** ① *T1300 473946, www.greyhound.com.au*. The Southern Cross Coach Station is the terminus for all services operated by **V-Line** ① *T136196, www.vline.com.au* and by **Firefly Express Coaches** ① *T1300 730740, www.fireflyexpress.com.au*, from Adelaide and Sydney.

Flinders Street Station is the main terminus for metropolitan **Metro** services, but is also the station for V-Line Gippsland services. Southern Cross Station is the main terminus for all other state **V-Line** services. All interstate trains, *The Overland*, *Ghan* (via Adelaide) and *XPT*, also operate from Southern Cross. For information on New South Wales (NSW) services refer to Great Southern Rail, www. gsr.com.au, and Cityrail, www.cityrail.com.au; for Queensland (QLD) refer to Queensland Rail, www.qr.com.au.

Getting around

All metropolitan services are operated by the Met and if intending to use public transport it's a good idea to head for the **Met Shop** ① *ground floor, Melbourne Town Hall, 103 Swanston St, Mon-Fri 0900-1700 Sat 0900-1300*. The shop has useful maps of tram, bus and train routes and timetables. For all train, bus and tram information, T131638 or refer to www.metlinkmelbourne.com.au and www.viclink.com.au.

Currently the ticketing system surrounding the Melbourne public transport system and trams, trams and buses combined has, to put it diplomatically, 'major issues'. Ask your

State phone codes and time difference

There are no area phone codes. Use a state code if calling outside the state you are in. These are: 02 for ACT/NSW (08 for Broken Hill), 03 for VIC and 07 for QLD. Note that NSW operates daylight saving, which means that clocks go forward one hour from October and March.

average Melbournian commuter about it an they will laugh and shake their heads. Traditionally a single Metcard fare system covered trains, trams and buses. Three zones covered greater Melbourne, but you would rarely need anything other than a Zone 1 ticket as this covered everything within about 10 km of the city centre. The city operated a system of saver cards. Most services operated every day, from early morning to around midnight.

This system was set to change with the introduction of the new and reputedly state-of-the-art 'Myki' ticketing system in 2010. But its development and introduction was nothing short of disastrous and has been plagued with technical and financial problems. So the best current travelling advice is to consult the Visitor Information Centre or Metshop as soon as you can upon arrival for the latest details. See Transport, page 76.

Tourist information

Melbourne Visitors' Centre ⓘ *Federation Sq, corner of Flinders St and St Kilda Rd, T03-9658 9658, www.visitmelbourne.com.au, 0900-1800*, offers information, brochures and bookings for Melbourne and the rest of the state. Also event ticketing, multilingual information and an ATM. The VIC runs one of the world's few **Greeter and Ambassador Services** ⓘ *T9658 9658, www.thatsmelbourne.com.au/greeter*, where local volunteer 'Ambassadors' (in distinctive red attire) are staked around the city centre to offer advice, while 'Greeters' take visitors on a free sightseeing walk of the city centre. Greeters and visitors are matched by interests and language (over 30 languages spoken). There are also information booths in the Bourke Street Mall and Flinders Street Station. Melbourne has a useful telephone interpreting service, offering assistance in communication in over 100 languages, T131450 (24 hours).

City centre → *For listings, see pages 62-78.*

Melbourne has some of the best museums, galleries, gardens and architecture in the country and recent developments will ensure that the city continues to possess the most impressive spread of cultural and sporting facilities in Australia. The main tourism and urban development areas within and on the fringes of the Central Business District (CBD) are Federation Square, Southbank and Docklands. Fed Square (as it is dubbed) is the most obvious and the most celebrated. Considered a city icon, it encompasses an entire city block next to the Yarra River and Flinders Street Station. The central plaza contains space for 10,000 people, and the square buzzes with restaurants, galleries and shops. In addition, the National Gallery of Victoria on the ground floor (which is one of two major venues) highlights the importance of arts to this city. Clearly in view beyond Fed Square is the Melbourne Cricket Ground, which is another great city icon. Often referred to as the 'G', it is Australia's most famous sporting venue. There is a well-developed walkway between the cricket ground and Fed square that has seen many a colourful procession over the years of both the victorious and the defeated.

Federation Square and the National Gallery of Victoria

Whether by design or location, or indeed both, Federation Square has become the main focus for visitors to Melbourne, and no matter what your movements around the city centre it always seems to draw you back. Initiated as an international architectural design competition in 1996, and finally opened in October 2002 at the mind-boggling cost of $450 million, it

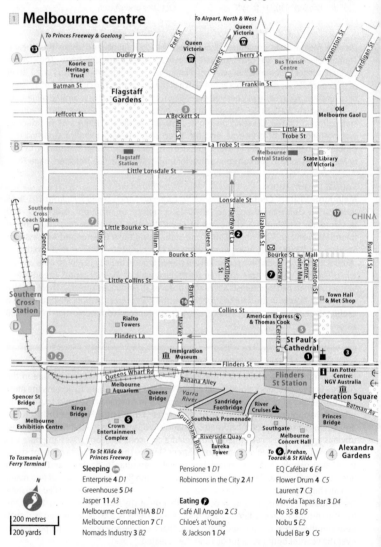

Melbourne centre

Sleeping 🛏

Enterprise 4 *D1*
Greenhouse 5 *D4*
Jasper 11 *A3*
Melbourne Central YHA 8 *D1*
Melbourne Connection 7 *C1*
Nomads Industry 3 *B2*

Pensione 1 *D1*
Robinsons in the City 2 *A1*

Eating 🍴

Café All Angolo 2 *C3*
Chloe's at Young
& Jackson 1 *D4*

EQ Cafébar 6 *E4*
Flower Drum 4 *C5*
Laurent 7 *C3*
Movida Tapas Bar 3 *D4*
No 35 8 *D5*
Nobu 5 *E2*
Nudel Bar 9 *C5*

remains one of the most ambitious construction projects undertaken in Australia. Covering an entire block, the ultra-modern city square is an intriguing combination of angular plates, steel girders and plate glass, all cleverly housing restaurants, cafés, performance spaces, the main VIC and the supremely well-endowed **Ian Potter Centre: NGV Australia** ⓘ *T8620 2222, www.ngv.vic.gov.au, daily 1000-1700, free except for special exhibitions*, which is one of two sites of the National Gallery of Victoria. This site houses the largest collection of Australian art in the world. Across the river, at 180 St Kilda Road, is the revamped **NGV International** (same details as NGV Australia), where the international collections are displayed. Especially impressive is the 19th-century European section, purchased during Melbourne's boom period.

Immigration Museum
ⓘ *Old Customs House, 400 Flinders St, T131102 or T9927 2700, www.immigration. museum.vic.gov.au, 1000-1700. $8, children and concessions free.*

A few blocks west of Fed Square is the late 19th-century former Customs House, which seems an appropriate spot for an immigration museum due to the relationship between this part of the river-bank and the city's earliest immigrants. Melbourne's culture has been heavily influenced by immigration, but this museum focuses on how the experience affected the migrants. Personal stories are told using photographs, recordings and letters, and there is even a mock ship to illustrate voyage conditions. Regular travelling exhibitions also explore the history and culture of migrants. Should you start suffering from information overload then you can always migrate to the onsite café.

Eureka Tower Skydeck
ⓘ *Riverside Quay, Southbank, T9693 8888, www.eurekalookout.com.au, daily 1000-2200, $16.50, children $9 (The Edge Experience an additional $12, children $8).*
Until mid-2006 Melbourne's tallest building was the 253-m Rialto Towers on Collins Street, but now, almost in its shadow and across the river, the Eureka

Melbourne maps
1 Melbourne centre
2 Melbourne inner suburbs, page 54
3 Around Melbourne, page 58

Rockpool Bar &
Grill 5 *E2*
Rosati 11 *D5*
Spencer 13 *A1*
Victoria Arts Centre 6 *B4*

Bars & clubs 🍸
Bridie O'Reilly's 14 *C5*
Hairy Canary 15 *C4*
Mitre 16 *D2*
Section 8 17 *C4*

City Circle Tram

Tower has surpassed it by 47 m. There is an impressive observation deck on the 88th floor. But it doesn't end there. Attached to the tower is 'The Edge', in essence, a see-through glass box that extends 3 m from the building's façade. Additional unique and impressive touches include walls that start opaque then gradually clear and soothing music that turns to the sound of grinding metal and breaking glass. There are also great views from the **Sofitel Hotel**, which takes up floors 35 to 50. The rooms are suitably impressive and there is also an excellent, if expensive, café and restaurant up on the 35th. If the budget doesn't allow for a sky-high meal then catch the lift up anyway for a brief glimpse, and make sure you pop to the toilet when you do.

Melbourne Aquarium

ⓘ *Yarra riverbank, T9620 0999, www.melbourneaquarium.com.au, open 0930-1800, $32, children $18.50, concessions $21.*

The Aquarium features the creatures of the Southern Ocean and offers the chance to get as close to these as most people would wish. Via a glass tunnel, visitors step into the Oceanarium, a large circular room with thick perspex walls. Sharks, stingrays, turtles and fish swim around and above you, so close that you can count the rows of teeth in the mouth of a 3-m-long shark. Several times a day divers get into the tank and feed the fish, and visitors can do the same (the sharks are kept well fed so they don't eat their tank mates). It is pricey, however: certified divers pay $150 and non-divers (who must complete a two-day resort dive course) $349. The Aquarium also has a simulated rollercoaster ride, café and shop.

Melbourne Museum and the Royal Exhibition Building

ⓘ *Carlton Gardens, 11 Nicholson St, T131102, www.melbourne.museum.vic.gov.au, 1000-1700, $8, children and concessions free.*

Due north of Fed Square is the vast and striking Melbourne Museum. Opened in 2000, it uses the most advanced display techniques to make the museum lively and interesting. Major exhibitions come and go, with some permanent features. The **Bunjilaka Aboriginal Centre** looks at the history of Aboriginal people since white invasion and the politics of displaying their possessions and artefacts. **Koorie Voices**, a photo gallery of Victorian Aboriginal people, is also fascinating for its contemporary recording of individual life stories. The **Mind and Body Gallery** examines humans in exhaustive detail, perhaps more than is palatable for the squeamish. Other highlights include the **Australia Gallery**, with its focus on the social history of Melbourne and Victoria, **Bugs Alive**, with its colourful inventory of live insects and spiders, and the **Children's Gallery**, where the little darlings can check out their weight and height in 'wombats'. The museum also has an excellent shop and lots of eating choices.

Facing the Melbourne Museum, and in striking architectural contrast, is the Royal Exhibition Building, a Victorian confection built for the International Exhibition of 1880. At the time it was Australia's largest building and grand enough to be used for the opening of the first Federal Parliament. The Victorian Parliament sat here for 26 years until it was able to move back into the Victorian Parliament House (see below). The building is still used as an exhibition centre, and the museum occasionally runs tours.

Old Melbourne Gaol

ⓘ *Russell St, T9663 7228, www.nattrust.com.au, 0930-1700, $21, children $11, concessions $16.*

Near Carlton Gardens is Melbourne Gaol, built in the 1850s when Victoria was in the grip of a gold rush. Like Tasmania's Port Arthur, the design was based on the Model Prison at

Pentonville in London, a system of correction that was based on isolation and silence. The three levels of cells now contain stories and death masks of female prisoners, hangmen and some of the 135 people hanged here. Visitors can also see the scaffold on which bushranger Ned Kelly was hanged in 1880, as well as his death mask and a set of Kelly Gang armour. The gaol comes alive on night tours when a tour guide acts as a prisoner from 1901 to explain the history of the gaol.

State Library of Victoria

ⓘ *328 Swanston St, corner of La Trobe St, T8664 7000, www.slv.vic.gov.au, Mon-Thu 1000-2100, Fri-Sun 1000-1800.*

Designed by Joseph Reed, who also designed the Town Hall and Exhibition Building, the doors behind the grand classical portico opened in 1856 with 3800 books chosen by the philanthropist Sir Redmond Barry. In 1913 a domed reading room was added, modelled on London's British Library and the Library of Congress in Washington. The library exhibits some of the treasures in its collection, such as Audubon's *Birds of America* (the library's most valuable book) and Ned Kelly's armour. The grassy forecourt is a popular meeting place and also serves as a sculpture garden.

Koorie Heritage Trust

ⓘ *295 King St, T8622 2600, www.koorieheritagetrust.com, daily 1000-1600, donation.*

On the northwestern fringes of the CBD is the Koorie Heritage Trust. 'Koorie' is the collective name given to the Aboriginal people of southeastern Australia. The trust preserves and celebrates the 60,000 year-old history and culture of the Koorie people of Victoria from their own viewpoint. The centre has some hard-hitting history displays on the shocking results of the arrival of Europeans in 1835. There are also exhibitions of contemporary art and crafts by local Koorie people, an extensive reference library and a small shop selling some original and reproduction art.

Parliament House

ⓘ *Spring St, T9651 8568, www.parliament.vic.gov.au, tours Mon-Fri when Parliament is not sitting, 40 mins, free. Call for sitting details.*

Due south of Carlton Gardens stands the extravagant colonnaded Parliament House, at the head of a group of government buildings and the manicured parkland of the Fitzroy and Treasury Gardens (see below). It was built at the height of the gold rush in 1856 and this is reflected in its grandeur and interiors lavished with gold. Victoria's Parliament House was also the first home of the Australian Parliament after Federation in 1901. When parliament is sitting visitors can watch from the public gallery.

Fitzroy and Treasury Gardens

Some Melbournians consider these gardens the best in the city for their small scale, symmetry and avenues of European elm trees. Nearby you can find **Cook's Cottage** ⓘ *T9414 4677, 0900-1700, $5, children $2.50, concessions $3*, a tiny stone house that used to belong to Captain James Cook's family and was transported from England in 1934 to commemorate the centenary of the State of Victoria. After sunset many possums come out of the trees in Treasury Gardens and are often fed by visitors.

Melbourne Cricket Ground and the National Sports Museum
① Jolimont St, T9657 8879, www.mcg.org.au, 0930-1630 (tours run from 1000-1500 on days without events), $15, children and concessions $11.

For some sports fans the 'G' – as the ground is universally known – approaches the status of a temple. Built in 1853, the ground became the home of the Melbourne Cricket Club and has hosted countless historic cricket matches and Aussie Rules (Australian football) games as well as the 1956 Olympics, rock concerts and lectures. Tours of the MCG are one of Melbourne's most popular attractions and include walking into a players' changing room, stepping on to the 'hallowed turf' and visiting the members' swanky Long Room. The tour also includes entry to the National Sports Museum (Gate 3, $15, children $8) a conglomerate of the Australian Gallery of Sport, Olympic Museum, Australian Cricket Hall of Fame and exhibitions on Aussie Rules and extreme sports. Interesting highlights include Don Bradman's cricket bat, Ian Thorpe's swimming costume, Cathy Freeman's running outfit, Olympic medals and memorabilia and the original handwritten rules, drafted in 1859, of the Aussie Rules game.

Southbank
Melbourne's Southbank is the heart of the cultural and entertainment precinct. At the western end the vast, shiny **Crown Entertainment Complex** – more commonly known just as 'the casino' – includes an enormous casino, hotel, cinema, over 35 restaurants, around 20 bars and nightclubs, and boutiques. To the west, beyond the Spencer Street Bridge, is the **Melbourne Exhibition Centre**, and the new precinct redevelopment surrounding it. On the river alongside the precinct is the *Polly Woodside*, an 1885 Belfast-built iron barque, which until recent years served as the main feature of the former Melbourne Maritime Museum.

At the eastern end of Southbank, by Princes Bridge, is the **Victorian Arts Centre** *① T9281 8000, www.theartscentre.net.au, Mon-Fri 0700-late, Sat 0900-late, Sun 1000-last show*, comprising the circular Concert Hall and the Theatres Building crowned by a steel net and spire. The arts centre also has free galleries, a café, quality arts shop and the city's best art and craft market, held on Sundays. It is possible to tour the complex. One of the most pleasant ways to see Southbank and the impressive border of the CBD is from the river. Many operators offer river cruises in front of Southgate; the cruises depart regularly and generally last about an hour, costing about $25.

Botanic Gardens
① Birdwood Av, South Yarra, T9252 2300, www.rbg.vic.gov.au, Apr-Oct daily 0730-1800; Nov-Mar 0730-2030, free. Visitors' Centre Mon-Sat 0900-1700, Sat-Sun 0930-1700.

The gardens are a large oasis just to the south of the CBD. Bordered by busy roads with the city's skyscrapers looming above, it's not easy to forget that you're in a city, but the emerald lawns, ornamental lakes and wide curving paths provide a soothing respite from crowds and concrete. The main entrance is at Observatory Gate, where there's a visitors' centre and the **Observatory Café**. A quieter and more upmarket tearoom, **The Terrace**, is by the lake. Check the Visitors' Centre for daily events, details on all the gardens' main features and in summer the outdoor theatre and cinema shows. There are several themed and specialist walking tours on offer. Consult the centre or visit the website for the latest details.

Going for gold

Melbourne boomed during the gold rushes of the 1850s. The population exploded and the money fuelled unbelievably fast growth. By 1861 the town had founded a university, built splendid municipal buildings including a public library and museum of art, and installed street lighting, clean water and gas supplies. It couldn't last though, and at the turn of the decade banks collapsed like cards, construction ground to a halt and unemployment soared. Nearly a quarter of all Melbournians were forced to leave the city between 1891 and 1900.

The resurgence came in 1956 when the city hosted the Olympic Games, the task that finally caused it to emerge from over half a century of relative inactivity. The next couple of decades were ones of consolidation rather than flair, while by contrast its northern rival was building its famous opera house. In the 1980s Melbourne realized it was rich once more, in both finances and its diverse multicultural bedrock. The vibrant culture of today began to take shape and the city experienced ambition not seen for a century.

As well as attaining the title of Australia's cultural capital, aggressive state governments set out to cement its reputation as the country's sporting centre, despite Sydney landing the 2000 Olympics. With the 2006 Commonwealth Games under its belt it has not only become the nation's sporting capital but is considered by many as the sports events capital of the world, period.

Sydney and Melbourne have been notoriously competitive for decades. The simple fact is that they are quite different. Sydney wins with aesthetics and Melbourne with character. Another emerging fact is that Melbourne is set to overtake Sydney in size in the coming years and as such may one day be considered the country's 'main centre', though most Sydneysiders would scoff at the very concept.

Inner suburbs → For listings, see pages 62-78.

The city centre has traditionally been thought of by visitors as the area enclosed by the circle tram, but it is far better to think of Melbourne city as a collection of inner city villages. Just to the north are Carlton, Fitzroy and Collingwood. Their proximity to the city meant that these were among the first areas to be developed as it expanded rapidly during the gold rush. **Carlton** is best known for being an area where Italian immigrants settled. It's now a middle-class area where yuppies enjoy the Italian food and cafés of Lygon Street. The neighbouring **Fitzroy** also has some fine boom-time domestic architecture but had become a slum by the 1930s. Cheap rents attracted immigrants, students and artists and the area gradually gained a reputation for bohemianism. Brunswick Street is still lively and alternative although increasingly gentrified. The alternative set now claim Smith Street in **Collingwood**, just a few blocks to the east, as their own. Johnston Street, crossing Brunswick, is the centre of Melbourne's Spanish community. These areas are the liveliest of the Melbourne villages and have some of the city's best cheap eating, edgy shopping, colourful street art and raw live music venues.

Just to the west of the CBD is a vast area known as **Docklands**, as big as the CBD itself. This was the city's major port until the 1960s when containers began to be used in world shipping and vast holding sheds were no longer needed. The area has undergone some

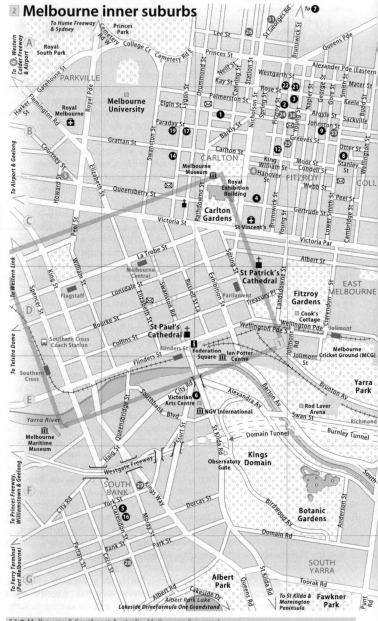

Melbourne inner suburbs

To Hume Freeway & Sydney

To Western Calder Freeway & Airport

To 6

To 7

Princes Park

Royal South Park

PARKVILLE

Cemetery Rd W

College Ct

Cemetery Rd E

Lee St

St Georges Rd

Brunswick St

Queens Pde

Gatehouse St

Royal Pde

Royal Melbourne

Harker St

Flemington Rd

Royal Melbourne

Princes St

Neill St

Kay St

Canning St

Station St

Westgarth St

Rose St

22 21

Alexander Pde (Eastern

Smith St

Mater St

George St

Gore St

Keele St

Palmerston St

Napier St

Budd St

Sackville

Elgin St

Lygon St

Nicholson St

Spring St

Fitzroy St

2 3

Argyle St

Johnston St

9

Faraday St

19 17

Barkly St

Greeves St

25

33

Grattan St

Swanston St

CARLTON

12

Otter St

8

Stanley St

14

Melbourne Museum

King William St

Condell St

Hanover St

FITZROY

Wellington St

COLL

Royal Exhibition Building

4

Brunswick St

Young St

Gertrude St

Lower Smith St

Cambridge St

Queensberry St

Rathdowne St

Carlton Gardens

Victoria St

St Vincent's

Webb St

Peel St

To Airport & Geelong

Courtney St

Elizabeth St

Howard St

Peel St

Victoria Par

King St

William St

Spencer St

La Trobe St

Melbourne Central

Lonsdale St

Spring St

Exhibition St

Albert St

St Patrick's Cathedral

Landsdowne St

Fitzroy Gardens

EAST MELBOURNE

Clarendon St

Flagstaff

To Western Link

Bourke St

Swanston St

Elizabeth St

Russell St

Parliament

Treasury Pl

Cook's Cottage

Jolimont

To Telstra Dome

Collins St

St Paul's Cathedral

Wellington Pde S

Wellington Pde

Jolimont Rd

Jolimont St

Melbourne Cricket Ground (MCG)

Southern Cross Coach Station

Flinders St

Flinders St

Federation Square

Ian Potter Centre

Yarra Park

Southern Cross

City Rd

Alexandra Av

Barton Av

Brunton Av

To Telstra Dome

Victorian Arts Centre

6

NGV International

Swan St

Rod Laver Arena

Richmond

Yarra River

Queensbridge St

Southbank

Southbank Blvd

St Kilda Rd

Domain Tunnel

Burnley Tunnel

Melbourne Maritime Museum

Haig St

Sturt St

Kings Domain

Observatory Gate

Westgate Freeway

SOUTH BANK

29

Kings Way

York St

5 16

Clarendon St

Moray St

Dorcas St

Birdwood Av

Botanic Gardens

To Princes Freeway, Williamstown & Geelong

City Rd

Ferrars St

Cecil St

Bank St

Park St

28

Albert Park

Albert Rd

Lakeside Dr

Lakeside Drive Formula One Grandstand

Albert Park Lake

Queens Rd

St Kilda Rd

Domain Rd

SOUTH YARRA

Toorak Rd

Anderson St

Fawkner Park

Punt Rd

To Ferry Terminal (Port Melbourne)

To St Kilda & Mornington Peninsula

To Maroondah Highway & Yarra Valley

Highway

Victoria Park

Perry St

INGWOOD
Collingwood

Langridge St

North Richmond

West Richmond

To Richmond, Maroondah Highway & Yarra Valley

Bridge Rd

Point Rd

To South Gippsland Highway, Phillip Island & Wilsons Promontory

Eastern Freeway

To Prahran, Toorak, Burwood Highway & Dandenongs

South Yarra

N

500 metres
500 yards

Melbourne maps

1 Melbourne centre, page 48
2 **Melbourne inner suburbs**
3 Around Melbourne, page 58

Sleeping

Melbourne Metro YHA **5** *B1*
Melbourne Oasis YHA **6** *A1*
Nunnery Accommodations **4** *B3*
Villa Donati **1** *E5*

Eating

Ablas's **1** *B3*
Babka **3** *B4*
Clarendon Fish & Chippers **5** *F2*
Cutler and Co **4** *C3*
EQ **6** *E3*
Gluttony It's a Sin **8** *B4*
Guru da Dhaba **9** *B4*
Kazen **12** *B3*
Mario's Café **2** *B3*
Moroccan Soup Bar **7** *A4*
Notturno **14** *B2*
Sakura Teppanyaki **16** *F2*
Shakahari **17** *B2*
Thresherman's Bakehouse **19** *B2*
Veggie Bar **21** *A4*
Viet Rose **22** *A3*

Bars & clubs

Bar Open **24** *B3*
Black Cat **25** *B3*
Brandon **26** *A3*
Limerick Arms **28** *G2*
Maori Chief **29** *F2*
Night Cat **30** *B4*
North Fitzroy Star **31** *A3*
Tote **33** *B4*

massive redevelopment in the last 10 years or so, transforming the area into an attractive waterfront precinct for inner city offices, apartments, restaurants, shops and entertainment venues. The flagship is the Etihad Stadium, a major venue for Aussie Rules football matches and Rugby League games. It is a great venue for a walk and views across the CBD.

Southeast of the centre, **Richmond** is the place to come for Vietnamese cuisine and offers the inner city's best range of factory outlet shopping on Bridge Road and Swan Street. Greeks populated the suburb before the Vietnamese and the community is still represented in the restaurants of Swan Street. South of the river, **Toorak** and **South Yarra** have long been the most exclusive residential suburbs and this is mirrored in the quality of the shops and cafés at the northern end of Chapel Street. The southern end becomes funkier and less posh as it hits **Prahran**, where Greville Street is full of second-hand clothes shops, bookshops and cafés and Commercial Street is the centre of the city's gay community. These suburbs are among the most fashionable and stylish and unsurprisingly Chapel Street is a wonderful destination for clothes shopping.

Down by the bay **St Kilda** has a charm all of its own. An early seaside resort that became seedy and run down, it's now a cosmopolitan and lively suburb but still has an edge. Only the well-heeled can afford to buy here and though some of them aren't too keen on living next to the junkies and prostitutes still seen on Grey Street, the picturesque foreshore makes this the most relaxed of the inner suburbs and a great place to base oneself for a few days. Here also is **Luna Park** ① *Cavell St, T9534 5764, www.lunapark.com.au, mid-Apr until mid- Sep Sat-Sun 1100-1800 and mid-Sep until mid-Apr Fri 1900-2300, Sat 1100-2300, Sun 1100-1800, from $35.95, children $25.95 and family $123*, a fairground with some impressive rides and an unmistakable front door.

The rural area northeast of Melbourne is promoted as a Valley of the Arts for its past and present links with artists' communities. A path winds along the Yarra River from the city centre to **Eltham** (25 km) so hiring a bicycle is a good way to explore these leafy and tranquil areas beyond the city. An important stop along the way is the **Heide Museum of Modern Art** ⓘ *7 Templestowe Rd, Bulleen, signposted from Eastern Freeway, T9850 1500, www.heide.com.au, Tue-Fri 0900-1700, Sat-Sun 1200-1700, $12, children free, concessions $8,* the former home of art patrons John and Sunday Reed during the 1930s and 1940s. The museum is set in beautiful bushland by the river and includes a sculpture garden with works by Anish Kapoor and Anthony Caro. The gallery has an exceptional collection of modern Australian art and hosts temporary exhibitions of contemporary art.

If you have your own transport and want to see something unique and Australian, head to the Bellbird Picnic Area (off Yarra Boulevard, location Melway 2D K6). You'll see a vast array of bizarre Christmas tree decorations there, as well as the largest **Flying Fox (fruit bat) colony** in Victoria.

Around Melbourne → For listings, see pages 62-78.

There is great variety of scenery and many activities around Melbourne, so even if you are short of time you can still see something of the state's attractions within a day. The Yarra Valley is a beautiful wine region with some of the most sophisticated cellar doors and accompanying restaurants in Australia. Nearby, Healesville has a wonderful wildlife sanctuary, and just beyond there is a very scenic winding drive through forest and ferns on the way to Marysville. The once beautiful sub-Alpine village of Marysville was effectively razed during the 'Black Saturday' bush fires of February 2009, with the loss of 47 lives and almost all man-made structures; see box, page 15. Although the bush is regenerating, little remains of the village itself and until it is rebuilt it is a sad testament to the devastation that bush fires can cause. Local natural sights still worth seeing include the 84-m Steavenson Falls (4 km from Marysville).

Heading south, the Dandenongs is a fine area in which to walk or drive through towering mountain ash forests, and if you're lucky you might just see an elusive lyrebird. The Mornington Peninsula, often just called 'the bay', has some great beaches as well as diving or swimming with dolphin trips, and the penguins of Phillip Island are among the region's most popular attractions.

Ins and outs

Mornington Peninsula VIC ⓘ *Point Nepean Rd, Dromana, T5987 3078, www.visitmornington peninsula.org, 0900-1700.* **Phillip Island VIC** ⓘ *1 km past the bridge on Phillip Island Tourist Rd, T5956 7447, www.visitphillipisland.com, open 0900-1700,* has a great range of local information. **Phillip Island Nature Park** ⓘ *T5951 2800, www.penguins.org.au,* manages most of the wildlife attractions. Saver tickets (the Nature Park Pass) can be bought at the VIC. **Dandenongs VIC** ⓘ *Burwood Highway, Upper Fern Tree Gully, T9758 7522, www.yarravalley tourism.com, 0900-1700.* They sell the Parks Victoria walking map for $2. **Yarra Valley VIC** ⓘ *The Old Courthouse, Harker St, Healesville, T5962 2600, www.visityarravalley.com.au, www.yarravalleytourism.asn.au.*

Mornington Peninsula → Colour map 1, B2

This is Melbourne's beach playground, where you can swim with dolphins, dive and sail, visit some world-class vineyards, play some of Australia's best golf courses, or take a trip to French and Phillip Islands. Both the peninsula's popularity and its proximity to Melbourne have resulted in a suburban sprawl creeping down as far as Rye, but beyond this things improve dramatically. The pristine south coast is protected by the Mornington Peninsula National Park; and the beaches and cafés of Sorrento and Portsea can make for a memorable stay.

Just east of the coastal suburb of Dromana is **Arthur's Seat**, a 300-m-high hill in Arthur's Seat State Park with striking views over Port Phillip Bay. At the top there are some pleasant, easy walks in the state park, as well as the Seawinds Botanic Gardens and a maze.

Near the tip of Mornington's curving arm is **Sorrento**, its shore lined with jetties, boats and the odd brightly coloured bathing box. The town has been popular for seaside holidays since the 1880s and consequently has many fine old limestone buildings along the main street, Ocean Beach Road. The Back Beach at Sorrento is also one of the best in the state with everything from views to rock pools ideal for snorkelling. A few kilometres further on is **Portsea**, a small suburb frequented by wealthy Melbournians and boasting the stunning Portsea Back Beach. Both Sorrento and Portsea are full of stylish cafés, pubs and shops. **Point Nepean** is the long, thin tip of the Mornington Peninsula, where it's possible to explore the gun emplacements, tunnels and bunkers of **Fort Nepean** ① *T5984 4276, 0900-1700, $8.10, children $3.90*. From the Visitors' Centre there is a short drive to Gunners car park; from here you can walk to the fort, about 3.5 km, with magnificent views over Bass Strait and the Bay, or you can take the visitors' bus ($17, children $10).

This long, straight strip of **Mornington Peninsula National Park** stretches from Portsea down to Cape Schank, protecting the last bit of coastal tea tree on the peninsula and the spectacular sea cliffs from the golden limestone at Portsea to the brooding black basalt around Cape Schank. There are picnic areas and a lighthouse at the cape and some good walks. There are also regular tours of the light station, and the lighthouse keepers' cottages have been renovated for holiday letting. There is a short walk with excellent views from the Cape Schank car park out to the end of the cape. For a longer walk, Bushrangers Bay Track is a great coastal route along the cliffs to the sublime and picturesque Bushranger Bay, ending at Main Creek (45 minutes one way).

The Mornington Peninsula is also well known for its world-class **vineyards**. Mornington wine production dates back to 1886 but was not begun in earnest until the early 1970s. The region is recognized as the home of Australian Pinot Noir, with around 200 vineyards and 50 cellar doors, many with quality restaurants or cafés attached. If you're short of time, don't miss what is arguably the most lauded of all the peninsula's vineyards, **Montalto** ① *33 Shoreham Rd, Red Hill, T5989 8412, www.montalto.com.au*. The VIC in Dromana can provide full details and tour options.

Peninsula Hot Springs ① *Springs Lane, T5950 8777, ww.peninsulahotsprings.com, daily 0730-2200, from$30*, is one of the most popular and unexpected attractions on the peninsula. Located in a peaceful bush setting just south of Rye, the 17-ha complex hosts a range of indoor and outdoor pools, a day spa and a café. Recommended.

Phillip Island → *Colour map 1, B3*

Phillip Island is one of Victoria's biggest attractions, with 3.5 million visitors a year. Connected to the mainland by a bridge, the island is 26 km long and 9 km wide. It certainly has its natural attractions, such as the rocky coves and headlands in the south and sunny north-facing beaches around Cowes, but the island has long since been tamed. Some wildlife continues to thrive, however, and this has been the lynchpin of the island's tourism success, particularly the rather overrated Penguin Parade. Other visitors come for the superb surfing breaks along the dangerous south coast and the safe swimming beaches on the sandy northern shores. There are some pleasant walking tracks throughout the island, particularly on **Cape Woolamai**. **Newhaven**, by the bridge, and **Cowes** are the main towns, while **Rhyll** has a quiet charm away from the crowds. **San Remo** is the gateway town, with accommodation a shade cheaper than on the island itself. The **Australian Motorcycle Grand Prix** is held here.

③ Around Melbourne

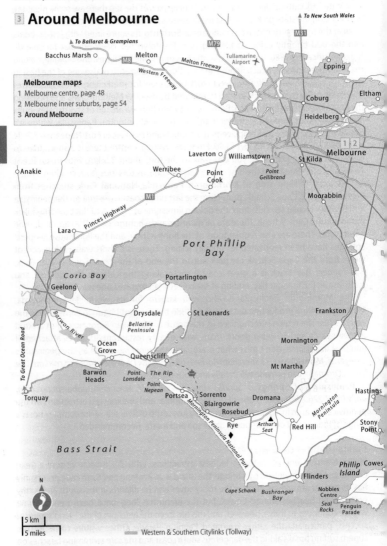

Melbourne maps
1 Melbourne centre, page 48
2 Melbourne inner suburbs, page 54
3 **Around Melbourne**

Western & Southern Citylinks (Tollway)

At the far end of the island are the **Nobbies**, a series of rocky islands joined to the coast at low tide, and beyond them **Seal Rocks**, home to Australia's largest fur seal colony. There is a new state-of-the-art visitors' centre and a series of boardwalks weave their way down past through penguin habitats to the rock shelf below. The seals can only be seen with powerful binoculars and a live webcam in the centre, but fairy penguins and gulls can often be seen sheltering under the boardwalks. The road out there is closed at dusk, when the **Penguin Parade** ⓘ *visitor centre, T5951 2800, www.penguins.org.au, from 1000, parade from dusk, $21.20, children $10.60, concessions $14.80,* gets into gear. Fairy penguins burrow in their thousands in the dunes along this stretch of coast, coming ashore in the darkness after a hard day at sea. Huge grandstands and powerful lights have been erected to allow thousands of visitors to watch the tired birds struggle out of the water and up the beach. Koalas are best seen at the **Koala Conservation Centre** ⓘ *Phillip Island Rd, 1000-1700, $10.60, children $5.30, concessions $7.40,* via an excellent series of elevated boardwalks through stands of gum trees. Other spots include **Swan Lake**, the island's only freshwater lake near Penguin Parade, **Cape Woolamai**, with its popular and pleasant walking tracks, and **Rhyll Inlet**, a wetland habitat favoured by migratory wading birds. Swan Lake and Rhyll both have boardwalks and bird hides.

Dandenong Ranges → *Colour map 1, B3*

Also referred to as the 'Dandenongs' or simply 'the mountain', these ranges comprise a hilly forested massif just to the east of Melbourne. They are a very popular destination for daytrippers, who swamp some parts at weekends and during school holidays. Several loosely connected chunks have been designated the **Dandenong Ranges National Park** and are crisscrossed with some wonderful walking tracks. Great views can be had from several points, the best over Melbourne being from the summit ⓘ *$2.20 per car, entry before 1600,* of Mount Dandenong itself. At the base of the mountain are the service towns of Fern Tree Gully and Belgrave. At the latter is the station for **Puffing Billy** ① *T9757 0700, www.puffingbilly.com.au, from 1030, $35, children $17.50 (return)*, the popular picturesque steam train that winds its way through scenic hilly country east to Gembrook, 24 km away. On the mountain itself **Sassafras** is the largest and most popular town, with a good range of facilities.

There are hundreds of interconnecting walking trails, and it is possible to organize circular walks from 10 minutes to three days in length, though longer walks may require short stretches on vehicular roads, and there is no camping on the mountain. Grants Picnic Grounds, just south of Kallista, is often inundated with cockatoos and crimson rosellas all keen to share your lunch and also serves as the start of several good loop tracks that pass through spectacular mountain ash forests and fern gullies. Lyrebirds live in these forests but are far more shy and difficult to spot than their assorted and cheeky pscittacine cousins. For an excellent circular walk through their territory, park at Cook's Corner and head down the Lyrebird Walk (7 km, two hours).

Yarra Valley and around → *Colour map 1, B23*

The Yarra Valley is one of Victoria's best known and most visited wine districts, but not content with creating great wine some of the wineries here have restaurants of the highest standard, and dining rooms and terraces that rank amongst the most striking and scenic in the country. In summer the valley gets very busy, particularly at weekends. Just east of the valley is another excellent reason to visit – Healesville Sanctuary, the best native wildlife park of its kind in Australia.

There are 40-plus wineries in the valley, most of which offer food. This is just a sample. **Rochford-Eyton** ① *Maroondah Highway, T5962 2119, www.rochford wines.com, wines $20-50, cellar door daily 1000-1700, lunches 1200-1500*, is striking for its modern architecture and has a fine dining room overlooking a lake. The excellent Merlot and the expensive modern Australian cuisine are regarded by many as the best in the valley. In summer, outdoor classical concerts add to the experience. At **Yering Station** ① *38 Melba Highway, T9730 0100, www.yering.com, wines $15-50, cellar door 1000-1700, lunches daily*, tastings and Yarra Valley produce are held in an old farm building, but don't miss a stroll around the new restaurant and cellars. This graceful sweep of stone and glass has the feel of a Bond movie, and the massive terrace has huge views. **McWilliam's Lilydale** ① *Davross Court, T5964 2016, wines $20-25, cellar door daily 1100-1700, flexible lunch hours*, is a small and very friendly winery with an octagonal conservatory dining room and vine-hung garden gazebo, both looking out over vines and gum woods. There are simple cheap platters and cook-it-yourself barbecue meals. The salad bar is balanced by the scrumptious puddings. **Domaine Chandon** ① *Maroondah Highway, T9739 1110, wines $25-50, cellar door daily 1030-1630*, is part of the Möet group, with a stylish but relaxed tasting room with a high arched window looking out over the valley. A small savoury platter is served with each $5-10 glass of bubbly. A couple are good for a snack lunch. There are no free tastings. Finally, **Long Gully** ① *Long Gully Rd, T9510 5798, wines $15-30, cellar door daily 1100-1700*, is a small easy-going winery with a very picturesque setting in its own mini-valley, making excellent and good value wines. Picnickers are welcome on the cellar door balcony.

Healesville Sanctuary ① *T5957 2800, www.zoo.org.au, 0900-1700, $25, children $13, concessions $18.50. A few buses daily from corner of Green St and Maroondah Highway, Healesville, Mon-Fri from 0925, Sat 0858, Sun 1133, 4 km from the little town of Healesville, on Badger Creek Road*, is devoted to the conservation, breeding and research of Australian wildlife. The appeal of this place is seeing animals being so well cared for, including species that are almost impossible to see in the wild, including Tasmanian devils, platypus, the endangered orange-bellied parrot, the lyrebird and Leadbeater's possum. The sanctuary has 30 ha of bushland with Badger Creek running through its centre. Visitors walk along a wide circular path (1.5 km), taking side loops to see the creatures that interest them. Highlights are the Animal Close-Up sessions, held several times a day, when you can get as close as is legally allowed to wombats and koalas. The star exhibit is the World of the Platypus, a nocturnal tunnel with glass windows where you can watch the little fellas swimming and hunting. The most recent addition to the zoo is the Australian Wildlife Health Centre. An impressive multi-million dollar facility, it cares for sick or injured native wildlife from all over Victoria and offers the visitor a unique live view of the working veterinary hospital.

Great Ocean Road → *For listings, see pages 62-78. Colour map 1, B1/2.*

The three great natural attractions of Australia are often said to be 'the road, the rock and the reef'. The 'road' is the Great Ocean Road, which runs west from Anglesea, round the treacherous Cape Otway, to Warrnambool. It is truly one of the great coastal routes of the world and has everything, from stylish villages such as Lorne and Apollo Bay, backed by a lush hinterland of forests and waterfalls inhabited by glow worms and platypuses, to Port Campbell National Park, whose famous golden rock stacks are seared into the minds of most travellers long before they see them for real.

Ins and outs

Getting around The road is congested all year, but especially in summer, when there is a procession of slow coaches. If you can, plan a route from west to east to avoid it all. Most traffic and tours travel west from Melbourne along the Great Ocean Road, then return eastwards to the city along the faster inland route, the Princes Highway. There are V-Line bus services along the Great Ocean Road to Warrnambool from Geelong, which stop regularly along the way. Backpacker buses from Melbourne also have a Great Ocean Road service (see page 76) and there are daily V-Line direct train services from Geelong to Warrnambool (two hours and 20 minutes).

Tourist information The **VIC** ⓘ *Princes Highway, Little River, north of Geelong, T1800 620888, www.greatoceanroad.org.au, 0900-1700*, is for the whole region, from Geelong to Port Fairy. There are also numerous VICs en route including Torquay, Beach Road, T1300 614219; Apollo Bay, 100 Great Ocean Road, T5237 6529, and Warrnambool, Merri Street, T1800 637725.

The route

Start off at **Lorne**, a glamorous coastal town of classy boutiques and fine restaurants surrounded by the thick forest, rivers and waterfalls of Angahook-Lorne State Park. Next up is **Apollo Bay**, a relaxed and friendly town and a good base from which to explore the **Otway National Park**, just to the west. Among the highlights of Otway National Park is Maits Rest Rainforest Walk. The towering mountain ash surrounding the upper edges of the gully are also impressive. Koala, swamp wallabies and yellow-bellied gliders live in the park, along with the rare spot-tailed quoll. The best place to see koala is in the roadside bush around the turn-off (left) to Blanket Bay Campsite, which in turn is along the main road to the Otway Lightstation.

West of the cape the sheer limestone cliffs have been eroded into a series of huge rock stacks, sculpted by the elements themselves into a series of arches, caves and tapering sails. The most famous group of stacks, the **Twelve Apostles**, was dramatically reduced to 11 when one of the stacks collapsed into the sea in June 2005, an event witnessed by a group of tourists (minus video camera, unfortunately). The most fascinating area of this stretch of the road is beautiful Loch Ard Gorge, named after the ship that was wrecked on Mutton Bird Island in 1878, killing 52 people on board. There is a walk from a lookout over the wreck site to the gorge and beach and then to the cemetery.

Beyond Port Campbell are more rock features, The Arch, London Bridge and The Grotto. The latter is probably the most interesting but London Bridge is famous for losing the arch connecting it to the mainland in 1990 and leaving some astonished tourists stranded on the far side. Adjoining Port Campbell, beyond the tiny settlement of Peterborough, is the Bay of Islands Coastal Park, an area of countless striking rock stacks. At Warrnambool the Great Ocean Road meets the Princes Highway. Only a stone's throw from here is the long, curving Lady Bay, with some of the coast's best swimming and boogie-boarding beaches, and the rugged low headlands and tiny bays that stretch away from the breakwater at its western end. The Thunder Point Coastal Walk runs along the top of these cliffs and at low tide offers the opportunity to wade out to Middle Island, with its rocky outcrops, caves and small fairy-penguin rookery. Just to the east of the town, across Hopkins River, there is a very good opportunity for seeing southern right whales from the free viewing platforms at Logans Beach (between mid-July and mid-September).

If you have the time, want to shed a few kilos and get really intimate with the coastline (and the odd koala) then consider doing the new Great Ocean Walk. Considered Victoria's premiere walking track, it stretches 104 km from Apollo Bay in the east to The Twelve Apostles. It can be tackled in whole or in part with a wide range of accommodation choices along the way, from luxury B&Bs to remote beachside campsites. For more information, consult Parks Victoria, the local Visitor Information Centres and the dedicated website.

● Melbourne and around listings

For Sleeping and Eating price codes and other relevant information, see Essentials pages 28-33.

Sleeping

Melbourne has a huge range of places to stay. The centre is first choice for most visitors, put off by the term 'suburbs', but the suburbs are only a 10-min walk away, boast an equally buzzing café society and nightlife and also offer better value and, in peak times, more choice. Most places are priced at a year-round rate, though some hostels will be cheaper in winter. St Kilda is something of a backpacking stronghold, though be aware that the quality of accommodation varies considerably. Almost everyone hikes their prices up for big events: the Melbourne Cup, Australian Open, Grand Prix and AFL Grand Final.

City centre *p47, map p48*
L-A Jasper, 489 Elizabeth St, T8327 2777, www.jasperhotel.com.au. Newly renovated and very slick. Good value double, twin and 2-bedroom suites. Pool, cable TV and Wi-Fi. Light or cooked breakfasts from $20. Discounted parking nearby.
L Robinsons in the City, 405 Spencer St, T9329 2552, www.robinsonsinthecity .com.au. A quality 4-star 6-bedroom boutique B&B in a former 1850s bakery. Contemporary decor, queen or king suites. Parking available with pre-booking.
A-B Pensione Hotel, 16 Spencer St, T9621 3333, www.pensione.com.au. Recently fully renovated and good value mid-range hotel.

B-C Enterprise, 44 Spencer St, T9629 6991, www.hotelenterprise.com.au. A modest contemporary chain hotel with good value en suite doubles, but sadly, no Captain Kirk, Scotty or beaming up from foyer to room. Undercover parking $25 per night.

C-D Nomads Industry, 198 A'Beckett St, T9328 4863, www.nomadsindustry.com. Modern and well-managed 'flashpackers' considered one of the best in the city. Relatively spacious doubles, some en suite and a female-only wing. Quality facilities include a cinema lounge, rooftop deck, bar and internet lounge. Recommended.

C-E Greenhouse, 228 Flinders Lane, T9639 6400, greenhouse@friendlygroup.com.au, and **C-E Hotel Bakpak**, 167 Franklin St, T9329 7525, www.bakpak group.com. Each has around 200 beds and a distinctly corporate feel, so these backpacker hostels are not a home-from-home, but are both modern, clean with good facilities and lots of organized events. Some doubles with en suite. Linen, pick-ups, free internet.

D-E Melbourne Central YHA, 562 Flinders St, www.yha.com.au. Newly renovated, 208-bed, 5-storey, heritage-listed building is ideally located in the Melbourne CBD and overlooks the North Shore of the Yarra. It has all the usual excellent modern YHA facilities and attention to detail, plus a few special features like rooftop terrace and funky ground-floor bar.

D-E Melbourne Connection, 205 King St, T9642 4464, www.melbourneconnection.com. One of the smaller city-centre hostels with around 80 beds, including simple but pleasant doubles, stripped wood floors and comfortable communal facilities (though the kitchen could be bigger). Usual facilities including satellite TV and Wi-Fi. Friendly and helpful owners also give the place a good atmosphere.

North of the centre *p53, map p54*
B-E Nunnery Accommodations, 116 Nicholson St, T9419 8637, www.nunnery.com.au. Friendly, funky backpacker hostel in a rambling Victorian terraced house with a seriously comfortable

front lounge. Free linen, breakfast and lots of laid-on activities. Range of doubles, twins, 3-beds and cheaper 12-bed dorms. There is also boutique accommodation available in newly refurbished premises in Fitzroy.

C-E Melbourne Metro YHA, 78 Howard St, T9329 8427, www.yha.com.au. Purpose-built, 350-bed hostel with mostly 4-bed dorms, doubles and twins, some en suite. All the usual YHA facilities, free use of bikes and car parking.

D-E Melbourne Oasis YHA, 76 Chapman St, T9328 3595, www.yha.com.au. This smaller , homely, backpackers has 120 beds, all in 4-bed dorms or smaller, good-value doubles. Modern and comfortable with a gazebo and garden, free bike hire and parking.

Southeast of the centre *p53*
LL-L The Prince, 2 Acland St, St Kilda, T9536 1111, www.theprince.com.au. Sleek boutique hotel, the height of hushed minimalist luxury with its own spa (see page 74). The 40 en suite rooms are seriously stylish and the pool and deck one of the city's finest posing spots. The smart fine dining restaurant, Circa, offers a business lunch for around $30. The basement Mink bar plays the tune to an Eastern bloc theme with leather couches and more varieties of vodka than a Russian distiller on speed.

L-A Villa Donati, 377 Church St, T9428 8104, www.villadonati.com. Charming and good value 4½-star boutique hotel located 2.5 km from the city centre. Chic, classy rooms with a mix of European and Asian furnishings. Fine café-style breakfast. On-street parking.

B-E Claremont, 189 Toorak Rd, Toorak, T9826 8000, www.hotelclaremont.com. Bottom end of the category, it has clean, bright but sparse rooms of good value and also 12 serviced apartments nearby. Mostly singles, doubles and twins. Linen, substantial continental breakfast, use of kitchenette.

C-D Olembia, 96 Barkly St, St Kilda, T9537 1412, www.olembia.com.au. Very comfortable and carefully planned hostel. 50 beds, including a dozen doubles and twins with shared bathroom facilities. Very competent, friendly and knowledgeable management create the classic homely environment. Bike hire, free off-street parking and secure bike shed.

C-E Habitat HQ St Kilda, 333 St Kilda Rd, St Kilda, T9537 3777, www.thehabitathq.com.au. Large, modern and well-facilitated place just a short stroll from the beach and those cake shops on Acland St. Usual room configurations from doubles (some en suite with TV) to 10-bed dorms. Car parking, cable TV, airport pick-ups.

C-F Base Backpackers, 17 Carlisle St, St Kilda, T8598 6200, www.basebackpackers.com. Hip and modern and part of the expanding Australasian chain. Women-only floor boasting hair straighteners, make-up boxes etc! Red laminate floors, futon-style beds, in-house bar, fast internet.

D-E Chapel St Backpackers, 22 Chapel St, Prahran, T9533 6855, www.csbackpackers .com.au. Right at the bottom of this street is this friendly, family-run hostel with 48 beds. Mostly doubles, twins and 4-bed dorms, some women only. Almost all are en suite with a/c, modest facilities. Linen and breakfast included.

D-E The Pint on Punt, 42 Punt St, St Kilda, T9510 4273, www.pintonpunt.com.au. Irish-style pub with good hostel accommodation upstairs. See also page 64.

Mornington Peninsula *p56*
L-C Oceanic Whitehall, 231 Ocean Beach Rd, Sorrento, T5984 4166, www.oceanic group.com.au. A grand old limestone guesthouse, traditional rooms with shared facilities, also some rooms with en suite, spa, open fire. Only a short stroll from Sorrento Back Beach, one of the best on the peninsula.

C Lighthouse keepers' cottages, Cape Schank, T5988 6184, capeschank@austpac inns.com.au. These have been renovated for holiday letting and can be booked by the room or as a whole.

C-D Bayplay Adventure Lodge, 46 Canterbury Jetty Rd, Blairgowrie, T5984 0888, www.bayplay.com.au. Good hostel run by dive operators (see page 75), with rooms, dorms, pool and café. Also offers transfers to and from

Melbourne. There is also a self-contained cottage (**A**) sleeping 4-6 at St Andrews Beach.

D Sorrento YHA, 3 Miranda St, Sorrento, T5984 4323, www.yha.com.au. Small, clean and very friendly hostel, owners help with arranging work (Apr-Jul) in local wineries and with tours and transport.

Phillip Island *p57*
Most of the accommodation for casual visitors is in Cowes, though there are a few options elsewhere on the island. There are dozens of motels and cheaper caravan parks. Most get booked out for long weekends and school holidays. Reserve a bed early.

L-B Cliff Top Boutique Accommodation, 1 Marlin St, , T5952 1033, www.clifftop.com.au. Secluded 1.2-ha oceanfront property with seven luxury rooms, some with spa. Regarded as one of the best establishments on the island. Recommended.

L-D Big 4 Phillip Island Caravan Park, 24 Beach Crescent, Newhaven, T5956 7227, www.big4.com.au. Motor park with good facilities handy for the visitors' information centre, San Remo shops and the beautiful Cape Woolamai.

C-D Beach Park Tourist Caravan Park, 2 McKenzie Rd, T5952 2113. Wide range of sites, cabins and units and camp kitchen.

D-E Amaroo Park YHA, 97 Church St, T5952 2548, www.yha.com.au. Of the 2 excellent and friendly backpacker hostels, this is by far the larger, with more facilities, very cheap breakfast and dinner (available to non-residents), a bar and pool. It also operates the Duck Truck and offers free transportation from Melbourne.

Dandenong Ranges *p59*
There are over 100 B&Bs on the mountain itself, with most catering for the high-end 4-poster open fire market. There are surprisingly no hostels or caravan parks and no camping facilities, though there are a couple of cheaper motels along Burwood Highway.

L Glen Harrow, Old Monbulk Rd, Belgrave, Dandenong Ranges, T9754 3232, www.glenharrow.com.au. Oozing character, it has 4 exquisite old gardeners' cottages, set in 8 ha of wild gardens. Completely self-contained and furnished mostly with antiques.

L-A Como Cottages, 1465 Mount Dandenong Tourist Rd, Olinda, T9751 2264, www.comocottages.com. A range of charming 1-3 bedroom self-contained cottages. The 4-poster, the fire and the spa are all at affordable mid-week prices. Go on – spoil yourselves.

Yarra Valley and around *p60*

The valley is awash with boutique hotel and B&B accommodation. Budget options are very thin on the ground, but there are a couple in Healesville.

A-B Art at Linden Gate, 899 Healesville Yarra Glen Rd, T9730 1861, erfrics@netstra.com.au. Single self-contained B&B apartment, with limited kitchen facilities, in the mud-brick house of a local sculptor. Isolated grounds encompass a hobby vineyard and a tiny wine cellar. The upstairs gallery has a range of contemporary work.

A-B Strathvea B&B, 755 Myers Creek Rd, T5962 4109, www.strathvea.com.au. Gracious 11-room B&B in its own wooded clearing adjacent to the state forest. Shared bathroom or en suite rooms. Fine cooked breakfast. Lots of wildlife and walking tracks nearby.

C-D Healesville Hotel, 256 Maroondah Highway, Healesville, T5962 4002, www.healesvillehotel.com.au. This pub has 7 funky, spacious and brightly coloured rooms upstairs with shared facilities and a good bistro with great country cooking (mid-range). Meals Thu-Mon 1200-1430, daily 1800-2030. Book ahead for rooms at weekends.

Great Ocean Road *p61*

Accommodation is very expensive in high season but Apollo Bay has a couple of gems.
L Queenscliff, 16 Gellibrand St, Queenscliff, T5258 1066, www.queenscliff hotel.com.au. At the southeasterly tip of the Bellarine Peninsula, southeast from Geelong, is the

graceful, genteel Edwardian seaside resort of Queenscliff. One of the grandest hotels in town, and a real window into Edwardian decadence, is this beautifully restored place. Not only is it a most sumptuous place to stay but the high standards are also reflected in what comes out of the kitchens. Lunches in the shop café, also bar meals, bistro and a separate dining room.

L-A Cape Otway Lighthouse, T5237 9240, www.lightstation.com. For something a bit different check out this large residence in the old keeper's cottage. It has 4 comfortable bedrooms and lounges with sofas and open fires, as well as the incredible position. Also 2 cheaper studio rooms for couples.

A-B Angel's Guesthouse, 7 Campbell Court, T5237 7085, www.angelasguesthouse .com.au. Spacious rooms with cheerful linen, spotless bathrooms and balconies. Angela's provides the warmest hospitality imaginable and the rooms are good value.

● Eating

Melbourne is foodie heaven. It boasts an incredible variety at inexpensive prices. In fact, the choice of restaurants can be overwhelming. A quarter of all Melbournians were born outside Australia and there are roughly 110 ethnic groups living in the city who have enriched Melbourne cuisine. Such is the breadth and quality of cuisine that the city can now claim to be ahead of Sydney – much to the latter's chagrin. The best option is to head for an 'eat street' or area known for a particular cuisine, such as Brunswick St in Fitzroy or the Vietnamese restaurants of Richmond, and stroll up and down to see what appeals. During the day look out for the Mon-Fri business lunches at some of the fancier restaurants: starter, main course and glass of wine for $25-35. Despite the vast number of seats, try to book in summer and at weekends.

City centre *p47, map p48*

City centre eating tends to be lunch-based. For greater choice in the evening most people head for the inner suburbs, although Chinatown (Little Bourke St) and the Southbank remain busy dinner spots. There are cheaper options on Russell St. Hardware Lane, to the west of Elizabeth St, has a strip of restaurants and cafés that buzz at lunchtimes. Centre Lane, off Collins St, at first glance looks like a grimy dark alley but is one of the best places in the city centre for a cheap lunch. ·

¶¶¶ **Flower Drum**, 17 Market Lane, T9662 3655, www.flower-drum.com. Mon-Sat 1200-1500, 1800-2300, Sun 1800-2230. Considered by many to be the best Chinese restaurant in Australia and well worth the painful hit to the wallet. The finest Cantonese cuisine in a light, elegant dining room, impeccable service and an excellent wine list. The Peking duck must be tried. Expect to spend about $150 for 2 without wine. Recommended.

¶¶¶ **Nobu**, Crown Complex, 8 Whiteman St, Southbank, T9292 7879, www.nobu restaurants.com. Lunch Mon-Thu 1200-1430, Fri-Sun 1200-1500; dinner Sun-Thu 1800-2230, Fri-Sat 1800-2300. Bar menu daily from 1730. Opened amid much hype and in partnership with actor Robert de Niro, the Nobu chain of classy Japanese restaurants has now arrived down under. The fact Melbourne was chosen over Sydney caused quite a stir – quite literally.

¶¶¶ **Rockpool Bar and Grill**, Crown Complex, Southbank, T8648 1900, www.rockpool melbourne.com. Sun-Fri 1200-1500, daily for dinner Sat. Multi award-winner and sister to the famous Sydney establishment. Home of lauded chef Neil Perry who is renowned for 'turning great produce into something memorable'. Steak is a house speciality.

¶¶ **EQ Cafébar**, Victorian Arts Centre, Riverside Terr, 100 St Kilda Rd, T9645 0644. Mon-Sat 1100-late. A little further south of the centre, for good casual Mediterranean food in a combined bar and café. Noisy but lively contemporary space.

¶¶ **No 35**, Level 35, Sofitel Hotel, 25 Collins St, T9653 7744. Daily from 0630-late. Ideal opportunity to get above the city mayhem and take in some great views. Modern à la carte Australian cuisine. Their buffet breakfasts are expensive but worth it.

¶¶ **Rosati**, 95 Flinders La, T9654 7772, www.rosati.com.au. Mon-Fri 0730-2200, Sat 1800-2200. Large, light Italian café-bar in an old glass-ceilinged warehouse that the owners have succeeded in giving a welcoming, classical feel.

¶¶ **Sakura Teppanyaki**, 331 Clarendon St, South Bank, T9699 4150. Mon-Fri 1100-1500, daily 1700-2300, later Fri-Sat. Leaving the centre southwards, the chefs throw their lively personalities into their cooking, and things can get pretty boisterous here. Good fun.

¶¶-¶ **Chloe's Lounge at Young and Jackson**, upstairs, corner Swanston St and Flinders St, T9650 3884, www.youngandjacksons.com.au. Lunch daily 1200-1430; dinner Sun-Thu 1730-2100, Fri-Sat 1730-2130 . Very conveniently located and quiet sanctuary amid the city chaos, above one of the city's best-known traditional pubs. Tapas for lunch and a quality full dinner menu. Arrive early for lunch or book ahead for a window seat, and don't miss the evocative portrait of 'Chloe'.

¶ **Café All Angolo**, corner of Hardware Lane and Little Bourke St, T9670 1411. Ideal for a fast and reliable bowl of pasta in simple and unpretentious surrounds, very popular with nearby office workers. Good value breakfasts.

¶ **Clarendon Fish and Chippers**, 293 Clarendon St. Daily by 1130, until at least 2100. Healthy fast food, one of the very best in Melbourne, with fresh fish and great chips. A bit south of the centre.

¶ **Laurent**, 306 Little Collins St, T9654 1011. Mon-Fri 0700-1900, Sat 0800-1800, Sun 0900-1700. An elegant Parisian-style patisserie that is begging for haute couture, but instead serves baguettes, coffee and exquisite pastries. Licensed.

¶ **Movida Tapas Bar**, 1 Hosier Lane. T9663 3038. Daily 1200-late. Considered by many as the best tapas venue in the city. Authentic and happening atmosphere.

Nudel Bar, 76 Bourke St, T9662 9100. Small and spartan, serving excellent noodle dishes and some pasta. Good vegetarian selection.

Pellegrinis, 66 Bourke St, T9662 1885. Mon-Sat 0800-2330, Sun 1200-2000. Melbourne's original Italian café – it opened in 1954 and hasn't really changed much since then. It still remains a vibrant, crowded small space serving wonderful coffee and cheap pasta dishes.

Spencer, 475 Spencer St, T9329 5111, www.hotelspencer.com.au. Food served Mon-Fri 1200-1500 and 1830-2100 (Sat 1830-2100). Victorian pub, now with a seriously smart, highly regarded and usually lively restaurant in the lounge area. The quality rubs off on the cheap counter meals, which are well worth the stroll from the city.

North of the centre p53, map p54

Carlton's Lygon St is sometimes called 'Little Italy' for its string of Italian restaurants. Brunswick St in Fitzroy is probably the most diverse eating street in Melbourne.

Abla's, 109 Elgin St, Carlton, T9347 0006. Thu-Fri 1200-1500, Mon-Wed and Sat 1800-2300. This small olive-green formal dining room consistently serves the best Lebanese food in town, with multi-course banquets.

Cutler and Co, 55 Gertrude St, Fitzroy, T9419 4888, www. cutlerandco.com.au. Dinner Tue-Sun from 1800; lunch Fri/Sat from 1200; bar Tue-Sun 1600-midnight.

Gluttony It's a Sin, 278 Smith St, Collingwood, T9416 0336. Tue-Sat 0830-2300, Sun 1000-2100. Rich food in a café atmosphere. Everything is oversized and over-indulgent, but exceptional quality is always maintained.

Shakahari, 201 Faraday St, Carlton, T9347 3848. Long-standing vegetarian restaurant with a warm, earthy but stylish interior. The limited but very fine menu will not disappoint. Multi award-winning restaurant/bar owned by celebrity chef Andrew McConnell. His former restaurant Three, One, Two in Carlton was his prelude to Cutler and Co and his

success continues unabated. Set in a former metalwork factory, the architecture successfully marries both the old and new creating a chic atmosphere that is both informal and relaxed. The brilliantly imaginative and inventive cuisine offers one of Australia's best dining experiences, provided you can get a booking!

Babka, 358 Brunswick St, Fitzroy, T9416 0091. Tue-Sun 0700-1900. Closed most of Jan. Friendly, unassuming and unpretentious bakery is perfection in everything it does.

Guru da Dhaba, 240 Johnston St, Fitzroy, T9486 9155. Very cheap but filling northern Indian dishes in a warm and noisy dining room with terracotta walls and simple black tables. BYO.

Kazen, 201 Brunswick St, T9417 3270. Tue-Sun 1200-1500, 1800-2230 (Sun 1800-2300 only). Small, Italian-influenced Japanese with dark, bluestone walls but a much lighter atmosphere. Excellent and interesting food, licensed but cheap corkage for BYO.

Mario's Café, 303 Brunswick St, Fitzroy, T9417 3343. Daily 0700-2400. Locally popular with a cosmopolitan clientele. Also good all-day breakfast and veggie options, licensed.

Moroccan Soup Bar, 183 St George's Rd, North Fitzroy, T9482 4240. Huge and superbly authentic Moroccan, with vegetarian meals.

Notturno, 179 Lygon St, T9347 8286. Daily 0600-0200. Of the many Italian cafés and restaurants in Lygon St, this large establishment is one of the least expensive. Good breakfasts, pasta, pizzas, cakes and coffee.

Thresherman's Bakehouse, 221 Faraday St, Carlton, T9349 2319. Daily 0630-2400. Spacious, relaxed café in an old car-repair shop. Great juices, soups and cafeteria meals as well as cakes and sandwiches.

Veggie Bar, 380 Brunswick St, T9417 6935. Daily 1100-2200, www.vegiebar.com.au. A relaxed, friendly vegetarian café-bar in a large old bare-brick warehouse. Great menu includes wood-fired pizzas, wraps, burgers and salads.

Viet Rose, 363 Brunswick St, T9417 7415. Generous quantities of laksa, vegetarian rolls and rice will defeat your stomach before your wallet.

Southeast of the centre *p53*

Richmond is one of the most international of the foodie suburbs. Most eateries are on Bridge Rd, but just to the north is Melbourne's 'Little Saigon', Victoria St, where there are around 50 Vietnamese restaurants. Greek food can be found on Swan St. In Prahran and Toorak there is no particular foodie area, the cafés and restaurants are dotted amongst the shops on Chapel St and Toorak Rd, but the choice is phenomenal. The eating in St Kilda has been traditionally clustered along Acland St and Fitzroy St, but since the ongoing renovation of St Kilda Baths, the choice on the foreshore has tripled. Italian predominates.

Richmond Hill Café and Larder, 48 Bridge Rd, East Melbourne, T9421 2808, thecafe@rhcl.com.au. Daily 0830-1700. Hugely indulgent café and restaurant with wonderful cheese shop attached. Lunch includes the cheese platter and dinners are a culinary event.

Borsch, Vodka & Tears, 173 Chapel St, Prahran, T9530 2694. Daily 1000-2130. Vibrant, friendly eastern European restaurant specializing in Polish broth and vodka … and tears (of laughter!). Live, gypsy-style music Mon, Wed and Sun. Evening bookings essential on music nights and weekends.

Flavours of India, 68 Commercial Rd, Prahran, T9529 7811. Small, smart curry bar, popular with locals for food of exceptional quality. Also takeaway.

Kanzaman, 458 Bridge Rd, Richmond, T9429 3402. Daily 1200-1500, 1800-2400. Excellent Lebanese with an exotic, richly decorated interior.

Mexicali Rose, 103 Swan St, Richmond, T9429 5550, www.mexicalirose.com.au. Fri 1130-1430, daily 1800-2100. Friendly, earthy Mexican with generous servings of all the classics, plus a few interesting variations.

Minh Tan 2, 192 Victoria St, Richmond, T9427 7131. Daily 1000-2230. One of the busiest and most respected Vietnamese restaurants, with a huge menu including fantastic mud crabs.

Stokehouse, 30 Jacka Blvd, St Kilda, T9525 5555, bar Mon-Fri 1200-2200, Sat 1100-2400, Sun 1000-2200, dining room daily 1200-1500, 1900-2200. With the best spot on the foreshore this award-winning bar-bistro is packed out year round. Simple ground floor bar and beach-facing terrace. Bookings not taken so arrive early for a good spot. Upstairs is an expensive, airy formal dining room, focusing on modern Australian seafood, which has the best balcony tables in Melbourne (bookings taken).

E Lounge, 409 Victoria St, Richmond, T9429 6060, elounge@tpg.com.au. Not an internet café, but some of the best thin and crispy wood-fired pizzas in the city. Very friendly, very orange. Also takeaway.

Greasy Joe's, 68 Acland St, St Kilda, T9525 3755. Daily 0700-2400. American retro bar and grill with excellent burgers, breakfasts and lots of pavement tables.

Il Fornaio, 2 Acland St, St Kilda, T9534 2922. 0700-2200. Small but warehousey, with lots of cheap eats and pavement tables, great for breakfast. French/Italian bakery.

Montalto, 33 Shoreham Rd, Red Hill, T5989 8412, www.montalto.com.au. One of many vineyard restaurants, Montalto is definitely one of the best, offering award-winning à la carte and a café alongside the cellar door. Outdoor and fine views add to the experience. Recommended.

Pier Pavilion, perched right at the end of St Kilda pier, St Kilda. 1000-sunset, 1000-2300 peak summer. Great spot for breakfast or simply one of the excellent coffees with a substantial slice of cake. Also cheap lunches.

Salona, 260 Swan St, Richmond, T9429 1460. Mon-Fri 1100-2200, Sat-Sun till 2300. The best of a small cluster of traditional Greek restaurants.

Topolinos, 87 Fitzroy St, St Kilda, T9534 4856. Well-established and always busy. Recommended for good value pizza and pasta.

Torch, 178 Swan St, Richmond, T9428 7378. Daily 0830-1800. Small and welcoming, this is one of a few excellent cafés on this street. Busy but relaxed with cheap light lunches and all-day breakfasts. Good value.

Mornington Peninsula *p56*

The Baths, on Sorrento foreshore overlooking a long skinny jetty, T5984 1500. Daily 0800-2100. For expensive but relaxed dining. Also a fish 'n' chip kiosk.

Continental, 1-21 Ocean Beach Rd, Sorrento, T5984 2201. A funky choice. Meals, including breakfast, are served in a large room hung with modern art. A nightclub operates upstairs on Sat.

Coppins Café, 250 Ocean Beach Rd, T5984 5551, Daily 1000-1630. Sits above Sorrento Back Beach and is a wonderful place for a casual lunch or tea and scones on a sunny afternoon.

Heronswood Café, 105 Latrobe Parade, Dromana, T5984 7318. A little hard to find but well worth it, this little-known gem of a café is located in the historic Heronswood Gardens estate. Try the lamb. Recommended.

Just Fine Food, 23 Ocean Beach Rd, Sorrento, T5984 4666. Gourmet deli and café with busy pavement tables.

Phillip Island *p57*

Foreshore Bar Café, 11 Beach Rd, Rhyll, T5956 9520. Thu-Mon 1000-2000. Facing the sea, the locals' favourite spot for fish and chips. It also has a funky bar serving platters and nibbles.

Mad Cows, the Esplanade 4, Cowes, T5952 2560. Also facing the water and convenient for the beach. The locals' favourite for coffee and breakfast.

Island Food Store, 75 Chapel St, Cowes. For high-quality cake and coffee or a salad, set back from Chapel St past the supermarket.

Terrazzo, 5 Thompson Av, Cowes, T5952 3773. Wed-Sun 1700-2030. Good cheap place for Italian.

Dandenong Ranges *p59*

As you would expect there are dozens of restaurants, cafés and bistros on the mountain. A couple of the best are almost opposite each other on the main road through Olinda, which is a good place to pick up picnic ingredients. A visit to **Ripe**, at 376 Mount Dandenong Tourist Rd, Sassafras, is also a must for any visitor.

Ranges, Olinda, T9751 2133. All day from 0900. Bright, large, cheerful and popular place for good value breakfasts, light lunches and, from Tue-Sat, mid-range Asian-influenced dinners.

Sky High Mount Dandenong, via Mount Dandenong Tourist Rd, T9751 0452. Daily. Bistro and café option at the Sky High complex. Memorable views. Open for breakfast, lunch or dinner.

View Point Tea Rooms, T9761 9902, opposite the Lookout at Kalorama, Five Ways intersection. Tue-Sun 0900. More wonderful views and divine breakfasts, baguettes, cakes and coffee.

Yarra Valley and around *p60*

Yarra Valley Dairy, just south of Yarra Glen on McMeikans Rd, T9739 0023, www. yarravalleydairy.com.au . As an alternative to a winery lunch (see page 60) try this place. It is a licensed, full-working dairy with a lively and relaxed café and views over cow-filled fields. Mid-range platters and light lunches, book ahead at weekends. Cheese tastings daily 1030-1700, café closes a little before.

Pasta Shop, next door to **Bodhi Tree**. Tue-Fri 0900-1730, Sat-Sun 0830-1700, restricted hours in winter. Cheery 2-room cottage café that does Healesville's best breakfast, tasty lunches and sells fresh handmade pasta and gourmet foods.

Bodhi Tree, 317 Maroondah Highway, Healesville, T5962 4407. Wed-Fri 1700-late, Sat-Sun 1200-late. Rustic, laid-back café with wholesome food and an assortment of tables in the large outdoor area, live acoustic music Fri nights.

♠ Bars and clubs

The city is bursting with watering holes, from the sleekest cocktail bar to the grungiest of Victorian-era pubs with sticky carpets. The city centre bars tend to be the most sophisticated, with many wine bars and cocktail bars crossing the line into club territory and a sprinkling of traditional pubs frequented by office workers during the week. The large student population to the north of the city means that Carlton, Fitzroy and Collingwood have the heaviest concentration of live band venues and alternative pubs and bars. The inner suburbs south of the Yarra have some of the most fashionable bars and respected live music venues. Many pubs and bars also serve good food at reasonable prices, and liberal licensing laws mean it is possible to get a drink well into the small hours. Many club nights move regularly and the clubs themselves open and close frequently. Entry is usually about $12-15. King St has a lot of clubs but is known for being slightly seedy. Most of the clubs listed are city based but Chapel St in South Yarra is also a hot spot.

Free newspapers, mostly catering for the clubbing and music scenes, come and go but currently include *Beat* and *Inpress. Bnews* and *MCV* cover the gay and lesbian scene. All are widely available in cafés and music shops. There are general listings and entertainment guides in the Thu *Herald Sun* and Fri *Age* newspapers.

City centre *p47, map p48*
Bridie O'Reilly's, 62 Little Collins St. Out-of-the-way Irish theme bar with 20-odd beers on tap. Pub grub 1200-1430, 1800-2100 and mainly Irish acoustic live music Tue-Thu, cover bands Fri-Sat.
Hairy Canary, 212 Little Collins St. Mon-Fri 0730-0300, Sat 1000-0300, Sun 1000-0100. A smart, trendy bar and café, serving food all day. Rocks into the early hours.

Limerick Arms, 364 Clarendon St, South Melbourne. Cheap meals daily 1200-1430, 1800-2100. Had a revamp a few years ago to reflect its name and cash in on the rise of Irish theme bars. This isn't too forced, however, and the result is a pleasant, traditional Aussie drinking bar with an Irish flavour. DJs Fri-Sat.
Maori Chief, corner of Moray St and York St, South Bank, T9696 5363. Meals 1200-1400 Mon-Fri, 1800-2130 Mon-Sat. Combines a groovily shabby bar, dimly lit and furnished with retro couches, with good cheap casual food.
Mitre, 5 Bank Place. A traditional British-style pub, now hemmed in by the high-rises, which has been quietly pulling pints since the 1860s.
Section 8, 27-29 Tattersalls Lane, T0422-972 656. Undoubtedly one of the city's most unusual pubs. Utilizing former parking spaces down a nondescript city centre lane and made out of a single shipping container, it also has to be one of the simplest. Section 8 is often the first place Melbournians take visitors for a night out to show them the city's unique and often raw laneway culture. No yuppified decor here, no comfy leather seats, just the basics, and it works remarkably well. Recommended.
Stork, 504 Elizabeth St, T9663 6237. Welcoming, relaxed front bar with pool table and open fire. Independent bands daily with a wide mix of styles. Seriously cheap, good quality bar food and cheap, surprisingly sophisticated bistro.

North of the centre *p53, map p54*
Bar Open, 317 Brunswick St, Carlton. Small, grungy bar with an open fire, armchairs and live music Wed-Sun.
Black Cat, 252 Brunswick St. Wed 1800-2300, Thu-Fri 1800-0100, Sat-Sun 1400-0100. Slick, seductive cabaret bar with live blues and jazz Thu-Sun.
Brandon, corner of Station St and Lee St, Carlton, T9347 2382. Goes out of its way to source real ales, both keg and bottled. Simple friendly front bar and large retro lounge. Equally simple pub grub, but with interesting touches.
Night Cat, 141 Johnston St, Fitzroy, T9417 0090. Lush, stylish bar with roomy couches and swing and salsa bands Thu-Sun.

North Fitzroy Star, 32 St George's Rd, Fitzroy, T9482 6484. Food daily 1100-2300. Contemporary, often exuberant styling in this traditional Victorian pub. Welcoming, with lots of nooks and crannies and open fires, the food is also well worth the trip. Cheap, inventive light lunches and bar nibbles and a mid-range set menu later on.

The Tote, 71 Johnston St, Fitzroy, www.thetotehotel.com. This isn't a gambling den, but is considered the most famous and influential of Melbourne's live music venues. For over 30 years the pub has hosted some of the best local talent, with many seasoned musos considering the place their second (or only) home. In 2010, due to new liquor licensing laws, the Tote's owner had no option but to close, but it would prove highly controversial and ultimately only temporary. The issue and the legislation drew such a massive backlash from the public that street protests were arranged and it drew intense media coverage. As a result, new investment was found and the Tote lives on, now more popular than ever.

Southeast of the centre p53

Dizzy's Jazz Club, 381 Burnley St, Richmond. Hosts live jazz; check the playlist on www.dizzys.com.au

Elephant and Wheelbarrow, 169 Fitzroy St, St Kilda. London-style pub with over 20 beers on tap, mostly British or Irish. Live music Wed-Sun and a 'meet-the-Neighbours' session (really) on Mon. Cheap, feel-good meals, including breakfast, daily 1100-1430, 1700-2100.

The Esplanade, Esplanade, St Kilda. Something of a Melbourne institution for live music, cheap food and a raucous atmosphere.

Frost Bites, corner of Chapel St and Simmons St, Prahran, T9827 7401, www.frostbites.com.au. *The* bar to be seen at. The cool warehouse look is complemented by industrial quantities of slush cocktails waiting on tap. Very cheap café meals and live music Wed-Thu and Sun. Late licence most nights.

George, corner of Fitzroy St and Grey St, St Kilda. Slick wine bar, in sharp contrast to the lively and grungy **gpb** beneath. The latter serves cheap pub grub daily 1200-0100, and there's interesting live music Sat 1600-1900 and Sun 1800-2100.

Greyhound, 1 Brighton Rd, St Kilda, T9534 4189, www.ghhotel.com.au. Relaxed comfortable pub and a good live venue for everything from roots to rock and Sun night karaoke.

The Local, 184 Carlisle St, St Kilda East, T9537 2633. A pub that takes beer very seriously. If you are an aficionado looking for fine choice, quality and a Euro-style atmosphere this is the place. Live music is also a regular feature.

The Pint on Punt, 42 Punt St, St Kilda, T9510 4273, www.pintonpunt.com.au. One of Melbourne's best drinking holes. A simple, warm country-Irish-style pub with open brick fires and bare wood floors. Accommodation upstairs (**D-E**), see page 64.

Prince of Wales, 29 Fitzroy St, St Kilda. A magnet for all types from the divine to the desperate and consequently has an unpredictable energy. Lots of pool tables, cheap pots on Mon and a busy live venue next door.

Vineyard, 71 Acland St, St Kilda, T9534 1942. Daily 1000-0300. The seriously laid-back and cool frequent this joint. A long, casual space that can be opened onto the side street on a sunny day. Also great café food.

🎭 Entertainment

Melbourne p46, maps p48 and p54

For details of events, visit the VIC and pick up a free copy of the *Official Visitor's Guide*, a useful rundown of highlights, and *Melbourne Events*, an excellent monthly publication that has details of every event and attraction in the city. See also Bars and clubs above for live music venues in pubs and bars. The main agencies are **Ticketek**, T132849, www.premier.ticketek.com.au, and **Ticketmaster**, T136100, www.ticket master.com.au. There is an outlet at the Athenaeum Theatre, 188 Collins St,

Mon-Fri 0900-1700, Sat 1000-1600. There is no telephone number – you have to go in person.

Cinema
Astor, 1 Chapel St, border of Prahran and St Kilda, T9510 1414. A different contemporary or classic movie every day, with lots of double bills.
George, 135 Fitzroy St, St Kilda, T9534 6922. Mainstream movies, cheap tickets for guests at some local hostels.
Village cinema, at the Jam Factory, 500 Chapel St, Prahran, T1300 555400, www.villagecinemas.com.au, and the Crown Complex, Southbank, T1300 555400.

Live music
Major acts play at the **Rod Laver Arena**, the **Melbourne Concert Hall**, the Etihad Stadium and the **MCG** and tickets for these events are usually sold through ticketing agencies. **Melbourne Concert Hall**, part of Victorian Arts Centre, is the home of the Melbourne Symphony Orchestra.

⊕ Festivals and events

Melbourne *p46, maps p48 and p54*
Melbourne puts on an extraordinary spread of festivals throughout the year. Many of these attract the best talent in the country and bring over prestigious international artists. To see what's on and how to buy tickets pick up a copy of the free monthly *Melbourne Events* from the VIC. For forward planning see www.thatsmelbourne.com.au. All of the festivals listed below are annual.

Sports fans should also watch out for the **Australian Open** in **Jan**, F1 Grand Prix in **Mar**, the Australian Football League Grand Final in **Sep** and the Spring carnival (Melbourne Cup) in **Nov**.
Jan Midsumma, T9415 9819, www.midsumma.org.au, is a gay and lesbian celebration of pride, presence and profile. Running for 3 weeks it involves street parties, events and the Midsumma Carnival.

Mar Melbourne Food and Wine Festival, T9823 6100, is a prestigious gastronomic celebration that showcases talent and the produce of the city and region. Events include master classes, food writers' forum, tasting tours and the 'world's longest lunch'. It's held over Labour Day weekend.

Moomba River Festival is an annual event that is over 50 years old and celebrates the city as a whole. The name derives from the aboriginal word meaning 'to get together and have fun'. Held alongside the Yarra in Alexandra Gardens, Birrarung Marr and the Waterfront City Piazza at Docklands, it includes live music, dance, a waterskiing competition, fireworks displays, the Moomba Parade along Swanston St and the wacky Birdman Rally.

Apr Melbourne International Comedy Festival, T9417 7711, www.comedyfestival .com.au, held over 3 weeks, is one of the world's largest laugh-fests. A month of comedy in every guise, from more than 1000 Australian and international performers.

Jul Melbourne International Film Festival, www.melbournefilmfestival.com.au, showcases about 350 of the best films from Australia and around the world. The 2-week festival includes features, documentaries, shorts and discussion sessions with film makers in 4 main theatre venues.

Sep-Oct Melbourne Fringe Festival, T9660 9600, www.melbournefringe.com.au, lasts for 10 days. It is an off-shoot of the main Melbourne Festival with a more anarchic spirit. Showcases new and innovative art in all fields and has lots of free events, parties and a legendary parade down Brunswick St, in Fitzroy.

Melbourne Festival, T9662 4242, www.melbournefestival.com.au, takes place over 3 weeks. It is the city's major arts festival showing the cream of local and overseas talent in theatre, dance, opera, music and the visual arts in indoor and outdoor venues all over Melbourne.

Oct-Nov Spring Racing Carnival, www.racingvictoria.net.au, is the horse-racing festival linked to several major races and race days. The highlight is 'the race the nation stops for', the Melbourne Cup (a public holiday in Melbourne), held at Flemington Racecourse. Traditionally celebrated with champagne, fancy frocks, oversized hats and a bet, it is run on the first Tue in Nov. Entry tickets cost about $60 from **Ticketmaster**, www.ticketmaster.com.au, and must be bought in advance.

O Shopping

Melbourne *p46, maps p48 and p54*
Art and crafts
There are some fine Aboriginal art galleries at the eastern end of Flinders Lane. There are a couple of upmarket shops on Bourke St, such as **Aboriginal Art**, at No 90, but there are also other options. **Koorie Heritage Trust** (see page 51) is one. Another is the **Aboriginal Handicrafts Shop**, the mezzanine part of the Uniting Church Shop at 130 Little Collins St, T9650 3277. It may be small, but they have an excellent range of affordable pieces, from bark and paper art to didgeridoos, carved wood and woven baskets. All profits go directly back to the originating communities. Open Mon-Fri 1000-1630.

Bookshops
Booktalk, 91 Swan St, Richmond. Mon-Sat 0830-1730, Sun 0900-1600. Also a café with good value breakfasts.
Brunswick Street Bookstore, 305 Brunswick, Fitzroy, T9416 1030. Daily 1000-2300. Large independent with a well-chosen range.
Dymocks, 234 Collins St, City. One of the largest chain stores with an excellent range, including music CDs, and knowledgeable staff. Open late on Fri.
Grub Street, 379 Brunswick St, Fitzroy. Great collection, covering a wide range of contemporary issues, non-fiction and fiction.
Readings, 701 Glenferrie Rd, Hawthorn, T9819 1917. Very popular and one of several outlets in the city. Café attached.

Information Victoria, 505 Little Collins St, T1300 366 356, www.vic.gov.au. Mon-Fri. Stocks an excellent range of maps and guides and offers good general advice. Mail order available.

Clothes
Melbourne is famous for its wonderful clothes shopping. People fly from all over Australia just to have a shopping weekend in Melbourne. **Crown Entertainment Complex** has some of the city's most exclusive boutiques, such as Armani and Versace. Equally swanky shopping can be found on **Collins St**, **Toorak Rd** and the city end of **Chapel St**, which is lined with designer label shops and chain stores, becoming steadily cheaper as you head south. In the city centre the eastern end of Collins St has expensive designer boutiques. More funky independent designers populate Little Collins St and Flinders Lane, such as the fascinating and colourful **Christine**, 181 Flinders Lane, and **Alice Euphemia**, Shop 6, 37 Swanston St, supporting Australasian design talent.

Brunswick St, Fitzroy, is still a good spot for finding choice second-hand articles, and it gets positively bargain basement over in neighbouring **Smith St**. South of Commercial Rd on Chapel St, Prahran, and on the side road Greville St, are a couple of dozen small and chic shops, including the wildly exuberant **Shag**, 130 Chapel St, daily 1200-1800, which is difficult to leave without having been tempted into buying something that'll turn heads. There are a couple of interesting shops on **Barkly St**, St Kilda, near the junction with Acland St, and on **Acland St** by the junction with Albert St.

Markets
Gleadell St Market, Richmond. Sat 0700-1300. A cheap, old-fashioned street market where few stallholders speak much English. Fruit, veggies, bread, flowers and fish.
Prahran Market, Commercial Rd. Dawn-1700 Tue, Sat, dawn-1800 Thu-Fri. Fabulous and fancy fresh-food market.

Queen Victoria Market 513 Elizabeth St. Tue, Thu 0600-1400, Fri 0600-1800, Sat 0600-1500, Sun 0900-1600. The market has expanded and evolved since the 1870s and now consists of a substantial brick building housing the meat and dairy sections and a vast area of open-air sheds, selling fruit and vegetables, clothing and souvenirs. The meat hall has fresh meat, fish and seafood and the dairy hall includes nearly 40 deli stalls selling bread, cheese, sliced meats, pickles, dips and sauces. The sheds can be a good place to find cheap leather goods but generally hold a lot of low-quality, mass-market junk. The food sections, however, are well worth a wander for the friendly banter of the stallholders and extremely tempting sights and smells. There is a food court and there are places in the dairy hall to grab a bite and sit down. There are also entertaining tours focusing on either history or tastes, such as the Foodies' Dream Tour, Tue, Thu-Sat 1000, $35 including samples along the way. Bookings essential, T9320 5822.

St Kilda Market takes place every Sun along the curve of the Esplanade. The stalls offer mostly craft and gifts with a few clothes stalls. **Victorian Arts Centre Market**, Southbank. High-quality art and craft stalls on Sun 1000-1800.

▲ Activities and tours

Melbourne *p46, maps p48 and p54*
Aerial tours
Melbourne Seaplanes, Williamstown's Gem Pier, T9547 4454, www.seaplane.com.au. Specializes in 4 main flights: a short 15-min loop around the city from $140, to a 55-min loop around Port Phillip Bay for $270, which, at an extra cost, can be broken by a stop in Sorrento for lunch. Minimum 2 people.

Ballooning
Despite its variable weather the city has a well-established reputation for early morning scenic flights.

Balloon over Melbourne, T9427 0088, www.balloonovermelbourne.com.au. Very experienced, departures from Richmond, including breakfast in the Observatory Café, Royal Botanical Gardens, from $330.
Go Wild, T9739 0772, www.gowild ballooning.com.au. Champagne breakfast flights of 1 hr from $350. Recommended.

Body and soul
Aurora Spa Retreat, part of **The Prince** boutique hotel (page 63), 2 Acland St, St Kilda, T9536 1130, www.aurorasparetreat.com. One of the country's largest and most decadent spa and treatment centres.

City tours
As you'd expect there are a wealth of city tour options from tours by bike to those for chocoholics. The visitor information centre has full listings and can book on your behalf.

Cricket
The annual highlight is the **Melbourne Boxing Day Test Match**. International test matches are played regularly in summer at the MCG, T136122, www.mcg.org.au. Tickets from **Ticketmaster**, www.ticketmaster.com.au.

Cycling
A great way to see some of the sights and parks of the city and inner suburbs is to cycle around them. **Real Melbourne Cycle Tours**, T417339203, biketours@internex.net.au or www.rentabike.net.au, provide the bike, refreshments and a guide for a variety of tours. Price around $99 for a half-day. They also offer independent hire from $15 ($35 day). Other outlets include **Borsari Cycles**, 193 Lygon St, Carlton, T9347 4100, **Freedom Machine**, 265 Bay St, Port Melbourne, T9681 8533, and **St Kilda Cycles**, 11 Carlisle St, T9534 3074.

Horse racing
The Spring Carnival's **Melbourne Cup** is one of the country's major events, held on the first Tue in Nov at Flemington Racecourse.

Grandstand tickets aren't cheap but ground entry is more reasonable (from $60). Tickets from **Ticketmaster**. For more information T1800 352229, www.racingvictoria.net.au.

Motor racing
The first Grand Prix of the F1 season is held at Albert Park in early Mar. Tickets cost about $100 for day entry, $160 for 4-day entry and from $350 for a 4-day reserved grandstand ticket. Note the Grand Prix is very much geared around the corporates so public access and views are limited. If you do not have a corporate ticket be prepared to be disappointed in what you see and where you can go. That said, in recent years entry has includes a post-race concert by a high-profile band such as Kiss and Simple Minds. See www.grandprix.com.au for more details. Tickets from **Ticketmaster**.

Penguin spotting
Penguin Waters, T9386 8488, www.penguinwaters.com.au. Sunset fairy penguin-watching tours departing from Southgate (2 hrs, $55). Barbecue and refreshments included.

Tour operators
Autopia Tours, T1800 000507, www.autopiatours.com.au. Day trips to Phillip Island, Great Ocean Rd and the Grampians (all around $125), plus 3-day trip options.
Go West, T1300 736551, www.gowest.com.au. This is one of the best day tours along the Great Ocean Rd. It picks up from about a dozen Melbourne backpacker hostels between 0715 and 0820 every day, returning about 2130. Tours cost around $125.
Wildlife Tours, T9741 6333, www.wildlifetours.com.au. This has similar options with a day tour of the Great Ocean Rd from $95, plus a trip to Ballarat, and another to the Dandenongs. Both companies offer a 2-day tour of the Great Ocean Rd plus the Grampians for around $169, and have backpacker bus routes to

Adelaide and Sydney. Larger coach companies (with larger coaches and slightly higher fares) such as **APT**, T1300 336932, www.aptours.com.au, **AAT Kings**, T1300 556100, www.aatkings.com.au, and **Gray Line**, T1300 858687, www.grayline.com, offer a wider range of day tours as far as Ballarat, Echuca, Mount Buller and the Yarra Valley.

Walking
For details of Melbourne's excellent free guided walks courtesy of the Greeter Service, see page 47. The VIC has free brochures and maps for a variety of self-guided walks, such as art walks along Swanston St and the Yarra River and heritage walks.
   The Golden Mile walk is a 4-km route through the city, which goes past the most significant architectural and historical features. It can be done as a self-guided walk ($4) or guided ($20, 2 hrs) on Wed and Fri-Sat at 1030 and 1330. Bookings essential, T1300 780045.

Mornington Peninsula *p56*
Diving
The diving is superb, with shipwrecks and j-class submarines, sheer-wall and fast-drift dives, leafy sea dragons and stingrays. Operators include:
Bayplay Adventure Lodge, 46 Canterbury Jetty Rd, Blairgowrie, T5988 0188, www.bayplay.com.au.
Dive Victoria, 3752 Point Nepean Rd, Portsea, T5984 3155, www.divevictoria.com.au.

Dolphin tours
Bottlenose dolphins live in Port Phillip Bay and swimming with them is becoming increasingly popular, from Oct-Apr.
Moonraker, T5984 4211, www.moonrakercharters.com.au. Offers day tours from Melbourne with dolphin watch or swim options (ex Sorrento) from $199. From Sorrento expect to pay around $100.

Horse trekking

Gunnamatta Trail Rides, T5988 6755, www.gunnamatta.com.au. Offers treks and gallops along the ocean beaches from 30 mins for $35 to full day from $190. Beginners welcome.

Hot pools and day spa

Peninsula Hot Springs, Springs Lane, T5950 8777, www.peninsulahotsprings.com, from $30. Daily 0730-2200. A range of indoor and outdoor pools, a day spa and a café. Recommended.

Surfing

Mornington Peninsula Surf School, T9787 6494, www.greenroomsurf.com.au. Offers surfing lessons.

Phillip Island p57
Seal spotting

The only way to get close to the seals is to take one of a range of excellent boat trips with **Wildlife Coast Cruises**, T5952 5583, www.wildlifecoastcruises.com.au, which operates out of Cowes ($67, 2 hrs). It also runs cruises out to French Island, Wilson's Promontory (see page 79), and operates whale-watching trips in winter.

Surfing

Out There, T5956 6450, or **Island**, T5952 2578. Would-be surfers can take a lesson with one of these outfits. Island also has 3 shops around the island and hires out equipment and wetsuits.

Tour operators

Afternoon or evening tours from Melbourne are offered by all the major operators. One of the best is **Autopia**, T9326 5536, www.autopiatours .com.au.

Yarra Valley and around p60

Several companies run day trips from Melbourne. **Tasting Tours Backpacker Winery Tours**, T9419 4444, www.backpacker winerytours.com.au, takes medium-sized groups out to 4 wineries including Domaine Chandon. From $100, including lunch, wine and afternoon tea. Pick-ups from Melbourne (Flinders St Station, Queensbury Hill and St Kilda).

If you fancy seeing the wineries from a hot air balloon rather than the bottom of a wine glass, check out **Global**, T1800 627661, or **Go Wild**, T9890 0339, www.gowildballooning .com.au. From $330.

⊖ Transport

Melbourne p46, maps p48 and p54
Most of the major sights can be reached on foot and using the free City Circle tram, which travels along Flinders St, up Springs St, along La Trobe St and around Telstra Dome down Harbour Esplanade.

Air

Flight information is available at www.melair.com.au or by ringing the relevant airline. See also page 46. **Qantas Virgin Blue Tiger Airways** and **Jetstar** are the principal suppliers of interstate flights with direct daily services to all state capitals. It's all very competitive so shop around on the net.

Bus

Local There is a bus for almost anywhere you could wish to go within Greater Melbourne, but the further out they travel the less frequently they go. City Saver, 2-hr and daily tickets can be bought on board and notes are accepted.
Long distance Greyhound has a service to **Sydney** and **V-Line** has a daily bus/train service to **Canberra** from Spencer St Station and also operates most state services to Victorian country towns, with a few Gippsland services from Flinders St Station.

Backpacker Autopia, T1800 000507, www.autopiatours.com.au, runs trips to **Sydney** (3½ days, from $445, including backpacker accommodation).

Car

The city has 3 arterial CityLink road tollways, www.citylink.com.au, which electronically read 'e-tags' in vehicles: great for residents, but a real pain for visitors. The road signs are marked in blue with orange text. Passes can be purchased in advance or until midnight the day after you travel (the fine for travelling without a pass is about $100), from the website, post offices and the CityLink Customer Centre, 67 Lorimer St, just off the Westgate Freeway. Buy passes (single use up to $4, 24 hr or weekend $11.30) over the phone with a credit card, 0800-2000, T132629, or via the website. Motorcyclists can use the CityLinks for free. To avoid the tolls when entering the city from the Westgate Freeway (Geelong, Highway 1) take the Kings Way exit for Richmond, Prahran and St Kilda, and the Power St exit for the city, Carlton and Fitzroy. From the South Eastern Freeway (the east, Highway 1) take the Toorak Rd exit and turn left for the city centre and suburbs. From the Calder/ Tullamarine Freeways (the northwest and the airport) take the first exit after the junction of the two freeways. This drops onto Bulla Rd, which eventually becomes Elizabeth St. Beware of metered parking in the city centre; it extends as late as 2400. If you are heading south to the Mornington Peninsula the fastest route is via the new Eastlink Tollway. A trip costs $5.50 and can be purchased online at www.breeze.com.au. Beware, however: do not exceed 100 kph as the bridges are littered with number plate ID cameras that double as speed cameras.

Car hire A cheap option is **Rent-a-Bomb**, T131553, T9696 7555 (South Melbourne depot), www.rentabomb.com.au, which hires out cars for $175 per week for use within 50 km of the city centre.

Ferry

Spirit of Tasmania, T1800 634906, www.spiritoftasmania.com.au. Operates nightly overnight ferries from Port Melbourne to Devonport in Tasmania (13 hrs, prices vary according to season and start at $99 per passenger and at $69 per car).

Taxi

Arrow, T132211; **Silver Top**, T131008; **Yellow 13 Cabs**, T132227.

Train

Local Used mostly to service the outer suburbs. Various networks extend regular services to destinations including **Belgrave** (the Dandenongs), **Frankston** (connections to the Mornington Peninsula), **Lilydale** (connections to the Yarra Valley and beyond), **Stony Point** (ferry connections to French and Phillip Islands), **Werribee** and **Williamstown**. Tickets must be bought at departure stations.

Tram

Trams are the main way to get about the city centre and inner suburbs. They operate more like a bus than a train so you'll need to hail one if you want to get on, and push the buzzer to indicate to the driver that you want to get off. The network of trams mostly radiates out from the city centre to the inner suburbs but some routes travel from suburb to suburb through the centre. **City Saver** and 2-hr tickets can be bought on board, but the dispensers take coins only. Daily tickets must be purchased in advance from a newsagent displaying the Metcard logo.

Mornington Peninsula *p56*
Bus

From **Frankston** station the **Portsea Passenger Bus Service**, T5986 5666, www.grenda.com.au, operates services (No 788) down the Port Phillip Bay coast, with stops including **Dromana**, **Sorrento** (stop 18, corner of Melbourne Rd and Ocean Beach Rd) and **Portsea** (stop 1, National Park entrance). Full run takes 1½ hrs. Mon-Fri services every 1-2 hrs, 0700-1900 (plus Fri 2040); every 2 hrs from 0800-2000 weekends. Last buses back from Portsea at Mon-Fri 1915, Sat 1800 and Sun 1735.

Ferry

A car ferry operates from **Sorrento** to **Queenscliff** on the Bellarine Peninsula. Ferries from 0700-1700, 50 mins, passenger $9, children and concessions $8, cars under 5.5 m $59 plus passengers $7 each, T5258 3244, www.searoad.com.au.

Dandenong Ranges *p59*
Bus/train

There are metropolitan train services daily between **Melbourne** City Circle stations, **Upper Fern Tree Gully** (1 hr) and **Belgrave**, running every 20-30 mins. **US Bus Lines**, T9754 1444, www.usbus.com.au, runs services between **Belgrave** station and **Olinda** (No 694), stopping at **Sherbrook** and **Sassafras**. Services at 0620, 0700 and 5 mins past the hour from Mon-Fri 1000-1500, and every 1-2 hrs Sat 0820-1620. They also have a service between **Upper Fern Tree Gully** and Olinda (No 698), following the commuter hours of 0730 and 0830, and 1610-1940 Mon-Fri only. Metropolitan fares apply, so get a day ticket in Melbourne. There are no local bus services on Sun.

Yarra Valley and around *p60*

There are metropolitan train services daily between **Melbourne** City Circle stations and **Lilydale** (40 mins), running every 20-30 mins. McKenzie, T5962 5088, www.mckenzies .com.au, runs less frequent daily bus services between **Lilydale**, **Yarra Glen**, **Healesville** and **Marysville**. Call for times.

● Directory

Melbourne *p46, maps p48 and p54*
Banks ATMs are on all the major shopping and eating streets. **American Express**, 233 Collins St, Mon-Fri 0900-1700, Sat 0900-1200. **Thomas Cook**, 257 Collins St, Mon-Fri 0900-1700, Sat 1000-1400. Also 261 Bourke St, near Swanston St, Mon-Sat 0900-1700, Sun 1100-1500. **Travelex**, 231 Collins St,

T1800 637642, Mon-Fri 0800-1830, Sat 0800-1730, Sun 1000-1630.
Health centres Travellers Medical and Vaccination Centre, Royal Melbourne Hospital, Royal Pde, T9347 7022. **City Health Care**, 255 Bourke St, T9650 1711. Mon-Fri 0900-1800, Sat 1000-1700, and **Acland St Medical Centre**, 171 Acland St, St Kilda, T9534 0635. Mon-Thu 0900-1900, Fri 0900-1800, Sat 0900-1200, are both visitor-friendly and bulk bill. Medicare at **Centre Point Mall**, corner of Bourke St and Swanston St, Mon-Fri 0900-1645. **Hospitals** Royal Melbourne, Grattan St, Parkville, T9342 7000; **St Vincent's**, 41 Victoria Pde, Fitzroy, T9288 2211. **Internet** Global Gossip, 440 Elizabeth St, city centre, daily 0900-2400. Net City, 404 Brunswick St, Fitzroy, daily 0930-2300. N2C, 100/Mid City Arcade, 200 Bourke St, City. **Pharmacies** Mulqueeny, corner Swanston St and Collins St, T9654 8569, Mon-Fri 0800-2000, Sat 0900-1800, Sun 1100-1800. **Sally Lew**, 41 Fitzroy St, St Kilda, T9534 8084, daily 0900-2100. Cheap film processing. **Post** Main Post Office, Elizabeth St, Mon-Fri 0815-1730, Sat 0900-1600. Poste Restante (take photo ID to collect mail) Mon-Fri 0900-1730, Sat 0900-1200. **Useful numbers** Police, 637 Flinders St, T9247 5347.

Phillip Island *p57*
Banks Most major banks have ATMs on Thompson St, Cowes. **Internet** Library, Thompson Av, T5952 2842, or Waterfront Computers, 130 Thompson Av (next to Mobil), T5952 3312. Mon-Fri 0900-1700, Sat 1000-1300. **Post** 73 Thompson Av.

Southeast Victoria

Lying east of Melbourne and extending from the mountains to the coast, Gippsland is the rural heartland of Victoria, a rich landscape of rolling green dairy pasture. In the far south is the main attraction, Wilson's Promontory, a low range of forest-covered granite mountains, edged with isolated sandy bays and golden river inlets and marked only by the occasional walking track. Carefully maintained as a wilderness, the 'Prom' offers intimate encounters with wildlife and is a stunning place to walk, swim, camp or simply laze about. In the centre of the region, the Gippsland Lakes system forms the largest inland waterway in Australia, where every small town has jetties festooned with yachts and fishing boats. Heading inland, the landscape rises to the limestone caves of Buchan and the rugged forest and gorges of the Snowy River National Park. Further east along the coast, is Croajingolong National Park, a wilderness of dense bush and river inlets, the largest of which is overlooked by one of Victoria's loveliest small towns, Mallacoota, an isolated and peaceful haven.

Ins and outs

Getting there and around
The main V-Line train line heads out from Melbourne through Dandenong and Warragul to Bairnsdale about three times daily. From here buses take over. The route heads east via Lakes Entrance, Orbost, Cann River and Genoa to the NSW border. From Dandenong there are connecting bus services to Bass then Newhaven and Cowes on Phillip Island; to Wonthaggi and Inverloch; and to Yarram via Leongatha, Fish Creek and Foster. There are also ferries to Cowes from Stony Point on the Mornington Peninsula. From Cann River there is a set-down-only service to Canberra and another up the coast to Batemans Bay.
▶▶ *See Transport, page 86.*

Tourist information
If heading east out of Melbourne along the Princes Highway you can stock up on information from the main Melbourne VIC. Within the region itself the main accredited VICs are to the east in Sale, the **Central Gippsland Information Centre** ⓘ *8 Forster St, T1800 677520, www.gippslandinfo.com.au*, or, if travelling south out of Melbourne towards Wilson's Promontory along the South Gippsland Highway, the **Prom Country Information Centre** ⓘ *on the highway in Korumburra, T5655 2233, infocentre@sgsc .vic.gov.au, 0900-1700*. The tourism website is www.inspiredbygippsland.com.au. Another option is **Bairnsdale and Lakes Entrance Information Centre** ⓘ *240 Main St Bairnsdale and corner Princes Highway and Marine Pde, Lakes Entrance T1800 637060, www.discovereastgippsland.com.au.*

Wilson's Promontory National Park → *For listings, see pages 83-86. Colour map 1, C4.*

The 'Prom', as it is known by Victorians, is one of the state's top attractions, with granite-capped mountains covered in forest sloping down to the purest of white sand beaches and tannin-stained rivers meandering down to the sea. The northeastern region is a wilderness area only accessible to bushwalkers and boats. The park's most accessible beaches and bushwalks are on the western coast near Tidal River, the only 'settlement', where parrots, wombats and kangaroos roam (and fly) around freely. The year 2005 saw two notable events on the Prom, first in summer when wildfires decimated the region, and then, ironically, the first snowfalls for years in August.

Ins and outs

There are two main routes down to the Prom. The more direct route heads through the heart of dairy country, taking in Koonwarra and Fish Creek. The longer route heads south to the coast via the 'Big Worm' and Wonthaggi. Tiny **Koonwarra**, 140 km from Melbourne and 80 km from Wilson's Promontory, is a worthy distraction thanks to the **Koonwarra Store** ① *daily 0800-1700*, a café/restaurant serving country breakfasts, lunches and dinners of the highest quality, and a takeaway. **Fish Creek** is another tiny and charming settlement. **Foster**, 30 km from Koonwara, is the closest major town to Wilson's Promontory and is well supplied with supermarkets and bakeries to fuel camping expeditions.

Visit the **Parks Office** ① *Tidal River, T5680 9555, www.parkweb.vic.gov.au, 0900-1700*, for permits, detailed notes on day and overnight walks and advice on activities in the park. Park entry at the gate is $9.50 per car per day.

Around the park

The park offers dozens of trail options. **Squeaky Beach**, **Picnic Bay** and **Whisky Bay** can be reached by very short walks from car parks but the best walk is to all of these beaches from Tidal River along the coast (9 km return). The best views of the Prom are from the top of **Mount Oberon**. The walk up from Telegraph Saddle car park, 3.5 km from Tidal River, is wide and easy with a few rock-cut steps at the top (7 km, two hours return). Sunrise is the best time for photographs of Norman Bay below. A good spot for sunset is Whisky Bay. A very popular day walk from the same car park is the track to **Sealers' Cove** (9.5 km, 2½ hours one way) passing through thick rainforest to the eastern side of the Prom. The cove has a long arc of golden sand, tightly fringed by bush. There is a basic campsite at Sealers' Creek. The cove is beautiful but the walk has little variety and the return leg can feel like a bit of a slog. A more interesting day's walk is the **Oberon Bay** loop that also starts from Telegraph Saddle (19 km, six hours). There is also an extended walk (38 km, two to three days) to the lighthouse that sits on a great dome of granite on the southern tip of the promontory. The **Lighthouse Trek** can be done independently or from October to May with a ranger guide ($300-450, including accommodation and meals). At the lighthouse you can stay in cottages that are equipped with bunks, kitchen and bathroom. The cottages can be booked by the bed or exclusively for groups (C-D).

Gippsland Lakes → *For listings, see pages 83-86.*

The break between central and eastern Gippsland is marked by a series of connected lakes, separated from the sea only by the long thin dune system of the eastern end of Ninety Mile Beach. This strip of sand, designated the Gippsland Lakes Coastal Park, is accessible only by boat and is relatively unspoiled, even in peak season. The main service town in the area is Bairnsdale, but there are some pretty settlements dotted around the margins of the lakes, and Metung is particularly picturesque. Soon after Yarram is the turning to Woodside Beach, which marks the start of Ninety Mile Beach, the long golden stretch of sand that curves all the way to Lakes Entrance.

Sale, the administration centre for Gippsland, has all the usual services available but offers few attractions for visitors. The **VIC** ① *Princes Highway, T5144 1108,* *www.gippslandinfo.com.au, 0900-1700,* is just west of the town centre. **Bairnsdale** is the largest town in the Lakes area, though it isn't actually on a lake shore itself. It is worth stopping here for the Aboriginal **Krowathunkalong Keeping Place** ① *Dalmahoy St, T5152 1891, Mon-Fri 0900-1200 and 1300-1700, $3.50, children $2.50, concessions $1.50,* which features chillingly frank descriptions of the brutal Gunnai massacres that took place in Gippsland during the 1830s-1850s. The excellent **VIC** ① *240 Main St, T5152 3444, www.discovereastgippsland.com.au, 0900-1700,* will help with information and bookings for the whole Lakes region as well as Bairnsdale.

Paynesville hugs a stretch of lake shore facing **Raymond Island**, a small haven for wildlife, especially koalas, with one of the country's most concentrated wild populations. It's not a park, however, and the Paynesville township effectively extends across the car ferry (every half an hour, $8.50 return, pedestrians free) to claim a portion of the island as a suburb. Further offshore, **Rotamah Island** is home to a **Bird Observatory** ① *T131963, rotamah@i-o.net.au.* Camping is possible; contact the observatory.

Metung is on a small spit only a few hundred metres wide, giving it the feel of a village surrounded by water. Most of the homes spreading up the low wooded hill to the rear overlook Bancroft Bay, lined with yachts and jetties. Well-heeled visitors are catered for here, with a couple of good restaurants, wonderful day and sailing options and some luxurious accommodation options.

Standing at the only break in the long stretch of dunes that separate the Gippsland Lakes from the sea is **Lakes Entrance**. Once a small fishing village, it has become a traditional Victorian coastal holiday resort, known for its pleasant and varied scenery, range of accommodation, eateries and water-based activities.

Over the footbridge is the **Entrance Walking Track**, a leisurely and rewarding two-hour return stroll through dunes and bush to **Ninety Mile Beach** and **Flagstaff Lookout**. Wyanga Park Winery, see page 85, runs popular day and evening cruises from the town's Club Jetty on their launch, the *Corque*. The **VIC** ① *corner Marine Pde and the Esplanade, T5155 1966, discovereastgippsland.com.au, 0900-1700.*

East to Mallacoota → *For listings, see pages 83-86.*

Orbost
The Yalmy Road continues down to Orbost, sitting at the point at which the Snowy River meets the Princes Highway. Though well placed to capitalize on the considerable tourist traffic, the small town offers little to the traveller except the cheapest petrol and last decent supermarkets until well into NSW, and a helpful **VIC** ① *The Slab Hut, Nicholson St, T5154 2424, orbostvic@bigpond.com, 0900-1700.*

Marlo and Cape Conran
The tiny fishing community of Marlo at the mouth of the Snowy River is a popular long-weekend destination for Victorians, with a variety of caravan and cabin accommodation but few facilities aside from a couple of small grocery shops, one doing takeaways, and an impressive pub with guesthouse facilities. There are several good marked walking trails around Cape Conran, where two beautiful sandy beaches are generally fine for swimming. Camping is available; see **Parks Victoria**, page 84.

Croajingolong National Park

This wonderful park, a narrow strip south of the Princes Highway that runs for 100 km west of the state border, is best known for its long stretch of wild coastline, but it also encompasses eucalyptus forests, rainforests, granite peaks, estuaries and heathland. The remoteness of much of the park has led to a wide diversity of flora and fauna, with over 1000 native plants and more than 300 bird species, and it has been recognized as a World Biosphere Reserve.

Point Hicks was the first land in Australia to be sighted by the crew of Captain's Cook's *Endeavour* in 1770 and mainland Australia's tallest lighthouse was built here in 1890. The track to Point Hicks (2.25 km) starts at the end of the road past Thurra River campsite, and passes Honeymoon Bay. There are fantastic views from the top of the **lighthouse** ① *T5156 0432, www.pointhicks.com.au, tours 1300 Fri-Mon*, and southern right whales are often seen just off shore in winter. For details of staying in the lighthouse or campsite see page 83. It is possible to walk the coast from **Bemm River** right over the NSW border into the **Nadgee Nature Reserve**. Trekking on the wild beaches makes up the bulk of the experience, but walkers will also encounter a range of spectacular coastal scenery. There are a number of campsites with facilities along the route, though water can get scarce and walkers need to carry a couple of days' supply. Numbers are restricted on all stretches of the trek, and permits are required. Contact the Cann River or Mallacoota Park's Victoria office ① *T5161 9500, www.parkweb.vic.gov.au*.

Mallacoota

Perched on the edge of the Mallacoota Inlet and the sea, Mallacoota is a beguiling and peaceful place. Surrounded by the Croajingolong National Park and a long way from any large cities, it's a haven for wildlife, particularly birdlife. The quiet meandering waters of the inlet are surrounded by densely forested hills. To the south are several beautiful coastal beaches, like **Betka Beach**, a popular local swimming beach. Spectacular layered and folded rocks can be seen at **Bastion Point** and **Quarry Beach**. There are almost unlimited opportunities for coastal walks, bushwalking, fishing and boating. Once a year in April there is an explosion of creativity at the Carnival in Coota – a week-long festival of theatre, visual arts, music and literature.

The **Mallacoota Walking Track** is a 7-km loop, signposted from the main roundabout, which goes through casuarina forest and heathland, along the beach to Bastion Point and back towards town past the entrance. To explore the inlet by water there are several options. Motor boats, canoes and kayaks can be hired from the caravan near the wharf. Several cruising boats are also based at the wharf: visit their kiosks for bookings. For details, see Activities and tours page 86. There are magnificent views of the area from **Genoa Peak**; the access road is signposted from the Princes Highway, 2 km west of Genoa. From the picnic and parking area there is a 1.5-km walking track to the summit, steep for the last 100 m. Further afield is tiny **Gabo Island**, home to one of the largest fairy penguin colonies in the country, plus one of the highest lighthouses. For local information, contact the **VIC** ① *main Wharf, T5158 0116, www.visitmallacoota.com.au, 0900-1700*.

Buchan and around → *For listings, see pages 83-86.*

Tiny Buchan is best known for its limestone caves but it is also just south of the Snowy River National Park. Consequently it is a good area for walking, canoeing and rafting as well as caving. There are over 300 caves in the region, the best of which are contained in the **Buchan Caves Reserve** ⓘ *entrance is just north of town, before the bridge, T131963, T5155 9264, Oct-Mar 1000, 1115, 1415 and 1530, Apr-Sep 1100, 1300 and 1500, $14, children $8, concessions $11.50*, which has two well-lit show caves with spectacular golden cave decorations. **Fairy Cave** and **Royal Cave** are famous for their pillars, stalactites, stalagmites, flowstone and calcite pools. There are 'adventure' caving tours, available during Easter and Christmas holidays or when numbers permit, and some good short walks. The 3-km **Spring Creek Walk** is a loop that heads uphill to Spring Creek Falls and passes through remnant rainforest, mossy rocks and ferns. Lyrebirds, kookaburras and parrots may be seen (or heard) on this track. Detailed walking notes and bookings for cave tours are available from the Parks Victoria office in the reserve. Limited information is available at the post office or general store in Buchan.

⊙ Southeast Victoria listings

For Sleeping and Eating price codes and other relevant information, see Essentials pages 28-33.

Sleeping

Wilson's Promontory National Park *p79*
The Prom is so popular that accommodation is allocated by ballot for Dec-Jan (including campsites). Even at other times, weekends may have to be booked a year in advance. Also, check out www.promaccom.com.au.
B Tingara View Tea House and Cottages, 10 Tingara Close, Yanakie, T5687 1488, www.promcountry.com.au/tingaraview. 3 pretty, colonial-style 1-room cottages with lovely views, cooked breakfast served in main house, also dinner and afternoon tea.
B-D Park cabin/campsite, T5680 9555, wprom@parks.vic.gov.au. The best place to stay is undoubtedly within the park itself. There is a good range of accommodation in cabins, units and huts.
Camping in the park is fantastic. There is an (unbookable) international campers area available for 1-2 nights.

Gippsland Lakes *p80*
In Bairnsdale there are a couple of caravan parks, and several motels and B&Bs. Accommodation may be plentiful in Lakes

Entrance, but if you're travelling over Christmas and January, book well ahead.
L-B Déjà Vu, just to the north of Lakes Entrance over the lake on Clara St, T5155 4330, www.dejavu.com.au. This modern, glass-filled, hosted B&B, set in 7 acres of wild lakeside country, has rooms with private lake-view balconies, and the first-class service is friendly and attentive, with some unexpected and unusual flourishes. Also a couple of suitably alluring self-contained properties fronting the lake. Book well in advance. Lovely.
A-B BelleVue, 201 Esplanade, Lakes Entrance, T5155 3055, www.bellevuelakes.com. A cracking little daytime café and decent mid-range seafood restaurant help make this very comfortably furnished, family-run motel stand out from the crowd.
A Anchorage, The Anchorage, Metung, T5156 2569, www.anchoragebedandbreakfast .com.au. Comfortable B&B with particularly wonderful wooden breakfast atrium.
C Arendell cabins, Metung, T5156 2507, www.arendellmetung.com.au. There are various spacious, self-contained options, set in lawned gardens.
C Bellbrae, 4 km out on Ostlers Rd, Lakes Entrance, T5155 2319, www.lakes-entrance .com/bellbrae. Similar cabins to **Arendell**, but cheaper and better spaced out in a forest setting.

C Lazy Acre, 35 Roadknight St, Lakes Entrance, T5155 1323, www.lazyacre.com. Several well-maintained and self-contained log cabins, one specifically designed for the disabled, each sleeping up to 6.

D Old Pub, Esplanade, Paynesville, T5156 6442. Five pub rooms, unusually all en suite, freshly decorated and furnished, continental breakfast, pleasant veranda. Bistro with a cheap menu, superb salad and veggie bar.

E Riviera Backpackers, 669 Esplanade, Lakes Entrance, T5155 2444, www.yha.com.au. Very well-run and well-equipped YHA hostel with a good range of rooms, including several doubles (some en suite), all at a good-value-per-head price. Cheap bike hire, pool. Friendly and knowledgeable owners.

East to Mallacoota p81

If using Orbost as a base for exploring the local national parks, the most interesting place to stay is out on the Buchan Road. Most of the accommodation in Mallacoota is self-contained holiday flats or caravan parks. Book ahead for Dec-Jan and during Carnival.

LL Point Hicks Lighthouse Keepers' Cottages, T5156 0432, www.pointhicks .com.au. In Croajingolong National Park, with verandas overlooking the sea, sleeps 8. Pricey, very comfortable and heavily booked at peak times. If free the managers may offer a 'rock-up rate' of $100 double or offer accommodation to backpackers in a simple bungalow. Call in advance to arrange an unlocked gate.

L-D Karbeethong Lodge, 16 Schnapper Point Dr, Mallacoota, T5158 0411, www.karbeethonglodge.com.au. Comfortable old guesthouse, 4 km north of the town centre, with wide verandas overlooking the inlet, 12 rooms, some with en suite, communal kitchen facility. Not suitable for kids.

B-C Marlo Hotel, 19 Argyle Pde, Marlo, T5154 8201. An impressive pub and guesthouse with en suites. An 11,000-ha, relatively undisturbed park extends from Cape Conran up to the Croajingolong.

B-D Adobe Mudbrick Flats, 14 Karbeethong Hill Av, just north of the Lodge, Mallacoota, T5158 0329, www.adobeholidayflats.com.au. 10 original and delightful hand-built self-contained flats with superb views of the inlet. Countless birds, possums and even koalas share this 28-ha property. The very welcoming, knowledgeable hosts help make a stay here a real experience.

C-F Parks Victoria, T131963/T5154 8438, www.parks vic.gov.au. Manages cabins at Cape Conran, sleeping up to 6 people, and a camping ground with fireplaces, toilets and bush showers. At peak times cabins are allocated by lottery, and campsites are booked months in advance.

D-E Mallacoota, 51 Maurice Av, Mallacoota, T5158 0455. Lively pub, particularly on a Fri, serves cheap light lunches and mid-range dinners, including a good range of vegetarian options. They have 20 motel rooms and also a few shared rooms designated for backpackers with a small but clean kitchen. Food daily 1200-1345 and 1800-2000.

Camping Campsites in Croajingolong National Park must be booked at the parks office. Book well in advance for Dec-Jan and Easter. The main camping areas are all situated where rivers and creeks meet the coast, **Thurra River** (46 sites) and **Wingan Inlet** (24 sites) both have stunning locations but the sites are close together and do get very busy in peak summer and holiday periods. It's still sleepy in comparison to the Prom though!

Mallacoota has excellent camping parks including the **D-E Foreshore**, T5158 0300, www.mallacootaholidaypark.com.au, the **D-E Shady Gully**, Lot 5, Mallacoota-Genoa Rd, T5158 0362 and the **D-E Wangralea**, 78 Betka Rd, T5158 0222. The latter has a camp kitchen.

Buchan and around p83

B Snowy River Wilderness, T5154 1923, www.snowyriverwildernest.com. An isolated 150-ha deer farm, 30 km towards Orbost, snuggled in a wooded valley on a beautiful stretch of the Snowy River, with 2 spacious but basic self-contained houses, sleeping 11 and 10. The cheap restaurant is in a rustic terrace by the main homestead that is friendly and cosy.

C **Buchan Valley Log Cabins**, Gelantipy Rd, just over the bridge, Buchan, T5155 9494, www.buchanlogcabins.com.au. Self-contained, 2-bedroom cabins, set on a hillside overlooking the valley. Serviceable furnishings, large deck.

E **Buchan Lodge**, Saleyard Rd, heading north, take first left after the bridge, Buchan, T5155 9421, www.buchanlodge.com. Excellent pine-log backpackers' hostel with warm, homely open kitchen and dining hall. Peaceful, rural location.

Camping D-F There is a camping ground in the Buchan Caves Reserve with cabins, bookings at the Parks Office, T5155 9264.

❶ Eating

Wilson's Promontory National Park *p79*
Places to eat in the park are limited to lacklustre fast food from the café at Tidal River or **Yanakie's Roadhouse**; the closest decent food is in Fish Creek or Foster. There is also a shop at Tidal River stocking a limited range of groceries and petrol.

♔ **Fishy Pub**, on the highway, Fish Creek, T5683 2404. Daily 1200-1400, 1800-2000. Excellent food, also live music most weekends.

♔ **Koonwarra Store**, Koonwarra, T5664 2285. Daily 0800-1700, wine bar and diner Fri-Sat 1830-2130. Café/restaurant serving country breakfasts, lunches and dinners of the highest quality, and a takeaway. Book for meals at weekends.

♔ **Rhythm**, 3 Bridge St, Foster, T5682 1612. Thu-Tue 0900-1700, daily 1800-2100 in peak summer. There aren't many places to eat but this café is excellent. Scrumptious breakfasts, casual lunches and cakes in a small, bright jazzy room.

Gippsland Lakes *p80*
♔♔ **Espas**, Raymond Island, near Paynesville, T/F5156 7275. Fri-Sat 1000-2030, Sun 1000-1700. Excellent modern food in this striking place with an outdoor deck facing Paynesville across the water.

♔♔ **Miriam**'s, 3 Bulmer St, Lakes Entrance, T5155 3999. 1800-2130. First-floor, funky restaurant, great balcony tables in summer, abundant candles and candelabras in the darker months. Good seafood.

♔♔ **Fisherman's Wharf Pavilion**, Paynesville, T5156 0366. Right on the water and a wonderful spot either summer or winter. A café by day with breakfasts and interesting light lunches, mid-range restaurant Thu-Sat to 2000.

♔♔ **L'Ocean Fish and Chips**, 19 Myer St, Lakes Entrance, T5155 2253. The best fish and chips in town.

♔♔ **Marrillee**, 50 Metung Rd, Metung, T5156 2121. Open breakfast, lunch and dinner. One of very few choices in the village, but good seafood none the less. Open fireplaces inside and out. Licensed.

♔♔ **Wyanga Park Winery**, 10 km north of Lakes Entrance on Baades Rd, T5155 1508, www.wyangapark.com.au. Tastings and a colourful, characterful café open daily 1000-1700, doubling as a restaurant, Thu-Sat 1800-2000.

♔ **Central**, Lakes Entrance. Daily 1200-1400, 1800-2000. A pub with a large bistro area. Surprisingly good meals, with a self-service salad and veggie bar.

♔ Other than that you will find plenty of traditional cafés and fish and chip shops along the Esplanade.

▲ Activities and tours

Wilson's Promontory National Park *p79*
Bunyip Tours, T9650 9680,
www.bunyiptours.com. An eco-friendly outfit
that takes small groups out to Wilson's
Promontory and Phillip Island. It offers 1- to
2-day guided or unguided treks, with hostel
stays (camping only at Wilson's Prom)
included (2 days Phillip Island and Wilson's
Prom, $280). Equipment – bar sleeping bags
and a backpack – and food included.
Wildlife Coast Cruises, T5952 5583,
www.wildlifecoastcruises.com.au. Runs
occasional day cruises from Port Welshpool
that include stops at Waterloo Bay, Refuge
Cove and cruising around the lighthouse,
Skull Rock and a seal colony (Port Welshpool,
$180, 7 hrs, half-day option $78).

Gippsland Lakes *p80*
Virtually all activity revolves around the water,
with several ways of getting out onto the
100s of square kilometres of lakes.
Clint's Ski School, Paynesville, T0427-825416.
Offers good-value private lessons, multiple runs
for the more experienced and ski-tube runs.
Equipment supplied.
Lakes Entrance Paddle Boats, over the
footbridge in Lakeside to the spit,
T0419-552753. Provides anything from a
body board to a small catamaran,
hourly/daily hire.
Riviera Nautic, Metung, T5156 2243,
www.rivieranautic.com.au. Highly regarded
operator offering various overnight
motor-cruisers and sailboats for hire, from
around $500 a day (minimum 2 days), which
is the best way to experience the lakes.
Victor Hire Boats, Marine Parade, T5155
3988. Motorboats can be hired from here.

East to Mallacoota *p81*
Mallacoota Explorer Tours,
T0408 315615/T5158 0116,
ww.mallacootaexplorer.com.au. Offers
popular 2-hr scenic and historic tours that
connect with V-Line Coach services, T136196,
in Genoa twice daily Tue, Thu and Sun.
To explore the inlet at Mallacoota: *MV
Lochard*, Mallacoota, T5158 0764, is an old
ferryboat taking larger groups on 2- to 3-hr
cruises around the inlet from $28, while *The
Porkie Bess*, Mallacoota, T5158 0109, is a
smaller wooden affair built in 1947, skippered
by a knowledgeable local.
The VIC can supply the latest charter listings,
T5151 0116.

Buchan and around *p83*
Adventurama, T9819 1311,
www.adventurama.com.au. Abseiling, caving
and rafting. Their full day rafting options range
from $155-$245, while the full 7-day Snowy
River experience will cost you around $1950;
full day abseiling and caving from $175.

☉ Transport

Wilson's Promontory *p79*
The 200-km drive from Melbourne via the
South Gippsland Highway, turning south at
Meeniyan and Fish Creek, or Foster, takes
about 3 hrs. Tidal River, where the main
visitor facilities are, is 30 km inside the park
boundary. There are limited services to the
Prom from Melbourne and Foster; for detailed
train information contact **V-Line**, T136196,
www.vline.com.au and for bus services
between Foster and Tidal River contact
Moon's Buslines, T5687 1249.

Gippsland Region *p80*
For bus service timetables and fares
throughout the Gippsland region contact
V-Line, T136196, www.vline
passenger.com.au, or the local VIC.

Contents

Footprint features

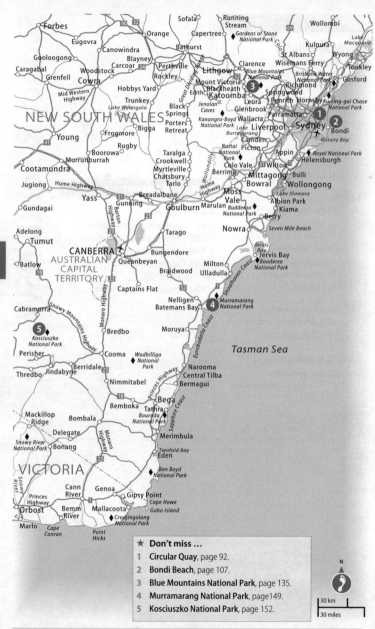

★ Don't miss ...
1 Circular Quay, page 92.
2 Bondi Beach, page 107.
3 Blue Mountains National Park, page 135.
4 Murramarang National Park, page149.
5 Kosciuszko National Park, page 152.

N

30 km
30 miles

Sydney has come a long way since January 1788, when Captain Arthur Phillip, commander of the 'First Fleet', weighed anchor in Port Jackson and declared the entire continent a British penal colony. Where once was a collection of sorry-looking shacks and lock-ups full of desperate, hopeless convicts, stands a forest of glistening modern high-rises. In their shadow, hordes of free-spirited, cosmopolitan city workers have every reason to be proud of their beautiful city, one that, in their eyes, is the 'real' capital of Australia.

One of the best things about Australia's largest city is that you are never too far away from water. To the south are the little-known coastal towns of Jervis Bay, Batemans Bay and Narooma, all of which act as gateways to the greatest concentration of parks in the state.

Less than two hours from Sydney is the Greater Blue Mountains region. Named after the visual effects of sunlight on eucalyptus oil released by the cloak of gum trees that liberally swathes the valleys and plateau, the 'Blueys' now attract over one million visitors a year, flocking to delight in the stunning vistas, walk the numerous tracks or simply relax in the many quaint and characterful hotels and B&Bs.

Sydney → *Colour map 2, A3*

Many adjectives and superlatives have been used to describe Sydney but the feelings stirred on seeing the city for the first time go beyond mere words. Seasoned travellers often complain that the world's great cities can seem a trifle disappointing; their icons somehow seeming smaller in reality than in the imagination. But not so Sydney. That first sighting of its majestic harbour from Circular Quay, with the grand Opera House on one side and the mighty Harbour Bridge on the other, is one that always exceeds expectations. Aussie writer and TV personality Clive James has described it as looking 'like crushed diamonds', but even without such analogies the marriage of natural and man-made aesthetics cannot fail to impress. Over the last decade vast sums have also been spent on inner-city rejuvenation, transportation and state-of-the-art venues to host high profile international sporting events like the 2000 Olympics and 2003 Rugby World Cup, both of which were resounding successes and only added to the city's global reputation. Yet even without such events, this is a city whose inhabitants know that their lifestyle is one of the best in the world and their metropolis one of the most impacting anywhere. It's hardly surprising then that Sydney also has a whole lot to offer tourists, from its fascinating museums and galleries and world-class restaurants and beaches to its renowned 24-hour entertainment. ▸▸ *For listings, see pages 111-132.*

Ins and outs

Getting there

Kingsford Smith Airport ① *9 km south of the city centre, www.sydneyairport.com*, has excellent facilities and its negotiation is straightforward. There is a **Tourism New South Wales** ① *T9667 9386*, information desk in the main arrivals concourse where help is at hand to organize transport and accommodation bookings, flight arrival information and airport facilities. There are ATMs, foreign exchange outlets, car hire, a post office and medical centre (open 0400-2300). The domestic terminal is a short distance west of the international terminal.

Public transport to the city centre is available within a short walk of the terminal building. The fastest and most convenient method is via the **Airport Link** rail service every 10-15 minutes ($15). Taxis are available outside the terminal (south). A trip to the centre takes 30 minutes, $50. Various independent shuttle operators and courtesy accommodation shuttles also operate door-to-door from outside the terminal building, including **Kingsford Smith Transport** ① *T9666 9988*, which runs every 20-30 minutes anywhere in the city ($14 one way and $23 return).

All interstate and NSW state destination trains arrive and depart from Sydney's **Central Railway Station** on Eddy Avenue, T131500. **Countrylink** ① *T132232, www.country link.info*, is the main interstate operator with a combination of coach and rail to all the main interstate and NSW destinations. They have a travel centre at Central Station (open 0630-2200), while Town Hall Station, Wynyard Station, Circular Quay and Bondi Junction all have on-the-spot **CityRail** information booths. The main **coach terminal** is in the Central Railway Station; **Greyhound** ① *T1300 473946, www.greyhound.com.au, daily 0730-1830*. Left luggage and showers are also available.

Getting around

Public transport in Sydney is generally efficient and convenient. The great hub of public transportation in the city centre revolves around Circular Quay at the base of the CBD. It is from there that most ferry (**Sydney Ferries**) and many suburban rail (**CityRail**) and bus (**Sydney Buses**) services operate. The State Transit Authority (STA) owns and operates the principal suburban ferry and bus services. Other principal terminals are Wynyard on York Street for northbound bus and rail services, Town Hall on George Street and the Central Railway Station. For information about all public transport, T131500 (0600-2200), www.131500.com.au. For discount passes, see box on page 130. Once in the city, ferry and rail route maps are available from information centres. The free leaflet *CBD Access Map Sydney*, available from the VICs or information booths, is a very useful map and guide for the disabled. ▸▸ *See Transport, page129.*

Tourist information

Beyond the visitor information booth at the airport international arrivals terminal, the first stop for any visitor should be the **Sydney Visitors Centre** ① *Level 1, corner Argyle St and Playfair St, the Rocks, T9240 8788, www.therocks.com.au, daily 0930-1730.* The centre provides information, brochures, maps and reservations for hotels, tours, cruises, restaurants and other city-based activities. There is another **VIC** ① *Darling Harbour, 33 Wheat Rd, T9240 8788, www.sydneyvisitorcentre.com.au.* It offers similar services to the Rocks centre but has an emphasis on sights and activities within Darling Harbour itself.

1 Sydney Harbour

Sydney maps
1 Sydney Harbour
2 Sydney centre, page 94
3 Kings Cross, page 105

Neither centre issues public transport tickets. Manly, Parramatta, Homebush Bay and Bondi also have local information centres while small manned information booths are located on the corner of Pitt Street and Alfred Street, Circular Quay; opposite St Andrew's Cathedral near the Town Hall on George Street; and on Martin Place, near Elizabeth Street.

The main daily newspaper in Sydney is the excellent *Sydney Morning Herald*, which has comprehensive entertainment listings daily (see the pull-out *Metro* section on Friday) and regular city features. There are some excellent, free tourist brochures including the *Sydney Official Guide*, *This Week in Sydney*, *Where Magazine*, the very interesting suburb-oriented *Sydney Monthly* and, for the backpacker, *TNT* (NSW Edition), www.tntdownunder.com. For entertainment look out for *Drum Media*, www.drummedia.com.au, and *3-D World*, www.threedworld.com.au. All these and others are available from the main VICs, city centre information booths or from cafés, newsagents and bookshops.

Circular Quay and the Rocks → *For listings, see pages 111-132.*

Sydney is without doubt one of the most beautiful cities in the world and the main reasons for this are its harbour, Opera House and Harbour Bridge. The first thing you must do on arrival, even before you throw your bags on a bed and sleep off the jet lag, is get yourself down to Circular Quay, day or night. Circular Quay also provides the main walkway from the historic and commercial Rocks area to the Opera House and the Botanical Gardens beyond. It's a great place to linger, take photographs or pause to enjoy the many bizarre street performers that come and go with the tides.

Sydney Opera House
ⓘ *Information T9250 7777, bookings T9250 7111, www.sydneyoperahouse.com, lines open Mon-Sat 0900-2030 for the latest schedules, and for tours, see below. See also page 123.*
Even the fiercest critics of modern architecture cannot fail to be impressed by the magnificent Sydney Opera House. Built in 1973, it is the result of a revolutionary design by Danish architect, Jorn Utzon, and every day, since this bizarre edifice was created, people have flocked to admire it. At times the steps and concourse seem more like the nave of some futuristic cathedral than the outside of an arts venue, with hordes of worshippers gazing in reverential awe. With such adoration it was perhaps inevitable that the great Aussie icon would join the international A-list of man-made creations, being awarded World Heritage Site status in 2007. The Opera House is best viewed not only intimately from close up, but also from afar. Some of the best spots are from Macquarie Point (end of the Domain on the western edge of Farm Cove) especially at dawn, and from the Park Hyatt Hotel on the eastern edge of Circular Quay. Also any ferry trip eastbound from Circular Quay will reveal the structure in many of its multi-faceted forms.

The Opera House has five performance venues ranging from the main, 2690-capacity Concert Hall to the small Playhouse Theatre. Combined, they host about 2500 performances annually – everything from Bach to Billy Connolly. The Opera House is the principal performance venue for Opera Australia, the Australian Ballet Company, the Sydney Dance Company, the Sydney Symphony Orchestra and the Sydney Theatre Company. There are two tours and three performance packages available. The **Essential Tour** ⓘ *every 30 mins, 1 hr, daily 0900-1700, $35, children and concessions $25*, provides an insider's view of selected theatres and foyers. The **Backstage Tour** ⓘ *T9250 7777, 2 hrs, daily 0700, $150*, as the name suggests, takes you behind the scenes and includes breakfast in the staff restaurant. Other performance packages combine a range of performance, dining and tour options.

Sydney Harbour's wildlife

Amidst all the human activity on Sydney Harbour you may be surprised to learn that it is not unusual to see a penguin dodging the wakes of boats in the inner harbour. Incredible as it may seem, little blue penguins live and breed in Sydney Harbour, and at the harbour mouth, in late winter and spring, migrating humpback whales are also regularly seen. Also, around the Rocks at dusk and after dark, keep your eye open for huge flying foxes (fruit bats). These sometimes stray from the large colony resident in the Botanical Gardens.

From the Opera House to the Rocks

At the eastern edge of the quay, the **Opera Quays** façade provides many tempting, if expensive, cafés and restaurants as well as an art gallery and a cinema. After dark and on a warm summer's evening this surely has to be one of the best places on the planet for a convivial beer or G&T. Look out for the **Writers Walk**, a series of plaques on the main concourse with quotes from famous Australian writers.

The **Justice and Police Museum** ① *corner of Albert St and Phillip St, T9252 1144, www.hht.nsw.gov.au, Sat-Sun 1000-1700, Sat-Thu in Jan, $8, children $4*, housed in the former 1856 Water Police Court, features a magistrates' court and former police cells, as well as a gallery and historical displays showcasing the antics and fate of some of Sydney's most notorious criminals. Nearby, facing the quay, is the former 1840 **Customs House** which now houses a major public library, several exhibition spaces, café-bars and on the top floor the long established and popular **Café Sydney**, see page 116. The ground floor – or city lounge as it is dubbed – comes complete with a newspaper and magazine salon, TV wall, internet access, information desk and a giant model of the Sydney CBD embedded beneath a glass floor.

At the southwestern corner of Circular Quay it is hard to miss the rather grand art deco **Museum of Contemporary Art** ① *T9245 2400, www.mca.com.au, 1000-1700, free with a small charge for some visiting exhibitions, tours Mon-Fri 1100 and 1300, Sat-Sun 1100, 1300 and 1500*. Opened in 1991, it maintains a collection of some of Australia's best contemporary works, together with works by renowned international artists like Warhol and Hockney. The museum also hosts national and international exhibitions on a regular basis.

A little further towards the Harbour Bridge is the rather incongruous **Cadman's Cottage**, overlooking the futuristic Overseas Passenger Terminal. Built in 1816, it is the oldest surviving residence in Sydney and was originally the former base for Governor Macquarie's boat crew. The cottage is named after the coxswain of the boat crew, John Cadman, who was transported to Australia for stealing a horse. The cottage is now the base for the **Sydney Harbour National Park Information Centre** ① *110 George St, T9247 5033, www.nationalparks.nsw.gov.au, Mon-Fri 0930-1630, Sat-Sun 1000-1630, free*, which is the main booking office and departure point for a number of harbour and island tours, see page 128.

The Rocks

Below the Bradfield Highway, which now carries a constant flow of traffic across the Harbour Bridge, is the historic Rocks village. It was the first site settled by European convicts and troops as early as 1788 and, despite being given a major facelift in recent decades (and losing its erstwhile reputation as the haunt of prostitutes, drunks and criminals), still retains

To North Sydney & Manly
Sydney Harbour Bridge
Sydney Harbour Tunnel

Walsh Bay

Dawes Point Park

Sydney Opera House

A

THE ROCKS

Hickson Rd
Pottinger
Lower Fort St
Bradfield Highway
George St
Hickson Rd

Clydebank
Windmill St
Argyle Pl
Argyle St

Rocks Discovery Museum

Sydney Visitors Centre

Cadman's Cottage

Circular Quay Ferry Terminal

Government House

Sydney Observatory

Susannah Place

Museum of Contemporary Art

Circular Quay Station

High St
Kent St
Cumberland St
Harrington St
Gloucester St

Cahill Expressway
Alfred St
Justice & Police Museum

Darling Harbour

Customs House

Conservatorium of Music

B

Grosvenor St

Bridge St
Loftus St
Young St

Museum of Sydney

Jamison St

George St

Spring St
Bent St
O'Connell St
Bligh St

Phillip St

Macquarie St

Royal Botanical Gardens

Tropical House

Margaret St
Bus Terminal

Wynyard Station

Carrington St

Hunter St

Chifley Square

State Library of New South Wales

Pyrmont Bay

National Maritime Museum

King St Wharf

Erskine St
Sussex St
Kent St
Clarence St
York St
Pitt St

Martin Pl
Martin Place Station

NSW Parliament House

Cahill Expressway

The Domain

C

To Star City Casino & Sydney Fish Market

Sydney Aquarium

NRMA

King St

Sydney Hospital

Royal Mint

Art Gallery of New South Wales

Sydney Wildlife World

Darling Park

Sydney (Centrepoint) Tower

St James Station

Hyde Park Barracks

Sir John
Art Gallery Rd

Harbourside

Pyrmont Bridge

Market
State Theatre

City Centre

Archibald Fountain

St Mary's Cathedral

PYRMONT

Cockle Bay
Cockle Bay Wharf

Queen Victoria Building

Park Plaza

Hyde Park

College St
Riley St
Crown St

Convention

Western Distributor

IMAX

Druitt St
Town Hall

St Andrew's Cathedral

Town Hall Station

Bathurst St

Museum Station

Australian Museum

William St

D

Western Distributor

Tumbalong Park

Liverpool St

World Square

Anzac War Memorial

Stanley St
Francis St

Eastern Distributor

Chinese Garden of Friendship

CHINATOWN

Exhibition Centre

Pier St

Darling Dr

Powerhouse Museum

Dixon St

Goulburn St

Wentworth Av
Poplar St
Pelican
Crown St
Oxford St

Macarthur St
Harris St

Haymarket

Hay St

Campbell St

Paddy's Market

Capitol Square

Hay St

To Central Station & Coach Terminal

Campbell St

Taylor Square
To Brett Whiteley Museum & Gallery

ULTIMO HAYMARKET

George St
Thomas St

To

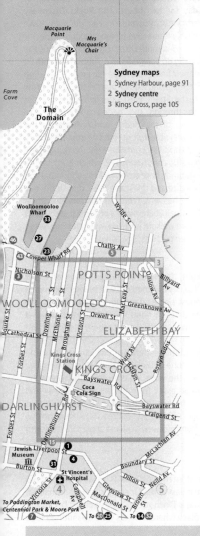

Sydney Harbour

Macquarie Point

Mrs Macquarie's Chair

Farm Cove

The Domain

Sydney maps
1 Sydney Harbour, page 91
2 **Sydney centre**
3 Kings Cross, page 105

Woolloomooloo Wharf

Cowper Wharf Rd

Challis Av

Nicholson St

POTTS POINT

WOOLLOOMOOLOO

Wylde St

Onslow Av

Billyard Av

MacLeay St

Greenknowe Av

Orwell St

Victoria St

Brougham St

Macleay St

McElhone St

Dowling St

Bourke St

Forbes St

Cathedral St

ELIZABETH BAY

Ward Av

Roslyn Gdns

Kings Cross Station

KINGS CROSS

Bayswater Rd

Coca Cola Sign

Bayswater Rd

Craigend St

DARLINGHURST

Darlinghurst Rd

Forbes St

Liverpool St

Jewish Museum

Burton St

St Vincent's Hospital

Campbell St

Victoria St

Glenview St

Boundary St

McLachlan Av

Dillon St

Neild Av

Macdonald St

Brown St

To Paddington Market,
Centennial Park & Moore Park

To 20 25

To 14 32

N

| 200 metres |
| 200 yards |

Sleeping
Alfred Park Budget
  Accommodation **4** D2
Australian Heritage
  Hotel **7** A2
B&B Sydney Harbour
  11 B2
Base Backpackers **20** D2
Capitol Square **3** D2
Challis Lodge **5** C4
Glasgow Arms **6** D1
Kangaroo Bakpak **1** D4
Lord Nelson **9** A1
Pensione **2** D2
Railway Square YHA
  23 D2
Royal Sovereign **15** D4
Russell **17** B2
Sydney Central YHA
  18 D2
Wake Up **22** D2
YHA The Rocks **7** B2
Y on the Park
  (YWCA) **21** D3

Eating
BBQ King **64** D2
Bill's Café **4** D4
Bill's Surry Hills **5** D3
Blackbird Café **6** C1
Botanical Gardens
  Café **8** B3
Brooklyn Hotel **9** B2
Café Sydney **12** B2
Casa Asturiana **13** D2
Chinta Ria – The
  Temple of Love **15** C1
Coast **16** C1
Dickson House
  Food Court **17** D2

Emperor's Garden
  Seafood **18** D2
Harry's Café de
  Wheels **23** C4
Hyde Park Café **24** D2
Indian Home Diner
  25 D4
La Renaissance **60** A2
Longrain **21** D3
Manta Ray **27** C4
MCA Café **28** B2
MG Garage **10** D3
MOS Café **30** B3
Oh! Calcutta! **31** D4
Otto Italiano **33** C4
Pavilion on the Park
  34 C3
Rocks Café **28** B2
Royal Hotel **14** D5
The Tearoom **38** C2
Una's **1** D4
Wharf **45** A2

Bars & clubs
Albury Hotel **7** D4
Cargo **11** C1
Cruise **19** A2
Durty Nelly's **20** D4
Harbour View
  Hotel **1** A2
Hero of Waterloo **26** A2
Lord Dudley **32** D5
Lord Nelson **44** A1
Mercantile **35** A2
Opera Bar **37** A3
Oxford Hotel **39** D3
Paddy McGuires **40** D2
Scruffy Murphys **41** D2
Scubar **42** D2
Tilbury **3** C4
Water Bar **46** C4
Woolloomooloo
  Bay Hotel **43** C4

Ⓛ LightRail Station
Ⓜ MonoRail Station

much of its original architectural charm. Old and new is married in an eclectic array of shops, galleries, arcades, cafés and some mighty fine pubs and restaurants.

By far the best way to see the Rocks properly is to join one of the official **Rocks Walking Tours**, which give an entertaining and informative insight into the past and present, see page 120. **Rocks Market**, held every weekend, is perhaps the most popular in Sydney. It features a fine array of authentic arts, crafts, bric-a-brac and souvenirs. For live entertainment head for the **Rocks Square** where you'll find jazz, classical or contemporary music every day from midday for two hours. The **Rocks Discovery Museum** ① *Kendal Lane, T9240 8680 www.rocksdiscoverymuseum.com.au, daily 1000-1700, free (Discovery Dig $5)*, houses various highly interactive historical exhibits specific to the Rocks. During school holiday periods the 45-minute Discovery Dig offers kids the chance to dress up as junior archaeologists and dig up objects in fake (rubber) soil with an expert on hand to unravel the stories behind their finds. To escape the crowds, head up Argyle Street, and the steps to Cumberland Street, taking a quick peek at the historic row of cottages at **Susannah Place**, 58-64 Gloucester Street, west side, below the popular Australian hotel and pub, before walking through the pedestrian walkway to **Observatory Park**. This offers some fine views of the bridge and is home to the **Sydney Observatory** ① *T9921 3485, www.sydneyobservatory.com.au, exhibition daily 1000-1700, free, space theatre daily Mon-Fri 1430 and 1330, Sat-Sun 1100, 1200, 1430 and 1530, $7, children $5, evening tour $15, children $10, concessions $12*, which is Australia's oldest (book ahead). There is an interesting exhibition here covering early aboriginal and European astronomy, as well as a 3D space theatre and telescope tours during the day and evening tours offering a chance to view the heavens. From Observatory Park it is a short walk further along Argyle Street to enjoy a small libation and a bite to eat at the **Lord Nelson**, Sydney's oldest pub, see page 119, before walking north down Lower Fort Street to **Dawes Point Park** with its dramatic bridge perspectives.

The Harbour Bridge

From near or far, above or below, day or night, the Harbour Bridge is impressive and imposing. The 'Coat Hanger', as it is often called, was opened in 1932, having taken nine years to build, and it remains one of the longest single-span bridges in the world. The deck supports eight lanes of traffic – accommodating around 150,000 vehicles a day – a railway line and a pedestrian walkway, and forms a crucial artery to the North Shore and beyond. For over six decades the best views from the bridge were accessed by foot from its 59-m-high deck, but now the **Bridge Climb** experience, which ascends the 134-m-high and 502-m-long span, has become one of the city's must-do activities, see page 128. Not as thrilling, but far cheaper, are the views on offer from the top of the **Southeastern Pylon Lookout**, which can be accessed from the eastern walkway and Cumberland Street, the Rocks. The pylon also houses the **Harbour Bridge Exhibition** ① *T9240 1100, www.pylonlookout.com.au, 1000-1700, $9.50, children $6.50*. From below, the best views of the bridge can be enjoyed from Hickson Road and Dawes Point (south side) and Milson's Point (north side).

Harbour Islands

Sydney Harbour is scattered with a number of interesting islands, most of which hold some historical significance. **Fort Denison**, just east of the Opera House, is the smallest, and by far the most notorious. Its proper name is Pinchgut Island – so called because it was originally used as an open-air jail and a place where inmates were abandoned for a week and supplied with nothing except bread and water. In 1796, the governor of NSW left a sobering warning to the new penal colony by displaying the body of executed murderer, Francis Morgan, from a gibbet on the island's highest point. The island was later converted to a fort in the 1850s (for fear of a Russian invasion during the Crimean War). There is a café and tours are available through the National Parks and Wildlife Services, from $27, T9247 5033. A little further east, off Darling Harbour, is **Clark Island**, a popular picnic retreat for those with their own transport (landing fee $6, must be pre-booked and pre-paid). East again, off Rose Bay, is **Shark Island**, so called because of its shape. It served as a former animal quarantine centre and public reserve, before becoming part of the Sydney Harbour National Park in 1975. Access is via Captain Cook Cruises leaving Circular Quay (Jetty 6) at the weekends (hourly from 0945-1645) $17 return, children $15, T9247 5033. West of the bridge is the largest of the harbour's islands, **Goat Island**, site of a former gunpowder station and barracks. For tours, contact the NPWS, T9247 5033, from $24.

City centre → *For listings, see pages 111-132.*

Many visitors find the city centre a chaotic place. It is cooler, owing to the high-rise blocks, but much noisier, disturbed by the collective din of corporate Sydney. Despite this, it is worth taking the plunge and joining the purposeful flood of humanity through its gargantuan corridors to discover some hidden gems.

Museum of Sydney
① *corner of Phillip St and Bridge St, T9251 5988, www.hht.nsw.gov.au, 0930-1700, $10, children $5, family $20.*
The Museum of Sydney (MOS) was opened in 1995 and is a clever and imaginative mix of old and new. Built on the original site of Governor Phillip's 1788 residence and incorporating some of the archaeological remains discovered there, it contains uncluttered and well-presented displays that explore the history and stories surrounding the creation and development of the city, from the first indigenous settlers, through the European invasion and up to the modern day. Art is an important aspect of this museum and as well as dynamic and temporary exhibitions incorporating a city theme there are some permanent pieces, the most prominent being the intriguing *Edge of the Trees*, a sculptural installation. There is also a shop and café.

Macquarie Street
Macquarie Street forms the eastern fringe of the CBD and is Sydney's most historic street and the site of many important and impressive buildings. Heading north to south, near the Opera House in its own expansive grounds is the **Government House** ① *T9931 5222, Fri-Sun 1030-1500, guided tours only every ½ hr from 1030, grounds open daily 1000-1600, free,* a Gothic revival building completed in 1837. The interior contains many period furnishings and features, giving an insight into the lifestyle of the former NSW governors and their families. Further up Macquarie Street, facing the Botanical Gardens, is the **State Library of New South Wales** ① *T9273 1414, www.sl.nsw.gov.au, Mon-Thu 0900-2200, Fri 0900-1700, Sat 1000-1700.* Its architecture speaks for itself, but housed within its walls are some very significant historical documents, including most of the diaries of the First Fleet. Also worth a look is the foyer floor of the **Mitchell Library** entrance, one of three Melocco Brothers' mosaic floor decorations in the city. The

library hosts visiting exhibitions that are almost always worth visiting and offers an ongoing programme of films, workshops and seminars. There is a shop and café on site.

Next door, the original north wing of the 1816 Sydney Hospital, formerly known as the Rum Hospital, is now the **NSW Parliament House**. Free tours are offered when parliament is not in session, and when it is you can visit the public gallery. The south wing of the hospital gave way to the **Royal Mint** ⓘ *small museum display, Mon-Fri 0900-1700, free*, in 1854 during the gold rush. The **Hyde Park Barracks**, on the northern edge of Hyde Park, were commissioned in 1816 by Governor Macquarie to house male convicts, and later utilized as an orphanage and an asylum. The renovated buildings now house a modern museum displaying the history of the Barracks and the work of the architect Francis Greenway. Various themed tours are available, from $10, children $5.

Central Business District (CBD)

Sydneysiders are very fond of the **Sydney (Centrepoint) Tower** ⓘ *100 Market St, T8223 3800, observation deck Sun-Fri 0900-2230, Sat 0900-2330, $25, children $15, family $65*. This slightly dated landmark, built in 1981, has a distinctive 2239-tonne golden turret. The view from one of Australia's highest buildings is mighty impressive. As well as enjoying the stunning vistas from the tower's observation deck, you can also experience a virtual 'Great Australian Expedition' tour or dine in one of two revolving restaurants. The more adventurous can even brave outdoors and experience **Skywalk** ⓘ *day, dusk or night from $65, T9333 9200, www.skywalk.com.au*, a glass-floored platform. Given the high price of entry to the observation deck alone, make sure that you keep an eye on the weather forecast and pick a clear day.

While you are on Market Street it is worth taking a peek at the impressive interior of the 1929 **State Theatre** ⓘ *49 Market St, T9373 6852, www.statetheatre.com.au*. Much of its charm is instantly on view in the entrance foyer, but the 20,000-piece glass chandelier and Wurlitzer organ housed in the auditorium steal the show. Just around the corner from the State Theatre, on George Street, taking up an entire city block, is the grand **Queen Victoria Building** ⓘ *T9264 9209, www.qvb.com.au, Mon-Wed and Fri-Sat 0900-1800, Thu 0900-2100, Sun 1100-1700, tours available with pre-booking*. Built in 1898 to celebrate Queen Victoria's Golden Jubilee and to replace the original Sydney Markets, the QVB (as it is known) is a prime shopping venue, containing three floors of boutique outlets, but the spectacular interior is well worth a look in itself. At the northern end is the four-tonne **Great Australian Clock**, the world's largest hanging animated turret clock. It is a stunning creation that took four years to build at a cost of $1.5 million. When activated with a $4 donation (which goes to charity), the clock comes alive with moving scenes and figurines. At the southern end is the equally impressive **Royal Clock**, which includes the execution of King Charles I. There are also galleries, historical displays, restaurants and cafés.

Across the street from the QVB is the **Town Hall** ⓘ *corner of George St and Druitt St, T9265 9819, 0900-1700, free, pre-booked tours T4285 5685*, built in 1888. It also has an impressive interior, the highlight of which is the 8000-pipe organ, reputed to be the largest in the world. Next door to the Town Hall is **St Andrew's Cathedral** ⓘ *T9265 1661, free*, built between 1819 and 1868, with regular choir performances.

Hyde Park and around

Hyde Park is a great place to escape the mania of the city and includes the historic grandeur of the 1932 Archibald Fountain and 1934 **Anzac War Memorial**. It's also great for people watching. At the northeastern edge of the park, on College Street, is **Saint Mary's Cathedral** ⓘ *crypt 1000-1600*, which is well worth a look inside. It has an impressive and wonderfully peaceful interior, with the highlight being the Melocco Brothers' mosaic floor in the crypt. Further south along College Street is the **Australian Museum** ⓘ *T9320 6000, www.austmus.gov.au, 0930-1700, $12, children $6, family $30 (exhibitions extra), Explorer bus, stop 6*, established in 1827, but doing a fine job of keeping pace with the cutting edge of technology, especially the modern Biodiversity and Indigenous Australians displays. Try to coincide your visit to the Indigenous Australians section with the live didgeridoo playing and informative lectures. Kids will love the Search and Discover section and Kidspace, a state-of-the-art mini museum for the under 5s.

Royal Botanical Gardens and Macquarie Point

The 30-ha **Botanical Gardens** ⓘ *0700-sunset, free*, offer a wonderful sanctuary of peace and greenery only a short stroll east of the city centre. They boast a fine array of mainly native plants and trees, an intriguing pyramid-shaped **Tropical House** ⓘ *1000-1600, small fee*, roses and succulent gardens, rare and threatened species and decorative ponds, as well as a resident colony of wild flying foxes (fruit bats). There is a visitors' centre and shop located in the southeastern corner of the park. There you can pick up a self-guided tour leaflet or join a free organized tour at 1030 daily. A specialist Aboriginal tour, exploring the significance of the site to the Cadigal (the original Aboriginal inhabitants) and the first European settlers' desperate attempts to cultivate the site, is available on request. The **Botanical Gardens Restaurant** is one of the best places to observe the bats. You'll see lots of tropical ibis birds around the gardens – the descendants of a tiny group that escaped from Taronga Zoo.

From the Botanical Gardens it is a short stroll to Macquarie Point, which offers one of the best views of the Opera House and Harbour Bridge. Mrs Macquarie's Chair is the spot where the first governor's wife came to reflect upon the new settlement. One can only imagine what her reaction would be now.

The Domain and the Art Gallery of New South Wales

ⓘ *Art Gallery Rd, The Domain, T9225 1744, www.artgallery.nsw.gov.au, 1000-1700 and Wed 1700-2100, free (small charge for some visiting exhibitions), Explorer bus stop 12.*
Inside its grand façade, Australia's largest gallery houses the permanent works of many of the country's most revered contemporary artists as well as a collection of more familiar international names like Monet and Picasso. The Yiribana Gallery, in stark contrast, showcases a fine collection of Aboriginal and Torres Strait Islander works and is a major highlight. The Asian Gallery is also well worth a look. The main gallery features a dynamic programme of major visiting exhibitions, and there is a great bookshop and café. Be sure not to miss the quirky and monumental matchsticks installation by the late Brett Whiteley, one of the city's most celebrated artists, behind the main building. More of his work can be seen at the Brett Whiteley Museum in Surry Hills, see page 104. The Domain, the pleasant open park between the Art Gallery and Macquarie Place, was declared a public space in 1810. It is used as a free concert venue especially over Christmas and during the **Sydney Festival**.

Darling Harbour and Chinatown → For listings, see pages 111-132.

Created to celebrate Sydney's Bicentennial in 1988, revitalized Darling Harbour was delivered with much aplomb and has proved such a success that even the waves seem to show their appreciation. Day and night, ferries and catamarans bring hordes of visitors to marvel at its modern architecture and aquatic attractions or to revel in its casino and trendy waterside bars and restaurants. Framed against the backdrop of the CBD, it is intricately colourful, urban and angular. In contrast, the Chinese Garden of Friendship towards the southwestern fringe provides a little serenity before giving way to the old and chaotic enclave of Chinatown, the epicentre of Sydney's Asian community and the city's most notable living monument to its cosmopolitan populace.

Sydney Aquarium

ⓘ *Aquarium Pier, T8251 7800, www.sydneyaquarium.com.au, 0900-2200, $35, children $18, concessions $23, Explorer bus stop 24.*

This modern, well-presented aquarium has over 650 species, but it's not all about fish. On show is an imaginative array of habitats housing saltwater crocodiles, frogs, seals, penguins and platypuses. The highlight of the aquarium is the Great Barrier Reef Oceanarium: a huge tank that gives you an incredible insight into the world's largest living thing. Of course, many visit the aquarium to come face-to-face with some of Australia's deadliest sea creatures, without getting their feet, or indeed their underwear, wet. There is no doubt that such beauty and diversity has its dark side, as the notorious box jellyfish, cone shell or rockfish will reveal.

Sydney Wildlife World

ⓘ *T9333 9288, www.sydneywildlifeworld.com.au, 0900-2200, $35, children $18, (VIP guided tours available from $185 for two), Explorer bus stop 24.*

Established in 2006, this highly commercial attraction has 65 exhibits hosting 100 native Australian species and offers a more convenient and less time-consuming alternative to Taronga Zoo. Far more compact, it showcases nine impressive habitat exhibits, from the 'Flight Canyon' to the 'Nocturnal', housing all the usual suspects from the ubiquitous koala to the lesser-known and eminently appealing bilby. Although commercial profit is of course the primary goal here, cynics can rest assured that Sydney Wildlife World, in partnership with the Australian Wildlife Conservancy, has established the Sydney Wildlife World Conservation Foundation, through which funds will be raised to help safeguard Australia's threatened wildlife and ecosystems.

National Maritime Museum

ⓘ *2 Murray St, T9298 3777, www.anmm.gov.au, 0930-1700, free except warship and submarine $20, children and concessions $10; heritage galleries and James Craig $12, children and concessions $7; heritage galleries and Endeavour $18, children $9; combination ticket (all attractions) $32, children and concessions $17. It is easily reached on foot across the Pyrmont Bridge, or by Monorail, LightRail or Explorer bus, stop No 21.*

The museum, designed to look like the sails of a ship, offers a fine mix of old and new. For many, its biggest attractions are without doubt the warship *HMAS Vampire* and the submarine *HMAS Onslow*, the centrepieces of a fleet of old vessels sitting outside on the harbour. Both can be thoroughly explored with the help of volunteer guides. The museum interior contains a range of displays exploring Australia's close links with all things nautical, from the early navigators and the First Fleet, to the ocean liners that brought many waves of immigrants. Don't miss the beautifully restored replica of the *Endeavour*, Captain Cook's famous ship of discovery, and the 1874 square-rigger, the *James Craig*, both of which are moored to the north of the museum at Wharf 7. Other museum attractions include a café, sailing lessons and a range of short cruises on historical vessels. Occasionally you can even take a multi-day voyage on board the *Endeavour* – but at a price!

Sydney Fish Market
ⓘ *T9004 1100, www.sydneyfishmarket.com.au, tours operate Mon, Thu and Fri from 0645, from $20, children $10 (book ahead on T9004 1143). Sydney Light Rail runs by, or catch bus 443 from Circular Quay or 501 from Town Hall, Explorer bus stop 19.*
For anyone interested in sea creatures, the spectacle of the Sydney Fish Market is recommended. Every morning from 0530, nearly 3000 crates of seafood are auctioned to a lively bunch of 200 buyers using a computerized clock system. The best way to see the action, and more importantly the incredible diversity of species, is to join a tour group, which will give you access to the auction floor. Normally the general public are confined to the viewing deck high above the floor. Also within the market complex are cafés, some excellent seafood eateries and a superb array of open markets where seafood can be bought at competitive prices.

Powerhouse Museum
ⓘ *500 Harris St, Ultimo, T9217 0111, www.powerhousemuseum.com, 1000-1700, $10, children $5, concessions $6. Monorail, LightRail or Explorer bus stop No 18.*
With nearly 400,000 items collected over 120 years, the Powerhouse is the state's largest museum and half a day is barely enough to cover its floors. Housed in the former Ultimo Power Station, there is an impressive range of memorabilia, from aircraft to musical instruments, mainly with an emphasis on Australian innovation and achievement, and covering a wide range of general topics from science and technology to transportation, social history, fashion and design. There's a shop and café on site.

Chinatown
The Chinese have been an integral part of Sydney culture since the gold rush of the mid-1800s, though today Chinatown is also the focus of many other Asian cultures, including Vietnamese, Thai, Korean and Japanese. The district offers a lively diversion, with its heart being the Dixon Street pedestrian precinct, between the two pagoda gates facing Goulburn Street and Hay Street. Here, and in the surrounding streets, you will find a wealth of Asian shops and restaurants. At the northwestern corner of Chinatown is the **Chinese Garden of Friendship** ⓘ *T9240 8888, www.chinesegarden.com.au, 0930-1700. $6, children $3, families $15,* which was gifted to NSW by its sister Chinese province, Guangdong, to celebrate the Australian Bicentenary in 1988. It contains all the usual beautiful craftsmanship, landscaping and aesthetics.

In stark contrast is **Paddy's Market** ⓘ *corner of Hay St and Thomas St, 0900-1700,* one of Sydney's largest, oldest and liveliest markets, though somewhat tacky.

Glebe
ⓘ *Bus from George St in the city (Nos 431 or 434).*
To the southwest of Darling Harbour, beyond Ultimo, and separated by the campus of **Sydney University** (Australia's oldest), are Glebe and Newtown. Glebe prides itself on having a New Age-village atmosphere, where a cosmopolitan, mainly student crowd sits in the laid-back cafés, browses old-style bookshops or bohemian fashion outlets or seeks the latest therapies in alternative health shops. The **Saturday market** ⓘ *Glebe Public School, Glebe Point Rd, T0419-291449, Sat 0930-1630*, provides an outlet for local crafts people to sell their work as well as bric-a-brac, clothes, etc.

Newtown
ⓘ *Bus from Loftus St on Circular Quay, or George St (Nos 422, 423, 426, 428). The Newtown Railway Station is on the Inner West/Bankstown (to Liverpool) lines.*
South beyond the university is **King Street**, the hub of Newtown's idiosyncratic range of shops, cafés and restaurants. Here you can purchase anything from a black leather codpiece to an industrial-size brass Buddha, drool over the menus of a vast range of interesting eateries, or simply idle over a latte and watch a more alternative world go by. A few hours' exploration, Sunday brunch or an evening meal in Newtown's King Street is recommended. Don't miss **Gould's Book Arcade** at 32 King Street, www.goulds books.com.au, which is an experience in itself.

Leichhardt
ⓘ *Bus Nos 436-438 or 440 from Circular Quay.*
Although receiving less attention than the eccentricities of Glebe and Newtown, Leichhardt is a pleasant suburb, famous for its Italian connections and subsequently its eateries and cafés. There are numerous places on Norton Street to enjoy a fine espresso, gelato or the full lasagne. Try Leichhardt institution **Bar Italia** at No 169.

Balmain
ⓘ *Bus from the QVB, Nos 441-444, or ferry from Circular Quay, Wharf 5.*
Straddling Johnstons Bay and connecting Darling Harbour and Pyrmont with the peninsula suburb of Balmain is Sydney's second landmark bridge, the **Anzac Bridge**, opened in 1995. It is a modern and strangely attractive edifice, which makes an admirable attempt to compete with the mighty Harbour Bridge. The former working-class suburb of Balmain has undergone a quiet metamorphosis to become an area with some of the most sought after real estate in Sydney. The main drag of **Darling Street** now boasts an eclectic range of gift shops, modern cafés, restaurants and pubs, which provide a pleasant half-day escape from the city centre. Try the cosy **Sir William Wallace Hotel**, 31 Cameron Street, or the more traditional and historic 1857 **Dry Dock Hotel**, corner of Cameron and College streets. There's a popular Saturday market in the grounds of St Andrew's Church.

Sydney Olympic Park
ⓘ *Centre, corner of Showground Rd and Murray Rose Av, near Olympic Park Railway Station, T9714 7888, www.sydneyolympicpark.com.au, 0900-1700, by train or RiverCat from Circular Quay (Wharf 5) to Homebush Bay Wharf.*

Although the vast swathes of Sydney's Western Suburbs remain off the radar for the vast majority of tourists, there are a few major and minor sights worth a mention. Topping the list is the multi-million-dollar Sydney Olympic Park, about 14 km west of the centre, with its mighty stadium, the centrepiece of a vast array of architecturally stunning sports venues and public amenities. Tours of the venues by bus or bike are available; see the visitors' centre at 1 Showground Road for details.

ANZ Stadium (formerly Stadium Australia) was the main focus of the games, being the venue for the opening and closing ceremonies, as well as track and field and soccer events. Although the Olympic flame has long been extinguished, it remains an important national venue for international and national Rugby Union, Rugby League, Aussie Rules football and soccer matches. Olympic Park was also the main venue for Catholic World Youth Day, and associated visit of Pope Benedict XVI in 2008, attracting well over 100,000 worshippers.

Next door is the state-of-the-art **Acer Arena**, which hosted basketball and gymnastics during the games and now offers a huge indoor arena for a range of public events from music concerts to Australia's largest agricultural show, the Royal Easter Show. Perhaps the most celebrated venue during the games was the **Aquatic Centre**, where the triumphant Aussie swimming team took on the world and won with the help of such stars as Ian Thorpe and Michael Klim. The complex still holds international swimming and diving events and is open to the public. The Olympic Park has many other state-of-the-art sports facilities and is surrounded by superb parkland. **Bicentennial Park** ① *T9714 7524*, is a 100-ha mix of dry land and conservation wetland and a popular spot for walking, jogging, birdwatching or simply feeding the ducks.

Parramatta and around

About 6 km further west from Homebush is Parramatta, often dubbed the city within the city, a culturally diverse centre that boasts some of the nation's most historic sites. After the First Fleeters failed in their desperate attempts to grow crops in what is now the city centre, they penetrated the upper reaches of the Parramatta River and established a farming settlement, first known as Rose Hill before reverting to its original Aboriginal name. The oldest European site is **Elizabeth Farm** ① *70 Alice St, Rosehill, T9635 9488, 0930-1600, $8, children $4, family $17*, a 1793 colonial homestead built for John and Elizabeth Macarthur, pioneers in the Australian wool industry. The homestead contains a number of interesting displays and is surrounded by a recreated 1830s garden. Also of interest is the 1799 **Old Government House** ① *T9635 8149, Tue-Fri 1000-1630, Sat-Sun 1030-1630, $9*, in Parramatta Park. It is Australia's oldest public building and houses a fine collection of colonial furniture. **Experiment Farm Cottage** ① *9 Ruse St, T9635 5655, Tue-Fri 1030-1530, Sat-Sun 1130-1530, $7*, is the site of the colonial government's first land grant to former convict James Ruse in 1791. The cottage itself dates from 1834. The **Parramatta River**, which quietly glides past the city, is without doubt its most attractive natural feature and it offers a number of heritage walking trails. These and many other historical details are displayed at the **Parramatta Heritage and VIC** ① *346a Church St, T8839 3311, www.parracity.nsw.gov.au, daily 0900-1700*.

Kings Cross

ⓘ *By bus Sydney Explorer stop No 9 or regular bus services Nos 311, 323-325, 327, 333.*

Even before arriving in Sydney you will have probably heard of Kings Cross, the notorious hub of Sydney nightlife and the long-established focus of sex, drugs and rock and roll. Situated near the navy's Woolloomooloo docks, 'the Cross' (as it's often called) has been a favourite haunt of visiting sailors for years. The main drag, **Darlinghurst Road**, is the focus of the action, while Victoria Street is home to a rash of backpacker hostels. At the intersection of both, and the top of William Street, which connects the Cross with the city, is the huge Coca Cola sign, a popular meeting point. The best time to visit the Cross is in the early hours when the bars, the clubs and the ladies of the night are all in full swing. It is enormously popular with backpackers and Sydneysiders alike and can provide a great night out. It is also a great place to meet people, make contacts, find work and even buy a car.

Amid all the mania there are a number of notable and more sedate sights in and around Kings Cross. **Elizabeth Bay House** ⓘ *7 Onslow Av, Elizabeth Bay, T9356 3022, www.hht.nsw.gov.au, Tue-Sun 1000-1630, $8, children $4, family $17,* is a revival-style estate built by popular architect John Verge for Colonial Secretary Alexander Macleay in 1845. The interior is restored and faithfully furnished in accordance with the times and the house has a great outlook across the harbour.

Woolloomooloo

To the northwest of Kings Cross, through the quieter and more upmarket sanctuary of Potts Point, is the delightfully named suburb of Woolloomooloo. 'Woo' is the main east coast base for the Australian Navy and visiting sailors also weigh anchor here, heading straight for the Kings Cross souvenir shops. Other than the warships and a scattering of lively pubs, it is the **Woolloomooloo Wharf** and a pie cart that are the major attractions. The wharf has a rash of fine restaurants that are a popular dining alternative to the busy city centre. If the wharf restaurants are beyond your budget, nearby is one of Sydney's best cheap eateries. **Harry's Café de Wheels**, near the wharf entrance (see page 118), is an institution, selling its own range of meat, mash, pea and gravy pies 24 hours a day (well, almost).

Darlinghurst and Surry Hills

The lively suburb of Darlinghurst fringes the city to the east, Kings Cross to the north and Surry Hills to the south. Both Darlinghurst and Surry Hills offer some great restaurants and cafés with Darlinghurst Road and Victoria Street, just south of Kings Cross, being the main focus. Here you will find some of Sydney's most popular eateries. The **Jewish Museum** ⓘ *148 Darlinghurst Rd, T9360 7999, www.sydneyjewishmuseum.com.au, Sun-Thu 1000-1600, Fri 1000-1400, $10, children $7,* has displays featuring the Holocaust and the history of Judaism in Australia. To get to Darlinghurst, take bus No 311.

Surry Hills is a mainly residential district and does not have quite the pizzazz of Darlinghurst, but it is well known for its traditional Aussie pubs, which seem to dominate every street corner. One thing not to miss is the **Brett Whiteley Museum and Gallery** ⓘ *2 Raper St, T9225 1881, Sat-Sun 1000-1600, free.* The museum is the former studio and home of the late Whiteley, one of Sydney's most popular contemporary artists. Both places can be reached on foot from the city via William Street, Liverpool Street or Oxford Street or by bus Nos 311-399.

3 Kings Cross

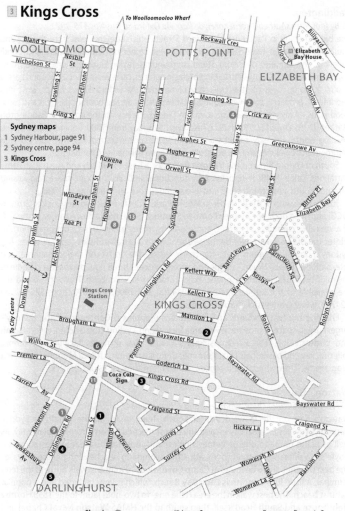

To Woolloomooloo Wharf

Rockwall Cres
Billyard Av
Onslow Pl
Elizabeth Bay House

WOOLLOOMOOLOO
Bland St
Nicholson St
Nesbit St
Dowling St
McElhone St
Pring St

POTTS POINT
ELIZABETH BAY
Onslow Av

Manning St
Crick Av
Victoria St
Tusculum St
Tusculum La
Macleay St
Greenknowe Av

Sydney maps
1 Sydney Harbour, page 91
2 Sydney centre, page 94
3 **Kings Cross**

Hughes St
Hughes Pl
Orwell St
Orwell La
Rowena Pl
Windeyer St
Brougham St
Hourigan La
Rae Pl
East St
Springfield La
Earl Pl
Baroda St
Birtley Pl
Elizabeth Bay Rd
Barncleuth La
Barncleuth Sq
Amos La
Dowling St
McElhone St

Kellett Way
Darlinghurst Rd
Kellett St
Ward Av
Roslyn La
Roslyn St
Roslyn Gdns

KINGS CROSS
Kings Cross Station
Brougham La
Mansion La
Bayswater Rd
William St
Premier La
Farrell Av
Goderich La
Kings Cross Rd
Bayswater Rd
Bayswater Rd
Craigend St

Coca Cola Sign

To City Centre
Dowling St
Kirketon Rd
Darlinghurst Rd
Victoria St
Kellett St
Caldwell St
Tewkesbury Av
Surrey La
Surrey St
Hickey La
Craigend St
Womerah Av
Womerah La
Oswald Av
Bacom Av

DARLINGHURST

N
100 metres
100 yards

Sleeping
Altamont 1
Barclay 3
Blue Parrot 4
De Vere 2
Eva's 5
Funk House 6
Jolly Swagman 7
Kanga House 8

Kirketon 9
L'Otel 11
Original Backpackers
  Lodge 13
Pink House 15
Victoria Court 17

Eating
Bar Coluzzi 1

Bayswater Brasserie 2
Café Hernandez 3
Govinda's 4
Le Petit Creme 5

Bars & clubs
Kings Cross Hotel 6

Paddington

ⓘ *By foot from southeast corner of Hyde Park via Oxford St, bus Nos 378-382.*

The big attraction in Paddington is **Oxford Street**, which stretches east from the city and southwest corner of Hyde Park to the northwest corner of Centennial Park and Bondi Junction. The city end of Oxford Street, surrounding Taylor Square, is one of the most happening areas of the city with a string of cheap eateries, cafés, restaurants, clubs and bars. It is also a major focus for the city's gay community. As Oxford Street heads west into Paddington proper it's lined with boutique clothes shops, art and bookshops, cafés and some good pubs. Many people coincide a visit to Oxford Street with the colourful **Paddington Market** ⓘ *395 Oxford St, T9331 2923,* held every Saturday from 1000. Behind Oxford Street, heading north, are leafy suburbs lined with Victorian terrace houses, interspersed with commercial art galleries and old pubs, all of which are hallmarks of Paddington.

South of Oxford Street is the **Victoria Barracks,** a base for British and Australian Army battalions since 1848. It remains fully functional and visitors can see a flag-raising ceremony, and a marching band and join a guided tour on Thursdays at 1000.

Just to the south of the Barracks, in **Moore Park**, is the famous **Sydney Cricket Ground (SCG)** and, next door, the **Sydney Football Stadium (SFS)**. The hallowed arena of the SCG is a veritable cathedral of cricket, considered by many as Australia's national sport. In winter the SCG is taken over by the Sydney Swans Australian Rules football team. The Sydney Football Stadium was, for many years, the focus of major national and international, Rugby Union, League and soccer matches but it now plays second fiddle to the mighty (and far less atmospheric) Telstra Stadium in Homebush. Tours of SCG and SFS are available to the public, Mon-Fri 1000, 1200 and 1400, Sat 1000, from $25, T1300 724737, www.sydneycricketground.com.au.

Fringing the two stadiums and Fox Studios Complex is **Centennial Park**, the city's largest green space. It provides a vast area for walking, cycling, horse riding, rollerblading and birdwatching. The Parklands Sports Centre also provides facilities for tennis, rollerhockey and basketball. In late summer there is a nightly outdoor **Moonlight Cinema** programme ⓘ *www.moonlight.com.au,* which often showcases old classics.

Watson's Bay

ⓘ *Ferry from Circular Quay, Wharves 2 and 4, or bus No 342 or 325.*

Watson's Bay, on the leeward side of **South Head**, guarding the mouth of Sydney Harbour, provides an ideal city escape and is best reached by ferry from Circular Quay. As well as being home to one of Sydney's oldest and most famous seafood restaurants – **Doyle's** – it offers some quiet coves, attractive swimming beaches and peninsula walks. The best beaches are to be found at **Camp Cove** about 10 minutes' walk north of the ferry terminal. A little further north is **Lady Bay Beach**, which is very secluded and a popular naturist beach. The best walk in the area is the one- to two-hour jaunt to the 1858 **Hornby Lighthouse** and South Head itself, then south to the **HMAS Watson Naval Chapel** and the area known as **The Gap**. The area also boasts some interesting historical sites. Camp Cove was used by Governor Phillip as an overnight stop before reaching Port Jackson in the Inner Harbour. **Vaucluse House** ⓘ *Wentworth Rd, T9388 7922, Tue-Sun 1000-1630, $8, children $4, family $17,* was built in 1827 and is a fine example of an early colonial estate. Many people spend a morning exploring Watson's Bay before enjoying a leisurely lunch at Doyle's, which sits just above the beach and ferry terminal on Marine Parade, or next door at the **Watson's Bay Hotel**, a more casual affair offering equally good views of the city skyline and a superb outdoor barbecue area (see page 119).

Bondi, Bronte and Coogee beaches

ⓘ *By car from the city, via Oxford St, by the Bondi and Bay Explorer, or buses Nos 321, 322, 365, 366 and 380. By rail go to Bondi Junction (Illawara Line) then take the bus (as above). For Coogee, bus Nos 372-374 and 314-315.*

Bondi Beach is by far the most famous of Sydney's many ocean beaches. Its hugely inviting stretch of sand is a prime venue for surfing, swimming and sunbathing. Behind the beach, Bondi's bustling waterfront and village offers a tourist trap of cafés, restaurants, bars, surf and souvenir shops. For years Bondi has been a popular suburb for alternative lifestylers and visiting backpackers keen to avoid the central city. It is also the place to see or be seen by all self-respecting beautiful people. If you intend swimming at Bondi note that, like every Australian beach, it is subject to dangerous rips, so always swim between the yellow and red flags, clearly visible on the beach. Watchful lifeguards, also clad in yellow and red, are on hand. Bondi Beach is the focus of wild celebrations on Christmas Day with one huge beach party, usually culminating in a mass naked dash into the sea.

To the south of Bondi Beach and best reached by a popular coastal walkway is the small oceanside suburb of **Bronte**. This little enclave offers a smaller, quieter and equally attractive beach with a number of very popular cafés frequented especially at the weekend for brunch. A little further south is **Clovelly**, which has another sheltered beach good for kids and snorkelling. Many people finish their walk at **Coogee**, which has a fine beach and bustling waterfront. Although playing second fiddle to Bondi, it is popular with those keen to stay near the beach and outside the centre.

City North → *For listings, see pages 111-132.*

North Sydney and surrounds

On the northern side of the Harbour Bridge a small stand of high-rise buildings with neon signs heralds the mainly commercial suburb of North Sydney. There is little here for the tourist to justify a special visit, but nearby, the suburb of **McMahons Point**, and more especially **Blues Point Reserve**, on the shores of Lavender Bay, offer fine city views. Another good vantage point is right below the bridge at **Milsons Point**. **Kirribilli** is a serene little suburb lying directly to the east of the bridge. **Admiralty House** and **Kirribilli House**, the Sydney residences of the governor general and the prime minister, sit overlooking the Opera House on Kirribilli Point. Both are closed to the public and are best seen from the water.

Mosman

ⓘ *By ferry from Circular Quay (Wharf 4) to Mosman Bay where buses run uphill to the commercial centre.*

Mosman has a very pleasant village feel and its well-heeled residents are rightly proud. Situated so close to the city centre, it has developed into one of the most exclusive and expensive areas of real estate in the city. However, don't let this put you off. Mosman, in unison with its equally comfy, neighbouring beachside suburb of **Balmoral**, are both great escapes by ferry from the city centre and offer some fine eateries, designer clothes shops, walks and beaches, plus one of Sydney's must-see attractions, **Taronga Zoo**.

Outback New South Wales

Some 1160 km west of Sydney, **Broken Hill**, or 'Silver City' as it is dubbed, is the most famous mining town in Australia, its gracious, dusty streets looking like something out of an Aussie version of Hollywood's Wild West. As well as all the obvious historical and mine-based attractions, Broken Hill is also home to a thriving arts community and numerous colourful galleries. There are tour operators to escort you to the surreal settlement of Silverton, as well as offering true outback adventures travelling to some superb regional national parks and lake systems. **Broken Hill VIC** ⓘ *corner of Blende St and Bromide St, T8080 3560, www.visitbrokenhill.com.au, 0830-1700*, has city and regional maps, a detailed, self-guided heritage walk and trail leaflet, and organizes two-hour guided tours.

First off, pay a visit to the **Miners' Memorial** ⓘ *T8087 1318, 0900-2200, access to memorial $2.50*, which tells the town's history. It stands atop the mullock heaps immediately to the east of the town centre.

The onsite **Broken Earth Café and Restaurant** is the best place to eat in town. **The Daydream Mine** ⓘ *20 km west of Broken Hill, signposted off Silverton Rd, T8088 5682, www.daydreammine.com.au, tours hourly 1000-1530, $20*, dating from 1882, has a walk-in mine.

Broken Hill artists create diverse works inspired by the landscapes, colours, light and perspectives of the outback. **Broken Hill Regional Art Gallery** ⓘ *Argent St, T8080 3440, www.broken hill.net.au/bhart/main, Mon-Sun 1000-1700*, is the oldest regional gallery in NSW and has a fine mix of local and national works. The **Living Desert and Sculpture Symposium** is a hilltop collection of sandstone sculptures, 12 km northwest of the town. There are numerous tours on offer from Broken Hill, from scenic flights and 4WD to local mine tours and even camel rides. The VIC has full details.

The tiny former mining town of **Silverton**, just a short journey from Broken Hill, is pure

Taronga Zoo

ⓘ *T9969 2777, www.zoo.nsw.gov.au, 0900-1700, $41, children $20, concessions $23. Zoo Pass combo ticket (including ferry transfers and zoo), $48, children $23. Best reached by ferry from Circular Quay (Wharf 2), every 30 mins Mon-Fri from 0715-1845, Sat 0845-1845, Sun 0845-1745.*

First opened in 1881 in the grounds of Moore Park, south of Centennial Park, before being relocated to Bradley's Head, Mosman, in 1916, Taronga contains all the usual suspects of the zoological world. It also has the huge added attraction of perhaps the best location and views of any city zoo in the world. You will almost certainly need a full day to explore the various exhibits on offer and there are plenty of events staged throughout the day to keep both adults and children entertained. The best of these is the Free Flight Bird Show, which is staged twice daily in an open-air arena overlooking the city. If you are especially interested in wildlife it pays to check out the dynamic programme of specialist public tours on offer. The Night Zoo tour after hours is especially popular. Taronga is built on a hill and the general recommendation is to go up to the main entrance then work your way back down to the lower gate. Or for a small additional charge on entry you can take a scenic gondola ride to the main gate.

outback, with wide, red, dusty roads and some mighty eccentric residents.

Silverton VIC ① *2 Layard St, T8088 7566, www.silverton.org.au, 0800-1700,* can assist with all the local detail.

The village and landscape is so typical of the perceived Australian outback aesthetic that it has featured in numerous magazine advertisements and as the backdrop to films, including *Mad Max II*. Right in its heart is the famous **Silverton Hotel**, featured in the film *A Town Like Alice*, which does a good lunch, has a fine atmosphere (ask if you can 'take the test') and has accommodation. There is no public transport to Silverton but it is on the agenda of most Broken Hill tour operators. There is no fuel on sale here.

⬭ Sleeping
LL Imperial Hotel, 88 Oxide St, T8087 7444, www.imperialfineaccommodation.com. Beautifully renovated with excellent en suites or shared facilities, with a historic feel.
C-F YHA Tourist Lodge, 100 Argent St, T8088 2086, brokenhill@yhansw.org.au. Deservingly popular is this friendly,
family-run lodge. It offers dorms, doubles/ twins with spacious facilities, pool and bike hire. The owners are local gurus on sights and activities.
D-E Silverton Hotel, T8088 5313. To this day, the hotel still plays host to Max fanatics. Good lunches, a fine atmosphere, hotel rooms and self-contained accommodation.

⬭ Transport
Broken Hill Airport is 4 km southwest of the town via Bonanza St. A taxi, T8087 2222, to/from the airport to the city centre costs $20. **Regional Express**, T131713, www.rex.com.au, and **Qantas** offer services to Sydney and Adelaide. Long-distance coaches stop at the coach terminal, T8087 2735, beside the VIC. **Countrylink**, T132232, provides regular coach/rail services to Sydney via Dubbo. Buses stop outside the VIC on Anson St. The train station is on Crystal St, T8087 1400. **Countrylink** and **Great Southern Railways**, T132147, www.trainways.com.au, offers Sydney and Perth (via Adelaide) services twice weekly.

Balmoral, Middle Head and Bradley's Head
Balmoral Beach is one of the most popular and sheltered in the harbour. Here, more than anywhere else in the city, you can observe Sydneysiders enjoying something that is quintessentially Australian – the early morning, pre-work dip. Balmoral Beach overlooks **Middle Harbour**, whose waters infiltrate far into the suburbs of the North Shore. On **Middle Head**, which juts out into the harbour beyond Mosman, you will find one of Sydney's best and most secluded naturist beaches – **Cobblers Beach**. The atmosphere is friendly and the crowd truly cosmopolitan, though less extrovert visitors should probably avoid the peninsula on the eastern edge of the beach. Access is via a little-known track behind the softball pitch near the end of Military Road. You can also walk to the tip of Middle Head, where old wartime fortifications look out across North Head and the harbour entrance, or enjoy the walk to the tip of **Bradley's Head**, below the zoo, with its wonderful views of the city.

Manly
① *By ferry from Circular Quay (Wharves 2 and 3), $6.40, children $3.20, 30 mins, or the JetCat, $8.20, 15 mins. Both leave daily on a regular basis.*
Manly is by far the most visited suburb on the North Shore and is practically a self-contained holiday resort, offering an oceanside sanctuary away from the manic city centre. The heart of the community sits on the neck of the **North Head** peninsula, which

guards the entrance of Sydney Harbour. **Manly Beach** is very much the main attraction. At its southern end, an attractive oceanside walkway connects Manly Beach with two smaller, quieter alternatives, **Fairy Bower Beach** and **Shelly Beach**. As you might expect, Manly comes with all the tourist trappings, including an attractive, tree-lined waterfront, fringed with cafés, restaurants and shops and a wealth of accommodation options.

Connecting Manly Beach with the ferry terminal and **Manly Cove** (on the western or harbour side) is the **Corso**, a fairly tacky pedestrian precinct lined with cheap eateries, bars and souvenir shops. Its only saving grace is the market held at its eastern end every weekend. **Oceanworld** ① *T8251 7877, www.oceanworld.com.au, 1000-1730, $19, children $10, concessions $14, regular tours available, 'Swim with the sharks' $250, sharks fed on Mon, Wed and Fri at 1100*, a long-established aquarium, although looking tired, is still worth a visit if you have kids or fancy a swim with the star attractions on the aquarium's unusual 'Swim with the sharks' tour. **Manly Art Gallery and Museum** ① *T9976 1420, Tue-Sun 1000-1700, free*, showcases an interesting permanent exhibition of historical items with the obvious emphasis on all things 'beach', while the gallery offers both permanent and temporary shows of contemporary art and photography. The 10-km **Manly Scenic Walkway** from Manly to Spit Bridge is an excellent scenic harbour walk, arguably the city's best. Meandering through bush and along beaches while gazing over the harbour, it's hard to believe that you are in the middle of Australia's biggest city. The walk starts from the end of West Esplanade, takes from three to four hours and is clearly signposted the whole way. Walk on a weekday if possible: Sundays can be very busy.

North Head

The tip of North Head, to the south of Manly, is well worth a look, if only to soak up the views across the harbour and out to sea. The cityscape is especially stunning at dawn. Just follow Scenic Drive to the very end. The **Quarantine Station** ① *T9466 1500, www.q-station.com.au, tours Wed-Sat at 1500, Sun at 1000 and 1300, 2 hrs, from $25; Ghost Tours (can include lunch from $70 or dinner from $99) Wed-Sun 1930, 3 hrs, from $44; Family Tour Thu and Sun at 1800, 2 hrs, from $34, children $22, bookings recommended, bus No 135 from Manly wharf*, taking up a large portion of the peninsula, was used from 1832 to harbour ships known to be carrying diseases like smallpox, bubonic plague, cholera and Spanish influenza to protect the new colony from the spread of such nasties. The station closed in 1984 and is now administered by the NSW Parks and Wildlife Service. Luxury accommodation is available at the Quarantine Station and there is a good-quality restaurant.

Northern beaches

The coast north of Manly is indented by numerous bays and fine beaches that stretch 40 km to **Barrenjoey Head** at Broken Bay and the entrance to the Hawkesbury River harbour. Perhaps the most popular of these are **Narrabeen**, **Avalon** and **Whale Beach**, but there are many to choose from. Narrabeen has the added attraction of a large lake, used for sailing, canoeing and windsurfing, while Avalon and Whale Beach, further north, are smaller, quite picturesque and more sheltered. A day trip to the very tip of Barrenjoey Head is recommended and the area is complemented by **Palm Beach**, a popular weekend getaway with some fine restaurants. This is also where most of the day-to-day filming takes place for the popular Australian 'soapie' *Home and Away*. There are many water activities on offer in the area focused mainly on **Pittwater**, a large bay on the sheltered western side of the peninsula. Whether you come for a day trip or a weekend stay get hold of the free *Northern Beaches Visitors' Guide* from the Sydney VIC. The L90 bus from Wynyard goes via all the main northern beach suburbs to Palm Beach, every 30 minutes.

For Sleeping and Eating price codes and other relevant information, see Essentials pages 28-33.

Sleeping

Sydney has all types of accommodation to suit all budgets. Most of the major luxury hotels are located around Circular Quay, Darling Harbour and the northern CBD. Other more moderately priced hotels, motels and small boutique hotels are scattered around the southern city centre and inner suburbs. It is worth considering this option as many in the suburbs provide attractive alternatives to the busy city centre. There are plenty of backpacker hostels scattered throughout the city with most centred around Kings Cross. The CBD is best for convenience, Kings Cross is best for social activities, or beachside resorts such as Manly or Bondi for the classic Sydney lifestyle. A less obvious option is a serviced apartment in the CBD. **Medina**, T1300 633462, www.medinaapartments.com.au, has several establishments throughout the city. At any time in the peak season (Oct-Apr) and especially over Christmas, the New Year and during major sporting or cultural events, pre-booking is advised for all types of accommodation. If you have not pre-booked the Rocks VIC is a good place to start.

Circular Quay and the Rocks
p92, map p94

L-B B&B Sydney Harbour, 140 Cumberland St, T9247 1130, www.bbsydneyharbour.com.au. Friendly B&B with a range of 10 rooms that capture something of the building's century-plus of history without sacrificing those little luxuries. Shared and en suite. Breakfast is served in the tucked-away courtyard.
L-B Russell, 143A George St, T9241 3543, www.therussell.com.au. Set right in the heart of the Rocks with views of the harbour, retaining a historic ambience and offering a good range of singles, en suites, standard rooms and suites. Also has an appealing rooftop garden.

A-B Lord Nelson Pub and Hotel, corner of Kent St and Argyle St, The Rocks, T9251 4044, www.lordnelson.com.au. This historic hotel has some very pleasant, new and affordable en suites above the pub. The added attraction here is the home-brewed beer, food and general ambience. The pub closes fairly early at night, so noise is not usually a factor.
B Australian Heritage Hotel, 100 Cumberland St, T9247 2229, www.australianheritagehotel.com. This hotel is a good B&B with 10 comfortable doubles (shared bathrooms) and a small rooftop terrace.
B-D YHA The Rocks, 110 Cumberland St, T8272 0900, www.yha.com.au. Hugely popular given its location and its views right across Circular Quay to the Opera House and beyond. Many of the multishare and double/twin en suites have views and the rooftop deck is something many 5-star hotels in the area cannot match. It has all the regular, reliable YHA features and facilities. Limited (paid) parking near the hostel. Recommended.

City centre *p97, map p94*

At the northern edge of the CBD, fringing Circular Quay, there are reliable chain hotels that still offer a peek across the harbour. Around Haymarket the hotels become cheaper and begin to be replaced by hostels.
A-B Capitol Square, corner of Campbell and George streets, T9211 8633, www.rydges.com. Right next door to the Capitol Theatre is this friendly boutique hotel. It has cosy en suite rooms, a good restaurant and is one of the best affordable 3-4-star hotels in the centre.
A-E Y on the Park (YWCA), 5-11 Wentworth Av, T9285 6288, www.yhotel.com.au. Pitched somewhere between a budget hotel and a hostel it welcomes both male and female clients, has a good range of clean, modern, spacious and quiet rooms and boasts all the usual facilities. It is also well placed between the city centre and social hub of Oxford St.
B-D Sydney Central YHA, corner of Pitt St and Rawson Pl, T9218 9000,

www.yha.com.au. Vast and very popular, next to Central Station and the main interstate bus depot, this huge heritage building has over 500 beds split into a range of dorms, doubles and twins, with some en suite. Naturally, it also offers all mod cons including, pool, sauna, café, bar, internet, mini-mart, TV rooms and employment and travel desks.

C-D Alfred Park Budget Accommodation, 207 Cleveland St, Redfern, T9319 4031, www.alfredpark.com.au. A good 10-min walk south of Central Station, down Chalmers St and across Prince Alfred Park, is this cross between a budget hotel and a backpackers, offering peace and quiet. It is well kept and clean, offering tidy dorms, and spacious singles, doubles and twins. Modern facilities and free guest parking.

C-D Base Backpackers, 477 Kent St, T9267 7718, www.basebackpackers.com. Modern chain backpackers right in the heart of the city. Large, spacious and with good facilities, it has fine doubles, twins and dorms.

C-D Railway Square YHA, 8-10 Lee St, T9281 9666, railway@yhansw.org.au. An excellent, modern 280-bed YHA hostel in the station area itself, with accommodation, including some en suite doubles, and facilities in railway carriages.

C-D Wake Up, 509 Pitt St, T9288 7888, www.wakeup.com.au. Opposite Central railway station with 24-hr check-in, this is huge, but convenient, safe, clean and well run. It has nicely appointed doubles and twins, some with en suite, and a range of dorms, plus kitchen facilities, café, bar, travel desk and employment information.

Darling Harbour and Chinatown
p100, map p94

A-C Pensione Hotel, 631 George St, T9265 8888, www.pensione.com.au. A no-nonsense modern hotel conveniently located on the edge of Darling Harbour. Choice of good value, European minimalist-style singles to quads, in-house restaurant/bar.

B Glasgow Arms Hotel, 527 Harris St, Ultimo, T9211 2354, www.glasgowarmshotel.com.au.

Good value, friendly, just on the edge of Darling Harbour, the hotel offers basic yet cosy rooms, entertaining bar and an affordable pub restaurant with a courtyard downstairs.

City West *p102*
Glebe
Glebe is especially popular as an alternative backpackers' venue offering a village-type atmosphere with interesting cafés, shops and pubs all within easy walking distance.

LL-L Trickett's Luxury B&B, 270 Glebe Point Rd, T9552 1141, www.tricketts.com.au. A beautifully restored Victorian mansion, decorated with antiques and Persian rugs and offering spacious, well-appointed en suites.

B-D Alishan International Guesthouse, 100 Glebe Point Rd, T9566 4048, www.alishan.com.au. Halfway between a small hotel and a quality hostel, this spacious, renovated Victorian mansion has spotless doubles, twins and family en suites, all with TV and fridge. Shared accommodation I s also available and overall the facilities are excellent. A great value budget option, especially for couples looking for a place away from the city centre. Limited off-street parking.

C-E Glebe Village Backpackers, 256 Glebe Point Rd, T9660 8878, www.glebevillage.com. A large, working backpackers' favourite and the management works hard to maintain its sound reputation. It offers a range of dorms and a few doubles (some en suite) and is friendly, laid-back and prides itself on finding work for guests. There's an-house café, pick-ups and regular day tours to beaches and other locations.

D Glebe Point YHA, 262 Glebe Point Rd, T9692 8418, www.yha.com.au. A popular option away from the CBD with a nice atmosphere, offering fairly small single, double, twin and 4-bed dorms and modern facilities throughout. Barbecues on the roof are a speciality. Regular shuttle to the city and transport departure points.

City East *p104, map p105*

There is no shortage of accommodation in Kings Cross and its surrounding suburbs, with everything from the de luxe 5-star hotels to the basic and affordable hostel. Most backpackers are located along Victoria St, Orwell St or on the main drag, Darlinghurst Rd. Others are scattered in quieter locations around the main hub, especially towards Potts Point.

Kings Cross

A-B The Barclay, 17 Bayswater Rd, T9358 6133, www.barclayhotel.com.au. Recently renovated and good value, with a touch of class. Restaurant, bar and nightclub.

D-E Funk House, 23 Darlinghurst Rd, T9358 6455, www.funkhouse.com.au. Set right on Darlinghurst Rd, this is definitely one for the younger party set. Zany artworks adorn the walls and doors. 3-4 bed dorms and double/twins all with fridge, TV and fan. Lots of freebies. Their legendary rooftop barbecues are a great place to meet others. Good job search assistance.

D-E Jolly Swagman, 27 Orwell St, T9358 6400, www.jollyswagman.com.au. Another buzzing hostel set in the heart of the action. Very professionally managed with all the usual facilities. TV, fridge and fan in most rooms. Excellent travel desk and job search assistance. Social atmosphere. 24-hr check-in, fast internet and free beer on arrival.

D-E Original Backpackers Lodge, 160-162 Victoria St, T9356 3232, www.originalbackpackers.com.au. Possibly the best hostel in Kings Cross if not the city and certainly one of the best in terms of facilities and management. The historic house is large and homely, well appointed and comfortable, offering a great range of double, twin, single, triple and dorm rooms all with TV, fridge and fans (heated in winter). There is a great open courtyard in which to socialize or enjoy a barbecue. Cable TV. The staff are always on hand to help with onward travel, job seeking or things to see and do. Book ahead.

D-E Pink House, 6-8 Barncleuth Sq, T9358 1689, www.pinkhouse.com.au. A historic mansion offering a homely feel that is lacking in many of the other Kings Cross hostels; deservingly popular, especially for those tired of the party scene. Lots of quiet corners and a shady courtyard in which to find peace of mind. Large dorms and some good doubles, cable TV and free internet.

Potts Point

LL-A Victoria Court, 122 Victoria St, T9357 3200, www.victoriacourt.com.au. This is a delightful and historic boutique hotel in a quiet location. It comes with period antiques, well-appointed en suites, fireplaces and 4-poster beds. The courtyard conservatory is excellent.

B-C De Vere Hotel, 44-46 Macleay St, T9358 1211, www.deverehotel.com.au. North, away from the mania of Kings Cross proper yet still convenient to eateries and nightlife, is one of the tidiest and best value standard hotels in the area. All rooms have a private bathroom and there are also self-contained options. Buffet breakfast.

C Challis Lodge, 21-23 Challis Av, T9358 5422, www.challislodge.com.au. A historic mansion, cheaper than **Victoria Court**, and therefore less salubrious, yet with a good range of singles, twins and doubles, some with en suites.

D-E Blue Parrot, 87 Macleay St, T9356 4888, www.blueparrot.com.au. Located towards Potts Point. Modern, clean and well managed, with an attractive courtyard garden to escape the hype of the Cross and open fires in winter. Free internet.

D-E Eva's, 6-8 Orwell St, T9358 2185, www.evasbackpackers.com.au. This is another clean and well-managed hostel that offers a distinctly homely feel. Arty rooms with some en suites. Rooftop space used for social barbecues and offering great views across the city.

D-E Kanga House, 141 Victoria St, T9357 7897, www.kangahouse.com.au. Offers a warm welcome and if you are lucky you may be able to secure a room with a view of the Opera House.

Darlinghurst, Surry Hills and Airport

Separated only by a river of traffic, Darlinghurst offers a fine alternative to Kings Cross. Surry Hills has few options.

LL L'Otel, 114 Darlinghurst Rd, Darlinghurst, T9360 6868, www.lotel.com.au. Classy, yet given its minimalist decor perhaps not everyone's cup of tea. Ultra hip and very much a place for the modern couple. Excellent personable service and a fine restaurant attached.

A Kirketon, 229 Darlinghurst Rd, Darlinghurst, T9332 2011, www.kirketon.com.au. Modern, chic and minimalist with a bar and restaurant.

A-B Altamont, 207 Darlinghurst Rd, Darlinghurst, T9360 6000, www.altamont.com.au. Classy, traditional hotel with beautiful spacious de luxe rooms with wooden floors and fittings. Some are fantastic value.

C Formule 1 Motel, 5 Ross Smith Av (300 m from domestic terminal), Mascot, T8339 1840, www.formule1.com.au. Cramped but affordable motel accommodation within walking distance of the domestic terminal and international terminal transfers.

C Royal Sovereign, corner of Liverpool St and Darlinghurst Rd, Darlinghurst, T9331 3672, www.darlobar.com.au. For something more traditional look no further than here. Quality refurbished rooms above the popular Darlo bar. Shared bathroom facilities.

C-E Kangaroo Bakpak, 665 South Dowling St, Surry Hills, T9319 5915, www.kangaroobakpak.com.au. A quiet backpacker option with a friendly family atmosphere. Good for longer stays.

Watson's Bay

LL Watson's Bay, T9337 5444, www.watsonsbayhotel.com.au. Set alongside the legendary seafood restaurant (see page 119) is this fabulous boutique hotel with 32 suites, each with its own breathtaking view from the balcony. Easily reached by ferry.

Bondi and Coogee

The older, well-established beachfront hotels in Bondi look a little garish but their interiors will not disappoint, and they are only metres from the world-famous beach. There are around a dozen backpackers. Coogee is steadily growing in popularity as a viable and often cheaper alternative to Bondi Beach.

LL-L Ravesi's, corner of Campbell Parade and Hall St, Bondi, T9365 4422, www.ravesis.com.au. Stylish and intimate with pleasant, good value 3-star standard rooms, standard suites and luxury split-level suites, most with balconies overlooking all the action. The balcony restaurant is one of the best in the area.

LL-A Coogee Bay Boutique Hotel, 9 Vicar St, Coogee, T9665 0000, www.coogeebay hotel.com.au. Very pleasant, boutique-style rooms in addition to good, traditional pub-style options. Well appointed, en suite, ocean views and good value. The hotel itself is a main social focus in Coogee both day and night.

A-B Bondi, 178 Campell Pde, Bondi, T9130 3271, www.hotelbondi.com.au. Traditional, with a popular public bar downstairs, a good café and a nightclub/performance space, **Zinc**, with live bands, DJs and pool competitions most nights.

B Bondi Beachouse YHA, corner of Fletcher St and Dellview St, Bondi, T9365 2088, www.yha.com.au. Art deco building with great ocean views from the rooftop deck. Usual YHA reliability and full room configurations, but no en suites. Café/restaurant and, of course, the odd surfboard.

B-E Coogee Beachside Backpackers, 178/172, Coogee Bay Rd, Coogee, T9315 8511, www.sydneybeachside.com.au. Just as good as **Surfside** (below) but smaller and with more character. There are 2 houses (Wizard of Oz and Beachside). The rooms, especially the doubles, are excellent. Good facilities, friendly staff with good work contacts. A 5-min walk to the beach. Ask about flat shares if you intend to stay long term.

C-E Surfside Backpackers, 186 Arden St, Coogee, T9315 7888, www.surfside backpackers.com.au. The largest of the several backpackers, beachside and very social with a solid reputation and modern facilities. 2-bedroom flats available for small groups with balcony and ocean view. They also run a sister facility at 35A Hall St, Bondi Beach, T9365 4900.

D-E Lamrock Lodge Backpackers, 19 Lamrock Av, Bondi, T9130 5063, www.lamrocklodge.com. Offers clean, modern facilities and all rooms – dorm, single, twin and double – have cable TV, fridge, kitchenette and microwave. Good value.

D-E Noah's Bondi Beach Backpackers, 2 Campbell Pde, Bondi, T9365 7644, www.noahsbondibeach.com. Perched on the hill, overlooking the beach as you descend to Bondi proper, is this large place, popular due to its position and price. As such it is certainly not the quietest. Former hotel rooms converted to dorms, twins and doubles (some with ocean view). Rooftop barbecue area offers great views.

City North *p107*
North Sydney and surrounds
The quiet yet central suburb of Kirribilli, across the water from the Opera House, is an excellent place to base yourself, with a short and spectacular ferry trip to the CBD. There is very little in the way of accommodation but that is part of its charm.

B-D Glenferrie Lodge, 12A Carabella St, T9955 1685, www.glenferrielodge.com. A vast, 70-room Victorian mansion with quality budget accommodation. The range of shared, single, twin, double, queen/king de luxe are above average with some having their own balconies. Cheap dinners are on offer nightly and there are B&B packages. Wi-Fi. Recommended.

Manly
Being a well-established resort within the city there is no shortage of accommodation in Manly. The VIC on the Forecourt beside the ferry wharf has detailed listings, maps and can help arrange bookings, T9976 1430, www.manlytourism.com.au.

L-B Manly Lodge Boutique Hotel, 22 Victoria Pde, T9977 8655, www.manly lodge.com.au. A homely option, popular and good value.

A-B 101 Addison B&B, 101 Addison Rd, T9977 6216, www.bb-manly.com. For a B&B option try this historic 1-bedroom gem. Open fire, grand piano; say no more! Book well ahead.

C-E Boardrider Backpackers, 63 Corso (rear), T9977 6077, www.boardrider.com.au. New purpose-built backpackers with all the usual amenities set in the heart of the action and only metres from the ferry and beach. Dorm, twin and doubles, some with en suite.

C-E Manly Backpackers Beachside, 28 Raglan St, T9977 3411, www.manly backpackers.com.au. Well-rated and busy with some en suite doubles and small dorms.

D Manly Bungalow, 64 Pittwater Rd, T9977 5494, www.manlybungalow.com. Bright and sunny budget accommodation with good value double and family rooms with kitchenettes.

Northern beaches
C-D Collaroy YHA (Sydney Beachhouse), 4 Collaroy St, Collaroy Beach, T9981 1177, www.sydneybeachouse.com.au. The Hilton of Sydney backpackers offers tidy dorms, twins, doubles and family rooms (some en suite) and great facilities, including a heated pool, spacious kitchen, dining areas, TV rooms, free equipment hire and organized day trips. When it comes to facilities it deserves its reputation as one of the best budget options in the city. Book ahead. Catch the L90 or L88 bus from Central, Wynyard or QVB.

D-E Pittwater YHA, via Halls Wharf, Morning Bay, via Church Pt, T9999 5748, www.yha.com.au. A real getaway located in the Ku-ring-gai National Park and accessible only by ferry. It has dorms and a few doubles. Plenty of walking and water-based activities or simple peace and quiet. Phone for details, take all your supplies and book ahead.

❶ Eating

When it comes to quality and choice there is no doubt that Sydney is on a par with any major city in the world and with over 3000 restaurants to choose from you have to wonder where on earth to start. As a general rule you will find the best of the fine dining establishments specializing in Modern Australian cuisine in and around Circular Quay, the Rocks, the CBD and Darling Harbour, though pockets of international speciality abound, from chow mein in Chinatown to pasta in Paddington. Sydney's thriving café culture is generally centred on the suburbs of Darlinghurst, Glebe, Newtown and the eastern beaches of Bondi and Bronte.

Circular Quay and the Rocks
p92, map p94

On the eastern side of the Quay you will find mid-range and expensive options with lots of atmosphere and memorable views under the concourse of the Opera House and within 'The Toaster'.

Australian Heritage Hotel, see page 111. Daily for lunch and dinner. Come here for a taste of Aussie pub life. It has a wonderful atmosphere and all the classic Australian beers. Good value and good alfresco and menu, which includes pizza, croc, emu and roo steaks.

Café Sydney, Level 5, Customs House, 31 Alfred St, T9251 8683. Daily for lunch, Mon-Sat for dinner. Set high above Circular Quay at the top of Customs House, this place offers superb views and alfresco dining. The food is traditional modern Australian with a good atmosphere and occasional live jazz.

The Wharf, Pier 4, Hickson Rd, Walsh Bay, T9250 1761. Lunch and dinner Mon-Sat. Off the beaten track and a firm local favourite is this option located at the end of one of the historic Walsh Bay piers. It has a great atmosphere and wonderful views of the busy harbour. Modern Australian.

MCA Café, 140 George St, T9241 4253. Lunch Mon-Fri and breakfast and lunch Sat-Sun. At the Museum of Contemporary Art, this café is ideally located next to all the action on Circular Quay. It is a bit expensive but worth it and the seafood is excellent.

La Renaissance, 47 Argyle St, The Rocks, T9241 4878. Head to this patisserie for a simple lunch. Authentic French baguettes and pastries in a quiet leafy courtyard or to takeaway.

Rocks Café, T9241 2883 daily 0800-2130. A cheaper option around the back of the MCA and also good.

City centre *p97, map p94*

The sheer chaos and noise that surrounds you in the CBD is enough to put anyone off eating. A retreat to the Botanical Gardens or Hyde Park is recommended.

Brooklyn Hotel, corner of George St and Grosvenor St, T9247 6744. Lunch Mon-Fri. Well known for its meat dishes, especially steak, and has plenty of inner city pub atmosphere.

Pavilion on the Park, 1 Art Gallery Rd, The Domain, T9232 1322. Opposite the Art Gallery, this place is the perfect escape from the city centre, offering alfresco dining with an eclectic modern Australian menu. Perfect for lunch after a tour of the gallery.

Botanical Gardens Café, Mrs Macquarie Rd, T9241 2419. Daily 0830-1800. For sublime tranquillity amidst the Botanical Gardens, the bat colony might not be everybody's cup of tea but for environmentalists and botanists it's really hard to beat.

Casa Asturiana, 77 Liverpool St, T9264 1010. Daily for lunch and dinner. In Sydney's Spanish quarter and well known for its Spanish cuisine, tapas in particular. Lots of atmosphere and regular live music.

Hyde Park Café, corner of Elizabeth and Liverpool streets, T9264 8751. Daily 0700-1630. A great spot for escaping the crowds, serving breakfast, light lunches, coffee and people watching.

¶ **MOS Café**, corner of Bridge and Phillip streets, T9241 3636. Mon-Fri 0700-2100 and Sat-Sun 0830-1700. Below the Museum of Sydney this congenial café offers good-value Modern Australian cuisine for lunch.

¶ **Tearoom**, on the top floor of the QVB, George St. Sun-Fri 1100-1700, Sat 1100-1500. If the shopping all gets too much escape to this gracious room where you can sink into a large comfy chair and have an enormous afternoon tea.

Darling Harbour and Chinatown
p100, map p94

¶¶ **Coast**, Roof Terrace, Cockle Bay Wharf, Darling Park, 201 Sussex St, T9267 6700. Lunch Mon-Fri and Sun, daily for dinner. Offers a fine range of Modern Australian dishes and has a formal, yet relaxed atmosphere and great views across Darling Harbour.

¶ **BBQ King**, 18 Goulburn St, T9267 2586. Daily 1130-0200. This Sydney institution is the first place to head for if you fancy Chinese. There's nothing special about the decor or service but the food is always excellent and good value.

¶ **Blackbird Café**, Mid Level, Cockle Bay Wharf, T9283 7385. Deservedly popular, congenial, laid back and good value with a huge selection from pasta to steak.

¶ **Chinta Ria – The Temple of Love**, Roof Terr, Cockle Bay Wharf, 201 Sussex St, T9264 3211, www.chintaria.com. Daily for lunch and dinner. With a name like that who can resist? Great aesthetics, buzzing atmosphere with quality Malaysian cuisine.

¶ **Dickson House Food Court**, corner of Little Hay St and Dixon St. Daily 1030-2030. Has a wealth of cheap Asian takeaways with generous meals for under $6.

¶ **Emperor's Garden Seafood**, 96 Hay St, T9211 2135, www.emperorsgarden.com.au. Daily 0800-0100. Moving into Haymarket is one of the most reliable of the Chinatown restaurants, always bustling, offering great service and value for money.

City West *p102*
Glebe

¶¶¶ **Boathouse on Blackwattle Bay**, Ferry Rd, T9518 9011, www.boathouse.net.au. Tue-Sun lunch and dinner. A quality upmarket (yet informal) seafood restaurant offering refreshingly different harbour views than those sought at Circular Quay and Darling Harbour. Here you can watch the lights of Anzac Bridge or the comings and goings of Sydney's fishing fleet while tucking into the freshest seafood.

¶ **Badde Manors**, 37 Glebe Point Rd, T9660 3797. Daily 0730 till late. Something of an institution in Glebe for many years, this student hangout can always be relied on for atmosphere and character, which is more than can be said for the service.

¶ **Iku Organic**, 25A Glebe Point Rd, T9692 8720. Mon-Fri 1130-2100, Sat-Sun 1130-2100. The first of what is now a chain of fine vegetarian and macrobiotic vegan cafés under the Iku banner, offering a delicious array of options.

¶ **Nawaz Flavour of India**, 142A Glebe Point Rd, T9692 0662. Quite simply Glebe's best Indian restaurant with lots of character, great service and value for money.

¶ **Toxteth Hotel**, 345 Glebe Point Rd, T9660 2370. Daily from 1100. Modern, traditional Australian pub serving mountainous plates of good pub grub at very cheap prices.

¶ **Well Connected**, 35 Glebe Point Rd, T9566 2655. Open 0700-2400. One of the city's first internet cafés. Laid back with a whole floor upstairs full of sofas dedicated to surfing the web. Not a bad cup of coffee either.

Newtown

¶ **Cinque**, 261 King St, Newtown, T9519 3077. Daily 0730-late. Another popular café located next to the Dendy Cinema and a small bookshop. Great all-day breakfasts, coffee.

¶ **Old Fish Shop Café**, 239A King St, T9519 4295. Daily 0730-2300. A charming little café and one of Newtown's best and most popular haunts, especially for breakfast and good coffee.

Thai Pothong, 294 King St, T9550 6277. Tue-Sun lunch, daily for dinner. On a street with more Thai restaurants than you can shake a chopstick at, this one stands head and shoulders above the rest. Good value, good choice and good service.

Thanh Binh, 111 King St, T9557 1175. Thu-Sun lunch, daily for dinner. Good value Vietnamese offering delicious dishes from simple noodles to venison in curry sauce.

City East *p104, map p105*
Kings Cross

As you'd expect there are a million and one fast food outlets here and other budget eateries catering for the cash-strapped backpacker and night owls.

Bayswater Brasserie, 32 Bayswater Rd, T9357 2177. Mon-Thu 1700-2300, Fri 1200-2300, Sat 1700-2300. A reliable choice and immensely popular for its laid-back yet classy atmosphere and imaginative Modern Australian cuisine. At the top end of this price range.

Café Hernandez, 60 Kings Cross Rd, T9331 2343. Great, eccentric 24-hr café serving Spanish fare, great coffee and with lots of character.

Govinda's, 112 Darlinghurst Rd, T9380 5155. Restaurant and cinema combo offering great value all-you-can-eat vegetarian buffet plus the movie ticket. Dinner is $19.80 and a further $10:00 for the movie/dinner package.

Woolloomooloo

The wharf has a growing reputation as one of the best places for fine dining in the city.

Manta Ray, 9 The Wharf, 6 Cowper Wharf Rd, T9332 3822. Mon-Fri lunch and daily for dinner. Classy seafood restaurant. Some say one of the best in the city.

Otto Italiano, 8 The Wharf, Cowper Wharf Rd, T9368 7488. Very trendy, quality Italian with all the necessary trimmings including extrovert waiters.

Harry's Café de Wheels, Cowper Wharf. Sun-Thu 0700-0200, Fri-Sat till 0300. Harry's is something of a Sydney institution, offering

the famously yummy pies with pea toppings and gravy. One is surely never enough, as the photos of satisfied customers will testify.

Darlinghurst and Surry Hills

Forty One, Chifley Tower, 2 Chifley Square, T9221 2500, www.forty-one.com.au. Enjoys an international reputation for quality fine dining. Stunning views across the Botanical Gardens and harbour. Intimate yet relaxed atmosphere. Book well ahead.

Bar Coluzzi, 322 Victoria St, Darlinghurst, T9380 5420. Daily 0500-1900. A well-established café that consistently gets the vote as one of Sydney's best. The character, the truly cosmopolitan clientele and the coffee are the biggest draws, rather than the food.

Bill's Café, 433 Liverpool St, Darlinghurst, T9360 9631. Mon-Sat 0730-1500, Sun 0830-1500. One of the city's top breakfast cafés with legendary scrambled eggs. Small and at times overcrowded but that's part of the experience. Also **Bill's Surry Hills**, at 359 Crown St, Surry Hills, T9360 4762. Daily 0700-2200.

Le Petit Creme, 118 Darlinghurst Rd, Darlinghurst, T9361 4738. Daily from 0800. Superb little French number with all the classics, from baguettes to cavernous bowls of café au lait. Great omelettes for breakfast or lunch.

Longrain, 85 Commonwealth St, Surry Hills, T9280 2888. Wed-Fri and Sun 1200-1430, dinner Mon-Sat 1800-2300. Without doubt one of the best Thai restaurants in the city. Housed in a century-old warehouse space, other than its cuisine, one of its most notable features the huge wooden tables deliberately designed to encourage Asian-style banquet dining. Recommended.

Oh! Calcutta!, 251 Victoria St, Darlinghurst, T9360 3650. Fri lunch and Mon-Sat dinner. An award-winning Indian restaurant and by far the best in the inner east. Book ahead.

Una's, 340 Victoria St, Darlinghurst, T9360 6885. Daily 0730-late. Local favourite offering generous hangover-cure breakfasts and

European-influenced lunches, including schnitzel and mouthwatering strudel.

Paddington
Indian Home Diner, 86 Oxford St, T9331 4183. You really can't go wrong here with the usual great value (if mild) Indian combo dishes and, on this occasion, a small courtyard out back.

Royal Hotel, 237 Glenmore Rd, T9331 2604. Lunch and dinner from 1200. One of the best choices at the increasingly popular Five Ways crossroads in Paddington. A grand old pub with gracious yet modern feel. Excellent modern Australian cuisine is served upstairs in the main restaurant or on the prized verandah. Perfect for a lazy afternoon.

Watson's Bay
Doyle's on the Beach, 11 Marine Pde, T9337 2007, www.doyles.com.au. Daily lunch and dinner. Sydney's best-known restaurant for years. It has been in the same family for generations and has an unfaltering reputation for superb seafood, atmosphere and harbour/city views, which all combine to make it one of the best dining experiences in the city, if not Australia. If you can, book well ahead and ask for a balcony seat. Sun afternoons are especially popular and you could combine the trip with a walk around the heads. Book well ahead.

Watson's Bay Hotel, 1 Military Rd, T9337 4299. Located right next door to the famous Doyle's, **Watson's** offers some stiff competition in the form of quality, value seafood alfresco, with lots of choice. You can even cook your own. Great for a whole afternoon, especially at the weekend.

Bondi, Bronte and Coogee
Icebergs Dining Room & Bar, 1 Notts Av, Bondi Beach, T9365 9000, www.idrb.com. Tue-Sat 1200-midnight, Sun 1200-2200. One of the trendiest dining spaces in the city, hanging over the beach and attracting a glamorous crowd to its modern Italian cuisine and sharp design. Expensive, but one to remember.

Ravesi's, corner Campbell Pde and Hall St, Bondi Beach, T9365 4422. Daily for dinner, Sat-Sun from 0900 for breakfast and brunch. A well-established favourite in Bondi, offering a combination of classy atmosphere, quality Modern Australian cuisine and fine views of the iconic beach.

Coogee Bay Hotel, corner of Coogee Bay Rd and Arden St, T6665 0000. The most popular spot in Coogee day or night, with multiple bars, huge open-air eating, value pub grub and live entertainment.

Jenny's, 485 Bronte Rd, T9389 7498. Daily 0700-1830. With competition on both sides, but consistently the café of choice on the 'Bronte strip'. Favourite breakfast spot at weekends and a great start (or finish) to the clifftop walk between Bronte and Bondi.

City North *p107*
Manly
Manly is blessed with numerous restaurants and cafés in a wide range.

Le Kiosk, Shelly Beach, T9977 4122. Daily lunch and dinner. Simple beach house ambience in a beautiful setting right on the beach. Reliable modern Australian cuisine.

Manly Wharf Hotel, T9977 1266. This fabulous redeveloped pub on the wharf is the hottest spot in Manly in summer. Classy food in a bustling, open space.

Bower, 7 Marine Pde, T9977 5451. Daily for breakfast and lunch, Thu and some weekends for dinner. Located right at the end of Marine Pde with memorable views back towards Manly Beach. Great spot for breakfast.

Out of Africa, 43 East Esplanade, Manly, T9977 0055. Daily for dinner, Thu-Sun for lunch. Good value, authentic African cuisine with all the expected furnishings. Seems oddly out of place in Manly, but remains refreshingly different.

Bars and clubs

Sydney has pubs to suit most tastes in both the city centre and the suburbs. Most are the traditional, street-corner Australian hotels, but there are lots of modern, trendy establishments, pseudo-Irish pubs and truly historic alehouses on offer. Many pubs, especially those along Oxford St and in Kings Cross, attract a distinctly metrosexual clientele. See also Entertainment, page 122, for gay nights. For the latest in club information and special events get hold of the free *3-D World* magazine, available in many backpackers, cafés or the clubs, www.threedworld.com.au.

Circular Quay and the Rocks
p92, map p94
Bars
The best single drinking area in Sydney is undoubtedly **The Rocks**, where history, aesthetics, atmosphere and most importantly darn good beer combine to guarantee a great night out.

Australian Heritage Hotel, see page 111. From the **Orient** negotiate the steady climb up to Cumberland St (the steps are located on the right, before the bridge behind the **Argyle Stores**) and reward yourself with an obligatory Australian beer. You may also like to sample a kangaroo, emu or crocodile steak for dinner.

Cruise, by the Passenger Terminal on the Rocks side, and **Harbour View Hotel**, 18 Lower Fort St, are both good choices with fine views.

Hero of Waterloo, 81 Lower Fort St, T9252 4553. Just around the corner from the **Nelson** is this smaller and characterful pub that can be a bit of a squeeze but is always entertaining.

Lord Nelson, see page 111. Past Observatory Park and down to Argyle St is Sydney's oldest pub. Within its hallowed, nautically themed walls, it brews its own ales and also offers some fine pub grub and accommodation.

Mercantile, 25 George St, T9247 3570. A chaotic Irish pub, it is often busy but offers a fairly decent pint of Guinness as well as great live traditional music until late.

Opera Bar, nestled in the lower concourse just short of the Opera House. This place is outdoors and serves great bar food, has regular live music and offers a truly world-class view. Expensive but worth it.

Clubs
Basement, 29 Reiby Pl, T9251 2797, www.thebasement.com.au. Ever popular.
Jacksons on George, 176 George St, T9247 2727. A huge club spread over 4 floors with 5 bars, dining, dancing, live bands and pool, open 24 hrs.

City centre *p97, map p94*
Bars
Paddy McGuires, on the corner of George and Hay, T9212 2111. Pretty authentic Irish pub that offers pleasant surroundings in which you can actually have a decent conversation or sample a fine range of beers. Live music.

Scruffy Murphy's, on the corner of Goulburn St and George St, T9211 2002. Open well into the early hours. Popular, well-established Irish pub that always draws the crowds. It's a great place to meet people and the live bands and beers are good, but there really is very little Irish or class about it.

Scubar, corner of Rawson Pl and Rawson Lane, T9212 4244, www.scubar.com.au. Popular backpacker-oriented pub that offers cheap beer, pizzas, pool, big TV screens and popular music until late.

Clubs
Chinese Laundry and Slip Inn, 111 Sussex St, T8295 9999. Has a solid reputation and one of the largest and best clubs in Australia.
Civic Hotel, 388 Pitt St, corner of Goulburn St, T8267 3185. Though essentially a pub, cocktail bar and restaurant, this is a traditional weekend haunt for a cosmopolitan crowd who repeatedly come to enjoy old anthems and classics. Cover charge.
Orbit Bar, Level 47, Australia Sq, 264 George St, T9247 9777. Upping the tone – and altitude – considerably is this retro revolving bar (and

expensive restaurant). Definitely a place to impress, and be impressed. Friendly service, great bar snacks and wonderful views.

Darling Harbour and Chinatown
p100, map p94

Bars
Cargo Bar, 52-60 The Promenade, Darling Harbour, T9262 1777. One of a few hip bars on Kings St Wharf with outdoor seating.

Clubs
Home, Cockle Bay Wharf, T9266 0600. Open 2200-0600. One of the country's largest, state-of-the-art nightclubs. Here, on 4 levels, you can get on down to house and trance. Every Sat there is a kinkidisco – the mind boggles. Cover charge.

City West *p102*
The Bank 324 King St, T8568 1988, just south of the railway station, Newtown. Always busy thanks to its dark and rambling succession of rooms and bars. It also has a great Thai restaurant in the beer garden.
Friend In Hand Pub, 58 Cowper St, Glebe, T9660 2326. 'World famous', it looks more like a venue for an international garage sale, but oozes character and also offers a bar-café and Italian restaurant. Look out – the cockatoo does bite!
Kuleto's Cocktail Bar, 157 King St, Newtown, T9519 6369, www.kuletos.com.au. Kuleto's offers something completely different.
Toxteth Hotel, 345 Glebe Point Rd, Glebe, T9660 2370. A far more modern, traditionally Australian affair. It is always pretty lively, has pool competitions and serves mountainous plates of good pub grub.

City East *p104, map p105*

Bars
Kings Cross is perhaps a little overrated when it come to pubs but Paddington has quite a few old traditional pubs (see below). If these are not to your taste you might like to try the more cutting-edge establishments with the music and atmosphere that the cosmopolitan and mixed gay and straight (but always

trendy) clientele hold dear. Some great examples are: **Bourbon**, 24 Darlinghurst Rd, T9358 1144, www.thebourbon.com.au; **Oxford Hotel**, 134 Oxford St, T9331 3467; and **Albury Hotel**, 6 Oxford St, T9361 6555.
Coogee Bay Hotel, 9 Vicar St, Coogee, T9665 0000. Beachside hotel with multiple bars and live music.
Durty Nelly's, 9 Glenmore Rd, Paddington, T9360 4467. The smallest, best and most intimate Irish pub in the city, offering pleasant surroundings and a grand congenial jam session on Sun evenings (last orders 2330).
Hotel Bondi, 178 Campell Pde, Bondi, T9130 3271. A popular bar with live bands and a nightclub attached.
Kings Cross Hotel, 248 William St, Kings Cross, T9358 3377. In the shadow of the huge Coca Cola sign is the bizarre interior of this rowdy backpacker favourite, open well into the early hours.
Lord Dudley, 236 Jersey Rd, T9327 5399, www.lorddudley.com.au. Deep in the Paddington suburbs is this grand historic rabbit warren with a distinct UK feel and some great, if expensive, pub grub on offer.
Royal Hotel, see page 119. There's a large atmospheric public bar downstairs and a fine restaurant on the 2nd floor.
Tilbury, southeast corner of Nicholson St and Bourke St, Woolloomooloo. Attracts a good-looking crowd to its slick, open spaces. Noisy thanks to the expanses of shiny chrome and pale timber but it's always humming.
Water Bar, just inside the Wharf at Woolloomooloo. Gorgeous, dark and groovy.
Woolloomooloo Bay Hotel, 2 Bourke St, Woolloomooloo, T9357 1177. Karaoke nights and regular DJs. When you can no longer pronounce its name it's definitely time to go home!

Clubs
Paddington's Oxford St is a major focus for nightlife and the main haunt for the gay and lesbian community. Kings Cross is the main focus for travellers, particularly backpackers, but is not necessarily the best venue in town.

Arq, 16 Flinders St, Paddington, T9380 8700. It has 2 large dance floors, plenty of space and a good balcony from which to watch a friendly crowd both straight and gay.

Le Panic, 20 Bayswater Rd, Kings Cross, T9368 0763, www.lepanic.com.au. Thu-Sun from 1900. Another intimate club come cocktail bar with a must-see eclectic decor. Again it concentrates on progressive house music. Fri nights are especially good.

Sapphire Suite, 2 Kellet St, Kings Cross, T9331 0058. 2200-0500. Modern and trendy, offering a fine range of expensive cocktails, acid jazz, house and rave. Cover charge.

World, 24 Bayswater Rd, Kings Cross, T9357 7700. Modern laid-back club set in grand surrounds and offering mainly UK house music, Fri-Sat cover charge after 2200.

⊙ Entertainment

Sydney p90, maps p91, p94 and p105

There is always a wealth of things to entertain in Sydney. For the latest information and reviews check the *Metro* section in the Fri *Sydney Morning Herald*. *The Beat* and *Sydney City Hub* are free weeklies that are readily available in restaurants, cafés, bars and bookshops in and around the city centre. On the net consult the websites already listed on page 91, or visit www.sydney.citysearch.com.au, www.whatsonsydney.com.

The usual ticket agent is **Ticketek**, City Box Offices at 50 Park St (corner Castlereagh), Mon-Fri 0900-1700, Sat 1000-1400, and Theatre Royal Sydney, MLC Centre, 108 King St, Mon-Fri 0900-1700, T132849, www.ticketek.com.au. It produces its own monthly events magazine *The Ticket*. **Ticketmaster7**, T136100, www.ticketmaster .com.au, also deals with sports events tickets.

Cinema

For listings see the *Sydney Morning Herald*. A movie ticket will cost from $17.50, children from $13. Cheaper tickets are often offered on Tue nights.

In the city centre most of the major conventional cinema complexes are to be found along George St between Town Hall and Chinatown. On Oxford St is **Chauvel**, corner of Oxford St and Oatley Rd, T9361 5398, www.chauvelcinema.net.au, which showcases more retro, foreign or fringe films.

Hayden Orpheum Cinema, 180 Military Rd, Cremorne, T9908 4344, on the North Shore. A wonderful art deco cinema offering a fine alternative to the modern city cinemas.

IMAX Theatre, Darling Harbour, T9281 3300, www.imax.com.au. A huge 8-storey affair showcasing 3D movies from 1000, from $20, children $15.

Moonlight Cinema, Centennial Park, www.moonlight.com.au (23 Nov-23 Feb). Old classics, take a picnic and cushions.

Open Air Cinema, Royal Botanical Gardens near Mrs Macquarie's Chair (summer only). New releases and smart deli food.

Contemporary music
Australian

You will almost certainly hear the bizarre and extraordinary tones of the didgeridoo somewhere during your explorations, be it the buskers on Circular Quay or in the many souvenir shops in the city.

Folk

All the Irish pubs offer folk jam nights early in the week and live bands from Wed to Sun. For some of the best try the **Mercantile Hotel**, 25 George St, The Rocks, **Scruffy Murphy's**, corner of Goulburn St and George St, T9211 2002, **O'Malley's Hotel**, 228 William St, Kings Cross, T9357 2211. Two excellent quieter options are **Paddy McGuires**, on the corner of George and Hay, T9212 2111, and **Durty Nelly's** (the best), on Glenmore Rd off Oxford St, which is a more intimate Irish pub offering low-key jam sessions on Sun afternoons.

Jazz and blues

Soup Plus, 383 George St, T9299 7728, **The Basement**, 29 Reiby Pl, Circular Quay, T9251 2797, www.thebasement.com.au, and the **Harbourside Brasserie**, Pier One, The Rocks, T9252 3000, are the major local jazz venues. **Zambezi Blues Room**, 481 Kent St, behind Town Hall Sq, T9266 0200, is a fine venue and free. For daily details of jazz gigs, tune into the *Jazz Gig Guide* at 0800 on Jazz Jam, 89.7 FM Eastside Radio, Mon-Fri. For **Sydney Jazz Club** call T9719 3876, www.sydneyjazzclub.com.

Rock

The three main rock concert venues are: the massive **Acer Arena**, Homebush Bay Olympic Park, T8765 4321, www.acerarena.com.au; the 12,000-seat **Sydney Entertainment Centre**, 35 Harbour St, City, T9320 4200, www.sydentcent.com.au; and **Metro Theatre**, 624 George St, T9550 3666. Tickets for a big international band will cost from $80-180.

Comedy

National or international comedy acts are generally hosted by the smaller theatres, like the **Lyric** and the **Belvoir** (see Performing arts below). A number of inner-city hotels have comedy nights once a week, including the **Roxbury Hotel**, 182 St Johns Rd, Glebe T9692 0822, and the **Marlborough Hotel**, 145 King St, Newtown, T9519 1222 (Tue), both of which are good. Other venues with more regular acts are the **Comedy Store**, Bent St, Fox Studios, T9357 1419, www.comedystore.com.au (nightly, from $12-30) and the **Laugh Garage**, B1, 60 Park St, Parramatta, T9264 1161, www.thelaughgarage.com.

Gambling

You will find that almost every traditional Australian hotel and pub in Sydney has the omnipresent rows of hyperactive pokies (slot machines), which to the uninitiated need a PhD in bankruptcy and visual literacy skills to play (whatever happened to a row of lemons or cherries?). The main focus for trying your luck in Sydney is the **Star City Casino**, 80 Pyrmont St, a coin's roll from Darling Harbour, T9777 9000, www.starcity.com.au. This vast arena has 200 gaming tables, 1500 pokies and lots of anxious faces. Open 24 hrs. Smart-casual dress mandatory.

Gay and lesbian

Sydney has a thriving gay and lesbian community that has reached legendary status through the **Mardi Gras Festival** held every Feb, which culminates in the hugely popular parade through the city on the first Sat of Mar, www.mardigras.org.au.

The main focus for social activity is Oxford St, especially at the western end between Taylor Sq and Hyde Park, while Newtown, in the inner west, is home to Sydney's lesbian scene. There are many clubs and cafés that attract a casual mix of both straight and gay. Some of the more gay-oriented bars are **Albury Hotel**, **Beauchamp Hotel** and **Oxford Hotel** on Oxford St, and the **Newtown Hotel**, 174 King St, Newtown. Some popular nightclubs for men are **Midnight Shift**, 85 Oxford St, and **Manacle**, 1 Patterson Lane, Darlinghurst, www.manacle.com.au. **DCM**, 33 Oxford St, T9267 7380, and the **Taxi Club**, 40 Flinders St, Darlinghurst, attract a mixed crowd. For more information and venues try the *Sydney Star Observer*, which is available at most gay-friendly restaurants, cafés and bookshops, especially on Oxford St. The **Bookshop**, 207 Oxford St, T9331 1103, is also a good source of information.

Performing arts

Naturally the focus for the performing arts in Sydney is the **Sydney Opera House**. It offers five venues: the Concert Hall, the Opera Theatre, the Drama Theatre, the Playhouse and the Studio. The Concert Hall is the largest venue and home to the Sydney Symphony Orchestra. The Opera House is the home of Opera Australia, the Australian Ballet and the Sydney Dance Company. The Drama Theatre is a performing venue for the Sydney Theatre Company while the Playhouse is used for small-cast plays, more low-key performances, lectures and seminars. The Studio is used for contemporary music and performance. Prices and seats range from about $35-200. For details call the box office, T9250 7777, or www.soh.nsw.gov.au. See also page 92.

Belvoir Theatre, 25 Belvoir St, Surry Hills, T9699 3444, www.belvoir.com.au. A less well-known venue with a good choice.

Capitol, 13 Campbell St, T1300 136166, www.capitoltheatre.com.au. The lovingly restored **Capitol** offers a diverse range of performances.

City Recital Hall, Angel Pl, City, T8256 2222, www.cityrecitalhall.com.au. Offers a programme of regular classical music performances from around $50.

State Theatre, 49 Market St, T9022 6258, T136100, www.statetheatre.com.au. This beautiful and historic venue offers a dynamic choice of specialist and mainstream performances and cinema.

Sydney Conservatorium of Music, near the Botanical Gardens, off Macquarie St, T9351 1222, www.music.usyd.edu.au.Also hosts occasional live performances.

Sydney Entertainment Centre, 35 Harbour St, City, T9320 4200, www.sydentcent.com.au. One of the city's largest and most modern performance venues, hosting a wide range of acts, shows, fairs and sporting events.

Theatre Royal, MLC Centre, 108 King St, T136166, www.mlccentre.com.au. Noted for its musicals and plays.

Wharf Theatre, Pier 4, Hickson Rd, The Rocks, T9250 1777, www.sydneytheatre.org.au. Home of the Sydney Theatre Company.

Bangarra are a contemporary Aboriginal dance group based at Wharf 4, Walsh Bay, The Rocks, T9251 5333, www.bangarra.com.au. The **Wharf Restaurant** next door is superb for pre-performance dining.

The **Lyric Theatre** and the **Showroom**, at the Star City complex, 80 Pyrmont St, T9777 9000, offer theatre, concerts, comedy, dance and musicals. From around $40-80 for a major performance.

⊕ Festivals and events

Sydney p90, maps p91, p94 and p105

Jan New Year kicks in with spectacular fireworks and celebrations that centre around The Rocks and the Harbour Bridge. Other good vantage points include Milsons Point, The Opera House and Cremorne Point.

Sydney Festival and Fringe Festival takes place through most of the month. It is a celebration of the arts including the best of Australian theatre, dance, music and visual arts and is held at many venues throughout the city. The highlights are the free open-air concerts in the Domain, including Opera in the Park and Symphony under the Stars, see www.sydneyfestival.org.au. The 26th sees the annual **Australia Day** celebrations with the focus being a flotilla of vessels flying the flag on the harbour, www.australiaday.com.au.

Feb Without doubt the most famous Sydney event is the legendary **Gay and Lesbian Mardi Gras Festival and Parade** held throughout the month. It is an opportunity for the gay community to celebrate, entertain and shock. The highlight is a good shake of the pants and codpieces (or very lack of them) during the spectacular parade from Liverpool St to Anzac Pde (held at the end of the festival), www.mardigras.org.au.

Mar The **Royal Agricultural Easter Show** is held every Easter and now uses the state-of-the-art facilities at Olympic Park as a venue, www.eastershow.com.au.

Apr The 25th sees the annual **Anzac Day** service at the Martin Place Cenotaph and a parade down George St.

May The annual **Sydney Morning Herald Half Marathon** is a great attraction, especially when it involves crossing the Harbour Bridge, www.halfmarathon.smh.com.au. **Australian Fashion Week** celebrations showcase some of the country's top designers. There is also another fashion week in Nov to preview the best of the winter collections.

Jun **Sydney Film Festival**, a 2-week fest for film buffs, runs more than 150 features from

40 countries, T9318 0999, www.sydneyfilmfestival.org.

Aug Sun-Herald City to Surf, a 14-km race from Bondi Beach to the city centre, T1800 555514, www.city2surf.sunherald.com.au.

Sep Festival of the Winds at Bondi Beach is a colourful festival of kites and kite flying, while the avid sports fans fight over tickets and take several days of drinking leave for the Rugby League and Rugby Union **Grand Finals**.

Oct The weekend **Manly Jazz Festival** is a gathering of Australia's best along with some fine foreign imports. Stages located in several public arenas including the beachfront and the Corso, as well as hotels, restaurants and bars, T9977 1088.

Dec Carols by Candlelight is the main festive public celebration of song in the Domain, while the wild and wicked grab a beer glass and a patch of sand at the **Bondi Beach Christmas Party**, which usually ends up as a mass streak into the waves. Far more serious is the **Sydney to Hobart** sailing race, which departs from the inner harbour, winds allowing, every Boxing Day.

O Shopping

Sydney *p90, maps p91, p94 and p105*
Sydney can offer a superb, world-class shopping experience. The most popular shopping venues are to be found in the city centre, but many of the suburban high streets also support a wide range of interesting outlets and some colourful weekend markets. In the city most of the large department stores, arcades, malls and specialist boutiques are to be found along **George St** and in the area around **Pitt St Mall**, **Castlereagh St** and **King St**. The suburbs of **Newtown** (King St) and **Glebe** (Glebe Point Rd) have some fascinating shops selling everything from codpieces to second-hand surfboards. **Double Bay**, **Mosman** and **Paddington** (Oxford St) are renowned for their stylish boutiques clothes shops and **The Rocks** is definitely the place to go for a didgeridoo or cuddly koala.

Art

For authentic Aboriginal art look out for the National Indigenous Arts Advocacy Association Label of Authenticity. For the best in authentic and original examples try: **Authentic Aboriginal Art Centre**, 45 Argyle St, The Rocks, T9251 4474, daily 1000-1700; **Aboriginal Dreamtime Fine Art Gallery**, Shop 8/199 George St, T9241 2953; **Coo-ee Emporium and Aboriginal Art Gallery**, Bondi, T9300 9233, www.cooeeart.com.au (by appointment); **Hogarth Galleries**, 7 Walker La, T9360 6839. Further afield try the **Boomalli Aboriginal Artists Co-operative**, 55 -59 Flood St, Leichhardt, T9560 2541, www.boomalli.org.au.

There are many art galleries showcasing some of the best Australian contemporary artists with most being in The Rocks or Paddington. Try to get hold of *Art Find* brochure from one of the galleries or the Sydney VIC. **Ken Done** is one of the most famous Sydney-based artists. He has a colourful style which you will either love or hate. His main outlet is at 1 Hickson Rd, The Rocks, T9247 2740, www.kendone.com.au.

Bookshops

Dymocks is the major player with outlets throughout the city. The largest is at 424 George St, T1800 688319, www.dymocks.com.au, Mon-Wed and Fri 0900-1800, Thu 0900-2100, Sat-Sun 0900-1700.

Gould's Book Arcade, 32 King St, Newtown. The largest and most bizarre second-hand bookshop in the city, it's a 'lost world'.

Travel Bookshop, 175 Liverpool St (southern edge of Hyde Park), T9261 8200. Mon-Fri 0900-1800, Sat 1000-1700. A good source of travel information, books and maps.

Clothes

You will find all the major labels in the main central city shopping streets, arcades and department stores (see section below). **Oxford St** in Paddington and also the suburbs of **Double Bay** and to a lesser extent **Chatswood** are renowned for their boutique clothes stores and Australian designer labels.

Names and labels to look for include Helen Kaminski, Collette Dinnigan, Morrissey, Bare, Isogawa and Bettina Liano. For designer bargains try the **Market City** above Paddy's Markets in Haymarket. Finally, if you are looking for something different then head for **King St** in Newtown.

You'll also find all the Aussie classics such as Akubra hats, RM Williams boots and Driza-Bone oilskin coats. These are all beautifully made and well worth the money. A pair of RM's boots for example will, provided you look after them, last a lifetime. **RM Williams clothing outlets** can be found at 389 George St and Shop 1-2 Chiefly Plaza, corner of Hunter St and Phillip St, www.rmwilliams.com.au.
Strand Hatters, Strand Arcade, 412 George St, T9231 6884. For Akubra hats and Driza-Bones.

Department stores and arcades
Queen Victoria Building, T9264 9209, www.qvb.com.au. Not to be missed. This vast and historic edifice has levels of retail therapy that are legendary, see also page 98. On Market St there are 3 great Sydney institutions, the characterful department stores of **Grace Bros**, T9238 9111, www.myer.com.au; **David Jones**, T9266 5544, www.davidjones.com.au; and **Gowings**, T9287 6394, www.gowings.com.au.

Food and wine
Australian Wine Centre, 1 Alfred St, Circular Quay, T9247 2755, www.australianwine centre.com. Open daily. If you are a novice or even a seasoned wine buff, before purchasing any Australian labels you might benefit from a trip here. The staff are very knowledgeable and are backed by a great collection of over 1000 wines. They also offer a worldwide delivery service.
David Jones department store, Market St, T9266 5544. For a taste of Australian foods visit the food hall in this elegant shop.
Sydney Fish Markets, Pyrmont. Even if you don't like seafood a trip here is fascinating,

with the stalls setting up their displays of Australia's best from 0800 (see page 101).

Handicrafts
Craft Australia Boutique, David Jones department store, Market St, 4th floor, T9266 6276. For unique Australian crafts.
Object, 417 Bourke St, Surry Hills, T9361 4511, www.object.com.au. Showcases the best in authentic Australian crafts.
The Rocks and the **weekend Rocks Market** sell a good range of souvenir products.

Jewellery
Given the fact Australia produces over 90% of the world's opals it is not surprising to find a wealth of specialist dealers. To ensure authenticity and good workmanship purchase opals only from retailers who are members of the **Australian Opal and Gem Industry Association Ltd** (AOGIA) or the **Jewellers Association of Australia**. Some of the best retailers include: **Flame Opals**, 119 George St, T9247 3446, www.flameopals .com.au, Mon-Fri 0900-1845, Sat 1000-1700, Sun 1130-1700; **Opal Minded**, 55A George St, T9247 9885, 1000-1800; and **Australian Opal Cutters**, Suite 10, 3rd floor, 295 Pitt St, T9261 2442. Pearls from the great Australian *Pinctada maxima* oyster, from gold to snow white, are also big business in Sydney and for some of the best and biggest look no further than **Bunda**, Shop 1, 488 George St , Hilton Hotel, T9261 2210.

Markets
There are plenty of weekend markets held in the inner city that offer a range of new and second-hand clothes, arts, crafts and foods.
Opera House concourse, every Sun. An uncluttered open-air market that focuses mainly on arts, crafts and souvenirs.
Paddy's Markets, Haymarket, Thu-Sun. The biggest in the city centre; fairly tacky and mildly amusing.
The Rocks Market, every Sat-Sun at the top end of George St. The most popular market. Good inner suburbs markets include:

Balmain Market at St Andrew's Church, corner of Darling St and Curtis St. Sat.
Bondi Markets, Campbell Pde. Sun.
Glebe Market, in the grounds of Glebe Public Schools, Glebe Point Rd. Sun.
Paddington Market, grounds of the church at 395 Oxford St. Sat.

Outdoor equipment
Kent St is the place to start looking for camping and outdoor equipment.
Mountain Equipment, 491 Kent St, T9264 5888, www.mountainequipment.com and **Paddy Pallin**, No 507 Kent St, T9264 2685, www.paddypallin.com.au.

▲ Activities and tours

Sydney *p90, maps p91, p94 and p105*
Sydney is the venue for some of the most important major national and international sporting events in Australia. The huge success of the 2000 Olympic Games has left the city some superb sporting venues. Most are to be found at the **Sydney Olympic Park**, see page 102. Test rugby, Aussie Rules and test cricket match tickets are often very hard to come by and any attempt must be made well in advance. A ticket will cost from $50-120 for a cricket test match and $50-150 for a rugby grand final. The usual ticket agent is **Ticketek**, T132849, www.ticketek.com.au. If you cannot secure tickets or don't rate your chances obtaining a spare ticket outside the venue (often possible), joining the throngs of Sydneysiders in the city pubs can be just as enjoyable and atmospheric.

Aerial tours and activities
Ballooning
Cloud 9, T1300 555711, www.cloud9balloon flights.com, and **Balloon Aloft**, T1800 028568, www.balloonaloft.com, offer early morning flights over the outer suburbs or in the Hunter Valley from $269.

Scenic flights
Palm Beach Seaplanes, based in Rose Bay (eastern harbour suburbs) and Palm Beach (Pittwater), T1300 720995, www.sydneyby seaplane.com.au. A 15-min flight around the harbour costs from $160, 30 mins from $240, while a 60-min trip taking in the harbour, beaches, Ku-ring-gai National Park and Hawkesbury starts at $495. A beach picnic will set you back $850. If you want to see the northern beaches from the air and to arrive in Palm Beach in style the one-way trip will cost you a hefty $450.

There are a number of scenic flight companies based at Bankstown Airport, T9796 2300. However, the adventurous should contact **Red Baron Scenic Flights** run by the Sydney Aerobatic School, T9791 0643, www.redbaron.com.au. It offers unforgettable aerobatic scenic harbour flights from an open cockpit Pitts Special from $440-660.

Sky diving
You can also test your courage sky diving in and around Sydney. Companies include **Simply Skydive**, CM12, Mezzanine, Centrepoint, T9223 8444, www.simplyskydive.com.au, and **Sydney Skydiving Centre**, based at Bankstown Airport, T9791 9155, www.sydneyskydivers. com.au. Jumps start from about $275.

Cruises
There are numerous harbour cruises on offer, with most being based at Circular Quay. Trips vary from a sedate cruise on a replica of the *Bounty* to paddle steamers and fast catamarans. In recent years whales have occasionally appeared in the inner harbour, which is believed to be a sign of improving water quality. For whale-watching cruises from Sydney Harbour, check out www.whalewatching sydney.net. Thanks to the increase of whale numbers, they can guarantee sightings on their cruises, which depart from Darling Harbour and Circular Quay from late May to early Nov. Vessels include the flagship *Ocean Dreaming*, a 34-m catamaran. Trips start at around $85, T9583 1199.

Tours
Bridge Climb
Bridge Climb, 3 Cumberland fSt, The Rocks, T8274 7777, www.bridgeclimb.com, 0700-1900. The most high-profile activity in the city is this award-winning climb. This involves the ascent of the 134-m Harbour Bridge span. The 3-hr climb can be done day or night and in most weather conditions apart from electrical storms. As well as the stunning views from the top the climb is most memorable. Although it is fairly easy going and is regularly done by the elderly, the sight and noise of the traffic below adds a special edge. You cannot take your own camera on the trip for safety reasons. Climbs during the week cost from $200, children $130, weekends $220, children $140. Twilight climbs cost from $260, children $190.

Cycling
Bonza Bike Tours, T9247 8800, www.bonzabiketours.com. Increasingly popular pedal power, guided or self-guided options of 2 hrs to half day. Independent hire also available.

Harbour Islands Tours
For all island access, tour information and bookings contact the **Sydney Harbour National Park Information Centre**, Cadman's Cottage, 110 George St, The Rocks, T9247 5033, www.nationalparks.nsw.gov.au, Mon-Fri 0900-1630, Sat-Sun 1000-1630.

Rocks Ghost Tour
Given the Rocks' sordid past there is plenty of material and also a child-friendly option. Again bookings (advised) can be made at the Sydney VIC, corner Argyll and Playfair streets, The Rocks, T9240 8788, or direct T1300 731971, www.ghosttours.com.au. Tours take 2 hrs, departing at 1845 (Apr-Nov) and 1945 (Nov-Mar). From $39.

Rocks Pub Tour
An excellent way to sample 3 of the Rocks' finest drinking establishments, T1300 458437, www.therockspubtour.com. 1700-1845.

Rocks Walking Tour
This is the best, most entertaining and informative way to get to know this area. Bookings (advised) can be made at the Sydney VIC, corner Argyll and Playfair streets, The Rocks, T9240 8788, or at the Walks Office, 23 Playfair St, T9247 6678, www.rockswalkingtours.com.au. Tours take 90 mins, departing Mon-Fri 1030, 1230 and 1430 and Sat-Sun 1130 and 1400. From $30, children $15, family $75.

Walking
The VIC has a number of free walking brochures including the detailed *Go Walkabout* produced by Sydney Ferries, *Sydney Harbour Foreshore Walks*, *Historical Sydney*, *Sydney Sculpture Walk* and the *Manly Scenic Walkway*. Another great book is *Sydney's Best Harbour and Coastal Walks* (Woodslane), available from most good bookshops.

Water sports
Diving
Although diving is best at the Barrier Reef, if you are heading north to Queensland, NSW and Sydney have some good diving. The southern beaches, La Perouse and the Botany Bay National Park offer the best spots. There are dive shops in the city and companies offering tuition and trips, including the popular **Dive Centre**.
Dive Centre, 10 Belgrave St, Manly, T9977 4355, and 192 Bondi Rd, Bondi, T9369 3855, www.divesydney.com. It offers shore and boat dive trips and Open Water Certificates with the latter from $395.
Pro Dive, T9255 0300, www.prodive.com.au. Offers local trips and training and stocks a good range of equipment.

Fishing
The VIC has listings of other charters based in Sydney, many of which also offer whale-watching trips Jun-Oct. Despite all the harbour activity, both the fishing and the water quality in Sydney Harbour is said to be pretty good. There are a number of fishing charters available including:

Charter One, Manly, T04-0133 2355, www.charterone.com.au. Trips range from a 3-hr jaunt from $95 to a full day, $135, with tackle hire.

Sailing

Sydney Harbour offers some of the best sailing in the world. On Boxing Day every year, at the start of the **Sydney to Hobart race**, the inner harbour becomes a patchwork of colourful spinnakers raised to the mercy of the winds.
Australian Spirit Sailing Company, T9878 0300, www.austspiritsailingco.com.au. Runs similar trips to **Sydney Mainsail** below.
Sydney by Sail, National Maritime Museum, T9280 1110, www.sydneybysail.com. Operates social day trips, introductory lessons and a 3-hr trip on the harbour from $150. The office is based below the lighthouse.
Sydney Mainsail, T9719 9077, www.sydney mainsail.com.au. Offers 3-hr trips 3 times daily with highly experienced skippers.

Sea kayaking

This is a great way to explore the backwaters and bays of the suburbs. The Middle Harbour, which branches off between Middle Head and Clontarf, snakes over 10 km into the lesser-known North Shore suburbs and is especially good. It offers a quiet environment and more wildlife.

Surfing

The famous surf spots are Bondi and Manly but some of the lesser-known Sydney beaches offer better surf. Try some of the northern beaches, such as Curl Curl (home to Layne Beachley), or see what the surf report recommends.
Manly Surf School, at the **North Steyne Surf Club**, Manly Beach, T9977 6977, www.manly surfschool.com. Good value daily classes from 1100-1300, 1-10 lessons from $60-340.

Swimming

Swimming is a popular pastime. South of the Heads, the beaches at Bondi, Bronte, Clovelly and Coogee are hugely popular while to the north, Manly, Collaroy, Narrabeen, Avalon,

Ocean Beach and Palm Beach are also good spots. Lifeguards patrol most beaches in summer and you are strongly advised to swim between the yellow and red flags. These are clearly staked out along the beach and placed according to conditions. Most of the city beaches also have safe, open-air, saltwater swimming pools to provide added safety, especially for children. **Bondi Icebergs pool** is a Sydney landmark but there are also quiet neighbourhood pools such the charming **McCallum Pool**, a small outdoor pool on Cremorne Point (off Milson's Road) with great views across the harbour.
Sydney Harbour Kayaks, 3/235 The Spit Rd, Mosman, T9960 4389, www.sydneyharbour kayaks.com.au. Runs guided trips and hires kayaks.

⊝ Transport

Sydney *p90, maps p91, p94 and p105*
Air
For information and details of arrivals and departures, T9667 6065, www.sydneyairport .com.au. See also page 90.

Bus
Local
The STA (**Sydney Buses**) is the principal operator with the standard buses being blue and white, the **Sydney Explorer** red and the **Bondi Explorer** blue. For information about suburban buses in Sydney, T131500, www.131500.com.au.
    Standard bus fares are between $2-6.30 depending on distance and zones crossed. If you intend to travel regularly by bus, a Travel Ten ticket is recommended ($16-50.40) while further savings can be also be made with the TravelPass and Sydney Pass system (see box, page 130). The Explorer buses cost $40 for the full return trip. There is an on-board commentary and you can hop on and off when you want. Both leave at regular intervals from Circular Quay. For all of the above bus fares children travel half price and there are

Ticket to ride

There are numerous popular travel pass systems in operation through the STA. The **MyMulti Day Pass** gives all-day access to Sydney's trains, buses and ferries within the suburban area from $20, children $10. Tickets can be purchased at any rail, bus or ferry sales or information outlet or on the buses themselves. **MyMulti Passes** allow unlimited, weekly, quarterly or yearly combined travel throughout designated zones or sections. A seven-day pass for the inner city, for example, costs $41,

children $20. For those staying only a few days, however, the best bet is the **Sydney Pass** which offers unlimited travel on ferry and standard buses as well as the Sydney and Bondi Explorer routes and the four STA Harbour Cruises. They are sold as a three-day ($116, children $58), five-day ($152, children $76) or seven-day ($172, children $86) package. Discount, 10-trip 'TravelTen' (bus) and 'FerryTen' passes are also available and recommended, from $16 (bus) and $41 (ferry), T131500, www.131500.com.au.

---

also family concessions. Note most Explorer buses operate between 0840 and 1722 only.

Drivers do not automatically stop at bus stops. If you are alone you must signal to the driver, or at night gesticulate wildly.

Long distance

Sydney Coach Terminal is in the Central Railway Station, Shop 4-7, Eddy Av, T131500 / T9281 9366, daily 0600-2230. Major interstate companies include **Greyhound** (National) T131499 (T1300 4739 46863), www.greyhound.com.au; **Murrays**, (Canberra, South NSW Coast), T132251, www.murrays.com.au; **Premier Motor Services** (national) T133410, www.premierms.com.au; and **Firefly** (Adelaide, Melbourne), T1300 730740, www.fireflyexpress.com.au. Typical interstate services and prices for 1-way from Sydney are: **Brisbane**, Greyhound, 5 daily, 20 hrs, $100; **Byron Bay**, Greyhound, 4 daily, 18 hrs, $90; **Cairns**, Greyhound, 5 daily, 46 hrs, $400; **Canberra**, Greyhound, 10 daily, 5 hrs, $25; **Melbourne**, Greyhound, 5 daily, 14 hrs 20 mins, $90.

Car/campervan

Travelling by car around Sydney is a nightmare with numerous tolls, expensive parking and omnipresent parking wardens. There really is no need to see the sights by car but if you must, take lots of change. The Sydney Harbour Tunnel

now has cashless tolls to improve traffic flow across the Harbour. To pay the toll, you need an electronic tag or an RTA E-Toll pass. If you use the Harbour Tunnel without a tag, register for an RTA E-Toll pass within 48 hours of your trip at myRTA.com or call T131 865. Additional fees apply for pass users. . The toll for the Harbour Bridge (Mon-Fri $4, Sat/Sun $3 southbound, free northbound) will remain payable by cash or E-Tag. **NRMA** are located at 74-76 King St, CBD, T9292 8292, T131122.

Car hire offices at the airport (Arrivals south) include **Avis**, T136333, **Budget** T132727, **Hertz** T1300 132607, **National**, T131390, **Red Spot**, T1300 668810 and **Thrifty** T136139. In the city try **Avis**, **Budget** and **Ascot** centred on or around William St, Darlinghurst. Cheaper options often include **Bayswater Rentals**, 180 William St, Kings Cross, T9360 3622, and **Dollar**, Domain Car Park, Sir John Young Cres, T9223 1444. Rates can get as low as $40 per day. Campervan hire from **Britz**, call T9667 0402, www.britz.com.au, and also **Maui**, T1300 363800, www.maui-rentals.com.

Secondhand car and campervan dealers include **Kings Cross Car Market**, Ward St Car Park, Kings Cross, T1800 808188, www.carmarket.com.au (good buying and selling), and **Travellers Auto Barn**, 177 William St, Kings Cross, T1800 674374, www.travellers-autobarn.com.au.

Cycling

The pace of cycling is perfect for sightseeing. Unfortunately the rest of the road users don't agree. Travel by bike within the city centre can be hairy to say the least. Several companies offer bike hire from about $40 per day or $200 per week, including **Inner City Cycles**, 151 Glebe Point Rd, Glebe, T9660 6605; the **Manly Cycle Centre**, 36 Pittwater Rd, Manly, T9977 1189; and **Wooly's Wheels**, 82 Oxford St, T9331 2671, www.woolyswheels.com. For general advice contact **Bicycle NSW**, Level 5, 822 George St, T9218 5400, www.bicyclensw.org.au. For *Sydney Cycle Ways* maps and information contact the RTA, T9218 6816.

Ferry

A trip on one of Sydney's harbour ferries is a wonderful experience and an ideal way to see the city, as well as accessing many of the major attractions and suburbs. The principal operator is **Sydney Ferries**, which operates the 'green and golds', also the fast **JetCats** to Manly and **RiverCat** to Homebush Bay and Parramatta. Several independent companies also operate out of Circular Quay offering cruises as well as suburban transportation and water taxis. See Cruises, page 127.

Like the buses, ferry fares are priced according to zone and start at a single trip for $5.20. If you intend to travel regularly by ferry then a FerryTen ticket (from $33.50) is recommended, while further savings can also be made with the TravelPass and Sydney Pass system, see box page 130. Various travel/entry combo tickets are offered to the major harbourside sights including Taronga Zoo (Zoo Pass $48, children $23.50) and Sydney Aquarium (Aquarium Pass $33, children $17.00). Children travel half price and there are also family concessions on most fares. For ferry information T131500, www.sydneyferries .com.au or www.sydneytransport.com.au. The main Sydney Ferries Information Centre is opposite Wharf 4, Circular Quay.

MonoRail and LightRail
MonoRail

MonoRail, www.metromonorail.com.au, runs in a loop around Darling Harbour and South Western CBD and provides a convenient way of getting from A to B. They run every 3-5 mins, Mon-Thu 0700-2200, Fri-Sat 0700-2400, and Sun 0800-2200. The standard fare (1 loop) is $4.90, a Day Pass costs $9.50. Children under 5 travel free and there are discounts for some major attractions.

LightRail

The **LightRail** network links Central Station with Lilyfield, via a number of stops within the southwest CBD and Darling Harbour, as well as the Casino, Fish Market and Glebe. It is a 24-hr service with trains every 10-15 mins from 0600-2400 and every 30 mins from 2400-0600. There are 2 fare zones starting at a single journey at $3.40. A Day Pass with unlimited stops costs $9. Children travel at half price. For information, T8584 5288, www.metromonorail.com.au.

Taxi
Land based

Sydney's once rather dubious taxi service was given a major revamp for the 2000 Olympics and it is now much improved. Ranks are located near every railway station, at Circular Quay and numerous spots in the CBD, otherwise hail one as required. From 2200-0600 higher tariffs apply. On short journeys tipping is not expected. There are several companies including **ABC** T132522, **Combined** T133300, **Legion** T131451, **Premier** T131017 and **RSL** T132211.

Water based

Water taxis operate all over the harbour with most being based on the western edge of Circular Quay. The main operators are **Water Taxis Combined**, Circular Quay, T9555 8888, and **Yellow Water Taxis** T1300 138840.

Train
Local
Sydney's 24-hr train services are a convenient way to reach the city centre and outlying areas, or to link in with bus and ferry services. Fares start at $3.20 and savings can be made with 'Off-Peak Tickets', which operate after 0900 on weekdays. Further savings can be made with the TravelPass and Sydney Pass (see box, page 130). There are coloured routes with the green/purple City Circle (Central, Town Hall, Wynyard, Circular Quay, St James and the Museum) and blue Eastern Suburbs Line (Central, Town Hall, Martin Place, Kings Cross, Edgecliff, Bondi Junction) being the most convenient. Tickets and information are available at major stations. For information about trains in Sydney, T131500, www.cityrail.info or www.131500.com.au.

Long distance
All interstate and NSW state destination trains arrive and depart from the Central Railway Station on Eddy Av, just south of the city centre. There is an information booth and ticket offices on the main platform concourse. **Countrylink** are the main interstate operators running with a combination of coach and rail to all the main interstate and NSW destinations, T132232 (daily 0630-2200), www.countrylink.info. You can find a **Countrylink Travel Centre** at the railway station, T9379 3800. First class and economy fares vary so you are advised to shop around and compare prices with the various coach operators. The railway station also houses the main interstate city coach terminal (**Greyhound**) and from there, or Pitt St and George St, you can pick up regular city and suburban buses. For information T131500, www.sydneytransport.net.au. **Countrylink** operates the 'XPT' Sydney to Brisbane (12 hrs daily, overnight, from $100) and Melbourne (11 hrs, twice daily, 1 overnight, from $90).

❶ Directory

Sydney *p90, maps p91, p94 and p105*
Banks
The major banks have ATMs. Foreign exchange is readily available on the arrivals concourse of Sydney Airport. In the city there are many outlets especially around Circular Quay and along George St.

Hospital
Prince of Wales Hospital, High St, Randwick, T9382 2222; **Royal North Shore Hospital**, Pacific Highway, St Leonard's, T9926 7111; **St Vincent's Hospital**, Victoria St, Darlinghurst, T9339 1111; **Sydney Children's Hospital**, T9382 1111.

Internet
Internet is widely available with the southern ends of George and Pitt streets (between Liverpool and Hay) and the western ends of Oxford St (between Crown and College) having many outlets. Most backpackers offer internet facilities and outlets, in the outer suburbs. **Global Gossip** has several Sydney outlets including 14 Wentworth Av, 790 George St in the CBD, and 37 Hall St, Bondi. Expect to pay from $5 to $10 per hr (be careful to confirm your start and finish time).

Post
Post shops are marked with a prominent red and white circular logo. The main General Post Office is located at 1 Martin Pl, T131318, Mon-Fri 0815-1730, Sat 1000-1400. Post Restante is based on the 3rd floor, 310 George St (across the road from the Wynyard Station entrance). Log your name into the computer to see if any mail awaits. The city centre poste restante code is NSW 2000. Open Mon-Fri 0830-1700.

Useful contacts
For the police, emergency T000, general enquiries T9690 4960. **City of Sydney Police Station**, 192 Day St, T9265 6499.

Around Sydney

One of the wonderful things about Australia's largest city is that you are never too far away from water or parks and nature reserves. To the west, a mere 70 km delivers you to the fringes of some of the state's largest and most celebrated national parks, all within the Greater Blue Mountains region. Once a major barrier to the exploration of the interior, until the route west was finally opened up in the first half of the 19th century, the 'Blues' now serve as a natural wonderland; a vast playground for over one million visitors a year who come to explore the eroded valleys, gorges, bluffs and amazing limestone caves.

Even closer to home is the Ku-ring-gai Chase National Park to the north and the Royal National Park to the south, the latter tragically destroyed by the terrible bush fires that have ravaged huge swathes of the country in successive recent years. Between Ku-ring-gai and what's left of Royal National Park is the tiny Botany Bay National Park, site of Captain Cook's first landing in April 1770.

Kamay Botany Bay National Park → *For listings, see pages 144-146. Colour map 2, A3.*

Botany Bay holds a very special place in Australian (European) history as the site of Captain Cook's first landing, in April 1770. The landing site is near what is now Kurnell on the southern shores of Botany Bay, which along with La Perouse on the northern shore, comes under the auspices of the 458-ha Kamay Botany Bay National Park. As well as possessing highly significant historical sites for both the European and Aboriginal cultures ('Kamay' is the indigenous Gweagal people's name for the area) it presents plenty of walking opportunities and ocean views.

Within the small northern sector of the park, around **La Perouse** on the northern headland, you can take a tour of **Bare Island Fort** ⓘ *T9247 5033, guided tours Sat-Sun, $8, children $6*, built in 1885 as a defence against the perceived threat of foreign invasion. Also located on the headland is **La Perouse Museum and Visitors' Centre** ⓘ *Cable Station, Anzac Parade, T9311 3379, Wed-Sun 1000-1600, $6, children $3.30*, on the actual site of the first landing of the First Fleet in 1788. The museum explores the great historical event and the fate of French explorer the Comte de La Pérouse, as well as local Aboriginal and European heritage.

The southern sector is larger and has the best walks including the short (1 km) **Monument Track** and the more demanding **Coast Walk** to Bailey lighthouse. It also hosts the **NPWS Botany Bay National Park Discovery Centre**, a good source of park and walks information with an interesting display surrounding Cook's landing.

Royal National Park → *For listings, see pages 144-146. Colour map 2, A3.*

The 15,080-ha Royal National Park was the first national park in Australia, gazetted in 1879. As well as providing over 100 km of walking tracks, many taking in terrific ocean views, there are some beautiful beaches and other activities ranging from swimming to scuba diving. However, the park is subject to the constant threat of fire and more than once in the last decade the Royal has been temporarily destroyed by bush fires. The main hub of human activity is historic **Audley** at the park's northern entrance, where you will find the **NPWS Royal National Park Visitors' Centre** ⓘ *Farnell Av, T9542 0648, 0930-1630*. **Wattamolla**, **Garie** and **Burning Palms** are three beautiful beaches and the choice of walks ranges from the 500-m (wheelchair-accessible) **Bungoona Track** to the 26-km **Coast Track** (Bundeena to Otford), which guarantees some glorious coastal views and on occasion (from June to September) the odd whale sighting. You can hire rowboats and canoes at the Audley Boatshed, near the visitors' centre, for a paddle up Kangaroo Creek. Mountain bikes are also available for hire but trail routes are limited and there is good surfing at the patrolled **Garie Beach**. Several freshwater pools also provide swimming. By car from Sydney take the Princes Highway south and follow signs for Audley (left, at Loftus on Farnell Avenue and McKell Avenue). Vehicle entry costs $11 per day.

Ku-ring-gai Chase National Park → *For listings, see pages 144-146.*

Though a few wealthy Sydney entrepreneurs might see Ku-ring-gai Chase as little more than 14,883-ha of wasted prime real estate, just 26 km north of Sydney, the rugged sandstone country that fringes the mighty Hawkesbury River, with its stunning views and rich array of native wild animals and plants, is thankfully safe from further suburban encroachment and has been since it was designated as a national park in 1894. As well as the stunning views across Pittwater and Broken Bay, the park offers some lovely bush walks, secluded beaches and regionally significant Aboriginal rock art. It is also a great place to see that much celebrated state flower, the warratah, in bloom. The highlight of the park is the **West Head Lookout**, high above the peninsula overlooking **Broken Bay** and the mouth of the **Hawkesbury River**. To the north is the beginning of the central coast and Brisbane Water National Park, while to the west is the tip of the northern beaches and the historic Barrenjoey Lighthouse. West Head is crisscrossed with walking

Around Sydney

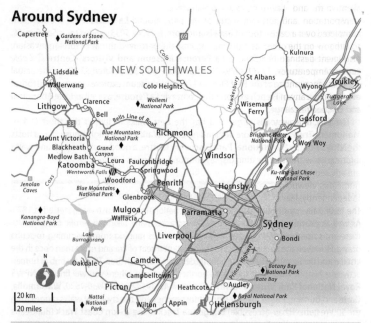

tracks that start from West Head Road. Aboriginal rock art can be seen along the **Basin Track** – which falls to the Basin Beach campsite and the arrival/departure point of the Palm Beach ferry – and the 3.5-km **Red Hand Track** (Aboriginal Heritage Track). **Bobbin Head** at the western end of the park is a popular base for water-based activities. Here, too, is the VIC, which can supply details on walks. **NPWS Bobbin Head Information Centre** ⓘ *Bobbin Inn, Bobbin Head Rd (western side of the park), T9472 8949, 1000-1600*, or the **Kalkari Visitors' Centre** ⓘ *Chase Rd, between Mount Colah and Bobbin Head, T9457 9853, 0900-1700*, can supply walks, camping information and maps. By car, access is via Bobbin Head Rd, via the Pacific Highway (from the south) or from Ku-ring-Gai Chase Road via F3 Freeway (from the north). Access to the eastern side (West Head Road and West Head Lookout) is from Mona Vale Road, Northern Beaches. Vehicle entry costs $11 daily.

Blue Mountains → *For listings, see pages 144-146. Colour map 2, A2.*

The 'Blues', as they are affectionately known, form part of the Great Dividing Range, 70 km, or two hours, west of Sydney, and contain no less than five national parks covering a total area of 10,000 sq km. They are not really mountains at all, but a network of eroded river valleys, gorges, and bluffs, that have formed over millions of years. The result is a huge wonderland of natural features, from precipitous cliffs, to dramatic waterfalls and canyons, not to mention the most dramatic limestone caves on the continent. Once the home of the Daruk Aboriginals, the Blue Mountains were seen by the first Europeans merely as a highly inconvenient barrier to the interior and for almost a quarter of a century they remained that way, before finally being traversed in 1813 by explorers Blaxland, Wentworth and Lawson. To this day the impenetrable geography still limits transportation and essentially the same two convict-built roads and railway line completed over a century ago reach west through a string of settlements from Glenbrook to Lithgow on the other side. For decades the 'Blues' have been a favourite weekend or retirement destination for modern-day Sydney escapees, who welcome the distinctly cooler temperatures and the colourful seasons that the extra elevation creates. But superb scenery and climate aside, there are some excellent walking opportunities, as well as abseiling, canyoning and rock climbing. Given the region's popularity there are also a glut of good restaurants and a wide range of places to stay from showpiece backpackers to romantic hideaways.

Ins and outs

Getting there Although public transport to and around the Blue Mountains is good you are advised to take your own vehicle or hire one, allowing you to make the most of the numerous viewpoints and sights within the region. Trains are the best way to arrive independently, leaving Sydney's Central Station (Countrylink and CityLink platforms) on the hour daily, stopping at all major towns through the Blue Mountains, T132232. The journey to Katoomba takes about two hours and costs around $30 for a day return. Numerous coach companies and hostels offer day sightseeing tours from Sydney. Some may allow overnight stops. The accredited VIC in Sydney can assist with the extensive choice and bookings. Most of the buses leave from Circular Quay.

Getting around The route through the Blue Mountains is easily negotiable. From the west (Sydney) you take the M4 (toll), eventually crossing the Neapean River, before it forms the Great Western Highway at Glenbrook (65 km). Then you pass through Blaxland,

Springwood, Faulconbridge and Woodford before arriving at Wentworth Falls. Here you reach the top of the main plateau at an average height of just above 1000 m. From Wentworth Falls the road then continues west through the northern edges of Leura and Katoomba, then north, through the heart of Blackheath and Mount Victoria. From Mount Victoria you then begin the descent to Lithgow (154 km). The rather peculiarly named Bells Line of Road provides another access point across the mountains from Windsor on the east to Mount Victoria on the Great Western Highway (77 km). Katoomba is the largest of the towns and has the best amenities. ▸▸ *See under the relevant destinations for further details.*

Tourist information The main accredited VICs are in **Glenbrook**, **Katoomba** ⓘ *Echo Point, T1300 653408, www.visitbluemountains.com.au, daily 0900-1700*, **Lithgow** ⓘ *Great Western Highway, T6350 3230, www.tourism.lithgow.com, 0900-1700*, and **Oberon** (west, near the Jenolan Caves). The main NPWS office is at the **Heritage Centre** ⓘ *near Govetts Leap, Blackheath, T4787 8877, www.nationalparks.nsw.gov.au*. If you are approaching from the east, stop at the Glenbrook VIC to begin with and stock up with the free visitor's guide and maps. All regional centres also offer a free accommodation bookings service. The NPWS stock a wide range of books covering the numerous walks within the national parks, as well as topographical maps.

The national parks

The Blue Mountains region contains five national parks which cover an area of 10,000 sq km, with half of that being considered 'wilderness area'. The largest, at an expansive 4876 sq km (and the second largest in the state after Kosciuszko National Park) is **Wollemi National Park**, to the north of the Bells Line of Road. It incorporates the state's most extensive officially recognized wilderness area and is very rugged and inaccessible. As well as its complex geology, topography, Aboriginal art sites and botanical features, it is also home to a rich variety of birds. Of all the parks in the region it is the one for the well-prepared modern-day explorer. There are basic NPWS campsites at Wheeny Creek, Colo Meroo, Dun's Swamp and Newnes. The main access is from Putty Road, 100 km northwest of Sydney or via Rylstone.

The most famous and accessible park is the 2470-sq-km **Blue Mountains National Park**, straddling the Great Western Highway and a string of mountain villages and towns, from Glenbrook in the east to Lithgow in the west. Only recently expanded in the 1980s, it contains natural features that range from deep canyons and forested valleys to pinnacles and waterfalls, as well as an abundance of flora and fauna. Although now receiving over one million visitors a year, much of the park remains extremely inaccessible, with over 500 sq km considered official wilderness area. Sadly, the Blue Mountains, like so many national parks in NSW, has suffered in recent years from the temporary impact of widespread bush fires. There are basic NPWS campsites at Euroka Clearing near Glenbrook, Ingar near Wentworth Falls and Perry's Lookdown near Blackheath. You can also camp anywhere within 500 m from roads and facilities. Access is from many points east and west off the Great Western Highway, or from the Bells Line of Road 70 km west of Sydney.

Next up is the beautiful 680-sq-km **Kanangra-Boyd National Park**, to the southwest of Katoomba. Fringed by the Blue Mountains National Park on all but one side it contains a similar geology and topography but is particularly famous for two natural features, the Jenolan limestone caves and the Kanangra Walls (a series of outstanding bluffs). Both are well worth visiting, with the latter considered one of the great walks in the region. There is a basic NPWS campsite at Boyd River. Access is via Mount Victoria and the Jenolan Caves 180 km west of Sydney.

To the southeast of Kanangra-Boyd and the Blue Mountains National Parks is the 860-sq-km **Nattai National Park**. It touches the region's largest body of water, Lake Burragorang, and contains the region's largest populations of eastern grey kangaroos as well as many rare plants and animals. NPWS camping near the lake. Access is 110 km south of Sydney between Warragamba Dam and Wombeyan Caves Road.

The smallest national park in the group is the 12,000-ha **Gardens of Stone National Park** north of Lithgow. Adjoining Wollemi it is most noted for its prominent and shapely limestone outcrops and sandstone escarpments. Birdlife is once again prolific. There are no campsites. Access is 30 km north of Lithgow via Mudgee Road.

Glenbrook to Wentworth Falls

Proud of its European roots and its railway heritage, the pretty village of Glenbrook, just beyond the Nepean River, acts as the unofficial gateway to the Blue Mountains. Along with Katoomba this is the main tourism administration and information centre for the Blue Mountains. **NPWS Conservation Hut** ① *Fletcher St (off Falls Rd), T4757 3827*, can provide walks information and has a small shop and café. **Glenbrook VIC** ① *off the Great Western Highway, T1300 653408, www.visitbluemountains.com.au, daily 0900-1700.*

Fringing the village, south of the highway, is the southern section of the Blue Mountains National Park and access to numerous attractions, including the **Red Hands Cave**, a fine example of Aboriginal rock art. The distinctive hand stencils made on the cave wall are thought to be over 1600 years old. You can reach the cave either by road or by foot (8 km return) from the Glenbrook Creek causeway, just beyond the park entrance. There are also shorter walks to the **Jellybean Pool** and the **Euroka Clearing**, a basic NPWS campsite and the ideal spot to see grey kangaroos, especially early or late in the day. To reach the park gate ($7 per day, walkers free), take Ross Road behind the VIC onto Burfitt Parade and then follow Bruce Road. The lookouts at **The Bluff**, at the end of Brook Road (slightly further east off Burfitt, then Grey), are also worth a look. North of the highway in Glenbrook you can also follow signs to the **Lennox Bridge**, the oldest in Australia, built by convicts in 1833.

Beyond Blaxland and Springwood is the small settlement of **Faulconbridge**, home to the **Norman Lindsay Gallery and Museum** ① *T4751 1067, www.norman lindsay.com.au, $10, children $5*. Lindsay (1879-1969) is just one of many noted artists who found the Blue Mountains conducive to their creativity and his studio remains very much the way he left it. For most, it is the stunning lookouts across **Wentworth Falls** and the **Jamieson Valley** that offer the first memorable introduction to the dramatic scenery of the Blue Mountains – assuming the weather is clear, of course. The car park is the starting point for some superb walking tracks, the best of which is the four-hour **Wentworth Pass Walk** that crosses the top of the falls and then descends precariously down to the valley floor. Then, if that were not enough, the track skirts the cliff base, through rainforest, before climbing back up via the dramatic **Valley of the Waters** gorge to the **Conservation Hut** (see above). From there it's an easy walk back to the car park. Another excellent walk is the five-hour **National Pass Walk** that follows a cutting halfway up the cliff, carved out in the 1890s. Both walks involve steep sections around cliff edges and laddered sections, but if you have a head for heights either one is highly recommended. Give yourself plenty of time and make sure you get maps from the Conservation Hut before you set out.

For something less demanding, try the **Den Fenella Track**, which will take you to some good lookouts, then you can return or preferably keep going (west) to the Conservation Hut along the **Overcliff Track**. Better still, is the magical **Undercliff Track** to **Princes Rock Lookout**.

Leura

Although the pretty village of Leura plays second fiddle to Katoomba, the two essentially merge into one. Possessing a distinct air of elegance, the residents of Leura are proud of their village and in particular their gardens. **Everglades Gardens** ⓘ *37 Everglades Av, T4784 1938, www.evergladesgardens.info, 1000-1700, $8, concessions $6, children $4,* provide the best horticultural showpiece and have done since the early 1930s. **Leuralla and NSW Toy and Railway Museum** ⓘ *36 Olympian Pde, T4784 1169, www.toyandrailwaymuseum.com.au, 1000-1700, $10, children $2,* is well worth a look, for kids and parents alike. There are several walks and lookouts around the cliff fringes in Leura with the best being the short 500-m walk to the aptly named **Sublime Lookout**, offering arguably the best view of the Jamieson Valley and Mount Solitary. Follow signs from Gladstone Road, west of the Mall.

Katoomba

Considered the capital of the Blue Mountains, the erstwhile mining town of Katoomba offers an interesting mix of old and new and a truly cosmopolitan ambience. As well as the wealth of amenities and activities based in the town, many come here simply to see the classic picture-postcard view of the Blue Mountains from the famous **Three Sisters lookout**. The steady stream of tourist traffic flows down Katoomba's main drag towards **Echo Point** to enjoy this view. It is little wonder the place is so popular. Built precariously 170 m above the valley floor, the lookout seems to defy gravity. Dawn and sunset are the best times to visit. From the lookout it is possible to walk around to the stacks and descend the taxing **Giant Stairway Walk** (30 minutes) to the valley floor. From there you join the **Federal Pass Track**, back through the forest below the cliffs to the **Katoomba Cascades** and **Orphan Rock** (a lone pillar that became separated from the nearby cliff over many centuries of erosion). From Orphan Rock it is a short walk to a choice of exits: the hard option, on foot, up the 1000-step Furbers Steps, or for the less adventurous, the Scenic Railway, see below. Give yourself three hours.

Katoomba presents many other excellent walking options, including the **Narrow Neck Plateau** (variable times) and the **Ruined Castle** (12 km, seven hours). The latter starts from the base of the Scenic Railway and can be made as part of an extended overnight trip to the summit of Mount Solitary. It's recommended, but go prepared. The **Grand Canyon** walk (5 km, four hours) from Neates Glen, Evans Lookout Road, Blackheath, is also a cracker.

West of Echo Point the junction of Cliff Drive and Violet Street will deliver you to the highly commercial **Scenic World** ⓘ *T4782 0200, www.scenicworld.com.au, 0900-1700, Railway Skyway and Cableway $28, Skyway $16,* with its unusual scenic transportations. The **Scenic Railway** option takes you on an exhilarating descent to the valley floor; on what is reputed to be the world's steepest 'inclined funicular railway'. At the bottom you can then take a boardwalk through the forest to see an old coal mine with an audiovisual display and bronze sculpture. In contrast, the **Scenic Skyway** provides a more sedate bird's-eye view of the valley floor and the surrounding cliffs. The last, and most recent, of the trio is the **Scenic Cableway**that takes you on a 545-m ride into – or out of – the World Heritage-listed rainforest of the Jamison Valley. Once at the bottom, you can take the Scenic Walkway to the base of the Scenic Railway. In all, there are just under 3 km of elevated boardwalk, 380 m of which is accessible by wheelchair. If you survive that there is also a cinema showing a Blue Mountains documentary on demand and a revolving restaurant.

Maxvision Edge Cinema ⓘ *225 Great Western Highway, T4782 8900, www.edge cinema.com.au, from 1020, from $14.50,* with its six-storey, 18-m high, 24-m wide screen, is worth visiting for its precipitous film of the Blue Mountains, *The Edge*.

Katoomba

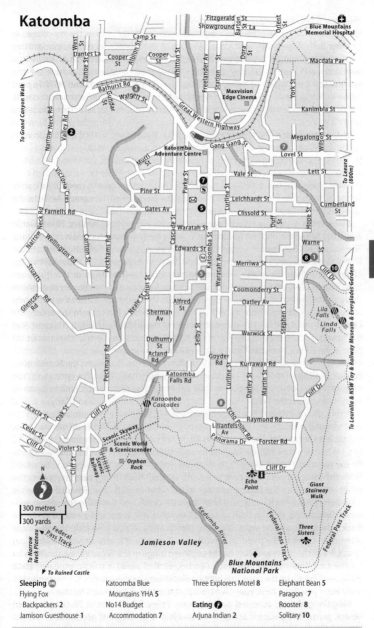

Sleeping 💤

Flying Fox
Backpackers **2**
Jamison Guesthouse **1**

Katoomba Blue
Mountains YHA **5**
No14 Budget
Accommodation **7**

Three Explorers Motel **8**

Eating 🍴
Arjuna Indian **2**

Elephant Bean **5**
Paragon **7**
Rooster **8**
Solitary **10**

Medlow Bath, Blackheath and Megalong Valley

From Katoomba the Great Western Highway heads north through the pretty villages of Medlow Bath, Blackheath and Mount Victoria. Although not as commercial as their bustling neighbour, all provide excellent accommodation, restaurants and are fringed both north and south by equally stunning views and excellent walks. To the east is the easily accessible **Megalong Valley**, particularly well known for its horse trekking, with **Grose Valley** to the west. **Evans** and **Govetts Leap Lookouts**, east of Blackheath, provide the best easily accessible viewpoints, but there are also some lesser-known spots well worth a visit.

In **Medlow Bath** is the historic **Hydro Majestic Hotel**, built in 1903 and the longest building in Australia at the time. Though a hotel in its own right, its original function was as a sanatorium, offering all manner of health therapies, from the sublime – mud baths and spas – to the ridiculous – strict abstinence from alcohol. At the time the rarefied air in the Blue Mountains was hailed as a cure-all for city ills and people flocked to the Hydro. Today, although the mud baths (and thankfully the prohibition) have gone, the hotel still provides fine accommodation and a great spot for afternoon tea.

Blackheath is a sleepy little village with a lovely atmosphere, enhanced in autumn when the trees take on their golden hues. There are two lookouts well worth visiting. The first, **Evans Lookout**, is accessed east along Evans Lookout Road and provides the first of many viewpoints across the huge and dramatic expanse of the Grose Valley. One of the best walks in the region, which we recommend, the **Grand Canyon Trail**, departs from Neates Glen, off Evans Lookout Road (5 km, five hours). From there you descend through the rainforest and follow Greaves Creek through moss-covered rock tunnels and overhangs, before climbing back up to Evans Lookout. The other lookout, **Govetts Leap**, is a stunner and has the added attraction of the **Bridal Veil Falls**, the highest (but not necessarily the most dramatic), in the Blue Mountains. Just before the lookout car park is the **NPWS Heritage Centre** ① *T4787 8877, www.npws.nsw.gov.au, 0900-1630*, which is worth a visit and can provide walking information, maps, guide and gifts. **Fairfax Heritage Track**, built to accommodate wheelchairs, links the centre with the lookout. From Govetts Leap you can walk either north to reach Pulpit Rock or south to Evans Lookout via the falls.

Although Govetts and Evans are both stunning, three other superb lookouts await your viewing pleasure and can be accessed from Blackheath. These are often missed, but no less spectacular. The first, **Pulpit Rock**, can be reached by foot from Govetts (2.5 km, 1½ hrs) or better still, by 2WD via (unsealed) Hat Hill Road. The lookout, which sits on the summit of a rock pinnacle, is accessed from the car park by a short 500-m walk. From the same car park then continue north to **Anvil Rock**, being sure not to miss the other short track to the bizarre geology of the wind-eroded cave. Perry Lookdown is 1 km before Anvil Rock and a path from there descends into the valley to connect with some demanding walking trails. Also well worth a visit is the aptly named **Hanging Rock**, which will, on first sight, take your breath away. Watch your footing and do not attempt to climb to the point, as tempting as it may be. It is also a favourite abseiling spot. Like all the other lookouts on the southern fringe of the Grose Valley, sunrise is by far the best time to visit. The rock can be reached along a rough, unsealed track (Ridgewell Road), on the right, just beyond Blackheath heading north. It is best suited to 4WD but if you don't have your own transport most local 4WD tours go there.

Megalong Valley, accessed on Megalong Valley Road, west of Blackheath town centre, provides a pleasant scenic drive and is one of the most accessible and most developed of the wilderness Blue Mountains valleys. **Megalong Australian Heritage Centre** ⓘ T4787 8188, www.megalong.cc, 0800-1730, offers a whole range of activities from horse trekking and 4WD adventures, to livestock shows.

Lithgow

Lithgow marks the western boundary of the Blue Mountains and was founded in 1827 by explorer Hamilton Hume. An industrial town and Australia's first producer of steel, its main tourist attraction is the remarkable Zig Zag Railway (see below), 10 km east in Clarence, as well as a scattering of historical buildings. The town also acts as the gateway to the Jenolan Caves and Kanangra-Boyd National Park to the south and the wilderness Wollemi National Park, to the north. Wollemi is one of the largest and the most inaccessible wilderness areas in NSW, a fact that was highlighted in no uncertain terms in 1994 with the discovery of the Wollemi Pine, a species that once flourished over sixty million years ago. The exact location of the small stand of trees is kept secret.

There are two fairly low-key museums in the town. **State Mine and Heritage Park and Railway** and **Lithgow Small Arms Museum**. **Eskbank House Museum** is a Georgian homestead built in 1842, complete with period furnishings and Lithgow pottery. The VIC can supply town maps and accommodation listings. Of far more natural and historic appeal are the derelict villages of **Newnes** and **Glen Davis**, to the north of Lithgow, between the scenic Gardens of Stone National Park and the western fringe of the Wollemi National Park. Both were once thriving villages supporting a population of thousands that worked in the two large oil-shale refineries during the early 1900s. South of Newnes an added attraction is the old 400-m rail tunnel that was once part of a busy line that connected the shale plants with Clarence Station. Now left dark and forbidding, the tunnel is the silent home of glow worms (gnat larvae), which light up its walls like a galaxy of stars. All along the unsealed roads to both Newnes and Glen Davis look out for the prolific birdlife.

In **Clarence**, 10 km east of Lithgow, you will find the **Zig Zag Railway** ⓘ T6351 4826, www.zigzagrailway.com.au, $28, concessions $22, children $14 (return), a masterpiece of engineering originally built between 1866 and 1869. Operated commercially up until 1910 as a supply route to Sydney it now serves as a tourist attraction with lovingly restored steam trains making the nostalgic 8-km (1½ hours) journey from Clarence to Bottom Points (near CityRail's Zig Zag Station). They leave Clarence on Wednesdays and at the weekend at 1100, 1300 and 1500. On other weekdays the less exciting motorized trains take over and leave at the same time. Request drop off if you are arriving by CityRail from Sydney/Katoomba at the Zig Zag Station.

Jenolan Caves

ⓘ T6359 3911, www.jenolancaves.org.au, the main caves can only be visited by guided tour, daily from 1000-2000. Cave combo tickets from $28-$40. Caving adventure tours are also an option, costing from $75-$200.

The Jenolan Caves, on the northern fringe of the Kanangra-Boyd National Park, south of Lithgow, comprise nine major (and 300 in total) limestone caves considered to be amongst the most spectacular in the southern hemisphere. After over 160 years of exploration and development – since their discovery in 1838 by pastoralist James Whalan – the main caves are now well geared up for your viewing pleasure with a network of paths and electric lighting to guide the way and to highlight the bizarre subterranean features. As well as guided cave tours, some other caves have been set

Canberra: Australia's capital city

Derived from the Aboriginal word *Kamberra* (meeting place), Australia's capital is, sadly, one of the most under-rated cities in the world. It lacks intimacy and is too modern to have developed a sense of history, but, if you can ignore the negative publicity, it's actually a pleasant place and offers a great deal to see and do. A sightseeing bus tour is a good way of experiencing the sights, particularly if you are short of time. Cycling is also a great way to get around, with many cycleways. An efficient bus service runs throughout the city and to the airport. Contact the **VIC** ⓘ *330 Northbourne Av, 3 km north of the centre, T1300 554 114 / T6205 0044, www.canberra tourism.com.au, Mon-Fri 0900-1700, Sat-Sun 0900-1600*, for more details and maps.

If you're short of time don't miss the National Museum, the New Parliament Building and the National Capital Exhibition, all of which are neatly contained within the National Triangle, or Parliamentary Triangle. Although the temptation is to head straight for the Triangle's crowning glory, the New Parliament Building, start your tour instead at the **National Capital Exhibition** ⓘ *Regatta Point, Commonwealth Park, T6272 2900, www.nationalcapital.gov.au, 0900-1700, free*, which imaginatively outlines the fascinating history of the nation's capital from its indigenous links to today's intriguing landscaped metropolis. The views across Lake Burley Griffin are memorable.

Completed in 1988, **New Parliament House** ⓘ *T6277 5399, www.aph.gov.au, 0900-1700, guided tours every 30 mins from 0900*, is the architectural showpiece of Canberra and one of Australia's great man-made wonders, like Sydney's Opera House and Harbour Bridge. Where else in the world is there such a building with its lawn on the roof? Once you have trampled all over it and taken in the angles, perspectives and views you can then turn to the interior. Along with more fascinating architecture the interior hosts precious Australian art and craft, including Arthur Boyd's impressive *Shoalhaven Tapestry*. When Parliament is sitting, access is allowed to 'Question Time' in the House of Representatives and begins at 1400. Tickets are free;

aside for adventure caving, and above ground, there is a network of pleasant bush trails. If you are short of time the **Lucas Cave** and **Temple of Baal Cave** are generally recommended. The **Chiefly Cave** is the most historic and along with the **Imperial Cave** it has partial wheelchair access. The **River Cave** is said to be one of the most demanding. On your arrival at the caves you immediately encounter the **Grand Arch**, a 60-m wide, 24-m high cavern that was once used for camping and even live entertainment to the flicker of firelight. Nearby, the historic and congenial **Caves House** has been welcoming visitors since 1898 (see Sleeping below).

Bells Line of Road

Bells Line of Road is named after Archibald Bell, who discovered the 'second' route through the Blue Mountains to Lithgow from Sydney, in 1823, at the age of 19. Starting just west of Richmond in the east, then climbing the plateau to fringe the northern rim of the Grose Valley, it provides a quieter, more sedate, scenic trip across the Great Divide. Just beyond the village of Bilpin, west of Richmond, the huge basalt outcrop of Mount Tomah (1000 m) make bookings through the Sergeant of Arms office. Facing Lake Burley Griffin, in the heart of the National Triangle, is the **Old Parliament House** completed in 1927, hub of the nation's political life until the New Parliament House took over in 1988. Immediately outside is the Aboriginal Tent Embassy that serves as a pertinent reminder that the Aboriginal people of Australia were living here for tens of thousands of years before the first acre of land was ever purchased. Sitting proudly on the shores of Lake Burley Griffin, the **National Museum of Australia** ① *Lawson Crescent, T6208 5000, www.nma.gov.au, 0900-1700, free (admission charge to some specialist displays)*, is superb, with a range of exciting displays and themed galleries that convey all things 'Aussie', all beautifully designed and presented.

● **Sleeping**

The VIC has listings and a bookings service, T1300 554 114, www.visitcanberra.com.au. **LL Kurrajong**, 8 National Circuit, Barton, T6234 4444, www.hotel kurrajong.com.au. One of

the capital's best boutique hotels. It is well positioned between the lively suburb of Manuka and the National Triangle.
A-D Canberra City YHA, 7 Akuna St, T6248 9155, www.canberracity accommodation.com.au. The best budget option, costing more than your average hostel but worth it. Kitchen, bar, pool and spa.

● **Transport**

The international airport, T6209 3336, www.canberraairport.com.au, is 8 km east of the centre via Morshead Drive. **QantasLink**, **Virgin Blue**, **Tiger Airways** and **Regional Express** fly to/from Sydney, Brisbane and Melbourne. Long-distance coaches stop at the Jolimont Tourist Centre, 65 Northbourne Av, Civic T02-6211 8545. **Greyhound** and **Premier Motor Services** have services to Sydney, Brisbane and Melbourne. The train station is in Kingston suburb, 6 km south of the centre, off Cunningham St, T6257 1576. **Countrylink**, T132232, runs regular daily services to/from Sydney and Melbourne (train/coach).

begins to dominate the scene and supports the 28-ha cool-climate annexe of the **Sydney Botanical Gardens (Mount Tomah)** ① *T4567 3000, 1000-1600, $5.50, children $4.40*. Opened in 1987, the garden's rich volcanic soils nurture over 10,000 species, including a huge quantity of tree ferns and rhododendrons. Although the gardens are well worth visiting in their own right, it is the views, the short walks and the restaurant that make it extra special. Just beyond Mount Tomah (right) is the **Walls Lookout**, with its expansive views across the Grose Valley. It requires a one-hour return walk from the Pierces Pass Track car park but the effort is well worth it. Back on the Bells Line of Road and just a few kilometres further west is the junction (north, 8 km) to the pretty village of **Mount Wilson** which is famous for its English-style open gardens. These include **Linfield Park** and **Nooroo**. Also of interest is the **Cathedral of Ferns** at the northern end of the village. The **Wynnes** and **Du Faurs Lookouts** can also be reached from Mount Wilson and are signposted, east and west of the village centre.

Around Sydney listings

For Sleeping and Eating price codes and other relevant information, see Essentials pages 28-33.

Sleeping

Ku-ring-gai Chase National Park *p134*
C-E Pittwater YHA, T9999 5748,
pittwater@yhansw.org.au. Take the ferry from
Church Point to this great place.

Blue Mountains *p135, Katoomba map p139*
Leura has many excellent historic B&Bs and
self-contained cottages and Katoomba has
plenty of choice. Wentworth also has plenty
of good B&Bs. If you prefer something a bit
quieter, the villages north of Katoomba –
Medlow Bath, Blackheath and Mount Victoria
– all provide some excellent accommodation.
There are plenty of places to stay in and
around Jenolan. Prices are higher at
weekends and you are advised to book ahead
at any time of year, especially winter.
L Jemby-Rinjah Eco Lodge, 336 Evans
Lookout Rd, Medlow Bath, T4787 7622,
www.jembyrinjah lodge.com.au. 1- or
2-bedroom, self-contained, modern cabins
(one with a Japanese hot tub) and log fires, all
in a beautiful bush setting close to the
lookout and walks. Dinner and bed and
breakfast packages are also available.
L-B Glenella Guesthouse, 56 Govetts Leap
Rd, Medlow Bath, T4787 8352,
www.glenellabluemountainshotel.com.au.
Well known and surprisingly affordable,
historic guesthouse, with a reputable
restaurant attached, plus all the comforts
including sauna, open fires and cable TV.
L-B Imperial, 1 Station St, Mount Victoria,
T4787 1878, www.hotel imperial.com.au.
Reputedly the oldest tourist hotel in Australia.
Beautifully restored, it is a fine place to soak
up the history and offers a wide range of
well-appointed rooms from the traditional to
the 4-poster with double spa. Breakfast
included, good restaurant, bar and live
entertainment at the weekends.

L-D Jenolan Caves Resort, Jenolan Caves,
T1300 763311, www.jenolancaves.com.
Grand, with a wealth of facilities, this resort
has the renowned Caves House. It offers a
range of rooms and suites, plus self-
contained cottages with a restaurant, bistro,
bar and a host of activities.
A-C Three Explorers Motel, 197 Lurline St,
Katoomba, T4782 1733, www.3explorers.
com.au. For a motel option try this
recommended and unconventional option.
They also offer a 2-bedroom cottage.
A-E Blackheath Caravan Park, Prince Edward
St, Blackheath, T4787 8101. In a quiet suburban
bush setting within walking distance of the
village. Onsite vans, powered and non-powered
sites, barbecue and kiosk, but no camp kitchen.
B Jamison Guesthouse, 48 Merriwa St,
Katoomba, T4782 1206, www.jamisonhouse
.com.au. One of the many fine historic B&Bs,
lodges and self-contained cottages in and
around Katoomba. This one is long-
established and large with plenty of old world
European-style charm, period decor, en
suites, a guest lounge with log fire and a
popular French restaurant attached (see
below). Close to all amenities.
B-C Jenolan Cabins, Porcupine Hill, 42 Edith
Rd, Jenolan Caves, T6335 6239,
www.jenolancabins.com.au. Self-contained
cabins sleep 6 with 1 queen size and bunks.
The owners also operate local tours.
B-E Katoomba Blue Mountains YHA, 207
Katoomba St, Katoomba, T4782 1416,
bluemountains@yhansw.org.au. Beautifully
renovated art deco building. A showpiece
hostel for the YHA and fast developing a
reputation as one of its best. It's modern,
spacious, friendly and has good facilities. Trips
arranged, also bike hire and internet.
C-E Flying Fox Backpackers,
190 Bathurst St, Katoomba, T02-4782 4226,
www.theflyingfox.com.au. Long-established
and sociable, spacious dorms and great bush
camping. Good advice on local activities and
transport to walking tracks.

D-E No14 Budget Accommodation,
14 Lovel St, Katoomba, T4782 7104,
www.bluemts.com.au/no14. Another fine
alternative, providing a peaceful, relaxed
atmosphere in a old former guesthouse with
double, twin, single and family rooms. Polished
floors and an open fire add to the atmosphere.

🍴 Eating

Blue Mountains *p135, Katoomba map p139*
Katoomba and the Blue Mountains generally
pride themselves in offering some classy
restaurants and fine cuisine. Book ahead for the
expensive places.
🍴🍴🍴 **Silk's Brasserie**, 128 The Mall, Leura,
T4784 2534. Daily for lunch and dinner (book
ahead). One of the many fine restaurants and
cafés in Leura, this one offers fine modern
Australian cuisine.
🍴🍴🍴 **Solitary**, 90 Cliff Dr, Katoomba, T4782
1164. Lunch Sat-Sun and public/school
holidays and dinner Tue-Sat. A classy award
winner with a fine reputation offering
imaginative modern Australian cuisine and
fine views across the Jamieson Valley.
🍴🍴 **Arjuna Indian**, 16 Valley Rd, Katoomba,
T4782 4662. Thu-Mon at 1800 (book ahead).
The best Indian restaurant in the region and
the views are almost as hot as the curry.
🍴🍴 **Rooster**, Jamieson Guesthouse, 48
Merriwa St, Katoomba, T4782 1206. Daily for
dinner and for lunch Sat-Sun. An old favourite
that serves good value French-influenced
cuisine, with fine views to boot. Also very
good accommodation.
🍴🍴 **Vulcans**, 33 Govetts Leap Rd, Blackheath,
T4787 6899. Fri-Sun for lunch and dinner.
Another well-known Blackheath institution;
the only drawback is the limited opening.
🍴 **Elephant Bean**, 159 Katoomba St,
Katoomba, T4782 4620. Wed-Mon
0800-1500. A fine café especially for lunch.
🍴 **Paragon**, 65 Katoomba St, Katoomba,
T4782 2928. Daily 0800-1700. If you have a
sweet tooth you just cannot afford to miss
out on this art deco Katoomba institution.

⛰ Activities and tours

Blue Mountains *p135, Katoomba map p139*
All based in Katoomba unless stated
otherwise. See the VIC for full listings.
Australian School of Mountaineering, 166
Katoomba St, T4782 2014,
www.asmguides.com. Hardcore professional
rock climbing and bush craft trips, plus others.
Blue Mountains Adventure Company, 84a
Bathurst Rd, T4782 1271, www.bmac .com.au.
A well-established local company with a fine
reputation, range of affordable options from
abseiling to mountain biking.
**Blue Mountains Explorer Double-decker
Bus**, T4782 1866, www.explorerbus.com.au.
A local service with 30 stops around
Katoomba and Leura, hourly between 0945
and 1645. An unlimited jump-on/off day pass
costs $36, concessions $30, children $18.
Blue Mountain Horseriding Adventures,
T4787 8188, www.bluemountainshorse
riding.com.au. Based in the Megalong Valley
west of Katoomba, offers hour/half/full and
multi day horse rides from $50.
Getabout 4WD Adventures, T8822 5656,
www.getabout.com.au. Professional day and
multi-day 4WD tours (Blue Mountains day
tour $685) with a tag-along options allowing
you to take your own vehicle.
High 'N' Wild, 3/5 Katoomba St, T4782 6224,
www.high-n-wild.com.au. Abseiling,
canyoning, rock climbing and mountain
biking trips.
Tread Lightly Eco-Tours, 100 Great Western
Highway, Medlow Bath, T4788 1229,
www.treadlightly.com.au. Very clued-up and
eco-friendly, great bushwalking and 4WD
tours throughout the region from $135.
Trolley Tours, 285 Main St, 1800-801577. A
29-stop historic trolley bus tour around the
sights of Katoomba and Leura. All-day travel
pass, daily 1015-1615, $20.

⊖ Transport

Kamay Botany Bay National Park *p133*
Access to the northern sector is via Anzac
Parade. **Sydney Buses**, T131500, runs regular
daily buses from Railway Sq (No 393) or
Circular Quay (No 394) in Sydney's CBD. To
get to the southern sector by car, follow
Princes Highway south, turn left on to The
Boulevarde, and then follow Captain Cook
Drive. Vehicle entry to the park costs $11. By
train from Sydney's Central Station, take
CityRail, T131500, to Cronulla (Illawarra line),
then **Kurnell Bus**, T9523 4047, No 987.

Royal National Park *p133*
By **train** take CityRail (Illawarra line) from
Central Station to Loftus (4 km from Audley),
Engadine, Heathcote, Waterfall or Otford. You
can also alight at Cronulla and take the short
crossing by ferry to Bundeena at the park's
northeastern corner, T9523 2990, www.cronulla
ferries.com.au, from $5.70, children $2.85.

Ku-ring-gai Chase National Park *p134*
The nearest public transport (western side) by
train is with **CityRail**, T131500 (Northern Line),
from Central Station to Berowa, Mount
Ku-ring-gai and Mount Colah, then walk to
Bobbin Head (3-6 km). A better option is to
catch a bus (No L90) to Palm Beach (eastern
side) then the ferry to Basin Beach. Ferries
also run to Bobbin Head (see page 135).

Blue Mountains *p135, Katoomba map p139*
Katoomba train station is off Main St, at the
northern end of Katoomba St. Trains leave
Sydney's Central Station on a regular basis.
Countrylink, T132232, offers daily services
to/from Sydney hourly. **CityRail**, T131500, with
Fantastic Aussie Tours, T4782 1866, also offer a
number of rail/coach tour options with Blue
MountainsLink, operating Mon-Fri and Blue
Mountains ExplorerLink, operating daily. Prices
include return transport and a tour on arrival in

Katoomba. **Greyhound** has coaches on the
westbound run from Sydney to Dubbo,
stopping behind the train station near Gearin
Hotel, Great Western Highway.
Blue Mountains Bus Co, T4751 1077,
www.bmbc.com.au. Operates a standard Hail
'n' Ride service around Katoomba, **Leura** and
Wentworth Falls. Mon-Fri 0745-2025, Sat
0800-1530, Sun 0915-1530, from $2.
Katoomba Radio Cabs, Katoomba, T4782
1311. Operates a 24-hr taxi service between
Mount Victoria and **Wentworth Falls**.

  Medlow Bath, **Blackheath** and **Mount
Victoria** are all on the main local bus/train
routes to/from Katoomba. The train station is
in the centre of town off the Great Western
Highway and on Station St.

  Lithgow is on the main local and
westbound bus/train route to/from
Katoomba and Sydney. See above for details
of tours and services. The train station is on
Main St, **Countrylink** and **CityRail**, both offer
regular daily services east and west.

  There is no public transport to the **Jenolan
Caves**, but tour operators in Katoomba and
Sydney run tours. A day tour to the caves will
cost about $120 exclusive of caves tour, $150
with a cave inspection and around $200 with a
cave inspection and a spot of adventure
caving. The VICs in Katoomba or Sydney have
full details. See Activities and tours, page 145.

ⓓ Directory

Katoomba *p138, map p139*
Banks Most bank branches with ATMs are
located along Katoomba St. **Hospital** Blue
Mountains District Hospital, Great Western
Highway (1 km east of the town centre),
T4784 6500. **Internet** Available at
Parakeet Café, 195b Katoomba St, T4782 1815.
Post Behind Katoomba St, at 14 Pioneer Pl,
2780, T4780 7304, Mon-Fri 0900-1700.

South Coast NSW

Few visitors have any idea that this little corner of NSW is just as beautiful as anywhere else in the state. Overshadowed by Sydney and the north coast, it has pretty much been left alone. But the south coast has over 35 national parks and nature reserves; more than any other region in the state and most are above the waterline. The south coast also has its fair share of beautiful unspoiled beaches and stunning coastal scenery. South of Wollongong and Kiama the coast is split into three quite distinct regions: the Shoalhaven Coast which extends from Nowra to Batemans Bay; the Eurobodalla Coast which stretches from Batemans Bay to Narooma; and the Sapphire Coast which idles its way to the Victorian border.

Wollongong and around → *For listings, see pages 153-157. Colour map 2, B2.*

Wollongong is a very attractive place, despite the stark industrial landscapes of Port Kembla to the south, and without doubt its greatest assets are its beaches, its harbour (with its historic lighthouse) and behind that, **Flagstaff Point** headland and the **Wollongong Foreshore Park**. Either side of Flagstaff Point over 17 patrolled beaches stretch from the Royal National Park in the north to Bass Point in the south, all providing excellent opportunities for sunbathers, swimmers and surfies. Wollongong serves as the gateway to the Illawarra region, an area renowned for its dramatic coastline and rugged mountain backdrop. It is also the first main stop along the 140-km 'Grand Pacific Drive' that encompasses some of the state's finest and most unspoilt coastline.

In the heart of the city the **Wollongong City Gallery** ① *corner of Kembla St and Burelli St, T4228 7500, www.wollongongcitygallery.com, Tue-Fri 1000-1700, Sat-Sun 1200-1600, free*, is definitely worth a visit. Considered one of the best and one of the largest regional galleries in NSW, it offers a wide range of media and an exciting programme of local, regional and interstate exhibitions. For train enthusiasts the **Cockatoo Run** ① *T1300 653801, www.3801limited.com.au, runs to Robertson every 2nd Sunday of the month and Kiama every 3rd Sunday, from $50, children $40, lunch an extra $25, bookings required*, is a scenic mountain railway that climbs through the Illawarra Ranges from Wollongong to Robertson in the Southern Highlands. Extended tours throughout the state are also on offer. South of the city centre, in the suburb of Berkeley, is Wollongong's unique attraction, the **Nan Tien Buddhist Temple** ① *Berkeley Rd, T4272 0600, www.nan tien.org.au, Tue-Sun 0900-1700, $4, also offers vegetarian lunches for $12 per person*. This is the Southern Hemisphere's largest Buddhist temple open to visitors and offers a varied programme of weekend workshops and accommodation, see Sleeping, page 153. Public transport to the temple is with Premier Illawarra Bus Company (No 34) from Marine Drive. Wollongong offers some excellent surfing with the best breaks on **North Beach**, just north of Flagstaff Point, and **Bulli Beach**, 12 km north of the centre. There are plenty of places to hire equipment; see Activities and tours, page 155. Find local information at the new **VIC** ① *Southern Gateway Centre, Princes Hwy, Bulli Tops, T4267 5910, www.southerngatewaycentre.com.au, Mon-Fri 0900-1700, Sat 0900-1600, Sun 1000-1600*.

The **Illawarra Ranges**, flanking Wollongong inland, have some excellent viewpoints that are well worth seeing, such as the **Mount Keira Lookout** in the Illawarra Escarpment State Recreation Area (left on Clive Bissell Road), and the **Bulli Lookout** (right), both off Highway 1 (Ousley Road), just north of the city. There are numerous fine beaches north of the city. **Bulli Beach** is perhaps the best, but it is a case of taking your pick, all the way from the city centre to **Otford** at the southern edge of the **Royal National Park**. Another great local attraction just to the south of the city, and beyond Port Kembla, is **Lake Illawarra**. Essentially a saltwater harbour, sheltered from the ocean by a narrow strip of land, it provides a haven for a wide range of water sports, from sailing to kayaking.

Kiama and Berry → For listings, see pages 153-157. Colour map 2, B2.

Just to the south of Lake Illawarra, the pretty coastal town of Kiama is the first of many that are encountered on the journey between Wollongong and the Victorian border. The centre of activity revolves around **Blowhole Point**, crowned by its 1887 lighthouse. During a good southeasterly, the surging waves can plough into the blowhole with awesome power, creating a thunderous roar and spout of mist, as if issued from some angry subterranean dragon. To the north of Blowhole Point is **Pheasant Point**, with its rock pool, and north again is **Bombo Beach**, a favourite amongst the local surf set. **VIC** ① *Blowhole Point Rd, T4232 3322, www.kiama.com.au, open 0900-1700.*

South, beyond the Mount Pleasant Lookout on the Princes Highway, is **Werri Beach**, which is a good one for surfing, then via Crooked River Drive, the headland villages of **Gerringong** and **Gerroa**. At Gerroa, the **Crooked River Winery** ① *11 Willow Vale Rd, 9 km south of Kiama, T4234 0975,* can provide a congenial stop with the added bonus of a fine café and coastal views. From the **Kingsford Smith Lookout** in Gerroa – which pays tribute to Australia's most famous aviator – it is hard to resist the temptation to explore the vast swathe of **Seven Mile Beach**, which beckons from below the rooftops. Inland, via the little village of **Jamberoo**, 10 km away, is the **Minnamurra Rainforest**, part of the **Budderoo National Park**. The popular **NPWS Minnamurra Rainforest Centre** ① *T4236 0469, www.nationalparks.nsw.gov.au, 0900-1700, $11 vehicle entry, café and shop,* is signposted off Jamberoo Mountain Road, heading west, acts as a base for explorations of the forest and the Minnamurra Falls.

Roughly halfway between Kiama and Nowra is the delightful little village of **Berry**, which is well worth a stretch of the legs to take a closer look. Almost impossible to miss is the bizarre façade and interior of the **Great Southern Hotel Motel**, 95 Queen Street. Not only is there a small fleet of rowboats on the roof and a signpost laden with markers to all conceivable destinations, there's also, next door, a bottle shop completely decked in shiny hubcaps. But it doesn't end there. Inside, the bar is decked with a wide array of objects including a centrepiece First World War torpedo set proudly above the pool table. During the great Pacific nuclear testing controversy in the mid-1990s, the said torpedo was actually rammed at admirable speed into the gates of the French Embassy in Canberra atop a VW Beetle. There are plenty of good cafés and restaurants along Berry's main drag.

Shoalhaven coast → For listings, see pages 153-157. Colour map 2, B2.

Beyond Berry you reach the Shoalhaven River and the twin towns of **Bomaderry** and **Nowra**. From here you are entering the south coast proper and an area known as Shoalhaven, which extends from Nowra to **Batemans Bay**. Although the town of Nowra is a fairly unremarkable introduction to the south coast, just to the east and especially around Jervis Bay and beyond, its true magic begins to be revealed, with some of the best beaches and national parks in the state. If you have time you may also like to consider some Tourist Drives inland to Kangaroo Valley and the Morton National park (Fitzroy Falls) or others that explore the coast in more detail. The VIC can provide all the details. Nowra is home to the **Shoalhaven VIC** ⓘ *corner of Princes Highway and Pleasant Way, T4421 0778, www.shoalhaven.nsw.gov.au, 0900-1630*, as well as the **NPWS office** ⓘ *55 Graham St, Nowra, T4423 2170*.

Paringa and Nowra Park, to the west of Nowra, fringes the riverbank and offers a riverside walk that takes in the 46-m **Hanging Rock Lookout** and a number of climbing sites. There are also river cruises.

Jervis Bay and around

Jervis Bay is a deep, sheltered bay that sits neatly in the embrace of the Beecroft Peninsula to the north and the exquisite Booderee National Park to the south. It is blessed with stunning coastal scenery, beautiful white beaches, a marine park with world-class dive sites and even a resident pod of over 60 playful dolphins, all of which combine to earn it the quiet reputation as the jewel of the NSW South Coast. Local information is available from **Huskisson Trading Post** ⓘ *1 Tomerong St, Huskisson, T4441 5241, www.tourismjervisbay.com.au, 0900-1700*.

The old shipbuilding town of **Huskisson** (known as 'Husky') and its neighbour **Vincentia** are the two main settlements on Jervis Bay and form the gateway to the bay's water-based activities. The diving in the **Jervis Bay Marine Park** in particular is said to be second only to the Great Barrier Reef and is well known for its marine variety and water clarity. A few companies offer activities like whale and dolphin watching, page 155.

Booderee National Park ⓘ *day fee (including and per car) costs $10 and camping fees (from $10-$20) must be paid on top of that, so if you intend staying overnight it does add up*, formerly known as the Jervis Bay National Park, takes up almost the entire southern headland of Jervis Bay and is, without doubt, one of the most attractive coastal national parks in NSW. Owned and administered by a collaboration of Parks Australia and the Wreck Bay Aboriginal Community, it offers a wealth of fine, secluded beaches, bush walks, stunning coastal scenery and a rich array of wildlife. Not to be missed are **Green Patch Beach**, the further flung **Cave Beach**, a good surf spot, and **Summercloud Bay**. The walking track to **Steamers Beach** (2.3 km) is also recommended although there are many fine options to choose from. Another unique attraction in the park is the 80-ha **Booderee Botanic Gardens** ⓘ *Mon-Fri 0800-1600, Sat-Sun 1000-1700, free with park entry fee*, created in 1952 as an annexe of the Australian National Botanic Gardens in Canberra. There are over 1600 species centred on the small freshwater Lake McKenzie, with most being coastal plants more suited to the local climate. There are a number of short walks and nature trails. The **VIC** ⓘ *Village Rd, T4443 0977, www.booderee.np.gov.au, 0900-1600*, at the park entrance, can supply detailed information about the park, its attractions, walks, amenities and its scattering of great campsites. Provisions can be bought at the **general store** ⓘ *0700-2100, or 1900 outside school holidays*, in Jervis Bay Village, off Jervis Bay Road, which is within the park boundary.

Murramarang National Park

ⓘ *Day-use vehicle entry costs $11, pedestrians free. Access to Pebbly Beach is via Mt Agony Rd (unsealed) right of the Princes Highway 10 km north of Batemans Bay. Depot Beach and Durras North are accessed via North Durras Rd off Mt Agony Rd. Pretty Beach and the Murramarang Aboriginal Area are accessed via Bawley Point and Kioloa on Murramarang Rd (sealed) off the Princes Highway 16 km south of Ulladulla.*

The 11,978-ha Murramarang National Park is most famous for its tame and extremely laid-back population of eastern grey kangaroos. Here they not only frequent the campsites and the foreshore but on occasion are even said to cool off in the surf. The park is a superb mix of forest and coastal habitat that offers a host of activities from swimming, surfing and walking to simple socializing with the resident marsupials. Of the beaches and campsites, **Pebbly Beach** and **Depot beach** are the most popular spots, but **Durras North**, south of Depot Beach and Pretty Beach to the north, is also great. There is a network of coast and forest walks available including the popular 'Discovery Trail' off North Durras Road, which skirts the edge of **Durras Lake**. There is also a fine coastal track connecting Pretty Beach with Pebbly Beach.

Eurobodalla Coast → For listings, see pages 153-157. Colour map 2, B2/C1.

The Eurobodalla coastal region stretches from Batemans Bay in the north to Narooma in the south. The bustling seaside resort of **Batemans Bay** provides an ideal stopover along the coastal Princes Highway. Most of the Bay's beaches are located southeast of the town centre and if you have time it is worth heading that way. Tomakin and Broulee offer the best surf and fishing sites and jet skis can be hired on Coriggan's Beach. On the river you can take a leisurely three-hour cruise upstream to the historic riverside village of Nelligen. The area offers some excellent sea kayaking. There are numerous excellent dive sites around the Bay. See Activities and tours, page 155, for details. Just off the Princes Highway near the town centre is the very helpful **VIC** ① *T4472 6900, www.naturecoast-tourism.com.au, 0900-1700.*

Nestled on a headland in the glistening embrace of the Wagonga River Inlet and surrounded by rocky beaches, national parks and the odd accessible island, **Narooma** has all the beauty and potential activities for which the south coast is famous. The biggest attraction is **Montague Island**, about 8 km offshore. Officially declared a nature reserve and administered by the National Parks and Wildlife Service, Montague has an interesting Aboriginal and European history and is crowned by a historic lighthouse built in 1881. But perhaps its greatest appeal are the colonies of fur seals and seabirds – including about 10,000 pairs of fairy penguins – that make the island home. Between October and December humpback whales can also be seen on their annual migration. There are tours of the island, see page 155.

Back on the mainland the immediate coastline has some interesting features including **Australia Rock**, which as the name suggests, looks like the outline of Australia. It is however not the rock that plays with the imagination but a hole in its middle. Access is via Bar Rock Road beyond the golf course, at the river mouth on Wagonga Head. Further south **Glasshouse Rocks** is another interesting geological formation. On the western side of town the Wagonga Inlet offers fishing and river cruises (see page 155). The **VIC** ① *off Princes Highway, T4476 2881, www.naturecoast-tourism.com.au, 0900-1700,* is at the northern end of town.

Sapphire Coast → For listings, see pages 153-157. Colour map 2, C1.

From Narooma to the Victorian border is a region known as the Sapphire Coast. Just south of Narooma, in the shadow of Gulaga Mountain, are the quaint and historic villages of **Central Tilba** and **Tilba Tilba** with a population of around 100. Now classified by the National Trust, they boast many historic cottages and also offer some of the South Coast's best cafés and arts and crafts outlets. Ask for a self-guided heritage leaflet from the VIC in Narooma. They can also provide listings for numerous cosy B&Bs in and around the two villages. **Tilba Valley Wines Vineyard** ① *off the Princes Highway, 5 km north of Tilba Tilba, T4473 7308, www.tilbavalleywines.com, open from 1000*, was established in 1978 and produces Shiraz, Semillon and Chardonnay. It offers tastings and has a small tavern-like restaurant.

Next along are the villages of **Bega** and **Tathra**. Bega's biggest tourist attraction is its famous **cheese factory** ① *Lagoon St, T6491 7762, www.begacheese.com.au, 0900-1700, free*. To the north and west of Bega is the 79,459-ha **Wadbilliga National Park**, a wilderness region of rugged escarpment and wild rivers. Along the road to the **Brogo River Dam** you can stay at **Fernmark Inn**, a perfect base from which to explore the park's rivers, perhaps best done by canoe (see page 155). From Bega you can then head straight for Merimbula or take a diversion to the coastal village of **Tathra**, where you can laze on the beach or explore the **Bournda National Park**. The 10-km Kangarutha Track from Tathra South to Wallagoot Lake is recommended. The **VIC** ① *at Bega Cheese Factory (see above), T6491 7645*, has information and listings.

Merimbula serves as the capital of the Sapphire Coast and receives most of its tourist traffic. Surrounded by fine beaches and bisected by Merimbula Lake (which is actually a saltwater inlet), it offers plenty to see and do, with **Main Beach**, south of the lake, being the most popular for swimming and body boarding. The lake itself is a great venue for boating, windsurfing and fishing. The surrounding coast also offers some good diving and is the happy home of a resident pod of dolphins. From September to December migrating whales join the party making cruising the town's speciality. On the northern bank of Merimbula Lake is the **VIC** ① *2 Beach St, T6495 1129, www.marimbulatourism.com.au, 0900-1700*, which has full details of diving, horse trekking and scenic flights; see also page 155. The **NPWS** ① *corner of Sapphire Coast and Merimbula Drive, T6495 5000, 0830-1630*, has a great Discovery Centre, offering parks and regional walks information, natural history displays, maps and gifts.

Ben Boyd National Park → *For listings, see page 154. Colour map 2, C1.*

Sheer wilderness, beautiful coastal scenery, sublime walks, strange, colourful geological features, great campsites and even a remote lighthouse all combine to make the Ben Boyd National Park one of the best coastal parks in NSW. The 9490-ha park straddles Twofold Bay and the fishing village of Eden.

Ins and outs

Access to the park is off Princes Highway (signposted). Roads within the park are both sealed and unsealed. Unsealed sections are badly rutted, but negotiable by 2WD when dry. Day-use vehicle entry to the park costs $6. NPWS office in Merimbula (see above) can provide detailed information on the park, its walks and its campsites.

Around the park

In the northern section of the park, the principal feature is **The Pinnacles**, a conglomerate of white and orange, sand and clay that has eroded into strange pinnacle formations over many thousands of years. They can be reached on a short 500-m-circuit walk from the car park off the 2 km Haycock Road, which is partly sealed and signposted off the Princes Highway. To the north, at the end of Edrom Road (16 km, signposted off the Princes Highway), is **Boyd's Tower**, which though very grand, never served its

Kosciuszko National Park

At over 600,000 ha, the Kosciuszko National Park is the largest in New South Wales and certainly one of the most beautiful. Home to the continent's highest peak, the 2228-m Mount Kosciuszko, the famous Snowy River and the country's best skiing and snowboarding resorts, the park also offers a plethora of year-round mountain activities, such as hiking, mountain biking, whitewater rafting, horse trekking and fishing. And with much of the park being wilderness, it also offers sanctuary to many rare native plants and animals. Jindabyne, at the eastern fringe of the park, is the main satellite town for the skiing and snowboarding resorts and has a huge range of accommodation and restaurants. It also hosts the NPWS Snowy Region Visitors' Centre, ① *just off Kosciuszko Rd, T6450 5600, www.environment.nsw.gov.au, 0830-1700*.

The best of the skiing and snowboarding resorts is Thredbo, set in a beautiful river valley, overlooked by the Crackenback Mountain Range. For a full list of the many activity and accommodation options, visit the excellent VIC ① *6 Friday Drive, T1300 020 589 / T6459 4100, www.thredbo.com.au, winter 0800-1800, summer 0900-1600*. Things don't grind to a halt after the snow disappears. In summer Thredbo becomes an alpine walking centre and the Valley Chairlift stays open, offering walkers the shortest route to the summit of Mount Kosciuszko.

⊖ Transport

Countrylink has daily coach services to Jindabyne from Sydney, while **V-Line** has services from Melbourne. To get to the ski fields, the 8-km long Skitube at Bullock's Flat, 20 km east of Jindabyne (Alpine Way), connects Thredbo Valley with Perisher Blue Resort and the summit of Blue Cow Mountain. It operates daily in winter on the hour from 0900-1500. A shuttle bus service runs between Jindabyne and Thredbo.

---

intended purpose as a lighthouse. Below the tower a clearing looks down to clear azure waters and the strange volcanic convolutions of the red coastal rocks. Another diversion off Edrom Road, to the west, takes you to the remains of the **Davidson Whaling Station**, created in 1818 and the longest-running shore-based station in Australia, ceasing operations in 1930. Further south off Edrom Road an unsealed, badly rutted road leads to the delightful and wildlife-rich **Bittangabee campsite** (15 km, then 5 km on the left), see page 154.

Back on the main track the Disaster Bay Lookout is worth a look before the track terminates at the 'must-see' **Green Cape Light Station** (21 km). Surrounding by strange, rust-coloured rocks, pounded by surf and home to laid-back kangaroos, it is a wonderful place to find some solitude. **City Rock**, accessed down a short badly rutted track, off the lighthouse road, is signposted also well worth seeing. The wave action against the rock platform is dramatic and a favourite haunt for sea eagles. The superb but demanding (30 km) **'Light to Light' Walking Track** connects the Green Cape Light Station with Boyd's Tower, passing the **Bittangabee** and **Saltwater Creek** campsites along the way. It is one of the best and most remote coastal walks in NSW.

For Sleeping and Eating price codes and other relevant information, see Essentials pages 28-33.

Sleeping

Wollongong and around *p147*

C Pilgrim Lodge, at the Nan Tien Buddhist Temple, Berkeley Rd, Berkeley, T4272 0500, www.nantien.org.au. For something completely different, this offers comfortable, modern en suite doubles, triples and family rooms, with meals if required. Specialist meditation weekend packages.

C-E Keiraview Wollongong YHA, 75-79 Keira St, T4229 1132, www.yha.com.au. The city's best backpackers with modern facilities, dorms, doubles and singles, most en suite, parking and internet.

Kiama and Berry *p148*

L-D Easts Van Park (Big 4), Ocean St, Easts Beach, Kiama, T4232 2124, www.eastvan parks.com.au. A spacious beachside motor park with above average facilities.

L Bellawongarah at Berry B&B, 869 Kangaroo Valley Rd, Bellawongarah, T4464 1999, www.accommodation-berry.com.au. Country home and cottage in an elevated bush setting only 10 mins from Berry. A former 1868 church now serves as a self-contained cottage, while the spacious, contemporary 3-storey house has 2 rooms with a shared bathroom and a loft suite with double spa bathroom. Wonderfully peaceful and a good change from coastal accommodation. 2-night minimum stay.

B-C Berry Hotel, 120 Queen St, Berry, T4464 1011, www.berryhotel.com.au. Good-value pub-stay rooms and an award-winning restaurant.

Shoalhaven Coast *p148*

L-F Rest Point Garden Village, Browns Rd (5 km south of Shoalhaven), T4421 6856, www.nowracaravanpark.com.au. The most modern motor park in the area with a range of accommodation including powered and non-powered sites.

Jervis Bay

LL-L Paperbark Lodge and Camp, 605 Woollamia Rd, T4441 6066, info@paperbarkcamp.com.au. An excellent eco-tourist set-up in a quiet bush setting with luxury en suite tent units, outdoor camp fire, good onsite restaurant (see Eating), tours and activities. Book ahead.

There's also a scattering of upmarket B&Bs, motels, pub-hotels, budget and motor park options in and around Huskisson, including:

A Huskisson Beach Tourist Resort, Beach St, Huskisson, T1300 733027, www.huskissonbeachtouristresort.com.au.

C Jervis Bay Backpackers, Owen St, T0402 109 912, www.jervisbaybackpackers.com.au. Centrally located, small but perfectly adequate.

Booderee National Park

All the campsites have groups of tame kangaroos and rosellas. Campsites of various sizes range in price from $10-20 for 5. Note the camping fee does not include vehicle entry ($10) so that does add extra cost, but it is well worth it! For bookings, T4443 0977, www.deh.gov.au/parks/booderee. Book well ahead during public holidays.

There are good campsites with hot showers at Green Patch, while Bristol Point, with similar facilities, is designed for groups. Camping with cold showers is available at Cave Beach (there is a 250-m walk to the site from the car park).

Murramarang National Park

LL-E Eco-Point Murramarang Resort, Banyandah St, South Durras, T4478 6355, www.murramarangresort.com.au. A top spot and although not in the park itself it has its own tame kangaroos and some sublime coastal scenery. Luxury cabins, en suite/standard powered and non-powered sites, pool, bar/restaurant, camp kitchen, activities and canoe and bike hire.

L-F Depot Beach, T4478 6582. Cabins, powered and non-powered sites with modern facilities.

C-F Pretty Beach, T4457 2019. Powered and non-powered sites with similar facilities.
F NPWS campsite, Pebbly Beach, T4478 6023, www.nationalparks.nsw.gov.au. Good facilities, with hot showers and fire sites. A warden collects fees daily. It's often busy so it's wise to book ahead.

Eurobodalla Coast *p150*
The VIC in Batemans Bay has full accommodation listings. There are several other motor parks located beachside along Beach Rd southeast of the centre as well as the one mentioned below. In Narooma there are plenty of standard motels for which the VIC has full listings. There are also a couple of options out of town that are worth the trip.

Batemans Bay
LL-A Big 4 Batemans Bay Beach Resort, 51 Beach Rd, T4472 4541. Five-star beachside holiday park with full facilities.
LL-A Bridge Motel, 29 Clyde St (200 m west of the bridge), T4472 6344. Well-placed motel accommodation.
L-B Comfort Inn Lincoln Downs, Princes Highway (on the right just beyond the bridge heading north), T4478 9200, www.lincolndowns.com.au. Excellent hotel with full facilities .
A-E Shady Willows Holiday Park, Old Princes Highway, corner of South St, T4472 4972, www.shadywillows.com.au. Backpackers and those in campervans should head here. It incorporates a YHA with dorm or onsite caravans for couples, fully equipped kitchen, pool, internet, bike hire.
F The best places for camping are the NPWS sites in the kangaroo-infested Murramarang National Park (see above).

Narooma
L-B Mystery Bay Cottages, 121 Mystery Bay Rd, Mystery Bay, 3 km off Princes Highway, 10 km south of Narooma, T4473 7431, www.mysterybaycottages.com. A good self-contained option in a rural setting close to the beach.

L-E Big 4 Island View Beach Resort, Princes Highway (5 km south of the town centre), T4476 2600, www.islandview.com.au. Convenient position with full motor park facilities including camp kitchen and internet.
A-B Priory at Bingie, Priory Lane, Bingie, 26 km north, T4473 8881, www.bingie.com. This delightful B&B is in a stylish modern home, offering 3 good double rooms, plenty of peace and quiet, an art gallery/workshop and great ocean views.

Sapphire Coast *p150*
There are plenty of motels and self-contained apartments in Merimbula. The VIC can supply full details.
L-E Merimbula Beach Holiday Park, Short Point Beach, east on Short Point, Merimbula, T6499 8999, www.merimbula beachholidaypark.com.au. One of the best-placed motor parks for peace and quiet, facilities and beach access. Camp kitchen.
A Fernmark Inn, 610 Warrigal Range Rd, Brogo, T6492 7136, www.fernmark.com.au. Worldly themed en suites, health treatments and fine cuisine, this place makes a good base to explore the surrounding area. Recommended.
C-E Wandarrah Lodge YHA, 8 Marine Pde, Merimbula, T6495 3503, www.wandarrah lodge.com. au. Excellent and purpose built, providing modern en suite dorms, double and family rooms, a well-equipped kitchen, 2 lounges, internet, free breakfast.
NPWS camping, Hobart Beach, off Sapphire Coast Drive, south of Tathra, T6495 5000.

Ben Boyd National Park *p151*
A-D Wonboyn Lake Resort, 1 Oyster Lane, 19 km off Princes Highway, T6496 9162, www.wonboynlakeresort.com.au. Self-contained en suite cabins, shop, spa and restaurant.
A-E Wonboyn Cabins and Caravan Park, Wonboyn Rd (33 km south of Eden), T6496 9131, www.wonboyncabins.com.au. Onsite vans, powered and non-powered sites.
F Saltwater Creek and **Bittangabee Bay**, T6495 5000. Basic (but delightful) camping.

Self-registration, fees apply. Book well ahead. There is also modern, self-contained accommodation available in the **lighthouse**, T6495 5000, fscr@environment.nsw.gov.au.

⊘ Eating

Wollongong and around p147
♦♦♦ **Aqua**, 17/54-58 Cliff Rd, T4225 9888. Daily for breakfast, lunch and dinner. A fine seafood and Modern Australian option with a classy ambience and wide-ranging menu clearly giving its neighbour some competition.
♦♦♦ **Beach House**, 16 Cliff Rd, T4228 5410. Lunch and dinner daily from 1200. A well-established seafood restaurant. Recommended.
♦♦♦ **Harbourfront**, 2 Endeavour Drive, T4227 2999. Lunch and dinner daily from 1200, breakfast Thu-Sun. Quality seafood with views to match.
♦♦ **Lagoon Seafood,** Stuart Park, corner George Hanley Drive and Kembla St, North Wollongong, T4226 1677. Daily 1000-0200. Local favourite overlooking Wollongong Beach.
Keira St is good for cheap eats, including:
♦ **Food World Gourmet Café**, 148 Keira St, T4225 9655. Great value Chinese.

Kiama and Berry p148
There are plenty of cafés and affordable eateries in Kiama with most located along Terralong St and Collins St or beside the harbour.
♦♦♦ **Cargo's**, on the Wharf, T4233 2771. Daily for lunch and dinner.
♦♦ **Chachi's Italian**, The Terraces, T4233 1144. Closed Tue.
♦♦ **Manning Street Deli**, 14 Manning St, T4232 4030. Daily for breakfast and lunch. Best bet for coffee and light meals.
♦♦ **Ritzy Gritz New Mexican Grill**, 40 Collins St, T4232 1853. Daily. Affordable option, locally popular and colourful.
There are many good cafés and restaurants along Berry's main drag, and if the pub food in the **Southern Hotel** is not sufficient, then try the award-winning **Coach House** in the Berry Hotel.

Shoalhaven Coast p148
In the centre of Nowra, Kinghorne St is the main drag and best place to browse menus.
♦♦♦ **Boatshed**, 10 Wharf Rd, south bank below the bridge, T4421 2419. Tue-Sat from 1800. For fine dining it's hard to beat.

Jervis Bay
♦♦♦ **Gunyah Restaurant**, Paperbark Camp (see page 153, daily for dinner). For fine dining (out of town). Recommended.
♦ **Husky Pub**, Owen St. No-nonsense, good value pub food.

Eurobodalla Coast p150
Batemans Bay
♦♦♦ **On the Pier**, Old Punt Rd, just north and west of the bridge, T4472 6405. Lunch and dinner, closed Mon. This one can always be relied on for excellent seafood as well as classy Modern Australian.
♦ **Boatshed**, Clyde St, T4421 2419. For fresh fish and chips with the seagulls on the waterfront.

Sapphire Coast p150
Market St and Beach St in Merimbula have numerous affordable cafés and restaurants.
♦♦ **Wharf**, overlooking the inlet at Merimbula Aquarium, Lake St, T6495 4446. Daily for lunch and Wed-Sat for dinner. Locally recommended.

▲ Activities and tours

Wollongong and around p147
Boat Shed, Windang, near the harbour entrance, T4296 2015. Rents boats, canoes and kayaks for Lake Illawarra.
Just Cruisin' Motorcycle Tours, T4294 2598, www.justcruisintours.com.au. Cruise the Illawarra and surrounds on a chauffeured Harley, from $90 per hour.
Skydive the Beach, T4225 8444, www.skydivethebeach.com.au. From $285 (cheaper for groups).
Sydney Hang Gliding Centre, T4294 4294, www.hanggliding.com.au. Trips around Stanwell Park and the Illawarra Ranges north of

Wollongong, 30 mins from $245. It is also the base for Australian champion Tony Armstrong, T04-1793 9200, www.hangglideoz.com.au, who will take you up tandem, from $220.

Shoalhaven Coast p148
Jervis Bay

Huskisson has several companies offering whale (Jun-Nov) and dolphin watching (year round) as well as standard bay or twilight barbecue cruises of 2-3 hrs from $30-$65:

Dolphin Explorer, 62 Owen St, T4441 5455.
Dolphin Watch, 50 Owen St (main drag), T4441 6311, www.dolphinwatch.com.au.
Jervis Bay Kayak Co, T4441 7157, www.jervisbaykayaks.com. Excellent half/full/weekend and multi-day sea kayaking trips in Jervis Bay or further afield from $100. Independent hire also available.
Pro Dive, 64 Owen St, T4441 5255, www.divejervisbay.com.au. This is a very knowledgeable, professional operation offering a range of diving options and courses. Bike hire also available.

Eurobodalla Coast p150
Batemans Bay

You can take a leisurely 3-hr cruise to the historic riverside village of Nelligen (30 mins stopover) on the locally built *Merinda*, at 1100, from $30, children $15 (lunch options available), T4472 4052.
Bay and Beyond Sea Kayaks, T4478 7777, www.bayandbeyond.com.au. Good half or full day and river and lake tours, from $55-110.
National Diving Academy, 5/33 Orient St, T4472 9930. Access, trips and gear hire.

Narooma

Island Charters, Bluewater Drive, T4476 8080, www.islandchartersnarooma.com. Independent sightseeing, fishing or dive charters from $65, Montague Island from $75, children $55.
NPWS, book at the VIC. 4-hr guided tour of Montague Island at 0930 and a 3½-hr evening tour at dusk. All tours are weather permitting

and numbers are limited, from $130, children $99. Tours depart from the town wharf on Blue Water Drive. Also offers 1- to 2-night island accommodation packages, T0407 909111.

The knowledgeable crew aboard the 90-year-old **Wagonga Princess**, T4476 2665, www.wagongainletcruises.com, offer 3-hr cruises up the river with an emphasis on wildlife and history. Departs 1300 daily in summer and Sun, Wed and Fri off season, from $33.

Sapphire Coast p150
Merimbula and around

Brogo Wilderness Canoes, T6492 7328, www.brogocanoes.com.au. Trips (including overnight camping), half day $25.
Cycle 'n' Surf, 1B Marine Parade, Merimbula, T6495 2171. Hires bikes, surf/body boards and fishing tackle.
Merimbula Marina, T6495 1686, www.merimbulamarina.com. Whale watching from $40, 2-hr dolphin cruise from $25, children $10. Fishing charters of 1-3 hrs at a very reasonable $35-55.
Ocean Wilderness Kayaking, T6495 3669. Quality ocean and lake trips, half-day to overnight, from $125. Whale sightings are possible from late Sep to late Nov.
Sapphire Eco-Tours, T6494 0283, www.sapphirecoastecotours.com.au (or book at the VIC). Ideal opportunity for visitors with hire cars to explore the region's rich and varied national parks aboard a 14-seater 4WD OKA vehicle. Half or full day trips.
Sinbad Cruises, Merimbula, T6495 1686, www.merimbulamarina.com/sinbad.html. Cruises on the Pambula River and Pambula Lake with afternoon tea ($20), lunch ($25) or dinner ($40).

Eden

Cat Balou Cruises, Eden, T0427-962027, www.catbalou.com.au. Whale-watching cruises (late Sep to late Nov) from $40 and year round 2-hr sightseeing trips along the Ben Boyd National Park (Twofold Bay) coastline, from $30, children $17.

⊖ Transport

Wollongong and around *p147*

Murray's, T132251, www.murrays.com.au. Daily service to **Canberra** and **Narooma** via **Batemans Bay**, from $26. Long-distance coaches stop at the Wollongong City Coach Terminal, corner of Keira St and Campbell streets, T4226 1022. Open Mon-Fri 0745-1730, Sat 0745-1415. **Greyhound**, T131499, and **Premier Motor Services**, T133410, offer daily services to **Sydney** (Brisbane) and **Canberra** (Melbourne) via the **Princes Highway**.

Taxi: Wollongong Radio Cabs, T4229 9311.

The train station is west of the city centre at the end of Burrelli St and Station St. **CityRail** offers regular daily services to/from **Sydney** to **Bomaderry** where the line ends.

Kiama and Berry *p148*

Kiama Coachlines, T4232 3466, operates services from the Bong Bong Rd train station to the **Minnamurra Rainforest**, daily at 1005. Long-distance coaches stop in the centre of town on Terralong St, or at the Bombo Railway Station, 1.5 km north. **Premier** and **Greyhound** both offer daily services between **Canberra** (Melbourne) and **Sydney** (Brisbane).

Bike hire is available with **Kiama Cycles and Sports**, 27 Collins St, T4232 3005.

Taxi T4464 1181.

The train station is off Bong Bong Rd in the centre of town. **CityRail**, T131500, offers regular daily services from **Sydney**.

Shoalhaven Coast *p148*

In **Nowra** numerous long-distance coach and local bus companies base their operations at the bus terminal on Stewart Pl. **Premier** and **Greyhound** offer daily services between **Canberra** (Melbourne) and **Sydney** (Brisbane).

Nowra Coaches, T4423 5244, operates regular daily bus services between **Nowra**, **Huskisson**, **Vincentia** and **Wreck Bay**.

Taxi T4421 0333.

Bomaderry train station is the end of the line from Sydney. **CityRail**, T131500, offers daily services via **Kiama** and **Wollongong**.

For bike hire contact **Pro Dive**, see page 155.

Access to **Booderee National Park** is via Jervis Bay Rd off Princes Highway and south of Huskisson and Vincentia.

Eurobodalla Coast *p150*
Batemans Bay

Long-distance coaches stop outside the Promenade Plaza on Orient St or the Post Office on Clyde St. **Premier**, **Greyhound** and **Priors**, T4472 4040, run daily services between **Canberra** (Melbourne) and **Sydney** (Brisbane). **Murray's**, T132251, also runs services to **Canberra**, north to **Nowra** and south to **Narooma**. The VIC or **Travelscene**, Shop 6, 8 Orient St, T4472 5086, assists with bookings.

Narooma

Long-distance coaches stop in the town centre on Princes Highway, with services between **Canberra** (Melbourne) and **Sydney** (Brisbane). **Murray's** also offers services to **Canberra** and north to **Nowra**.

Sapphire Coast *p150*

From Merimbula, **Deane's Buslines**, T6299 3722, www.deanesbuslines.com.au, runs local daily services to **Bega**, **Eden** and **Pambula**. Long-distance coaches stop at the Ampol Service Station in the town centre. **Premier** and **Greyhound** offer daily services between **Melbourne** and **Sydney** (Brisbane). **V-Line**, T136196, operates additional services to **Melbourne**.

Contents

Footprint features

Central & North Coast NSW

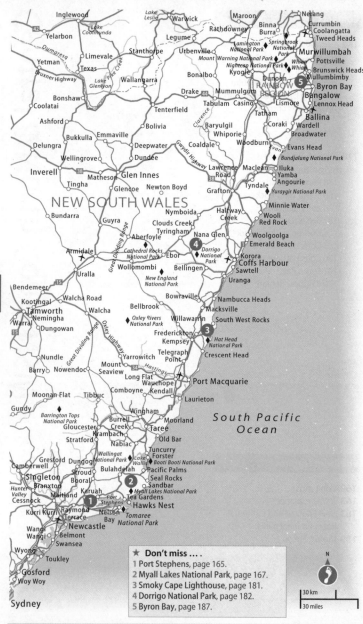

★ **Don't miss ....**
1 Port Stephens, page 165.
2 Myall Lakes National Park, page 167.
3 Smoky Cape Lighthouse, page 181.
4 Dorrigo National Park, page 182.
5 Byron Bay, page 187.

30 km
30 miles

The north coast of New South Wales stretches almost 900 km from Sydney to Tweed Heads, a seemingly endless string of beautiful beaches, bays and headlands, blue sea and national parks. There are so many stunning natural features that, after a while, they all seem to merge into one golden memory of sun-drenched sands and crystal clear waters, with the constant soundtrack of rolling surf.

Such appeal, however, has its downside, and the weak-willed traveller may suffer from severe option paralysis, especially with so many activities to choose from: surfing, sea kayaking, diving, sailing, fishing, kite boarding and koala spotting are all here in abundance.

As a general guide, from south to north, extended stops in Nelson Bay (Port Stephens), Myall Lakes National park, Port Macquarie, South West Rocks, Coffs Harbour, Bundjalung National Park, and, of course, Byron Bay, are all recommended.

Also, try to break up the journey with the odd trip inland, especially to Bellingen, the Dorrigo and New England National Parks and the numerous other superb national parks in the Rainbow Region, inland from Byron Bay.

Sydney to Port Macquarie

With the lure of Byron Bay to the north, few take the time to explore the coast and national parks between Sydney and Port Macquarie. But to do so is to miss out on some of the best coastal scenery in the state. Myall Lakes National Park offers a superb diversion, and a couple of days exploring the beaches and lakes is highly recommended. Just inland are the vineyards of Hunter Valley, a name synonymous with fine wines and world-class vineyards – a little piece of Australia that conjures up images of mist-covered valleys and rolling hills, clothed in a patchwork of grape-laden vines. Although not necessarily producing the best wines in Australia, this is one of the best venues in the country to learn something of the process or sample that classic vineyard ambience and enjoy the congenial conviviality of fine wine, fine food and fine accommodation. To the north are the high and secluded river valleys of the Barrington Tops National Park, an area renowned for its unpredictable climate and diverse wildlife, while back on the coast is Nelson Bay, an ideal stopover on the route north and gateway to the beautiful Tomaree Peninsula.

Newcastle and the Hunter Valley → *For listings, see pages 170-177. Colour map 2, A3.*

As one of the most industrialized cities in Australia – with a main drag and a city centre mall as inspiring as a bowl of week-old porridge – Newcastle has limited tourist appeal. It is mostly used as a base from which to visit the Lower Hunter Valley, home to dozens of wineries, which provide one of the finest 'winery' experiences in the world. From Newcastle, the Hunter River becomes increasingly scenic, with rolling hills draped in vineyards backed by wilderness forest, given over to the vast Wollemi (pronounced 'Wollem eye') National Park.

Ins and outs

Getting there and around The nearest main airport to Hunter Valley is at Newcastle. Shuttles ferry people to and from the airport to the Valley. There are plenty of coaches and tours from Sydney, Newcastle and Port Stephens and trains arrive at Maitland and Scone. From Newcastle there are regular coach and train connections with the main surrounding cities and tourist centres, with frequent daily services from Sydney and Port Stephens. ▸▸ *See Transport, page 175.*

Tourist information Hunter Valley (Wine Country Tourism) VIC ① *455 Wine Country Drive (4 km north of the town centre), T4990 0900, www.winecountry.com.au, Mon-Thu 0900-1730, Fri 1800, Sat 1700, Sun 1600,* is the principal centre, well set up with a café and winemaking display. It provides detailed and objective vineyard information as well as accommodation and tour bookings. You are strongly advised to pick up the free detailed maps from the VIC. **Newcastle VIC** ① *361 Hunter St, opposite the Civic Rail Station, T4974 2999, www.visitnewcastle.com.au, Mon-Fri 0900-1700, Sat-Sun 1000-1500.*

Newcastle

Newcastle grew from its humble beginnings as a penal colony to become one of the largest coal ports in the world, shipping vast amounts of the black stuff from the productive Hunter Valley fields. Major steel production followed, until its rapid decline in the late 20th century. To add insult to injury, in 1989 the city suffered Australia's worst earthquake in modern times. Despite this, the city still boasts some very fine and gracious

A vine romance

With so many vineyards, choosing which to visit can be tough. There are many tours on offer, but for those with little prior knowledge it is advisable to mix some of the large, long-established wineries and labels with the smaller boutique affairs. Although many of the biggest names are well worth a visit, you will find a more, relaxed and personalized service at the smaller establishments. Also be aware that almost every vineyard has received some award or another and this is not necessarily a sign that one is better than the next. The following wineries are recommended and often considered the must-sees but it is by no means a comprehensive list.

Of the large long-established vineyards (over a century old), **Tyrells,** www.tyrrells.com.au, **Draytons,** www.draytonswines.com.au and **Tullochs**, www.tulloch.com.au. (all in Pokolbin) are recommended, providing fine wine and insight into the actual wine-making process. Tyrells also has especially nice aesthetics. **Lindemans**, www.lindemans.com, **McGuigans**, www.mcguiganwines.com.au (again in Pokolbin), and **Wyndhams**, www.wyndhamestate.com (Branxton), are three of the largest and most well-known labels in the region, offering fine vintages and a broad range of facilities. McGuigans and Wyndhams also offer guided tours. Of the smaller boutique wineries, **Oakvale**, www.oakvalewines.com.au, **Tamburlaine**, www.tamburlaine.com.au, and **Pepper Tree** – with its classy restaurant and former convent guesthouse added attractions – are also recommended. All are located in Pokolbin. Then, for a fine view as well as vintage, head for the **Audrey Wilkinson Vineyard**, DeBeyers Road, Pokolbin, www.audreywilkinson.com.au, or **De Luliis**, Lot 21, Broke Road, www.dewine.com.au, with its lookout tower. The VICs have details.

Given the fact that copious wine tasting and responsible driving do not mix, organized tours are by far the best way to tour the vineyards. All day jump-on-jump-off services are also available around the main vineyards. Another fine alternative is to visit the various vineyards by bike. For details of the various tours on offer, see page 174.

historical buildings, including the 1892 **Christ Church Cathedral**, the 1890 **Courthouse** and several classics on and around Hunter and Watt streets such as the **post office** (1903), **railway station** (1878) and **Customs House** (1877).

The **Newcastle Regional Art Gallery** ⓘ *Laman St*, is worthy of investigation, while history buffs will enjoy the newly renovated **Maritime and Military Museum** ⓘ *T4929 3066, www.fortscratchley.org.au, Wed-Mon 1000-1600, entry fee, full site tours from $12, tunnel tour $10*. Serving as the city's main museum, Fort Scratchley has been extensively redeveloped in recent years and not surprisingly places a special emphasis on the town's military history as well as its infamous earthquake. The fort itself was first established in 1882 and at the risk of making it sound like the local McDonalds it houses an impressive range of 'muzzle loaders' from a 20-pounder to the full 80-pounder. It's enough to work up quite an appetite.

The beaches on the eastern fringe of the city are superb and well known for their excellent surfing, swimming (patrolled in summer) and fishing, while 6 km inland the 180-ha **Blackbutt Reserve** ⓘ *daily 0900-1700, free*, is an excellent nature reserve that presents a fine opportunity to see wild koala. By car there are four main entrances into Blackbutt Reserve. These include off Carnley Avenue (Blackbutt Picnic Area), Freyberg Street (Richley Reserve), Queens Road and Lookout Road. Buses (Nos 317 and 224) pass by Orchardtown Road and Lookout Road.

Hunter Valley

This is really two distinct regions, the Lower Hunter Valley and Upper Hunter Valley, with the vast majority of the vineyards (over 80) in the lower region. The Hunter River and the New England Highway bisect both. The Lower Hunter Valley encompasses the area from Newcastle through Maitland to Singleton, with Cessnock to the south considered the 'capital' of the Lower Hunter Valley's vineyards, which are concentrated in a few square kilometres to the northwest. Though the region's true heritage lies below the ground, in the form of coal, it is vineyards that dominate the economy these days, producing mainly Shiraz, Semillons and Chardonnays. They range from large-scale producers and internationally recognized labels to low-key boutiques. Despite the sheer number, the emphasis in the Hunter Valley is definitely on quality rather than quantity. Though the vineyards are all comprehensively signposted around Cessnock, you are strongly advised to pick up the free detailed maps from the VIC. See also box, page 163.

For many, their first introduction to the great wine growing region is the drab and disappointing former mining town of **Cessnock**. Head north and west, however, and things improve as you reach the vineyard communities of **Pokolbin**, **Broke** and **Rothbury**.

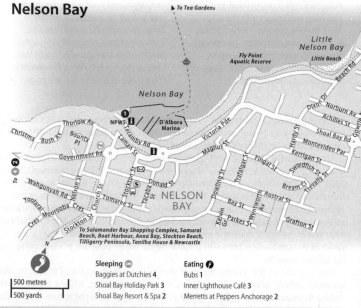

Nelson Bay

Sleeping
Baggies at Dutchies 4
Shoal Bay Holiday Park 3
Shoal Bay Resort & Spa 2

Eating
Bubs 1
Inner Lighthouse Café 3
Merretts at Peppers Anchorage 2

Nelson Bay and around → *For listings, see pages 170-177. Colour map 3, C1.*

Nelson Bay is the recognized capital of an area known as Port Stephens, a name loosely used to describe both the natural harbour (Port Stephens) and the string of foreshore communities that fringe its southern arm. Nelson Bay is fast developing into a prime New South Wales coastal holiday destination and provides an ideal first base or stopover from Sydney. Other than the stunningly beautiful views from Tomaree National Park and from Tomaree Heads across the harbour to Tea Gardens and Hawks Nest, there are an ever-increasing number of activities on offer in the area, from dolphin watching to camel rides.

Ins and outs

Getting there The nearest airport is at Newcastle (Williamtown), 30 km away, with regular connections to main centres. Coaches serve Nelson Bay from Sydney direct or connect with interstate services in Newcastle. ▶▶ *See Transport, page 175.*

Getting around Nelson Bay is small enough to navigate on foot. Local regional buses connect the town with surrounding attractions of Port Stephens.

Tourist information **Port Stephens VIC** ① *Victoria Pde, T4980 6900, www.portstephens.org.au, Mon-Fri 0900-1700, Sat-Sun 0900-1600*, has a guide. **NPWS** ① *12B Teramby Rd (Marina Complex), T4984 8200, hunter@npws.nsw.gov.au*, has national parks and camping information.

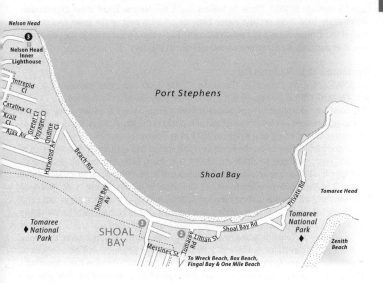

Sights

Even if you do nothing else around the Nelson Bay area except laze about on its pretty beaches, do climb to the summit of **Tomaree Head**, at the far east end of Shoal Bay, which is particularly spectacular at sunrise or sunset. The views that reward the 30-minute strenuous ascent are truly memorable.

The best beaches in the area are to be found fringing the national park, east and south of Nelson Bay. To the east, **Shoal Bay** is closest to all amenities while farther east still, within the national park boundary, **Zenith Beach**, **Wreck Beach** and **Box Beach** all provide great surfing, solitude and scenery. Two kilometres south of Shoal Bay the glorious beach that fringes **Fingal Bay** connects Point Stephens with the mainland. You can access the headland and its fine walking tracks at low tide. South of Fingal Bay, though not connected to it by road, **One Mile Beach** is a regional gem while **Samurai Beach**, just north of that, is the local naturist beach. West of One Mile Beach **Boat Harbour** gives way to **Anna Bay** which forms the northern terminus of **Stockton Beach**, stretching for over 30 km all the way down to Newcastle. It's well worth a visit simply to see the endless sweep of dunes. If you have 4WD you can 'let rip' but a permit must be obtained from the Council (or the VIC). See also Activities and Tours page 174.

There is a healthy suburban population of **koalas** in the region and the best places to see them are the fringes of Tomaree National Park or wooded areas of the Tilligerry Peninsula (via Lemon Tree Passage Road, off Nelson Bay Road, 30 km south of Nelson Bay). There are guided walks, see Activities and Tours page 174. While you are in the area you may also be tempted to visit **Tanilba House** ① *Caswell Corner, Tanilba, T4982 4866, Wed, Sat-Sun 1030-1630, admission charge*, one of the oldest homesteads in Australia, built by convicts in 1831. Closer to Nelson Bay is the **Nelson Head Inner Lighthouse**, *T4984 9758, 1000-1600*, set just above Little Bay, 1.5 km east of the town centre, with guided tours, great views and a small café. Little Bay is also a great place to see pelicans as they wait patiently for fishermen's handouts late in the day.

Barrington Tops National Park

① *NPWS office, 59 Church St, Gloucester, T6538 5300, gloucester@npws.nsw.gov.au, Mon-Fri 0830-1700, is the nearest to the park. There is also an office in Nelson Bay.*

The 40,453-ha Barrington Tops National Park encompasses a 25-km long plateau extending between a series of extinct volcanic peaks in the Mount Royal Ranges, north of the Hunter Valley. Rising to a height of 1577 m at Polblue Mountain, the plateau forms one of the highest points on the Great Dividing Range and contains a diverse range of habitats, from rainforest to alpine meadows, with many waterfalls and glorious views. The high elevation also results in unpredictable weather year round and an annual rainfall of over 2 m, with sub-zero temperatures and snow in winter. Given its geographical position, the park hosts a diverse range of species including lyrebirds, bandicoots and spotted-tailed quolls. At the very least you are almost certain to encounter kangaroos as well as small squadrons of elegant and very vocal black cockatoos.

The scenery and wildlife alone make a day trip well worthwhile, but given the many excellent B&Bs, campsites, walks and activities available you may well be tempted to extend your stay. The Great Lakes VIC in Forster (see page 169) handles Barrington Tops information. Look out for the free brochure, *Barrington Tops World Heritage Area*, and also visit www.barringtons.com.au. If you have your own transport there are various routes. From the south and east, the park and the two main fringing communities of Dungog and Gloucester are best reached from Bucketts Way Road (Highway 2) which heads northwest off the Pacific Highway 33 km north of Newcastle. Alternatively, the northern sector of the park (and Gloucester) can be accessed west off the Pacific Highway at Nabiac, 160 km north of Newcastle. If you have 2WD and your time is limited, the drive up the Gloucester River Valley to Gloucester Tops is recommended. Take the Gloucester Tops Road off Bucketts Way Road, 10 km south of Gloucester. The climb to the plateau begins at the Gloucester River Camping Area (see Sleeping, page 172). The northern sector of the park offers a more extensive 78-km scenic drive (mostly unsealed) from Gloucester to Scone via Scone Road and then Barrington Tops Road, west of Gloucester. Sadly, the best views from Carey's Peak and its surrounding campsites can only be reached by 4WD south off Forest Road, just west of the Devils Hole Camping Area. The southern sector of the park is accessed 40 km northwest of Dungog, via Salisbury and the Williams River Valley Road.

Myall Lakes National Park → *For listings, see pages 170-177. Colour map 3, C2.*

Myall Lakes National Park, or Great Lakes as it is known, combines beautiful coastal scenery with a patchwork of inland lakes, waterways and forest to create one of the best-loved eco-playgrounds in NSW. Just four hours north of Sydney, the only drawback is its inevitable popularity during holidays and weekends. However, given the sheer scale of the area (21,367 ha), of which half is water, there is always somewhere to escape the crowds. The main settlements fringing the national park are Tea Gardens and Hawks Nest on the northeastern shores of Port Stephens, Bulahdelah on the Pacific Highway to the northwest and the popular surf spots of Bluey's Beach and Pacific Palms to the north. If you have at least two days to spend here, the route below, from Tea Gardens in the south to Pacific Palms in the north, or vice versa, is recommended. A day fee per vehicle of $7 applies to the park.

Ins and outs
Getting there Myall is best explored by car though there are regional bus services between Taree and Sydney. ›› *See Transport, page 175.*

Getting around For navigation, whether on foot, by car or paddle, the *Great Lakes District Map* ($10) is not only recommended but essential. Copies can be bought in the VIC. There are daily local bus services around the area, paddleboat hire and houseboat hire.

Tourist information Great Lakes VIC in Forster serves as the region's main centre. Local VICs are in Tea Gardens ① *209 Myall St, T4997 0749, 1000-1600*; Bulahdelah ① *corner of Pacific Highway and Crawford St, T4997 4981, www.greatlakes.org.au, Mon-Fri 0900-1700, Sat-Sun 0900-1500*, and Pacific Palms ① *Boomerang Drive, Bluey's Beach, T6554 0123, 1000-1600*. All can provide NPWS information; the nearest NPWS office is in Nelson Bay. Also see www.greatlakes.org.au.

Tea Gardens and Hawks Nest
The little-known but fast-developing coastal settlements of Tea Gardens and Hawks Nest, on the northeastern shores of Port Stephens, serve not only as excellent holiday destinations in themselves but as the main southern gateway to the Myall Lakes National Park. Straddling the Myall River and surrounded by beautiful beaches, headlands, coastal wetlands and forest, these twin towns offer a wealth of activities from surfing to koala spotting, though most people come here simply to escape the crowds, relax and enjoy the beautiful scenery and laid-back atmosphere.

The place to be is **Bennetts** (Ocean Beach) at the southeastern end of Hawks Nest. From there you can access the **Yaccaba Walk** (3 km return) to the summit of the Yaccaba Headland, affording some memorable views across the mouth of Port Stephens and the numerous offshore islands. To reach Bennetts Beach, cross the bridge from Tea Gardens on Kingfisher Avenue, turn right on Mungo Brush Road, then left to the end of Booner Street. The bridge connecting the two towns is often called 'The Singing Bridge' because of its tendency to 'sing' in strong winds.

Another excellent but far more demanding walk is the **Mungo Track** that follows the Myall River through coastal forest to the **Mungo Brush Campsite** (15 km one way). It starts on the left, off Mungo Brush Road, 600 m past the national park boundary. The detailed booklet, *Walkers' Guide to The Mungo Track*, breaks the entire walk into sections with additional alternatives and is available from the VIC Tea Gardens, NPWS or Hawks Nest Real Estate on Tuloa Avenue. Look out for koalas along the way, especially late in the day. Dolphin-watching cruises, diving, golf, fishing charters and boat, sea kayak, canoe and surf ski hire are all readily available in the twin towns. Tea Gardens VIC (see Tourist information above) has full listings.

Hawks Nest to Bulahdelah

From Hawks Nest, Mungo Brush Road heads north, parallel with the Myall River, to meet the southern boundary of the Myall National Park (4.5 km). From there the road remains sealed and cuts through the littoral rainforest and coastal heath for 15 km to the Mungo Brush Campsite beside the Bombah Broadwater, the second largest of the Great Lakes.

Before reaching Mungo Brush consider stopping and walking the short distance east to the long swathe of deserted beach. **Dark Point**, about 5 km north of the southern boundary at Robinson's Crossing, is an interesting rocky outcrop and the only significant feature along this 44 km of beach between Hawks Nest and Seal Rocks. It is an interesting spot and the site of a midden (ancient refuse tip) used by the Worimi Aboriginal peoples for centuries before invading European cedar cutters displaced them. This particular example is thought to be at least 2000 years old. Lying tantalizingly offshore is **Broughton Island**, which is accessible by day trip from Nelson Bay.

From Mungo Brush the road skirts the northern shores of **Bombah Broadwater**, turning inland past increasingly thick stands of paperbark trees to reach the Bombah Point ferry crossing which – provided there is enough water – runs daily every half an hour from 0800 to 1800. There is a small fee. **Bombah Point** is dominated by the large yet unobtrusive **EcoPoint Myall Shores Resort**. On the same road, 10 km from Bulahdelah, are the **Bombah Point Eco Cottages**. See page 172 for details.

Bulahdelah, Seal Rocks and Sanbar

From Bombah Point 16 km of partly sealed roads takes you to the small community of **Bulahdelah** and the Pacific Highway. Bulahdelah has a helpful VIC and is the main venue for houseboat hire for the region. Four kilometres north of Bulahdelah, the Lakes Way – the main sealed access road through the Great Lakes region – heads east, eventually skirting Myall Lake, the largest of the lakes. Before reaching the lake, however, you may consider the short diversion 5 km north along **Stoney Creek Road**. Some 38 km into the southern fringe of the Bulahdelah State Forest, along Wang Wauk Forest Drive, is the **Grandis**, a towering 76-m flooded gum reputed to be the highest tree in NSW.

Back on the Lakes Way, between Myall Lake and Smiths Lake, Seal Rocks Road (unsealed) heads 11 km southeast to reach the coast and the pretty beachside settlement of **Seal Rocks**. The residents of this sublime little piece of wilderness know all too well that it is the jewel in the Myall and do not really want to advertise the fact. There is a superb beach and short rainforest and headland walks; the 2-km stroll to the **Sugarloaf Point Lighthouse** past the **Seal Rocks Blowhole** is well worth it. The views from the lighthouse (no public access to the interior) are excellent and Lighthouse Beach to the south is more than inviting. Seal Rocks lie just offshore and serve as a favourite regional dive site (they are home to numerous grey nurse sharks). Since 1875 there have been 20 shipwrecks, with the SS Catterthun being one of the nation's worst with the loss of 55 lives.

Back on the Lakes Way, just before **Smiths Lake**, look out for signs to the **Wallingat National Park**. If it is a fine day, an exploration (4WD and map required) of the forest is recommended, with the steep climb to **Whoota Whoota Lookout** providing fine views north over the lakes and coast.

Sandbar, 1 km past the turn off to Smiths Lake village, is also a sight for sore eyes. Here you'll find some excellent, quiet beaches (500-m walk), good birdwatching along the sandbar that holds the lake back from the sea and many lakeside activities based at the delightful caravan park.

Pacific Palms and Bluey's Beach

Four kilometres north of Smiths Lake is the small community of **Pacific Palms** fringing the southern shores of Lake Wallis. Two kilometres east are the delightful little communities of **Bluey's Beach**, **Boomerang Beach** and **Elizabeth Beach**. While Pacific Palms boasts its lakeside charms and activities, Bluey's and its associates are something of a local surfing mecca. Bluey's Beach itself is idyllic and further north, beyond Boomerang Point, Boomerang Beach is only marginally less attractive. Further north, the rather unfortunately named Pimply Rock and Charlotte Head give way to **Elizabeth Beach**, which is an absolute stunner.

Forster-Tuncurry and around → For listings, see pages 170-177. Colour map 3, C2.

The twin coastal towns of Forster-Tuncurry, which straddle Wallis Lake and the Cape Hawke Harbour, are a favourite domestic holiday destination forming the northern fringe of the park and providing the northern gateway to the superb Great Lakes Region. Although the towns themselves have some fine beaches and numerous water-based activities, it is the lakes, beaches and forests of the Booti Booti and Myall Lakes National Parks to the south that keep visitors coming back. As one of the most appealing coastal regions between Sydney and Byron Bay, a few days here are highly recommended. For all the necessary amenities Forster is the place to stay but there are some superb alternatives in the national park and coastal villages to the south; see Myall Lakes National Park, page 167.

Ins and outs

The **Great Lakes VIC** ⓘ *beside the river on Little St, Forster, T6554 8799, www.greatlakes.org.au, daily 0900-1700*, serves Forster-Tuncurry and the Great Lakes (Myall) Region as far south as Tea Gardens and Hawks Nest. To find your way around the twin towns and region ask for the free *Cartoscope Great Lakes Region Map*. The Great Lakes District Map ($12) is recommended if you intend to explore the Myall Lakes and National Park fully. The VIC also supplies NPWS camping and national parks information.
▸▸ *See Transport, page 175.*

Sights

Many short-term visitors find ample satisfaction on Forster Beach, which sits at the mouth of the Hawke Harbour Inlet, just north of Forster's main drag, Head Street, but better beaches await your attention further east. **Pebbly Beach**, only a short walk along the coast from Forster Beach (or alternatively accessed by car, just beyond the junction of Head Street and MacIntosh Street), is a great spot for families and despite the name does possess some sand. At the western end of town, **One Mile Beach** is the town's true favourite, offering great views and good surfing at its northern end. It is best accessed via Boundary Street, south off Head Street/Bennetts Head Road, then east down Strand Street. **Bennetts Head**, at the terminus of Bennetts Head Road, also provides good views south along One Mile Beach, north to Halliday's Point and straight down into almost unbelievably clear waters.

If you can drag yourself away from the town beaches, the **Booti Booti National Park**, straddling the Lakes Way and the distinctly svelte strip of terra firma between Lake Wallis and the ocean, is well worth investigating. At the park's northern fringe, head east along Minor Road (just south of Forster, off the Lakes Way) and climb to the top of **Cape Hawke** where there is a lookout tower (40 minutes return). **McBride's Beach** sits in almost perfect isolation below and is one of those beaches that instantly has you mesmerized. It is as good as it looks and the ideal place to escape for the day, provided you are up for the 20-minute walk from the parking area just west of the lookout car park. To the south **Seven Mile Beach** stretches to **Booti Hill**, **The Ruins** and **Charlotte Head**. The Ruins has a good NPWS campsite and the southern edge of the park offers some excellent walks, with the 7-km track from The Ruins to Elizabeth Beach being recommended. **Elizabeth Beach** is another regional gem that has the habit of detaining all who visit – sometimes for days! On the western side of Lakes Way, **Wallis Lake** provides saltwater swimming, fishing, boating and numerous picnic sites.

● Sydney to Port Macquarie listings

For Sleeping and Eating price codes and other relevant information, see Essentials pages 28-33.

Sleeping

Newcastle and Hunter Valley *p162*
Newcastle has a wide range to suit all budgets and is a good venue to base yourself to enjoy the laid-back beach culture while still within range of the Hunter Valley. There are dozens of B&Bs, guesthouses, self-contained cottages and restaurants set amongst the vineyards of Hunter Valley, mainly around Pokolbin and Rothbury. If you are on a budget or searching for a bargain, aim to stay midweek, when accommodation is cheaper. In and around Cessnock you will find operators have to offer lower rates due to

the huge competition in and around the vineyards. Contact the Hunter Valley (Wine Country Tourism) VIC, see page 162.
LL Casuarina Restaurant and Country Inn, 1014 Hermitage Rd, Pokolbin, T4998 7888, www.casuarinainn.com.au. One of several world-class establishments combining fine accommodation with fine dining. It offers 9 beautifully appointed, themed suites from the 'French Bordello' to the 'British Empire'.
LL Peppers Guest House, Ekerts Rd, Pokolbin, T4993 8999, www.peppers.com.au. 48 de luxe rooms, suites and a private homestead. All beautifully appointed and with a tariff to match. The homestead has all the usual extras, including pool, spa and the obligatory open fire. The in-house **Chez Pok Restaurant**, see page 173, is widely regarded as one of the best restaurants in the area.

L-B Newcastle Backpackers, 42 & 44 Denison St, Newcastle, T4969 3436, www.backpackersnewcastle.com.au. Traditional home-style hostel with excellent welcoming and helpful hosts. Well located and with the added plus of a heated pool. Free pick-ups from bus or train.

A Hunter Country Lodge, 1476 Wine Country Drive, North Rothbury, T4938 1744, www.huntercountrylodge.com.au. A quirky motel/restaurant combo with log cabin-style rooms. **Shakey Tables** restaurant, page 173, is equally quirky and adds to the attraction.

B-E Hunter Valley YHA, 100 Wine Country Drive, Nulkaba (near Cessnock), T4991 3278, www.yha.com.au. A purpose-built hostel set on 26 acres in the heart of vineyard country. Offers spacious dorms, doubles and twins (some en suite). Sauna, pool, outdoor barbecue and wood-fired pizza oven. It also offers its own wine tours and bike hire.

B-E Newcastle Beach YHA, 30 Pacific St, Newcastle, T4925 3544, www.yha.com.au. Housed in a gracious heritage building, complete with chandeliers, ballroom, large open fireplaces and leather armchairs. Deservingly popular, it offers numerous spacious dorms and doubles and the odd family and single room. Also on offer is internet, free use of surf/boogie boards. An added attraction is the weekly all-you-can-eat barbecues and pizza nights. Parking (metered) can be a problem during the day.

C-D Cessnock Hotel, 234 Wollombi Rd, Cessnock, T4990 1002, www.huntervalley hotels.com.au. Traditional town hotel-cum-pub with 18 comfy rooms and a popular bistro. Good value and a fine chance to meet the locals.

Nelson Bay and around *p165, map p164*
There is plenty of choice in and around Nelson Bay, from resorts and modern self-contained apartment blocks to tidy B&Bs and koala-infested hostels.

L-A Shoal Bay Resort and Spa, Shoal Bay Rd, T4981 1555, www.shoalbayresort.com.au. Enjoying a solid reputation, this resort has apartments, suites, family and standard rooms (all en suite) with B&B or half board, pool, à la carte, casual dining and a top-quality day spa. Located overlooking the bay and near to all amenities.

L-B Baggies at Dutchies, 9 Burbong St, Nelson Bay, T4984 9570, www.dutchies.com.au. Very tidy, self-contained apartments with both standard units and a de luxe unit with good deck views across the harbour and a spa.

L-E Shoal Bay Holiday Park, Shoal Bay Rd, T4984 3411, shoalbay@ beachsideholidays.com.au. Excellent beachside, modern and friendly motor park. It is close to all amenities and offers the full range of accommodation options, including camping. Great camp kitchen.

C-E Samurai Beach Bungalows, corner of Frost Rd and Robert Connell Close, approach from Nelson Bay Rd, Anna Bay, T4982 1921, samurai@nelsonbay.com. This eco-friendly YHA affiliate is recommended. Although on the bus route, it is some distance from Nelson Bay (5 km) but its position amidst bush at the edge of the Tomaree National Park gives it a more relaxed atmosphere. Accommodation options range from dorm to en suite double bungalows (with TV and mini kitchen). The general facilities are also excellent. Free sand, surf and boogie board hire, bike hire and pick-ups. Recommended.

Barrington Tops National Park *p166*
The local VICs have full accommodation listings including the numerous quaint B&Bs that surround the park. The NPWS can also supply details of the many campsites.

L-B Barringtons Country Retreat, 1941 Chichester Dam Rd, 23 km north of Dungog, T4995 9269, www.thebarringtons.com.au. A popular bush resort offering comfortable lodges, à la carte (BYO) restaurant, pool, spa and organized activities such as horse riding.

L-B Salisbury Lodges T4995 3285, www.salisburylodges.com.au. On the southern slopes of the national park about 40 km northwest of Dungog, this establishment gets consistently good reviews. Peaceful, good facilities with spas and log fires in 3 lodges, a de luxe spa room and very cute cabin. Also in-house restaurant.

F Gloucester River Camping Area, Gloucester Tops Rd, T6538 5300. Fine riverside spot at the park boundary and comes complete with tame kangaroos but no showers. No bookings required.

Myall Lakes National Park *p167*
LL-L Bombah Point Eco Cottages, 10 km from Bulahdelah on the same road as Eco Point Myall Shores Resort (see below), Bombah Point, T4997 4401, www.bombah.com.au. Consists of 6 very classy, self-contained, modern eco-friendly cottages in a peaceful setting. Very popular, so book ahead.

LL-F EcoPoint Myall Shores Resort, Bombah Point, T4997 4495, www.ecopoint.com.au. Provides a range of accommodation from luxury waterfront villas, en suite cabins and budget bungalows to shady powered and non-powered sites. There is also a small licensed restaurant, café/bar, fuel, a small store, boat and canoe hire.

L-E Sandbar Caravan Park, 3434 The Lakes Way, Sandbar, T6554 4095, sandbar@paspaley.com.au. This lakeside park offers self-contained cabins, powered and non-powered sites, barbecue, kiosk, fuel, canoe and bike hire and a 9-hole golf course.

A-C Bluey's by the Beach, 186 Boomerang Dr, Pacific Palms, T6554 0665, www.blueys bythebeach.com.au. A good motel option with 9 tidy units, an outdoor pool and spa, all within a short stroll from the beach.

A-E Seal Rocks Camping Reserve, Kinka Rd, Seal Rocks, T4997 6164, www.sealrocks campingreserve.com.au. Out of the 3 campsites in and around Seal Rocks, this has the best facilities. It overlooks the main beach and offers a handful of self-contained cabins, powered and non-powered sites.

B BreakFree Moby's Beachside Retreat, Redgum Rd (off Boomerang Drive), Pacific Palms, T1800 655322, www.breakfreemobys.com.au.

Boutique-style, contemporary 1- to 3- bedroom villas, with a smart restaurant, pool and spa. Also convenient for surf beaches.

Forster-Tuncurry and around *p169*
L-A Tokelau guesthouse, 2 Manning St, T6557 5157, www.tokelau.com.au. Opposite the bridge on the north bank (Tuncurry). Historic and beautifully renovated heritage home offering 2 cosy en suites, with spa or a traditional clawfoot bath.

L-E Forster Beach Caravan Park, Reserve Rd, T1800 240632, www.forsterbeachcaravan.com.au. Centrally placed park right beside the Harbour Inlet and Forster Beach, within walking distance of Forster town centre. It has a good range of cabins and barbecues but lacks privacy.

C-E Lanis Holiday Island, 33 Lakes Way (near Bright St Intersection), T6554 6273, www.toptouristparks.com.au. Holiday park with good facilities located on the banks of Wallis Lake and boasting its own 25 ha bushland island for tent sites. There are spas in the self-contained cabins, en suite powered sites, pools and Wi-Fi.

F NPWS Ruins campsite, beneath Booti Hill at what is known as the 'Green Cathedral' about 20 km south, T6591 0300. The best bet out of town. Great position, beach or lakeside, with good coastal and forest walks. Self-registration, hot showers, but no fires allowed.

Eating

Newcastle and Hunter Valley *p164*
The main venues for fine dining in Newcastle are Queens Wharf and the Promenade beside the river, while Beaumont St in the suburb of Hamilton has the widest selection of lively and affordable cafés and pubs. In the Lower Hunter Valley the best restaurants are mostly found in the hotels of the vineyards. You can expect to pay more for a meal here (most often with a main between $25-35), but the quality almost always makes up for it. Book well in advance.

Chez Pok at Peppers Guest House , Ekerts Rd, T4998 7596, www.peppers.com.au. Daily for breakfast, lunch and dinner. Popular, top-class restaurant, offering local fare with a French, Asian and Italian edge. Booking essential.

Scratchley's, 200 Wharf Rd, on the Promenade, Newcastle, T4929 1111, www.scratchleys.com.au. Mon-Sat 1130 for lunch and 1730 for dinner, and open all day Sunday from 1130. Something of a regional institution over the last decade combining excellent cuisine – mainly seafood and steak – with great views across the river. Again, book ahead.

The Cellar Restaurant, Broke Rd, Pokolbin, T4998 7584, www.the-cellar-restaurant.com.au. Daily for lunch, Mon-Sat for dinner. Highly regarded.

Queens Wharf Brewery, 150 Wharf Rd, Newcastle, T4929 6333. Located on the city's foreshore this is one of its most popular hotels, with good food and live entertainment on Sun afternoons.

Shakey Tables, Hunter Country Lodge, 220 Cessnock-Branxton Rd, North Rothbury, T4938 1744, www.shakeytables.com.au. Daily for dinner and Sun from 1230. An unusual and colourfully decorated place for a tasty meal.

Kent Hotel, 59 Beaumont St, Newcastle, T4961 3303. One of many traditional and often historic pubs in the city, which can provide quality, quantity and good value. This hotel also hosts live gigs most evenings.

Nelson Bay and around *p165, map p164*
Most of Nelson Bay's eateries are to be found in the D'Albora Marina Complex on Victoria Pde.

Merretts at Peppers Anchorage, Corlette Point Rd, Corlette, T4984 0352. Daily for breakfast, lunch and dinner. This is a fine dining, award-winning option. It's fully licensed, has a varied traditional Australian menu and comes recommended, especially for seafood or set lunches.

Bubs, 1 Teramby St (just west of D'Albora Marina Complex), Nelson Bay, T4984 3917. Daily 1100-1800. Good fish and chips.

Inner Lighthouse Café, Nelson Head, above Little Beach, T4984 2505. Daily 1000-1600. A decent café with great harbour views. For something different consider the dinner cruise options with **Moonshadow**, from $65, see Activities and tours, page 174

Myall Lakes National Park *p167*
Oyster Hut, Marine Pde, Tea Gardens, T4997 0579. This is the place to sample local fare, such as fresh, locally harvested oysters.

Forster-Tuncurry and around *p169*
Other than the fish and chip shops at **Beach St Seafoods** 1 Wallis St, you will find more value seafood and pub grub at the popular **Lakes and Ocean Hotel**, 10 Little St, T6555 6005. Across the bridge, the **Fisherman's** Co-operative on the riverbank (right, heading north) is also a good bet.

Bella Bellissimo, Memorial Drive, T6555 6411. Good value Italian dining, friendly family atmosphere. Lake views.

Paradise Café, 51 Little St, T6554 7017. Tues-Sun 0800-1600. A regular award winner set overlooking Wallis Lake and one that seems to maintain its good reputation beyond just the location.

⊛ Festivals and events

Newcastle and Hunter Valley *p164*
The highlight of the busy events calendar is the wonderfully hedonistic and convivial **Lovedale Long Lunch**, held over a weekend every **May** where several top wineries and chefs combine with music and art, www.lovedalelonglunch.com.au.
Other top events include the **Jazz in the Vines Festival**, www.jazzinthevines.com.au; **Opera in the Vines** and the **Newcastle Mattara and Maritime Festival**, www.mattarafestival.org.au, all held in **Oct**.

▲ Activities and tours

Newcastle and Hunter Valley p164
Harbour cruises
Moonshadow, T4984 9388,
www.moonshadow.com.au. Modern
catamaran company offering lunch and
dinner cruises, dolphin watching 1-3 hrs from
$26, children $13.50.
Nova Cruises, T0400-381787, www.nova
cruises.com.au. Whale watching or harbour
cruises and Hunter Valley tours. All
entertaining and good value. Whale watching
cruises Wed, Sat and Sun 1000 from $60,
children $35.

Hot air balloon tours
Balloon Aloft, Rothbury, T4991 1955,
www.balloonaloft.com. From around $299.
Hunter Valley Hot Air Ballooning, T1800
818191, www.huntervalleyhotair
ballooning.com.au.

Wine tours
If you have the time, the best way to
experience the area's delights is to splash out
on 3 days of relaxation, vineyard tours, fine
dining and a stay at one of its many cosy
B&Bs. However, for most a day tour taking in
about 5 wineries with numerous tastings and
the purchase of 1 or 2 bottles of their
favourite vintage will have to suffice. There
are numerous tour operators offering a whole
host of options and modes of transport, from
the conventional coaches and mini-vans to
horse-drawn carriages and bikes. Most of the
smaller operators will pick you up from your
hotel and many can arrange lunch or dinner.
Hunter Valley Cadillac Tours, T4966 4059,
www.cadillactours.com.au. Tours in restored
classic Cadillac convertibles.
Hunter Valley Classic Carriages, T4991 3655,
www.huntervalleyclassiccarriages.com.au. More
horse, less power, half day from $50, full $85.
Hunter Valley Cycling, T0418-281480,
www.huntervalleycycling.com.au. For
traditional pedal power, from $30.

Vineyard Shuttle Service, T4991 3655,
www.vineyardshuttle.com.au. Local mini-van
firm offering flexibility and good value, from $42.

Nelson Bay and around p165, map p164
The VIC has a comprehensive list of daily
tours and excursions and can assist with
bookings. The main activities are cruising
with dolphin, whale-watching and island
trips, 4WD and horse trekking excursions to
the vast Stockton Bight sand dunes as well as
diving and fishing. Tour schedules are
reduced in winter.

Diving
Pro Dive, D'Albora Marina, Teramby Rd, T4981
4331, www.prodivenelsonbay.com, and **Feet
First**, T4984 2092, www.feetfirstdive.com.au,
both offer local dive and snorkelling trips in the
Fly Point Aquatic Reserve, 1 km east of the
town centre.

Dolphin and whale watching
Dolphin watching (year round) and whale
watching (Jun-Nov) are top of the agenda,
with numerous vessels operating.
Imagine, T4984 9000, www.imagine
cruises.com.au. Comfortable and less
crowded cruises of 1½-4 hrs on a sail
catamaran. Options include dolphin
swimming, from $30-229. Recommended.
Moonshadow, Shop 3, 35 Stockton St, T4984
9388, www.moonshadow.com.au. The
biggest operator with the largest, fastest and
most comfortable vessels (Supercats). They
offer daily cruises from 1½-4 hrs in search of
sea mammals (1030, 1330 and 1530 from
$26/$60), 7-hr trips to Broughton Island off
the Myall Coast (Tue-Thu and Sun 1000 from
$75) and twilight dinner and entertainment
trips around the port, from 1900, $65.

6WD, 4WD, quad bike and horse
trekking tours
Stockton Beach, south of Nelson Bay, with its
incredible dune habitat and wrecks, provides
a major playground for 4WD and quad bike
tours, as well as horse trekking.

Moonshadow 4WD Tours, T4984 4760, www.moonshadow4wd.com.au. Standard 4WDs, a 6X6 and sand-boarding shuttles, 1-3 hrs, from $23-78. Their extended 3-hr trip takes in the *Sygna* shipwreck and 'Tin City', a hidden ramshackle settlement, threatened by the encroaching sand.

Johno's Getaways Beach Fishing, T0412688873, johno@nelsonbay.com. Dune adventures with fishing as the main activity.

Quad Bike King, T4919 0088, www.quadbikeking.com.au. As the name suggests, quad-bike tours of the dunes with sand-tobogganing, 2 hrs from $75. A great all-weather activity.

Rambling Sands Horse Treks, Janet Pde, off Nelson Bay Rd, Salt Ash, T4982 6391. Bush and dune treks of 1½-2 hrs, from $80.

Sahara Trails Horse Riding and Farmstay, T4981 9077, www.saharatrails.com. 1-2 hr bush, coast and beach rides from $50-120. Stay and ride packages are also an option.

Sea kayaking

Blue Water Sea Kayaking, T0405-033518, www.kayakingportstephens.com.au. Guided day or sunset trips suitable for beginners and for the more experienced. Tours start from 1 hr, $25, and they offer pick-ups.

Surfing

Surfing lessons are available with ex-pro **Port Stephens Learn to Surf** at Fingal Bay, T0401-214455, www.portstephens learntosurf.com. Group 2 hrs from $50, private $70, 3-day $135.

Forster-Tuncurry and around *p169*
Boat tours

All manner of watercraft, from barbecue boats to canoes, can be hired along the waterfront.

Dive Forster Cruises, Fisherman's Wharf, T6554 7478, www.diveforster.com.au. Swimming with dolphins. Tours, from $70, $45 non-swimmers, children $25.

Tikki Boatshed, 15 Little St, T6554 6321, opposite the VIC.

Diving

There are several excellent dive sites in the region including Seal Rocks, the *SS Satara* wreck dive, Bennetts Head and the Pinnacles, which are all well known for their grey nurse sharks. There are several local dive operators including **Forster Dive Centre**, 11-13 Little St, T6555 4477, www.forsterdivecentre.com.au, and **Action Divers**, Shop 4, 1-5 Manning St, Tuncurry, T6555 4053, www.actiondivers.com.au.

⊖ Transport

Newcastle and Hunter Valley *p162*
Air

Newcastle Airport, T4928 9800, www.newcastleairport.com.au, is 24 km north of the city centre. **Jet Star**, T131538, www.jetstar.com.au; **Qantas Link**, T131313, www.qantas.com.au; **Regional Express**, T131713, www.rex.com.au; and **Virgin Blue**, T136789, www.virginblue.com.au, offer regional services from Sydney and other destinations.

Port Stephens Coaches, T4982 2940, www.pscoaches.com.au, stops off at the Williamtown (Newcastle) Airport ($6.60) while **Happy Cabby**, T4976 3991, www.happycabby.com, offers transfers to and from **Newcastle** and **Sydney** from $35.

Cessnock-based **Vineyard Shuttle Service**, T4991 3655, operates shuttle services from the airport to **Hunter Valley** accommodation.

Bus and ferry

Local Newcastle Bus and Ferry, T131500, www.newcastlebuses.info, provides local bus and ferry services. Fares start at $3.30 and allow an hour's unlimited travel with an all-day pass costing $9.80. Bus/ferry and train/bus/ferry passes are available.

Ferry Services, T131500, link central **Newcastle** (Queens Wharf) with **Stockton** Mon-Sat 0515-2400, Sun 0830-2200, one way $3, tickets on board. Rover Coaches, 231 Vincent St, Cessnock, T4990 1699, www.rovercoaches.com.au, runs services between **Newcastle** and **Cessnock** as well as an all-day jump-on-jump-off service around the vineyards from $40.

Long distance Coaches stop next to the train station in Newcastle. **Greyhound**, T131499, runs daily **Sydney** and north/southbound services. They stop at all major towns along the **New England Highway**. Countrylink Travel Centre (see under Train below) acts as a booking agent. Port Stephens Coaches, T4982 2940, www.pscoaches.com, also provides daily services to **Sydney** and **Port Stephens**, while **Rover Coaches**, T4990 1699, www.rovercoaches.com.au, covers the **Hunter Valley**. If you intend to pass through the Great Lakes Region and Myall National Park, **Busways**, T4997 4788, runs a daily regional bus service between **Taree** and **Sydney** via **Forster-Tuncurry**, **Bluey's Beach**, **Hawks Nest** and **Newcastle**.

Taxi
If you want to avoid driving between your accommodation and restaurant **Vineyard Shuttle Service**, T4991 3655, in Cessnock, offers local transfers or call a conventional taxi, T4990 1111. **Newcastle Taxis** T133300.

Train
The main train station is located at the far end of Hunter St. **Cityrail**, T131500, has regular daily services to **Sydney**. **Countrylink**, T132232, has a travel centre at the station (daily 0900-1700) and luggage storage. Note state-wide service connections are from Broadmeadow, 5 mins west. The nearest train station for Hunter Valley is Maitland, which links with **Newcastle** and **Sydney**'s Cityrail, T131500. Countrylink, T132232, offers state-wide services to **Queensland** via **Scone**.

Nelson Bay and around *p165, map p164*
Air
The nearest airport is near Newcastle (Williamtown), 30 km south (see page 165).

Bus
Local Port Stephen's Coaches, T4982 2940, www.pscoaches.com, has regular bus services between the airport and Port Stephens and local bus services.
Long distance Coaches stop on Stockton St in Nelson Bay. Port Stephens Coaches, Local above, serves Nelson Bay from Sydney direct. Another alternative is to use the more frequent Newcastle-bound services (see above), then catch the regular daily service from Newcastle to Nelson Bay.
If you intend to pass through the **Great Lakes Region** and **Myall National Park**, Busways, T4983 1560, www.busways.com.au, has daily services between **Taree** and Sydney via **Tuncurry-Forster**, **Bluey's Beach**, **Hawks Nest** and **Newcastle**.

Car
Car hire from **Avis**, Newcastle Airport, T136333.

Ferry
Ferry services, T4126 2117, link **Nelson Bay** with **Tea Gardens**, 4 times daily from Nelson Bay, return $25, children $12.

Train
Train services to **Newcastle** with onward bus connections.

Barrington Tops National Park *p166*
Bus
The only way to access the park by public transport is with the **Forster Bus Service** (No 308), T6554 6431, www.forsterbus.com.au, which accesses **Gloucester**, Mon-Fri, from **Forster-Tuncurry**.

Myall Lakes National Park *p167*
Bus
Busways, T4983 1560, and **Forster Bus Service**, T6554 6431, operate daily local bus services around **Tea Gardens** and **Hawks Nest** and south as far as **Pacific Palms**, **Bluey's Beach** and **Smith Lake** (Mon-Fri). Busways also runs regional bus services between **Taree** and **Sydney** via

Forster-Tuncurry, Bluey's Beach, Hawks
Nest and Newcastle.

Ferry
Port Stephens Ferry Services, T4126 2117,
links **Nelson Bay** with **Tea Gardens**, daily
(from Nelson Bay 0830,1200, 1530 and 1630),
return $25, children $12. Boat hire in **Tea
Gardens** and **Hawks Nest**.

Forster-Tuncurry and around *p169*
Bus
Forster Bus Service, T6554 6431,
www.forsterbus.com.au, operates daily local
bus services around the twin towns Mon-Fri.
Long-distance buses stop outside the VIC on
Little St. The VIC also acts as a booking
agent. **Greyhound**, T131499, services from
Sydney or **Port Macquarie**. Busways, T4983
1560, www.busways .com.au, also offers
services between **Taree** and **Sydney** via
**Tuncurry, Forster, Bluey's Beach, Hawks
Nest** and **Newcastle**.

Train
The nearest train station is at Taree.
Countrylink, T132232, offers daily services
north and south. **Busways** (see above) or
Eggins Coaches, Taree, T65522700, provide
links between the train station and Forster.

Directory

Newcastle and Hunter Valley *p162*
Banks Most of the major banks with ATMs
can be found along the Hunter St Mall in
Newcastle. **Internet** Regional Library,
Laman St, T4974 5300, Mon-Fri 0930-1700, Tue
0930-200, Sat 0930-1700. Book ahead. **Patsans**,
301 Hunter St, T4925 3996. **Post
office** Ground floor, 1 Market St, Mon-Fri
0830-1700. **Useful numbers** Police, corner
of Church and Watt streets, T4929 0999.

Nelson Bay and around *p165, map p164*
Banks Most of the major branches with
ATMs are to be found along Stockton or
Magnus St, Nelson Bay. **Internet** AACF,
Shop 2, 106 Magnus St, T4984 3225. Until
2100. **Tomaree Library**, Salamander
Shopping Centre, T4982 0670. Mon, Wed, Fri
1000-1800, Tue, Thu 1000-2000, Sat
0930-1400. **Police** Government Rd, Nelson
Bay, T4981 1244. **Post office** 97 Magnus St.
Mon-Fri 0900-1700.

Myall Lakes National Park *p167*
The main amenities such as **post offices**,
service stations and **supermarkets** can be
found on Marine Drive in Tea Gardens,
Mungo Brush Rd and Booner St in Hawks
Nest and Boomerang Drive in Bluey's Beach.

Forster-Tuncurry and around *p169*
Internet Available at library on Breeze Pde,
T6591 7256 (Tue-Sat), or the **Leading Edge**,
16 Beach St, T6554 5006.

Port Macquarie to Byron Bay

There are some great stops on this route. Port Macquarie itself is often unfairly overlooked. The fast developing coastal town of South West Rocks near Smoky Cape and the sublime coastal Hat Head National Park are relaxing places to explore. For many the main destination on the north NSW coast is laid-back Byron Bay, which is usually the last port of call before crossing the state border. It's well worth diverting inland, however, especially to the arty village of Bellingen, a pleasant stop on the way to the Dorrigo and New England National Parks, both of which offer some superb views and bush walks.

Port Macquarie → *For listings, see pages 192-204. Colour map 3, C2*

Officially declared as possessing the best year-round climate in Australia and blessed with a glut of superb beaches, engaging historic sites, wildlife-rich suburban nature reserves and water-based activities, the former penal colony of Port Macquarie is rightfully recognized as one of the best holiday destinations to be found anywhere in NSW. Due perhaps to more domestically oriented advertising, or simply the 6 km of road between the town and the Pacific Highway, it seems the vast majority of international travellers miss Port Macquarie completely as they charge northwards towards more high-profile destinations such as Byron Bay. But if you make the effort and short detour, you will not be disappointed.

Ins and outs

Getting there Port Macquarie is 10 km east of the Pacific Highway along the Oxley Highway. The airport is 3 km away. Long-distance buses serve the town and there is a train station 18 km away with connecting buses to the town centre. ▸▸ *See Transport, page 202.*

Tourist information There is a **VIC** ⓘ *The Glasshouse, corner of Clarence St and Hay St, T6581 8000, www.portmacquarieinfo.com.au, Mon-Fri 0830-1700, Sat-Sun 0900-1600.* **NPWS** ⓘ *152 Horton St, T6586 8300, midnorthcoast.region@environment.nsw.gov.au, Mon-Fri 0900-1630.*

Sights

Allman Hill on Stewart Street is home to the settlement's first cemetery (where the gravestones reveal the hardships and life expectancies). Nearby is Gaol Point Lookout, site of the first gaol, now offering pleasant views across the harbour and Town Beach. If you would like to quietly search the heavens, visit the **Observatory** ⓘ *Rotary Park on William St, www.pmobs.org.au, viewing nights Wed and Sun 1930 EST, 2015 DST, $8, children $7.* On the eastern side of Rotary Park is Town Beach, the most convenient for swimming with good surfing at the northern end. South of here, the **Maritime Museum** ⓘ *6 William St, T6583 4505, daily 1000-1600, $4, children $2,* is worth a look for a delve into the coast's history.

The 1869 **Courthouse** ⓘ *corner of Clarence St and Hay St, T6584 1818, Mon-Sat 1000-1500, $2,* served the community for over a century and has been refurbished faithfully. Across the road is the **Historical Museum** ⓘ *$5,* housed in a former convict-built store (1835) and containing 14 rooms of historical artefacts.

St Thomas's Church ⓘ *corner of Hay St and William St, T6584 1033, Tue-Fri 0930-1200 and 1400-1600, donation welcome,* is the fifth oldest Anglican Church still in use in Australia, built by convict labour in the late 1820s. Its most interesting feature actually lies

Port Macquarie

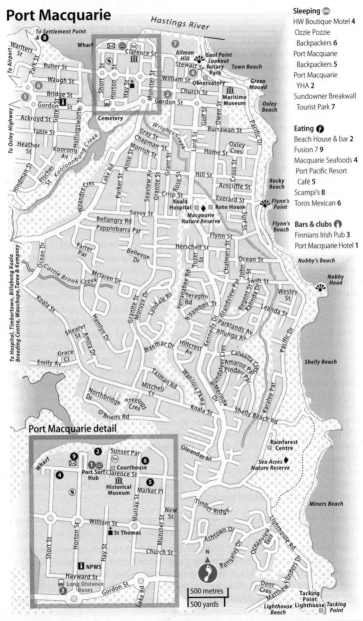

Hastings River

To Settlement Point & 8

Wharf

Warlters St
Park St
To Airport
Buller St
Waugh St
Short St
Horton St
Clarence St
Stewart St
Munster St
Hay St
Allman Hill Lookout
Gaol Point Rotary Park
Town Beach
Observatory
William St
Church St
Bridge St
Gordon St
Gore St
To Oxley Highway
Ackroyd St
Hollingsworth
Cemetery
Maritime Museum
Green Mound
Oxley Beach
Table St
Heather St
Hindmans
Pictts St
Koorong Av
Kooloonbung Creek
Lake Rd
Wrights Creek
Gray St
Chapman St
Morrish St
Gordon St
Burrawan St
Golf St
Lord St
Owen St
Pacific Dr
Nyandra Cres
Parker St
Anne St
Seaview Av
Granite St
Rose St
Grant St
Hill St
Home St
Oxley Cres
Rocky Beach
Arncliffe St
Cross St
Crisp St
Koala Hospital
Roto House
Everard St
Flynn's Point
Savoy St
Bellangry Rd
Pappinbarra Par
Macquarie Nature Reserve
Flynn's Beach
Farrer Par
Bellevue Dr
Flynn St
Herschell St
Tozer St
Chalmers St
Ocean Dr
Cattle Brook Creek
Ocean Dr
Mclaren Dr
Granite St
Monya Dr
Lyndale Av
Yarranabee Rd
Teraglin Rd
Boambee St
John St
Grandview Par
Swift St
Regent St
Kalinda St
Westey St
Leanda St
Nobby's Beach
Nobby Head
Koala St
Shearer St
Hamlyn Dr
Anita Dr
Braemar Dr
Hillcrest Av
Kennedy Dr
Parklands Av
Atlunga Av
Calwalla Cres
Amaroo Par
Pindar Par
Pacific Dr
Karalee Par
Shelly Beach
Grace Cl
Emily Av
Tasman Rd
Mitchell Ct
Wanjara Pkwy
Bundarra Cres
Belinda
Northbridge Dr
Treetops Cres
O'Briens Rd
Koala St
Shelly Beach Rd
To Hospital, Timbertown, Billabong Koala Breeding Centre, Wauchope, Taree & Kempsey
Oleander Av
Rainforest Centre
Sea Acres Nature Reserve
Miners Beach

Port Macquarie detail

Wharf
Sunset Par
Courthouse
Port Surf Hub
Clarence St
Historical Museum
Market Pl
Short St
Horton St
Hay St
Murray St
William St
Munster St
St Thomas
New St
Church St
NPWS
Hayward St
Long Distance Buses
Gordon St
Lake Rd
Timber Ridge
Ashtown Dr
Bangalay Dr
Oceanview Terr
Lighthouse Rd
Flinders Dr
Matthew Flinders Dr
Dent Cres
Tacking Point
Lighthouse Beach
Lighthouse
Tacking Point

N

500 metres
500 yards

Sleeping
HW Boutique Motel 4
Ozzie Pozzie Backpackers 6
Port Macquarie Backpackers 5
Port Macquarie YHA 2
Sundowner Breakwall Tourist Park 7

Eating
Beach House & bar 2
Fusion 7 9
Macquarie Seafoods 4
Port Pacific Resort Café 5
Scampi's 8
Toros Mexican 6

Bars & clubs
Finnians Irish Pub 3
Port Macquarie Hotel 1

buried beneath one of the pews, in the form of one Captain Rolland – the port's former gaol supervisor – who died from sunstroke. He was buried inside to avoid his body being dug up by vengeful convicts.

A healthy suburban population of koalas lives in the area's nature reserves and parks and numerous roadside signs are testament to this. In town, one of the best places to spot a wild koala is in Sea Acres Nature Reserve (see below), but if you have no joy there is always the **Koala Hospital** ① *Lord St, T6584 2399, www.koalahospital.org.au, daily, donation welcome*, in the Macquarie Nature Reserve. Although you cannot see any sick marsupials, some of the pre-released critters are usually on display. Feeding takes place daily at 1500 and 1630. There's also the **Billabong Koala Breeding Centre** ① *61 Billabong Drive, 10 km from the town centre, T6585 1260, www.billabongkoala.com.au, 0900-1700. $18, children $11*, which not only provides copious koala patting (1030, 1330 and 1530) but also the usual array of Australian natives such as wallabies, wombats and rainbow lorikeets in 2.5ha of landscaped gardens, with a café, barbecue and picnic areas. Step back in time with a visit to **Timbertown Wauchope** ① *Oxley Highway, west of Wauchope, T6586 1940, www.timbertown.com.au, about 20 mins' drive west of Port Macquarie, daily 0930-1530, $5, children $3, family $12,* where you can ride the steam train, watch the bullock team display, observe the timber craftsmen at work and smell the coals of the blacksmith's fire.

The beaches that fringe the western suburbs of the town from the Hastings River mouth south to Tacking Point and beyond are simply superb, offering excellent swimming, fishing, surfing, walks and views. Whale-watching tours operate from June to November; prices start from $40 per person. For further details, contact **Greater Port Macquarie VIC** ① *T1300 303155*. North of the town, the great swathe of **North Beach**, stretching 15 km to Point Plomer, fringed by the diverse coastal habitats of Limeburners Creek Nature Reserve, provides almost total solitude. South, beyond Green Mound, Oxley Beach and Rocky Beach are less accessible. Beyond those, Flynn's Beach and Nobby's Beach are two other favourite spots with great views and good swimming as well as fossicking and snorkelling on the extensive rock platforms.

South of Nobby Head the coastal fringe gives way to Shelly Beach and the 72-ha coastal **Sea Acres Nature Reserve** ① *T6582 2930, 0900-1630, $6, children $3, under 7s free, family $15,* one of the best places in town to spot wild koalas (particularly in the late afternoon). This sublime piece of rainforest is preserved with a 1.3 km boardwalk providing the ideal viewpoint. The boardwalk starts and finishes at the Rainforest Centre, which itself houses an interesting range of displays, a café and shop. Guided tours are available and recommended. Then it is on to Miners Beach, reached by coastal paths from the same car park. This is a favourite spot for naturists. At the terminus of Lighthouse Road is Tacking Point, named by Matthew Flinders in 1802, and the pocket-sized Tacking Point Lighthouse built in 1879. From there you are afforded great views south along Lighthouse Beach towards Bonny Hills and North Brother Hill.

South West Rocks and Hat Head → *For listings, see pages 192-204. Colour map 3, B2*

South West Rocks is the best-kept secret on the NSW north coast. It has everything that Byron Bay has, except the footprints. Long swathes of golden sand, great fishing and swimming, a cliff-top lighthouse, stunning views and a superb local national park – Hat Head – combine to make South West Rocks the ideal place to get away from it all for a few days. Here, you can watch dolphins surfing rather than people. South West Rocks is best reached and explored using your own transport.

Ins and outs

South West Rocks Visitors' Centre ① *1 Ocean Av, T6566 7099, www.kempsey.nsw.gov.au, 0900-1700.* **Kempsey VIC** ① *South Kempsey Park, off Pacific Highway, Kempsey, T6563 1555, www.kempsey.midcoast.com.au, daily,* is a good source of information. They have NPWS national parks information.➤ *See Transport, page 203.*

Sights

South West Rocks sits at the southern bank of the Macleay River mouth and the western end of Trail Bay, where the colourful, wave-eroded rocks that earned the village its name form the perfect playground for swimmers and snorkellers. At the eastern end of Trial Bay the charming settlement of **Arakoon** fringes the Arakoon State Recreation Area and Laggers Point, site of the pink granite monolith of **Trial Bay Gaol** ① *T6566 6168, 0900-1700, $8,* built in 1886 and now housing a small museum that offers an insight into the torrid existence of its former inmates. Trial Bay was named after *The Trial,* a vessel that was stolen by former convicts and wrecked in the bay in 1816. Several other vessels with more conventional crews were wrecked in Trial Bay in the 1970s. A few rusting remnants still reach out from their sandy graves. At the terminus of Wilson Street, at the western end of Arakoon, is **Little Bay,** with its sublime, people-free beach. The car park also provides access to the **Graves Monument walking track** (2 km return) which provides memorable views back across Trial Bay and the Trial Bay Gaol. **Gap Beach,** accessed a little further south, is another fine spot, especially for the more adventurous surfer. South of Arakoon (3 km), Lighthouse Road provides access to the northern fringe of the **Hat Head National Park, Smoky Beach** and the **Smoky Cape Lighthouse.** The 1891 lighthouse is one of the tallest and oldest in NSW and provides stunning views south to Crescent Head and north down to the beckoning solitude of North Smoky Beach.

South of South West Rocks, accessed via Hat Head Village Road and Kinchela, the small village and headland of **Hat Head** sits in the heart of the national park separating the long swathes of Smoky Beach north and Killick Beach to the south. The village has a caravan park, limited amenities and walking access to Hat Hill, Korogoro Point, Connor's Beach and the Hungry Hill Rest Area.

Bellingen and Dorrigo National Park → *For listings, see pages 192-204. Colour map 3, B2.*

Away from the coast, sitting neatly on the banks of the Bellinger River in the heart of the Bellinger Valley, is the pleasant country village of Bellingen, renowned for its artistic and alternative community, its markets, music festivals and laid-back ambience. Simple relaxation or country walks are the name of the game for travellers here, before they continue further inland to explore the superb national parks of Dorrigo (see page 182), and Oxley and New England (see page 183), or resume the relentless journey northwards up the coast. The village has its own nickname used affectionately by the locals – Bello.

Ins and outs

Getting there There are no long-distance connections to Bellingen – you must travel to Nambucca Heads or Urunga and then get a connection.➤ *For transport details for Dorrigo National Park, see page 202.*

Tourist information **Bellingen Shire VIC** ⓘ *T6655 5711, www.bellingen.com, Mon-Sat 0900-1700, Sun 1000-1400,* is beside the Pacific Highway in Urunga, just south of the Bellingen turn-off. Ask for a free street map of the town. In Bellingen itself you will find the **Waterfall Way VIC** ⓘ *29 Hyde St, T6655 1522, www.waterfallway.com, T6655 5711, www.bellingen.com, Mon-Sat 0900-1700, Sun 1000-1400.* Further afield the **Dorrigo VIC** ⓘ *Hickory St, T6657 2486, www.dorrigo.com.au, 1000-1600,* offers local listings. Ask for a free street map. **NPWS Dorrigo National Park Rainforest Centre** ⓘ *Dome Rd, T6657 2309, www.nationalparks.nsw.gov.au,* supplies details on national parks, walks and other local information.

Bellingen

Bellingen's peaceful tree-lined streets are lined with some obvious heritage buildings, many of which are protected by the National Trust. The small **Bellingen Museum** ⓘ *Civic Sq, Hyde St, T6655 0289, Mon and Wed-Fri 1000-1200,* contains a low-key collection of photos and artefacts from the mid-1800s. The **Old Butter Factory** ⓘ *Doepel Lane, 0930 to 1700,* on the western approach to the village, and the unmistakable **Yellow Shed** ⓘ *2 Hyde St, 0930 to 1700,* are the two main arts and crafts outlets in the village, selling everything from opals to wind chimes. The Old Butter Factory also has a café and offers a range of relaxation and healing therapies including iridology, massage and a flotation tank. The colourful **Bellingen craft and produce market** is considered one of the best in the region and is held in the local park on the third Saturday of the month. The village also hosts a top quality **Jazz Festival** ⓘ *www.bellingenjazzfestival.com.au,* in mid-August, and the equally popular **Global Carnival** ⓘ *www.globalcarnival.com,* which is an entertaining celebration of world music held in the first week in October.

Nature lovers should take a look at the large (and smelly) flying fox (fruit bat) colony on **Bellingen Island** (which is now no longer an island) beside the river, within easy walking distance of the village. The best place to see the bats is from the Bellingen Caravan Park on Dowle Street (cross the Bridge off Hyde, on to Hammond then turn right into Dowle), while the best time is around dusk when they depart to find food. But even during the day it is an impressive sight indeed as they hang like a thousand fuzzy Christmas decorations from almost every tree.

Dorrigo and Dorrigo National Park

Provided the weather is kind and the clouds do not blind you, you are in for a scenic treat here. Even the **Dorrigo National Park Rainforest Visitors Centre** ⓘ *T6657 2309, 0900-1700,* has amazing views. Sitting right at the edge of the escarpment, the view across the forested slopes and across the Bellinger Valley towards the coast is even better from the slightly shaky 100-m **Skywalk** that projects like a jetty out across the rainforest canopy. From its end you can survey the glorious scene and listen to the strange and distant calls of elusive rainforest birds. You may also see the odd python curled up in a branch or right next to the handrail. The visitors centre itself has some good interpretative displays and a small café. The main office and shop can provide the necessary detail on the excellent rainforest walks (ranging from 400 m to 5 km) that begin from the centre and descend to the very different world beneath the forest canopy.

From the Rainforest Centre it is then a short, scenic 10-km drive along the edge of the escarpment to the **Never Never Picnic Area,** which is a fine network of rainforest walks, including the 5.5-km **Rosewood Creek Track** to **Cedar Falls,** the 4.8-km **Casuarina**

New England and Cathedral Rocks National parks

The 71,207 ha New England National Park is breathtaking. What makes it so special is not only its sense of wilderness and rich biodiversity, but its stunning vistas, Point Lookout being the most popular and accessible viewpoint, and truly memorable. Do not venture here expecting to see those views automatically however. What adds an atmospheric and unpredictable edge to this viewpoint is its height, which, at over 1564 m, often results in a shroud of mist or worse still, sheets of rain. It really can be a glorious day in Armidale and along the coast and yet Point Lookout is like Edinburgh Castle in midwinter. Still, if you can afford a couple of days, the camping, the views and the varied walks around Point Lookout (2.5 km to a full day) are well worthwhile.

Just north of Point Lookout Road, Round Mountain Road (8 km) ventures into the heart of Cathedral Rock National Park. The main feature here is the magnificent granite tors – Cathedral Rocks – and in spring, vivid displays of wild flowers. The 6-km Cathedral Rock Track from the Barokee Rest Area is a circular route with a 200-m diversion to the Rocks.

The VIC and NPWS offices in Armidale and the Dorrigo Rainforest Centre ① T6657 2309, www.environment.nsw.gov.au, stock the relevant leaflets and information surrounding the parks, their walks, camping and self-contained accommodation. To reach the New England and Cathedral Rocks National Parks, Point Lookout Road is unsealed and accessed (signposted) off Waterfall Way, 5 km south of the Waterfall Way/Guyra Road Junction (3 km west of Ebor). It is then 11 km to the park boundary and a further 3 km to Point Lookout.

Falls Track and the 6.4-km **Blackbutt (escarpment edge) Track**. Before heading into Dorrigo township itself, it is worth taking the short 2-km drive to **Griffith's Lookout** for its memorable views across the Bellinger Valley. The road to the lookout is signposted about 1 km south of Dome Road off the Waterfall Way. Just north of Dorrigo (1.5 km), the **Dangar Falls** may prove a disappointment after long dry periods but after rain can become a thunderous torrent of floodwaters.

Coffs Harbour → For listings, see pages 192-204. Colour map 3, B2.

Roughly halfway between Sydney and Brisbane and the only spot on the NSW coast where the Great Dividing Range meets the sea, Coffs Harbour is a favourite domestic holiday resort and the main commercial centre for the northern NSW coast. Surrounded by rolling hills draped in lush banana plantations and pretty beaches, it's a fine spot to kick back for a couple of days. The main activities in town are centred around the attractive marina where regular fishing, whale- and dolphin-watching cruises are on offer, together with highly popular diving and snorkelling trips to the outlying Solitary Islands. The island group and surrounding coast is gazetted as a marine park and considered to have one of the largest marine biodiversities in NSW. Other principal attractions include Muttonbird Island, guarding the entrance to the harbour and offering sanctuary to thousands of burrowing seabirds and, in complete contrast, the kitsch Big Banana complex on the northern edge of the town. Often overlooked is the fast developing, but still pleasant, beachside community of Sawtell, which is worth the trip.

Information

VIC ⓘ *corner of Elizabeth St and Maclean St, T6648 4990, www.coffscoast.com.au, 0900-1700.* Ask for the free Coffs Coast visitors' guide.

Sights

The rather unsightly and uninspiring main drag, **Grafton Street**, has seen something of an improvement recently, with the creation of the Palms Centre Arcade and redevelopment of the Mall and Park Avenue, which, combined, form the hub of the town centre. From the end of the Mall, **High Street** heads 3 km southeast to the **harbour**, which is hemmed in by the town's three main beaches: **Park Beach**, which straddles Coffs

Coffs Harbour

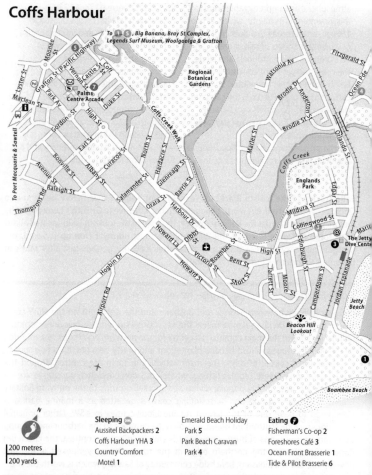

To ① ④ ⑤, Big Banana, Bray St Complex, Legends Surf Museum, Woolgoolga & Grafton

Regional Botanical Gardens

Coffs Creek Walk

Coffs Creek

Englands Park

The Jetty Dive Centre

Jetty Beach

Beacon Hill Lookout

Boambee Beach

N

| 200 metres |
| 200 yards |

Sleeping 🛏
Aussitel Backpackers **2**
Coffs Harbour YHA **3**
Country Comfort Motel **1**

Emerald Beach Holiday Park **5**
Park Beach Caravan Park **4**

Eating 🍴
Fisherman's Co-op **2**
Foreshores Café **3**
Ocean Front Brasserie **1**
Tide & Pilot Brasserie **6**

Creek to the north, **Jetty Beach** beside the harbour and **Boambee Beach** to the south. Park Beach is the most popular and is regularly patrolled in summer. Jetty Beach is considered the safest. The view from **Beacon Hill Lookout**, at the end of Camperdown Street, off High Street, offers fine 360-degree views across the harbour, the coast, and the green rolling hills of the Great Dividing Range to the west. There are also numerous other, excellent beaches, stretching 20 km north all the way to Woolgoolga.

Linked to the mainland by the marina's 500-m sea wall is **Muttonbird Island Nature Reserve**, which offers more than just a pleasant walk and some memorable views back towards the town. From October to April Muttonbird Island and others in the Solitary Island group are home to thousands of breeding wedge-tailed shearwaters (muttonbirds) that nest in a warren of burrows across the entire island. The birds are best viewed just after dusk, when they return in number to feed their mates or chicks hiding deep within the burrows. Although the birds were once easily harvested for food, they are now, thankfully, fully protected. For obvious reasons, do not stray from the main pathway. Also keep a lookout for humpback whales which are often spotted just offshore from June to September.

The **Solitary Islands** offer some fine dive sites with such evocative names as Grey Nurse Gutters and Manta Arch, a wealth of marine life (90 species of coral and 280 species of fish) and the densest colonies of anemones and anemone fish (clown fish) in the world. For more details contact the VIC, see above. Coffs Harbour is one of the cheapest places on the NSW coast to get certified for diving. For details of diving and snorkelling trips, see page 201.

It's incredible that by building an oversized banana next to the main highway, you attract people like bees to honey. Coffs' famous icon and monument of marketing genius, the **Big Banana** ① T6652 4355, www.bigbanana.com, 0900-1600, located just north of the town on the Pacific Highway, fronts a banana plantation that has 'grown' over the years and now hosts a new 'World of Bananas' attraction. As you can imagine it showcases just about all you need to know about bananas, plus a number of long-established activities, from a lookout (free) to toboggan rides, snow-tubing, ice

South Pacific Ocean

Park Beach

Marina Booking Centre
6
2

Marina

◆ Muttonbird Island Nature Reserve

Bars & clubs ⋒
Ex-servicemen's Club **7**
Plantation **5**

skating and the obligatory café and shop selling lots of souvenir banana-meets-koala kitsch. It is, however, perhaps entertainment enough to sit in the café and watch people posing for photos in front of the Big Banana. This in itself will without doubt prove the age-old suspicion that human beings are indeed really weird.

Also north of town is the **Legends Surf Museum** ⓘ *T6653 6536, Gauldrons Rd, left off the Pacific Highway, 1000-1600, $8, children $4*, run by enthusiastic and enigmatic Scott Dillon, ex-master of the waves. There are over 120 classic boards on display as well as the odd canoe, photos and other such enlightening memorabilia.

Sawtell, a seaside village 6 km south of Coffs Harbour, is blessed with some fine beaches and a pleasant laid-back atmosphere that has quietly attracted domestic holidaymakers for years. Now the secret is well and truly out; like most of the East Coast's beachside communities the influx of city 'sea changers' may well prove its very demise. Other than the obvious attractions of the beach, the **Cooinda Aboriginal Art Gallery** ⓘ *Shop 1/4, First Av, T6658 7901, www.cooinda-gallery.com.au*, relocated from Coffs Harbour, is well worth a look. It showcases some excellent examples of the unique and spiritually loaded 'dot-style'.

Coffs Harbour to Byron Bay → *For listings, see pages 192-204. Colour map 3, A3/B2.*

Ins and outs
Clarence Coast Visitor Centre ⓘ *Ferry Park, just south of the turn-off for Yamba, and 2 km south of Maclean, T6645 4121, www.clarencetourism.com, 0900-1700*, has full accommodation, events and activities listings for the region.

Yamba, Angourie and Yuraygir National Park (North)
The coastal fishing town of **Yamba**, 13 km east of the Pacific Highway (exit just before the Clarence River bridge) and on the southern bank of the Clarence River mouth, is famed for its prawn industry and its fine surf beaches. Serving mainly as a domestic holiday destination, it offers the opportunity to spend two or three days away from the mainstream tourist resorts further north. **Main Beach**, below Flinders Park, is the most popular of Yamba's many golden strands but **Turners Beach**, between the main breakwater and lighthouse, **Covent Beach**, between Lovers Point and Main Beach, and **Pippie Beach**, the most southerly, are all equally good. **Clarence River Delta** and **Lake Woolooweyah**, 4 km south, provide boating, fishing and cruising opportunities. The Yamba-Iluka ferry shuttles back and forth daily, providing access to some sublime beaches and bluffs, a stunning rainforest reserve and the wilderness of Bundjalung National Park.

Iluka and Bundjalung National Park
If you can give yourself at least two to three days to explore the Iluka area, you won't regret it. Other than the superb coastline contained within the southern sector of the Bundjalung National Park and one of the best campsites on the northern NSW coast at **Woody Head**, the big attraction at the sleepy fishing village of **Iluka** is the World Heritage Rainforest Walk through the **Iluka Nature Reserve**. The 136-ha reserve contains the largest remaining stand of littoral rainforest in NSW – a rich forest habitat unique to the coastal environment and supporting a huge number of species such as the charmingly named lily pilly tree and noisy pitta bird. The 2.5-km rainforest walk can be tackled either

from the north at the Iluka Bluff Car Park (off the main Iluka Road opposite the golf club) or from the caravan park at western edge of the village (Crown Street).

Iluka Beach is another fine quiet spot reached via Beach Road (head west from the end of Iluka Road). Further north, just beyond Iluka Bluff, **Bluff Beach** and **Frazer's Reef** are popular for swimming and fishing. The Whale Viewing Platform on Beach Road can guarantee panoramic views of the area and the possibility, in season (June to November), of seeing mainly humpback whales migrating up and down the coast.

Two kilometres north of Iluka and Woody Head, the 18,000-ha wilderness of **Bundjalung National Park** with its 38 km of beaches, littoral rainforest, heathlands, unusual rock formations, lagoons, creeks and swamps is an eco-explorer's paradise. Sadly, access from the south is by 4WD only ($16 permit), or on foot. There is better access from the north along the 21-km unsealed road. Go up to Gap Road, off the Pacific Highway, 5 km south of Woodburn, to the Black Rocks campsite. Accommodation and park information, maps and internet are available at the Clarence Coast Visitor Centre (see page 186 for details).

Lennox Head

The small, beachside settlement of Lennox Head is world famous for the long surf breaks that form at the terminus of Seven Mile Beach and Lennox Point. Even without a board, the village offers a quieter, alternative destination in which to spend a relaxing couple of days, away from the clamour of Byron Bay. Just south of the village the eponymous head offers excellent views north to Cape Byron and is considered a prime spot for hang-gliding and dolphin and whale spotting. The **Lennox Reef**, below the head, known as 'The Moat', is also good for snorkelling. At the northern end of the village **Lake Ainsworth** is a fine venue for freshwater swimming, canoeing and windsurfing. **Lennox Head Sailing School**, beside the lake on Pacific Parade, hires water sports equipment and offers lessons. The lake edge also serves as the venue for the coastal markets that are held on the second and fifth Sundays of the month.

Byron Bay → *For listings, see pages 192-204. Colour map 3, A3.*

Anything goes in Byron Bay. This town would love to have its own passport control to prevent entry to anyone who is remotely conservative or thinks surfing is something you do in front of a computer. Only three decades ago 'Byron' was little more than a sleepy, attractive coastal enclave. Few strayed off the main highway heading north except a few alternative lifestylers who found it an ideal escape and the land prices wonderfully cheap. But news spread and its popularity exploded. It lacks the glitz of the Gold Coast and the conformity of many other coastal resorts, but there is little doubt it is perilously close to the level of popularity that can turn to a love-it-or-hate-it experience. Despite all this, however, it remains a beautiful place (no high-rise hotels here) and boasts a wonderfully cosmopolitan mix of humanity. Few people leave disappointed.

Ins and outs

Getting there The two nearest airports are Coolangatta (north) and Ballina (south) with good daily services and shuttle buses to town. There are plenty of long-distance buses and trains from Sydney, Cairns, Brisbane, etc. Both the train station and bus station are in the centre of town.

Getting around You can enjoy all the offerings of Byron Bay on foot, or, to cover more ground, hire a bike. There are local bus services for getting around town and also to sights around Byron Bay such as Ballina and Lennox Head. ▸▸ *See Transport, page 203.*

Tourist information **Byron Bay VIC** ⓘ *80 Jonson St, T6680 8558, www.visitbyron bay.com, 0900-1700.* See also page 201, for tour operators.

Sights
The main attractions in Byron, beyond its hugely popular social and creative scene, are of course the surrounding beaches and the stunning Cape Byron Headland Reserve. There are over 37 km of beaches, including seven world-class surf beaches stretching from Belongil Beach in the west to Broken Head in the south. Byron also hosts an extensive array of organized activities to lure you from your beach-based relaxation. Surfing is the most popular pastime. For details, see page 202.

Only metres from the town centre, **Main Beach** is the main focus of activity. It is patrolled and safest for families or surfing beginners. West of Main Beach, **Belongil Beach** stretches about 1 km to the mouth of Belongil Creek. About 500 m beyond that (accessed via Bayshore Drive), there is a designated naturist beach. East of the town centre, Main Beach merges with **Clark's Beach**, which is no less appealing and generally much quieter.

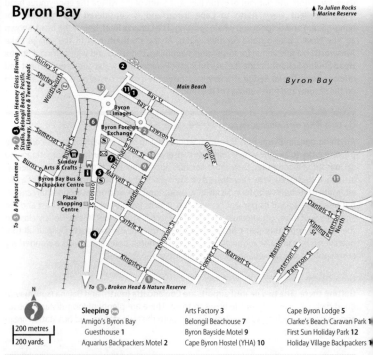

Byron Bay

↑ To Julian Rocks
│ Marine Reserve

Sleeping	Arts Factory **3**	Cape Byron Lodge **5**
Amigo's Byron Bay	Belongil Beachouse **7**	Clarke's Beach Caravan Park **1**
Guesthouse **1**	Byron Bayside Motel **9**	First Sun Holiday Park **12**
Aquarius Backpackers Motel **2**	Cape Byron Hostel (YHA) **10**	Holiday Village Backpackers **1**

Beyond Clark's Beach and the headland called **The Pass** – a favourite surf spot – **Watego's** and **Little Watego's Beaches** fringe the northern side of Cape Byron, providing more surf breaks and some dramatic coastal scenery. South of Cape Byron, **Tallow Beach** stretches about 9 km to Broken Head and is a great spot to escape the crowds (but note that it is unpatrolled). Several walks also access other more remote headland beaches within the very pretty **Broken Head Nature Reserve**. In the heart of Byron Bay itself, 2.5 km from the shore, is the small and clearly visible rocky outcrop known as **Julian Rocks Marine Reserve**. It is listed as one of Australia's top 10 dive sites, with over 400 species of fish, including sharks and manta ray, and turtles and dolphins often joining the party. If you are not a certified diver, a snorkelling trip to the rocks is recommended.

Crowning the **Cape Byron Headland** is the **Byron Bay Lighthouse** ⓘ *T6685 5955, 0800-1930 (1730 in winter), 30 mins' walk from the town, 40-min tours available.* Built in 1901 it sits only metres away from Australia's easternmost point. As well as the dramatic coastal views east over Byron Bay and south down Tallow Beach to Broken Head, the headland provides some excellent walking opportunities, with the track down from the lighthouse to Little Watego's Beach being the most popular. Humpback whales can often been seen offshore during their annual migrations in midwinter and early summer, while dolphins and the occasional manta ray can be spotted in the clear waters below the cliffs year round.

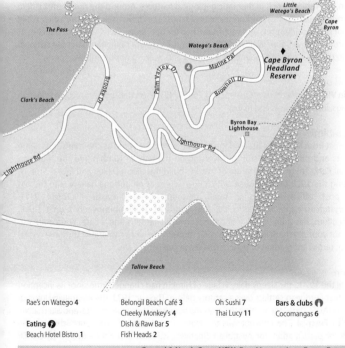

Rae's on Watego **4**

Eating ⑦
Beach Hotel Bistro **1**

Belongil Beach Café **3**
Cheeky Monkey's **4**
Dish & Raw Bar **5**
Fish Heads **2**

Oh Sushi **7**
Thai Lucy **11**

Bars & clubs ⑪
Cocomangas **6**

The town has a number of galleries worth seeing including the **Colin Heaney Glass Blowing Studio** ① *6 Acacia St, www.colinheaney.com,* and the superb works of local photographer John Derrey, at **Byron Images** ① *on the corner of Lawson St and Jonson St, www.johnderrey.com*. The VIC has full gallery listings. Byron also hosts an arts and crafts market on the first Sunday of the month on Butler Street.

Rainbow Region → *For listings, see pages 192-204. Colour map 3, A3.*

Inland from Byron Bay lies the so-called Rainbow Region, a collection of bohemian, arty villages famous for their alternative lifestyle. This very pleasant, scenic area, often called the Northern Rivers, stretches from Murwillumbah in the north to Kyogle in the west, Lismore and Ballina in the south and Byron Bay on the coast to the east.

Geologically the region is dominated by the Mount Warning shield volcano and its vast caldera (crater), the largest of its type in the southern hemisphere. The huge volcano, which erupted about 23 million years ago, produced a flat shield-shaped landform with its highest point rising almost twice the height of **Mount Warning** (1157 m), which is all that remains today of the original magma chamber and central vent. If viewed from the air the huge eroded bowl of the caldera can be seen stretching almost 60 km inland from the coast, with the dramatic peak of Mount Warning in its middle. The original lava flows reached as far as Canungra in the north, Kyogle to the west, Lismore and Ballina in the south and almost 100 km out to sea. Today, after millions of years of wind and water erosion, the region is rich in dramatic geological features. Around the rim of the caldera and fringing plateaux lush rainforest-covered landscapes have risen from the ashes, while the floor of the caldera acts as a vast watershed for the Tweed River, which debouches at the border of New South Wales and Queensland. There are no fewer than nine national parks in the area, offering magnificent scenery and walking opportunities.

Ins and outs

Nimbin VIC ① *northern end of Cullen St (71), T6689 1453*, offers transport and accommodation bookings, internet access and maps.

Mullumbimby

Northwest from Byron, the little village of Mullumbimby is about as charming as its name suggests and offers a fine stop or diversion on the way to Nimbin and the Nightcap National Park. There is a scattering of historic buildings along Dalley and Stuart Streets, including the 1908 **Cedar House**, which now serves as an antique gallery, and the old 1907 post office housing a small museum. **Crystal Castle** ① *T6684 3111, www.crystalcastle.com.au, 1000-1700, free*, south of Mullumbimby on Monet Drive, Montecollum, has a fine display of natural crystals, gardens and a café. You could also check out your psychedelic colours as seen through the 'aura camera' or try some crystal healing, tarot card reading or sip a herbal tea in the Lotus Café.

Nimbin

Up until the 1970s, the sleepy dairy village of Nimbin had changed little since its inception by the first European settlers over a century before. Then, in 1973, the Australian Union of Students (AUS) chose the Nimbin Valley as the venue for the 'experimental and alternative' **Aquarius Festival**. The concept was to create 'a total cultural experience, through the lifestyle of participation' for Australian creatives, students and alternative lifestylers. Of course, with many of that generation eager to maintain the ideologies and practices of the sixties, the very concept became like a red rag to the proverbial 'alternative' bull, and when the time arrived it all inevitably went into orbit. In many ways Nimbin never got over the invasion, the excitement or indeed the hangover, and its more enlightened long-term residents have been joined by a veritable army of society's dropouts, man.

In many ways the colourful main street of Nimbin, **Cullen Street**, is the single collective sight in the village and one that speaks very much for itself. Amidst a rash of laid-back cafés, alternative health and arts and craft shops, is **Nimbin Museum** ⓘ *61 Cullen St, T6689 1123, www.nimbinmuseum.com, 0900-1700, $2.* Entirely true to the unconventional and the alternative ideology, it goes deliberately beyond any conventional concepts. It is perhaps simply unique in its creative, historical and often humorous interpretations and expressions of the village, its inhabitants and Australia as a whole.

On the other side of Cullen Street, the loudly advertised **Hemp Embassy** ⓘ, *www.hempembassy.net free,* is also worth a look but, as you can imagine, has little to do with gardening or fashion wear. As well as supporting the multifarious and controversial uses of hemp, the Nimbin Valley is also well known for fruit growing and permaculture. For the visitor the **Djanbung Gardens Permaculture Centre** ⓘ *74 Cecil St, www.permaculture.com.au, T6689 1755, Tue-Fri 1000-1500, Sat-Mon 1000-1200, tours Tue and Thu 1030, Sat 1100,* offers garden tours, herbal crafts, environmental workshops and an organic café.

The most obvious volcanic feature around Nimbin is the **Nimbin Rocks**, which are estimated to be over 20 million years old. There is a lookout on **Lodge Road**, 3 km south of the village. If you fancy a further investigation try a bicycle tour, see page 201 for details.

Nightcap National Park and Whian Whian State Forest

The World Heritage 8145-ha Nightcap National Park is located on the southern rim of the Mount Warning caldera and adjacent is the Whian Whian State Forest Park. Combined, they offer a wealth of volcanic features including massifs, pinnacles and cliffs eroded by spectacular waterfalls and draped in lush rainforest. Some unique wildlife also resides in the park, including the red-legged pademelon (a kind of wallaby), the Fleay's barred frog and the appealingly named wompoo fruit dove.

The main physical features of the park are **Mount Nardi** (800 m), 12 km east of Nimbin; **Terania Creek** and the **Protestors Falls**, 14 km north of the Channon; and **Whian Whian State Forest** and 100-m **Minyon Falls**, 23 km southwest of Mullumbimby. The 30-km Whian Whian Scenic Drive (unsealed), which can be accessed beyond the Minyon Falls, traverses the forest park and takes visitors through varied rainforest vegetation and scenery including the memorable **Peates Mountain Lookout**. Nightcap National Park also holds the rather dubious accolade of receiving the highest mean rainfall in the state.

Popular long walking tracks include the moderate-to-hard 7.5-km **Minyon Loop**, which starts from the Minyon Falls Picnic Area and takes in the base of the falls and the escarpment edge, and the moderate-to-hard 16-km **Historic Nightcap Track**, which follows the former pioneer trails that once connected Lismore and Mullumbimby. Other shorter and easier possibilities are the 3-km **Mount Matheson Loop** and 4-km **Pholis Gap walks**, which both start from Mount Nardi, and the 1.5-km **Big Scrub Loop**, which starts from the Gibbergunyah Range Road in Whian Whian State Forest. It is said to contain some of the best remnant rainforest in the region. Protestors Falls, which were named after a successful six-week protest to prevent logging in the late 1970s, are reached on a 1.5-km return track from the Terania Creek Picnic Area.

The Mount Nardi section of the park is accessed via Newton Drive, which is off Tuntable Falls Road west out of Nimbin. The Terania Creek and Protestors Falls are reached via Terania Creek Road north out of the Channon, and the Minyon Falls and Whian Whian State Forest are reached via Dunoon or Goonengerry southwest of Mullumbimby.

Murwillumbah

The pleasant sugar cane town of Murwillumbah sits on the banks of the Tweed River, at the eastern edge of the Mount Warning caldera, and serves as a major gateway to the Rainbow Region. Most people who visit the town gather what information they need from the World Heritage Rainforest Centre (see below) and then 'head for the hills'; however, if you can spare an hour or so, the small **Tweed Regional Art Gallery** ① *Mistral Rd, T6670 2790, Wed-Sun 1000-1700*, is worth a look. As well as its permanent collection of Australian and international art, it features some fine works by local artists and also hosts the lucrative Doug Moran National Portrait Prize. Murwillumbah VIC shares its office with the NPWS and the **World Heritage Rainforest Centre** ① *corner of Tweed Valley Way and Alma St, T6672 1340, www.tweedtourism.com.au, open till 1600*. Combined they offer insight and information surrounding the region and the parks.

Mount Warning National Park

The 1157-m peak of Mount Warning is all that remains of the magma chamber and vent that formed the vast caldera that shaped much of the Northern Rivers region. Other than its stunning scenery and rich flora and fauna, the great appeal of Mount Warning is the pilgrimage to the summit to see the first rays of sunlight to hit the Australian mainland. The moderate to hard 4.4-km ascent starts from the Breakfast Creek Picnic Area, 17 km southwest of Murwillumbah at the terminus of Mount Warning Road. To ensure you reach the summit for sunrise you are advised to set off about 2½ hours beforehand. Murwillumbah, see above, serves as an overnight stop for those undertaking the dawn ascent. For the less energetic, Lyrebird Track crosses Breakfast Creek before winding 200 m through palm forest to a rainforest platform. Access to Mount Warning is via Mount Warning Road, 11 km south of Murwillumbah on the main Kyogle Road.

⊚ Port Macquarie to Byron Bay listings

For Sleeping and Eating price codes and other relevant information, see Essentials pages 28-33.

Sleeping

Port Macquarie *p178, map p179*
There are plenty of accommodation options in and around Port Macquarie, from basic NPWS campsites to luxury resorts. During holiday periods and in the high season you are advised to book ahead.
L-A HW Boutique Motel, 1 Stewart St, T6583 1200, www.hwmotel.com.au. For a really chic motel in the ideal position, look no further than this. The rooms are well appointed with

most offering views across the river mouth and Town Beach.
L-E Sundowner Breakwall Tourist Park, beside the river mouth, 1 Munster St, T6583 2755, www.sundowner.net.au. Of the many motor parks in the area this one is hard to beat for position. It has vast and good facilities including a pool and camp kitchen.
B-E Port Macquarie YHA, 40 Church St, T6583 5512. Closest hostel to the beaches, offering tidy dorms, twins and family rooms, spacious facilities, free bikes, internet, pick-ups from the bus station.
C-E Ozzie Pozzie Backpackers, 36 Waugh St, T6583 8133, www.ozziepozzie.com. More

modern, activity-oriented backpackers than **Port Macquarie Backpackers**, well in tune with travellers' needs, good facilities, dorms, doubles/twins, internet, pick-ups, free use of boogie boards, bikes and fishing gear.

C-E Port Macquarie Backpackers, 2 Hastings River Drive, T6583 1791, www.portmacquariebackpackers.com.au. A friendly, family-run historic house with lots of character, dorms, twins and doubles, pool, 24-hr kitchen and TV room, free use of boogie boards, fishing gear, bikes, pool table, internet and pick-ups.

Remote NPWS camping is available at Big Hill and Point Plomer in the Limeburners Creek Nature Reserve, T6586 8300.

South West Rocks and Hat Head p180

L Smoky Cape Lighthouse B&B, T6566 6301, www.smokycapelighthouse.com. The most unusual accommodation in the area has to be these former keepers' quarters. A totally refurbished interior provides self-contained or B&B options, modern facilities, 4-poster and stunning views south across the national park. Two-night stay minimum. Book well in advance.

L-A Rockpool Motel, 45 McIntyre St, T6566 7755, www.rockpoolmotorinn.com.au. Modern motel complex 1 km east of the town centre.

A-B Bay Motel, 1 Livingstone Av, T6566 6909. Another motel only older and cheaper, right on the main shopping street.

A-E Horseshoe Bay Beach Park, Livingstone St, T6566 6370, www.horseshoebaypark.com.au. Overlooks the river, ocean and the sheltered Horseshoe Bay Beach and is within metres of the town centre. Busy and beautifully placed, this motor park offers cabins, onsite vans and powered sites (some en suite). Hugely popular with locals so book well in advance.

D Arakoon State Recreation Area, T6566 6168, Laggers Point, beside the Trial Bay Gaol. Equally fine aesthetics and more seclusion can be secured here. It's a great spot and the best for camping.

F Hungry Rest Area, south of Hat Head village. Self-registration including day-use fees apply, T6584 2203. Contact for both sites. A good basic NPWS campsite with pit toilets, no water and fires are permitted.

F Smoky Rest Area, near the lighthouse, see Hungry Rest Area for contact details. Excellent for wildlife, a good basic NPWS campsite.

Bellingen p181
There are plenty of good B&Bs and self-contained cottages in verdant country settings.

L Promised Land Cottages, 934 Promised Land Rd, T6655 9578, www.promisedland cottages.com.au. Good value quality self-contained options 15 mins outside of the village. Recommended.

L-A Monticello Countryhouse, 11 Sunset Ridge Drive, (2 km), T6655 1559, www.monticello.com.au. Popular B&B, with classy, good value double, twin and singles, within easy reach of the village.

A Fernridge Farm Cottage, 1673 Waterfall Way (4 km west), T6655 2142, www.fernridge.com.au. Peaceful, cosy, self-contained accommodation in a 19th-century 'Queenslander' cottage on a 120-ha alpaca farm.

B Rivendell guesthouse, 12 Hyde St, T6655 0060, www.rivendellguesthouse.com.au. A historic guesthouse with 3 queen rooms situated right in the heart of the village.

B-F Bellingen YHA Backpackers, 2 Short St, T6655 1116, www.yha.com.au. Consistently receives rave reviews and deservedly so. Housed in a beautifully maintained 2-storey historic homestead in the heart of the village, with large decks overlooking the river valley, it oozes character and has a great social, laid-back atmosphere. It has a range of dorms, double/twins, family rooms and camping facilities, internet, musical instruments, hammocks and entertaining trips to Dorrigo National Park. Lining the hallways are tasteful photographs of over 200 guests willing to get buck naked in the name of art.

Dorrigo National Park

B Fernbrook Lodge, 470 Waterfall Way, 6 km west, T6657 2573, fernbrooklodge@mid coast.com.au. Traditional and homely B&B with great views.

B-C Historic Dorrigo Hotel, corner of Hickory St and Cudgery St, T6657 2016, www.hotelmoteldorrigo.com.au. Traditional pub rooms at affordable prices in the centre, some with spa bath.

C-D Gracemere Grange, 325 Dome Rd, 2 km from the Rainforest Centre, T6657 2630, www.gracemeregrange.com.au. Another comfortable B&B option close to the Dorrigo National Park visitor centre.

C-F Dorrigo Mountain Resort, on the southern edge of the town, Waterfall Way, T6657 2564, www.dorrigomountainresort.com.au. Standard self-contained cabins, powered and non-powered sites, barbecues, but no camp kitchen.

New England National Park p183

B-D Moffat Falls Cottage, T6775 9219, Point Lookout Rd, www.moffatfalls.com.au. Comfortable, self-contained option in New England National Park with a wood fire and 2 bedrooms. There is also a self-contained room in the lodge and cheaper, value cabins on the property.

Coffs Harbour p183, map p184

There is a rash of motels and resorts located along the Pacific Highway on the north and south approaches and along the waterfront on Ocean Pde. There are plenty of motor parks in the area with the best located north or south of the town. The hostels are lively places – very activity- and party-oriented.

L Friday Creek Retreat, 267 Friday Creek Rd, Upper Orara, 17 km west of town, T6653 8221, www.fridaycreek.com. Sheer luxury, as well as complete peace and quiet in a country setting is offered here. There are 9 superb fully self-contained cottages with spas, open fires, hammocks and great views, free bike hire, complimentary breakfast and dinner by arrangement.

L-F Park Beach Caravan Park, Ocean Pde, T6648 4888, www.parkbeachholidaypark.com.au. If you must stay in the town itself this is the beachside motor park with the best facilities.

A-C Country Comfort Motel, 353 Pacific Highway, T6652 8222, www.countrycomfort.com.au. Next to the Big Banana, this modern, convenient and good value motel is a good choice if you are merely passing through. Pool, sauna and spa.

A-E Emerald Beach Holiday Park, Fishermans Drive, Emerald Beach, T6656 1521, www.ebhp.com.au. 18 km north of Coffs, this motor park has luxury villas, standard cabins, onsite vans, powered and shaded non-powered sites in a bush setting with shop, café and pool. The beach is only metres away and is simply superb with headland walks nearby. Recommended.

A-E Sawtell Beach Caravan Park, 5 Lyons Rd, Sawtell (6 km), T6653 1379, www.sawtell beachcaravanpark.com.au. South of town is this motor park close to the surf beach and local amenities with camp kitchen.

C-E Coffs Harbour YHA, 51 Collingwood St, T6652 6462. Friendly, spotless and well managed. Recently relocated to a spacious modern facility in a suburban setting close to the beach, offering dorms, doubles/twins and family rooms (with en suite), pool, internet, cable TV and free bikes, surf/body boards and pick-ups. Recommended.

C-F Aussitel Backpackers, T6651 1871, www.aussitel.com. Also near the beach at 312 Harbour Drive, this a social place with emphasis on discounted activities and its own attractive dive packages a speciality. Dorms, twins and doubles, large kitchen, common area, internet, pool, bikes, surf/body boards, wetsuits, etc.

Coffs Harbour to Byron Bay p186

Most of Yamba's amenities can be found along its main drag, Wooli St, or Yamba St off Wooli St, which terminates at Pippie Beach.

LL-A Surf Motel, 2 Queen St, Yamba, T6646 2200. Modern, well-appointed motel option right next to Main Beach.

LL-E Blue Dolphin Holiday Resort,
Yamba Rd, Yamba, T6646 2194,
www.bluedolphin.com.au. This 5-star resort
offers luxury/standard self-contained cabins,
en suite/standard powered and non-powered
sites, café, pool and camp kitchen.

B-E Lake Ainsworth Caravan Park,
Pacific Pde, Lennox Head, T6687 7249,
www.lake-ainsworth-holiday-park.nsw.big4.
com.au. For campers and campervans this
option is ideally located next to the lake and
offers en suite/standard cabins, powered
and non-powered sites but no camp
kitchen. Activities include windsurfing,
sailing and canoeing.

C-E Lennox Head Beach House YHA, 3 Ross
St, T6687 7636, www.yha.com.au.
Purpose-built hostel with a great laid-back
friendly atmosphere, near the beach and Lake
Ainsworth. Dorms and small doubles and free
use of surf/boogie boards, bikes and fishing
gear. Free sailing and windsurfing lessons can
also be arranged and there is a natural
therapies (massage) clinic onsite, as well as
their legendary chocolate cake.

D-F Woody Head Campsite, beside the
beach off Iluka Rd, 14 km west of the Pacific
Highway, 4 km north of Iluka, T6646 6134,
www.nationalparks.nsw.gov.au. This NPSW
campsite is simply superb. Non-powered
sites, toilets, water, hot showers, boat ramp
and fires permitted, plus 3 cabins with
cooking facilities. Book well ahead.

Byron Bay p187, map p188

There is certainly plenty of choice in Byron,
with the emphasis on backpacker hostels and
upmarket boutique hotels, B&Bs and
guesthouses. There are over a dozen very
competitive backpackers in town, all having
to maintain good standards. Mostly the
choice comes down to availability – book
well ahead for all accommodation but
particularly the backpackers. If the options
below don't suffice, the VIC has an excellent
accommodation booking service. See
www.byron-bay.com and
www.byronbayaccom.net.

LL Rae's on Wategos, overlooking Watego's
Beach, T6685 5366, www.raes.com.au. This
sits firmly at the top of this price category and
is the most luxurious hotel in Byron. It was
voted in *Condé Naste Traveller* magazine (and
others) as being in the top 50 worldwide.
Although location has a lot to do with that
accolade, the place itself is superb and cannot
be faulted. It has an in-house restaurant that
is also excellent and open to non-guests.

L-D Belongil Beachouse, 25 Childe St
(Kendal St, off Shirley St), T6685 7868,
www.belongilbeachouse.com.
East of the town centre, in contrast to the
Arts Factory this option offers a wide range
of modern, well-appointed options, from
dorms and private double/twins with
shared facilities, to luxury motel-style rooms
with spas, or two-bedroom self-contained
cottages. Quiet setting across the road from
the beach. Onsite Balinese-style café and
float/massage therapy centre. Internet, bike,
body/surf board hire and courtesy bus.

L-E Broken Head Caravan Park, Beach Rd,
Broken Head (8 km), T6685 3245,
www.brokenhd.com.au. Further afield and
much quieter, the appeal of this motor park is
its friendly atmosphere, beachside position
and proximity to the Broken Head Nature
Reserve. It has cabins, powered and
non-powered sites, small shop, barbecue and
camp kitchen.

L-E Clarke's Beach Caravan Park,
off Lighthouse Rd, T6685 6496,
www.clarkesbeach.com.au. Further west,
with prettier surroundings and right beside
Clark's Beach, this motor park offers
self-contained and standard cabins, powered
and shady non-powered sites, but no camp
kitchen, just barbecues.

L-E First Sun Holiday Park, Lawson St
(200 m east of the Main Beach Car Park),
T6685 6544, www.bshp.com.au/first. The
most convenient for the town centre and
Main Beach, it offers a range of self-
contained/standard cabins, powered and
non-powered sites, camp kitchen.

A Byron Bayside Motel, 14 Middleton St, T6685 6004, www.byronbaysidemotel.com.au. This budget 3-star motel is well placed in the heart of town, modern and good value.

A-B Amigo's Byron Bay Guesthouse, corner of Kingsley St and Tennyson St, T6680 8662, www.amigosbb.com. Doubles (one en suite, one with shared bathroom), bike and body board hire.

A-E Aquarius Backpackers Motel, 16 Lawson St, T6685 7663, www.byron-bay.com/aquarius. Large and lively complex offering dorms, doubles and spa suites (all en suite, with 'proper beds'), pool, good value licensed café/bistro, internet, free boogie boards, bikes, pool tables and courtesy bus.

The YHA operates two hostels in Byron Bay:
A-E Byron Bay YHA, 7 Carlyle St, T6685 8853, www.yha.com.au. Very similar and just as reliable.

A-E Cape Byron YHA , corner Byron St and Middleton St, T6685 8788, www.yha.com.au. Offers modern, clean dorms, double and twins (some en suite and a/c) set around a large courtyard with pool. Well managed and friendly. Good kitchen facilities, café, free barbecue nights, large games room, internet and tours desk. Dive shop next door.

A-E Holiday Village Backpackers, 116 Jonson St, south of town centre, T6685 8888, www.byronbaybackpackers.com.au. Offers modern dorms, doubles and motel-style apartments (some en suite with TV), large courtyard with pool, spa, well-equipped kitchen, all-you-can-eat barbecues, internet, free surf/body boards, scuba lessons, bike hire.

A-F Arts Factory, Skinners Shoot Rd (via Burns St, off Shirley St), T6685 7709, www.artsfactory.com.au. This place takes some beating for the quintessential 'alternative' Byron experience. It offers a wide range of 'funky' accommodation, from the Love Shack and Island Retreats, to the Gypsy Bus, tepees and campsites. Excellent amenities, pool, sauna, internet, café (plus vegetarian restaurant nearby), bike hire, tours desk and unusual arts, relaxation, yoga or music-based activities including didgeridoo

making and drumming. It even has its own recording studio should you feel a Susan Boyle coming on. The Byron Lounge Cinema and Buddha Gardens Day Spa are also within the village. It may not be everybody's cup of herbal tea, but for an experience it is recommended.

C-E Cape Byron Lodge, 78 Bangalow Rd (1 km from the town centre), T6685 6445, www.capebyronlodge.com. Very congenial hostel that more than meets the stiff competition with all the usual facilities and a good atmosphere. Also free shuttle into town and dawn trips to the lighthouse.

Rainbow Region p190
LL Crystal Creek Rainforest Retreat, Brookers Rd, Murwillumbah, T6679 1591, www.crystalcreekrainforestretreat.com.au. This award-winning retreat is located on the edge of the Numinbah Nature Reserve, about 23 km west of Murwillumbah, with modern design, well-appointed self-contained bungalows, spa baths, excellent cuisine, local forest walks and even the odd hammock across the creek. Transfers from Murwillumbah by arrangement.

LL Ecoasis, near the village of Uki, Mt Warning, T6679 5959, www.ecoasis.com.au. These luxury couple-oriented bush chalets are an excellent choice. Indulge yourself.

B-E Mount Warning Caravan Park, about 3 km up Mt Warning Rd, T6679 5120, www.mtwarningholidaypark.com. Camping is available at this privately run caravan park. It has cabins, onsite vans, powered and non-powered sites (some with fires) and a camp kitchen.

B-F Midginbil Hill Country Resort, near Murwillumbah, T6679 7033, www.midginbilhill.com.au. Also has a full range of accommodation from B&B to camping with the added attraction of in-house canoe trips and horse riding.

C-E Mount Warning/Murwillumbah YHA, 1 Tumbulgum Rd, Murwillumbah (first right across the bridge, 200 m, across the river from the VIC), T6672 3763, www.yha.com.au. This is the best budget option. Located right next to the river and with a deck overlooking Mt Warning, it is a friendly and homely place, run by a caring and dedicated manager. Dorms and double/twins, free use of canoes and transport to Mt Warning if you stay 2 nights.

C-F Nimbin Rox YHA, 74 Thorburn St, Nimbin, T6689 0022, www.yha.com.au. Deservingly popular, this YHA is set in a 10-ha elevated position just west of the village, offering great views across Nimbin Rocks (hence the name). Offers the full range of rooms and modern facilities, including the obligatory tepee for that essential Nimbinesque ambience. Internet, pool and bike hire. Camping sites also available.

C-F Rainbow Retreat Backpackers, 75 Thorburn St, Nimbin, T6689 1262, www.rainbowretreat.net. You are invited to 'Live the Nimbin Dream' at this unusual, good value and suitably laid-back backpackers. Not surprisingly, it provides a wide choice of highly unconventional accommodation options from Malay-style huts to VW Kombis, dorms and secluded campsites, all set in a quiet 7-ha site near the edge of the village. Both the facilities and atmosphere are excellent with regular musical jam sessions, visiting chefs preparing cheap meals, alternative practitioners and performers, not to mention the odd platypus in the creek or harmless python up a tree. Overall, it provides the ideal way to experience the true spirit of Nimbin. Recommended.

D-E Nimbin Caravan and Tourist Park, 29 Sibley St, Nimbin, T6689 1402. Basic facilities, onsite vans, powered and non-powered sites, within easy walking distance of the village.

🍴 Eating

Port Macquarie *p178, map p179*
Seafood rules in Port Macquarie, from the full plate of oysters to humble fish and chips. The main outlets can be found at the Wharf end of Clarence St. The vineyards are also worth considering, especially for lunch.

🍴🍴🍴 **Fusion 7**, 124 Horton St, T6584 1171. Daily for lunch and dinner. Relaxed atmosphere and value, quality Australian cuisine from lauded chef Lindsey Schwab.

🍴🍴🍴 **Scampi's**, Port Marina, Park St, T6583 7200. Daily from 1800. The best venue for quality à la carte seafood in congenial surroundings.

🍴🍴 **Beach House**, 1 Horton St, T6584 5692. Daily breakfast, lunch and dinner. The most popular venue for locals given the location, with a good atmosphere. Standard pub-style fare with pizza a speciality.

🍴🍴 **Ca Marche**, 764 Fernbank Creek Rd (corner of Pacific Highway), T6582 8320. Daily 1030-1600. Out of town a little but worth the journey is this small, award- winning French/Mediterranean restaurant at the Cassegrain Winery, with a congenial atmosphere and good views across the vines.

🍴🍴 **Toros Mexican**, 22 Murray St, T6583 4340. Long-established and good value venue that does a wicked fajita.

🍴 **Macquarie Seafoods**, corner of Clarence St and Short St, T6583 8476. Daily 1100-2100. Great fish and chips.

🍴 **Port Pacific Resort Café**, 14 Clarence St, T6583 8099. Breakfast for around $12.

South West Rocks and Hat Head *p180*
🍴🍴 **Geppy's**, corner of Livingstone St and Memorial Av, South West Rocks, T6566 6196. Well known for good seafood, Italian and modern Australian cuisine. Live jazz and blues on Wed.

🍴🍴 **Pizza on the Rocks**, 134 Gregory St, South West Rocks, T6566 6626. Locally recommended.

🍴🍴 **Trial Bay Kiosk**, Arakoon, overlooking the Trial Bay Gaol and beach, T6566 7100. Daily for breakfast and lunch 0800-1600 and Thu, Fri and Sat for dinner. Superb location, alfresco dining and quality, though fairly pricey, fare. Good breakfasts and coffee.

Bellingen *p181*
🍴🍴 **No 2 Oak St**, T6655 9000. Tue-Sat, from 1800. Recommended for fine dining. Housed

in a 1910 heritage cottage it offers an excellent and innovative menu. Book ahead.

Old Butter Factory Café, 1 Doepel La, T6655 2150. Breakfast and lunch. Good breakfast or light meal venue with indoor or outdoor seating overlooking the golf course. The added attraction is the arts and crafts (see above).

Café Bare Nature & Pizza, 111 Hyde St, T6655 1551. Daily from 1700. For gourmet pizza.

Lodge 241 Gallery Café, Masonic Hall, T6655 2470. Daily 0800-1700. Overlooking the river valley is this café and gallery combined, serving fine local cuisine and good coffee.

Dorrigo and Dorrigo National Park
Misty's, 33 Hickory St, T6657 2855. Wed-Sat from 1800 and Sun from 0730 for brunch. For fine dining.

Historic Dorrigo Hotel, corner of Hickory St and Cudgery St, T6657 2016. Classic pub grub.

Coffs Harbour *p183, map p184*
Tide and Pilot Brasserie, Marina Drive, T6651 6888. Daily for breakfast, lunch and dinner from 0700. Quality alfresco dining at this award-winning and friendly restaurant can follow a pre-dinner walk to Muttonbird Island.

Ocean Front Brasserie, Coffs Harbour Deep Sea Fishing Club, Jordan Esplanade, T6651 2819. Daily 1200-1430 and 1800-2030. Good value and great views across the harbour.

Fisherman's Co-op, 69 Marina Drive, T6652 2811. Daily until 1800. *The* place for fish and chips.

Foreshores Café, Jetty Strip, 394 High St, T665 23127. Daily. Good breakfast, coffee and lunch. Locals swear by this place.

Coffs Harbour to Byron Bay *p186*
Yamba
Pacific Hotel, 18 Pilot St, T6646 2466. Overlooking the ocean, an old favourite for good value bistro meals daily. Also has budget accommodation.

Iluka
Golf Club, Iluka Rd, T6646 5043. Tue-Sun. The best of a poor selection.

Sedger's Reef Bistro, 5 Queens St, T6646 6119. One of very few open daily.

Lennox Head
Lennox Head Pizza and Pasta, 2/56 Ballina St, T6687 7080. A good option.

Byron Bay *p187, map p188*
Although Jonson St and the various arcades host some good restaurants and cafés, most folk gravitate towards Bay Lane where you will find plenty of atmosphere.

Dish Restaurant, corner of Jonson St and Marvell St, T6685 7320. An award-winning, very chic place with fine innovative international and Australian cuisine. Also runs the **Marvell Bar**.

Beach Hotel Bistro, Bay Lane, T6685 6402. Lunch and dinner 1200-2100. Never fails to attract the crowds and wins hands down for atmosphere. Little wonder it sold for 'Good Lord, how much' in 2007 and will probably do the same in another decade.

Oh Sushi, 90 Jonson St, T6685 7103. Daily 1200-2200. Sushi fans should look no further.

Thai Lucy, Bay Lane, T6680 8083. Daily 1200-1500 and 1730-2200. Offers excellent dishes, good value and lots of atmosphere, but book ahead.

Belongil Beach Café, Childe St, T6685 7144. Daily 0800-2200. If a beach stroll is in order you'll find a good coffee and generous breakfasts at this friendly café.

Buddha Bar and Restaurant and **Zula** (Arts Factory Village), Skinners Shoot Rd (5 mins west of the town centre), T6680 8038. Daily from 1600. Both good value and always a cosmopolitan crowd. You could combine a visit with a film at the **Lounge Cinema** next door, T5685 5828.

Cheeky Monkey's, 115 Jonson St, T6685 5886. Mon-Sat 1900-0300. Backpacker specials are regularly on offer in order to tempt you to stay late at the bar and nightclub.

Fish Heads, 7 Jonson St, T6685 7810. Best bet for takeaway fish and chips, then head for the beach.

Market forces

One of the great tourist attractions in the Rainbow Region is its colourful weekend markets. These operate in a circuit throughout the region, mostly on Sundays. Byron Bay Market is held in the Butler Street Reserve on the first Sunday of the month, while Lismore hosts a regional Organic Produce Market at the Lismore Showgrounds every Tuesday between 0800-1000, as well as the Lismore Showground Markets every second Sunday. The excellent Channon Craft Market, kicks off in Coronation Park on the second Sunday, while the Aquarius Fair Markets in Nimbin are on the third and fifth Sunday and Bangalow holds its market in the local showgrounds on the fourth Sunday.

Rainbow Region *p190*
Nimbin
♔♔ **Rainbow Café**. The oldest of the alternative eateries in Nimbin.

Murwillumbah
♔ **Imperial Hotel**, 115 Main St, T 6672 1036. Good value pub lunches and dinners. Pub rooms also available.

◑ Bars and clubs

Port Macquarie *p178, map p179*
For up-to-date listings, pick up the free weekly *Hastings Happenings* at the VIC.
Beach House, on the Green, 1 Horton St, T6584 5692. Nightly, free entry until 2300. Modern and popular nightclub with occasional jazz on Sun afternoons.
Finnians Irish Pub, 97 Gordon St. For a quieter night out try this friendly pub which stages live bands at weekends.
Port Macquarie Hotel, corner of Clarence St and Horton St, T6580 7888. Perhaps the most popular pub in town.

Coffs Harbour *p183, map p184*
Ex-servicemen's Club, Vernon St, T6652 3888. A popular haunt for cheap food and drinks, especially on Fri night, but ID is required for entry.
Plantation, 88 Grafton St. A firm local favourite with regular live entertainment, staying open well into the wee small hours.

Byron Bay *p187, map p188*
Beach Hotel, facing the beach off Bay St, T6685 6402. Huge and the place to see and be seen, popular both day and night, with the lively atmosphere often spilling out onto beer garden. Live bands Thu-Sun.
Cocomangas, 32 Jonson St. 2100-0300, free entry before 2330. Retro 80s on Wed and disco funk and house on Sat.
♔ **Buddha Bar and Restaurant**, for details see Eating, above.

✹ Festivals and events

Byron Bay *p187, map p188*
Easter Blues and Roots Festival, www.bluesfest.com.au. The most lauded annual festival in Byron is a popular affair attracting its fair share of international stars, wannabes or has-beens.

◑ Shopping

Byron Bay *p187, map p188*
Byron offers a wealth of 'alternative' and arts and crafts shops selling everything from futons to $300 hand-painted toilet seats. With so many image-conscious backpackers around, the town is also becoming saturated with lingerie shops. See also box above.
Byron Bay Camping and Disposals, Plaza, Jonson St, T6685 8085. Camping gear and supplies.

Byron Images, corner Lawson St and Jonson St, T6685 8909, www.johnderrey.com.au. For a lasting image of Byron, see John Derrey's photography work.

▲ Activities and tours

Port Macquarie *p178, map p179*
Boat trips and cruises
Port Macquarie River Cruise (Port Venture), Clarence St, T6583 3058, www.portventure .com.au. Over 200 passengers can be carried on board the *MV Venture* for a scenic 2-hr river cruise, most days 1000 and 1400, from $25, children $12; 5-hr barbecue cruise at 1000 Wed, from $60, children $20, and a 3½-hr barbecue cruise, from $40, children $20.
Settlement Point Boat Hire 1 Settlement Point Rd (North Shore), T6583 6300. Independent boat hire.

Horse and camel riding
Bellrowan Valley Horse Riding, 35 mins from Port Macquarie, T6587 5227, www.bellrowanvalley.com.au. Professional outfit offering rides of 1 or 2 hrs, $60/85 including refreshments and pick-ups from Wauchope (transfer from the Port $10). Trek with dinner and overnight accommodation $125.
Port Macquarie Camel Safaris, Lighthouse Beach, T0437 672 080, www.portmacquariecamels.com.au. Daily except Saturday 0930 and 1300, from $30, children $25.

Skydiving and paragliding
Coastal Skydivers, T0428-471227, www.coastalskydivers.com. Offers 10,000-ft tandem skydives for $320.
High Adventure Air Park, Pacific Highway, Johns River, T0429-844961, www.high adventure.com.au. Tandem paragliding (30 mins from $160).

Water sports
Port Macquarie Surf School, T6585 5453, www.portmacquariesurfschool.com.au. Lessons from $40 per hour.
Stoney Park, Telegraph Point, T6585 0080, www.stoneypark.com.au. Specialist water-skiing and wakeboarding complex offering single lessons from $60 or day packages from $199. Recommended. Accommodation also available.

South West Rocks and Hat Head *p180*
This area is renowned for its excellent dive sites including the 120-m Fish Rock Cave. The entrance to the Macleay River offers good snorkelling at peak tide.
South West Rocks Dive Centre, 5/98 Gregory St, T6566 6474, www.southwest rocksdive.com.au. Offers both trips and rooms with dives to see grey nurse sharks and the Fish Rock Cave.

Bellingen *p181*
This is a fine base from which to explore the numerous excellent rainforest walks of the Dorrigo National Park. The river also offers some exciting opportunities either by canoe or on a river cruise.
Bellingen Canoe Adventures, 4 Tyson St, T6655 9955, www.bellingen.com/canoe. Half-day guided trips from $48, full-day trips from $90, 1 hr sunset tour from $25 and independent hire from $15 per hr.
Hinterland Tours, T6655 2957, www.hinterlandtour.com.au. Informative and English/German speaking multi-day eco-walks/tours of the Dorrigo Plateau and national park with accommodation options.

Coffs Harbour *p183, map p184*
The VIC has full activity listings and can offer non-biased advice. **Marina Booking Centre** based at the marina also acts as booking agent for most regional activities and cruises, T6651 4612.

Diving
Jetty Dive Centre, 398 High St, T6651 1611, www.jettydive.com.au. Small group PADI certification from $395, double dives at the Solitary Islands from $115 and snorkelling trips from $65.

Dolphin, whale watching and fishing
Pacific Explorer , T6652 8988, www.pacificexplorer.com.au. Whale and dolphin watching aboard a catamaran, which being quieter often has the advantage of closer viewing, 2½ hrs, from $40.
Various operators and vessels based at the marina offer entertaining fishing trips from around $125 for a half day. Big game fishing is also an option.
Spirit , T6650 0155. Good value whale-watching trips in season (Jun to end of Nov) at 0830 and 1330, from $40.

Horse trekking
Valery Trails, T6653 4301, www.valery trails.com.au. Award-winning outfit suited to advanced and beginners, 13 km south of Coffs. It offers 1-2-hr breakfast; barbecue, moonlight and camp ride-outs from $50.

Skydiving
Coffs City Skydivers, T6651 1167, www.coffsskydivers.com.au. Tandem skydiving, 3000 m, from $325.

Water sports
East Coast Surf School, T6651 5515, www.eastcoastsurfschool.com.au. Lessons at Diggers Beach (near the Big Banana) 1030-1230, private lessons, from $70 per hr, group from $55.
Liquid Assets, T6658 0850, www.surfrafting.com. An exhilarating range of aquatic adventures, including half or full day whitewater rafting on the Goolang River (grade III) and the Nymbodia River (a scenic grade III-V), from $85/$170. Sea kayaking, half day from $50. Surf rafting, half-day from $50 and flat water kayaking in Bongil Bongil

National Park, half day from $50. Surfing lessons from $50 and evening trips to observe platypus from $95.

Coffs Harbour to Byron Bay *p186*
Yamba Kayak Tours, Yamba, T6646 1137, www.yambakayak.com.au. 3-hr guided trips exploring the Islands and beaches inside the mouth of the Clarence River, from $70 and half-day or full-day tours on demand.

Byron Bay *p187, map p188*
Diving
Byron Bay Dive Centre, 9 Marvell St, T6685 8333, www.byronbaydive centre.com.au. A range of diving and snorkelling trips from full to half day exploring the wonderful biodiversity of the Cape Byron Marine Park.
Sundive, opposite the Court House on Middleton St, T6685 7755, www.sundive.com.au. Courses, half-day introductory dives from $150 and snorkelling from $50.

Health and spa therapies
There are now numerous alternative and conventional health therapies available including the 2 spas below, and the VIC has full listings.
Buddah Gardens Balinese Day Spa, 21 Gordon St, T6680 7844, www.buddhagardensdayspa.com.au.
Byron Bay Yoga, T8007 5128, www.byron bayyoga.com. Yoga classes.
Quintessence, 6 Fletcher St, T6685 5533, www.quintessencebyron.com.au.

Kiteboarding
Byron Bay Kiteboarding, T0402-008926, www.byronbaykiteboarding.com. Half, 2- or 3-day packages to master the increasingly popular art of kiteboarding, introductory session $49, full day from $250.

Mountain biking
Mountainbike Tours, T0429-122504, www.mountainbiketours.com.au. Great range of informative eco-based biking

adventures in the hinterland national parks, full day from $99, coastal half day from $59.

Sea kayaking
Dolphin, T6685 8044, www.dolphinkayaking.com.au. Good trips around the headlands with chance encounters with dolphins, half day departing daily at 0830, from $60.

Skydiving and gliding
Byron Bay Gliding, Tyagarah, T6684 7572, www.byronbaygliding.com. Entertaining trips in a 'motorglider', a sort of glider and microlight cross, of 20 mins to 1½ hrs from $95 to $395.
Byron Bay Skydiving Centre, based near Brunswick Heads, T1800 800840, www.skydivebyronbay.com. Owned by Australian world representative 'skysurfer' Ray Palmer. The team offers a range of professional services including tandems. The views from the jump zone across Byron Bay to the headland and beyond are stunning. Jumps are pretty cheap and range from $239 (2750m) to $324 (4250m).

Surfing
With so many superb surf breaks around Byron there is no shortage of surfing opportunities for pros and grommets alike. Most operators offer surf hire with short boards starting at about $15 per hr, $20 for 4 hrs and around $30 for 24 hrs.
Byron Bay Surf School, T1800 707274, www.byronbaysurfschool.com. 1-, 3- and 5-day packages, from $65 (3-day $165, 5-day $235, private 2-hr lesson from $130).
Style Surfing, T6685 5634, www.stylesurfingbyronbay.com. 3½-hr beginner's package or advanced courses daily at 0900, 1100 and 1300, from $60, or private lessons for 2 hrs, from $180.
Surfaris, T1800 634951, www.surfaris.com.au. This operation is for real enthusiasts or serious learners. Week-long Sydney–Byron trip from $499 or a 4-day/3-night Byron–Noosa–Hervey Bay trip, from $365.

Tour operators
Byron Bay Wildlife Tours, T0429 770 686, www.byronbaywildlifetours.com. Excellent trips to view all the favourite natives, from the ubiquitous koala to flying foxes (bats) and sea eagles. Also offers evening platypus and wildlife photography tours. All tours 5 hrs and great value from $70. Recommended.
Grasshoppers Nimbin Eco-Explorer Tour, The Hub, 9 Marvel St, T0438 269 076. Recommended if you want to see some of the hinterland's best sights, from $45. Transport to the Nimbin backpackers is an additional option.
Jim's Alternative Tours, T6685 7720, www.jimsalternativetours.com. A wide array of entertaining options from simple lighthouse or market trips to dolphin watching and national park ecotours. Day tour departs daily at 1000.

⊖ Transport

Port Macquarie p178, map p179
Bus
To access the eastern beaches jump on Nos 334, 332 or 324. Long-distance buses stop at the bus terminal on Hayward St. **Busways**, 6 Denham St, T6583 2499, www.busways.com.au, runs both local and regional bus services between **Sydney** and **Yamba**. Greyhound, T1300 473946, www.greyhound.com.au, offers daily state-wide services. **Keans Coaches**, T6543 1322, runs a service from Port Macquarie to **Scone** (via the **Waterfall Way**, **Dorrigo**, **Bellingen**, **Armidale** and **Tamworth**) on Tue, Thu and Sun. **Premier Motor Service** has a booking office at the terminal, T6583 1488, T133410, www.premierms.com.au Mon-Fri 0830-1700, Sat 0830-1200.

Train
The nearest train station is at Wauchope, 19 km west of the city, T132232. The connecting bus to Port Macquarie is included in the fare.

South West Rocks and Hat Head p180
Bus
Busways, T1300 555611, runs **Kempsey** (Belgrave St) to **South West Rocks** (Livingstone St) route 350, Mon-Sat.

Bellingen and Dorrigo National Park p181
Bus
Busways, T1300 555611, runs between **Nambucca Heads**, **Urunga**, **Coffs Harbour** and **Bellingen** several times a day Mon-Fri. See above for **Keans Coaches** service from **Scone** to **Port Macquarie** and **Coffs Harbour**. Long-distance buses do not make the detour to Bellingen. The nearest stop is Nambucca Heads or Urunga.
The nearest train station is in Urunga. Countrylink, T132232, operates state and interstate services.
From local towns you can catch local services to the national parks.

Coffs Harbour p183, map p184
Bus Busways, T1300 555611, www.busways.com.au, is the local suburban bus company with daily half-hourly services from 0715-1730. To get from Park Av in the town centre to the jetty, take 365E. Ryan's Buses, T6652 3201, offers local services Mon-Sat to **Woolgoolga** and **Grafton**. Sawtell Coaches, T6653 3344, offers daily local services to **Sawtell**, No 364.
Long-distance buses stop beside the VIC on Elizabeth St. Greyhound, T131499 and Premier, T133410, offers daily interstate services. See under Port Macquarie for **Keans Coaches** service to **Scone**.
Cycle/scooter Hire from Bob Wallis Bicycle Centre, corner of Collingwood and Orlando streets, T6652 5102, from $25 per 24 hrs ($50 deposit).
Train The station is at the end of Angus McLeod St (right off High St and Camperdown St), near the harbour jetty. Countrylink, T132232, runs daily services to **Sydney** and **Brisbane**.

Coffs Harbour to Byron Bay p186
Bus
Busways, T6645 8941, provides daily services for **Grafton-Yamba-Maclean-Iluka**.

Ferry
The **Iluka-Yamba** ferry, T6646 6163, departs 4 times daily from the River St Wharf, Yamba, from $6.50.

Byron Bay p187, map p188
Air
The closest airports to Byron Bay are **Coolangatta** to the north (90 km, Gold Coast), see page 218, and **Ballina** to the south (31 km). Both are served by Jetstar, T131538; QantasLink, T131313; Regional Express, T131713, www.rex.com.au; Tiger Airways, T03-9335 3033, www.tigerairways.com.au; and Virgin Blue, T136789, www.virginblue.com.au. Airporter Shuttle, T04-1460 8660, and Airport Transfers, T6685 8507, www.airporttransfers byronbay.com, serve Coolangatta and Ballina from about $40 one way.

Bus
Local Blanch's Buses, T6686 2144, www.blanchs.com.au, runs local services within **Byron Bay** (No 637) and also south to **Ballina** via **Lennox Head** (No 640) and north to **Mullumbimby** (No 640).
Long distance The long-distance bus stop is located right in the heart of town on Jonson St. Greyhound, T131499, and Premier Motor Services, T133410, run daily interstate services north/south.
Northern Rivers Buslines, T6622 1499, run services to **Ballina** and inland to **Lismore** and **Mullumbimby**.
Kirklands, T6622 1499, runs services to **Brisbane**, **Ballina**, **Lismore** and **Coolangatta**. The VIC acts as the local booking agent. Also of note is the Brisbane Express, T1800 626222, www.brisbane2byron.com, which operates 2-hr transfers to the city centre for $34 (**Brisbane Airport** $46) and J and B Byron

Bay Express, T5592 2655, www.byronbay express.com.au, which operates daily services to **Coolangatta** and **Surfers Paradise** from $25 one-way.

Car/motorcycle
Byron Car Hire, corner of Lawson and Butler streets, T6685 6638. **Byron Bus Transit Centre**, T6685 5517, and **Hertz**, 5 Marvell St, T6621 8855. Car servicing at **Bayside Mechanical**, 12 Banksia Drive, T6685 8455

Cycling
Surf and Bike Hire, 1/31 Lawson St, T6680 7066, www.byronbaysurfandbikehire.com.au and **Byron Bay Bicycles**, T6685 6067. See also Mountain biking, page 201.

Train
The station is located in the heart of town, just off Jonson St. **Countrylink**, T132232, runs daily services south to **Sydney** and beyond, and north (with bus link) with Queensland Rail, T132232, to **Brisbane**.

Rainbow Region p190
Bus
Northern Rivers Buslines, T6622 1499, run services to **Lismore** and **Mullumbimby**. For **Brisbane**, Kirklands, T1300 367077, and interstate **Greyhound**, T132030, stop outside **Tweed Valley Travel**, on the corner of Main St and Queen St. Northbound buses and trains both stop in **Murwillumbah**. Nimbin Shuttle Bus, T6680 9189, operates daily, departing from Jonson St, Byron Bay at 1100, returning at 1700, from $40 return.

Train
Murwillumbah station is opposite the VIC and is served by **Countrylink**, T132232.

Port Macquarie *p178, map p179*
Banks All major branches with ATMs can be found along Clarence St and Horton St.
Internet Port PC & Electronic Services, 2/ 15 Short St, T6583 9399. Daily until around 1900. **Medical services** Port Macquarie Base Hospital, Wright Rd, T6581 2000. **Post office** Shop 2, Palm Court Centre, 14-16 William St. Mon-Fri 0900-1700. Postcode 2444. **Useful numbers** Police, 2 Hay St, T6583 0199.

Coffs Harbour *p183, map p184*
Banks Major branches with ATMs can be found on the Mall or along Grafton St and Park Av. **Internet** The Internet Room, Shop 21, Jetty Village Shopping Centre, T6651 9155. Mon-Fri 0900-1800, Sat-Sun 1000-1600, or **Jetty Dive Centre**, 398 High St, T6651 1611. **Medical services** Hospital, T6656 7000. **Post office** Palms Centre Arcade, 35 Harbour Dr. Mon-Sat 0830-1700. Postcode 2450. **Useful numbers** Police, Moonee St, T6652 0299.

Byron Bay *p187, map p188*
Banks Most major branches with ATMs are represented along Jonson St or Lawsons St. Currency exchange is readily available including **Byron Foreign Exchange**, Shop 4 Central Arcade, T6685 7787. 0900-1800.
Car hire Earth Car Rentals, Shop 3A, 1 Byron St, T6685 7472, www.eathcar.com.au. The first carbon neutral car hire company in Australia, with a percentage of the rental fee going to Cool Planet.
Internet Omnipresent, including Wicked Travel, 29 Jonson St, T1800 555339. 0800-2400. **Medical services** Bay Centre Medical, 6 Lawson St, T6685 6206, www.byronmed.com.au. **Post office** 61 Jonson St. Mon-Fri 0900-1700. Postcode 2481. **Travel agents** Backpackers World, Shop 6, Byron St, T6685 8858. **Useful numbers** Police, 2 Shirley St, T6685 9499.

Contents

Footprint features

Brisbane & South Coast QLD

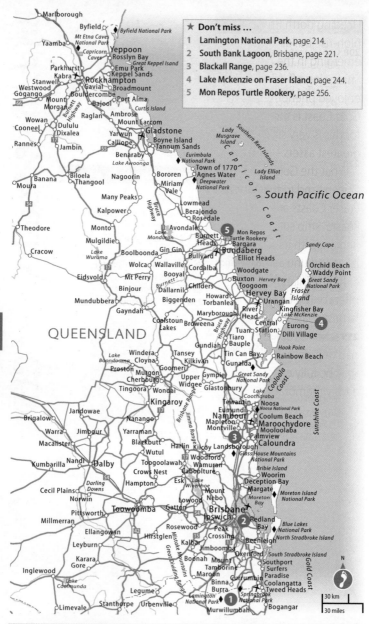

★ **Don't miss ...**

South Pacific Ocean

QUEENSLAND

30 km
30 miles

Heading north from New South Wales, you pass the forest of high-rise buildings strung along the infamous Gold Coast before emerging in the relaxing embrace of the state capital, Brisbane. Shrugging off its non-progressive reputation, Brisbane has enjoyed phenomenal growth in recent years and along with the Gold Coast is the fastest developing region in Australia. The reason for this is very simple and revolves almost entirely around its greatest assets – climate and lifestyle.

What the Gold Coast is to glitz and theme parks and Far North Queensland to the Barrier Reef and rainforests, the Sunshine and Fraser Coasts are to sand, surf and sunshine. North of Noosa the coastal strip succumbs to the vast expanses of the Great Sandy Region, with its ancient coloured sands, sand blows, freshwater lakes and unusual wildlife.

The mainland (Cooloola) section is well worth investigating but offers only a taste of something even better: Fraser Island, the largest coastal sand island in the world. Fraser is the biggest tourist attraction in Southern Queensland. With its unique range of habitats, natural features and rich biodiversity, all of which can only be fully explored by 4WD, Fraser presents the opportunity for a truly memorable eco-experience.

Gold Coast → *Colour map 4, C2.*

With almost five million visitors a year the 'Coast with the Most' is Australia's most popular domestic holiday destination and for some inexplicable reason is seen by some native Australians as the perfect piece of real estate. Like any place that is bold and brash, the Gold Coast's reputation precedes it and no doubt those who have never been will already have formed a strong opinion. Sure it's a concrete jungle and a womb of artificiality, but for lovers of the laid-back beach lifestyle, socialites seeking a hectic nightlife, theme park and thrill ride junkies and shopaholics, it can promise more than just a surfers' paradise. For those of you just itching to scratch the mighty Gold Coast from your travelling agenda at the mere prospect of such a place, think again. Even for the greatest cynic, the worst (or the best) of the Gold Coast can prove utterly infectious and lead to a thoroughly enjoyable experience. Turning your back on the coast, only an hour away is one of the Gold Coast's greatest assets and the 'Green behind the Gold', in the form of the Springbrook and Lamington National Parks, two of Queensland's best, and perfect retreats from all the chaos.

Currumbin to Surfers Paradise

Just off the Gold Coast Highway is **Currumbin Wildlife Sanctuary** ① *T5534 1266, www.currumbin-sanctuary.org.au, 0800-1700, $40, children $24*, one of the most popular parks in the area. A small train takes you into the heart of the park where you can investigate the various animal enclosures housing everything from Tasmanian devils to tree kangaroos. But the highlight is the rainbow lorikeet feeding. To either partake or be a spectator at this highly colourful and entertaining 'avian-human interaction spectacular' is truly memorable and thoroughly recommended. Just before feeding time the air fills with the excited screeching of the birds and the trees are painted in their radiant hues, while the human participants below are each given a small bowl of liquid feed. Given that 80% of Australia's native wildlife is nocturnal, the Wildnight tour programme (1920-2145, from $71) is well worth considering. It includes an Aboriginal dance display.

Burleigh Heads, an ancient volcano, forms one of the few breaks in the seemingly endless swathe of golden sand and offers fine views back towards Surfers. There are also world-class surf breaks and several good walking tracks through the Burleigh Heads National Park. West of Burleigh Heads, **David Fleay Wildlife Park** ① *signposted 3 km west of Gold Coast Highway on Burleigh Heads Rd, T5576 2411, 0900-1700, $17, children $8*, is home to all the usual suspects (koalas, crocs, kangaroos and cassowaries), and some less well-known species, like bilbies, brolgas and dunnarts. Overall it offers a fine introduction to Australia's native species. The park is especially well known for its nocturnal platypus displays, breeding successes and care of sick and injured wildlife.

Surfers Paradise → *For listings, see pages 215-219. Colour map 4, C2.*

From its humble beginnings as a single hotel four decades ago, Surfers Paradise has mushroomed and now epitomizes all the worst aspects of the Gold Coast. An endless line of high-rise apartment blocks towers over shopping malls and exclusive real estate properties, and a thousand and one tourist attractions, many of them planted firmly and unashamedly at the kitsch end of the market, provide round-the-clock entertainment.

State phone codes and time difference

There are no area phone codes. Use a state code if calling outside the state you are in. These are: 02 for ACT/NSW (08 for Broken Hill), 03 for VIC and 07 for QLD. Note that NSW operates daylight saving, which means that clocks go forward one hour from October to March.

Ins and outs

Getting there and around As the transport hub of the Gold Coast, there are frequent links with all major towns and cities. The airport is at Coolangatta, 22 km south, with regular shuttles to Surfers, which is a small place with most of the action focused in and around the Cavill Avenue Mall and adjacent nightclub strip, Orchid Avenue. *▸▸ See Transport, page 218.*

Tourist information **VIC** ① *2 Cavill Av Mall, T5538 4419, www.goldcoasttourism.com.au, Mon-Fri 0830-1700, Sat 0830-1700, Sun 0900-1600,* is an incredibly small affair. Try to get a copy of the official *Gold Coast Holiday Guide*.

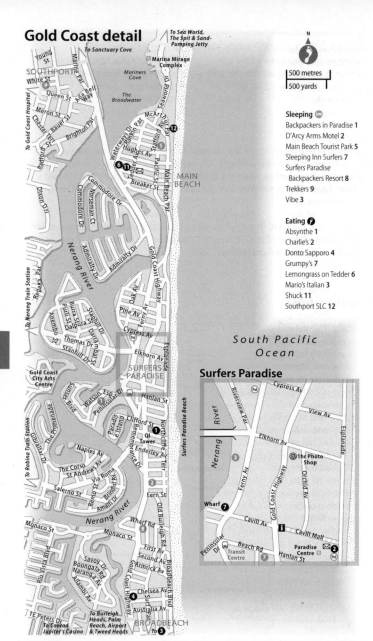

Gold Coast detail

To Sea World,
The Spit & Sand-
Pumping Jetty

To Sanctuary Cove

Marina Mirage
Complex

Mariners
Cove

SOUTHPORT

The
Broadwater

MAIN
BEACH

Nerang River

Gold Coast
City Arts
Centre

SURFERS
PARADISE

QI
Tower

Surfers Paradise Beach

South Pacific
Ocean

Nerang River

BROADBEACH

To Burleigh
Heads, Palm
Beach, Airport
& Tweed Heads

To Conrad
Jupiter's Casino

N

| 500 metres |
| 500 yards |

Sleeping
Backpackers in Paradise **1**
D'Arcy Arms Motel **2**
Main Beach Tourist Park **5**
Sleeping Inn Surfers **7**
Surfers Paradise
  Backpackers Resort **8**
Trekkers **9**
Vibe **3**

Eating
Absynthe **1**
Charlie's **2**
Donto Sapporo **4**
Grumpy's **7**
Lemongrass on Tedder **6**
Mario's Italian **3**
Shuck **11**
Southport SLC **12**

Surfers Paradise

Nerang River

@1hr Photo
Shop

Wharf

Transit
Centre

Paradise
Centre

Sights

Surfers Paradise Beach is, of course, the big draw. If you can, take a stroll at sunrise along the 500-m sand-pumping jetty at the end of The Spit, north of Sea World. It opens at 0600 and for $1 you can walk out to the end and take in the memorable view of the entire beach and the glistening high-rises disappearing into the haze, all the way down to Tweed Heads.

One high-rise building stands out above the rest: **Q1** ⓘ *Paradise Blvd, T5582 2700, Fri-Sat 0900-midnight, Sun-Thu 0900-2100, from $19, children $11 (day and night pass $29/$16.50)*. It's marketed as the world's highest residential building. As you might expect you can of course take in the elevated views from its 77th floor observation deck both day and night, which is well worth a look. On Friday and Saturday nights its swish QBar serves up cocktails, live music and the odd high-altitude DJ to enhance the view.

Gold Coast City Art Centre ⓘ *135 Bundall Rd, 3 km west of Surfers, T5581 6500, www.gcac.com.au, Mon-Fri 1000-1700, Sat-Sun 1100-1700, free*, presents a dynamic programme of local contemporary work as well as a more wide-ranging historical collection. It is also home to one of Australia's longest running art prizes, now titled the Conrad Jupiters Art Prize, which has provided an exciting overview of contemporary Australian Art since 1968. The outdoor sculpture walk is also worth looking at.

Between Surfers Paradise and The Spit, **Main Beach** fringes the southern shores of Broadwater Bay and the Nerang River Inlet. The Marina Mirage shopping complex contains some of the best restaurants in the region, most of which offer alfresco dining overlooking Mariners Cove, the departure point for scenic cruises and helicopter flights.

The Gold Coast is often labelled as Australia's **Theme Park** capital, with millions visiting annually. The stalwarts are Sea World, Dreamworld and Movie World, with other less high-profile parks like Wet'n'Wild and the Australian Outback Spectacular providing back-up. Entry for each is expensive, from $72 (children $47), but that usually includes all the rides and attractions. Note also there are any number of combination passes with which to make life easier, or indeed, more complicated. To visit three parks over five days will cost around $150. And you thought this was a holiday? The VIC can help secure the latest complex discounts, or you can contact Myfun direct on T133386. For cheaper online bookings (and to complete your organizational odyssey) see www.myfun.com.au.

Sea World ⓘ *Main Beach (1 km), T5588 2205, www.seaworld.com.au, 1000-1700, $72, children $47*, has been successfully developing its sea-based attractions for over 30 years, picking up numerous awards along the way and earning a reputation as one of the world's best theme parks. The main attractions are the dolphin and seal shows, thrill rides and water ski stunts, resident polar bears (!) and multi-million dollar Shark Bay, which guarantees to get you up close and personal with the beasts. You can also go on whale and dolphin cruises or helicopter scenic flights.

Movie World ⓘ *Pacific Highway, T133386, www.movieworld.com.au, 1000-1730, $72, children $47*, is perhaps the most popular of all the theme parks. Even if you are not a great fan of Scooby Doo and co, cartoons or science fiction generally, a peek at the sets, props and costumes from the latest big release will certainly impress. Aside from the special effects of the main exhibits, thrill seekers can hit the water on the Wild West Adventure Ride, or even risk the rollercoaster.

As the name suggests, the **Australian Outback Spectacular** ⓘ *Entertainment Road at Oxenford, T133386, www.outbackspectacular.myfun.com.au, Tue-Sun 1930, show and dinner $100, children $70*, is all 'yee haw' horses, Akubra hats and cracking whips. Although both commercial and expensive it is certainly highly entertaining and dinner is included. However, what a crusty ol' station owner in Tittybong or Mount Buggery would have to say about all the hyperbole is an entirely different matter…mate.

Coolangatta and Tweed Heads → For listings, see pages 215-219. Colour map 4, C2.

What Surfers Paradise is to rollercoasters and shopping malls, Coolangatta is to sand and surf. Its greatest attraction is undoubtedly its beaches and the mighty surf that breaks upon them. The coast around Coolangatta and Tweed Heads is not only renowned as one of the world's premier surf spots, it has also produced many world-class surfers such as the legendary Michael Peterson 'MP', and ex-world champions Peter Townend 'PT' and Wayne 'Rabbit' Bartholomew. Such a reputation has led to something of a population boom in the Coolangatta region and this, coupled with an increase in the popularity of surfing, has caused a massive increase in the numbers of surfers in the water on any good day.

Ins and outs
Getting there and around The airport is 2 km from Coolangatta. Major bus companies have services to the town, which is small enough to navigate on foot, with local bus services to surrounding sights. ▶▶ *See Transport, page 218.*

Tourist information **Gold Coast (Coolangatta) VIC** ① *Shop 22, Showcase on the Beach, Griffith St, T5569 3380, www.goldcoasttourism.com.au, Mon-Fri 0800-1700, Sat 0900-1500.* **Tweed Heads VIC** ① *corner of Bay St and Wharf St, Tweed Heads, T5536 6737, www.tweedcoolangatta.com.au, Mon-Sat 0900-1630, Sun 0930-1600.* There is a town map in the useful, free brochure *Tweed-Coolangatta Visitor's Guide.*

Sights
Coolangatta is fringed with superb beaches that surround the small peninsula known as Tweed Heads. The tip of the peninsula, named **Point Danger** by Captain Cook in 1770, provides a fine starting point from which to survey the scene. Below and to the right is **Duranbah Beach**, which flanks the sea wall at the mouth of the Tweed River. Like all the beaches around the heads it is a popular surf spot, and Point Danger provides a good vantage point if you want to watch.

To the left is **Snapper Rocks**, one of the most popular surf spots on the southern Gold Coast. It's a great place to watch the surfers as you can literally sit on the rocks beside the 'launch zone' only metres away from all the action. Just to the west of Snapper Rocks is the pretty little beach called **Rainbow Bay**, which is the first of the beaches that combines good surfing with safe swimming. Continuing west, Rainbow Bay is then separated from **Greenmount Beach** by a small headland that offers fine views from **Pat Fagan Park**. Greenmount Beach then merges with Coolangatta Beach, both of which are idyllic, excellent for swimming and enormously popular with families. At the western end of Coolangatta Beach, **Kirra Point** also provides great views back down Greenmount and Coolangatta beaches and north, beyond **North Kirra Beach**, to Surfers Paradise. Between Snapper Rocks and Kirra Point is the famed surfers' Superbank, see box opposite.

Making waves

Between Snapper Rocks and Kirra Point is the so-called Superbank, a man-made phenomenon that has created one of the world's greatest point breaks and most incredible surfing experiences. In the early 1990s a scheme was proposed to remove sand from the mouth of the Tweed and relocate it to the northerly points. This was finished in 2001 and sand is now pumped from the mouth of the river, underground, to spots at Froggies Beach – just to the south of Snapper – Rainbow Bay and Kirra. However, no one expected the scheme to produce such an amazing sandbank or to have such a profound effect on the surf. On a perfect day, machine-like waves roll along the shallow sandbank in one unending steam-train. The Superbank is capable of producing rides of 2 km in length and multiple 10-second barrel rides, making it one of the most popular breaks on the entire Australian East Coast.

Gold Coast hinterland → For listings, see pages 215-219. Colour map 4, C2.

Less than an hour's drive from the Gold Coast are its greatest inland attractions, the national parks of Lamington, Springbrook and Mount Tamborine. Labelled 'the Green Behind the Gold', they provide their own natural wonderland of pristine subtropical rainforest, waterfalls, walking tracks and stunning views. The weather here can also be dramatically different from that on the coast with much more rain and the coolest temperatures in the state.

Ins and outs

Tourist information The principal QPWS offices are located within the parks ① Springbrook, T5533 5147, and Lamington, T5544 0634, www.derm.qld.gov.au. Walking track guides with maps and details are available from each office. For vineyard information, visit www.goldcoastwinecountry.com.au. ▸▸ See Transport, page 218.

Springbrook National Park

This 2954-ha park, 29 km south from Mudgeeraba on the Pacific Highway, is the most accessible for the coast and sits on the northern rim of what was once a huge volcano centred on Mount Warning (see also page 192). The park is split into three sections: **Springbrook Plateau**, **Natural Bridge** and the **Cougals**. The Natural Bridge section of the park is accessed from the Nerang to Murwillumbah Road.

Springbrook offers a rich subtropical rainforest habitat of ancient trees and gorges, interspersed with creeks, waterfalls and an extensive system of walking tracks. In addition, the park is well known for its many spectacular views including **Canyon**, **Wunburra**, **Goomoolahara** and the aptly named **Best of All**. Other attractions include the **Natural Arch** (1-km walk), a cavernous rock archway that spans **Cave Creek**, and the 190-m **Purling Brook Falls** (4-km walk). Natural Arch also plays host to a colony of glow worms. See Tour operators, page 218, if you don't have your own transport.

Mount Tamborine

Mount Tamborine is a name used loosely to describe the 17-section **Tamborine National Park** and the picturesque settlements of **Mount Tamborine**, **Tamborine Village** and

Eagle Heights. Combined, they offer an attractive escape from the coast with fine coastal views, walking tracks, vineyards, B&Bs, teahouses and arts and crafts galleries. One of the most popular sections is the **Witches Falls**, first designated a national park in 1908, making it Queensland's oldest. Other popular spots include **Cedar Creek** section, with its pleasant 3-km walk to some pretty waterfalls, or the **Joalah** section, where, if you are lucky, you may see – or more probably hear – one of its best-known residents, the mimicking lyrebird.

Mount Tamborine is accessed via the Oxenford-Tamborine Road (Oxenford turn-off) or the Nerang-Tamborine Road (Nerang turn-off) both on the Pacific Highway. There is no public transport to Mount Tamborine but various tours are available.

The biggest attraction here is the new **Tamborine Rainforest Skywalk** ⓘ *333 Geissmann Drive, North Tamborine, T5545 2222, www.rainforestskywalk.com.au, daily 0930-1600, $18.50, children $9.50.* This attraction aims to echo the success of other elevated forest walkways in The Otways in Victoria and in Tahune Forest in Tasmania. The idea is identical in that you can experience the forest and its many inhabitants from a unique viewpoint high above the forest floor. The walk takes about 45 minutes and there is an interpretative centre, shop and café.

Bushwacker Eco Tours ⓘ *T1300 559355, www.bushwacker-ecotours.com.au,* and **JPT Day Tours** ⓘ *T1300 363436, www.daytours.com.au,* both offer package deals from Brisbane.

The VICs can supply information on other attractions in the area, while the **Doughty Park Information Centre** ⓘ *off Main Western Rd, North Tamborine, T5545 3200, www.tamborinemtncc.org.au,* stocks walks and parks information. There are no QPWS campsites in the park.

Lamington National Park

The 20,500-ha Lamington National Park sits on the border of Queensland and New South Wales and comprises densely forested valleys, peaks straddling the **McPherson Range** and an ancient volcanic area known as the **Scenic Rim**, about 60 km inland from the Gold Coast. The park is essentially split into two sections: the **Binna Burra** to the east and the **Green Mountains** (O'Reilly's) to the west. Combined, they offer a wealth of superb natural features and a rich biodiversity that can be experienced on over 100 km of walking tracks. The Green Mountains were first settled in 1911 by the O'Reilly family, who established a number of small dairy farms before consolidating their assets in 1915 with the opening of their now internationally famous guesthouse (see page 216). Other than the sense of escape and surrounding beauty, its most popular draw is the treetop canopy walkway: an ideal way to see the rainforest habitat. There are also some excellent walking tracks offering spectacular views and numerous waterfalls. Guided tours are available, along with a broad range of places to stay. The Green Mountains (O'Reilly's) section is accessed from Canungra.

The most accessible section is Binna Burra, 35 km south west of Nerang on the Pacific Highway. From Brisbane you can travel south via Nerang or via Mount Tamborine and Canungra. If you don't have your own transport, there are numerous tour operators, see page 218. Like the Green Mountains, Binna Burra offers a wealth of excellent rainforest walking opportunities and plays host to another historic guesthouse (see page 216). Guided tours are available from the lodge and there is a QPWS centre and campsite.

Gold Coast listings

For Sleeping and Eating price codes and other relevant information, see Essentials pages 28-33.

Sleeping

Surfers Paradise *p208, map p210*
The Gold Coast has accommodation of all types to suit all budgets. But even with the 60,000 odd beds currently available you are advised to book in advance. Prices fluctuate wildly between peak and off-peak seasons. Standby deals and packages are always on offer so you are advised to shop around and research thoroughly. Booking at least 7 days in advance will usually work out cheaper.

Here we list a small selection. For a much greater choice pick up the free Qantas and Sunlover Gold Coast brochures available from travel agents. Accommodation agents include the **Gold Coast Accommodation Service**, Shop 1, 1 Beach Rd, Surfers, T5592 0067, www.goldcoastaccommodation service.com.au. The Gold Coast City Council operates a number of excellent facilities up and down the coast. Look out for their free *Gold Coast City Council Holiday Parks* brochure or visit www.gctp.com.au.
L Vibe Hotel, 42 Ferny Av, Surfers Paradise, T5539 0444, www.vibehotels.com.au. Quality contemporary boutique hotel in a central location. Plenty of style and a good choice if you want to indulge.
A-E Main Beach Tourist Park, Main Beach Pde, T5581 7722, www.gctp.com.au. This park offers cabins, en suite/standard powered and non-powered sites, with good facilities and camp kitchens, all nestled quietly amongst the high-rise blocks and across the road from the main beach.
C D'Arcy Arms Motel, 2923 Gold Coast Highway, corner of Frederick St, Surfers, T5592 0882, www.darcyarms.com.au. Fine Irish hospitality, good value modern units and a good pub/restaurant (see page 216).
C-E Backpackers in Paradise, 40 Peninsular Drive, just west of the Transit Centre, T5538

4344, www.backpackers in-paradise.com. Lively, colourful, friendly and well equipped. Dorms and 3 spacious doubles (en suite), café, bar, pool, excellent kitchen, broadband internet, tour desk and a comfy TV lounge with a huge screen.
C-E Sleeping Inn Surfers Hostel and Apartments, 26 Peninsular Drive, T5592 4455, www.sleepinginn.com.au. Modern facilities with a wider choice of room options than most: from dorms and singles to doubles, twins and self-contained units with TV and living room. It can also throw a good party. They also have a modern apartment complex (**L**) consisting of 1, 2 and 3 bedroom, twin or double rooms at 2963 Surfers Paradise Blvd, T5539 0090.
C-E Surfers Paradise Backpackers Resort, 2837 Gold Coast Highway, T5592 4677, www.surfersparadisebackpackers.com.au. Lively and popular purpose-built place on the border of Surfers and Broadbeach. It offers tidy en suite dorms, units (some self-contained with TV) and good facilities, including well-equipped kitchen, bar, free laundry, pool, sauna, gym, volleyball pitch, cable TV/games room, internet, party and activity tours, pick-ups and off-street parking.
C-E Trekkers, 22 White St, Southport, 2 km north of Surfers, T5591 5616, www.trekkersbackpackers.com.au. The best backpackers in the region. Small traditional suburban Queenslander, offering cosy, well-appointed rooms including en suite doubles with TV, good pool and garden. Great atmosphere, friendly, family-run business with the emphasis on looking after each guest rather than the turnover.

Coolangatta and Tweed Heads *p212*
A-E Kirra Beach Tourist Park, Charlotte St, off Coolangatta Rd, T5667 2740, www .gctp.com.au. Spacious, with good facilities, offering powered and non-powered sites, cabins, camp kitchen and saltwater pool.

B-D Sunset Strip Budget Resort,
199-203 Boundary St, T5599 5517,
www.sunsetstrip.com.au. Much closer to the
beach and the town centre, this is an old,
spacious hotel with unit-style singles,
doubles, twins, quads and family rooms with
shared bathrooms, excellent kitchen facilities,
large pool and within metres of the beach.
Basic but spacious, good value. Fully
self-contained 1- and 2-bedroom
holiday flats also available.
C-E Coolangatta/Kirra Beach YHA,
230 Coolangatta Rd, T5536 7644,
booking@coolangattayha.com. Near the
airport and facing the busy Pacific Highway,
offers tidy dorms, doubles/twins, pool, bike
and surfboard hire, internet. Free shuttle to
the beaches and Greyhound bus terminal.

Gold Coast Hinterland *p213*
LL Binna Burra Mountain Lodge, Binna
Burra Rd, Beechmont (via Nerang),
Lamington National Park, T5533 3622,
www.binnaburralodge.com.au. The most
accessible of the Lamington National Park
medium to luxury options. Well-appointed en
suite cabins with fireplace (some with spa),
activities, meals included.
LL The Mouses House, 2807 Springbrook
Rd, Springbrook, T5533 5192, www.mouses
house.com.au. Characterful luxury eco-resort
with themed bush chalets with spa. Very
romantic and cosy. Recommended.
LL-L O'Reilly's Rainforest Guesthouse,
Lamington National Park Rd (via Canungra),
Lamington National Park, T5544 0644,
www.oreillys.com.au. A range of room
options from luxury suites to standard, pool,
sauna, spa and restaurant. Package includes
meals and some tours.
QPWS campsites for Lamington National
Park at both Binna Burra, T5533 3584, and
Green Mountains (200 m from O'Reilly's) with
water, hot showers and toilets. Fees apply,
book ahead with the ranger or information
centres at each location. Also at Purling Brook
Falls, Springbook National Park, T5533 5147.

● Eating

Surfers Paradise *p208, map p210*
There are too many good restaurants to list
here; it's best to browse the menus at your
leisure. The Marina Mirage in Main Beach is a
favourite haunt, but don't expect a cheap
deal. Further north, Sanctuary Cove is a fine
spot for lunch but is also expensive. To the
south, Burleigh Heads has superb views,
while the many surf lifesaving clubs offer
great value as do the dinner cruises.
¶¶¶ **Absynthe**, ground floor, Q1, Hamilton Av,
T5504 6466, www.absynthe.com.au. Chic
new French/Australian restaurant where
award-winning Chef Meyjitte Boughenout
gets creative. Try the degustation menu.
¶¶¶ **Lemongrass on Tedder**, 6/26 Tedder Av,
T5528 0289. Of the many Thai options, this
one stands out for quality and value for
money, but book ahead.
¶¶ **D'Arcy Arms Irish Pub and Motel**, see page
215. Mon-Sat from 1800. Offers traditional
wholesome pub food at reasonable prices.
¶¶ **Donto Sapporo**, 2763 Gold Coast
Highway, T5539 9933. Considered one of the
best Japanese restaurants in the city.
¶¶ **Grumpy's**, at the river end of Cavill Mall (Tiki
Village), T5531 6177. Well known for its
affordable seafood, casual atmosphere and
pleasant views.
¶¶ **Mario's Italian**, Oasis Shopping Mall,
Broadbeach, T5592 1899. A fine reputation
and good value takeaway pizza.
¶¶ **Shuck**, Shop 1-4/20 Tedder Av, T5528
4286. Daily from 1200. Award-winning
seafood restaurant with an imaginative and
wide-ranging menu, good service and chic,
contemporary decor. Try the signature dish:
sand crab lasagne.
¶ **Charlie's**, Cavill Mall, T5538 5285. Decent
meals 24 hrs a day and good breakfast.
¶ **Southport SLC**, McArthur Pde, Main Beach,
T5591 5083, and the **Palm Beach SLC**, 7th Av
and Jefferson Lane, Palm Beach, T5534 2180,
are two of many surf lifesaving clubs (SLCs)
along the coast, with great value meals.

Coolangatta and Tweed Heads *p212*

♥♥ Cooli Steak and Seafood Restaurant,
Shop 1, Blue C Resort, 3 McLean Street,
northern end of Marine Pde , T5536 8808.
Breakfast Sat-Sun from 0700; lunch Fri-Sun
1200-1400; dinner daily from 1730. Best
option for affordable steak and seafood. Tue
specials: buy one main meal and get one of
equal value free.

♥♥ Fisherman's Cove Seafood Taverna, at
Oaks Calypso Resort, Griffith St, T5536 1646.
Affordable and fine fishy fare.

♥ Coffee Club, 120 Marine Pde, T5599 4755.
Value light meals and quality coffee
overlooking the beach.

🎧 Bars and clubs

Surfers Paradise *p208, map p210*
If you are staying at any of the hostels you will
be well looked after by the staff and will only
need to go with the flow. If not, Orchid Av, off
Cavill Mall, is the main focus for clubbing,
with most places staying open until about
0300. Dress is smart casual, carry ID and be
prepared to kiss your money goodbye. Entry
ranges from $12-20, which is manageable,
but drinks are expensive. For a more
sophisticated night out, try the QBar, at the
top of the Q1 tower; see page 211.

🎭 Entertainment

Surfers Paradise *p208, map p210*
Conrad Jupiter's Casino, off Hooker Blvd,
Gold Coast Highway, Broadbeach, T5592
8100, www.conrad.com.au. 2 floors of
gaming tables and pokies (slot machines).
Open 24 hrs. There is a cinema and theatre at
the Arts Centre, 135 Blundall Rd, T5588 4008,
and other mainstream cinemas in the malls.

✦ Festivals and events

Surfers Paradise *p208, map p210*
The Gold Coast hosts a number of exciting
annual events most of which involve lots of
money, fireworks and parties, festivals, races
and sporting spectaculars. Although listed
under Surfers, many of these are spread out
along the coast. For a detailed calendar, visit
www.verygoldcoast.com.au.
Feb kicks off with Conrad Jupiter's Magic
Millions, a 10-day horseracing event with a
very popular fashion event.
Mar The beach is the main focus for the
Australian Surf Life Saving Championships,
arguably the Gold Coast's most famous event.
It attracts over 7000 national and
international competitors, all trying to out
swim, run and row each other, to win the
prestigious Iron Man or Iron Woman trophy.
Jul Gold Coast Marathon is considered to be
Australia's premier long-distance running event.
Oct It's green for go with the ever-popular
Nitro Super GP, when the streets of Surfers
are alive to the sound of racing cars and, in
the evenings, to the heady beat of parties,
parades and the mardi gras.
Numerous food festivals are also held
throughout the year, including the Gold
Coast Food Festival in Sep, the Broadbeach
Festival in Oct and the Gold Coast Signature
Dish Competition in Dec.

○ Shopping

Surfers Paradise *p208, map p210*
The Gold Coast offers a healthy dose of retail
therapy with some 3500 shops, all of which
contribute to over $3 billion of visitor
spending per annum.
Marina Mirage, Main Beach and Sanctuary
Cove. More upmarket than the Paradise
Centre but lacking atmosphere.
Paradise Centre, Cavill Av. A focus for mainly
tourist-based products and more bikinis than
an episode of *Baywatch*.

▲▲ Activities and tours

Surfers Paradise p208, map p210
Other than the beach, shopping and the theme parks, Surfers presents a mind-blowing array of additional activities way beyond the scope of this guide. Visit the VIC for the full list. If anything is to be recommended, it has to be a rainforest tour to the stunning Lamington and Springbrook national parks (see below), an hour's drive inland. The resorts on South Stradbroke Island offer a suitable coastal escape (see Moreton Bay, page 224).

Tour operators
Tour Gold Coast, T5532 8687, www.tourgc.com.au. Specialist eco-operator offering trips to see the Natural Bridge and its glow-worm tours in the Springbrook National Park and whale watching cruises.
Bushwacker Ecotours, T3720 9020 , www.bushwacker-ecotours.com.au. Day walking tours and overnight camping trips to Lamington and Moreton Island from $249.

Water sports
For anything water based, including self-hire, shop around at the Cruise Terminal, at Mariners Cove (Main Beach) or the wharf at the western end of Cavill Av.
For surfing lessons try **Cheyne Horan**, T1800 227873, www.cheynehoran.com.au.

Gold Coast Hinterland p213
Tour operators
Several tour operators offer day trips to Springbrook from both Brisbane and the Gold Coast including **Bushwackers Ecotours** (day and night tours, see above), and **Scenic Hinterland Tours**, T5531 5536, www.hinter landtours.com.au, from $75. The VIC has full listings.

⊖ Transport

Getting around the Gold Coast is generally very easy, with 24-hr local bus transport, numerous companies offering theme park/airport transfers and car, moped, and bike hire.
Surfside Buslines Tourist Shuttle, T5574 5111, www.gcshuttle.com.au, is the principal local operator and sells a Freedom Pass of 3-14 days, from $67 (children $34). Surfside also offers airport (Coolangatta) transfers from $21.
Note that for regular local use Surfside Buslines use Translink's GoCard Ticketless system. GoCard is a travel card that stores up to $200 so you can travel seamlessly on all TransLink buses.
Airtrain, T1800 119091, www.airtrain.com.au, operates suburban rail services and theme park and airport transfers ($45) from Robina and Nerang, 0830-2245 (main trunk services from Coolangatta to Southport 24 hrs).

Surfers Paradise p208, map p210
Bus
Active Tours, T5527 4144; **Coachtrans**, T3358 9700 (T1300 664700), www.coachtrans.com.au, and **Con-X-ions**, T5556 9888, www.con-x-ion.com, offer regular shuttles to and from **Brisbane** city, Brisbane and Coolangatta airports and the theme parks.
The long-distance terminal is on the corner of Beach Rd and Remembrance Drive. Most of the major coach companies have offices within the complex (0600-2200). **Premier Motor Services**, T133410, www.premierms.com.au, and **Greyhound**, T1300 473946, www.greyhound.com.au, offer daily interstate services. **Coachtrans**, T1300 664700, www.coach trans.com.au, are recommended for **Brisbane** city and airport transfers. **Kirklands**, T1300 367077, www.kirklands.com.au, and **Suncoast Pacific**, T131230, and several Byron Bay-based local operators offer regular services to **Byron Bay** and the **NSW coast**.

Cycling

Bike hire is available from **Red Rocket Rent-A-Car**, 16 Orchid Av, T5538 9074, www.redrocketrentals.com.au.

Mopeds/jeeps

Rent-A-Jeep, corner Ferny Av and Ocean Av, Surfers Paradise, T1800 228085. Small jeeps and microscopic Smart cars, starting from about $75 per day.
Yahoo, 88 Ferny Av, T5592 0227. From $50 for mopeds.

Train

Both Robina and Nerang train stations (15 km and 10 km southwest and west of Surfers respectively) are served by **Airtrain**, T1800 119091, www.airtrain.com.au, from **Brisbane** (with connections to Brisbane airport), from $45, children $22. **Airtrain Connect**, T1800 119091, and **Surfside Buslines** T5571 6555 (Nos 2 and 11), then offer road transport to the coast.

Coolangatta and Tweed Heads *p212*
Air

Gold Coast Airport is near Coolangatta, 22 km south of Surfers, T5589 1100, www.goldcoastairport.com.au. **Jet Star**, T131538, www.jetstar.com.au; **Qantas**, T131313, www.qantas.com.au; **Tiger**, T03-9355 3033, www.tigerairways.com.au; and **Virgin Blue**, T136789, www.virgin blue.com.au, all offer domestic services (and/or international connections).
Con-X-ions, T5556 9888, www.con-x-ion.com, and **Surfside Buses**, T5571 6555, offer local transfers, from $15, children $7.

Bus

Premier Motor Services, T133410, and **Greyhound**, T5531 6677, operate daily interstate services, while **Coachtrans**, T1300 664700, www.coachtrans.com.au, runs regular shuttles up and down the coast, to **Brisbane** and to/from the airport. Kirklands,

T1300 367077, www.kirklands.com.au, and **Suncoast Pacific**, T131230, have regular services to **Byron Bay** and the **NSW coast**. For other Byron Bay-based operators see page 203.

Surfside Buslines, T131230, www.gcshuttle.com.au, is the main suburban bus company with regular links north to **Surfers**.

Taxi

For a taxi, T5536 1144.

Gold Coast Hinterland *p213*

Coolangatta Coachlines Mountain Coach, T1300 762665, www.mountaincoach.com.au, run transportation to and from the **Gold Coast** (via Mount Tamborine) to **Tamborine Mountain** and **O'Reilly's Resort** in the Lamington National Park.

Binna Burra Mountain Lodge (Binna Burra section) uses Limousine Hire from both the Gold Coast and Brisbane, T1300 249622.

❶ Directory

Surfers Paradise *p208, map p210*
Banks All major branches with ATMs and currency exchange are around the Cavill Mall-Gold Coast Highway intersection.
Hospitals **Gold Coast Hospital**, 108 Nerang St, Southport, T5571 8211. **Paradise Medical Centre**, Shop 135 Hanlan Street, Surfers Paradise, T5538 8099 (24-hr).
Internet widely available including **The Chat Room Café** , Shop 37, 3240 Gold Coast Highway, T5539 0062. **Pharmacy** Day and Night, Piazza on the Boulevard (ANA Hotel), 3221 Gold Coast Highway, Surfers, T5592 2299, open 0700-2200. **Post** Centro Shopping Centre, Shop 165. Postcode 4217. Mon-Fri 0830-1730, Sat 0900-1230. **Useful numbers** Police, 68 Ferny Av, T5570 7888. **Surfers**, T5581 2900. **RACQ**, 239 Nerang St, Southport, T5588 7777.

Brisbane and Moreton Bay→ *Colour map 4, C2.*

Brisbane has come an awfully long way since its days as a penal settlement. A lot of money was pumped into the city for its Expo 88 and Brissie has never looked back. South Bank, especially, represents the very essence of modern-day Brisbane with numerous cultural attractions and even its own inner-city beach. Australia's only true tropical city also enjoys a near-perfect climate. Wherever you go, alfresco restaurants, cafés and outdoor activities dominate. Nearby, the sand islands of Moreton Bay offer a wonderful opportunity to enjoy some peace and quiet.

▸▸ *For listings, see pages 226-234.*

Ins and outs

Getting there Trains and buses connect the CBD with both airport terminals: **Airtrain**, T3216 3308, www.airtrain.com.au, departs from Central (top end of Edward Street), Roma (Transit Centre) and Brunswick Street (Fortitude Valley) four times per hour from $14.50, children free. **Coachtrans** (SkyTrans service), T1300 664700, www.coachtrans.com.au, departs from Roma Street Transit Centre every 30 minutes (0500-2100) from $15. Accommodation pick-ups cost $2 extra. A taxi to the airport costs about $45. There are frequent long-distance buses and trains to the city from major centres and cities. ▸▸ *See Transport, page 232.*

Getting around There is an efficient transport system with the river playing a large part in navigating the city. The main centre is within walking distance. The city tours, see page 230, are a great way to get around and see the sights, especially if short of time.

Tourist information Brisbane VIC ⓘ *Queen Street Mall, Albert St and Edward St, T3006 6290, www.experiencebrisbanetourism.com, Mon-Thu, 0900-1730, Fri 0900-1900, Sat 0900-1700, Sun 0930-1630,* offers free city maps and assists with tours and accommodation. **QPWS main office** ⓘ *3rd floor, 400 George St, T1300 130372, Mon-Fri 0830-1700.*

Sights

Central Brisbane

A number of historical buildings stand out amidst the glistening high-rise blocks. At the top end of Albert Street is **City Hall** ⓘ *T3403 8888, 0800-1700 guided tours available, lift free, Mon-Fri 1000-1500,* with its 92-m Italian renaissance clock tower. Built in 1930, it became known as the 'Million Pound Town Hall' due to its huge and controversial construction cost. The ride in the old lift to the top for the views is a highlight but the interior of the building is also worth a look. On the ground floor is the **Museum of Brisbane (MoB)** ⓘ *daily 0900-1700, free,* which showcases the various aspects of contemporary social history and culture with a heavy emphasis on local writers and artists. Around the corner on George Street and the riverbank is the grand 19th-century façade of the former **Treasury Building**, now a casino.

To the east beside the Botanical Gardens (note there are two in the city, see page 224 for the Botanical Gardens-Mount-Coot-tha) is the 1868 French Renaissance-style **Parliament House** ⓘ *T3406 7562, www.parliament.qld.gov.au, Mon-Fri 1030-1430, free,* which was commissioned when Queensland was declared a separate colony in 1859.

Visitors can join tours conducted by parliamentary attendants. Nearby is the **Old Government House** ⓘ *2 George St, T3864 8005, www.ogh.qut.edu.au, 1000-1600, free*, built in 1862 as the official residence of the state's governors and now housing the HQ of the National Trust. It is currently undergoing interior refurbishment and will reopen to the public in 2009.

Further north, beyond the modern architecture and chic restaurants of Waterfront Place, Eagle Street Pier and the Riverside Centre, is **Customs House** ⓘ *399 Queens St, T3365 8999, www.customshouse.com.au, Mon-Fri 0900-1700, tours Sun*. Built in 1889, it resembles a miniature version of St Paul's Cathedral in London. Directly opposite the Customs House is the city's best-known and most-photographed sight – the **Story Bridge**. It was built between 1935 and 1940 and due to the lack of bedrock has some of the deepest (42 m) foundations of any bridge in the world. Recently Brisbane has emulated Sydney's highly successful Harbour Bridge Bridge climb experience and, although far less dramatic, the Story Bridge Adventure Climb still offers great views and may appeal. The dawn or dusk trip is recommended (see page 231).

Overlooking the high-rise blocks on the southern bank of the Brisbane River is the remarkable 17-ha 'oasis in the city' that is known as the **South Bank** ⓘ *www.visitsouthbank.com.au*. Built primarily as the showpiece for Expo 88, the 1-km stretch of parkland remains a fascinating and functional recreational space and includes riverside walks, shops, restaurants and a swimming lagoon with its very own beach. This area is also the venue for the colourful **South Bank Lifestyle Markets** ⓘ *every Fri night, Sat and Sun*.

At the northwestern end of the park, straddling Melbourne Street, is the **Queensland Cultural Centre**, encompassing the State Library, Queensland Museum, Queensland Art Gallery, Gallery of Modern Art and Queensland Performing Arts Complex. **Queensland Art Gallery** ⓘ *T3840 7303, www.qag.qld.gov.au, Mon-Fri 1000-1700, Sat-Sun 0900-1700, free, tours available daily*, is Brisbane's premier cultural attraction, featuring a huge and diverse collection of Aboriginal, European, Asian and contemporary Australian art. Early works include paintings by John Russell and Rupert Bunny, two of the nation's most noted expat artists, as well as more familiar international names such as Rubens, Degas, Picasso and Van Dyck. The **Gallery of Modern Art** ⓘ *T3840 7303, www.qag.qld.gov.au, Mon-Fri 1000-1700, Sat-Sun 0900-1700, free, tours available daily*, is Australia's largest dedicated to the genre and includes the first Australian Cinémathèque, purpose-built to showcase the art of film.

Next to the art gallery is the **Queensland Museum** ⓘ *T3840 7555, www.qm.qld.gov.au, 0930-1700, free*, which is noted for its prehistoric and natural history displays. The museum also has entertaining and educational interactive exhibits, guaranteed to keep little Einsteins amused for hours. On the opposite side of Melbourne Street is the **Queensland Performing Arts Complex**, which houses several theatres and concert venues. At the southeastern end of the South Bank you can find the **Queensland Maritime Museum** ⓘ *T3844 5361, www.maritimemuseum.com.au, 0930-1630, $8, children $3.50*, with all the usual relics from anchors to lifebuoys. Most of the larger vessels, including the Second World War warship *The Diamantina*, sit forlornly in the adjacent dry dock. All this is best viewed from the futuristic **Goodwill Bridge**, built in celebration of the 2001 Goodwill Games.

Brisbane

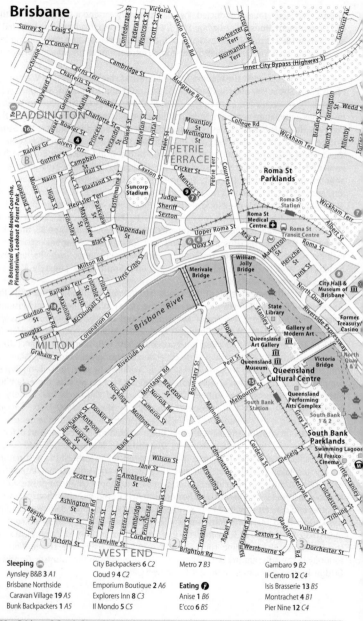

Sleeping 🛏
Aynsley B&B **3** A1
Brisbane Northside
  Caravan Village **19** A5
Bunk Backpackers **1** A5
City Backpackers **6** C2
Cloud **4** C2
Emporium Boutique **2** A6
Explorers Inn **8** C3
Il Mondo **5** C5
Metro **7** B3

Eating 🍴
Anise **1** B6
E'cco **6** B5
Gambaro **9** B2
Il Centro **12** C4
Isis Brasserie **13** B5
Montrachet **4** B1
Pier Nine **12** C4

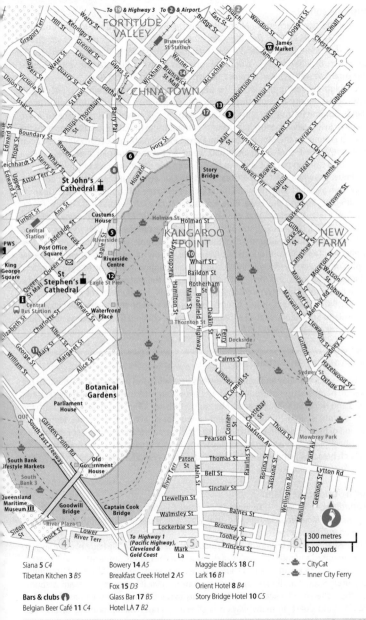

Siana **5** *C4*
Tibetan Kitchen **3** *B5*

Bars & clubs 🎵
Belgian Beer Café **11** *C4*

Bowery **14** *A5*
Breakfast Creek Hotel **2** *A5*
Fox **15** *D3*
Glass Bar **17** *B5*
Hotel LA **7** *B2*

Maggie Black's **18** *C1*
Lark **16** *B1*
Orient Hotel **8** *B4*
Story Bridge Hotel **10** *C5*

- - • - CityCat
- - 🛥 - Inner City Ferry

Brisbane suburbs

West of the city, reached via Milton Road, is the **Botanical Gardens-Mount-Coot-tha** ① *T3403 2535, 0830-1730, free, tours Mon-Sat 1100 and 1300 or pick up a free self-guided leaflet*, considered Queensland's finest subtropical gardens, featuring over 20,000 specimens of 5000 species. Within the grounds is also a **Planetarium** and **Lakeside Restaurant** as well as picnic facilities, library and gift shop (0900-1700).

Set high above the gardens is the **Mount Coot-tha Lookout**, which offers superb views across the city and out across Moreton Bay to Moreton, North Stradbroke and Bribie Islands. **Summit Restaurant** and **Kuta Café**, see page 228, provide an ideal place for lunch, dinner or just a glass of vino while soaking up the sun and the city vistas. Backing onto the lookout complex is the **Mount Coot-tha Forest Park** which consists of 1500 ha of open eucalyptus forest containing over 350 weird and wonderful native species, with a network of walking tracks. Catch bus No 471 from Ann Street or join a City Sights Tour.

Almost anywhere east of the Great Divide in Queensland, it seems you are never far away from a wildlife sanctuary and the opportunity to see (or cuddle) a koala. Brisbane is no different, hosting the **Lone Pine Koala Sanctuary** ① *Jesmond Rd, Fig Tree Pocket (southwest via Milton Rd and the western Freeway 5), T3378 1366, www.koala.net, 0830-1700, $30, children $21*, the oldest and the largest in the world. Having opened in 1927 and now housing around 130 of the famously adorable, yet utterly pea-brained tree dwellers, it offers a fine introduction, or reminder, of how unique Australia's wildlife really is. Also on display are the equally ubiquitous and marginally more bush-wise wombats, echidnas, kangaroos and the latest addition, 'Barak' the platypus. Bus No 430, from the 'koala platform' in the Myer Centre, Queen Street, will get you there, or hop aboard the Mirimar Boat Cruise on Cultural Centre Pontoon (located on the boardwalk outside the Queensland State Library) at 1120, which costs $55, children $33 (including admission) and returns at 1445, T1300 729742.

Moreton Bay and islands → *For listings, see pages 226-234.*

Brisbane's Moreton Bay and islands are easily accessible and remarkably unspoilt. Of the 300-odd islands scattered around the bay, the two largest and most popular are Moreton Island and North Stradbroke Island. Moreton, which lies 37 km northeast of the Brisbane River mouth, is almost uninhabited and famous for its 4WD opportunities, shipwrecks and pod of friendly dolphins. Further south, North Stradbroke is the largest of the islands, a laid-back place with world-class surf beaches, awesome coastal scenery and the chance to watch breaching whales and dolphins and manta rays gliding past beneath the waves. ▸▸ *For further details, see page 233.*

North Stradbroke Island

① *Stradbroke VIC, Shop 1 Kennedy Drive, Point Lookout, T3415 3044, www.stradbroke tourism.com, Mon-Fri 0830-1700, Sat-Sun 0830-1500. It stocks island maps and can assist with general information.*

Wedge-shaped North Stradbroke, or 'Straddie' as it is affectionately known, is the largest, most inhabited and most accessible of the Moreton Bay Islands. Some 30 km southeast of Brisbane, it is 36 km long and 11 km at its widest point. Separated from its southerly neighbour, South Stradbroke, by a fierce cyclone in 1896, it has become a magical tourist attraction often overlooked due to its proximity to the competing attractions of Brisbane and the Gold Coast. In many ways it is similar to Fraser Island, offering diverse and unspoilt coastal scenery and a rich biodiversity that is so typical of sand islands. The three picturesque villages of Dunwich, Amity Point and Point Lookout offer a broad range of accommodation, excellent beaches and plenty of water-based activities. Surfing is the obvious speciality.

Dunwich, a former penal colony and quarantine station, is on the west mid- section of the island and the main arrival point. The small museum ① *Welsby St, open Wed and Sat*, explores the island's rich aboriginal and early settler history. **Amity Point**, first settled in 1825, sits on the northwest corner, 17 km from Dunwich, while **Point Lookout**, the main focus for today's tourist accommodation, sights and activities, is 21 km away on the northeast corner. If you only have one or two days on the island the place to be is Point

Moreton Bay

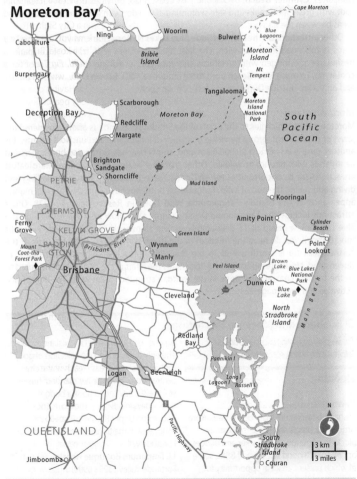

Lookout, with its golden surf beaches and dramatic headland. At the terminus of East Coast Road is the start of the **North Gorge Headlands Walk** (1 km one way). Before you set off take a look at **Frenchman's Bay** below, which gives you a flavour of the dramatic scenery to come. Follow the track, through wind-lashed stands of pandanus palms, to **The Gorge**, a narrow cleft in the rock that is pounded endlessly by huge ocean breakers. Further on, **Whale Rock** provides an ideal viewpoint from which to spot migrating humpback whales between June and October. Manta rays, turtles and dolphins are also a familiar sight all year round. At the far end of the walk the vast swathe of **Main Beach** hoves into view, stretching 34 km down the entire length of the island's east coast. It offers some excellent 4WD action, fishing, surfing and a few mosquito-infested campsites. **Cylinder Beach**, back along East Coast Road, provides the best recreational spot with great surf breaks and safe swimming. If you do swim always stick to patrolled areas between the flags.

Other attractions on the island include **Blue Lakes National Park**, which is reached via Trans Island Road from Dunwich. The lake itself, a 2.5-km walk from the car park, is freshwater and fringed with melalucas and eucalypts, providing the perfect spot for a cool swim. To reach Main Beach from there requires a 4WD. **Brown Lake**, which is bigger and only 2 km outside Dunwich, is a less popular spot.

Moreton Island

Moreton Island, which lies to the north of the Stradbroke Islands, is often considered the jewel of the Moreton group by virtue of its lack of inhabitants and unspoilt beauty. It is another sand mass: almost 20,000 ha of long, empty beaches, dunes, forest, lagoons and heathlands with abundant wildlife. Other than the beauty and solitude, the greatest attractions are its opportunities for 4WD trips, fishing, camping, wreck snorkelling and diving and seeing the pod of 'wild' Tangalooma bottlenose dolphins that put in a nightly appearance at the island's **Tangalooma Wild Dolphin Resort**, see page 228. Other attractions include the Tangalooma Desert, a large sand blow near the resort, and the Blue Lagoons, a group of 15 deliberately sunken shipwrecks, which provide excellent snorkelling. If you do have the freedom of the island with a 4WD, Cape Moreton at the northeastern tip is worth a visit to see the 1857 lighthouse, which is the oldest in Queensland. Mount Tempest (285 m) dominates the heart of the island and is reputed to be the highest coastal sand dune in the world; a strenuous 5-km walk. For details, see Activities and tours page 231.

◉ Brisbane and Moreton Bay listings

For Sleeping and Eating price codes and other relevant information, see Essentials pages 28-33.

Sleeping

Central Brisbane *p220, map p222*
Brisbane boasts more than 12,000 beds, from large 5-star hotels and modern apartment blocks to numerous backpacker and budget options plus a good selection of B&Bs, some of which present an ideal opportunity to

experience a traditional Queenslander house. The only thing lacking is a selection of good motor parks within easy reach of the city centre. Although there are plenty of hostels you are still advised to book a budget bed at least 2 days in advance. There are good options on Upper Roma St, just 500 m southwest of the transit centre, and around Fortitude Valley.
LL Emporium Boutique Hotel, 1000 Ann St, Fortitude Valley T3253 6999,

www.emporiumhotel.com.au. Set in the heart of the Valley this hip contemporary place offers the full range of studio suites, from standard to king spa, an outstanding cocktail bar and a rooftop pool.

L-B Il Mondo Boutique Hotel, 25 Rotherham St, T3392 0111, www.ilmondo.com.au. Across the river on Kangaroo Point, this modern and chic hotel offers 1-3 bedroom suites and self-contained apartments, interesting aesthetics and relative peace from the centre. It is also within walking distance of all the action via a typical Brizzie ferry ride from the Holman St Wharf. In-house contemporary alfresco restaurant and a lap pool.

A Explorers Inn, 63 Turbot St, T3211 3488, www.explorers.com.au. One of the better value (and certainly the best placed) of the budget hotel options. Friendly, it offers tidy (if small) doubles, twins, family rooms and singles and has a cheap but cheerful restaurant/bar. It is only 500 m from the transit centre and Queens St.

B-C Metro Inns, 239 Wickham St, T3832 1412, www.metroinns.com.au. Sits high on the hill, like a transparent pepper pot, overlooking the CBD and offering 3-4 star standard rooms, each with a balcony to soak up the views. In-house licensed restaurant.

D-E Bunk Backpackers, corner of Ann St and Gipps St, T3257 3644, www.bunkbrisbane.com.au. This large modern establishment is well placed in the heart of the Valley. It offers doubles, twins, singles and dorms on themed floors. Modern facilities, including a pool and bar. Fast internet and travel/jobs desk.

D-E City Backpackers, 380 Upper Roma St, 500 m southwest of the transit centre, T3211 3221, www.citybackpackers.com. Deservedly popular and well managed, it has spotless en suite doubles and dorms, modern kitchen, excellent security, roof decks, pool, internet and a great bar. It's a very sociable place that can throw a great party at the weekend.

D-E Cloud 9, 350 Upper Roma St, City, T3236 2300, www.cloud9backpackers.com.au. If you

are looking for a smaller, modern establishment near the transit centre then this is the best bet. Recently opened, it offers modern facilities throughout with dorms, twins and doubles (some en suite), fast internet, free pick-ups and off-street parking. The city views from the rooftop deck add to the appeal.

Brisbane suburbs *p224, map p222*

L-E Brisbane Northside Caravan Village, 763 Zillmere Rd (off Gympie Rd), on the northern approach, 12 km from the CBD, T3263 4040, www.caravanvillage.com.au. This is the best motor park, offering a wide range of options from luxury cabins, en suite/standard powered and non-powered sites, pool, store, internet and an excellent camp kitchen.

A-B Aynsley B&B, 14 Glanmire St, Paddington, T3368 2250, www.aynsley.com.au. Traditional Queenslander with good value, queen or twin en suites, parking and pool.

Moreton Bay and islands *p224*
North Stradbroke Island

There is a broad range of accommodation available on Straddie, with the vast majority being based in Point Lookout. Nevertheless, pre-booking is recommended in the summer, and on public/school holidays.

L-A Domain Stradbroke Resort, Home Beach, Point Lookout, T3415 0000, www.stradbrokedomain.com. Stylish modern beach shacks and villas overlooking Home Beach, with an excellent in-house café, shop, pool and gym.

L-A Stradbroke Island Beach Hotel and Spa Resort, East Coast Rd, Point Lookout, T3409 8188, www.stradbrokeislandbeachhotel.com.au. The former 'Straddie' has recently been fully redeveloped and now offers ultra-modern facilities all overlooking the surf beach. Great place to indulge.

B-F Stradbroke Holiday Parks Adder Rock, East Coast Road, Point Lookout (17 km from Dunwich) T1300 551253. Located in Point Lookout it offers de luxe villas, standard cabins, powered and non-powered sites, saltwater pool, barbecue and camp kitchen. **D-E Manta Lodge YHA and Scuba Centre** (above and part of the Dive Shop), 1 East Coast Rd, T3409 8888, www.mantalodge.com.au. Friendly and near the beach, with focus on dive trips. Pick-ups from Brisbane.

Moreton Island
LL-D Tangalooma Wild Dolphin Resort, T3637 2000, www.tangalooma.com. A fine resort offering a wide range of beachside accommodation, from luxury self-contained apartments and standard rooms/units to new backpacker/budget beds, a restaurant, bistro/bar café, pools, an environmental centre, with dolphin feeding and watching, and many water sports and other activities; see page 231. **QPWS campsites**, T3408 2710, www.derm.qld.gov.au. Available at The Wrecks, Ben-Ewa, Comboyuro, North Point and Blue Lagoon. The Wrecks campsite is about a 2-km walk from the resort. Each has toilets, limited supplies of water and cold showers. Fees apply.

✪ Eating

Brisbane offers a vast choice. Outside the city centre and the Riverside (Eagle St) areas the suburbs of Fortitude Valley, New Farm (east), South Bank, the West End (south of the river) and Paddington (west) are well worth looking at. The main focuses for Brisbane's café scene are Brunswick St Mall in Fortitude Valley, South Bank parklands, West End (Boundary St) and Petrie Terrace/Paddington (Caxton and Given Terrace). Worth checking out are the stunning views from the **Summit Restaurant** at Mount Coot-tha (see page 228); or a leisurely lunch or dinner cruise on a paddle steamer (see page 230). And for something uniquely Brisbane, try the famed Moreton Bay Bug (a delicious and very weird-looking lobster).

Central Brisbane p220, map p222
E'cco, 100 Boundary St, T3831 8344, www.eccobistro.com. Tue-Fri for lunch, Tue-Sat for dinner. Home of internationally acclaimed chef, Philip Johnson. Other than the food itself another great attraction is the unpretentious nature of the place, the bustling atmosphere and the staff.
Il Centro, Eagle St Pier, T3221 6090, www.ilcentro.com.au. Sun-Fri for lunch, Thu-Sun for dinner. Large Italian restaurant renowned for its riverside location and stunning sand crab lasagne.
Pier Nine, Eagle St Pier, T3226 2100, www.piernine.com.au. Mon-Fri from 1130, Sat from 1700. Another riverside restaurant, a Brisbane institution famous for quality seafood.
Siana, Riparian Plaza, 71 Eagle St, T3221 3887, www.siana.com.au. Mon-Fri lunch and dinner and from 1600 Sat. Quality mix of Thai, Chinese and Indian cuisine in stylish surroundings overlooking the river.

Brisbane suburbs p224, map p222
Anise, 697 Brunswick St, New Farm, T3358 1558, www.anise.com.au. Tue-Sun for lunch, daily for dinner. Small and congenial wine bar/restaurant with a French- influenced menu, lengthy wine list and great foie gras.
Gambaro, 33 Caxton St, Petrie Terrace, T3369 9500. Sun-Fri for lunch, Mon-Sat for dinner. An old favourite offering good seafood.
Isis Brasserie, 446 Brunswick St, south towards New Farm, T3852 1155. Tue-Fri for lunch, Tue-Sun for dinner. Causing something of a stir, winning awards and maintaining a loyal following, who swear by the class and quality of both environment and cuisine consistently created by its youthful owners.
Montrachet, 224 Given Terrace, Paddington, T3367 0030, www.montrachet.com.au. Mon-Fri lunch and dinner. A friendly French restaurant, home of acclaimed chef and extrovert character Thierry Galichet. Lots of French flair and ambience. Recommended.
Summit, Mount Coot-tha, T3369 9922. Daily for lunch/dinner and on Sun for brunch. Further afield and well worth the trip is this

Brisbane classic with its superb views across the city and Moreton Bay.

Ⅲ Tibetan Kitchen, 454 Brunswick St, Fortitude Valley, T3358 5906. Plenty of character offering traditional Tibetan and Nepalese fare and considered by many as the best venue for samosas and curries in town. It caters well for vegetarians.

Moreton Bay and islands *p224*
North Stradbroke Island

Ⅲ Amis, 21 Cumming Pde, Pandanus Palms Resort Point Lookout, T3409 8600. Wed-Sun. Casual fine dining with excellent views.

Ⅲ Seashells Café, 21 Ballow St, Amity Point, T3409 7886 , T3415 3390. Daily 0800-2200. New establishment earning a good reputation. Open for breakfast, lunch or dinner with alfresco seating and bar.

Ⅲ Stradbroke Island Beach Hotel and Spa Resort, East Coast Rd, Point Lookout, T3409 8188, www.stradbrokeislandbeach hotel.com.au. Daily for breakfast lunch and dinner from 0730. A popular spot for good value bistro meals with a large outdoor deck space overlooking Cylinder Beach.

🕈 Bars and clubs

Brisbane *p220, map p222*
Belgian Beer Café, 169 Mary St, City, T3221 0199, www.belgianbeercafebrussels.com.au. Try the traditional mussels and *frites* with a choice of 30 of the nation's finest. It also has one of the city's best beer gardens.
Bowery, 676 Ann St, Fortitude Valley T3252 0202, www.thebowery.com.au. Hailed as the best cocktail joint in the city, this New York-style bar offers class and a quiet, cosy ambience.
Breakfast Creek Hotel, 2 Kingsford Smith Drive, Breakfast Creek, T3262 5988, www.breakfastcreekhotel.com. Although a bit of a trek, this 115-year-old enterprise is something of a Brisbane institution. It retains a colonial/art deco feel, has a large Spanish beer garden and serves excellent steaks.

Fox, corner of Hope St and Melbourne St, T3844 2883. Historic place with good old-fashioned service. Also has a quality Italian restaurant attached.
Hotel LA, corner of Petrie Terrace and Caxton St, Paddington, T3368 2560. Attracts the loud and pretentious and if you can get past the over-ambitious 'fashion police' on the door, it stays open well into the wee small hours.
Lark, 1/267 Given Terrace, T3369 1299, www.thelark.com.au. Closed Mon. A colonial-style cottage converted into a quality cocktail/ wine bar, proving something of a hit for both food and drink.
Orient Hotel, corner of Queen St and Ann St, City, T3839 4625. Thu-Sat nightly until 0300. A traditional street corner Australian. It's well known for its live rock music.
Story Bridge Hotel, 200 Main St, Kangaroo Point, T3391 2266, www.storybridgehotel.com.au. In the shadow of its namesake edifice, this is a firm favourite at any time, but most famous for hosting the annual Australia Day cockroach races and the Australian Festival of Beers in Sep.

🕊 Entertainment

Brisbane *p220, map p222*
Fortitude Valley (The Valley) enjoys international acclaim (recently recognized as 'a new global hotspot' by *Billboard* magazine) and is the best place to check out the latest local rock bands, with its many pubs hosting bands from Thu-Sat. **Fortitude Valley**, the **Riverside Centre** (Eagle St, City) and **Petrie Terrace** are the main club and dance venues. For up-to-date listings and entertainment news consult the free street press publications, *Rave*, *Time Off* and *Scene*.

Live music
Brisbane Jazz Club, 1 Annie St, Kangaroo Point, T3391 2006. A loyal following with regulars playing on Sat-Sun, from 2030 (cover around $15).
Glass Bar, 420 Brunswick St, Fortitude Valley, T3252 0533, www.glassjazz.com.au. This is another good venue.

⊕ Festivals and events

Brisbane *p220, map p222*
An up-to-date events listing is available at www.ourbrisbane.com/whats-on/events.
New Year The year begins with a bang with celebrations and a fireworks display over the river beside the South Bank parklands. This is repeated with even more zeal on **26 Jan, Australia Day**, with other hugely popular and bizarre events including the annual cockroach races; see box opposite.
Easter The **Brisbane to Gladstone Yacht Race** leaves Shorncliffe.
May **Queensland Racing Festival** and **Valley Jazz Festival**.
Jun Annual **Queensland Day** celebrations.
Jul **Brisbane International Film Festival** at the end of the month. **Mid-July** also sees the start of the 18-day **Brisbane Festival** with an international programme featuring artists from contemporary dance, opera, theatre and music from all over the globe performing alongside outstanding Australian artists.
Late Aug/Sep The 2-week **River Festival** celebrates the 'city's lifeblood' with food, fire and festivities.
Oct Fortitude Valley's Chinatown and Brunswick St become the focus for the lively **Valley Fiesta**.

O Shopping

Brisbane *p220, map p222*
Brisbane is *the* Queensland capital for retail therapy, with over 1500 stores and 700 shops in and around the Queens Street Mall. Two department stores, 6 shopping centres and a rash of malls and arcades all combine to provide a vast array of choice from fashion to furnishings. The city also hosts a few good markets including the **South Bank markets** on Fri night, Sat and Sun, the **Riverside and Eagle St Pier markets** on Sunday and **The Valley markets** (Brunswick St) on Sat and Sun. The new **James Market** in New Farm (2nd

and 4th Sat of the month) is excellent for fresh produce and deli products and is surrounded by good cafés.

⚠ Activities and tours

Brisbane *p220, map p222*
City Bus tours
There is a free **City Loop Bus** service around the CBD Mon-Fri 0700-1800 with departures every 10 mins. **CitySights**, www.citysights.com.au, also offers city tours of 1½ hrs, from $35, children $20, T131230, taking in a total of 19 stops in the inner city. Tours leave every 45 mins from Post Office Square, from 0900-1545. It's a great way to see the inner city and the views from Mount Coot-tha, with the added bonus of free bus and CityCat travel.

River cruises
Although there are a number of specialist cruise companies and a range of vessels, one of the best ways to see the sights is to utilize the hop-on/hop-off, all day Translink services ticket with **CityCat**, T131220, www.translink.com.au, from $4.60.
Kookaburra River Queen paddle steamers, T3221 1300, www.kookaburrariverqueens .com. A familiar sight on the river offering a range of sightseeing/dining options: 2-hr lunch Sat/Sun, from $55; 3-hr dinner Tue, Thu-Sun 1900, from $75.
Mirimar Boat Cruises, T3221 0300, www.mirimar.com, depart daily from Cultural Centre Pontoon (located on the boardwalk outside the Queensland State Library) at 1000, from $55, children $33 (including admission, returns at 1445). Combines a cruise upriver with a visit to the Lone Pine Koala Sanctuary.

Other activities
Riverlife Adventure Centre, T3891 5766, www.riverlife.com.au. Operates from the Naval Stores at the base of Kangaroo Point Cliffs and offers abseiling and rock climbing (from $39),

Roach runners

Twenty years ago (or so the story goes) two Brisbanites were sitting in a bar arguing about whose suburb had the biggest, fastest cockroaches. Unable to reach a settlement, the following day they captured their very best and raced them. And with that the annual 'Cockroach Races' were born. (And who said Queenslanders are not as mad as cut snakes?) Now, every Australia Day (26 January), the Story Bridge Hotel in Kangaroo Point hosts the infamous and truly unique cocky races. Of course, the races, along with many other events and live entertainment (much of it involving the removal of girls' blouses), is merely an excuse to get utterly inebriated. Picture the scene for a second … small grandstands surround a central ring, bursting with rowdy punters, many with faces painted in national colours and wearing flags (often as the only item of clothing). The race is called

and from deep within the crowd comes the sound of badly played bagpipes, heralding the arrival of the lovable little competitors. Then the sea of spectators parts and the scene is set. On the count of three, the plastic container, which covers the eager cockies in the middle of the ring, is lifted and off they run – in all directions. The crowd goes wild. The more squeamish onlookers scream as the insects run under bags, shoes and into sandwiches. As soon as the winner is declared (if, indeed, it can ever be found) it's drinks all round – and again – and again, until no one can remember who won. To say it is an experience is an understatement and it's not to missed if your visit coincides with the event. Just don't plan on doing anything the following day, except perhaps checking the contents of your shoes. Check out details at www.storybridgehotel.com.au.

or kayaking (from $35). Bike and rollerblade hire (1½ hrs from $20) also available.
Story Bridge Adventure Climb, T3514 6900, www.storybridgeadventureclimb.com.au. This is emulating the success of the Sydney Bridge Climb. The secure 2½-hr climb offers dramatic views across the city from the 80-m span, with the dawn or dusk climbs adding that aesthetic edge, from $89-130.

Moreton Bay and islands p224
North Stradbroke Island
The VIC has all details of activities and operators and can book on your behalf.
Kingfisher Tours, T3409 9502, www.straddie kingfishertours.com.au, offer excellent and informative 4WD tours.
Manta Lodge YHA and Scuba Centre, 1 East Coast Rd, Point Lookout, T3409 8888, www.mantalodge.com.au. Daily boat dives to try to track down manta ray, turtle and dolphin. Snorkelling, 4WD tours and sea kayaking can also be arranged. Surf and body board hire.

Straddie Adventures, T3409 8414, www.straddieadventures.com.au. An exciting range of backpacker-based tours and activities, including sand boarding, sea kayaking, surf lessons and snorkelling, full day 4WD tours.

Moreton Island
Dolphin Wild, T3880 4444, www.dolphin wild.com.au. Backpacker-oriented day cruises to Moreton Island from Redcliffe. From $115, children $65. Transfers are available from Brisbane for $25 extra.
Tangalooma Wild Dolphin Resort, T1300 652250, www.tangalooma.com, see page 228. Full day tour options (from $45), with dolphin feeding/watching from $95 (see page 226), an excellent range of island excursions and activities from sand boarding, quad biking, snorkelling and diving to scenic helicopter flights. Daily whale-watching cruises are also available Jun-Oct, from $110, children $85.

⊖ Transport

Brisbane *p220, map p222*
For all public transport enquiries, T131230,
www.translink.com.au.

Air

Brisbane's international and domestic airports
are 16/18 km northeast of the city centre. **Jet
Star**, T131538, www.jetstar.com.au; **Qantas**,
T131313, www.qantas.com.au; **Tiger Airways**,
T9335 3033, www.tigerairways.com.au; and
Virgin Blue, T136789, www.virginblue.com.au,
all fly regularly to all main centres and some
regional destinations.

Bus

Local The Central Bus Station is downstairs
in the Myer Centre, Queen St. There is a free
City Loop Bus service around the CBD
Mon-Fri 0700-1800 with departures every
10 mins. Other service fares work on a zone
system from $2.30, children $1.20. For
attractive day or weekly saver passes in
conjunction with the CityCat, ask at a ticket
office. TransLink also operates a travel card
called GoCard, which stores up to $200 so
you can travel seamlessly on bus, train and
ferry services. You can travel on participating
buses, trains and ferries using your GoCard or
other valid TransLink ticket. Fares are
calculated according to the number of zones
travelled in a journey. All Brisbane's CityCat
and CityFerry stops are within TransLink's
zones 1 and 2.
Long distance All interstate and local
buses stop at the multi-level Roma St
Transit Centre, Roma Street, 0530-2030.
Most of the major bus companies have
internal offices on Level 3 (Coach Deck)
and there are also lockers, internet and
a visitors' information desk, T3236 2528,
www.brisbanetransitcentre.com.au. Various
food outlets and showers are available on
Level 2. **Greyhound**, T1300 473946,
www.greyhound.com.au, and **Premier Motor
Services**, T133410, www.premierms.com.au,

both operate north/southbound interstate
and regional services.

Coachtrans, T3358 9300,
www.coachtrans.com.au, runs 4 daily services
to the **Gold Coast** (including the airport) and
'Unlimited Travel Passes' for city sights, airport
and Gold Coast. **Crisps Coaches**, T4661 8333,
www.crisps.com.au, offers south and
westbound services from Brisbane to
Toowoomba/Tenterfield. Sunshine Coast
Sunbus, T5450 7888, www.sunbus.com.au,
also runs regular daily services to the
Sunshine Coast. Brisbane Bus Lines, T3355
0034, also services the **Sunshine Coast** and
South Burnett Region.

CityCat and ferry

Brisbane's famous, sleek blue-and-white
CityCats glide up and down the river from
Bretts Wharf (Hamilton) in the east, to the
University of Queensland (St Lucia) in the west,
stopping at selected wharfs on both sides of the
river, daily from 0530-2230. The round trip takes
about 2 hrs. Fares start at $2.30. A day ticket
costs from $4.60, children $2.30, depending on
zone covered. Day tickets and off-peak saver
tickets also apply in conjunction with TransLink
city bus services, ask at the ticket office. **CityFerry**
operates an inner city and cross-river service
(every 15-20 mins) at various points along the
river. Fares are determined by the number of
sectors crossed and start at $2.30. Pick up a copy
of the *Brisbane River Experience Guide*, which
highlights the main attractions and specialist
tours on offer. General enquiries, T131230,
www.translink.com.au.

Cycling

Brisbane is very well geared up for cyclists
with over 350 km of city cycleways. Most of
these have been established around the edge
of the CBD along the riverbank, providing an
excellent way to take in the sights and to get
from A to B. VICs can supply the free and
comprehensive *Brisbane Bicycle Maps* booklet.
Hire from **Riverlife Adventure Centre**, T3891
5766, www.riverlife.com.au (see page 230).

Taxi
Black and White Cabs, T131008, or Yellow Cabs, T131924.

Train
Queensland Rail Travel Centre is located on the ground floor, Roma St Transit Centre, T3236 2528, www.brisbanetransit centre.com.au; for general enquiries T132232, 0600-2000. **Citytrain**, T131210, www.citytrain.com.au, services greater Brisbane with networks to the Gold Coast. The main city stations are Central (top end of Edward St), Roma (Transit Centre), South Bank (South Brisbane) and Brunswick St (Fortitude Valley). Fares are based on a zone system and start at $2.30, 'one-day unlimited ticket', from $4.60. **Airtrain**, T1800 119091, www.airtrain.com.au, services the airport and Gold Coast from the city centre stations from $14.50 one-way, Gold Coast from $25.

Northbound services include the **Tilt Train**, www.tilttrain.com.au, the express service between **Brisbane** and **Rockhampton** (6½ hrs), which is recommended for those travelling to **Noosa** via Nambour or **Hervey Bay** via Maryborough (free bus connection). It departs Sun-Fri 1100 and 1700 (Rockhampton $107 and Bundaberg $67 single). **Sunlander** (**Brisbane** to **Cairns**) departs 4 times weekly from Brisbane – Sun and Thu to Cairns, First Class from $430, economy from $218. **Spirit of the Outback** travels from Brisbane to **Rockhampton** where it heads west to **Longreach**. Departs Tue 1825 and Sat 1310, from $190.

Moreton Bay and islands *p224*
North Stradbroke Island
The ferry terminal is at Toondah Harbour, Cleveland. From Brisbane take the **Citytrain** from the Roma St Transit Centre, where a **National Bus** (T3245 3333) provides pick-ups to the ferry terminal, T131230. **Stradbroke Ferries**, T3488 5300, www.stradbrokeferries.com.au, operate a car/passenger and passenger water taxi every

hour from Cleveland Mon-Fri 0600-1915, Sat-Sun 0600-1845, return from $17, children $10. **Sea Stradbroke Big Red Cat** T3488 9777, www.seastradbroke.com, runs a vehicle and passenger service from the same harbour roughly every hour, from $135 return for a car including passengers (foot passengers $11, children $6, bikes $4). The crossing for both services takes 30 mins. **North Stradbroke Flyer** (Gold Cats), T3286 1964, www.flyer.com.au, also offers a fast passenger service (end of Middle St, Cleveland), daily every half hour from 0530-1830, return from $19. Its bus meets the Cleveland train.

Once on the island, **North Stradbroke Bus Services**, T3415 2417, www.stradbrokebuses.com, meet every scheduled ferry arrival or departure and operate between Dunwich, One Mile, Amity and Point Lookout daily 0700-1900. The return fare for Dunwich to Point Lookout is about $10.

Moreton Island
Moreton Island Ferries (miCat), T3909 3333, www.moretonventure.com.au, run a vehicle and passenger service from Howard Smith Drive, Brisbane (refer to website for detailed directions) to **Tangalooma Wrecks** (1 km from the resort). Depart Mon-Sun 0830, returning at 1530 with additional sailings Fri 1830, Sun 1430 (and on public holidays), from $190 return (for a 4WD and 2 adults) and from $50 return for passengers, bikes $15. The crossing takes 30 mins.

There are no sealed roads on Moreton and independent access is by 4WD only ($44 fee for 1 month). **Moreton Island Ferries (miCat)** operates a minibus around the island as a guided day trip package only, with island activities, from $115, children $95.

For those without a 4WD vehicle the best way to reach the island is through the **Tangalooma Resort**, T1300 652250, www.tangalooma.com, which offers accommodation, day trips, tours and independent transfers, see pages 228 and 231. Its launch leaves from the terminal on the northern bank of the Brisbane River, at the end of Holt St, daily 0730 and 1000, from $45, children $25 (75 mins). Full day dolphin feeding from $95, whale watching in season (Jun-Oct) from $110. A courtesy coach operates from Roma St Transit Centre and most CBD hotels, from $10, T1300 652250.

❶ Directory

Brisbane *p220, map p222*
Banks All major bank branches with ATMs are found in the city centre, especially in the Queen St, Edward St and Eagle St malls. Foreign exchange also from **American Express**, 260 Queen St, T 1300 139060. **Travelex**, 261 Queen St, T1800 637642; Shop 149F, Queen St Mall. **Hospital** Mater Hospital (24 hr), Raymond Terrace, Woolloongabba, T3840 8111. **Roma St Medical Centre**, Transit Centre, T3236 2988. Travellers Medical Service, Level 1, 245 Adelaide St, T3221 3611, www.travellersmedicalservice.com.

Internet Cyber Room, Level 1, 25 Adelaide St, T3012 9331. **State Library**, South Bank, T3840 7666, 30 mins free, book a day in advance, Mon-Thu 1000-2000, Fri-Sun 1000-1700. **Pharmacy** Day and Night, 245 Albert St, T3221 8155. **Post** The central post office is at 261 Queen St, opposite Post Office Sq. Mon-Fri 0830-1730, Sat 0900-1230. Post restante post code 4000. **Useful numbers** **Police**, corner of Queen St and Albert St and opposite the Roma St Transit Centre, 67 Adelaide St, T3224 4444. **Emergency** T000. **RACQ**, 261 Queen St, T3872 8465.

Moreton Bay and islands *p224*
North Stradbroke Island
Banks The post offices in Dunwich, Amity and Point Lookout all act as Commonwealth Bank agents. Eftpos is available in shops and resorts. There is an ATM at the **Stradbroke Island Beach Hotel and Spa Resort**, Point Lookout. **Internet** Manta Lodge YHA and **Scuba Centre**, 1 East Coast Rd, Point Lookout, T3409 8888. **Post** Dunwich, Point Lookout (Megerra Pl).

Sunshine and Fraser coasts

Just an hour north of Brisbane, the spellbinding volcanic peaks known as the Glass House Mountains herald your arrival at the aptly named Sunshine Coast. For those who can drag themselves away from the coast, the hinterland promises a wealth of more unusual attractions, while north of Noosa the coastal strip gives way to the Great Sandy Region, the largest coastal sand mass in the world, with Fraser Island, the largest coastal sand island in the world.

Noosa → *For listings, see pages 245-254. See also map, page 236. Colour map 4, B2.*

To some the former surfing backwater of Noosa is now little more than an upmarket suburb of Brisbane. However, it does have one of the finest surf beaches in Queensland, a climate that is 'beautiful one day, perfect the next' and it is fringed with two unspoilt national parks. In the last three decades, the string of coastal communities known as 'Noosa' has metamorphosed into one of the most desirable holiday resorts and residential areas on the entire east coast with a corresponding population growth rate. Many Melbournians in particular have bought holiday properties here to escape the southern winter. But, if you can turn a blind eye to the pretentiousness of the place, it makes a worthwhile stop on your way north.

Sights

Noosa Heads is the main focus of activity with the main surf beach at **Laguna Bay** and the chic tourist shops, accommodation and restaurants along Hastings Street. To the south is **Noosa Junction**, with Sunshine Beach Road providing the main commercial shopping area. From **Noosa VIC** ① *Hastings St, Noosa Heads, T5430 5000, www.visitnoosa.com.au, 0900-1700*, get hold of the free *Noosa Guide* with a detailed road and locality maps.

To the west of Noosa Heads is the pretty 454-ha **Noosa National Park**, which offers an escape from all the sand and surf as well as some fine walks. The most popular of these is the 2.7-km **coastal track**, which starts beside the information office at the end of Park Road (T5447 3243) and takes in a number of idyllic bays and headlands, before delivering you at **Alexandria Bay**. From there you can return the way you came, explore the interior of the park, continue south to the very plush northern suburbs of **Sunshine Beach** or simply spend the day on the beach in relative isolation. Bear in mind that all the beaches that fringe the national park are unpatrolled and swimming is not recommended.

The Noosa River runs both west and south from Noosa Heads in a tangled mass of tributaries to join **Lake Weyba** (south) and **Lakes Cooroibah and Cootharaba** (west and north). **Gympie Terrace**, in Noosaville, runs along the southern bank of the river and is the focus for most river- and lake-based activities.

Sunshine Coast hinterland → *For listings, see pages 245-254.*

With a name like 'Sunshine Coast' it is hardly surprising that the vast majority of travellers head straight for the beach. But though the swathes of golden sand will not disappoint, if you allow some time to explore the hinterland you will find colourful markets, quaint villages, giant 'walk-in' fruits and, topping the lot, the late Steve Irwin's famous Australia Zoo. This area is best visited on a tour from Brisbane or Noosa (see pages 230 and 249) or in your own vehicle. The **Noosa VIC** ① *T5430 5000*, can provide information on the major attractions, along with accommodation listings and maps.

Eumundi

The historic 19th-century former timber town of Eumundi, 1 km off the Bruce Highway and 23 km west of Noosa, is pretty enough in its own right, but timing your visit to coincide with the town's famous markets is highly recommended. Every Saturday and, to a lesser extent, Wednesday morning, Eumundi becomes a creative extravaganza of over 300 arts, crafts and produce stalls, all offering excellent quality, as well as lots of atmosphere and colour. Everything, it seems, is on offer, from kites and bandannas to massages and boomerangs. The markets kick off at about 0700 and start winding up about 1500. The best time to go is early on Saturday before the day heats up and the tourist buses arrive. It can get busy and a little stressful. There are plenty of food outlets and cafés on hand for coffee and breakfast.

Blackall Range Tourist Drive

Blackall Range Tourist Drive, from **Nambour**, a busy agricultural service centre, to the Glass House Mountains, is highly recommended, offering everything from national parks with waterfalls and short rainforest walks to fine coastal views and cosy B&Bs.

Noosa

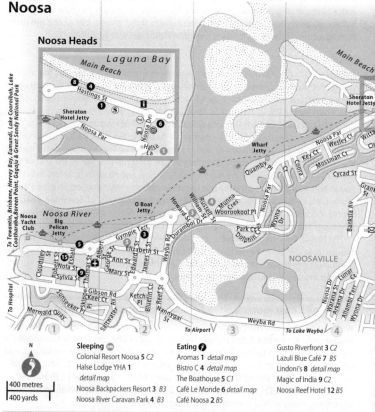

N

400 metres
400 yards

Sleeping 🛏
Colonial Resort Noosa **5** *C2*
Halse Lodge YHA **1**
  detail map
Noosa Backpackers Resort **3** *B3*
Noosa River Caravan Park **4** *B3*

Eating 🍴
Aromas **1** *detail map*
Bistro C **4** *detail map*
The Boathouse **5** *C1*
Café Le Monde **6** *detail map*
Café Noosa **2** *B5*

Gusto Riverfront **3** *C2*
Lazuli Blue Café **7** *B5*
Lindoni's **8** *detail map*
Magic of India **9** *C2*
Noosa Reef Hotel **12** *B5*

Driving west from Nambour, you begin the ascent up the Blackall Range to reach the pleasant little town of **Mapleton**. As well as its own great views and attractive B&Bs, Mapleton is the gateway to **Mapleton Falls National Park**. The heady views of the 120-m falls can be accessed 17 km west on Obi Obi Road. Nearby, the 1.3-km Wompoo Circuit walk winds through rainforest and eucalypts providing excellent views of the Obi Obi Valley. Obi Obi was a noted Aboriginal warrior and *wompoo* refers to a beautiful native pigeon.

From Mapleton the road heads south along the range through **Flaxton village** and the **Kondalilla National Park**. This 327-ha park is accessed and signposted 1 km south of Flaxton and offers views of the 90-m Kondalilla Falls, from the 2.1-km Picnic Creek trail and the 2.7-km Kondalilla Falls circuit, which winds its way down through rainforest to the base of the falls. Neither of the parks offers camping facilities.

First settled by fruit growers in 1887, historic **Montville**, 5 km south of Flaxton, is the main tourist hub along the Blackall Range. With its European-style historic buildings, chic cafés, galleries and souvenir shops, it provides a pleasant stop for lunch or a stroll. Nearby, Lake Baroon also offers a pleasant spot for a picnic. Although undoubtedly very touristy, Montville has not yet been spoiled and remains a delightfully quaint contrast to the coast. From Montville the road continues south taking in the **Gerrard** and **Balmoral Lookouts**. Both offer memorable coastal views from Noosa Heads in the north to Caloundra and Bribie Island in the south.

Turning inland you then arrive at the equally pretty town of **Maleny** which, like Montville, offers many interesting arts and crafts galleries, good B&Bs and a winery. At the far end of the town turn left down the narrow Maleny–Stanley Road to access Mountain View Road (left). Heading back towards the coast you are then almost immediately offered the first stunning views of the Glass House Mountains to the south from **McCarthy's Lookout**. A few kilometres further on is the 41-ha **Mary Cairncross Scenic Reserve**, named after the 19th-century environmentalist. Here you can admire the views, visit the environmental centre (T5499 9907), or take a stroll through the rainforest (1.7 km). From the Cairncross Reserve, the road descends towards **Landsborough**, which is the northern gateway to the Glass House Mountains.

Glass House Mountains National Park

The Glass House Mountains are indeed a wonderful sight but they do nothing for safe driving. These 13 volcanic peaks that dominate the skyline from all directions are utterly absorbing and will, if you are not careful, have you swerving off the road. Gradual weathering by wind and water over the last 20 million years created their distinctive shapes and earned them their unusual name from Captain Cook, who thought they resembled the glass furnaces in his native Yorkshire. The highest peak is **Mount Beerwah** (556 m), while everybody's favourite has to be the distinctly knobbly **Mount Coonowrin** (377 m). Although the best views are actually from Old Gympie Road – which runs north to south, just west of Landsborough, Beerwah and Glass House Mountains Village – there is an official lookout on the southern edge of the park, 3 km west off Old Gympie Road. When it comes to bush walking and summit climbing, **Mount Ngungun** (253 m) is the most accessible (Fullertons Road off Old Gympie or Coonowrin roads) while **Mount Tibrogargan** (364 m) and Mount Beerwah also offer base viewpoints and two or three rough summit tracks. Sadly, pointy Mount Coonowrin is closed to public access due to the danger of rock falls. There is no camping allowed in the park, though several companies offer walking and climbing adventures (see Activities and tours, page 249).

Australia Zoo

ⓘ *Glass House Mountains Rd, Beerwah, T5436 2000, www.crocodilehunter.com.au, 0830-1600, $57, children $34. Free transportation is available daily from Noosa, Maroochy, Mooloolaba and Caloundra. Phone for details.*

Of all Queensland's many wildlife attractions, it is the Australia Zoo that seems to arouse people's enthusiasm the most. The reason for this is the hype and exposure of the late TV celebrity Steve Irwin (alias Crocodile Hunter), his widow Terri and daughter Bindi, to whom the zoo is official home-base. Founded by Steve's father, the collection – thanks to his son's antics – developed faster than a crocodile could clamp its jaws around a dead chicken. The zoo houses a wide array of well-maintained displays exhibiting over 550 native and non-native species, ranging from mean-looking wedge-tailed eagles and insomniac wombats to enormous 6-m pythons and senescent Galápagos tortoises. Of course, the biggest attractions are the numerous crocodiles, or more precisely, the croc feeding, enthusiastically demonstrated daily at 1330. But what lets the place down is the sheer megalomania so apparent in the shop, with its talking Steve and Terri dolls and personal clothing lines (which even include a special kids' line after Bindi). Truly nauseating and a sad testament to modern celebrity marketing hype.

Cooloola Coast → *For listings, see pages 245-254. Colour map 4, B2.*

With access limited to 4WD only from Noosa from the south and a 76-km diversion from Gympie on the Bruce Highway from the north, the mainland – Cooloola Coast – section of the Great Sandy National Park, and its delightful, neighbouring coastal communities of Rainbow Beach and Tin Can Bay, are all too often missed by travellers in their eagerness to reach Hervey Bay and Fraser Island. As well as the numerous and varied attractions and activities on offer within the 56,000-ha park – including huge sand blows, ancient coloured sands and weathered wrecks – Tin Can Bay offers an opportunity to feed wild dolphins. Rainbow Beach is an ideal rest stop off the beaten track, as well as providing southerly access to Fraser Island.

Ins and outs

Rainbow Beach VIC ⓘ *8 Rainbow Beach Rd, T5486 3227, www.rainbow-beach.org, 0900-1700. Also in Tin Can Bay* ⓘ *T5486 4855, www.tincanbay tourism.org.au. For information on Fraser Island refer to the VIC or call T131304, www.epa.qld.gov.au.* ⏩ *See also Transport, page 253.*

Great Sandy National Park

Along with Fraser Island, Great Sandy National Park forms the largest sand mass in the world. For millennia, sediments washed out from the river courses of the NSW coast have been steadily carried north and deposited in vast quantities. Over time the virtual desert has been colonized by vegetation that now forms vast tracts of mangrove and rainforest, which in turn provide a varied habitat for a rich variety of wildlife.

The most notable feature of the park is the magnificent multi-coloured sands that extend from Rainbow Beach to Double Island Point. Over 200 m high in places and eroded into ramparts of pillars and groves, with a palette of over 40 colours, from blood red to brilliant white, they glow in the rays of the rising sun. Carbon dating of the sands has revealed some deposits to be over 40,000 years old. It is little wonder that they are steeped in Aboriginal legend. According to the Kabi tribe, who frequented the area long before the Europeans, the mighty sands were formed and coloured by the Rainbow Spirit who was killed in his efforts to save a beautiful maiden. Other features of the park include the Carlo Sand Blow, just south of Rainbow Beach, a favourite haunt for hang gliders, and the wreck of the cargo ship *Cherry Venture*, which ran aground in 1973. The views from the lighthouse on Double Island – which is actually a headland, falsely named by Captain Cook in 1770 – will also prove memorable. All the features of the park can be explored by a network of 4WD and walking trails. At the southern end of the park (accessed from Noosa), the lakes Cootharaba and Cooroibah are popular for boating and canoeing.

Rainbow Beach and Tin Can Bay

Located at the northern edge of the park, the laid-back, yet fast developing, seaside village of Rainbow Beach provides an ideal base from which to explore the park and as a stepping-stone to Fraser Island. Inskip Point, 14 km north, serves as the southerly access point to the great island paradise. Tin Can Bay, west of Rainbow Beach on the banks of the Tin Can Bay Inlet, is a popular base for fishing and boating but by far its biggest attraction is the visiting wild dolphin called 'Mystique' who appears, religiously, for a free handout, usually early each morning around the Northern Point boat ramp.

Hervey Bay → *For listings, see pages 245-254. Colour map 4, B2.*

The sprawling seaside town of Hervey Bay, the main gateway to Fraser Island, may lack 'kerb appeal', but more than makes up for this in the huge numbers of visitors who flood in to experience two mighty big attractions – Fraser Island and the migrating whales that use the sheltered waters of the bay as a temporary stopover. Considered by many to be the whale-watching capital of the world, Hervey Bay tries hard to stand on its own as a coastal resort and retirement destination, but – despite its low-key attractions, activities and ubiquitous sweep of golden sand – it fails. The concerted attempts to keep people on the mainland for anything more than a day or a night seem futile and, as a result, it has become one of Queensland's most depressing tourist transit centres.

Ins and outs

For objective information (rare in these parts) visit the accredited **Maryborough Fraser Island VIC** ① *City Hall, Kent St, T4190 5742, www.visitmaryborough.info*, and 1 km before Hervey Bay (signposted) ① *Maryborough/Hervey Bay Rd, T4124 7626, www.visitherveybay.info, daily 0900-1700.*

Sights

Hervey Bay is one of Australia's fastest growing cities and is the main gateway to Fraser Island, the world's largest sand island. Essentially a beachfront conglomerate of north-facing suburbs, from Point Vernon in the east, through Urungan, Torquay, Scarness and Pialba in the west, it is however a popular holiday destination in its own right and in season (July-November) is arguably Australia's best venue for whale watching. Almost all major amenities are to be found along the Esplanade from the junction with Main Street in Pialba to Elizabeth Street, Urungan. The main Fraser Island ferry and whale-watching terminal is just south of Dayman Point in Urungan. The Esplanade has a footpath and cycle track, which offers a convenient way to soak up the seaside atmosphere.

History buffs will enjoy the city's **Historical Village and Museum** ① *13 Zephyr St, Scarness, open Fri-Sun, small entry fee.* It includes over 8000 exhibits and an impressive collection of buildings including a traditional slab hut, a former church and a railway station. Blacksmith and treadle lathe demonstrations are available at weekends. In Pialba is the **Regional Gallery** ① *161 Old Maryborough Rd, Tue-Sat 1000-1600*, which showcases the work of an increasing number of local artisans and also hosts national touring exhibitions.

The 1.5-km-long **Urungan Pier** offers a pleasant breezy stroll and good fishing. Keep your eyes open for the aptly named soldier crabs on the beach at low tide.

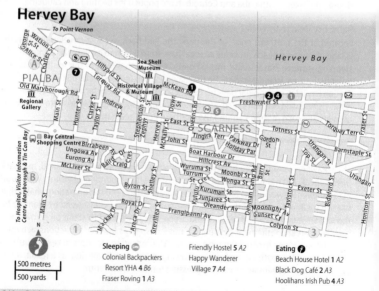

Hervey Bay

500 metres
500 yards

Sleeping 🛏
Colonial Backpackers
Resort YHA **4** *B6*
Fraser Roving **1** *A3*

Friendly Hostel **5** *A2*
Happy Wanderer
Village **7** *A4*

Eating 🍴
Beach House Hotel **1** *A2*
Black Dog Café **2** *A3*
Hoolihans Irish Pub **4** *A3*

Fraser Island → *For listings, see pages 245-254. Colour map 4, B3.*

Jutting out from the eastern Australian coast is the astounding 162,900-ha land mass known as Fraser Island – the biggest sand island in the world. Part of the Great Sandy National Park, which extends across to the mainland to the south, Fraser is now fully protected and was afforded World Heritage status in 1992. It is a very special place: a dynamic 800,000-year-old quirk of nature blessed with stunning beauty and a rich biodiversity. For the vast majority of visitors, the island may come as something of a surprise. Beyond a few sand blows and long, seemingly endless, stretches of beach, this is no Sahara. Blanketed in thick rainforest, pockmarked with numerous freshwater lakes and veined by numerous small streams, it surely confounds the preconceived notions of even the most experienced environmentalist. As well as its stunning beauty, sheer scale and rich wildlife, Fraser presents a great opportunity to try your hand at four-wheel driving and also plays host to one of the best resorts in the country. And despite the fact the island attracts over 300,000 visitors annually, it is still possible – only just – to find a little peace and solitude.

Ins and outs
Getting there
Vehicle and passenger ferries depart daily for Fraser Island from both Hervey Bay and Rainbow Beach. For details and the latest schedules, contact Maryborough VIC, see page 240, or see www.frasercoastholidays.info. ▸▸ *See Transport, page 253.*

Getting around
By far the best way to experience Fraser Island is to stay for at least three days and hire your own 4WD. Other than the freedom, this allows an ideal opportunity to get a feel of what an expensive 4WD is all about. Having said that, walking is hard to beat –

RSL **7** *A1*
Salt Café at Peppers Pier
  Resort **3** *B6*

to experience the sights, sounds and smells that would otherwise be missed. There is an eight-day walking trail and many short walk options. But with wheels or your walking boots you are advised to take detailed maps, which are available from the VIC or QPWS. Fraser is a big island.

Tourist information VICs and QPWS offices on the mainland – such as Maryborough Fraser Island VIC, see page 240 – can provide most of the necessary information.

QPWS Great Sandy Information Centre ① *240 Moorindil St, Tewantin T5449 7792, www.derm.qld.gov.au/parks/fraser*. There is also an office at **Rainbow Beach** ① *Rainbow Beach Rd, T5486 3160, www.derm.qld.gov.au*.

On the island there are QPWS ranger stations at Eurong (T4127 9128), Central Station (T4127 9191), Dundubara (T4127 9138) and Waddy Point (T4127 9190). All have variable opening times so call ahead. The resorts, especially **Kingfisher Bay**, are also valuable sources of information.

East Beach Highway (Eurong to Orchid Beach)

Fringed by pounding surf on one side and bush on the other, barrelling up and down the 92-km natural highway of East Beach is an exhilarating experience in itself. The main access point for those arriving on the west coast is Eurong, where you can fuel up and head north for as far as the eye can see. Of course you will not be alone and at times the beach looks like a 4WD version of a bikers' meet on their way to a rock'n'roll gig.

There are a number of sights as you head north, the first of which is **Lake Wabby**, 4 km north of Eurong. Reached by foot – 4 km return on soft sand – Lake Wabby is one island lake that is at war with an encroaching sand blow, creating a bizarre landscape and the potential for lots of fun partaking in sand surfing and swimming. For a really stunning elevated view of the scene you can head inland for 7 km, on Cornwells Road, 2 km north of the beach car park. In itself will test your 4WD skills. A walking track (5 km return) connects the lookout car park with the lake.

Next stop is **Eli Creek**, which offers a cool dip in crystal clear waters. Some 3 km beyond Eli Creek the rusting hulk of the *Maheno* – a trans-Tasman passenger liner that came to grief in 1935 – provides an interesting stop and a welcome landmark along the seemingly endless sandy highway. A further 2 km brings you to the unusual **Pinnacles** formation, an eroded bank of sand of varying gold and orange hues that looks like some bizarre sci-fi film set. Just south of the Pinnacles, the 43-km Northern Road circuit ventures through ancient rainforest known as **Yidney Scrub**, taking in views of the huge **Knifeblade Sand Blow**, the pretty, small **Lake Allom** and **Boomerang Lakes**, which, at 130 m above sea level, are the highest dune lakes in the world.

Back on East Beach, the colourful sandbanks continue to the **Cathedral Beach Resort** and the **Dundubara campsite**, offering the fit and adventurous walker the chance to explore the turtle-infested **Lake Bowarrady** (16 km return). From Dundubara it is another 19 km to **Indian Head**. One of the very few genuine rocks on the island, the head offers a fine vantage point from which to view the odd shark and manta ray in the azure waters below (demonstrating why swimming in the sea is ill advised around Fraser). Just beyond Indian Head, at the start of Middle Head, the track turns inland providing access to **Orchid Beach** and **Champagne Pools**. Named for their clarity and wave action, they provide perfect saltwater pools for swimming amongst brightly coloured tropical fish. Beyond the settlement of Orchid Beach and Waddy Point, travel with a 4WD becomes more difficult, with most hire companies banning further exploration north. But if you have your own

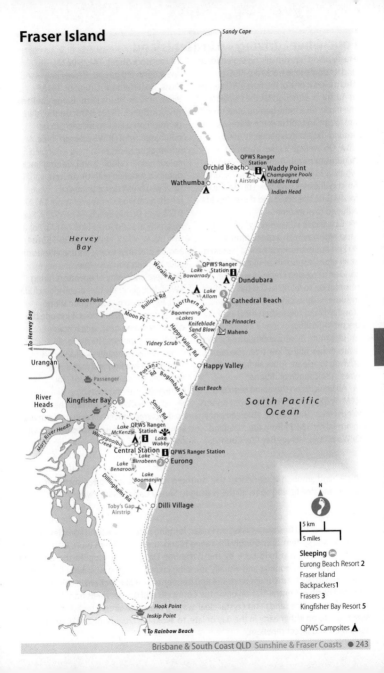

Fraser Island

Sandy Cape

QPWS Ranger
Station
Orchid Beach ○   🚹   Waddy Point
                Champagne Pools
Wathumba ○   ⊹Airstrip   ▲ *Middle Head*
    ▲   *Indian Head*

*Hervey
Bay*

        Woralie Rd   QPWS Ranger
            Lake   Station
        Bowarrady   🚹
            ▲ ○ Dundubara
Moon Point   Bullock Rd
              Lake   ❸
            ▲ *Allom*   ○ Cathedral Beach
  Moon Pt   ❶
        *Boomerang
Lakes*
          Knifeblade   *The Pinnacles*
          Sand Blow   ☒ Maheno
    Yidney Scrub

To Hervey Bay

Urangan ○
    🚢 *Passenger*   ○ Happy Valley
            East Beach
River
Heads ○
Kingfisher Bay ○ 🚢 ❺   *South Pacific
Ocean*

Mary River Heads
        Smith Rd
      Lake   QPWS Ranger
    McKenzie   Station
          🚹   ❄ *Lake
                Wabby*
  Wanggoolba   Central Station
  Creek   *Lake*   QPWS Ranger Station
    Lake   *Birrabeen*   🚹
  Benaroon   ❷ ○ Eurong
        *Lake
      Boomanjin*
  Dillinghams Rd   ▲
      Toby's Gap   ⊹
      Airstrip   ○ Dilli Village

Northern Rd   Eli Creek   Happy Valley Rd   Postans Rd   Bogimbah Rd

Hook Point
  🚢
Inskip Point
To Rainbow Beach

N

⊕

|5 km|
|5 miles|

Sleeping 🛏
Eurong Beach Resort **2**
Fraser Island
Backpackers **1**
Frasers **3**
Kingfisher Bay Resort **5**

QPWS Campsites ▲

Four-wheel driving on Fraser Island

Fraser Island has virtually no sealed roads and its single-lane tracks are 4WD only. This makes it one of the best 4WD venues in Australia. Although for the layperson the tracks take some getting used to and are rough and soft in some places, access around the island is generally good, if slow. On average it takes about 30 minutes to travel 10 km on inland roads where a 35 kph speed limit is in force. Strict guidelines have been put in place for 4WD on the island and these should be adhered to at all times.

→ East Beach is, essentially, a 90-km sand highway with a speed limit of 80 kph but extreme care must be taken at all times, especially at high tide, in soft sand and crossing creeks. Avoid the temptation to let rip as this has resulted in some nasty accidents. Also apply standard road rules when meeting oncoming traffic.

→ Optimum driving conditions are two hours either side of low tide. You are also advised to release some air from your tyres in soft sand conditions.

→ All vehicles on the island require a RAM 4WD permit to be displayed on the windscreen. They can be obtained prior to arrival for $38.25 from the mainland QPWS offices, Hervey Bay City Council,

77 Tavistock Street, T4125 0222, www.derm.qld.gov.au, Hervey Bay Marina Kiosk, Boat Harbour, Urungan, T4128 9800, or River Heads Kiosk-Barge Car Park, Ariadne Street, T4125 8473. On the island permits cost a little more and can be purchased from QPWS Eurong Office. An information pack containing a detailed colour guide, camping and walking track details is supplied with the permit.

→ If you break down there are mechanical workshops at Eurong, T4127 9173, and Orchid Beach, T4127 9220. For mechanical assistance, T4127 9173. For a tow truck, T4127 9449 or T0428-353164, and be prepared to wave the contents of your bank account bye bye.

→ There are plenty of operators hiring 4WDs, but generally hire does not include fuel, ferry, food or accommodation/ camping permits, nor does it include the cost of camping gear, which is an additional expense. The more professional companies will also give you a thorough briefing and maps. See Activities and tours, page 251, for companies offering tours.

→ To hire a 4WD you must at least 21, hold a current driver's licence and provide around $500 bond or credit card imprint and a permit.

vehicle, and enough experience, the northern peninsula can offer some welcome solitude and fine fishing spots all the way up to **Sandy Cape**, 31 km away.

The lakes

There are over 100 freshwater lakes on Fraser, forming part of a vast and complex natural water storage system. Surprisingly for a sand island, there is 20 times more water stored naturally here than is held back by the Wivenhoe Dam, which supplies the whole of Brisbane. The most popular and visually stunning lakes are scattered around the island's southern part. By far the most beautiful and frequented is **Lake McKenzie**, which can be accessed north of Central Station or via the Cornwells and Bennet roads from East Beach. With its white silica sands and crystal clear waters, it is quite simply foolish not to visit. Make sure to go either early in the day or late, to avoid the crowds. Also take sunglasses, sunscreen and insect repellent.

Further south, **Lakes Birrabeen** and **Benaroon** offer fine swimming and are quieter than McKenzie but do not share quite the same beauty. Further south still is **Lake Boomanjin**, the largest 'perched' lake in the world, which means it ranks high on the humus podsol B Horizon with a large pH – it's very brown, in other words.

Central Station

For those arriving on the west coast, Central Station provides the first glimpse of just how wooded Fraser Island really is. Shaded by towering bunya pine and satinay and thick with umbrella-like palms, this green heart of Fraser has its own unique biodiversity. In the 50-m canopies many of the island's 240 recorded species of birds reside, from brightly coloured lorikeets and honeyeaters to tiny fairy wrens. On the ground echidna and dingoes roam and beneath it there are earthworms as long as your arm! One of the most pleasant features of Central Station are the crystal clear waters and white sandy bed of **Wanggoolba Creek**, which is the main feature on the 450-m boardwalk. Central Station also serves as the departure point for some excellent walking tracks to Lake McKenzie and the Pile Valley, where you will find yourself gazing heavenwards wondering if the trees could possibly grow any taller.

⊙ Sunshine and Fraser coasts listings

For Sleeping and Eating price codes and other relevant information, see Essentials pages 28-33.

Sleeping

Noosa *p235, map p236*

Noosa is very much like a mini Gold Coast without the high-rise blocks, yet with the same massive range of 4-star resort complexes, self-contained holiday apartments and backpacker options. Here we simply skim the surface. If you have a specific idea about what you want there are various agencies who can oblige including: **Accommodation Noosa**, T1800 072078, www.accomnoosa.com.au; **Noosa Holidays**, T1800 629949, www.noosare.com.au; and **Peter Dowling**, T5447 3566, www.peterdowlingnoosa.com.au. For something a little different, try a houseboat, T5449 7611, www.luxuryafloatnoosa.com.au.

L Eumarella Shores, 251 Eumarella Rd, T5449 1738, www.eumarellashores.com.au. Next to Lake Weyba. Offers something far removed from the resorts and tourist hype. Fully self-contained colonial and log cabin-style cottages and contemporary 'eco-pavilions' sleeping 2-6 in a bush setting overlooking the lake. Minimum 2-night stay.

A Colonial Resort Noosa, 239-245 Gympie Terr, Noosaville, T5455 8100, www.colonialresortnoosa.com.au. In the heart of Noosaville and overlooking the river. Stylish fully self-contained rooms with decks, spa and all the usual facilities such as heated pool and secure parking.

C-F Gagaju, Boreen Point, T5474 3522, www.travoholic.com/gagaju. Characterful eco-backpackers-cum-bush-camp, located between Lakes Cooroibah and Cootharaba, on the Noosa River. Everything is built from recycled timber with dorms and shaded campsites (campfires allowed), full kitchen facilities, TV lounge room and excellent in-house half, 1 and 3-day canoe trips on the river. Pick-ups are offered from Noosa Heads.

D-E Halse Lodge YHA, 2 Halse Lane, Noosa Heads, T5447 3377, www.halselodge.com.au. At the other end of the scale is this spacious lodge, which is only a short walk from the long-distance bus stop. It is a historic 1880s Queenslander offering a good range of rooms from 6/4 dorms to doubles, twins and triple, all with shared bathrooms, bistro/bar, large quiet deck and social areas, good tour and activities desk and surf/body board hire.

D-E Noosa Backpackers Resort, 9-13 William St, Noosaville, T5549 8151, www.noosabackpackers.com. This is the main backpacker option west of Noosa Heads. It offers tidy 4-bed dorms, en suite doubles, pool, cheap meals, cable TV and internet. Free use of surfboards and kayaks.

E-F Noosa River Caravan Park, 4 Russell St, Noosaville, T5449 7050. This is the best motor park/camping option in the area. Hugely popular given its riverside location and views but sadly becoming the preserve of 4WD fashionistas, which reflects the rapid influx of wealth and snobbery in the area. Powered and non-powered sites, modern amenities and barbecue. Book at least 2 days in advance.

Sunshine Coast hinterland p235

L Eyrie Escape B&B, 316 Brandenburg Rd, Bald Knob, Mooloolah, T0414-308666, www.eyrie-escape.com.au. A 'spa with a view' at this incredible and aptly named place.

L-B Montville Mountain Inn, Main St, Montville, T5442 9499, www.montvilleinn.com.au. Central and affordable option.

Cooloola Coast p238

C-E Dingo Backpackers, 20 Spectrum St, Rainbow Beach, T1800 111126, www.dingosatrainbow.com. Modern, purpose-built option that offers en suite singles, doubles, dorms, bar/restaurant, pool and internet. Despite its location it is a busy place with an excited atmosphere (at the prospect of visiting Fraser). Book ahead.

E Rainbow Beach YHA, 18 Spectrum Av, Rainbow Beach, T5486 8885, www.frasersonrainbow.com. Just down the road from **Dingo Backpackers** is the other backpackers, which is older but comfortable, with motel-style dorms, doubles and twins, all with en suite. Facilities include internet, pool, a large well-equipped kitchen and a bar. There are also budget meals on offer and plenty of assistance with organizing a trip to

Fraser or onward travel via the Cooloola beaches to Noosa.

QPWS campsites can be found at Great Sandy National Park (Cooloola). There are 20 varied sites. The main one is the Freshwater camping area, 20 km southeast of Rainbow Beach. It provides water, showers and toilets, but fires are banned. Access is by 4WD only. Booking centre, T5486 3160, Mon-Fri 1300-1500, otherwise contact the QPWS office on Rainbow Beach Rd in Rainbow Beach.

Bush camping is available just north of Rainbow Beach at Inskip Peninsula. Sealed roads provide easy access to both bay or surf side campgrounds but the only facilities are composting toilets. Phone the QPWS for more details.

Hervey Bay p239, map p240

The range and quality of accommodation in Hervey Bay caters for all budgets and tastes, from 5-star apartment resorts to hotels, motels, and backpacker hostels. There are also many holiday parks including four beachfront sites at Pialba, Torquay, Scarness and Burrum Heads administered by the local council. During the whale-watching season and public holidays book well ahead.

A-E Colonial Backpackers Resort YHA, corner of Pulgul St and Boat Harbour Drive (820), T4125 1844, www.yha.com.au. Closest to the harbour, this excellent backpackers has a fine range of options from luxury villas and 1-2 bedroom cabins, to en suite doubles and dorms, a good bistro/bar, pool, spa, internet, bike hire and tours desk.

A-E Happy Wanderer Village, 105 Truro St, Torquay, T4125 1103, www.happywanderer.com.au. For a motor park with an excellent range of options and facilities stay here. It offers good value fully self-contained duplex villas, studio/standard units, cabins, onsite vans (shared amenities), en suite/standard powered sites and non-powered sites, pool, camp kitchen. Backpacker cabins are also available.

C-E Fraser Roving, 412 the Esplanade, T4125 3879, www.fraserroving.com.au. Enjoys a

solid reputation with excellent and well-maintained facilities. Full range of rooms, spacious double en suites. Attractive package deals to Fraser Island in shocking pink 4WDs.
C-E Friendly Hostel, 182 Torquay Rd, T4124 4107, www.thefriendlyhostel.com. You are certain to get fine hospitality and some peace and quiet in this hostel. It is small and comfortable and more like a B&B, with tidy dorms (with single beds no bunks), doubles/twins and well-equipped kitchen facilities.

Fraser Island p241, map p243
LL-L Kingfisher Bay Resort, T4120 3333, www.kingfisherbay.com.au. This multi-award-winning resort is one of the best resorts in Australia. More an eco-village than a resort, it is highly successful in combining unique and harmonious architecture with superb facilities and a wide variety of accommodation options (fully self-contained holiday villas, lodges and luxury hotel rooms) centred on a spacious central lodge with landscaped pools and gardens. Within the main lodge are two excellent, if pricey, restaurant/bars, with a separate bistro/pizzeria and shopping complex nearby. The resort also offers a wide range of activities and tours and hires out 4WD vehicles. There are regular daily ferry services from Urungan Boat Harbour. The resort also offers budget accommodation in its Wilderness Lodge but only through a multi-night stay option and in conjunction with its wide range of activities, tours and 4WD hire.
LL-A Eurong Beach Resort, east coast, T4127 9122, www.eurong.com. Traditional resort with a full range of options from tidy self-contained apartments, motel-style units and cabins to budget A-frame houses that can accommodate up to 8. Other budget units are also available. There is a spacious, yet fairly characterless, restaurant/bar, a pool and organized tours and activities. A well-stocked shop, café and fuel are on site. Comfortable and well situated for East Beach.
A-E Fraser Island Backpackers, T1800 446655, www.fraserislandco.com.au. The

traditional backpackers on the island, located midway up East Beach. Offers twins, doubles and dorms in individual en suite timber lodges. Bar and bistro, pool, internet, bottle shop and general store.
C-E Frasers at Cathedral Beach, Cathedral Beach is located 10 km north of Eli Creek, T4127 9177. This place offers tidy cabins, onsite tents and vans, all with fully equipped kitchens and non-powered sites with hot showers and a shop at Cathedral Beach.
QPWS campsites are at Central Station, Lake Boomanjin, Lake McKenzie, Lake Allom, Wathumba, Waddy Point and Dundubara. Facilities include toilets and cold showers. There are coin ($0.50/$1) operated hot showers at Central Station, Waddy Point and Dundubara.
Beach camping is permitted all along the east coast and on a few selected sites on the west coast. A nightly fee of $5 ($20 per family) applies to all campsites (Dundubara and Waddy Point must be pre-booked, all others cannot be pre-booked). QPWS fees do not apply to private resorts or campsites. And don't feed the dingoes!

🍴 Eating

Noosa p235, map p236
There are almost 200 restaurants in the Noosa area with around 30 along Hastings St alone. Over the years many top national chefs have set up kitchen in the region, fed by their desire to escape the big cities and the stiff competition. Many foreign chefs have also followed suit, adding a distinctly cosmopolitan range of options. Other than the expensive offerings on Hastings St in Noosa Heads, the main culinary hotspots are along Gympie Terrace and Thomas St in Noosaville. The best budget options are to be found along lower Noosa Drive and Sunshine Beach Rd in Noosa Junction.
♥♥♥ Café Le Monde, 52 Hastings St, Noosa Heads, T5449 2366, www.cafelemonde.com. Daily 0600-late. One of the most popular

socially with its large, covered, sidewalk courtyard and live entertainment 5 nights a week. It serves generous international and imaginative vegetarian dishes and is also popular for breakfast.

♥♥♥ Lindoni's, 13 Hastings St, Noosa Heads, T5447 5111, www.lindonis.com.au. Daily 1800-2230. Of the Italian restaurants in Noosa, this place has the finest reputation, a good atmosphere and entertaining, Italian-speaking staff.

♥♥ Bistro C, on the Beachfront Complex, 49 Hastings St, Noosa Heads, T5447 2855, www.bistroc.com.au. Daily 0730-2130. This classy restaurant offers a good traditional Australian/seafood menu and a welcome escape from the main drag overlooking the beach. Excellent for breakfast.

♥♥ Boathouse Restaurant, 1945 Gympie Terrace, Noosaville, T5440 5070, www.boathouserestaurant.com.au. Tue-Sun from 1000. Contemporary bistro-style cuisine including seafood, steaks and wood-fired pizzas overlooking the river. Try the much-lauded seafood platter.

♥♥ Gusto Riverfront, 2/257 Gympie Terrace, Noosaville, T5449 7144, www.gustonoosa.com.au. Mon-Sat from 1100-late, Sun from 0800. One of the most popular restaurants in the region, offering cuisine which locals describe as 'honest and fresh' and for which they keep coming back time and again. Seafood, meat and vegetarian dishes. Book ahead.

♥ Aromas, 32 Hastings St, Noosa Heads, T5474 9788. Daily 0700-late, Fri-Sat until 0100. Spacious and modern with a Mediterranean-influenced menu. Also excellent coffee, and the streetside location is a great spot to watch the world go by.

♥ Café Noosa, 2/1 Sunshine Beach Rd, Noosa Heads, T5447 3949. Mon-Thu 1600-midnight, Fri-Sun 1300-midnight. Popular BYO pizza café with casual indoor or outdoor seating. Takeaway orders welcome.

♥ Lazuli Blue Café, 9 Sunshine Beach Rd, towards Noosa Junction, T5448 0055. Good vegetarian dishes and value breakfasts.

♥ Magic of India, across the road from **Thai Breakers**, Noosaville, T5449 7788. Reputed to be the best Indian takeaway in Noosa. Also open for sit-in meals Tue-Sun from 1730.

♥ Noosa Reef Hotel, towards Noosa Junction, on Noosa Drive, T5430 7500. Fine views, value for money and especially good for families.

Sunshine Coast hinterland p235

♥♥ King Ludwig's German Restaurant & Bar, 401 Mountain View Rd, Maleny, T5499 9377. Wed-Sun lunch, Wed-Sat dinner. Overlooking the Glass House Mountains. Excellent food and a good atmosphere.

♥♥ Tree Tops Gallery, Kondalilla Falls Rd, near Flaxton, T1800 444350, www.treehouses.com.au. Also has equally excellent cabin-style accommodation.

Hervey Bay p239, map p240

Many of the upmarket resort complexes have restaurants offering fine dining. Cheaper eateries are to be found along the Esplanade in Torquay, Scarness and Pialba.

♥♥ Beach House Hotel, 344 Esplanade, Scarness, T4128 1233. Deservedly popular for both lunch and dinner, offers a good range of pub /café-style options overlooking the beach. They also have live entertainment and pool tables.

♥♥ Black Dog Café, corner of Esplanade and Denman Camp Rd, between Scarness and Torquay, T4124 3177. Wed-Mon 1030-1500, daily for dinner. A modern, classy restaurant with good-value Japanese dishes.

♥♥ Hoolihans Irish Pub, 382 Esplanade, T4194 0099. Daily from 1100. A wide range of traditional offerings with an Irish flavour. Servings are generous and it's pricey, but then there is always the quality beer!

♥♥ Salt Café, Shop 5, 569 Esplanade Peppers Pier Resort, Urangan, T4124 9722, www.saltcafe.com.au. Stylish contemporary café amid the Peppers complex, considered one of the best venues for fine dining.

♥ RSL, 11 Torquay Rd, Pialba, T4128 1133. Daily. At the other end of town, this place can always be relied on for value for money and sedate entertainment.

Fraser Island *p241, map p243*
Resorts have restaurants/bistros and some campsites have fully equipped kitchens. See page 247. Food on the island is expensive, so if you're camping you're advised to bring all your supplies from the mainland.

♪ Bars and clubs

Noosa *p235, map p236*
Reef Hotel, 19 Noosa Drive, Noosa Heads, T5430 7500. This is highly regarded and hosts 2 popular bars on two levels, with Level 1 offering a live entertainment each weekend - from resident and visiting DJs.

▲ Activities and tours

Noosa *p235, map p236*
Aerial pursuits
Dimona Motor Glider Flights, based at the Sunshine Coast Airport, Maroochy, T1300 667042, www.comegliding.com.au. Trips (50 mins to 1 hr 45 mins) in something between a light aircraft and a glider, from $265-395.
Epic Horizon Paragliding, T0428-185727, www.epic-horizon.com. Tandem flights from $100.
Noosa and Maroochy Flying Services, T5450 0516, www.noosaaviation.com. Range of scenic flights from coastal trips to Fraser Island and reef safaris, $100-550.
Skydive Ramblers, T5446 1855, www.ramblers.com.au. Has a drop zone on Coolum Beach with 'photo specialist' tandems at around $350.
Sunshine Coast Skydivers, Caloundra Airport, T5491 1395, www.scskydivers.com. Large and reputable operator providing 3650- to 4250-m tandems, including the unusual 'night' tandem from $369 (night $460).

Camel safaris
Camel Safaris, based on Noosa North Shore, T0408-710530, www.camelcompany.com.au. Safaris of 1-2 hrs along Forty Mile Beach (Great Sandy National Park/Cooloola) from $60, overnight camping $220.

Cruises and boat hire
There are numerous operators along the riverbank from whom you can hire U-Drive Boats, barbecue boats, speedboats, kayaks and jet skis at competitive prices. There are also plenty of operators offering sedate cruises up and down the Noosa River from Noosa Heads to Tewantin and beyond.
Noosa Everglades Discovery, T5449 0393, www.noosaevergladesdiscovery.com.au. A variety of cruise options exploring the upper reaches of the Noosa River (from $99, children $70) and 4WD trips along the forty Mile Beach 'sandy highway' to see the coloured sands (from $155/$105). Informative, comfortable and entertaining. Recommended.
Noosa Ferry Cruise, T5449 8442, www.noosaferry.com. Runs regular services between all these stops, daily, from 0915-1800 (later at weekends), from $13 one way, children $6, family $45. An all-day pass costs $19.50. Sunset Cruise $19.50.
The main ferry terminals are (from west to east): Tewantin Noosa Marina (7/2 Parklyn Ct, Tewantin), Noosa Yacht Club, Big Pelican, O Boat Jetty, T Boat jetty, Noosa Wharf, Sheraton Hotel jetty.

Cycling/mountain biking
Noosa Bike Hire and Tours, T5474 3322, bikeon.com.au. Stylish outfit offering customized or scheduled guided trips according to your fitness and level of skill, as well as independent hire outlets throughout the area. Main outlet Noosa Tour Centre, Noosa Drive and Halse Lane, Noosa Heads, T5447 3845. Expect to pay around $40 per day, $20 for 2 hrs.

Horse trekking

Clip Clop Horse Treks, 249 Eumarella Rd, Lake Weyba, T0429-051544, www.clipclop treks.com.au. Wide range of exciting adventures on the waterways of the Great Sandy National Park (Cooloola), from half day (from $70), to 5-day/4-night (from around $1100). Independent hire and accommodation is also available from 2-hr treks to 4-day adventures. Prices on application.

Kayaking and canoeing

Elanda Point Canoe Company, T5485 3165, www.elanda.com.au.
Kayak Noosa , The Boathouse, 194 Gympie Terrace, Noosaville, T0448-567321, www.kayaknoosa.com. Coastal or river kayaking with the chance of encountering dolphins from $55 (2-hr sunset trips available). Independent hire from 1hr $20 to $55 per day.

Motorcycle tours

Aussie Biker Tours, 4/15 Venture Drive, Noosaville, T5474 1050, www.aussiebiker.com.au. Hire and self-guided trips.

Sightseeing tours

Fraser Island Adventure Tours, T5444 6957, www.fraserislandadventuretours.com.au. Exciting 4WD day trip to Fraser Island from Noosa, taking in the main sights of the Great Sandy National Park (Cooloola) along the way, from $145, children $110.
Noosa 4WD Eco Tours, T5449 8252, www.noosa4wdtours.com.au. Full- and half-day tours throughout the week to the Great Sandy Marine Park (Cooloola), from $95-129.
Noosa Hinterland Tours, T5448 6111, www.noosahinterlandtours.com.au. Tours throughout the week to the Hinterland taking in a winery and the Glass House Mountains, from $55, children $35; the Eumundi Markets (Wed and Sat), from $20, children $10; and the Australia Zoo on demand, from $49, children $29 (discounted zoo entry).

Spas

No doubt after a few hours on a camel or a horse your weathered cheeks and other bodily parts would greatly benefit from a spa or a massage. **Ikatan Balinese Day Spa**, 46 Grays Road, Doona, T5471 1199, www.ikatanspa.com, is a little bit out of Noosa but well worth it, or visit the **Noosa Spa** (South Pacific Resort), 167 Weyba Rd, T5447 1424, www.noosaspa.com.au.

Surfing and kitesurfing

There are more learn-to-surf operators on Main Beach than there are beach umbrellas. Generally they are all very professional and run by pros and/or experts. 2-hr session starts at about $65.
Wavesense, T0414-369076, www.wavesense.com.au, **Learn to Surf**, with world champ Merrick Davies, T0418-787577, www.learntosurf.com.au, 2 hrs from $60 and, for girls only, the **Girls Surf School**, T0418-787577, www.learntosurf.com.au.
Kitesurf, T5455 6677, www.kite-surf.com.au, and **Wind 'n' Sea**, T5455 6677, will introduce you to the world of kite surfing, from $150 for 2 hrs.
Noosa Longboards, Shop 4, 64 Hastings St, T5447 2828. Hires long/short surfboards and body boards, from $35 for 4 hrs.

Cooloola Coast *p238*

Horse trekking, diving, paragliding, canoeing and fishing all feature in the growing list of available activities and Cooloola VIC can provide detailed operator details. It is however 4WD tours that dominate, with options both north to Fraser Island and south to the Cooloola Section of the Great Sandy National Park.

4WD tours

Aussie Adventure 4WD, T5486 3599. If you want to go it alone, come here to hire 2-9 seater 4WD vehicles.

Dolphin watching

Dolphin Ferry Cruise, T0428-838836. Departs Carlo Point daily for the dolphin

A whale of a time

Every year from August to November the waters around Hervey Bay echo to the haunting symphonies of whale song. These whales spend the warmer summer months in Antarctic waters feeding on krill before starting their annual migration north to the central and southern Great Barrier Reef where calves are born in the warm waters. Finding temporary haven in the bay's calm waters, pods of humpback whales stop to socialize and play, often breaching the surface or slapping it with fins and tail, before moving on to the far more serious business of returning to their feeding grounds in Antarctica. Other marine animals, including dolphins, turtles and occasionally dugongs, also join the fray and can be seen all year round. See below for tours.

feeding at Tin Can Bay, from $20. For Fraser Island ferry services, see page 252.

Hervey Bay *p239, map p240*
Whale watching
The high number of visiting whales, the calm water conditions and the variety of cruises on offer has ensured Hervey Bay is the best location on the East Coast for experiencing whales up close. The choice of cruises range from 3-hr fast catamaran trips, to morning, afternoon half-day or full-day excursions that include lunch and refreshments. There are numerous operators based at the Urungan Boat Harbour and you are advised to take a look at the various boats and compare their itineraries. With so many operators, other than cruise time, the differences really come down to minor details like the size of the group. See also box above.
Blue Dolphin, T4124 9600, www.blue dolphintours.com.au. 'Whales by sail', half-day and sunset cruise option, from $70.
Mikat Whale Watch Safari, T4125 1522, www.mikat.com.au, and **Whalesong**, T4125 6222, www.whalesong.com.au, both operate cruises on large catamarans. 6-hr cruises with Mikat from $125. **Whalesong** do specialist year-round dolphin cruises, half day from $75, children $50.
Spirit of Hervey Bay, T1800 642544, www.spiritofherveybay.com. This one has the added luxury of underwater viewing rooms.

Tasman Venture II, T1800 620322, www.tasmanventure.com.au. Offers whale watching but also something different with a West Coast day tour which explorers the quiet and largely inaccessibly beaches of Fraser's west coast, with snorkelling and perhaps a bit of dolphin watching along the way, from $125.

Fraser Island *p241, map p243*
As you might expect, there are many tours on offer to Fraser from as far away as Brisbane and Noosa. To get the most from the island you really need at least 3 days, so a day tour should only be considered if you are hard pressed for time. If you want to explore the island in a short space of time try the excellent guided tour and accommodation packages on offer through the resorts, especially **Kingfisher Bay**, T1800 072555, www.kingfisherbay.com.au. Daily tours start at $169, children $99.
Air Fraser Island, T4125 3600, www.airfraser island.com.au. Recommended if you're on your own or are a couple. They will fly you out to Eurong, where you are supplied with a small, economical 4WD (with camping gear if required, fuel not included) from around $275 per day. The only drawback is that the vehicle must stay on the island and be dropped off again at Eurong. This option does avoid the expensive vehicle ferry fees and is fine if you want to fly back, but it can present problems if you wish to stay at the **Kingfisher Bay Resort** and/or get the ferry back as foot passengers from the island's west coast.

Noosa

Fraser Explorer Tours, T4194 9222, www.fraserexplorertours.com.au. Day or 2-day trips departing from either Hervey Bay or Rainbow Beach, from $165, children $99 ($309/$209).

Fraser Island Adventure Tours, T5444 6957, www.fraserislandadventuretours.com.au. Exciting 4WD day trip to Fraser Island ex Noosa, taking in the main sights of the Great Sandy National Park (Cooloola) along the way, from $145, children $110.

Fraser Island Trailblazers Tours, T5499 9505, www.trailblazertours.com.au. Good value 'down-to-sand' 3-day camping safari, via the Great Sandy National Park (Cooloola section), from $360 (2-day from $280).

Hervey Bay

Fraser Experience & Safari 4WD, 102 Boat Harbour Rd, T4124 4244, www.safari 4wdhire.com.au. For those wishing to get a group together and go independently, this is one of the most professional. They offer a range of models from $140-200 a day, camping kits from $20 per day and hire/ accommodation packages are also available. Their guided Fraser Experience departs Hervey Bay to Rainbow Beach then Fraser Island, 2-day tour from $285.

Fraser Explorer Tours, T4194 9222, www.fraserexplorertours.com.au. Day tour from Hervey Bay, starting at $165.

Fraser Island Company, T4125 3933,, www.fraserislandco.com.au. Offers a good range of safaris, 1 day from $145, children $85, 2 days from $269.

Nomads, T4125 3601, www. nomadshostels.com, and **Palace**, T1800 063168, are 2 backpackers offering their own vehicles, guides and budget packages (camping), from around $155. Other companies worth looking at are **Aussie Trax**, 56 Boat Harbour Drive, T4124 4433, www.fraserisland4wd.com.au, and **Fraser Magic**, 5 Kruger Court, Urangan, T4125 6612, www.fraser4wdhire.com.au.

⊖ Transport

Noosa *p235, map p236*
Air
The nearest airport is the Maroochydore (Sunshine Coast) Airport, www.sunshine coastairport.com, which is 6 km north of Maroochydore. **Jet Star**, T131538, www.jetstar.com; **Qantas**, T131313, www.qantas.com.au; **Tiger Airways**, T9335 3033, www.tigerairways.com; and **Virgin Blue**, T136789, www.virginblue.com.au, provide daily services from national centres including **Brisbane**. Local northbound bus services stop at the airport and a taxi to **Noosa Heads** will cost about $70.
Henry's, 12 Noosa Drive, T5474 0199, www.henrys.com.au, offers express (non-stop) services between Brisbane Airport/Maroochydore Airport and Noosa Heads 7 times daily, from $25 each way.

Bus
Local Sunshine Coast Sunbus, T5450 7888, www.sunbus.com.au, has services to Noosa Heads/Tewantin north/ southbound to the Sunshine Coast west to Eumundi/Cooroy/Nambour. A free council-run bus service every 15 mins between Tewantin and Noosa Fair is available and the information centre can provide times and routes.

Long distance The long-distance terminal is on the corner of Noosa Pde and Noosa Drive, Noosa Heads. **Greyhound**, T1300 473946, and **Suncoast Pacific**, T131230, offer daily north/southbound services and regular services to **Tin Can Bay**. **Harvey World Travel**, Shop 2, Lanyana Way, Noosa Heads, T5447 4077, and **Palm Tree Tours**, Bay Village, Hastings St, T5474 9166, act as local booking agents.

Car
Avis, Shop 1, Ocean Breeze Resort, corner Hastings St and Noosa Drive, T5447 4933. **Budget**, 52 Mary St, Noosaville, T5474 2820. If you wish to explore the Great Sandy National

Park there are several 4WD hire companies including **Thrifty**, 66 Noosa Drive, T5447 2299; and **Pelican 4WD Hire**, 66 Noosa Drive, T1800 144294.

Ferry
The **Tewantin car ferry**, T5447 1321, www.noosacarferries.com, crosses the Noosa River (end of Moorindil St) and provides access to the national park. It operates Nov-Jan Sun-Thu 0530-2230, Fri-Sat 0530-0030 and Feb-Oct Mon-Thu 0600-2230, Fri 0600-0030, Sat 0500-0030 and Sun 0500-2230, from $6.

Train
The nearest train station is at Cooroy, T132232. **Sunbus** offers services from there to Noosa Heads (No 12).

Cooloola Coast *p238*
Bus
Greyhound, T131499, and **Suncoast Pacific**, T131230, operate daily coach services to **Tin Can Bay** and **Rainbow Beach**.

Car
Rainbow Beach is 76 km east of the Bruce Highway at Gympie and the road is sealed all the way. Alternative access is by 4WD only from Tewantin, 3 km east of Noosaville, Noosa River ferry 0600-2200, from $6.

Hervey Bay *p239, map p240*
Air
Hervey Bay airport, T1800 811728, has daily scheduled flights to **Brisbane** and **Sydney** with Jetstar, T131538, Qantas, T131313, and **Virgin Blue**, T136789. The airport shuttle meets all flights, T4194 0953. Taxi T131008.

Bus
Local **Wide Bay Transit**, T4121 3719, www.widebaytransit.com.au, runs local hail and ride bus services between Maryborough (including the railway station) and Hervey Bay (No 5), taking in a circuit of the town along the Esplanade to Urangan and back via Boat

Harbour Drive. Nos 16 and 18 also cover the main centres and Urangan Marina.
Long distance The long-distance bus terminal is in the Bay Central Shopping Centre, Boat Harbour Rd, Pialba, T4124 4000. Greyhound, T1300 473946, and **Premier Motor Services**, T133410, offer daily services north/south and to **Tin Can Bay** and **Rainbow Beach**.

Car
Car hire from **Hervey Bay Rent A Car**, T4194 6626, and **Nifty Rent A Car**, 463 Esplanade, T4125 6008.

Train
The nearest train station is in Maryborough, Lennox St, T4123 9264. **Queensland Rail**'s fast Tilt Train (**Brisbane** to **Rockhampton**) offers regular services north and south, T132232. Wide Bay Transit No 5 service connects with every Tilt Train for transfers to and from **Hervey Bay**, T4123 1733. **Hervey Bay Travel Centre**, Bay Central Shopping Mall, Torquay, T1800 815378, can act as booking agents.

Fraser Island *p241, map p243*
Air
There are 2 small airfields on Fraser – Toby's Gap and Orchid Beach – but most light aircraft land on East Beach at Eurong or Happy Valley.
Air Fraser Island, T4125 3600. Daily services from around $100, www.airfraserisland.com.au. It also offers packages and scenic flights, see page 251.

Boat
There are several barge options to Fraser island: **Fraser Island Barges and Ferry** have several services daily from River Heads, south of Hervey Bay, Rainbow Beach and Urangan Boat Harbour, T4194 9300, www.fraserislandferry.com.au; the **Fraser Venture Barge** also departs River Heads to Wanggoolba Creek. Both barges operate continuously between dawn and dusk departing Inskip Point daily, landing at the most southern tip of Fraser, Hook Point.

Crossing time takes approximately 10 mins, from $90. The **Kingfisher Bay (Resort)**, T1800 072555, www.kingfisherbay.com.au, also operates its own passenger/4WD ferry to the resort from $85. The **Fraser Dawn Barge** operates from Urangan Boat Harbour to Moon Point– crossing time approximately 55 mins. Moon Point is directly opposite Happy Valley on Fraser Island's west coast.

ⓘ Directory

Noosa *p235, map p236*
Banks Most branches/ATMs are on Hastings St, Noosa Heads or Sunshine Beach Rd, Noosa Junction. Currency exchange at **Harvey World Travel**, Shop 2, Lanyana Way, Noosa Heads, T5447 4077.
Hospitals **Noosa Hospital**, 111 Goodchap St, T5455 9200; **Noosaville Medical Centre**, corner of Thomas St and Mary St, T5442 4922, Mon-Thu 0800-2000, Fri-Sun 0800-1800.
Internet Travel Bugs, Shop 3/9, Sunshine Beach Rd, Noosa Junction, T5474 8530, daily 0800-2200. **Urban Mailbox**, Ocean Breeze Resort, Shop 4, Noosa Drive, Noosa Heads, T5473 5151, daily 0900-1900 (2200 high season). **Pharmacy** Night and Day, 32 Hastings St, daily 0900-2100. **Post** 91 Noosa Drive, T5473 8591, Mon-Fri 0900-1730, Sat 0900-1230. Postcode 4567.

Hervey Bay *p239, map p240*
Banks Most branches/ATMs are in the Central Avenue Plaza, Pialba.
Hospital Nissen St, T4120 6666.
Pharmacy Pialba Place Main St, Pialba, T4128 1140. **Post** Post Office, 414 Esplanade, Torquay, Mon-Fri 0830-1700, Sat 0830-1200 and Central Av, Pialba, T131318. Postcode 4655. **Useful numbers** Police, 142 Torquay Rd, T4128 5333.

Fraser Island *p241, map p243*
Food, hardware, fuel and telephones are available at the **Eurong Beach Resort, Fraser Island Retreat** (Happy Valley), **Kingfisher Bay Resort, Cathedral Beach Resort** and **Orchid Beach**. Additional telephones are located at Ungowa, Central Station, Dundubara, Waddy Point and Indian Head. There are no banks or ATMs on the island but most major resorts accept EFTPOS. There are no medical services on the island. QPWS ranger stations and resorts all have basic first aid and can call in an air ambulance in an emergency, T000. For mechanical assistance on the island contact: Eurong T4127 9173 and T0427-279173; Orchid Beach T4127 9220. For tow truck services contact: Eurong, T4127 9449 and T0428-353164; Yidney Rocks, T4127 9187 and T0427-279167; Orchid Beach T4127 9220. For taxi service: Eurong, T4127 9188 and T0429-379188.

Capricorn Coast

Capricorn Coast begins north of Hervey Bay, where the great sand masses of the Fraser Coast give way to fields of sugar cane and, offshore, the start of the Great Barrier Reef. Near Bundaberg – or 'Bundy' – is Mon Repos, one of the world's most important and accessible mainland turtle rookeries. The once remote towns of 1770 and Agnes Water serve as gateway to the stunning southern reef island of Lady Musgrave, while even more beautiful Heron Island is accessed from the industrial port of Gladstone. East of Rockhampton, Queensland's 'beef capital', are the coastal resorts of Yeppoon and Emu Park, while just offshore Great Keppel Island offers many tourists their first taste of Queensland's many beautiful tropical island resorts.

Bundaberg and Southern Reef Islands → For listings, see pages 262-268. Colour map 4, A2.

Little Bundaberg sits beside the Burnett River amidst a sea of sugar cane. The city relies far more on agriculture than tourism to sustain it and as a result is usually absent from most travel agendas. Many refer to the town as 'Bundy', though this affectionate nickname is most often used to describe its famous tipple, rum, which has been faithfully distilled in Bundaberg since 1883. Not surprisingly, the wonderfully sweet-smelling distillery is the biggest tourist attraction, while others nearby include the southern reef islands of Lady Musgrave and Elliot, both of which offer excellent diving, and the fascinating seasonal action at the Mon Repos Turtle Rookery.

Ins and outs

Getting there and around Bundaberg's airport is 3 km from the city centre. All the main bus companies operate services to the city from the north and south. The **Tilt Train** is the major train service from Brisbane. The reef ferries depart from the Bundaberg Port Marina, on the lower reaches of the Burnett River, about 19 km northeast of the centre. The coastal resorts of Bargara, Burnett Heads and the Mon Repos Turtle Rookery are 15 km east. Local coach operators run regular services. See Transport, page 266.

Tourist information There are two VICs, with little difference between them. The accredited centre is at ⓘ *271 Bourbong St, T4153 8888, www.bundabergregion.org, 0900-1700.*

Bundaberg

Before filling the nostrils with the sweet smell of molasses and titillating the taste buds with the dark nectar at the distillery, it is perhaps worth taking a quick, and sober, look at one or two of the historical buildings dominating the city centre. Most prominent is the 30-m clock tower of **Post Office building**, on the corner of Bourbong Street and Barolin Street, which has been in continuous operation since 1890. A few doors down is the 1891 **Old National Australia Bank**, with its distinctive colonnades and spacious verandahs embellished with cast iron balustrades.

An equally popular retreat is the city's **Botanical Gardens Complex** ⓘ *1 km north of the city centre, corner of Hinkler Av and Gin Gin Rd, T4152 0222, 0730-1700, $5, children $2, museums 1000-1600.* Added to the obvious botanical attractions and landscaped ponds and gardens are the **Fairymead House Sugar Museum**, which documents the history of the region's most important industry, and the **Hinkler House Memorial Museum**, T4130

Coral Sea Islands

Lying 70 km east of the industrial town of Gladstone, just beyond the horizon, is one of the most beautiful of the picture-postcard Coral Sea Islands – Heron Island. As well as being a fairly accurate representation of most people's tropical fantasy, Heron is also considered one of the best dive sites on the reef. All this perfection comes at a price. Even getting there is an expensive business. Heron Island is 2 hours by launch or 30 minutes by helicopter. The resort launch leaves daily at 1100 from the Gladstone Marina on Bryan Jordan Drive in Gladstone and costs from $240 return. Contracted helicopters fly daily from Gladstone Airport for around $555 return. Contact the resort direct (below) or the VIC at the Marina in Gladstone, T4972 4000, www.gapdl.com.au for bookings.

Accommodation is limited to the exclusive **LL Heron Island Resort**, T1300 233432, www.heronisland.com. Newly refurbished, the resort offers luxury suites to beach houses, pool, an à la carte restaurant, bar, dive shop and a host of other activities.

4400, which celebrates the life and times of courageous local pioneer aviator, Bert Hinkler. Born in Bundaberg in 1892, Hinkler was the first person to fly solo from Australia to England, in 1928. Sadly, after going on to break numerous other records, he then died attempting to break the record for the return journey in 1933. There is also a working steam train that clatters round the gardens on Sundays.

Although a relatively small operation, the **Bundaberg Distillery** ⓘ *Avenue St (4 km east of the city centre, head for the chimney stack), T4131 2999, www.bundabergrum.com.au, tours daily on the hour Mon-Fri 1000-500, Sat-Sun 1000- 1400, from $25, children $15*, established in 1883, provides a fascinating insight into the distilling process. The one-hour tour begins with a short video celebrating the famous Bundy brand before you are taken to view the various aspects of the manufacturing process. First stop is a huge 5-million-litre well of sweet-smelling molasses, which is gradually drawn through a maze of steel pipes, fermenters, condensers and distillers, before ending up in mighty vats within the maturing warehouses. With one vat alone being worth $5 million ($3 million of which goes to government tax) it is hardly surprising to hear the solid click of lock and key and to be mildly aware of being counted on the way out! Then, with a discernibly quickening pace, you are taken to an authentic bar to sample the various end products. Generous distillers they are too, allowing four shots, which is just enough to keep you below the legal driving limit.

Mon Repos Turtle Rookery

ⓘ *Grange Rd, off Bundaberg Port Rd, T4159 1652 or T4153 8888, www.epa.qld.gov.au. Turtle viewing Oct-May, 1900-0600 (subject to activity), information centre open daily 24 hrs Oct-May and 0600-1800 Jun-Sep, $9.60, children $5.10.*

Supporting the largest concentration of nesting marine turtles on the eastern Australian mainland and one of the largest loggerhead turtle rookeries in the world, the Coral Coast beach, known as Mon Repos (pronounced 'Mon Repo'), is a place of ecological reverence. It can be found 12 km east of Bundaberg, near the coastal resort of Bargara. During the day Mon Repos looks just like any other idyllic Queensland beach and gives absolutely no indication of its conservation value. Yet at night, between mid-October and May, it takes on a very different aura. Hauling themselves from the waves, just beyond the tideline, with a determination only nature can display, the female turtles (often quite elderly) each dig a large pit in the sand and lay over 100 eggs before deftly filling it in and disappearing beneath the waves, as if they had never been there at all. To watch this happen, all in the space of about 20 minutes, is a truly magical experience. And it doesn't end there. Towards the end of the season, from January to March, the tiny hatchlings emerge from the nest and make their way as fast as they can, like tiny clockwork toys, towards the relative safety of the water. Watching this spectacle is moving and, strangely, hilarious, despite the knowledge that only one in 1000 of the hatchlings will survive to maturity and return to the same beach to breed. Of course, like any wildlife-watching attraction, there are no guarantees that turtles will show up on any given night, so you may need a lot of patience. While you wait at the Information Centre to be escorted in groups of about 20 to watch the turtles up close, you can view static displays, or better still, join in the staff's fascinating question-and-answer sessions, where you can learn all about the turtles' remarkable natural history, and sadly, the increasing threat that humans are posing to them. Best viewing times for nesting turtles are subject to night tides between November and February. Turtle hatchlings are best viewed from 1900 to 2400, January to March.

Southern Reef Islands

Lady Musgrave Island, 83 km northeast of Bundaberg, is part of the Capricornia Cays National Park and the southernmost island of the Bunker Group. With a relatively small 14 ha of coral cay in comparison to a huge 1192-ha surrounding reef, it is generally considered one of the most beautiful and abundant in wildlife, both above and below the water. The cay itself offers safe haven to thousands of breeding seabirds and also serves as an important green turtle rookery between November and March. Then, between August and October, humpback whales are also commonly seen. With such a large expanse of reef, the island offers some excellent snorkelling and diving as well as providing a pleasant escape from the mainland.

Lady Elliot Island, about 20 km south of Lady Musgrave, is one of the southernmost coral cays on the Barrier Reef. It's larger than Musgrave and though the surrounding reef is smaller, it is very similar in terms of scenery and marine diversity. The island is also a popular diving venue with numerous wrecks lying just offshore (about $30 a dive). ▸▸ *For further details see Tours, page 265, and Transport, page 266.*

Agnes Water, 1770 and around → *For listings, see pages 262-268. Colour map 4, A2.*

With the dawning of the new millennium it was already obvious that both 1770 and Agnes would be changed from being fairly inaccessible, sleepy coastal neighbours into the next big thing on the southern Queensland coast. Sadly, this seems to have happened and they have fallen victim to the great East Coast property development phenomenon. As predicted, the money has moved in and the locals have moved out. Where wooded hillsides once created a soft green horizon, designer holiday homes owned by absentee landlords have appeared. Where once dunescapes created pockets of soporific seclusion, sterile and exclusive apartment resorts look set to dominate. Despite the decline, the two towns are still extremely picturesque and hemmed in by two fine national parks, Eurimbula and Deepwater. The Town of 1770 also acts as gateway to Lady Musgrave Island, an undeniable gem located 50 km offshore.

Ins and outs

Getting there and around There are long-distance bus services from Rockhampton or Bundaberg and a train station at Miriam Vale, 55 km east. ➤➤ *See Transport, page 266.*

Tourist information **Miriam Vale VIC** ⓘ *Bruce Highway, Miriam Vale, T4974 5428, www.gladstoneholidays.info, Mon-Fri 0830-1700, Sat-Sun 0900-1700*, and **Discovery Centre** ⓘ *Captain Cook Drive, Agnes Water, T4902 1533, Mon-Sat 0830-1700*, are the two main sources of local information. **QPWS** ⓘ *Captain Cook Drive, Agnes Waters, T4902 1555, www.qld.gov.au, Mon-Fri 0900-1630.*

Agnes Water and the Town of 1770

Agnes Water has a beautiful 5-km beach right on its doorstep, which offers good swimming and excellent surfing. More remote beaches offering more solitude and great walking opportunities can be accessed within the national parks. The small **museum** ⓘ *Springs Rd, Sat-Sun 1000-1200, Wed 1300-1500, $2*, touches on Aboriginal settlement, Cook's visit and the subsequent visitations by explorers Flinders and King, as well as more recent maritime and European settlement history.

The Town (village) of 1770 nestles on the leeward side of Round Hill Head and along the bank of the Round Hill Inlet, 6 km north of Agnes, and is a popular spot for fishing and boating. It also serves as the main departure point for local national park and reef island tours and cruises, see page 265.

Deepwater and Eurimbula national parks

Deepwater National Park, 8 km south of Agnes, presents a mosaic of coastal vegetation including paperbark, banksias and heathland fringed with dunes and a sweeping beach studded with small rocky headlands. As well as fishing and walking, there are fine opportunities for birdwatching and it is often used as a nesting site by green turtles between January and April. The roads within the park are unsealed so 4WD is recommended.

To the northwest of Agnes is Eurimbula National Park. Indented by the Round Hill Inlet and Eurimbula Creek, it is an area covered in thick mangrove and freshwater paperbark swamps. It is less accessible than Deepwater and best explored by boat. Other than the interesting flora and fauna, highlights include the panoramic views of the park and coastline from the Ganoonga Noonga Lookout, which can be reached by vehicle 3 km from the park entrance, 10 km west of Agnes Water. Again a 4WD is recommended, especially in the wet season.

Rockhampton and around → *For listings, see pages 262-268. Colour map 5, C3.*

Straddling both the Tropic of Capricorn and picturesque Fitzroy River, Rockhampton – or 'Rocky' as it is affectionately known – is the dubbed the 'beef capital' of Australia. First settled by Scots pioneer Charles Archer in 1855 (yet strangely bestowed the anglicized suffix 'Hampton', meaning 'a place near water'), the city enjoyed a brief gold rush in the late 1850s before the more sustainable bovine alternative finally sealed its economic fate. Although most visitors stay only very briefly, on their way to sample the coastal delights of Yeppoon and Great Keppel Island, Rocky has a truly diverse range of tourist attractions, from the historical and cultural to the ecological and even subterranean. Then, of course, there is the town's legendary gastronomic delight, in the form of a steak the size of a small European country.

Ins and outs

Tourist information **Capricorn Region VIC** ① *Gladstone Rd, Rockhampton, T4927 2055, www.capricorntourism.com.au, daily 0900-1700*, is in the Capricorn Spire, which marks the point of the Tropic of Capricorn (23.5° south), and caters for city and region. **Rockhampton VIC** ① *208 Quay St, T4922 5625, www.rockhamptoninfo.com, Mon-Fri 0830-1630, Sat-Sun 0900-1600*, is housed in the grandiose 1902 Customs House. ▸▸ *See Transport, page 266.*

City centre

With its mineral and agricultural heritage, there are numerous historical buildings dominating the city centre. These include the 1902 **Customs House**, which now houses the VIC, the 1895 **Post Office**, on the corner of East Street and Denham Street, the 1890 **Criterion Hotel**, on Quay Street, and the 1887 **Supreme Court**, on East Lane, which has

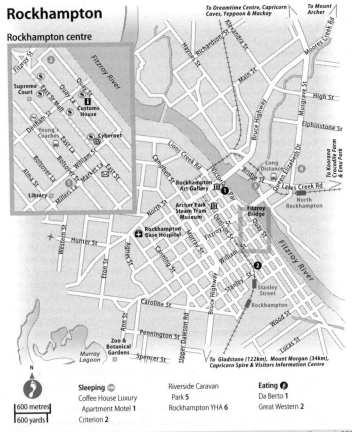

Rockhampton

Sleeping 🛏
Coffee House Luxury
Apartment Motel **1**
Criterion **2**

Riverside Caravan
Park **5**
Rockhampton YHA **6**

Eating 🍴
Da Berto **1**
Great Western **2**

600 metres
600 yards

been in continuous use now for over a century. As well as its numerous historical buildings, Rockhampton also boasts six bull statues, in celebration of its status as the beef capital of Australia.

Train enthusiasts will enjoy the **Archer Park Steam Tram Museum** ① *Denison St, T4922 2774, www.steamtram.rockhampton.qld.gov.au, Sun-Fri 1000-1600, $7.30, children $4.20, tram operates Sun 1000-1300*. The town also has a number of art galleries. Best of the lot is the **Rockhampton Art Gallery** ① *62 Victoria Pde, T4927 7129, Tue-Fri 1000-1600, Sat-Sun 1100-1600, free*, which displays a long-established collection of mainly 1940-1970s Australian works as well as some more recent contemporary acquisitions.

The small but tidy **Rockhampton Zoo** ① *T4922 1654, 0800-1700, free*, on Spencer Street, has many natives on hand including koala and tame kangaroos and a charming pair of chimps called Cassie and Ockie (as in Dokie). Almost next door are the spacious **Botanical Gardens** ① *0600-1800*, first established in 1869. Amongst its leafy avenues of palms and cycads are a fernery, a Japanese garden and the peaceful garden tearooms. **Murray Lagoon** is also a fine place to stroll around.

Around the city

Though not quite on a par with the Tjapukai Aboriginal park near Cairns (see page 303), the **Dreamtime Centre** ① *6 km north of the Rockhampton city along the Bruce Highway, T4936 1655, www.dreamtimecentre.com.au, Mon-Fri 1000-1530, $13.50, children $6.50, guided tours start daily at 1030*, is an entertaining introduction to Aboriginal and Torres Strait heritage using a wide range of displays and hands-on activities. Set in 12 ha of parkland just off the Bruce Highway, 6 km north of the city centre, a guided or self-guided tour allows you to witness some masterful didgeridoo playing, before exploring the various displays outside in the Torres Strait Islander Village. These include traditional gunyahs (shelters) and the giant Dugong Complex, with artefacts and building materials. There is also a native plant garden where you can learn about their use as food and medicine. For many the highlight of their visit is the opportunity to throw a boomerang so it actually comes back.

Established over 20 years ago, **Koorana Crocodile Farm** ① *Coowonga Rd, Emu Park, 33 km east of the city, T4934 4749, www.koorana.com.au, 1000-1500, $22, children $11, tours at 1030-1200 and 1300-1430, no public transport*, was the first private croc farm in Queensland and is home to some mighty large characters. Tours are available and there is an interesting video presentation that will avail you of many facts, the most memorable being that crocodile dung was once used for contraception (though quite how, thankfully, remains an enigma). **Mount Morgan**, 38 km southwest of the city, has a steam railway and a small but well-presented museum ① *1000-1600, $5, children $1*, celebrating its highly productive gold and copper mining heritage. There is also a bat-infested cave nearby where dinosaur footprints were discovered in 1954. **Mount Archer**, which looms large at 604 m above Rocky's northeastern suburbs, has a fine summit walk and lookout. Access is from the end of Moores Creek Road, north of the Bruce Highway. Vehicular access to the summit is from Frenchville Road, off Norman, which is off Moores Creek Road.

Capricorn Caves

① *Olsen's Caves Rd, T4934 2883, www.capricorncaves.com.au, 0900-1600, standard tours $22, children $11; 3-hr caving from $60 (1300); 2-hr geological fossil tour from $35. Accommodation packages also available.*

This limestone cave system, 23 km north of Rockhampton, is well worth a visit. Privately owned and open to the public for over a century, the caves offer a memorable combination of subterranean sights and sounds and are home to an array of unusual wildlife. An entertaining guided tour takes you through numerous collapsed caverns, beautifully lit caves and narrow tunnels, to eventually reach a natural amphitheatre where stunning acoustics are demonstrated with classical music and then, utter silence. The venue is so special it is often used for weddings and Christmas carol concerts. During December and January, exiting visitors can witness a brilliant natural light spectacle created by the rays of the sun.

The cave system has been home to tens of thousands of bats and the odd harmless python for millennia, and although very few are seen, it adds that essential Indiana Jones edge. The more adventurous can go on an exhilarating two- to four-hour caving tour and come face to face with the bats and pythons while squeezing through the infamous 'Fat Man's Misery'. Also on offer is a new specialized cave geo tour revealing an ancient geological landscape and the marine fossils encrusted on the cave walls, evidence of the coral reef that existed 390 million years ago.

Yeppoon and around → For listings, see pages 262-268. Colour map 5, C3.

Blessed by a cooling breeze and a string of pretty beaches, the small seaside settlements of Yeppoon, Rosslyn Bay and Emu Park are the main focus of the Capricorn Coast and the region's principal coastal holiday resorts. Yeppoon – the largest – offers a wealth of affordable accommodation and safe swimming, while 7 km south, Rosslyn Bay provides the gateway to Great Keppel Island. One of the highlights of the area is the vast coastal wilderness of the **Byfield National Park** – a sanctuary a rich variety of water birds and venue for some fine 4WD adventures.

Although most non-natives stop only briefly on their way to Great Keppel Island, the surrounding coastline offers plenty to see and do. There are beaches and headlands dotted all along the 16-km stretch of road between Yeppoon and Emu Park. South of Yeppoon the small national parks of **Double Head**, above Rosslyn Harbour, and **Bluff Point**, at the southern end of Kemp Beach, provide short walks and viewpoints across to Great Keppel Island. South of the Bluff, **Mulambin Beach** stretches south to **Pinnacle Point** and the entrance to **Causeway Lake**, a popular spot for fishing and boating. From there the road skirts **Shoal Bay** and **Kinka Beach**, considered by many as the best in the region, before arriving in Emu Park.

West of Yeppoon, just off the main highway, is the knobbly volcanic peak known as **Mount Jim Crow** (221 m). Who Mr Crow was exactly remains a mystery, but the peak was steeped in Aboriginal legend well before his arrival and can be climbed, with a bit of scrambling, from the old quarry.

To the north of Yeppoon, the seemingly boundless **Byfield Coastal Area** is one of the largest undeveloped regions on the east coast of Australia and, although the vast majority of it is taken up by the inaccessible Shoalwater Bay Military Training Area, the biodiversity of **Byfield National Park**, on its southern fringe, offers plenty of opportunity for camping, walking, boating, fishing, birdwatching and 4WDs. The heart of the park is reached via the Byfield Road and Byfield State Forest, but you'll need a 4WD, especially if you want to reach Nine Mile Beach. This is perhaps what makes the park so special. If such luxuries are beyond your budget then you can still get a feel for the place from the 'wetlands' west of the Rydges Capricorn Resort, or the Sandy Point Section of the park, to the north. Although the road is unsealed it is easily negotiable by 2WD and offers numerous access points to Farnborough Beach where you can have a stretch of pristine sand almost entirely to yourself. **Rydges Capricorn Resort** itself is also well worth a look, see page 264.

Great Keppel Island → *For listings, see pages 262-268. Colour map 5, C3.*

Great Keppel Island (1400 ha) is the largest of 18 islands in the Keppel group, which sits within easy reach of Rosslyn Bay. For many, Great Keppel provides the first real taste of Queensland's idyllic tropical islands. Although not quite on a par with Magnetic Island, it has a wealth of beautiful sandy beaches, walks and activities, with a good range of places to stay.

Despite having 17 beaches to choose from, few visitors venture beyond the main hub of activity at **Fisherman's Beach**, which fronts the main resort and provides ferry access. You are far better to be more adventurous and seek out the quieter spots. A 20-minute walk south is **Long Beach**, which in turn provides access to **Monkey Beach**, 35 minutes away, across the headland to the west. North of the resort, beyond the spit, is **Putney Beach**, which offers pleasant views across to Middle Island. There are numerous walks around the island, with the most popular being the 45-minute trek to **Mount Wyndham**, the highest point on the island. Longer excursions of around 1½ hours will take you to the realms of solitude and the island's northeastern beaches, including **Svendsen's**, **Sandhill** and **Wreck Beach**, or further still to the unremarkable light beacon on the island's southeast coast. Walking maps and descriptions are readily available from the ferries and resorts. With so many walks and beaches you will probably have very little time for anything else, but do check out the tame and beautiful rainbow lorikeets that frequent the resort's **Keppel Café**.

While Great Keppel Island is the main focus of activity, some of the other, smaller islands in the group offer more solitude, good snorkelling and camping. **Middle Island**, lying north of Great Keppel, is home to an underwater observatory that sits above a sunken Taiwanese wreck teeming with monster cod and other bizarre sea creatures. There is a QPWS campsite, but you will need to take your own water and gas stove. Other QPWS campsites are located at **Considine Beach**, **North Keppel Island**, and **Humpy Island**, renowned for its good snorkelling. Both sites have seasonal water supplies and toilets. For more details and permits contact the QPWS office ① *Yeppoon Courthouse, Normanby Street, Yeppoon, T4939 5385, Mon-Fri 0900-1630.* All the islands have a complete fire ban. **Pumpkin Island** (6 ha), just to the south of North Keppel, is privately owned but offers some accommodation.

Capricorn Coast listings

For Sleeping and Eating price codes and other relevant information, see Essentials pages 28-33.

Sleeping

Bundaberg and Southern Reef Islands *p255*

Beyond the usual rash of motels, Bundaberg has little choice. The town is short on quality backpackers with most catering for workers seeking cheap long stays. If you have your own transport you are advised to head for the seaside resort of Bargara (12 km east) where you will find a number of pleasant low-key resorts and beachside motor parks.

L-C Kacy's Bargara Beach Hotel and Motel, corner of Bauer St and the Esplanade, Bargara, T4130 1100, www.bargaramotel.com.au. A range of apartment and standard rooms and a in-house restaurant.

A Villa L'sha, 6 Albatross Court, Moore Park Beach, Bundaberg, T4154 8220, www.villa-l-sha.com. Contemporary villa B&B, set in a tropical garden and near the beach. Queen en suite, kitchenette and pool. Excellent value.

B-E Big 4 Cane Village Holiday Park, Twyford St (2 km south of Bundaberg, off Takalvan St), T4155 1022, www.cane-village-holiday-park.qld.big4.com.au. The best motor park in town, it has en suite/standard cabins, powered and non-powered sites and a camp kitchen.

C-F Bargara Beach Caravan Park, the Esplanade, Bargara, T4159 2228, www.bargarabeach.com.au. Spacious option near the amenities in Bargara, has good facilities and a camp kitchen.

D Bargara Gardens Motel and Villas, 13 See St, Bargara, T4159 2295, www.bargarabeachvillas.com.au. A good budget motel option with self-contained villas in a quiet tropical garden setting and near the beach.

E Feeding Grounds Backpackers, 4 Hinkler Av, North Bundaberg, T4152 3659, www.footprintsadventures.com.au. Tempting to say with a name like that it has to be good; however, despite the name this is a reputable, quality establishment and the recent adjunct to a well-established tour company specializing in entertaining tours to the turtle rookery.

QPWS campsite, T4971 6500 (Gladstone), on Lady Musgrave Island. No water, and fires banned. Bookings essential and needs to be arranged well in advance.

Agnes Water, 1770 and around *p257*
There is a good range of accommodation but both towns are getting increasingly busy, especially around Christmas and public holidays, so book ahead.

L-A Beachshacks, 578 Captain Cook Drive, 1770, T4974 9463, www.1770beach shacks.com. Characterful, spacious, modern, fully self-contained bungalows complete with thatched roofs and decks overlooking the beach and next door to the local store and bottleshop.

A-F Captain Cook Holiday Village, 300 m further inland on Captain Cook Drive, 1770, T4974 9219, www.1770holidayvillage. Set in the bush and offers a good range of options from self-contained en suite cabins to campsites and a good bistro/bar. Fires are permitted and there is access to Agnes Water main beach.

C-E Beachside Backpackers 1770, 12 Captain Cook Drive, Agnes Water, T4974 7200, www.1770beachsidebackpacker.com.au. This is the newer of the 2 backpackers in Agnes and offers self-catering and luxury apartments as well as the usual hostel-style dorms all with modern facilities including internet café, pool and yoga classes. The Freckles Bar and Grill is a popular feature of the complex and offers cheap backpacker meals.

C-E Cool Bananas 2 Springs Rd, Agnes Water, T4974 7660, www.coolbananas.net.au. Of the 2 backpackers in Agnes, this has the most activity. It is a fine place, and very popular, with modern, purpose-built facilities, fast internet, off-street parking and a wealth of organized activities, including surf lessons from $17 and even flying lessons (yes, as in plane) from $50. Excellent staff. Free pick-ups from Bundaberg on Mon, Wed and Fri.

E-F 1770 Camping Grounds, in 1770, T4974 9286. This is the most popular camping ground. It sits beachside on Captain Cook Drive and has powered and non-powered sites, a small camp kitchen and a shop. Fires are permitted.

QPWS campsites, at Wreck Rock, Deepwater National Park, 11 km south of Agnes, with toilets, rainwater supply and a cold shower, self-registration (fires are banned) and Bustard Beach, Eurimbula National Park, with bore water and toilets, self-registration; fires are banned. For more information on both parks contact the QPWS in Agnes Water, T4902 1555.

Rockhampton *p258, map p259*
There are plenty of good places in the centre of the city, and numerous motels and motor parks scattered around the outskirts and along the Bruce Highway.

L-B Coffee House Luxury Apartment Motel, corner of Williams St and Bolsover St, T4927 5722, www.coffeehouse.com.au. A tidy, modern establishment with well-appointed, fully self-contained apartments, executive and standard rooms. A fine café and internet.

B-E Rockhampton YHA, located across the river on MacFarlane St, T4927 5288, www.rockhamptonbackpackers.com.au. Rather plain but well maintained and good facilities, it has standard doubles, some with en suite and dorms, new en suite cabins, a well-equipped kitchen, internet and tours desk. Onward trips to the coast and Great Keppel a speciality.

B-F Capricorn Caves Eco-Lodge and Caravan Park, Capricorn Caves, 23 km north of the city, T4934 2883, www.capricorncaves.com.au. Handy for visiting the caves.

C-D Criterion, Quay St, T4922 1225, www.thecriterion.com.au. Try this for a traditional, historical edge, overlooking the river, old fashioned and characterful rooms at good rates.

E Riverside Caravan Park, next to the river just across the Fitzroy Bridge, 2 Reaney St, T4922 3779. Basic, 3-star park. Convenient to the city centre, but only has powered and non-powered sites with limited facilities.

Yeppoon and around p261

LL Rydges Capricorn Resort, Farnborough Rd, T4925 2525, www.capricornresort.com.au. This hugely popular resort is set in the perfect beachside spot on the fringe of the Byfield National Park. The focus of its popularity is not surprisingly its superb pool, golf courses and huge range of activities. It offers slightly ageing apartments, suites and rooms with all the usual facilities, including 2 restaurants, a bistro and café. Although designed for extended package holidays it often offers attractive short-stay deals, especially on weekdays and in the low season. Bookings essential.

A-E Big 4 Capricorn Palms Holiday Village, Wildin Way, Mulambin Beach (1 km south of Rosslyn Bay), T4933 6144, www.capricorn-palms-holiday-village.qld.big4.com.au. This is the best motor park in the area with everything from deluxe villas to non-powered sites, a good camp kitchen and pool.

A-F Ferns Hideaway Resort, located near Byfield, 50 km north of Yeppoon, T4935 1235, www.fernshideaway.com.au. Set deep in the rainforest, in near perfect isolation beside a creek, this colonial-style resort lodge offers log cabins with open fires and spa, basic budget rooms, campsites and a licensed bar and restaurant.

C-D Sunlover Lodge, 3 Camellia St, T4939 6727, www.sunloverlodge.com.au. Further afield in Kinka Beach is this excellent lodge, with a fine range of quiet, modern, fully self-contained cabins and villas, some with spa and all within a short stroll of the beach.

Great Keppel Island p262

The island is well known for offering a broad range of accommodation from luxury to budget. Before making a decision on island accommodation budget travellers should look into the numerous packages available, including those from Rockhampton/Yeppoon backpackers. This will save considerably on independent travelling costs.

A-E Great Keppel Island Holiday Village ('Geoff and Dianna's Place'), T4939 8655, www.gkiholidayvillage.com.au. A laid-back place with everything from a self-contained house to cabins, doubles, twins, dorms and custom-built tents. Fully equipped kitchen, free snorkel gear and organized kayak trips.

A-E Self-contained cabins, Pumpkin Island, T4939 4413, www.pumpkinisland.com.au. Each of the 5 cabins sleep 5-6 (from $350), camping area with fresh water, toilet, shower and barbecue (from $25).

🍴 Eating

Bundaberg and Southern Reef Islands p255

🍴 **Bargara Beach Hotel and Motel**, corner of Bauer St and the Esplanade, Bargara, T4130 1100. Good bistro restaurant with Australian/Chinese, wood-fired pizza.

🍴 **Viva Italia**, corner Bourbong and Bingera streets, T4151-1117. Licensed Italian restaurant offering value pastas and pizzas.

🍴-🍴 **Grand Hotel**, corner of Targo St and Bourbong St, T4151 2441. Modern, licensed restaurant offering traditional pub grub, value breakfasts and good coffee.

Ann's Kiosk, the Botanical Garden, Bundaberg, T4153 1477. Daily 1000-1600. Ideal for a light lunch in quiet surroundings.

Agnes Water, 1770 and around *p257*
Agnes Water Tavern, 1 Tavern Rd, Agnes Water, T4974 9469. Daily for lunch and dinner. A popular haunt with long-term locals (now becoming an endangered species). Offers good value meals and has a pleasant garden bar.

Deck, Captain Cook Holiday Village, 1770 (see page 263). Tue-Sat for lunch and dinner. Good value, local seafood, great views and a nice atmosphere.

Rockhampton *p258, map p259*
Unless you're a strict vegetarian, then you hardly need a menu in Rocky. Big around here (literally) are the steaks.

Criterion, see page 264, and the **Great Western**, 39 Stanley St, T4922 1862, are the best bets for steaks. Both are open daily from about 1100-late.

Da Berto, 62 Victoria Pde, T4922 3060. Open daily for lunch and dinner. Quality contemporary Italian option overlooking the river. Mon night specials.

Yeppoon and around *p261*
Causeway Lake Kiosk, beside the Causeway Bridge (between Rosslyn Bay and Kinka Beach). Daily until about 2000. The best fish and chips in the area.

Keppel Bay Sailing Club, above the beach on Anzac Parade, T4939 9500. Daily for lunch and dinner. Good value and a great view.

Shorething Café, 1/6 Normanby St, Yeppoon, T4939 1993. Good breakfasts, coffee and internet.

Great Keppel Island *p262*
Other than the resort eateries (see Sleeping, page 264) there is **Keppel Island Pizza**, on the waterfront, T4939 4699, Tue-Sun 1230-1400, 1800-2100.

The resorts have limited groceries and they are pricey so you are advised to take your own food supplies.

▲ Activities and tours

Bundaberg and Southern Reef Islands *p255*
Day trips (by air) from Bundaberg to Lady Elliot Island cost from $299, children $162, T5536 3644, www.ladyelliot.com.au.
Bundaberg Dive Academy, Shop 3A, Targo St, T4152 4064, www.bundabergdiveacademy.com. This place offers a fine range of land- and water-based accommodation and diving course packages that are good value for money compared with the high-profile operators further north.
Footprints Adventures, T4152 3659, www.footprintsadventures.com.au. For local tours look no further than the dedicated team here. Turtle rookery night trips (Jan to late Apr) from $50.
Lady Musgrave Barrier Reef Cruises, departs Town of 1770 (transfers from Bundaberg), T1800 072110, www.lmcruises.com.au. Day trips daily (0800-1745), from $160, children $80. Certified diving is available, from $40, introductory dives from $75. Whale-watching trips operate between Aug-Oct. Camping transfers from $320.

Agnes Water, 1770 and around *p257*
1770 Environmental Tours, 1770 Marina, T4974 9422, www.1770larctours.com.au. An exciting and unique eco/history tour/cruise on board an amphibious vehicle (LARC), along the coast north of 1770 to Bustard Head and Pancake Creek. There are 2 tours on offer: **Paradise Tour** (Mon, Wed and Sat 0900-1600) explores the beaches, Aboriginal middens and the stunning views from the Bustard Head Light Station and neighbouring cemetery, with a spot of sand boarding en route, from $148, children $88. **Afternoon Cruise** (on demand, 1630) is a 1-hr

exploration of Round Hill Creek and Eurimbula National Park, from $35, children $16. Book ahead.

1770 Great Barrier Reef Cruises, based at the Marina, T4974 9077, www.1770reefcruises.com. Day trips and camping transfers to Lady Musgrave Island (51 km east of 1770), from $160, children $80 (plus $5 reef tax). The cruise, dubbed the 'See More Sea Less' allows a whole 6 hrs on the reef, including a stop on a floating pontoon that acts as an ideal base for snorkelling, diving and coral viewing. Departs daily at 0800. Lunch included and bookings essential. A shuttle bus is available from Bundaberg. Camping transfers to the island cost $320. For more information on Lady Musgrave Island, see page 257.

Rockhampton *p258, map p259*
Farm stays
There are several renowned farm/station stays in the region, where you can go horse riding, on 4WD adventures, help to rehabilitate abandoned or injured kangaroos and even learn how to milk a cow. These include **Myella Farmstay**, 125 km southwest of the city, T4998 1290, www.myella.com..

Sightseeing tours
Mt Etna Little Bent-Wing Bat Tours, T4936 0511. Guided tours to see tens of thousands of cave dwelling bats in the 'bat cleft' located in the Mt Etna Caves National Park. Dec-Jan only, 1730 on Mon, Wed, Fri and Sat, from $9, children $5. Own transport required.
Mount Morgan Guided Tours, T4938 1823. Trips of 2 hrs taking in the town, mine and some Jurassic caves, from $27, children $12.

Yeppoon and around *p261*
Rydges Capricorn Resort, Farnborough Rd, T1800 075902, www.capricornresort.com.au. Offers horse treks (from $80), eco-tours (from $45) and canoe trips (from $55).

Great Keppel Island *p262*
All the main places to stay offer their own range of activities and tours but day trippers can access a huge variety of water-based activities and equipment from the beach hut directly opposite the ferry drop-off point. The island also has fine snorkelling and diving.
Freedom Flyer Cruises, T4933 6244, www.keppelbaymarina.com.au. Range of cruise packages beyond their basic transfers to Great Keppel. Transfers from $47, children $27. Coral cruise in a glass-bottom boat with fish feeding, boom netting and snorkelling, from $23, children $15. All day from $135. Coach transfers from Rockhampton are available. Book ahead.
Great Keppel Island Holiday Village, T4939 8655. Excellent sea kayaking and snorkelling trips from $55.
Keppel Reef Scuba Adventures, Putney Beach, T4939 5022, www.keppeldive.com. Dive shop just beyond the Spit. Qualified dive from about $85 including gear, introductory dive from $100, depart 0830 daily. Also offer island and beach drop-offs.

⊖ Transport

Bundaberg and Southern Reef Islands *p255*
Air
Bundaberg airport is 3 km south of the city centre via the Isis Highway. **Qantas**, T131313, flies daily to **Brisbane**, **Rockhampton**, **Mackay** and **Townsville**.
    For **Lady Elliot Island**, SeAir, T5536 3644, www.ladyelliot.com.au, offers flight transfers from **Bundaberg** and **Hervey Bay** from $254, children $136. See also Activities and tours above (and for Lady Musgrave Island).

Bus
Local services run by **Duffy's Coaches**, 28 Barolin St, T4151 4226, www.duffysbuses.com.au around the city, the Coral Coast, Rum Distillery, Bargara, Burnett Heads, Bundaberg Port Marina, several times daily. The long-distance bus terminal is at 66 Targo St, between Woondooma St and Crofton St. **Greyhound**, T1300 473946, and

Premier Motor Services, T133410, offer interstate services north and south.

Train
The station is in the heart of the city on the corner Bourbong St and McLean St. The **Tilt Train** is the preferred service between **Brisbane** and **Rockhampton** but other north/southbound services pass through daily, T132235. **Stewart and Sons Travel**, 66 Targo St, T4152 9700, acts as booking agents for air, bus and train operators.

Agnes Water, 1770 and around *p257*
Bus
Greyhound, T1300 473946, offers part-transfers to Agnes (from the Bruce Highway) stopping at the Fingerboard Junction Service Station (about 30 km south of Agnes and 20 km east of Miriam Vale). There is a transfer bus from there. **Bananas Backpackers** offer their own pick-ups from Bundaberg.

Car/4WD
The twin towns are best accessed from the Bruce Highway at Miriam Vale (55 km), or from the south via Bundaberg (120 km).

Train
The nearest station is in Miriam Vale, T132232.

Rockhampton *p258, map p259*
Air
Rockhampton Airport is 4 km west of the city centre. **Jet Star**, T131538; **Qantas**, T131313; **Tiger Airways**, T03-9335 3033; and **Virgin Blue**, T136789, have regular schedules to main centres north, south and west. A taxi to town costs about $20.

Bus
Capricorn Sunbus, T4936 2133, www.sunbus.com.au, is the local suburban bus company. **Young**'s Coaches, 274 George St, T4922 3813, www.youngsbus service.com.au, runs regular daily services to the train station, **Yeppoon** (No 20); **Rosslyn**

Bay (cruise boats); **Emu Park** and **Mount Morgan** (No 22). The main local terminal is on Bolsover St. The long-distance bus terminal, T4927 2844, is located at the Mobil service centre, George St. **Greyhound**, T1300 473946, and **Premier Motor Services**, T133410, offer north/southbound services.

Train
The station is 1 km south of the city centre at the end of Murray St (off Bruce Highway). **Tilt Train** is the preferred daily service to **Brisbane**. Other slower services north/southbound are the budget **Sunlander** and luxury **Queenslander**. **Spirit of the Outback** heads west to **Longreach** Tue and Sat. There is a travel centre at the station, T132232.

Yeppoon and around *p261*
Bus
Young's Coaches, 274 George St, T4922 3813, have regular daily services to Yeppoon (Route 20), **Rosslyn Bay** (cruise boats) and **Emu Park**.

Great Keppel Island *p262*
Air
Great Keppel has its own airfield but services vary. For details, contact the VIC.

Bus
Young's Coaches, T4922 3813, run regular daily services from **Rockhampton** to **Rosslyn Bay** (No 20).

Ferry
Both the major ferry companies are based at Rosslyn Bay Harbour, 7 km south of Yeppoon. **Freedom Fast Cats**, T4933 6244, www.keppelbaymarina.com.au, are based at the new Keppel Bay Marina. They have a travel centre, shop, café and internet. Yacht charters are also available. The basic return fare to Great Keppel (30 mins) is $47, children $27. Ferries depart daily at 0900, 1130 and 1530. See also Activities and tours, page 265. To reach the other islands, Rosslyn Bay ferry

companies offer cruises daily to Middle Island. Other than Middle Island, all water transport must be arranged privately through the **Keppel Bay Marina**, T4933 6244.

⊕ Directory

Bundaberg and Southern Reef Islands *p255*

Banks All the major branches have ATMs and can be found on Bourbong St. **Hospitals** After Hours Medical Clinic, Mater Hospital, 313 Bourbong St, T4153 9539. Mon-Fri 1800-2300, Sat 1200-2300, Sun 0800-2300. **Bundaberg Base Hospital**, Bourbong St, T4150 1222. **Internet** Cosy Corner, Barolin St (opposite the post office), T4153 5999, Mon-Fri 0700-1930, Sat 0700-1700, Sun 1100-1700. **Pharmacy** Amcal, 128 Bourbong St, T4151 5533. **Post** 157b Bourbong St, T131318. Mon-Fri 0900-1700, Sat 0830-1200. Postcode 4670. **Useful numbers** Police, 254 Bourbong St, T4153 9111.

Agnes Water, 1770 and around *p257*

Banks There is a **Westpac Bank** and ATM facilities in the Agnes Water's Shopping Complex. **Internet** Bananas Backpackers, 2 Springs Rd.

Rockhampton *p258, map p259*

Banks All the main branches with ATMs are centred in and around the CBD on East St. **Commonwealth Bank** offers currency exchange services. **Hospital** Rockhampton Base Hospital, Canning St, T4920 6211. **Internet** Cybernet, 12 William St, T4927 3633. Mon-Fri 1000-1730, or the Library, corner of William St and Alma St, T4936 8265, Mon, Tue, Fri 0915-1730, Wed 1300-2000, Thu 0915-2000, Sat 0915-1630. Book in advance. **Post** 150 East St, Mon-Fri 0830-1730. Postcode 4700. **Useful numbers** Police, corner of Denham St and Bolsover St, T4932 3500.

Contents

Footprint features

Central & Far North QLD

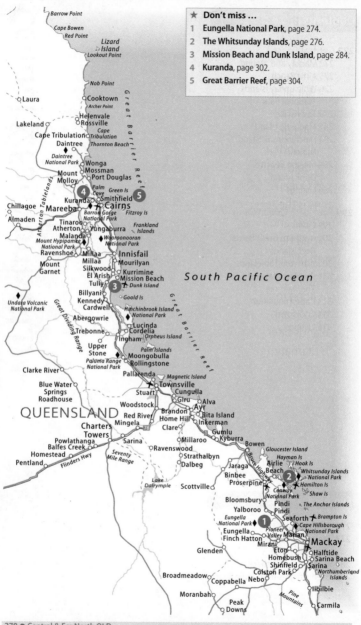

Barrow Point
Cape Bowen
Red Point
Lizard Island
Lookout Point

Nob Point

Laura

Cooktown
Archer Point
Helenvale
Rossville
Lakeland
Cape Tribulation
Cape Tribulation
Daintree
Thornton Beach
Daintree National Park
Wonga
Mount Molloy
Mossman
Port Douglas

Palm Cove
Green Is
Kuranda
Smithfield
Mareeba
Cairns
Chillagoe
Barron Gorge National Park
Fitzroy Is
Almaden
Tinaroo
Atherton
Yungaburra
Frankland Islands
Atherton Tablelands
Malanda
Wooroonooran National Park
Mount Hypipamee National Park
Ravenshoe
Millaa
Innisfail
Mount Garnet
Millaa
Mourilyan
Silkwood
El Arish
Kurrimine
Mission Beach
Tully
Dunk Island
Billyani
Goold Is
Kennedy
Cardwell
Undara Volcanic National Park
Hinchinbrook Island National Park
Abergowrie
Lucinda
Trebonne
Cordelia
Ingham
Orpheus Island
Upper Stone
Palm Islands
Moongobulla
Paluma Range National Park
Rollingstone
Clarke River
Pallarenda
Magnetic Island
Blue Water Springs Roadhouse
Townsville
Stuart
Cungulla
QUEENSLAND
Woodstock
Giru
Alva
Charters Towers
Red River
Brandon
Ayr
Rita Island
Mingela
Home Hill
Inkerman
Powlathanga
Clare
Gumlu
Balfes Creek
Sarina
Millaroo
Kyburra
Homestead
Ravenswood
Bowen
Pentland
Flinders Hwy
Strathalbyn
Gloucester Island
Seventy Mile Range
Dalbeg
Jaraga
Hayman Is
Hook Is
Airlie Beach
Whitsunday Islands National Park
Binbee
Proserpine
Hamilton Is
Lake Dalrymple
Scottville
Conway National Park
Shaw Is
The Anchor Islands
Bloomsbury
Pindi Pindi
Brampton Is
Yalboroo
Eungella National Park
Seaforth
Cape Hillsborough National Park
Eungella
Pioneer Valley Marian
Finch Hatton
Mirani
Mackay
Glenden
Eton
Halftide
Homebush
Sarina Beach
Shinfield
Sarina
Broadmeadow
Colston Park
Nebo
Northumberland Islands
Coppabella
Moranbah
Peak Downs
Pine Mountains
Ilbilbie
Carmila

South Pacific Ocean

Great Barrier Reef

Great Dividing Range

Blue Highway

For many, the Central and North Coasts of Queensland are the raison d'être of an Australian holiday. Here are the sublime Whitsunday Islands, the effortlessly appealing Magnetic Island, heart-achingly beautiful Hinchinbrook and luscious Lizard Island. But it's not all about beaches, coral reef and tropical islands. Eungella National Park boasts slopes draped in lush rainforest and cloaked in rain-bearing clouds that in turn give rise to wonderful waterfalls and unusual wildlife, while inland from Townsville, the historic gold-mining town of Charters Towers gives many their first taste of Queensland outback.

Cairns is the region's tourist heart and gateway to the Great Barrier Reef and Wet Tropics Rainforest. Nowhere else on earth do two World Heritage-listed ecosystems meet.

North of Cairns is the small and sophisticated resort of Port Douglas, gateway to the wonderful Daintree National Park and the exhilarating route north to the wilds of Cape Tribulation.

West of Cairns the lush, green plateau known as the Atherton Tablelands offers relief from the heat and humidity of the coast and a dramatic change in landscape.

Central Coast

This is the home straight on the long trek north to Cairns and there's still an awful lot to pack in. The town of Mackay is the base from which to explore the reef island groups of Brampton, Newry and Carlisle. Inland, the lush slopes of Eungella National Park are home to wonderful waterfalls and unusual wildlife. Back on the coast the rush is on to reach the fast developing resort of Airlie Beach, gateway to the sublime Whitsunday Islands. Further north, Magnetic Island lives up to its name, attracting tourists with its beautiful beaches, while inland the historic gold-mining town of Charters Towers offers many their first taste of Queensland 'outback'. North again is Mission Beach, like a mainland version of Magnetic Island, while, offshore, as always, are the tropical reef islands.

Mackay and around → *For listings, see pages 286-299. Colour map 5, B2.*

Driving towards Mackay at night in early summer is a surreal experience. For miles around, sugar cane fields are awash with the orange glow of flames. Although the sugar cane industry is in crisis, and the burning of harvested cane fields in preparation for the next crop a less frequent sight, when it does happen it looks like the world is on fire. After Scots pioneer John Mackay recognized the region's agricultural potential in 1862 it grew to become the largest sugar-producing area in Australia and still hosts the biggest bulk processing facilities in the world. Although not tourist-oriented, Mackay provides a welcome stop halfway between Brisbane and Cairns and is also the gateway to several Barrier Reef and Whitsunday Islands and a fine base from which to explore the superb Eungella and Cape Hillsborough national parks.

Ins and outs

Mackay VIC ⓘ *320 Nebo Rd (Bruce Highway), T4944 5888 www.mackay region.com, Mon-Fri 0830-1700, Sat-Sun 0900-1600*, housed in a former sugar mill, offers booking services for local and island accommodation and tours. There is a smaller VIC in the Town Hall ⓘ *63 Sydney Rd, T4951 4803*. **QPWS** office ⓘ *DPI Building, 30 Tennyson St, T4944 7800, www.epa.qld.gov.au, Mon-Fri 0830-1700*, offers information and permits for island and national park camping. ▸▸ *See Transport, page 295.*

Mackay

Although most of Mackay's attractions are to be found beyond the city limits, the centre, with its palm-lined main street and pleasant river views, is worth a look. The heart of the city boasts some notable historical buildings, including the impressive façades of the **Commonwealth Bank** (1880) ⓘ *63 Victoria St*, the former **Queensland National Bank** (1922) ⓘ *corner of Victoria St and Wood St*, the **Town Hall** (1912) ⓘ *63 Sydney St*, which houses the VIC and a small historical display, and the old **Customs House** (1902) ⓘ *corner of Sydney St and River St*. The VIC stocks a free *Heritage Walk* leaflet.

The **Artspace Mackay** ⓘ *Gordon St, Civic Centre Precinct, T4961 9722, www.artspacemackay.com.au, Tue-Sun 1000-1700, free*, is a recent and welcome architectural addition to the city, housing an art gallery and museum showcasing the social and natural history of the region. The sugar industry features heavily but this is interspersed neatly with many contemporary displays including the school trophies of the city's most famous daughter, Olympic gold medal runner Cathy Freeman.

The beaches north of Mackay are well known for their tropical beauty and fine swimming and are a great place to recharge the travel batteries. The best spots are at **Black's Beach**, **Dolphin Heads** (Eimeo Beach) and **Bucasia Beach** and are best accessed from the Mackay–Bucasia Road off the Bruce Highway.

Aside from the lure of the beach, there is an opportunity to visit to one of the local sugar mills. The **Polstone Sugar Cane Farm** ① *Masottis Rd, Homebush, T4959 7298, offers tours Mon, Wed and Fri at 1330, Jun-Nov, from $16, children $7.*

Brampton and Carlisle islands

The islands of Brampton (464 ha) and Carlisle (518 ha) are part of the **Cumberland Islands National Park**, which lies 32 km northeast of Mackay. Both are practically joined by a sandbank that can be walked at low tide and have a rich variety of island habitats, rising to a height of 389 m on Carlisle's Skiddaw Peak and 219 m on Brampton's namesake peak. The waters surrounding both islands are part of the Mackay/Capricorn Section of the Great Barrier Reef Marine Park, offering some excellent dive sites. There are 11 km of walking tracks on Brampton giving access to Brampton Peak as well as several secluded bays and coastal habitats. In contrast walking on Carlisle Island is rough, with no well-formed paths. Instead you are better to explore the beaches or take to the water with a snorkel and mask, especially in the channel between the two islands. Day trips aren't available and the minimum stay is one night.

Newry Islands

The Newry group, also part of the Great Barrier Reef Marine Park, consists of six national park islands 50 km northeast of Mackay. Like the Cumberlands, they are hilly, diverse in coastal habitat types and rich in wildlife, including sea eagles, ospreys, echidna and bandicoots. Green sea turtles also nest between November and January on the largest of

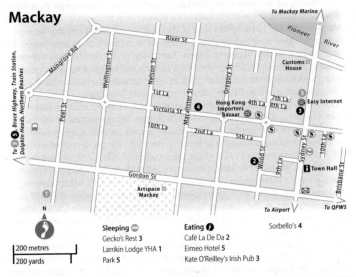

Mackay

Sleeping 🛌
Gecko's Rest **3**
Larrikin Lodge YHA **1**
Park **5**

Eating 🍴
Café La De Da **2**
Eimeo Hotel **5**
Kate O'Reilley's Irish Pub **3**
Sorbello's **4**

the group – Rabbit Island. There are 2 km of walking tracks on Newry Island leading through rainforest and open forest to elevated viewpoints.

Cape Hillsborough National Park

Although positively petite compared to most of Queensland's other mainland national parks, Hillsborough is no less impressive, boasting some superb coastal habitats, views and beaches. It is also particularly famed for its tame, beach-loving wildlife such as kangaroos, the aptly named pretty-faced wallabies and the distinctly more ugly scrub turkeys. There are four diverse walking tracks ranging from 1.2 km to 2.6 km in length, including the Juipera Plant Trail, which highlights the food plants once utilized by the Juipera Aboriginal people.

Eungella National Park and Pioneer Valley

The 80-km inland excursion from Mackay via the Pioneer Valley to Eungella (pronounced 'young-galah') offers an excellent diversion from the coast and access to what the Aboriginal people once called 'the land of the clouds'. Whether shrouded in mist or gently baking under the midday sun, Eungella and its exquisite national park possess a magic as special as the wildlife that lives there and the Aboriginals who once did.

Immediately west of Mackay, the Mackay–Eungella Road branches off the Peak Downs Highway and follows the southern bank of the Pioneer River to the small sugar cane town of **Marian**. In **Mirani**, 10 km further west of Marian, you can find out why the two were so called, and if they were indeed sisters, at the small museum on Victoria Street. Just beyond Mirani is the **Illawong Fauna Sanctuary** ① *T4959 1777, www.illawong-sanctuary.com, 0930-1730, $15, children $6.* It's a fairly low-key affair but worth stopping to take a walk through enclosures full of emus, wallabies and roos. The sanctuary also has accommodation, a café and its own tour company, **Gum Tree Tours**.

A further 29 km past Mirani, beyond the small hamlet of Gargett and 1 km east of Finch Hatton Township, is the turn-off to the **Finch Hatton George section** of the Eungella National Park. In the dry season the 10-km road is suitable for 2WD, but in the wet, when several creek crossings are subject to flooding, the final 6-km gravel road often requires 4WD. At the gorge there is a private bush camp (see page 287), picnic site and access to the memorable **Wheel of Fire Falls** (5 km return) and **Araluen Falls walks** (3 km return).

Back on the main highway, the road head towards the hills before climbing up dramatically 800 m to the small, pretty township of **Eungella**. At the crest of the hill, past a few worrying gaps in the roadside barriers, is the historic **Eungella Chalet**, with its spacious lawns, swimming pool and views to blow your wig off; see page 286. As well as being an ideal spot for lunch, it is also a popular launch pad for hang-gliders.

From the chalet the road veers 6 km south, following the crest of the hill, before arriving at Broken River. Here you will find a picnic area, QPWS campsite and the **Eungella National Park Ranger Station** ① *T131304, 0800-0900, 1130-1230 and 1530-1630.* They will give you all the necessary detail on the numerous excellent short walks in the vicinity. There is also a platypus viewing platform nearby but bear in mind they can only be seen around daybreak. The park is also home to a host of other unique species including the Eungella honeyeater, the brown thornbill and the infinitely wonderful Eungella gastric brooding frog. The latter, as its name suggests, has the unenviable habit of incubating its eggs in its stomach before spitting the young out of its mouth.

Airlie Beach → *For listings, see pages 286-299. Colour map 5, A1.*

From a sleepy coastal settlement, Airlie Beach and its neighbouring communities of Cannonvale and Shute Harbour (known collectively as Whitsunday) have developed into the main gateway to the Whitsunday Islands. With over 74 islands, many idyllic resorts and a long list of beaches, including Whitehaven, which is often hailed as among the world's best, it comes as no surprise that little Airlie has seen more dollars spent in the name of tourism in recent years than almost anywhere else in the state. With all the offerings of the Whitsunday Islands lying in wait offshore, most people use Airlie simply as an overnight stop but the town itself can be a great place to party or just relax and watch the tourist world go by.

Airlie Beach

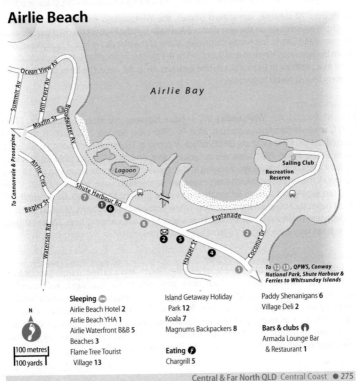

Sleeping 🛏
Airlie Beach Hotel **2**
Airlie Beach YHA **1**
Airlie Waterfront B&B **5**
Beaches **3**
Flame Tree Tourist
   Village **13**

Island Getaway Holiday
   Park **12**
Koala **7**
Magnums Backpackers **8**

Eating 🍴
Chargrill **5**

Paddy Shenanigans **6**
Village Deli **2**

Bars & clubs 🍸
Armada Lounge Bar
   & Restaurant **1**

Ins and outs

Getting there and around The nearest airports are at Proserpine and Hamilton Island. Long-distance bus services run from Cairns and Sydney, stopping at all major centres and cities along the way. Both north and south services run three times weekly. The train station is at Proserpine. The main centre is small and easily explored on foot. See page 292 for tours to the Whitsundays and below for tourist information details. ▸ *See Transport, page 296.*

Sights

Right in the heart of town, and the focus for many, is the new and glorious **lagoon** development. In the absence of a proper beach (and the accompanying threat of marine stingers between October and May) it has to be said that the local authorities have created a fine (and safe) substitute. In anticipation of going out to the islands you can secure some good views of them in the **Conway National Park** between Airlie and Shute Harbour. There is a self-guided 6.5-km circuit walk through mangrove forest on the way to a lookout on the summit of Mount Rooper offering a slightly obscured view of Hamilton, Dent, Long and Henning Islands.

Whitsunday Islands National Park → *For listings, see pages 286-299. Colour map 5, A2.*

With over 70 sublime, sun-soaked islands, the Whitsundays are not only the largest offshore island chain on the east coast of Australia but the biggest tourist draw between Brisbane and Cairns. It is hardly surprising. Many of the islands are home to idyllic resorts, from the luxurious Hayman and Hamilton to the quieter, more affordable, South Molle, as well as a plethora of beautiful, pristine beaches. Here, for once, the term paradise is not merely tourist board hyperbole.

Ins and outs

Tourist information **Whitsunday VIC** ⓘ *Bruce Highway, 192 Main St, Proserpine, T4945 3711, www.whitsundaytourism.com, Mon-Fri 0900-1700, Sat-Sun 1000-1600,* is the main accredited VIC for the islands. **QPWS office** ⓘ *corner of Shute Harbour Rd and Mandalay St, Airlie Beach, T4946 7022, www.epa.qld.gov.au, Mon-Fri 0900-1700, Sat 0900-1300,* is very helpful. Operators are always changing in the region so you are advised to visit the VIC first to get all the very latest information, especially surrounding water transport logistics. The VIC can supply all camping information and issue permits. Note, to obtain a permit you must have proof of return transportation. **Island Camping Connections**, T4946 5255, offers independent transportation by water taxis and hires out camping gear. Shute Harbour scheduled ferry services stop on most major island resorts. ▸ *See Transport, page 296.*

South Molle Island

South Molle (405 ha) is one of three little Molles (South, Mid and North) sitting about 8 km from Shute Harbour. Being in such close proximity to the mainland, and therefore relatively cheap to reach, South Molle is popular with day trippers. With its varied habitats and hilly topography, the island offers some excellent walking and sublime views. The best of these is undoubtedly the 6-km **Spion Kop walk** that climbs through forest and over open grassland to some superb viewpoints across to the outer islands. The resort on the island is both pleasant and casual (see Sleeping, page 288).

Whitsunday Islands

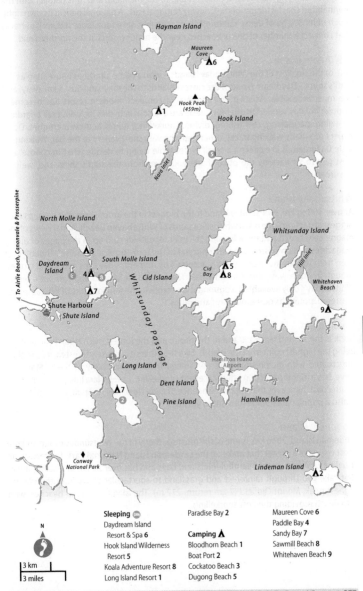

Hayman Island

Maureen Cove
▲6

Hook Peak
(459m)▲

Hook Island

▲1

Naia Inlet

North Molle Island

Whitsunday Island

▲3

Daydream
Island

South Molle Island

Cid Island

Cid
Bay

▲5
▲8

Hill Inlet

Whitehaven
Beach

To Airlie Beach, Cannonvale & Prosserpine

4▲

Shute Harbour

Shute Island

Whitsunday passage

9▲

Long Island

Hamilton Island
Airport

Dent Island

▲7

Pine Island

Hamilton Island

Conway
National Park

Lindeman Island

▲2

N

3 km

3 miles

Sleeping
Daydream Island
  Resort & Spa **6**
Hook Island Wilderness
  Resort **5**
Koala Adventure Resort **8**
Long Island Resort **1**

Paradise Bay **2**

Camping ▲
Bloodhorn Beach **1**
Boat Port **2**
Cockatoo Beach **3**
Dugong Beach **5**

Maureen Cove **6**
Paddle Bay **4**
Sandy Bay **7**
Sawmill Beach **8**
Whitehaven Beach **9**

Long Island

Aptly named Long Island is the closest island to the mainland and runs parallel with the uninhabited coastal fringes of the Conway National Park. A national park in its own right, much of its 800 ha of dense rainforest is inaccessible, save for a loose network of tracks that connect a number of pretty beaches near the major resorts at the northern end.

Daydream Island

One of the smallest of the Whitsunday Islands – with a name almost as nauseating as the staff's shirts – Daydream is one of the closest islands to the mainland (just 5 km away) and the most accessible. As such its congenial, if compact, modern resort has become a popular holiday venue. On offer for guests are a host of activities including sail boarding, jet-skiing, parasailing, reef fishing, diving, snorkelling, tennis and even croquet. Don't expect too many walking tracks, other than the very short variety to the bar. Walking on little Daydream is like circling a small buffet table trying to decide what to choose. It is best just to sit back by the pool, shade your eyes from the staff's shirts and, well … daydream.

Whitsunday Island

At over 100 sq km, Whitsunday Island is the biggest in the group, boasting perhaps their biggest attraction – the 6-km white silica sands of **Whitehaven Beach**. Aerial views of this magnificent beach and the adjoining Hill Inlet repeatedly turn up in the pages of glossy magazines and on postcards as the epitome of the term 'tropical paradise'. Though best seen from the air, the beach is easily accessed by numerous day trips and island cruises, though in many ways this is its downfall. Thankfully uninhabited and without a resort, Whitsunday's only available accommodation comes in the form of eight QPWS campsites scattered around its numerous bays and inlets.

Hook Island

Hook is the second largest island in the group and the loftiest, with Hook Peak (459 m) being the highest point of all the islands. Like the others it is densely forested, its coastline punctuated with picturesque bays and inlets. The most northerly of these, **Maureen Cove**, has a fringing reef that offers excellent snorkelling. Lovely Nara Inlet, on the island's south coast, has caves that support evidence of early Ngalandji Aboriginal occupation. It is also a popular anchorage for visiting yachties.

Lindeman Island

Lindeman Island, 20 sq km, is one of the most southerly of the Whitsunday group and the most visited of a cluster that make up the **Lindeman Island National Park**. It offers all the usual natural features of beautiful inlets and bays and has over 20 km of walking tracks that take you through rainforest and grassland to spectacular views from the island's highest peak, Mount Oldfield (7 km return, 212 m). The island has seven beaches, with Gap Beach providing the best snorkelling.

Townsville → *For listings, see pages 286-299. Colour map 6, C2.*

Considered the capital of Queensland's north coast and the second largest city in the state, Townsville attracts a considerable number of both domestic and international visitors drawn by its enviable tropical climate and the huge range of activities on offer, not to mention the considerable attraction of Magnetic Island lying offshore. If you are short of time Townsville presents a fine opportunity to venture briefly outback with the grand old gold-mining town of Charters Towers less than a two-hour drive west.

Ins and outs

Tourist information The **VIC** ① *T4778 3555, 0900-1700,* is several kilometres south of town on the Bruce Highway. There is an information booth in the Flinders Mall ① *T4721 3660, Mon-Fri 0900-1700, Sat-Sun 0900-1300,* and next to the Museum of Queensland ① *70-102 Flinders St East, T4721 1116, www.townsvilleholidays.info, Mon-Sun 0900-1700.* **QPWS** ① *Marlow St, T4796 7777.* ►► *See Transport, page 297.*

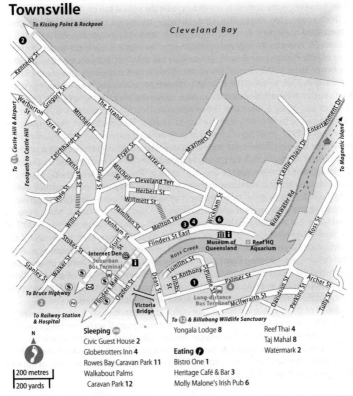

Townsville

Sleeping 🛏
Civic Guest House **2**
Globetrotters Inn **4**
Rowes Bay Caravan Park **11**
Walkabout Palms
  Caravan Park **12**
Yongala Lodge **8**

Eating 🍴
Bistro One **1**
Heritage Café & Bar **3**
Molly Malone's Irish Pub **6**
Reef Thai **4**
Taj Mahal **8**
Watermark **2**

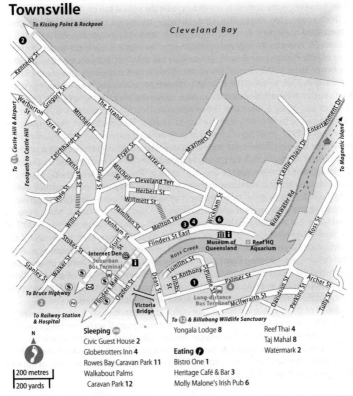

Sights

SS Yongala is a passenger ship that sank with all 121 crew – and a racehorse called Moonshine – during a cyclone in 1911. Located about 17 km off Cape Bowling Green, it is often touted as one of Australia's best dives, offering diverse habitats and a huge range of species, including enormous manta rays, colourful coral gardens and even the odd human bone. Since the wreck sits at a depth of 29 m and is subject to strong currents, the dive presents a challenge and requires an above average level of competency. See Activities and tours, page 294 for details.

The long-established **Reef HQ Aquarium** ① *2-68 Flinders St East, T4750 0800, www.reefhq.org.au, 0930-1700, $25, children $19,* is not on a par with Sydney Aquarium's remarkable Reef Exhibit, but it still provides an excellent introduction to the reef. The centrepiece is a huge 750,000-litre 'Predator Exhibit', complete with genuine wave action, a part replica of the famous (local) *Yongala* wreck, an 'interactive island' and myriad colourful corals, fish and the obligatory sharks. Feeding takes place on most days at 1500, but equally interesting is the 'Danger Trail', a guided presentation (daily at 1300) that introduces some of the most deadly and dangerous creatures on the reef, such as the nasty box jellyfish (see box, page 37, for more on this charming creature). The star of the show, however, is the stonefish, which has to be the ugliest fish on the planet.

Next door to Reef HQ, the newly renovated **Museum of Tropical Queensland** ① *Flinders St East, T4726 0600, www.mtq.qld.gov.au, 0930-1700, $14, children $8,* provides an impressive insight into the region's maritime history, with the story of *HMS Pandora*, the British 17th-century tall ship that is closely linked with that of the better known *HMS Bounty*. It was the *Pandora* that was dispatched by the British Admiralty in 1790 to bring the Bounty mutineers to justice, but her own voyage to the South Pacific proved no less notorious. After capturing 14 of the mutineers on the island of Tahiti and going in search of those who remained on the *Bounty*, the *Pandora* ran aground on the Barrier Reef, with the loss of 31 crew. The wreck was rediscovered near Cape York in 1977, resulting in a frenzy of archaeological interest, and the many exhibits and artefacts are on show in the museum today. There is an interactive science centre to keep the less nautically inclined suitably engaged. The café has fine views across the river.

Fringing the shoreline east of the city centre is **The Strand**, which, along with the Museum of Queensland, is the new showpiece of the city and part of its recent multi-million dollar facelift. Said by some to be the most attractive public waterfront development in Australia, it provides an ideal spot to soak up the rays, take a stroll or break a leg on rollerblades. It is also designed to serve as protection against cyclones, but you won't find any signs advertising the fact. One of the most attractive features of the Strand is the collection of 50-year old Bunyan fig trees that look like columns of melted wax. At its westerly terminus – **Kissing Point** – there is a man-made rockpool, which provides safe swimming year round and complete protection from the infamous 'marine stingers'. There is also a popular fish and chip shop and seafood restaurant next to the pool, but unless you want an enforced hunger strike while you wait in line, it is best avoided.

As well as the enigmatic sugar shaker building, Townsville's skyline is dominated by **Castle Hill**, which glows orange in the rays of the rising sun. If you cannot drag yourself out of bed to see for yourself, then you can always make the climb to the summit by car or on foot and take in the memorable views, day or night. Access by car is at the end of Burk Street, off Warburton Street. The Goat Track to the summit is off Stanton Street, at the end of Gregory Street, also off Warburton.

Billabong Wildlife Sanctuary ⓘ *17 km south of the city, next to the Bruce Highway, T4778 8344, www.billabongsanctuary.com.au, 0800-1700, $30, children $19,* is one of the best in Queensland. Fringing an authentic billabong (water hole or stagnant pool), it houses an extensive collection of natives, from the leggy cassowary to the sleepy wombat. There are many tame roos and emus lazing on paths around the park, as well as more dangerous individuals such as crocs and poisonous snakes. Various shows and talks throughout the day give you an opportunity to learn about the animals and, if you wish, to handle the more docile serpents and baby crocs. Don't miss the smelly fruit bat colony next to the lake.

Magnetic Island → *For listings, see pages 286-299. Colour map 6, C2.*

Magnetic Island is Townsville's biggest tourist attraction and the most easily accessible tropical island bolthole on the reef. Lying only 8 km offshore and baking in over 320 days of sunshine a year, 'Maggie' has always been a popular holiday spot, but its discreet permanent population also adds charm and an authenticity lacking in most of the resort-style islands. In fact, it is considered by many in the region as the most desirable suburb in Townsville. With its amenities concentrated in the eastern and northeastern fringes of the island, Maggie boasts a much larger area of wild and fairly inaccessible terrain giving an overall impression of wilderness and escape. With over half the island given over to national park, encompassing over 40 km of walking tracks, 20 picture-postcard bays and beaches, as well as a wealth of activities and some great budget accommodation, not to mention a resident population of koalas, the island certainly does earn its name in the number of visitors it attracts, though the real derivation is from Captain Cook (who else?) whose compass had a small fit as he passed by in 1770.

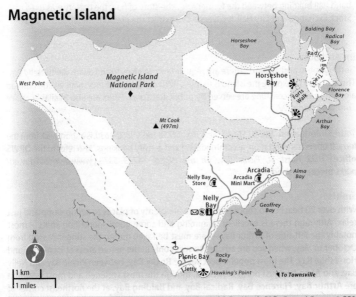

Magnetic Island

Queensland Outback

The former gold-mining settlement of Charters Towers, 132 km west of Townsville, offers a great outback experience and is only two hours away, via the sealed Flinders Highway. This was the second largest city in Queensland at the turn of the 20th century – a place known as 'The World', where people's wildest dreams of wealth could come true. In its heyday, its gold mines yielded over six million ounces ($25 million) of the precious metal. Nowadays it's better known for its beef production than its mineral resources, but is a fascinating example of a quintessential outback town.

With the help of the National Trust, Charters Towers has made some sterling efforts in the restoration of its heritage buildings and mining relics. The Ghosts of Gold Heritage Trail begins at the VIC ① *74 Mosman St, T4761 5533, www.charterstowers.qld.gov.au, 0900-1700,* which is housed in the former band hall building between the former Stock Exchange and City Hall. It covers a number of venues throughout the city and helps to bring to life the colourful stories, legends, incredible feats and the characters of the gold rush.

The trail includes the old Stock Exchange Building ① *0900-1500*, built originally as a shopping arcade in 1888 and converted into a stock exchange in 1890 before being fully restored in 1970. Next door is the magnificent former 1892 Australian Bank of Commerce building. The unusually named Ay Ot Lookout, on the corner of Hodgkinson Street and the High Street, was built in 1896 and reflects the architectural excellence of the era. Guided tours of the interior are conducted throughout the week, 0800-1500.

On the outskirts of the city, east via Gill Street and Millchester Road, are the remains of the Venus Battery Mill ① *0930-1630, guided tours on the hour, $12, child $6,* the largest surviving battery relic in Australia. Interactive displays tell the story of how the battery was used to extract the precious metal, and as you

Ins and outs

Getting there and around There are regular ferry services from Townsville to Nelly Bay. The best way to explore the island is to hire a 4WD or moke. The four main villages spread along its eastern coastline are served by public transport. Tours are also available. » *See Transport, page 297.*

Tourist information VIC ① *Shop 1, Nelly Bay, T4758 1862, 0800-1630,* is a short walk from the ferry. It offers transportation, accommodation and activity bookings. Also refer to the **QPWS office** ① *22 Hurst St, Picnic Bay, on the island, T4778 5378, www.derm.qld.gov.au/ parks/magnetic-island/index.html.*

Sights

With over 20 beaches to choose from there are plenty of places to set up camp and just relax. Although there is excellent swimming and some good snorkelling spots – most notably the left side of Arthur Bay – care must be taken during the stinger season from October to May, when you are advised to swim only in the netted areas at Picnic Bay and Horseshoe Bay. The most popular beaches are **Rocky Bay**, between Picnic Bay and Nelly Bay, and **Alma Bay**, just north of Arcadia, though the most secluded and most beautiful are **Arthur Bay**, **Florence Bay**, **Radical Bay** and **Balding Bay**, at the northeast corner of wander around its eight huge stampers and former cyanide ponds it certainly stirs the imagination back to the days when it was in full production. Just south of the city on the Flinders Highway are the Dalrymple Sale Yards, one of the largest stock sale yards in the state with countless head of beef cattle transported in by monstrous road trains — a true reminder that you are now in real outback country.

Nearby, Towers Hill has superb views across the city, especially at sunrise or sunset. At an open-air amphitheatre in the evening the film *Ghosts After Dark* is screened. Access is from the south end of Mosman Street, off Black Jack Road. Film tickets from the VIC. The VIC can also book an excellent city tour.

🛌 Sleeping

A-D Aussie Outback Oasis Big4 Holiday Park, 76 Dr George Ellis Drive, T4787 8722, www.aussieoutbackoasis.com.au. One of several motor parks with good facilities in the town that offers the full range of accommodation options. Charters Towers is the stepping stone to popular outback stations, with comfortable accommodation and the quintessential outback experience. Charters Towers VIC has details.

A-D Bluff Downs, T4770 4084, www.bluffdowns.com.au. A historic 40,000-ha working cattle station, set on the spectacular deepwater lagoons of the Basalt River, 80 km north of the city. A range of activities, from mustering to fossil hunting, and a/c backpackers' quarters, homestead rooms and a cottage.

🚌 Transport

Daily **Greyhound** bus service to/from Townsville, 1 hr 40 mins, from $44. The Inlander train service operates twice-weekly services from Townsville to Mount Isa, Sun and Thu from $27. The station is on the corner of Gill St and Enterprise Rd, Charters Towers, T132232, www.traveltrain.com.au.

the island. All four are accessed via the unsealed Radical Bay Track, 8 km north of Picnic Bay (but note that all vehicle hire companies place restrictions on unsealed roads, so you may have to walk). Beyond these bays is **Horseshoe Bay**, the biggest on the island and a popular spot for swimming and water sports.

There are many excellent walking tracks on the island with the two most notable being the Horseshoe Bay to Arthur Bay track (3 km, two hours one way) and in the same vicinity, the **Forts Walk** (2 km, 1½ hours return). The Horseshoe Bay to Arthur Bay track can be tackled in either direction and takes in all the secluded bays and some low-lying bush. Many allow themselves extended stops at one of the beaches since it can be very difficult to drag yourself away. The Forts Walk starts at the Radical Bay turn-off and follows the ridge past some old gun emplacements to the old observation tower lookout. This track is also one of the best places to observe koalas. Late afternoon (when they are awake and feeding) is the best time to see them. Another short walk to **Hawking's Point lookout** above Picnic Bay is also worthwhile. It starts at the end of Picnic Street (600 m, 30 minutes). To visit the more remote areas on the south and west coast requires your own 4WD, a boat or a very long trek. The unsealed track west starts from Yule Street, Picnic Bay, beside the golf course. Sadly, the island's highest peak Mount Cook (497 m) is inaccessible. Magnetic Island is a superb and relatively cheap venue to learn to dive. There are also some excellent dive sites around the island, including the wreck of the *Yongala*.

From the moment you first see it, Hinchinbrook Island casts its irresistible spell. Even from afar, the green rugged peaks possess a dramatic air of wilderness. Heading north from Townsville, the Bruce Highway passes Ingham before crossing the Herbert River. It then climbs to reach the breathtaking lookout across to Hinchinbrook, its mountainous outline and velvety green cloak of rainforest seemingly almost connected to the mainland by the huge expanse of impenetrable mangrove swamps and smaller islands.

Ins and outs

The beachside town of **Cardwell** is the jumping-off point for Hinchinbrook. It is fast developing into a tourist resort and provides a welcome stop on the route north. The lengthy main drag, Victoria Street, hosts most amenities, accommodation and numerous operators offering fishing, cruising, flightseeing or wildlife-watching activities, as well as the **QPWS Rainforest and Reef Centre** ① *by the jetty, T4066 8601, www.great greenwaytourism.com and www.epa.qld.gov.au, Mon-Fri 0830-1630, Sat-Sun 0900-1500*, which provides local tourist information and details of seasonal eco-cruises and issues permits for Hinchinbrook Island National Park.

Around the island

At almost 40,000 ha, Hinchinbrook is the largest island national park in the world and, having changed little since white settlement in Australia, remains one of the most unspoilt. Crowned by the 1142 m peak of Mount Bowen, it is a wonderland of sheer cliffs, forested slopes and pristine beaches inhabited with some of the state's weirdest and most dangerous wildlife. And unlike many of its peers along the Queensland coast, Hinchinbrook presents more of a challenge than a relaxing excursion. Most who choose to visit the island do so for a day, but you can stay longer at one of two designated campsites or in the lap of luxury at its one and only (expensive) resort, **Hinchinbrook Island Wilderness Lodge & Resort**, see page 290. For true explorers, though, there is only one mission – the famed **Thorsborne Trail**. This 32-km, 4-day (minimum) bushwalk, also known as the East Coast Trail, is one of the best in the country and takes in a wide range of habitats along the east coast, from Ramsay Bay in the north to George Point in the south. Given its obvious popularity, only 40 intrepid souls are allowed on the track at any one time and you must book, sometimes up to a year in advance. The best time to do it is from April to September, which avoids the very wet and the very dry, but the topography of Hinchinbrook can create inclement weather at any time. The track is not graded and in some areas is rough and hard to traverse and insect repellent is an absolute must. The QPWS centre, see Ins and outs above, provides detailed information on the track and issues the relevant camping permits. Its excellent broadsheet *Thorsborne Trail* is a fine start.

Mission Beach and Dunk Island → *For listings, see pages 286-299. Colour map 6, B2.*

Taking its name from a former Aboriginal mission established in the early 1900s, Mission Beach is the loose term given to an idyllic 14-km stretch of the Queensland coast from Bingil Bay in the north to the mouth of the Hull River to the south. The area is not only noted as the main tourist centre between Townsville and Cairns, but for the importance of its rainforest biodiversity, being home to many unique plants and animals. These include the umbrella-like licuala palm and the rare cassowary. There is plenty to see and do here, but it is as much a place to relax from the rigours of the road, as it is to explore its many natural delights. The superb offshore resort of Dunk Island is no exception.

Ins and outs

Tourist information **Mission Beach VIC** ⓘ *El-Arish-Mission Beach Rd, Porter Promenade, T4068 7099, www.missionbeachtourism.com, 0900-1700,* is a powerhouse of information, fuelled with the great enthusiasm of both the management and volunteers. The area is hard to navigate, so be sure to secure the free *Street and Business Directory*. ▸▸ *See also Transport, page 298.*

Mission Beach

Wet Tropics Environmental Centre ⓘ *next door to the VIC, 1000-1700,* offers a fine introduction to the rainforest ecology and habitats of the region. If you plan on doing any rainforest walks, this is the place to get directions and all the relevant details. The centre also acts as a nursery for rainforest plants, collected, by all accounts, from cassowary droppings! Also of note are the records kept of the great bird's all-too-frequent disagreements with local automobiles. Before leaving this area, take a look at the large tree just to the south of the VIC and Environmental Centre. It is the seasonal home to a large colony of metallic starlings and in spring (August) becomes a hive of activity when the birds return to their own extensive and exclusive piece of real estate, in the form of countless, beautifully woven nests.

The main tracts of accessible rainforest are to be found in the **Tam O'Shanter State Forest** that dominates the region and contains one of the largest tracts of coastal lowland rainforest in northern Queensland. There are a number of excellent walks on offer, but take plenty of insect repellent. The best and the most moderate of these is the **Licuala Walk**, accessed and signposted off the Tully-Mission Beach Road. It's a 1.2-km stroll under the canopy of the rare and beautiful licuala palms. On a hot day the torn lily pad-like leaves offer a cool and quiet sanctuary. There is also a special 350-m section designed for kids, where they can 'follow the cassowary footprints' to find a surprise at the end of the walk. If you are fit enough for a longer walk, the 7-km (two hours) **Licuala-Lacey Creek Track** also starts at the car park. This track cuts through the heart of the Tam O'Shanter Forest and links Licuala with Lacey Creek, taking in the upper Hull River, a giant fig and lots of mosquitoes on the way. At Lacey Creek there is another short rainforest walk (1.1 km, taking 45 minutes), accessed and signposted off the El-Arish-Mission Beach Road. Just north of Mission Beach and Clump Point is the 4-km (2 hours) **Bicton Hill Track**. It is a stiff, yet pleasant climb to the summit though views are rather disappointing once you get there. Yet another option is the historic, 8-km (4 hours' return) **Kennedy Track** (named after local explorer Edmund Kennedy), which heads from South Mission Beach to the mouth of the Hull River.

Other than the rainforest and Dunk Island, the big attractions in these parts are the beaches. There are over 65 to choose from, blending together into one 14-km long stretch of glorious, soft sand backed by coconut palms. While sunbathing here might be heavenly enough, you may also be tempted into the water to swim and to snorkel. But if your visit is between October to May, play it safe and stick within the netted areas off Mission and South Mission beaches, in order to avoid 'stingers'.

Dunk Island

Once named (far more suitably) Coonanglebah by the Aboriginals, meaning 'The Island of Peace and Plenty', this island was renamed Dunk by Captain James Cook in 1770 after Lord Dunk, First Lord of the Admiralty. But whatever its official label, this 730-ha national and marine park, lying less than 5 km off Mission Beach, certainly offers plenty and is one of the most beautiful island parks and resorts north of the Whitsundays. What is perhaps most attractive for the visitor is the fact that it is so easily accessible.

Whether staying at the resort or as day visitors, the vast majority come to relax big style, but if you can drag yourself away from the beautiful stretch of palm-fringed beach either side of the wharf in **Brammo Bay**, you can experience the island's rich wildlife or sample some of the many activities on offer. The island has 13 km of walking tracks and the reception in the main resort building can provide free maps and information. There are plenty of options, from the short 15-minute stroll to see **Banfield's Grave** at the eastern end of the resort complex, to a complete Island Circuit (9.2 km, three hours) that takes in the remote **Bruce Arthur's Artists Colony/Gallery** ⓘ *Mon-Thu 1000-1300, $4*. The energetic may also like to attempt the stiff climb (5.6 km, three hours' return) to the summit of Mount Kootaloo (271 m), the island's highest peak.

The resort itself offers a day visitor's package that includes lunch and access to the bar, some sports facilities and the attractive **Butterfly Pool** (from $40), tickets available at **Watersports**, next to the wharf. If you really want to push the pampering boat out, book a session at the heavenly **Spa of Peace and Plenty** where you can choose from a wide range of alluring treatments, with such evocative names as the Floral Rain or Taste of Tahiti. Also book at **Watersports**.

● Central Coast listings

For Sleeping and Eating price codes and other relevant information, see Essentials pages 28-33.

Sleeping

Mackay and around *p272, map p273*
L-B Broken River Mountain Retreat, Broken River (for Eungella National Park), Eungella Dam Rd, T4958 4000, www.brokenrivermr.com.au. A range of studio, 1- and 2-bedroom self-contained cabins, restaurant (open to the public) and an exciting range of in-house activities from night spotting to canoeing.
A-D Historic Eungella Chalet Mountain Resort, Chelmer St, Eungella, T4958 4509, www.eungellachalet.com.au. As well as the magnificent views it has a wide range of options, from self-contained cabins with open fires to motel rooms and backpacker (weekday only) beds, an à la carte restaurant, public bar and pool.

B-E The Park, Bruce Highway Mackay, T4952 1211, www.toptouristparks.com.au. In the south, 6 km to the city centre and handy for the main highway, this 3-star motor park offers villas, cabins, powered and non-powered sites, and a good camp kitchen in a garden setting.
B-F Bucasia Beachfront Caravan Park, 2 Esplanade, Bucasia Beach, T4954 6375. Some 10 km north of the city, this is one of several good motor parks in the area. It has 3 stars and has self-contained villas, cabins, powered and non-powered sites and memorable views across to the Whitsunday Islands.
B-F Cape Hillsborough Nature Resort, Casuarina Bay in Cape Hillsborough National Park, T4959 0152, www.capehillsborough resort.com.au. Beachfront cabins, motel units or powered and non-powered sites. Fires permitted. There is a small store, pool, restaurant and bar lounge with internet.

B-F Eungella Holiday Park, North St (take the first right beyond the chalet), Eungella, T0437479205, www.eungella-holidaypark.com.au. Self-contained cabin, powered and non-powered sites.

D-E Gecko's Rest 34 Sydney St, T4944 1230, www.geckosrest.com.au. Centrally located, purpose-built hostel with a/c singles, dorms, singles, doubles and twins. Free shuttle.

D-E Larrikin Lodge YHA, 32 Peel St (200 m south of the bus terminal), T4951 3728, www.larrikinlodge.com.au. Backpackers will find a warm welcome here, the city's budget mainstay for some time now. It offers standard dorms, doubles and one family room with all the usual facilities in a traditional 'Queenslander'. Internet and entertaining in-house tours to Eungella National Park. A 3-night 'tour' package with 1 night in Mackay and 2 at the Eungella Chalet costs a very reasonable $180.

D-F Platypus Bush Camp, Finch Hatton Gorge Rd (for Eungella National Park), T4958 3204, www.bushcamp.net. Created by a friendly and laid-back bushman called Wazza, it gets mixed reviews and features a characterful collection of basic open-air huts and campsites, set amongst the bush and beside the river. The huts range from single, through doubles to the notably more distant Honeymoon Hut, with its exclusive platypus-spotting opportunities. Other camp features include an open-air communal kitchen and sauna (all constructed from local cedar wood) and a fine swimming hole. Campfires are authorized. A bit pricey, but certainly different.

QPWS campsites At Broken River (for Eungella National Park), with toilets, drinking water, showers and gas barbecues, permits available at the Ranger Station (T4958 4552) which has a small food kiosk attached. Also at **Newry Island** and **Outer Newry Island**. The latter has a hut (maximum of 10 at any one time). **Rabbit Island** has a QPWS campsite with toilets and a seasonal water tank. Also available at **Smalley's Beach** at the western end of Cape Hillsborough

National Park, T4944 7800, limited fresh water. There's a basic site at **Carlisle Island**, all supplies must be imported, seasonal water tank but a back-up supply should be taken anyway. Basic bush campsites are also on Goldsmith, Scawfell, Cockermouth, Keswick and St Bee's Islands. Permits and fees apply to all sites. Book ahead with the QPWS, 30 Tennyson St, Mackay, T4944 7800, www.epa.qld.gov.au.

Airlie Beach *p275, map p275*

Despite having numerous smart resorts, apartments and backpackers aplenty, Airlie can hardly keep pace with its own popularity and you are advised to book ahead. Many backpackers offer accommodation and activity combo deals, often booked from afar, but though these can be attractive in price, they can severely limit your choice.

L-A Airlie Waterfront B&B, corner of Broadwater Av and Mazlin St, T4946 7631, www.airliewaterfrontbnb.com.au. This is one of the best B&Bs in the region and certainly the best located for all amenities.

L-B Airlie Beach Hotel, corner of Esplanade and Coconut Grove, T4946 1999, www.airliebeachhotels.com.au. No-nonsense centrally located hotel with recently renovated standard rooms, motel-style units and self-contained suites. Cable TV, internet, 2 restaurants, bar and off-street parking.

B-F Flame Tree Tourist Village, 2955 Shute Harbour Rd, T4946 9388, www.flametreevillage.com.au. Further east near the airfield, low-key in a quiet bush setting, with a camp kitchen and within easy reach of the ferry terminal.

B-F Island Getaway Holiday Park, a short walk east of the town centre (corner of Shute Harbour Rd and Jubilee Pocket Rd), T4946 6228. This 4-star motor park is a popular option offering value units, cabins, camp-o-tels and powered and non-powered sites. Good camp kitchen and some very tame possums.

C-E Airlie Beach YHA, 394 Shute Harbour Rd, T4946 6312. YHA members will get the usual discounts at this friendly motel-style option.

C-E Bush Village Backpackers Resort, 2 St Martins Rd, Cannonvale, T4946 6177, www.bushvillage.com.au. For a little bit of peace and quiet this is an excellent option. It is friendly with tidy and spacious self-catering cabins with a/c, en suite doubles, dorms, pool and a regular shuttle into town.

C-F Koala, Shute Harbour Rd, T4946 6446, www.koalaadventures.com, and

C-E Magnums Backpackers, 366 Shute Harbour Rd, T4946 6266, www.magnums.com.au, are the main players when it comes to the major party- oriented backpackers located right in the heart of the town. In many ways they are the heart of the town! At the end of the day (or night) they are all pretty similar and certainly fiercely competitive, always trying to outdo each other on the small details. But in essence they all have the full range of dorms, singles and doubles, boast lively bars, nightclubs, a pool, good value eateries and internet. They can also advise on activities and trips (though this advice will not be completely objective).

Whitsunday Islands *p276, map p277*

LL Daydream Island Resort and Spa, T4948 8426, www.daydreamisland.com. Daydream is the closest island to the mainland and one of the smallest, making it a popular base. This 4-star luxury resort is modern, offering attractive multi-night package deals and good facilities including a luxury spa, open-air cinema and organized activities.

LL Paradise Bay, Long Island, T4946 9777, www.paradisebay.com.au. In almost perfect isolation on the island's western side, this is an architect's dream realized. It strives very successfully to create a relaxing eco-friendly retreat with a focus on the place rather than the amenities. Although basic and expensive, visitors very rarely leave disappointed. The accommodation is in comfortable en suite beachfront units. The hosts are very

professional and friendly and there is a moody yet enchanting pet kangaroo. The lodge has its own yacht which is part of an optional, and comprehensive, daily activities schedule. 3-night packages available.

L-D Long Island Resort and Barefoot Lodge, Long Island, T4946 9400, www.longislandresort.com.au. Offering its guests the perfect arrival point in Happy Bay, both atmosphere and amenities are casual but stylish. There are 2 options: the standard resort and the budget Barefoot Lodge that has access to resort facilities.

A-B Koala Adventure Island Resort, South Molle Island, T1800 466444, www.southmolleisland.com.au. A pretty relaxed place aimed at the younger set, offering a full range of accommodation from beach bungalows to dorms, all with the usual mod cons and allowing day trippers access to the pool, bar/bistro and some activities. It is also noted for its evening entertainment.

A-E Hook Island Wilderness Resort, Hook Island, T4946 9470, www.hookislandresort.com. Located towards the southeastern end of the island, this is a low-key resort popular with budget travellers. It offers en suite and standard cabins and dorms along with numerous activities, an underwater observatory, café-bar, pool and spa.

QPWS campsites Whitsunday Island
There are 8 QPWS campsites here. The most popular is Whitehaven Beach, southern end. It can accommodate up to 60 and has toilets, but no water supply. The only campsites with water are Sawmill Beach and Dugong Beach, both of which fringe Cid Bay on the island's western side. They are connected by a 1-km walking track.

Hook Island There are 5 QPWS campsites here, with Maureen Cove and Bloodhorn Beach (Stonehaven Bay) being the most popular. None has a water supply.

Lindeman Island The only campsite here is at Boat Port, with toilets but no water.

Long Island This has a campsite on the western side of the island at Sandy Bay. It is a fine, secluded spot backed by rainforest, through which there is a track allowing you to explore and reach viewpoints overlooking the other islands. There are toilets but no water supply.

South Molle 2 campsites, at Sandy Bay and Paddle Bay with toilets but no water supply. There are 2 other sites on small offshore islands and at Cockatoo Beach on North Molle, but if the resort cannot offer you a lift in one of its vessels, independent access must be arranged. Cockatoo Beach site has seasonal water supplies.

Townsville *p279, map p279*

B-E Rowes Bay Caravan Park, west of the Strand on Heatley's Parade, T4771 3576, www.rowesbaycp.com.au. Close to town and beach, offering villas, cabins, powered and non-powered sites and camp kitchen.

B-E Walkabout Palms Caravan Park, 6 University Rd, Wulguru, T4778 2480, www.walkaboutpalms.com.au. This 4-star park has good facilities and is connected to the 24-hr petrol station. Although not central to the city (7 km away) it's in a good position for the transitory visitor right on the main north-south highway.

C Yongala Lodge, off the Strand on Fryer St, T4772 4633, www.historicyongala.com.au. Named after the famous local shipwreck, offers a range of contemporary motel units from single to 2-bedroom, a pleasant Mediterranean/international restaurant and is a pebble's throw from the waterfront.

C-E Civic Guest House, 262 Walker St, T4771 5381, www.backpackersinn.com.au. A little less conveniently situated, but the pick of the bunch. It has a wide range of rooms (some with en suite and a/c), good general facilities, a spa and interesting in-house trips.

D-E Globetrotters Inn, 121 Flinders St East, T4771 5000. Choice of modern 4-share rooms or your own en suite motel-style room with TV and fridge. Pool and internet café. Dive/stay packages a speciality.

Magnetic Island *p281, map p281*

Picnic Bay, the main arrival point, offers many amenities but most of the accommodation is evenly spread down the east coast. There is plenty of choice, from luxury poolside apartments to a hammock, and most are virtually self contained. For full listings contact the VIC. Book ahead for budget accommodation and during school and public holidays.

L-C Magnetic Island Tropical Resort, 56 Yates St, Nelly Bay, T4778 5955, www.magnetic islandresort.com. An excellent choice, offering modern, A-frame self-contained chalets with good facilities. Restaurant/bar, pool and spa, amidst a bush setting. Recommended.

B-C Marshall's B&B, 3-5 Endeavour Rd, Arcadia, T4778 5112. This eco-friendly option, next door to Magnetic North Apartments, offers basic, but good value singles and doubles in a traditional Queenslander house and is surrounded by spacious gardens with the odd friendly wallaby for company. Fans. Free night standby special (ie buy 2, get 3) Oct-Jun.

C-E Base Backpackers, 1 Nelly Bay Rd, Nelly Bay, T4778 5777, www.stayatbase.com. South of Nelly Bay on the beach, this newly branded backpackers is regaining popularity after renovation. It has an interesting range of accommodation options, from dorms to ocean-view *bures* (traditional South Pacific thatched huts). Modern facilities, café, dive shop and home to the notorious full moon parties.

C-F Bungalow Bay Koala Village (YHA), 40 Horseshoe Bay Rd, Horseshoe Bay, T4778 5577, www.bungalowbay.com.au. Set in spacious grounds, offering everything from a/c chalets (some en suite) and en suite multi-share to camp and powered sites with camp kitchen. Regular, mass lorikeet feeding. Lively place with popular late night bar and bistro, pool, spa and internet but a little further away from the beach.

D-F Magnums, 7 Marine Pde, Arcadia, T4778 5177, www.magnums.com.au. A busy, sprawling place with 30 a/c motel-style units (including dorms) close to all local amenities. Pool, spa, restaurant/bar and bistro. Internet.

Hinchinbrook Island National Park *p284*
There are as yet limited accommodation options in Cardwell. Hinchinbrook VIC can help with finding accommodation.

LL-L Hinchinbrook Island Wilderness Lodge and Resort, Hinchinbrook Island, T4066 8270 www.hinchinbrookresort.com.au. This exclusive place offers an excellent, though somewhat expensive, sanctuary, with an eco-friendly setting and all mod cons. Don't expect a party atmosphere or a place overrun with activities as this is a resort that is proudly in tune with the wilderness and environment that surround it. A perfect place at which to indulge, relax and pamper yourself.

A-E Kookaburra Holiday Park and Hinchinbrook Hostel (YHA), 175 Bruce Highway (north of the jetty), Cardwell, T4066 8648, www.kookaburraholidaypark.com.au. YHA affiliated, this has everything from self-catering villas to campsites as well as dorms, doubles and twins in the hostel section. Good facilities, including a pool, tours and activities bookings, internet and free bike hire for guests.

Camping Facilities on Hinchinbrook Island are at Scraggy Point (The Haven), on the island's northwest coast, and Maucushla Bay, near the resort. Toilets and gas fireplaces.

Bush camping sites on Hinchinbrook Island have been established along the Thorsborne Trail with Zoe Bay offering toilets and water. Open fires are not allowed and you will require a gas stove and water containers. Camping permits for all sites must be obtained from the QPWS Rainforest and Reef Centre, see page 284 for contact details, or email to hinchinbrookcamp@env.qld.gov.au.

Mission Beach and Dunk Island *p284*
Although there is a smattering of resorts in the area, the many excellent and characterful B&Bs and self-contained accommodation are recommended.

LL-A Sejala, 1 Pacific St, Mission Beach, T4088 6699, www.sejala.com.au. 5-star luxury in the form of a stunning beachfront villa with private pool or a choice of 3 arty (and cheaper) self-contained beach huts with shared plunge pool.

LL-L Dunk Island Resort, Brammo Bay, Dunk Island, T4068 8199, www.dunk-island.com. This 4-star resort offers a delightful range of units and suites, excellent amenities and a wealth of activities and sports on offer. Book well ahead. Children welcome.

L-F Beachcomber Coconut Caravan Village, Kennedy Esplanade, Mission Beach South, T4068 8129, www.beachcomber coconut.com.au. There are several motor parks in the area including this very tidy beachside option. Recommended.

L-F Hideaway Holiday Village, 60 Porters Prom, Mission Beach village, T4068 7104, www.missionbeachhideaway.com.au. This motor park is a little sterile but has good facilities and is very handy for the beach and village amenities. Pool, camp kitchen and internet.

B Dragonheart B&B Resort, Bingil Bay, T4068 7813, www.dragonheartbnb.com. A friendly welcome and separate accommodation in Balinese-style cottages (with en suite) set in the rainforest. It also has a pool. A good choice and good value.

B-C Licuala Lodge, 11 Mission Circle, Mission Beach, T4068 8194, www.licuala lodge.com.au. Excellent award-winning pole house B&B with doubles, singles, and a memorable 'jungle pool' and spa. Dinner available on request.

B-C Sanctuary Retreat, 72 Holt Rd, Bingil Bay, T4088 6064, www.sanctuaryatmission .com. An interesting eco-retreat; wildlife enthusiasts will love it. The minimalist and secluded forest huts are in a setting designed to nurture and attract the local wildlife rather than scare it away. Restaurant, internet and pick-ups. Good value.

C-D Treehouse YHA, Frizelle Road (off Bingil Bay Road), Bingil Bay, T4068 7137, www.treehousehostel.com.au. Always popular, this pole house has doubles, twins and dorms a pool and all the usual amenities. Its only drawback is its distance from the beach but shuttle buses regularly ply the route.

C-E Absolute Backpackers, 28 Wongaling Beach Rd, Wongaling Beach, T4068 8317, www.absolutebackpackers.com.au. Newly renovated, popular place with a social atmosphere, offering 10-, 8- and 4-bed dorms and separate doubles with fans or a/c and a well-equipped kitchen. It is also close to the happening bar in the **Mission Beach Resort** and the main shopping complex.

C-E Beach Shack, 86 Porter Promenade, 1 km north of Mission Beach village, T4068 7783, www.missionbeachshack.com. This complex is a colourful 2-storey house opposite the beach and within walking distance to the village centre. It offers tidy dorms and doubles, 2 kitchens, spas and a relaxed, friendly atmosphere.

C-E Scotty's Beach House Hostel, 167 Reid Rd, Wongaling Beach, T4068 8676, www.scottysbeachhouse.com.au. Closer to the beach than **Mission Beach Backpackers Lodge**, this is a well-established and popular place, offering a range of unit-style dorms and doubles surrounding a fine pool, a very relaxed atmosphere, restaurant and reputedly the best bar in town.

QPWS camping ground, Dunk Island, is discreetly located next to the resort. Permits can be purchased from **Watersports** on the island. Barbecues and showers.

❶ Eating

Mackay and around p272, map p273
♔ **Sorbello's** , 166B Victoria St, T4957 8300. Daily 1200-2000. The best Italian restaurant in town.
♔♔ **Café La De Da**, 70 Wood St, T4944 0203. New establishment; good quality and value.
♔ **Eimeo Hotel**, Mango Av, Dolphin Heads, 12 km away, T4954 6106. Daily 1200-2000. Cheap counter meals with spectacular views over Eimeo Beach and the Whitsunday Islands.
♔ **Hideaway Café**, just beyond the chalet, Eungella, T4958 4533. Daily 0800-1700. Well worth a stop. The delightful Suzanna has single-handedly created her own little piece of paradise, with spacious gardens,

home-made pottery and a wishing well. Take a tour of the imaginative and truly international menu while supping a coffee and soaking up the views across the valley.
♔ **Kate O'Reilley's Irish Pub**, 38 Sydney St, T4953 3522. The best for pub grub.

Airlie Beach p275, map p275
♔♔ **Beaches Backpackers** and **Magnums** (see page 289), have popular bar/bistros offering a wide variety of good-value dishes (including the obligatory roo burgers) and a lively atmosphere. The 2-for-1 pizzas in the **Magnums** complex are also a bargain. Both are open for lunch and dinner.
♔♔ **Chargrill**, 382 Shute Harbour Rd, T4946 6320. Popular for seafood and meat dishes and has live entertainment most nights until 0300.
♔♔ **Paddy Shenanigans**, 352 Shute Harbour Rd, T4946 5055. This Irish pub also offers good value bar meals and is a fine place to remain for a night out.
♔ **Village Deli**, 366 Shute Harbour Rd, T4946 5745. Tucked away at the back of the shopping complex, opposite the post office, good coffee, healthy snacks, fruit smoothies and breakfast in peaceful surroundings.

Townsville p279, map p279
There are reputable, upmarket restaurants in most major hotels and motels. Palmers St has taken over from Flinders St East as the preferred venue of the local gourmand, offering a wide range of international, mid-range options.
♔ **Bistro One**, 30-34 Palmer St, T4771 6333. Popular, especially for seafood.
♔ **Molly Malone's Irish Pub**, corner of Wickham St and Flinders St East, T4771 3428. For pub grub, tidy surroundings and congenial atmosphere.
♔ **Reef Thai** , 455 Flinders St, T4721 6701. Daily 0530-late. Takeaway service. Locally recommended, with a seafood edge.
♔ **Taj Mahal**, 2/235 Flinders St East, T4772 3422. Good Indian cuisine.
♔ **The Watermark**, 72-74 The Strand, T4724 4281. Modern Australian cuisine amid chic and contemporary surrounds and great ocean views.

Heritage Café and Bar, 137 Flinders St East, T4771 2799. Nice atmosphere, varied and good value blackboard of dishes.

Magnetic Island *p281, map p281*
The restaurants and cafés on Maggie tend to be casual affairs and close early. Most of the major resorts and backpackers have cafés, bistros, or à la carte restaurants all open to the public. Self-caterers will find grocery stores in all the main centres mostly open daily until about 1900.

Man Friday, 37 Warboys St, Nelly Bay, T4778 5658. Wed-Mon from 1800. Mexican, traditional Australian and international dishes with vegetarian options.

Noodies, on the waterfront, Horseshoe Bay, T4778 5786. Another place offering fine seafood and overlooking the beach.

Sandbar Restaurant, 11 Cook Rd, Arcadia, T4778 5477. Good atmosphere and seafood.

Mission Beach *p284*
Most eateries are concentrated in and around the Village Green Shopping Complex on Porter Promenade in Mission Beach village, but between here and Wongaling Beach you won't be short of choice.

Mission Beach Restaurant and Bar, corner of Banfield Rd and Wongaling Beach Rd, Wongaling Beach, T4068 8433. Daily for dinner except Wed. For fine dining with an international menu try this classy joint. Cleverly designed in typical, though modern, Queenslander style, on poles and open plan, it is stylish with food to match. Recommended.

Greek Tavern, corner of Webb St and Banfield Parade, T4068 8177. As the name suggests, predominantly Mediterranean oriented cuisine, but also some Asian and Australian options. Great views over Wongaling Beach and good for a quiet romantic dinner.

Café Gecko, Shop 6, The Hub, Porter Promenade, T4068 7390. Daily 0900-1700. Seems to change management regularly but maintains quality when it comes to a caffeine fix.

Scotty's Beachhouse Bar and Grill, 167 Reid Rd, off Cassowary Drive, Wongaling. This place has a lively atmosphere and offers budget bistro meals.

Bars and clubs

Airlie Beach *p275, map p275*
Beaches Backpackers and **Magnums** (see page 289) have streetside bars that are popular and the best place to meet others for the obligatory wild night out.
M@ss, at **Magnums**, is a nightclub that rips it up well into the wee hours (sometimes quite literally, with wet T-shirt competitions and foam parties).

Magnetic Island *p281, map p281*
The major backpackers provide most of the island's entertainment and have late bars.
Magnums, Arcadia (see page 289). Live bands most nights and full-on pool competitions.
Picnic Bay Hotel has pool competitions every Tue.

Activities and tours

Mackay and around *p272, map p273*
Jungle Johno Tours, T4951 3728, www.larrikinlodge.com.au/ jungle-tours. A popular option, offering entertaining eco-tours and camping trips to Eungella National Park and the Finch Hatton Gorge. Platypus spotting is a speciality. A 3-night 'tour' package with 1 night in Mackay YHA and 2 nights at the Eungella Chalet costs a very reasonable $180.
Mackay Reeforest Tours, T4959 8360, www.reeforest.com. Wider range of day tours to Hillsborough and Eungella National Parks and in season the Farleigh Sugar Mill Tour, from $145, children $95.

Scenic flights from Airlie Beach

There are several options for scenic flights from Airlie Beach. Most of the operators are based at the airfield between Airlie and Shute Harbour. Helicopter flights are also offered from the waterfront in Airlie; a 10-minute scenic flight around the bay costs from $95. In general, a flight of 5-20 minutes over the town and inner islands (South Mole, Long and Daydream islands) will cost around $130. A scenic trip to Whitehaven with no stopover will cost around $290, while a 40-minute Whitehaven Beach flight with 2-hour stopover will cost from $399. Extended trips to the outer reef with stopovers will cost up to $530. **HeliReef Whitsunday**, T4946 8249, www.avta.com.au, has a range of flight-seeing options by helicopter, fixed-wing and floatplane. **Air Whitsunday**, T4946 9111, www.airwhitsunday.com.au, and **Island Air**, T4946 9120, www.avta.com.au, both have a fleet of fixed-wing land and seaplanes and offer both tours and island transfers, from $130.

Airlie Beach *p275, map p275*

With numerous dive shops, umpteen cruise operators, over 74 islands and almost as many vessels, the choice of water-based activities and trips is mind blowing. The 2 most popular trips are Whitehaven Beach and Fantasea's floating Reefworld pontoon, which offers the chance to dive, snorkel or view the reef from a semi-submersible or underwater observatory. Note that both options are also the most commercial and most crowded. The main ferry companies also offer island transfers and island day tripper specials with South Molle being a popular and good value choice.

Cruises

All offer a wide array of day cruises to the islands, the outer reef, or both. A day cruise will cost from $95-200.
Fantasea (Blue Ferries) Cruises, T4967 5455, www.fantasea.com.au. The major player with fast catamarans.
Whitehaven Express, T4946 1585, www.whitehavenxpress.com.au. Well-established operator offering day trips to Whitehaven from $150.

Diving

The outer reef offers the clearest water and most varied marine life. There are numerous options with all local dive shops and most of the larger cruise companies offering day or multi-day trips and courses.
Dive Australia, Sugarloaf Rd, T4946 1067, www.scubacentre.com.au. A range of 3-day liveaboard Open Water Courses from $649.
Reefjet, Shop 2, Abel Point Marina, T4946 5366, www.reefjet.com.au. Excellent day cruise to the Bait Reef (outer reef) and Whitehaven Beach with dive and snorkelling options from $140.

Fishing

MV Moruya, T4948 1029, www.fishingwhitsunday.com.au. Entertaining half, full and multi-day trips from Shute Harbour, from $150.

Kayaking

Salty Dog Sea Kayaking, T4946 1388, www.saltydog.com.au. Half day guided trips from $70, full day from $125, overnight (from $360) or 6-day (from $1490), island camping adventures and independent kayak hire from $50 per day. The trips guarantee plenty of beautiful scenery as well as a spot of island bushwalking and snorkelling.

Ocean rafting

Ocean Rafting, T4946 6848, www.ocean rafting.com.au. Runs a 6½-hr fast cruise around the islands and Whitehaven Beach on board their rigid inflatable. Includes snorkelling, guided rainforest and Aboriginal cave walk from $108, children $69.

Sailing

Again the choices are mind-boggling. A whole host of vessels from small dinghies to world-class racing yachts are available for day, night or multi-day adventures. Depending on the vessel type, as well as accommodation and food, a day cruise will cost about $150 while a 2-day/2-night will cost from $350-550; a 3-day/2-night trip around $450-700 and a 3-day/3-night from $550-1000.

Townsville p279, map p279
Diving

There are several companies in Townsville or on Magnetic Island (which is often the preferred location) offering a wide variety of trips for certified divers wishing to experience the *Yongala*. It's best to shop around.
Adrenalin Dive, 9 Wickham St, T4724 0600, www.adrenalinedive.com.au. Range of courses/trips to the *Yongala* wreck, from $220.

Sightseeing tours

Kookaburra Tours, T0448 794798, www.kookaburratours.com.au. Range of tours including entertaining full day trips to the Wallam Falls (Australia's tallest) on Tue and Charters Towers on Wed from $125.

Magnetic Island p281, map p281
Cruises/sailing

Jazza's Sailing Tours, 90 Horseshoe Bay Rd, T4778 5530, www.jazza.com.au. Good value, 6-hr cruise aboard the 12-m *Jazza* from $100, children $50 (includes lunch).
Tropic Sail, T4772 4773, www.tropicsail.com.au. Hire of yachts from $440 per night and day sailing trips from Townsville.

Diving

Pleasure Divers, 10 Marine Pde, T4778 5788, www.pleasuredivers.com.au. Reputable 2-4

day course/trips (including *Yongala* wreck) from $220.

Flights

Red Baron Sea Planes, Horseshoe Bay, T4758 1556, www.redbaronseaplanes.com. A unique opportunity to fly in a Grumman Sea Cat (used in the film *The Phantom*) and the only one of its type in the world, from $350.

Golf

Magnetic Island Country Club, Picnic Bay, T4778 5188, www.magvac.com. Small 9-hole golf course, visitors welcome, $14 ($20 for 18 holes).

Horse trekking

Bluey's Ranch, 38 Gifford St, Horseshoe Bay, T4778 5109, www.horseshoebayranch.com.au. Horse treks from 2 hrs to half day, from $100.

Sightseeing tours

Magnetic Island Bus Service, Nelly Bay, T4778 5130. 3-hr guided tours from Nelly Bay, 0900 and 1300, from $35, children $18, family $88.
Tropicana Guided Adventure Company, Harbour Terminal, T4758 1800, www.tropicanatours.com.au. Multifarious award-winning 4WD trips with entertaining and multi-talented guides. Full day (8 hrs) '7-days-in-1' trip recommended from $198, children $99.

Water sports

Magnetic Island Sea Kayaks, Horseshoe Bay, T4778 5424, www.seakayak.com.au. Half-day sea kayaking adventures from $85, which also includes a beach breakfast.

Hinchinbrook Island National Park p284
Hinchinbrook Ferries Eco-Tours,
Cardwell, T4066 8585, www.hinchinbrookferries.com.au. Full day national park discovery trips from $125. See also Transport, page 295.

Mission Beach and Dunk Island *p284*
Many of the Mission Beach operators incorporate Dunk Island in their kayak and jet ski tours. Snorkelling on Dunk is poor compared to the reef.

Skydiving
Jump The Beach, T4031 5466, www.jumpthebeach.com. Great value tandem jumps on to Mission Beach or Dunk Island: 2750 m and 3350 m from $210, 4250 m from $295.
Paul's Parachuting, based in Cairns, T1800 005 006, www.paulsparachuting.com.au. Tandems with landings on Mission Beach at similar prices.

Water sports
Calypso Dive and Snorkel, 20 Wongaling Beach Rd, T4068 8432, www.calypsodive.com. Purpose-built dive centre in Mission Beach; as well as a full range of courses it offers wreck dives and a blast around Dunk Island on jet skis from $230.
Coral Sea Kayaking, T4068 9154, www.coral seakayaking.com. Full day sea kayaking voyages to Dunk Island with plenty of time to explore and a fine lunch from $128 (half-day coastal exploration, $77).
Dunk Jet Sports, T4068 8432, www.dunkjet sports.com. 2-hr circumnavigation of Dunk Island on jet ski, from $230, or full day including lunch with plenty of time to relax and explore Dunk itself. From $330. Departs South Mission Beach 0830.
Watersports, next to the wharf on Dunk Island. Offers independent day visitors a host of equipment and water-based activities from a mask and snorkel hire to windsurfing, waterskiing and parasailing.

☉ Transport

Mackay and around *p272, map p273*
There is no public transport to Eungella, though it is possible to make arrangements with local tour operators (see page 292).

Air
Mackay Airport, T4957 0255, is 2 km south of the city centre, along Sydney St and is served by **Jet Star**, T131538; **Qantas**, T131313; **Tiger Airways**, T9335 3033, www.tigerairways .com; and **Virgin Blue**, T136789. All have daily services throughout Queensland and New South Wales.
Air Whitsunday, T4946 9111, www.airwhitsunday.com.au, has shuttle services to **Proserpine** and **Hamilton Island**. Taxis meet all flights and cost about $20 into town.
For **Brampton and Carlisle islands**, local companies also fly to and from Hamilton Island and daily to and from Mackay. A launch service for resort guests is available Thu-Mon at 1130 from Mackay Marina, T4951 4499. Campers can take a scheduled launch and walk to the QPWS campsite or arrange to be ferried directly to the island through the resort. **Qantas** flies to Brampton from Australian state capitals. For more information contact the QPWS office, Mackay.

Boat
For the Newry Islands access is by private boat from the boat ramp at Victor Creek, 4km west of Seaforth. For details contact **QPWS**, T1300 130372, www.derm.qld.gov.au/ parks/newry-islands/index.html.

Bus
Local Mackay Transit, Casey Av, T4957 3330, www.mackaytransit.com.au, is a hail 'n' ride bus service to Northern Beaches (Mon-Fri, No 7) and Mirani (No 11). Day Rover tickets are available.
Long distance Greyhound, T1300 473946, stops at the terminal on Milton St, between Victoria and Gordon St, T4951 3088.

Taxi
Mackay Taxis (24 hrs), T131008.

Train
The station is 5 km southwest of the city centre on Connor's Rd, between Archibald St and Boundary Rd off the Bruce Highway. Queensland Rail, T132332. Taxis meet most

trains and cost $20 in to the centre. Regular buses leave from Nebo Rd (Bruce Highway).

Airlie Beach *p275, map p275*
Air
The nearest airports are in Proserpine, 36 km west, and Hamilton Island in the Whitsunday Islands. Both are served by Qantas, T131313, and **Island Air Taxis**, T4946 8249, www.avta.com. au, who provide local island transfers from **Mackay**, **Proserpine** or **Shute Harbour**. Whitsunday Transit buses meet flights in Proserpine.

Bus
Local Whitsunday Transit, T4946 1800, www.whitsundaytransit.com.au, offers daily buses from **Proserpine Airport** to **Shute Harbour** (through Airlie) from $8.50 (Explorer Pass). Buses between **Cannonvale** and **Shute Harbour** operate daily between 0600-1845, from $5 one way. Day pass, $8.50.
Long distance Buses stop beside the lagoon in the heart of town or next to the Sailing Club in the Recreation reserve. Either way most accommodation is within walking distance or you will be met by private shuttle. **Greyhound**, T1300 473946, runs regular daily services.

Taxi
Whitsunday Taxis, T131008.

Train
The nearest station is in Proserpine, 36 km west of Airlie, with 8 trains weekly including the **Brisbane-Cairns Tilt Train**. For bookings, call **Queensland Rail**, T132232. The station is served by Whitsunday Transit, T4946 1800, linking Proserpine with Airlie Beach and Shute Harbour, which meets all arrivals.

Whitsunday Islands *p276, map p277*
Air
Proserpine Airport, 36 km west of Airlie Beach, on the mainland, and Hamilton Island Airport, provide air access. Both are serviced by Qantas, T131313. **Lindeman** is the only other island with an airfield.

Island Air Taxis, T4946 9102, www.avta.com.au, provides local island transfers by fixed-wing or helicopter from **Mackay**, **Proserpine** or **Shute Harbour**. Air Whitsunday, T4946 9111, www.airwhit sunday.com.au, also offers fixed-wing and seaplane services. All local fixed-wing, helicopter and seaplane companies also offer scenic flights (see box, page 293).

Boat
Shute Harbour, east of Airlie Beach, is the main departure point for ferry services to the Whitsunday islands. Ask at the VIC for the latest transfer services and day packages. **Cruise Whitsundays**, Abel Point Marina, Airlie Beach, T4946 4662, www.cruise whitsundays.com, offers an island resort transfer service to Hamilton, Daydream Island Resort and Spa, Long Island, and the Koala Adventure Resort on South Molle. Cruise Whitsundays also operates a connecting service from Whitsunday Coast Airport (Proserpine) through to Daydream and Long Islands. The average transfer cost is around $45. They also offer day packages, day trips to Whitehaven Beach (from $165) and their own Reef Pontoon at Knuckle Reef (from $199). Fantasea , T4967 5455, www.fantasea.com.au, offers daily services and day packages to **Hamilton** (6 daily, from $45 return). They too offer a range of day tripper and adventure cruises that include their 'Reefworld' pontoon out on the reef; the island resorts (with use of resort facilities and lunch) are also on offer from $225. Their main office is at the ferry terminal, with another office at Shop 11, Shute Harbour Rd, Airlie Beach, T4967 5455. Ferry schedules are available at the VICs. **Whitehaven Express**, T4946 6922, www.whitehavenxpress.com.au, runs a daily trip to Whitehaven Beach from Abel Point Marina (Cannonvale) at 0900, from $150, children $75. **Island Camping Connections**, T4946 5255, based at the ferry terminal, runs island transfers for campers by water taxi, from $45-150. Book ahead.

Bus

Whitsunday Transit, T4946 1800, www.whit
sundaytransit.com.au, has regular daily
services from **Proserpine** to **Shute Harbour**
(through Airlie Beach).

Townsville *p279, map p279*
Air

Townsville is serviced from all major cities by
Qantas, **Jet Star**, and **Virgin Blue**. The airport,
T4727 3211, is about 5 km west of the city in
the suburb of Garbutt.

Bus

Local Townsville's Sunbus, T4725 8482,
www.sunbus.com.au, runs regular daily
suburban services. Fares are from $2.50, day
pass from $10.
Long distance Premier Motor Services,
T133410, and **Greyhound**, T1300 473946.
Westbound destinations include Charters
Towers. Most coaches stop at the Sunferries
Terminal, Breakwater, Sir Leslie Thiess Drive,
T4772 5100. Daily 0600-1930.

Car

Main companies at the airport. **Network**, 25
Yeatman St, T4725 3210.

Train

The station, Blackwood St, just south of the
Flinders Mall, next to the river, has a travel
centre, T4772 8546 (confirmations and
timetable), T132232 (bookings),
www.traveltrain.qr.com.au. The **Sunlander** and
Tilt Train operate regular services between
Brisbane and **Cairns**; the **Spirit of the Tropics**
operates a twice-weekly service from **Brisbane**
to **Townsville** and the **Inlander** runs
twice-weekly services to **Mount Isa**.

Magnetic Island *p281, map p281*
The island speed limit is a strict 60 kph. Fuel is
available around the island.

Bus

Interstate buses stop in the centre of **Cardwell**
off the Bruce Highway on Brasenose St.

Magnetic Island Bus Service, T4778 5130,
runs up and down the east coast, between
Picnic Bay to Horseshoe Bay every hour or so
from 0600-2340. Tickets are sold on the bus
from $2.50. 1-day ($15) and 2-day ($18)
unlimited passes are generally the preferred
option. They also offer 3-hr guided tours from
Picnic Bay at 0900 and 1300 from $40,
children $20.

Cycle and scooter hire

Magnetic Island Photos, Picnic Bay Mall,
T4778 5411, rents bikes. **Road Runner
Scooter Hire**, 64 Kelly St, T4778 5222,
scooters. Bikes can also be hired from
some hostels.

Ferry

Passenger ferries arrive at the Nelly Bay
wharf. Vehicular ferries arrive at Geoffrey Bay,
Arcadia. **Fantasea Ferries**, Ross St,
Townsville South, T4796 9300,
www.magneticislandferry.com.au, have
regular sailings to Nelly Bay, Mon-Fri
0520-1805, Sat-Sun 0710-1805, from $164
(vehicle with up to 6 passengers) return.
Passenger only $26. **Sunferries Magnetic
Island**, T4726 0800, www.sunferries.com.au,
offers regular daily sailings from the
Bayswater Terminal to Nelly Bay 0535-1840
and from $29 return, children $15.

Moke and 4WD

One of the highlights of Maggie is exploring
the island by mini-moke or toy-like 4WDs.
Moke Magnetic, based at 112 Sooning St,
Nelly Bay, T4778 5377, www.moke
magnetic.com, hires mokes and vehicles
seating up to 8 from about $75 per day, with
60 km of fuel for free. Deposit $200. **Tropical
Topless Car Rentals**, 138 Sooning St, T4758
1111, has a fleet of colourful (and topless)
4WD, comfortable, good value and
economical, from about $75 per day, flat rate,
unlimited kilometres. Credit card deposit.

Hinchinbrook Island p284

Hinchinbrook Island Ferries, Cardwell, T4066 8270, www.hinchinbrookferries.com.au, is the main operator in Cardwell and provides the northerly access to the island (including the resort, $85). It also offers day cruises from $125, children $65. Irregular schedule Nov-May. Hinchinbrook Wilderness Safaris (Bill Pearce) T4777 8307, www.hinchinbrook wildernesssafaris.com.au, provide southerly access from Lucinda (from $46 one-way, $57 return), east of Ingham, and a range of day tours and cruises. Most people doing the Thorsborne Trail attempt it from north to south using Hinchinbrook Island Ferries for the northerly drop-off and Hinchinbrook Wilderness Safaris for southerly pick-up. Sailings vary according to season.

Mission Beach and Dunk Island p284

Air

Dunk has its own airport and regular flights are available via Cairns from major Australian cities. Qantas Link from Cairns several times daily with onward connection with Hinterland Aviation, T4035 9323,www.hinterlandaviation.com.au.

Boat

Quickcat, T4068 7289, www.quickcatcruises.com.au leaves Clump Point for Dunk daily at 0830, 1000 and 1400, from $56 return. Quickcat also visit the outer reef and Beaver Cay which is a beautiful spot offering much better snorkelling than Dunk Island, from $138. Quickcat offers coach pick-ups from Cairns. Prices vary, so do shop around. Dunk Island Express, T4068 8310, departs from the beach opposite their office on Banfield Parade, Wongaling Beach, 5 times daily, from $30, children $15 return. Quick Cat Cruises and Dunk Island Express offer local courtesy pick-ups.

Bus

Mission Beach Bus and Coach, T4068 7400, run the daily Bingil Bay to South Mission Beach service, single fare $3, day ticket $12,

children $6. Greyhound, Premier Motor Services and Coral Coaches have regular daily services from north and south stopping outside the post office on Porter Promenade in Mission Beach. Mission Beach Connections, T4059 2709, offers daily shuttles from Cairns (departing 0730 arriving at 0925 and departing Mission Beach 0730 arriving Cairns 0945) from $47 single. It links up with the Tilt Train in Tully.

⊙ Directory

Mackay and around p272, map p273

Banks Branches at Victoria St and Sydney St. **Hospital** Mackay Base Hospital, Bridge Rd, T4968 6000. **Internet** Easy Internet, 22 Sydney St, T4953 3331, Mon-Fri 0830-1730, Sat 0800-1300. Hong Kong Importers Bazaar, 128 Victoria St, T4953 3188, Mon-Fri 0845-1715, Sat-Sun 0900-1400. **Pharmacy** Night and Day, 65 Sydney St (next door to the post office). 0800-2100. **Post** 69 Sydney St. Open Mon-Fri 0800-1700. Postcode 4740. **Useful numbers** Police, Sydney St, T4968 3444.

Airlie Beach p275, map p275

Banks Most (with ATMs) on Shute Harbour Rd in Airlie and Cannonvale. Currency exchange at Magnums. **Medical** services Whitsunday Diving Medical Centre, 257 Shute Harbour Rd, T4946 6241. **Pharmacy** Night and Day, 366 Shute Harbour Rd, Airlie, T4946 7000. **Post** Shop 6A/366-370 Shute Harbour Rd. Mon-Fri 0900-1700. **Useful numbers** Police, 8 Altmann Av, Cannonvale, T4946 6445.

Townsville p279, map p279

Banks Most in and around the Flinders Mall. Currency exchange at Westpac Bank, 337 Flinders Mall. **Hospital** Townsville Hospital, 100 Agnes Smith Drive, T4796 1111. **Internet** Internet Den, 265 Flinders Mall, T4721 4500, Mon-Fri 0900-2100, Sat-Sun 1000-2000. **Post** Sturt St, T4760 2020,

Mon-Fri 0830-1730. **Useful numbers**
Police, corner of Sturt and Stanley streets,
T4759 7777.

Magnetic Island *p284, map p281*
Banks The post office, Nelly Bay, acts as
Commonwealth Bank agents. There are ATMs
at Picnic Bay Hotel, Magnums Resort and
Horseshoe Bay Store. **Internet** VIC, Nelly
Bay, free with bookings and in Picnic Bay at
most backpackers. **Medical
services** Sooning St, Nelly Bay, T4778 5614.
Pharmacy Magnetic Island Pharmacy,
Shopping Centre, 55 Sooning St Nelly Bay,
T4778 5375, Mon-Fri 0900-1730, Sat
0900-1300. **Post** 98 Sooning St, Nelly Bay.

Mon-Fri 0830-1700, Sat 0900-1100. Postcode
4819. **Useful numbers** Police, T4778 5270.

Mission Beach and Dunk Island *p284*
Bank/Post Post office, Porter Promenade,
Mission Beach, is Commonwealth Bank Agent.
ATMs in the **Mission Beach Supermarket** and at
Comfort Resort Mission Beach.
Internet Piccalo Paradiso, Shop 3/ 41 David
St, Mission Beach, and **Mission Beach
Information Station**, shop 4, **Mission Beach
Resort Shops**, Wongaling Beach. **Medical
services** Medical Centre, Cassowary Drive,
Mission Beach, T4068 8174. **Useful
numbers** Police, corner of Cassowary Drive
and Web Rd, Mission Beach, T4068 8422.

Far North Queensland

*Far North Queensland offers more to see and do than any other region in Australia. The bustling
tourist centre of Cairns is the gateway to the Great Barrier Reef and Wet Tropics Rainforest that,
between them, offer a seemingly endless choice of activities, from world-class diving to wilderness
outback tours. West of Cairns the lush, green plateau of the Atherton Tablelands is a cool retreat
from the coast, while to the north, Cape Tribulation and Port Douglas are popular excursions. Few
venture beyond Port Douglas but those adventurous souls who try will experience the very best that
4WD has to offer, and be exposed to some of Australia's true wilderness.*

Cairns → *For listings, see pages 315-327. Colour map 6, A1.*

Wedged between rolling hills to the west, the ocean to the east and thick mangrove
swamps to the north and south, Cairns is the second most important tourist destination in
Australia, only after Sydney. With the phenomenal Great Barrier Reef on its doorstep,
Cairns was always destined to become a major tourist hotspot, but the attractions don't
end there. With the ancient rainforest of Daintree National Park just to the north, this is
one of the very few places on earth where two such environmentally rich and diverse
World Heritage listed national parks meet.

Ins and outs
Getting there Many hotels and hostels provide shuttle services to and from the airport,
on the northern outskirts of the town, www.cairnsairport.com.au. **Coral Reef Coaches**
ⓘ *T4098 2800, www.coralreefcoaches.com.au*, offers regular services to and from the city
and throughout the region, from $15. **Cairns City Airporter (Australia Coach)** ⓘ *T4087
2900*, runs services to the city and to/from Port Douglas, Cape Tribulation and Mission
Beach. A taxi costs about $20, T131008. The interstate coach terminal is next to the Reef
Fleet Terminal on Spence Street. Cairns Railway Station is located beside Cairns Central
Shopping Complex. Coach and rail services from all major towns nearby, Brisbane and
beyond. ►► *See Transport, page 326.*

Cairns

To 6 To 4 To 14 29 , Airport, Skyrail Rainforest Cableway, Kuranda Scenic Railway, Tjapukai, Tanks Art Centre, Northern Beaches & Port Douglas

Trinity Bay

Charles St
Charles St
Charles St

Gelting St

Beryl St

Sheridan St

Digger St

Lake St

Esplanade

Grove St

Dunn St

McLeod St

(Captain Cook Highway)

Grafton St

Cairns Base Hospital

Gatton St
Gatton St
Gatton St

Kerwin St

Abbott St

Draper St

Martyn St

Parramatta St

Mary St

Nellie St

Water St

Upward St

Minnie St

9

20

St Monica's Cathedral

10

Maranoa St
Maranoa St

Florence St

Water St

Centre for Contemporary Arts

To 32 & Mission Beach

Mulgrave Rd

Prewitt St

Warrego St

Aplin St

8 2

4

Library

Esplanade

Cairns

Grimshaw St

Terminus St 13

16
26

Scott St

Cairns Central Shopping Complex

Lake St

Abbott St

10
7

Lagoon Complex

Shields St

13

Bunda St

McLeod St

12 18

Transit Centre

15 S

III Cairns Regional Art Gallery

11

Tourism Tropical North Queensland

i

27

S

Lumley St

3 10

Spence St

6 13

Sheridan St

5 Reef Teach

S

Pierpoint Rd

Reef Fleet Terminal

Draper St

Grafton St

Rainforest Dome & Casino

19

Interstate Terminal

Wharf St

Trinity Wharf

1

2 QPWS i

3

4

N

| 200 metres |
| 200 yards |

Sleeping 🛏
Bohemia Resort **4** *A2*
Cairns Coconut Caravan
  Resort **32** *E1*
Cairns Holiday Park **6** *A1*
Cairns Rainbow Inn **9** *C2*
Caravella Hostels **10** *D4, E4*
Dreamtime Travellers
  Rest **13** *F1*
Fig Tree Lodge & Willie
  McBride's **14** *A2*
Geckos **16** *F1*
Gilligan's Backpackers
  Resort **27** *F3*
Hides **18** *F3*
Kookas B&B **29** *A2*
Njoy **20** *D2*
Nomads Beach House **5** *A2*
Travellers Oasis **26** *F1*

Eating 🍴
Adelphi's Greek Taverna **8** *E3*
Barnacle Bill's **1** *F4*
Café China **3** *G3*
Dundee's **5** *G3*
Fish D'Vine **19** *G3*
Fusion Organics **2** *E3*
Gaura Nitai's Vegetarian **6** *G3*
International Food Court **7** *F4*
Mudslide Café **4** *E3*
Red Ochre Restaurant **13** *F3*

Bars & clubs 🍸
Cairns Rhino Bar
  & Bistro **10** *F3*
Courthouse Hotel **11** *F4*
PJ O'Briens **12** *F3*
Trybox **13** *G3*
Tropos **10** *F3*
Woolshed **18** *F3*

Harbour

Pier Complex

Marlin Marina

Trinity Inlet
5

To Green Island,
Fitzroy Island &
Frankland Islands

Getting around The centre of Cairns is compact and easily negotiable on foot. The waterfront with its new lagoon complex serves as the social focus of the city during the day along with the many hostels, hotels, shops and restaurants along the Esplanade and in the CBD. South of the CBD, the new Lagoon and Trinity Pier complex gives way to Trinity Inlet and Trinity Wharf, where the reef ferry and interstate coach terminals are based. Local bus operators serve the outskirts of the city. Bike hire is readily available. Buy maps from **Absells Map Shop**, Main Street Arcade off Lake Street (85), T4041 2699.

Tourist information The number of independent commission-based information centres and operators in Cairns is famously out of control. For objective information and advice on accommodation and especially activities, visit the accredited **Tourism Tropical North Queensland** ⓘ *Gateway Discovery Centre, 51 the Esplanade, T4051 3588, www.tropicalaustralia.com.au, 0830-1730.* The **QPWS office** ⓘ *5B Sheridan St, T4046 6602, www.epa.qld.gov.au, Mon-Fri 0830-1630,* has detailed information on national parks and the Barrier Reef Islands, including camping permits and bookings. Also useful are www.wettropics.gov.au and www.greatbarrierreef.org.

Sights
The majority of tourist activities in Cairns are focused on the Great Barrier Reef. The choice is vast and includes diving and snorkelling, cruising, sailing, kayaking and flightseeing. On land the choices are no less exciting with everything from bungee jumping to ballooning. See page 321 for details. The city itself also has many colourful attractions.

The **Lagoon Complex**, which overlooks the mudflats of Trinity Bay, is the city's biggest attraction and its new social hub. Cleverly designed and with shades of the popular Brisbane and Airlie Beach urban lagoons, it is now the place to see and be seen. A café and changing rooms are onsite.

Cairns Regional Art Gallery ⓘ *corner of Abbott St and Shields St, T4046 4800, www.cairnsregionalgallery.com.au, Mon-Sat 1000-1700, Sun 1300-1700, $5, free for children*, is housed in the former 1936 Public Curators Offices. Since 1995 the gallery has been an excellent showcase for mainly local and regional art as well as national visiting and loan exhibitions. The **KickArts Centre of Contemporary Arts** ⓘ *96 Abbott St, T4050 9494, www.kickarts.org.au, Tue-Sat 1000-1700, café and bar from 1100-late, free*, intriguingly guarded on the outside by five man-sized jelly babies, is home to three resident arts companies and is never short of artistic programmes. Visiting international exhibitions also feature. Also worth a visit is the **Tanks Art Centre** ⓘ *46 Collins Av, T4032 6600, www.tanksartscentre.com, Mon-Fri 1000-1600*, on the northern outskirts of the city. Three former diesel storage tanks are now used as a dynamic exhibition and performance space for the local arts community.

The **Rainforest Dome** ⓘ *T4031 7250, www.cairnsdome.com.au, 0800-1800, $22, children $11*, housed in the glass rooftop dome of the **Reef Hotel Casino**, is a strange mix of hotel, casino and small zoo, but once you are inside the dome itself it soon proves a very enjoyable experience and a far better bet than $20 on the card tables downstairs. There are over 100 creatures, from the ubiquitous koalas to 'Goliath' the salty croc. For some divine inspiration head for **St Monica's Cathedral** ⓘ *183 Abbott St, entry by donation*, to see the unique stained glass windows known as the 'Creation Design'. The huge and spectacularly colourful display even includes the Great Barrier Reef, complete with tropical fish. Leaflets are on hand to guide you through the design.

If you know very little about the reef and its myriad fascinating and colourful inhabitants, and especially if you are going snorkelling or are a first-time reef diver, you would greatly benefit from an appointment with **Reef Teach** ⓘ *2nd floor, Mainstreet Arcade, between Lake St and Grafton St, T4031 7794, www.reefteach.com.au, Tue-Sat show at 1830, $15*. Created by the rather over-animated Irish marine biologist and diver Paddy Cowell and his equally enthusiastic staff, it offers an entertaining two-hour lecture on the basics of the reef's natural history, conservation and fish/coral identification.

Skyrail Rainforest Cableway and Kuranda Scenic Railway
Skyrail ⓘ *T4038 1555, www.skyrail.com.au, daily 0815-1715, $42 one way ($61 return), children $21 ($31), price excludes Cairns transfers*. **Kuranda Scenic Railway** ⓘ *T4036 9333, www.ksr.com.au, departs Cairns 0830 and 0930 (except Sat), departs Kuranda 1400 and 1530, $45 single ($68 return), children $23*.

The award-winning Skyrail Rainforest Cableway, 15 minutes north of Cairns on the Captain Cook Highway, is highly recommended in both fine or wet weather and is perhaps best combined with a day tour package to Kuranda via the Kuranda Scenic Railway (see below). The once highly controversial Skyrail Gondola project was completed in 1995 and at 7.5 km is the longest cable-gondola ride in the world. It gives visitors the unique opportunity to glide quietly above the pristine rainforest canopy and through the heart of the World Heritage listed **Barron Gorge National Park**.

From the outset the mere prospect of such an intrusion into the ancient forest caused international uproar. Botanists and conservationists the world over were immediately up in arms and high-profile local demonstrations took place. But for once, all the fears and protestations proved groundless and now Skyrail has proved a highly impressive project that encompasses environmental sensitivity and education, with a generous dash of fun thrown in for good measure.

The journey includes two stops: one to take in the views and guided rainforest boardwalk from Red Peak Station (545 m) and another at Barron Falls Station where you can look around the entertaining Rainforest Interpretative Centre before strolling down to the lookouts across the **Barron River Gorge** and **Barron Falls**. The interpretative centre offers a range of displays and some clever computer software depicting the sights and sounds of the forest both day and night, while the short walkway to the falls lookout passes some rather unremarkable remains of the 1930s Barron Falls hydroelectric scheme construction camp. A word of warning here: prepare to be disappointed. Ignore the postcards or promotional images you see of thunderous, Niagara-like falls. They only look like that after persistent heavy rain and/or during the wet season. Sadly, for much of the year – from April to December – the falls are little more than a trickle. From the Barron Falls Station you then cross high above the Barron River before reaching civilization again at the pretty Kuranda Terminal. When crossing the rainforest you may be lucky enough to see the unmistakable Ulysses butterfly, which has now become a fitting mascot symbolic of the North Queensland rainforest.

The Kuranda Scenic Railway wriggles its way down the Barron Gorge to Cairns and provides an ideal way to reach the pretty village of Kuranda (see page 306). To add to the whole experience, you are transported in a historic locomotive, stopping at viewpoints along the way (which provides respite from the rambling commentary). Skyrail can be combined with the Kuranda Scenic Railway for around $88, children $44. Tickets available on the web, from travel agents, tour desks, hotels, motels, caravan parks and at the VIC.

Tjapukai
① T4042 9900, www.tjapukai.com.au, 0900-1700, day rates $35, children $17.50; night rates $99, children $50.
Tjapukai, pronounced 'Jaboguy', is an award-winning, multimillion dollar Aboriginal Cultural Park lauded as one of the best of its kind in Australia. It is the culmination of many years of quality performance by the local Tjapukai tribe. The 11-ha site, located next to the Skyrail terminal in Smithfield, offers an entertaining and educational insight into Aboriginal mythology, customs and history and, in particular, that of the Tjapukai. The complex is split into various dynamic theatres that explore dance, language, storytelling and history and there is also a mock-up camp where you can learn about traditional tools, food and hunting techniques. For many, the highlight is the opportunity to learn how to throw a boomerang or to play a didgeridoo properly without asphyxiating. To make the most of the experience give yourself at least half a day. Tjapukai also offers a new 'Tjapukai by Night experience', which begins at 1930 with an interactive, traditional and dramatic *corroboree* ritual, which is followed by an impressive buffet of regional foods and an entertaining stage show. Transfers are readily available for an extra charge and there's a shop and quality restaurant.

Other excursions
North of the airport the thick mangrove swamps give way to the more alluring northern beaches and the expensive oceanside resorts of **Trinity Beach** and **Palm Cove**. Both make an attractive base to stay outside the city or a fine venue in which to swing a golf club or to catch some rays. The VIC has listings. Other than Trinity Beach and Palm Cove the most northerly of the beaches, **Ellis Beach** is recommended. The northern beaches are also home to the **Cairns Tropical Zoo** ① Clifton Beach, 22 km, T4055 3669, www.cairnstropical zoo.com, 0830-1730, $32, children $16, which houses crocs, snakes, wombats and a range of species unique to tropical North Queensland. It is very touchy-feely and there are various shows on offer with everybody's favourite – the 'Cuddle a Koala Photo Session' – taking place daily at 0930 and 1430, $16 extra.

Some 40 km north of Cairns, on the road to Port Douglas, is **Hartley's Crocodile Adventures** ① *T4055 3576, www.crocodileadventures.com, 0830-1700, $32, children $16*, one of the best wildlife attractions in the region. Long-term resident and near octogenarian croc 'Charlie', was, until his death in September 2000, the star exhibit. Despite his demise, the park has been greatly enhanced by a recent relocation and impressive renovations, and still hosts plenty of heavyweights (fed daily at 1100 and 1500). There are plenty of other animals in evidence, including the ubiquitous koala, wallabies and cassowaries. There's also a restaurant and shop. Just north of Hartley's Creek is the Rex Lookout from where you can get your first glimpse of Port Douglas and the forested peaks of the Daintree National Park and Cape Tribulation in the distance.

Northern Great Barrier Reef islands → *For listings, see pages 315-327. Colour map 6, A2/B2.*

Cairns is the principal access point to the some of the top attractions of the Great Barrier Reef. The GBR is sometimes referred to as the largest single living entity on earth and is certainly the largest coral reef on the planet, stretching 2000 km from Cape York to the Tropic of Capricorn and up to 250 km at its widest point. Diving is the great attraction here, but if that's not your thing, then you should at least take a day cruise to one of the islands to sample the good life and go snorkelling. If you seek solitude there are a number of islands that can be visited independently and where camping is permitted, but you must arrange all transportation. Bookings and permits are essential. For information contact the QPWS Office in Cairns. For Lizard Island, see page 314.

Green Island
Once you arrive in Cairns it won't take long before you see postcards of Green Island, a small outcrop of lush vegetation, fringed with white sand and surrounded by azure and green reefs. The island, named after Charles Green, the chief observer and astronomer on board Captain Cook's ship, *Endeavour*, is a textbook cay – formed by dead coral – and will fulfil most people's fantasy of a tropical island. Only 45 minutes (27 km) away by boat, and part of the inner reef, it is the closest island to Cairns and, at 15 ha, one of the smallest islands on the reef. It is home to an exclusive resort but is designed more the day tripper in mind, with concrete pathways leading to food outlets, bars, dive and souvenir shops, a pool and some well-trodden beaches.

Despite its size, you can still grab a snorkel and mask and find a quiet spot on the bleached white sand. The best place to snorkel is by the pier itself, where the fish love to congregate around the pylons. Here you may see what appears to be a large shark. It is, in fact, a shark ray or 'bucket mouth', a charming and friendly bottom feeder and totally harmless. Another fine set of dentures can be seen at **Marineland Melanesia** ① *T4051 4032, 0930-1600, $15, children $7.50*, in the heart of the island, with its small collection of aquariums and marine artefacts, all presided over by Cassius, a crocodile with plenty of attitude. If you are unable to go diving or snorkelling, you can still experience the vast array of colourful fish and corals from a glass-bottom boat or a small underwater observatory ($6) both located by the pier. Although nothing remarkable, the latter was reputedly the first underwater observatory in the world.

There are a number of tour options for Green Island, giving you the opportunity to combine, diving and/or snorkelling to the outer islands with a few hours exploring the island. Or you may just want to pay the ferry fare and use the island's facilities, go snorkelling or laze on the beach. You can walk right round the island (1.5 km) in 20 minutes.

Fitzroy Island

Fitzroy, part of the inner reef, just 6 km off the mainland and 25 km south of Cairns, is a large 339-ha continental island surrounded by coral reef. It is mountainous and offers more of an escape than the others, with pleasant walking tracks through dense eucalyptus and tropical rainforests rich in wildlife. One of the most popular walks is a 4-km circuit to the island's highest point, 269 m, with its memorable views and modern lighthouse. A scattering of quiet beaches provide good snorkelling and diving. The best beach is **Nudey Beach** which is not, as the name suggests, a base for naturists. It can be reached in about 20 minutes from the island's resort. Fitzroy was used by the Gunghandji Aboriginal people as a fishing base for thousands of years and in the 1800s by itinerants harvesting bêche-de-mer, or sea cucumbers. It is named after Augustus Fitzroy, Duke of Grafton, who was the British prime minister when the *Endeavour* left England.

Frankland Islands

A further 20 km south of Fitzroy Island is the Frankland Group, a small cluster of continental islands of which 77 ha are designated a national park. The islands are covered in rainforest and fringed with white sand beaches and coral reef. They offer a wonderfully quiet retreat in comparison to the larger, busier islands. There are QPWS camping areas on Russell and High Islands. Permits and bookings can be obtained through the QPWS in Cairns.

Atherton Tablelands → *For listings, see pages 315-327. Colour map 6, B1.*

The Atherton Tablelands extend inland in a rough semi-circle from the Cairns coast to the small mining settlements of Mount Molloy in the north, Chillagoe in the west and Mount Garnet in the south: in total an area about the size of Ireland. At an average height of over 800 m, and subsequently the wettest region in Queensland, the Atherton Tablelands are most extraordinary: here, you'll find lush fields and plump cattle, tropical forests busting with birdsong, huge brimming lakes, high – and at times thunderous – waterfalls and even kangaroos that live in trees (see page 310). The further west you go the drier it gets until, at the edge of the Great Divide Range, the vast emptiness of the outback takes over. Given their inherent beauty, the Tablelands, especially the small and pretty settlements like Yungaburra, are the favourite retreat of Queensland's coastal dwellers, as well as tourists in search of peace and quiet, greenery and, above all, cooler temperatures.

Ins and outs

Getting there and around If you are short of time the best way to see the region is as part of a tour from Cairns. Otherwise, the Tablelands are best explored using your own transport. There are four access roads from the coast: from the south via Palmerston Highway (north of Innisfail) through the scenic tropical rainforests of Wooroonooran National Park and Millaa Millaa; from Cairns, south via Gordonvale and the steeply climbing Gillies Highway; north via Smithfield, the Kuranda Range Road and Kuranda; and from Port Douglas via the Rex Range Road and Kennedy Highway. **Trans North**, T4095 8644, www.transnorthbus.com, provides daily services to Atherton, Yungaburra, Mareeba and Kuranda. To arrive via Kuranda Scenic Railway or Skyrail Gondola, see page 302. ▸▸ *See Transport, page 326.*

Tourist information Research the region from the VIC in Cairns. **Tropical Tableland Promotion Bureau** ⓘ *corner of Silo Rd and Main St, Atherton, T4091 4222, www.athertontableland.com*, is the principal accredited regional body. For parks information contact the QPWS office in Cairns. **Kuranda VIC** ⓘ *Centenary Park, Therwine St, T4093 9311, www.kuranda.org, 1000-1600*, has maps and accommodation, tours and activities details.

Kuranda

The small, arty settlement of Kuranda has become the main tourist attraction in the Atherton Tablelands, thanks to its proximity to Cairns, a scenic railway and its markets. But while there's no doubting its appeal, particularly the spectacular means of access, Kuranda has, to a large extent, become a victim of its own popularity. The town was first put on the map in 1891 with the completion of the railway, providing a vital link between the Hodgkinson Gold Fields and the coast.

Kuranda's main attraction is its permanent markets: **Heritage Markets** ⓘ *just off Veivers Drive, daily 0900-1500*, and the nearby **Original Markets** ⓘ *Therwine St, daily 0900-1500*. Other stalls and permanent shops are also strung along the village's main drag, **Coondoo Street**. The emphasis is on souvenirs, with much of it being expensive and tacky, but there are some artists and craftspeople producing pieces that are both unusual and good quality, so shop around. In addition to the markets themselves, the **Australis Gallery** ⓘ *26 Coondoo St*, is worth a look, showcasing some fine work by local artists.

Below the Heritage Markets is **Koala Gardens** ⓘ *T4093 9953, www.koalagardens.com, 0900-1600, $16, children $8*, which offers the inevitable photo sessions for $16 on top of the admission price. Also next to the Heritage Markets is **Birdworld** ⓘ *T4093 9188, www.birdworldkuranda.com, 0900-1600, $16, children $8*, which is a free-flight complex showcasing some of Australia's most colourful (and audible) avian species. There is much emphasis on the endangered cassowary, though the numerous parrots and lorikeets will provide the best photo opportunities.

Another wildlife attraction is the **Australian Butterfly Sanctuary** ⓘ *8 Veivers Drive, T4093 7575, www.australianbutterflies.com, 1000-1600, $16, children $8*. It is reputedly the world's largest and houses about a dozen of the country's most brilliant and beautiful Lepidoptera in a huge free-flight enclosure, well landscaped like a rainforest complete with stream and waterfalls. A bright red or white hat is recommended.

To complete the tour of all things winged and wonderful you could also consider a visit to **Batreach** ⓘ *T4093 8858, www.batreach.com.au, Tue-Fri and Sun 1030-1430, entry by donation*, an independent wild bat rescue and rehabilitation hospital at the far end of Barang Street. Here you will get close up and personal with a number of species, most notably, the huge flying fox – a sort of startled-looking dog on a hang-glider. Those who think bats are vicious creatures, invented by witches and horror movie makers, will have their ideas changed here. There is a large local colony of flying foxes in the **Jum Rum Creek Park**, off Thongon Street. Follow the noise – and the unmistakable musty smell.

The award-winning **Rainforestation Nature Park** ⓘ *T4085 5008, www.rainforest.com.au, 0900-1600, attractions $40, children $20, transportation and tours extra*, is located a few kilometres east of Kuranda on the Kuranda Range Road. Set amidst a rainforest and orchard setting it offers yet another chance to experience aboriginal culture and mingle with captive native animals. There is also an exhilarating one-hour tour of the complex and rainforest in an amphibious army vehicle.

If you did not arrive in Kuranda via the Skyrail or railway and it is the wet season then take a look at the **Barron Falls**, which can be accessed via Barron Falls Road (Wrights Lookout) south of the town. In 'the Wet' the floodgates are opened above the falls and the results can be truly spectacular.

Chillagoe

Given its isolation, yet easy access, from Cairns, the former mining settlement of Chillagoe presents an ideal opportunity to experience the outback proper, without having to embark on a long and difficult 4WD journey from the coast. It's a fascinating little place, somewhat out of character with the rest of the Atherton Tablelands, and combines mining history with natural limestone caves and Aboriginal rock paintings. Chillagoe was a cattle station before the discovery of gold in the late 1880s dramatically transformed both the settlement and the landscape. The establishment of a rail link in 1900 led to a sharp increase of incomers and for the next 40 years the area produced almost 10 tonnes of gold and 185 tonnes of silver, as well many more tonnes of copper and lead. Those boom days are long gone and the population has declined dramatically, but the town retains a hint of its former importance in the sun-baked mining relics that remain.

The **Hub Interpretative Centre** ⓘ *Queen St, T4094 7111, www.chillagoehub.com.au, 0800-1700*, is the best source of local information and introduction to the settlement's mining history and can provide directions to the most obvious mining relics. **QPWS** ⓘ *on the corner of Cathedral St and Queen St*, offers guided tours of three of the local limestone caves. There are more caves and old copper mines about 10 km west of the town at **Mungana**, also the location of some Aboriginal rock paintings.

Lake Tinaroo and Danbulla Forest

Barron River Tinaroo Dam was completed in 1958, creating a vast series of flooded valleys that now make up Lake Tinaroo and provide the region with essential irrigation. The lake itself has an astonishing 200 km of shoreline and is a popular spot for water sports, especially barramundi fishing. Indeed, some say the lake contains the biggest 'barra' in Australia. The Danbulla Forest that fringes its northern bank is bisected by 28 km of unsealed scenic road that winds its way from the dam slipway, at Tolga, to Boar Pocket Road, northeast of Yungaburra.

Other than the various campsites, viewpoints and walks on offer, highlights include **Lake Euramoo**, a picturesque double explosion crater lake, **Mobo Creek Crater**, something of a geological odyssey, and the unmissable **Cathedral Fig**. Signposted and reached by a 5-minute walk, this example of the strangler fig species is indeed a sight to behold. The tree – though it is hard to see it as such – is 500 years old, over 50 m tall and 40 m around the base and is worth visiting at dawn, when its many avian inhabitants are full of chatter. Several types of nocturnal possum also inhabit the tree and are best seen with a torch after dark.

From the Cathedral Fig you emerge from the forest onto Boar Pocket Road. The short diversion to the **Haynes Lookout**, left on Boar Pocket Road, heading from the forest towards Gillies Highway, is worthy of investigation. The track passes through beautiful woodland before emerging at the edge of the mountain and the memorable views across the **Mulgrave River Valley** and **Bellenden Ker Range**. When the winds are right the site is often used by hang-gliders. Check out the message written on the launch pad.

For more information on the Danbulla Forest scenic drive and self-registration campsites ($2), contact the **QPWS** ⓘ *83 Main St, Atherton, T4091 1844, or their Tinaroo Office, T4095 8459*. The area is best explored in your own vehicle or on a regional tour.

Around Cairns & the Atherton Tablelands

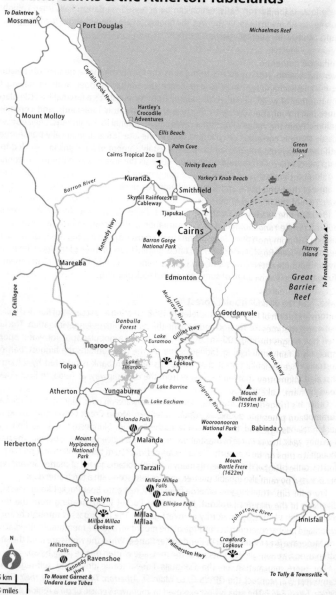

Yungaburra and around

While Kuranda may be the most visited and high profile town in the Atherton Tablelands, sleepy little Yungaburra is the main event. Formerly called Allumba, it has changed little in over a century and offers a wonderful combination of history, alternative lifestyle and a cool and tranquil retreat from the coast. As well as an impressive gathering of listed historical buildings, it has good places to stay, eat and shop and is surrounded by some of the best scenery in the Tablelands. Lakes Tinaroo, Barrine and Eacham, see below, are all within a short drive and provide the focal point for a number of walks, scenic drives and water-based activities. The most spectacular way to reach Yungaburra is via the Gillies Highway and Mulgrave River Valley just south of Cairns. From the valley floor the road climbs almost 800 m up to the top of the Gillies Range. There is currently no official visitor information centre in the village, but the locals are always glad to help. There is also a useful website, www.yungaburra.com. The local **QWPS** office ① *Lake Eacham, T4095 3768*, provides information about campsites and all things environmental.

Most of the listed historical buildings were built from local wood, between 1910 and 1920. Two of the finest examples are **St Mark's** and **St Patrick's churches**, on Eacham Road. Other fine examples are evident on Cedar Street, next to the Lake Eacham Hotel. Look out for the *Yungaburra Heritage Village* leaflet, available from the VICs in Cairns and Atherton, or from most local businesses. Just a few minutes southwest of the village, on Curtain Fig Tree Road, is the 800-year-old **Curtain Fig Tree**, another impressive and ancient example of the strangler species (*Yungaburra* is Aboriginal for fig tree).

Yungaburra is also one of the best, and most accessible, places in the country in which to see that surreal quirk of nature, the duck-billed platypus. **Peterson Creek**, which slides gently past the village, is home to several pairs. The best place to see them is from the bottom and north of Penda Street, at the end of Cedar Street, and the best time is around dawn or sometimes at dusk. Sit quietly beside the river and look for any activity in the grass that fringes the river or on its surface. They are generally well submerged but once spotted are fairly obvious. Provided you are quiet they will generally go about their business, since their eyesight is fairly poor.

A few kilometres east of the village are two volcanic lakes, **Lake Barrine** and **Lake Eacham**. Lake Barrine is the largest and has been a tourist attraction for over 80 years. It's fringed with rainforest and circled by a 6-km walking track. Two lofty and ancient kauri pines, amongst Australia's largest species, are located at the start of the track. The long-established **Lake Barrine Rainforest Cruise and Tea House** ① *T4095 3847, www.lakebarrine.com.au*, is nestled on the northern shore and offers 40-minute trips on the lake ($15, children $8). Just south of Lake Barrine and accessed off the Gillies Highway, or from the Malanda Road, is Lake Eacham. Once again it is surrounded by rainforest and a 3.5-km walking track and is a favourite spot for a picnic and a cool dip. The most southerly fingers of Lake Tinaroo can also be accessed northeast of the village via Barrine Road.

Malanda and Millaa Millaa

The little village of Malanda marks the start of the famous Tablelands waterfalls region. Malanda has its own set of falls but they are actually amongst the least impressive in the group and the village is more famous for milk than water. Dairying has always been the raison d'être in Malanda. The first herds of cattle were brought by foot from the north of NSW – a journey that took a gruelling 16 months. Today, there are over 190 farmers in

Undara Lava Tubes

The Undara Lava Tubes, on the edge of the Undara Volcanic National Park, 150 km south of Ravenshoe via Mount Surprise, are an amazing 190,000-year-old volcanic feature and well worth the journey. The unusual volcanic feature was formed during a massive eruption around 200,000 years ago when lava flowed down a dry riverbed. As the top layer of lava gradually cooled and hardened, the bottom layer flowed on, forming the so-called tubes. There are regular guided tours available, also available from Cairns, as well as a restaurant, pool and accommodation ranging from charming train carriages to a swag tent village and powered sites, YHA affiliated. **Undara Experience**, T4097 1900, www.undara.com.au, runs day trips and excellent package deals by coach, self-drive or rail to see the lava tubes, with activities and accommodation. Their Wildlife at Sunset tour (of the lava tubes) starts at $46.

the region producing enough milk to make lattes and shakes from here to Alice Springs. The main attraction, other than a cool dip in the swimming hole below the falls, is the neighbouring **Malanda Falls Environmental Centre and Visitors Information** ⓘ *T4096 6957, 0930-1630*, which has some interesting displays on the geology, climate and natural history of the Tablelands.

A further 24 km south of Malanda is the sleepy agricultural service town of Millaa Millaa, which also has waterfalls and is surrounded by fields of black and white Friesian cattle. The **Millaa Millaa Falls** are the first of a trio – the others being the **Zillie Falls** and **Ellinjaa Falls** – which can be explored on a 16-km circuit accessed (and signposted) just east of the town on the **Palmerston Highway**, which links with the Bruce Highway just north of Innisfail. There are a few lesser-known waterfalls on the way and Crawford's Lookout, on the left, with its dramatic view through the forest to the North Johnstone River – a favourite spot for rafting.

The **Millaa Millaa Lookout** (at 850 m) just to the west of Millaa Millaa on the recently upgraded East Evelyn Road, is said to offer the best view in North Queensland. On a clear day you can see 180 degrees from the Tablelands to the coast, interrupted only by the Bellenden Ker Range and the two highest peaks in Queensland, Mount Bartle Frere (1622 m) and Mount Bellenden Ker (1591 m).

South of here are the impressive volcanic Undara Lava Tubes, see box above.

Mount Hypipamee National Park

Mount Hypipamee National Park is a small pocket of dense rainforest with a volcanic crater lake, waterfalls and some very special wildlife. During the day the trees are alive with the sound of many exotic birds such as the tame Lewin's honeyeaters, but it is at night that it really comes into its own. Armed with a torch and a little patience (preferably after midnight) you can see several of the 13 species of possum that inhabit the forest, including the coppery brush tail, the green ringtail, and the squirrel glider who leaps and flies from branch to branch. If you are really lucky you may also encounter the park's most famous resident, the Lumholtz's tree kangaroo, one of only two species of kangaroo that live in trees.

The 95,000-year-old **Crater Lake** – which is, in fact, a long, water-filled volcanic pipe blasted through the granite – is a 10-minute walk from the car park. With its unimaginable depths, algae-covered surface and eerie echoes it is quite an unnerving spectacle, like some horrific natural dungeon. The park has picnic facilities but no camping.

Port Douglas and the Daintree → For listings, see pages 315-327. Colour map 6, A1.

Almost since their inception the coastal ports of Cairns and Port Douglas, just 70 km apart, have slugged it out as to which is the most important. Although Cairns has gone on to become a world-famous tourist heavyweight, lesser-known Port Douglas has always known been sure it is a classier option, with its boutiques, fine restaurants and upmarket accommodation. Given its proximity to the Barrier Reef, the Mossman Gorge, Daintree and Cape Tribulation, Port Douglas has never had a problem attracting tourist dollars, though the building of massive developments and multimillion dollar resorts will result in it losing its village feel and much of its charm.

Ins and outs
Port Douglas Tourist Information Centre ① 23 Macrossan St, T4099 5599, www.pddt.com.au, 0830-1800. Mossman has the nearest **QPWS office** ① 1 Front St, T4098 2188, www.epa.qld.gov.au. **Daintree Tourist Information Centre** ① Stewart St, T4098 6120, www.daintree village.asn.au. For Daintree and local walks information contact the QPWS office in Cairns, see page 301, or visit www.port-douglas-daintree.com.

Port Douglas
Like Cairns, Port Douglas places great emphasis on reef and rainforest tours, with only a few attractions in the town itself pulling in the crowds. See page 321 for details of the activities available in the area. About 6 km from the centre of town, at the junction of Captain Cook Highway and Port Douglas Road, the **Rainforest Habitat Wildlife Sanctuary** ① T4099 3235, www.rainforesthabitat.com.au, 0800-1730, $30, children $15, is well worth a visit, offering a fine introduction to the region's rich biodiversity and natural habitats. There are over 180 species housed in three main habitat enclosures – wetlands, rainforest and grassland – with many of the tenants being tame and easily approachable. 'Breakfast with the Birds' (0800-1100, $44, children $22, see page 324) is an enjoyable way to start the day, while 'Habitat After Dark' offers a truly unique dining experience.

Port Douglas is rather proud of its lovely **Four Mile Beach**, which attracts cosmopolitan crowds of topless backpackers and the more conservative resort clients. Many water-based activities are on offer for those not satisfied with merely sunbathing or swimming. A net is placed just offshore to ward off box jellyfish and other stingers and lifeguards are usually in attendance (always swim between the flags). Before picking your spot on the sand you might like to enjoy the picture-postcard view of the beach from **Flagstaff Hill**: turn right at the bottom of Mossman Street, then follow Wharf Street on to Island point Road. **Anzac Park** hosts a market every Sunday. It is a colourful affair and offers everything from sarongs to freshly squeezed orange juice. More expensive permanent boutiques are housed in the delightfully cool **Marina Mirage Complex**, Wharf Street. For further information, see www.portdouglasmarina.com.au.

Mossman Gorge and the Daintree Wilderness National Park
Built on the back of the sugar cane industry in the 1880s, **Mossman** sits on the banks of the Mossman River and has one of the world's most exotic tropical gardens at its back door in the form of the Daintree Wilderness National Park. Although the 80-year-old, fern-covered tall raintrees that form a cosy canopy on its northern fringe are a sight in themselves, it is the Mossman Gorge, some 5 km west of the town, that is its greatest attraction. Here, the Mossman River falls towards the town, fringed with rainforest and

Port Douglas

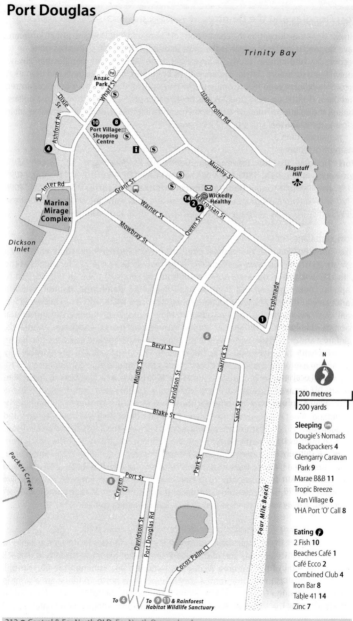

Trinity Bay

Anzac Park

Dixie St

Ashford Av

Wharf St

Island Point Rd

Port Village Shopping Centre

Murphy St

Flagstaff Hill

Inlet Rd

Marina Mirage Complex

Grant St

Warner St

Wickedly Healthy

Macrossan St

Owen St

Dickson Inlet

Mowbray St

Esplanade

Beryl St

Mudia St

Davidson St

Garrick St

Sand St

Blake St

Park St

Packers Creek

Port St

Craven Cl

Davidson St

Port Douglas Rd

Cocos Palm Cl

Four Mile Beach

To ④ To ⑨ ⑪ & Rainforest Habitat Wildlife Sanctuary

N

200 metres
200 yards

Sleeping
Dougie's Nomads
  Backpackers **4**
Glengarry Caravan
  Park **9**
Marae B&B **11**
Tropic Breeze
  Van Village **6**
YHA Port 'O' Call **8**

Eating
2 Fish **10**
Beaches Café **1**
Café Ecco **2**
Combined Club **4**
Iron Bar **8**
Table 41 **14**
Zinc **7**

networked with a series of short walks. Many combine a walk with another big attraction – the cool swimming holes. Although the walks are excellent, you should also try following the river upstream for about 2 km – if you are fit. This will give you an ideal opportunity to see the region's most famous mascot – the huge Ulysses blue butterfly.

The tiny, former timber town of **Daintree** sits at the end of the Mossman–Daintree Road, sandwiched between the western and eastern blocks of the Daintree National Park. The village exudes a quaint and original charm and consists of an enormous model barramundi fish, a general store, a small timber museum, a couple of restaurants, a school and a caravan park. At the edge of the village is the biggest local attraction – the croc-infested **Daintree River**. Visitors can embark on a cruise on the river in search of these gargantuan saltwater crocodiles. There are several cruise operators to choose from, all of whom ply the river from Daintree village to the coast several times a day. You can either pick up the cruise near the village itself or at various points south to the Daintree/Cape Tribulation ferry crossing, but most people arrive on pre-organized tours. For independent choice and bookings call in at the general store (T4098 6146).

Cape Tribulation → *For listings, see pages 315-327. Colour map 6, A1.*

Although Cape Tribulation is the name attributed to a small settlement and headland that forms the main tourist focus of the region, the term itself is loosely used to describe a 40-km stretch of coastline within Daintree National Park and the start of the Bloomfield Track to Cooktown. It was Captain Cook who bestowed the name 'Tribulation', just before his ship *Endeavour* ran aground here in 1770. This and other names, such as Mount Sorrow, Mount Misery and Darkie's Downfall, are indeed fitting for a place of such wild and, at times, inhospitable beauty. People come to this remote wilderness not only to witness a rainforest rich in flora and fauna, but also to experience nature in the raw.

Ins and outs

Tourist information Detailed information can be obtained from the VICs in Port Douglas or Cairns. Local information is available from Daintree Discovery Centre or Bat House (see page 314). For walks information contact the **QPWS** office in Cairns, see page 301. The **Australian Rainforest Foundation** website, www.wettropics.com.au, is also useful.

Sights

Five kilometres beyond the ferry crossing, the Cape Tribulation Road climbs steadily over the densely forested Waluwurriga Range to reach **Mount Alexandra Lookout**, offering the first glimpse of the coast and the mouth of the Daintree River. Turning back inland and 2 km past the lookout, is the turn-off (east) to the **Daintree Discovery Centre** ① *T4098 9171, www.daintree-rec.com.au, 0830-1700, $28, children $14*, with excellent displays on the local flora and fauna, and the added attraction of a 400-m boardwalk where guided walks are available as well as a 25-m canopy tower offering a bird's-eye view of the forest canopy. There's also a pleasant café from which to sit back and let the forest wildlife pervade the senses. Back on Cape Tribulation Road and just beyond the centre is the settlement of **Cow Bay** with its attractive bay and beach that can be reached by road 6 km to the east on Buchanan Creek Road.

Continuing north you are then given another interesting reminder that you are in the tropics by passing a well-manicured tea plantation before crossing Cooper Creek and hitting the coast below Mount Emmett. Oliver Creek then sees the first of a duo of excellent boardwalks, which provide insight into the botanical delights of the forest and mangrove swamps. **Marrdja boardwalk** takes about 45 minutes and is well worth a look. From here it is about 9 km to the settlement of Cape Tribulation. Here, too, is the second and equally interesting 1.2-km **Dubuji boardwalk**, taking about 45 minutes.

The headland at Cape Tribulation is also well worthy of investigation, as are its two beautiful beaches – **Emmagen** and **Myall** – that sit either side like two golden bookends. The Kulki picnic area and lookout is at the southern end of Emmagen Beach and is signposted just beyond the village. Just beyond that, the Kulki turn-off – 150 m – is the start of the **Mount Sorrow track**, a challenging 3.5-km ascent rewarded with spectacular views from the 650-m summit.

While in Cape Tribulation be sure to visit the **Bat House** ① *T4098 0063, Tue-Sun, 1030-1530, $4 donation at least*, opposite PK's Backpackers. Although you won't encounter the saviour of Gotham City, you will find the saviours of the local bat population, in the form of volunteers who tend the needs of injured and orphaned flying foxes. A range of interesting wildlife displays are also on view.

Beyond Cape Tribulation the road gradually degenerates to form the notorious, controversial blot on the landscape known as **Bloomfield Track**. From here you are entering real 'Tiger Country' and a 4WD is essential. A 2WD will get you only as far as Emmagen Creek, which offers a limited incursion into the fringes of the dense rainforest and some good swimming holes – thankfully, too clear and shallow for local crocodiles.

Cooktown → *For listings, see pages 315-327. Colour map 6, A1.*

Like Cairns and Port Douglas, Cooktown has grown in stature as an attractive lifestyle proposition and a popular tourist destination. There is plenty to see and do here, with the James Cook Museum the undeniable highlight. **Cookshire Council** ① *T4069 5444*, and **Nature's Powerhouse** ① *Finch Bay Road, T4069 6004, www.cooktowns.com*, cover visitor information services.

A good place to start is from the **Grassy Hill Lighthouse**, which is reached after a short climb at the end of Hope Street, north of the town centre. Here you can take in the views of the coast and town from the same spot Captain Cook reputedly worked out his safe passage back through the reef to the open sea. The old corrugated iron lighthouse that dominates the hill was built in England and shipped to Cooktown in 1885. For decades it served local and international shipping before being automated in 1927 and becoming obsolete in the 1980s. From Hope Street it is a short walk to the **James Cook Museum** ① *corner of Furneaux St and Helen St, T4069 5386, Apr-Jan 0930-1600 (reduced hours Feb-Mar), $8, children $3*, housed in a former convent built in 1889 and touted as one of the most significant museums in Australia. The museum is not dedicated solely to Cook; it also houses interesting displays covering the town's colourful and cosmopolitan history. Other sites of historical interest include the Cooktown Cemetery, at the southern edge of town along Endeavour Valley Road, where many former pioneers are buried.

Lizard Island is home to Australia's most northerly, and most exclusive, reef island resort (see page 319). The island lies 27 km off Cooktown and is almost 1000 ha, with the vast majority of that being national park. Tranquil and pristine with fantastic diving and snorkelling, it makes for a great trip. All the delights of the other popular islands are on offer without the hordes of tourists. There are over 24 tranquil beaches, backed by lush forests, mangroves and bush, all abundant in wildlife, while just offshore, immaculate, clear water reefs offer superb diving and snorkelling. The famous Cod Hole is considered one of the best dive sites on the reef and the island is also a popular base for big game fishermen in search of the elusive black marlin. A delightful walking track leads to Cook's Look, which at 359 m is the highest point on the island and the place where Captain Cook stood in 1770 trying to find passage through the reef. The island was named by Joseph Banks, the ship's naturalist, who must have kept himself busy searching for lizards as Cook struggled to find a way back out to the ocean.

Far North Queensland listings

For Sleeping and Eating price codes and other relevant information, see Essentials pages 28-33.

Sleeping

Cairns *p299, map p300*

There is plenty of choice and something to suit all budgets. Most of the major hotels and countless backpackers are in the heart of the city, especially along the Esplanade, while most motels are located on the main highways in and out of town. If you are willing to splash out, want access to a proper beach and wish to escape the city, ask at the VIC about the numerous apartment and resort options at Palm Beach and other northern beach resorts (about 20 mins north of the city). Prices fluctuate according to season, with some going through the roof at peak times (May-Sep). Prices are often reduced and special deals are offered through 'the Wet' (Jan-Mar). Despite the wealth of accommodation pre-booking is still advised. Cairns and TNQ Accommodation Centre, corner of Sheridan St and Alpin St, T4051 4066, www.accomcentre.com.au, can also be of assistance.

B&Bs

A Kookas B&B, 40 Hutchinson St, Edge Hill, T4053 3231, www.kookas-bnb.com. Some 10 km from city centre, a traditional modern home in an elevated position, 3 en suites tastefully decorated, friendly owners and lots of visiting kookaburras.

B-C Fig Tree Lodge, 253 Sheridan St, T4041 0000, www.figtreelodge.com.au. More like a motel than a lodge, but fine facilities, a warm welcome and a bar.

Backpackers

There is plenty of choice of backpackers with over 30 establishments, almost all within easy reach of the city centre. Most people gravitate towards the Esplanade where a string of places sit, virtually side by side, but you are advised to look into other options too. Another small cluster of quieter hostels lies just west of the railway station. All offer the usual facilities and range of dorms, twins and doubles. Look for rooms with a/c or at least a powerful fan and windows that open, and check for approved fire safety regulations.

C-D Gilligan's Backpackers Hotel and Resort, 57 Grafton St, T4041 6566, www.gilligansbackpackers.com.au. Causing something of a stir in backpacking circles, this is one of a new breed, pitched somewhere between a backpackers and modern 3-star hotel. There is no doubting its class or range of facilities. It has a large pool, internet café, chic bar with dance floor and big screen TV. Rooms vary from spacious doubles with TV and futon lounge to traditional dorms.

C-E Caravella Hostels, at 77 the Esplanade, T4051 2159, and 149 the Esplanade, T4051 2431, www.caravella.com.au. Both are modern, with good facilities, a/c doubles and free meals.

D-E Bohemia Resort, 231 McLeod St, T4041 7290, www.bohemiaresort.com.au. A little further out of the centre is this modern, excellent option. It is more like a tidy modern motel with great doubles and a pool. Regular shuttles to town.

D-E Dreamtime Travellers Rest, 4 Terminus St, T4031 6753, www.dream timetravel.com.au. Homely and friendly with a great atmosphere, well equipped with good facilities and a great pool and spa, as well as proper beds, not bunks.

D-E Geckos, 187 Bunda St, T4031 1344, www.geckosbackpackers.com.au. Rambling and spacious Queenslander with good facilities and caring staff. Rooms are spacious, have fans rather than a/c but are well ventilated. Good for doubles.

D-E Njoy, 141 Sheridan St, T4031 1088, www.innthetropics.com. A quality option with single rooms, good motel-style doubles. Good pool. Also suitable for families.

D-E Nomads Beach House, 239 Sheridan St, T4041 4116, www.cairnsbeachhouse.com.au. North of the centre is this popular option with all the usual facilities, especially noted for its pool, beer/bistro garden and party atmosphere. Courtesy coach into town.

D-E Travellers Oasis, 8 Scott St, T4052 1377, www.travoasis.com.au. A large place that still maintains a pleasant quiet atmosphere, offering a good range of a/c rooms including value doubles ($64) and pool.

Motels, motor parks and apartments
There are endless motel and apartment options, with the vast majority offering the standard clean, spacious rooms and usual facilities, including the almost obligatory tropical flower paintings and palm tree-fringed swimming pools. Most motels are located on the main drag in and out of town (Sheridan St). If you are looking for a caravan park you are advised to base yourself in the northern beaches.

L-F Cairns Coconut Caravan Resort, on the Bruce Highway (about 6 km south, corner of Anderson Rd), T4054 6644, www.coconut.com.au. Offering sheer class and with all mod cons, this is one of the best in the country.

A Hides, 87 Lake St, T4051 1266, www.hideshotel.com.au. Historical and well-placed apartments offering budget options with shared facilities.

A-B Cairns Rainbow Inn, 179 Sheridan St, T4051 1022, www.rainbowinn.com.au. A colourful good value motel with standard room options, restaurant, pool and spa.

C-E Cairns Holiday Park, corner of James St and Little St, T4051 1467, www.cairnscamping.com.au. If you prefer to be in the city this is the best placed for sheer convenience and has been recently redeveloped to include a pool, TV and internet room and modern camp kitchen.

Atherton Tablelands *p305, map p308*
Although Kuranda attracts the tourist hordes like bees to honey, once the last train leaves and peace returns it can be a wonderful place to stay away from the usual coastal haunts. However, there aren't too many options and for something more luxurious you have to look further afield than Kuranda.

LL Allumbah Pocket Cottages, 24-26 Gillies Highway, Yungaburra, T4095 3023, www.allumbahpocketcottages.com.au. A cluster of spacious and well-appointed, 1-bedroom and fully self-contained cottages complete with spa. The friendly and welcoming owners also offer 2 other exceptional 2-bedroom cottages, at 7/9 Pine St, ideal for romantic couples.

LL Canopy Rainforest Tree Houses, between Malanda and Millaa Millaa (2.5 km on Hogan Rd east of Tarzali), T4096 5364, www.canopytreehouses.com.au. Five charming, fully self-contained pole houses set in wildife-rich bush offering real peace and quiet and all mod cons including a spa. There is also a fully self-contained 3-bedroom unit attached to the main building. Spa treatments and packages provide an added attraction.

L-E Kuranda Resort and Spa, 3 Greenhills Rd, Kuranda, T4093 7556, www.kuranda resortandspa.com. Just 2 km southwest of the village this attractive new resort has a fine range of villas, a self-contained apartment and a multi-share budget option. Excellent facilities with a gym, spa, a spectacular pool, massage therapies and a fine restaurant. Recommended.

A Curtain Fig Motel, 16 Gillies Highway, Yungaburra, T4095 3168, www.curtainfig.com. Good value, spacious self-contained units and a large fully self-contained apartment in the heart of the village.

A-E Kuranda Rainforest Accommodation Park, 88 Kuranda Heights Rd, Kuranda, T4093 7316, www.kurandarainforest park.com.au. This 3-star place has cottages, cabins, powered and non-powered sites. Facilities include kitchen and pool.

C Pteropus House B&B, corner of Carrington Rd and Hutton Rd, Atherton, T4091 2683, www.tolgabathospital.org. An excellent and unusual place to say (provided you love bats). Kind host Jenny Maclean runs not only a quality B&B with 2 tidy self-contained apartments, but a (separate) working fruit bat hospital. There is the opportunity to see some of the patients and sometimes assist in their care. Book ahead.

C-E Lake Eacham Caravan Park, Lakes Drive, 1 km south of Lake Eacham, T4095 3730, www.lakeeachamtouristpark.com. The nearest motor park to Yungaburra. Basic but good value, it has cabins, powered and non-powered sites.

C-E Millaa Millaa Tourist Park, Malanda Rd, T4097 2290, www.millaapark.com. Closest park to the falls, 3-star, with cabins, powered and non-powered sites, pool, camp kitchen and café.

D-E Kuranda Backpackers Hostel, 6 Arara St, Kuranda, T4093 7355, www.kuranda backpackershostel.com. Near the train station, this renovated 1907 traditional Queenslander is a fine if basic retreat with dorms, doubles, singles and good facilities. Pool, bike rental and pick-ups from Cairns.

D-F On the Wallaby Backpackers, 34 Eacham Rd, Yungaburra, T4095 2031, www.onthewallaby.com. The best budget option is this excellent little backpackers offering dorms, doubles and camping for $10 (pair $15). The decor is all wood and stone, giving it a cosy ski lodge feel, very different to the bustling modern places in Cairns. Plenty of activities are on offer including an exciting range of wildlife and day/night canoeing tours on Lake Tinaroo from $30. Mountain bikes for hire. 2-day/1-night package with tour, canoeing and mountain biking for $169. Pick-ups from Cairns daily.

Port Douglas and the Daintree
p311, map p312

There is plenty of choice in Port Douglas and though the emphasis is on 4-star resorts and apartments, budget travellers are also well catered for with a number of good backpackers, cheap motels and motor parks. Rates are naturally competitive and more expensive in the high season but at any time you are advised to shop around for special rates, especially in 'the Wet' (Dec-Mar).

Port Douglas

B Papillon B&B, 36 Coral Sea Drive, Mossman Gorge, T4098 2760, www.papillonstays.com.au. Contemporary wooden-pole house, set in a tropical garden near the Mossman Gorge. 2 well-appointed rooms with their own deck overlooking a heated pool. Both have a king-size double bed, en suite shower, a/c, fan, TV, DVD player, Wi-Fi and locally grown tea and coffee. Great hosts and excellent value.

B-C Marae B&B, Lot 1, Ponzo Rd, Shannonvale, T4098 4900, www.marae.com.au. This B&B provides an ideal sanctuary, yet is still within reach (15 km north) of Port Douglas. It is a beautiful eco-friendly place offering a cabana-style king room, close to the pool or another king within the house. Both have their own bathrooms.

B-F Glengarry Caravan Park, Mowbray River Rd, just short of Port Douglas, off the captain Cook Highway, T4098 5922, www.glengarry park.com.au. This motor park has fully self-contained en suite cabins, powered/non-powered sites, with a good camp kitchen and a pool.

C-E Tropic Breeze Van Village, 24 Davidson St, closer to the centre of town, and only a short stroll from Four Mile Beach, T4099 5299. A 3-star motor park, it offers cabins, powered/non-powered sites and a camp kitchen.

D-E YHA Port 'O' Call Eco Lodge, Port St, just off Davidson St, T4099 5422, www.portocall. com.au. One of 2 good backpackers in town. Motel-style with en suite doubles/twins, budget dorms and a fine restaurant/bar, pool and internet. Free pick-ups from Cairns.

D-F Dougie's Nomads Backpackers, 111 Davidson St, T4099 6200, www.dougies.com.au. The other good backpacker in town, this one has a/c doubles/twins, dorms and van/campsites, bar, bike hire and internet. Again, it offers free pick-ups from Cairns.

Mossman Gorge and the Daintree Wilderness National Park

LL Daintree Eco Lodge and Spa, 20 Daintree Rd, 3 km south of Daintree village, T4098 6100, www.daintree-ecolodge.com.au. This is an international multi-award winner and enjoys a good reputation, offering 15 luxury, serviced villas set in the rainforest, a specialist spa, Aboriginal and eco-based activities and a top-class restaurant. If you are looking to indulge for once – then this is it. Recommended.

LL Silky Oaks Lodge, Finlayvale Road, north of Mossman, T4098 1666 www.silkyoakslodge.com.au. The most upmarket place in the immediate area. It offers de luxe designer 'riverhouses' fronting the Mossman River and superb 'treehouses' with spa. 5-star facilities including spa treatments and a fine restaurant. Complimentary activities and pick-ups are also available.

B-C Red Mill House, Daintree village, T4098 6233, www.redmillhouse.com.au. One of a few good B&Bs in the heart of the village is this very pleasant and friendly option offering well-appointed rooms, some with shared facilities and some with en suites (separate from the main house). The place has a wonderfully peaceful atmosphere with lovely gardens and plenty of wildlife that you can watch from the deck. Good value.

D-F Daintree Riverview Caravan Park, 2 Stewart St, Daintree village, T4098 6119, www.daintreeriverview.com. En suite cabins, powered and non-powered sites right in the heart of the village. Modern amenities block.

Cape Tribulation *p313*

There is a wide range of accommodation in and around the Cape, though prices are well above the norm for north Queensland.

A-E Cape Trib Beach House, Cape Tribulation Rd, T4098 0030, www.capetribbeach.com.au. At the top end of Cape Tribulation this new and very congenial option. It offers a range of modern cabins (some en suite) from dorm to 'beachside'. The most attractive aspects are the bush setting, its quiet atmosphere, the communal bar and bistro (with internet) all right next to the beach. A wide range of activities and tours are also available. The only drawback is the inability to park your vehicle near the cabins. This is definitely the best budget option for couples.

A-F Lync Haven, T4098 9155, www.lynchaven.com.au. Some 4 km north of Cow Bay Village, this park is very eco-friendly with plenty of wildlife around and also has a reputable restaurant.

B-D PK's Jungle Village, Cape Tribulation Rd, in Cape Tribulation village, T4098 0040, www.pksjunglevillage.com.au. This is a well-established, mainstream hostel, popular with the social and party set. It has all the usual facilities including a lively bar, restaurant, pool and a host of activities.

C-D Ferntree Rainforest Resort, Camelot Close, T4041 6741, www.ferntreerainforestlodge.com.au. Just to the south of Cape Tribulation, this large complex has fine facilities and, for a resort, a pleasantly quiet and intimate feel. The wide range of rooms, villas and suites are well appointed, the bar/restaurant is a fine place to relax and the pool is truly memorable. Occasional good deals on offer and budget accommodation with full access to facilities.

D-E Crocodylus Village, near Cow Bay Village, along Buchanan Creek Rd, and the beach, T4098 9166, www.crocodyluscapetrib.com. YHA-affiliated backpacker. By far the most ecologically in tune, this is essentially a glorified bush camp, with an interesting array of huts (some en suite) set around a large communal area and a landscaped pool. The only drawback is the 3-km distance from the beach. Regular shuttle buses are run, as are regular daily Cairns and Port Douglas transfers, tours and activities including local canoe trips.

Cooktown *p314*
L-A Sovereign Resort Hotel, on the corner of Charlotte St and Green St, T4043 0500, www.sovereign-resort.com.au. The most upmarket place in town offering 4-star rated modern 2-bedroom apartments, de luxe and standard units. It also has a reputable à la carte restaurant and a fine pool.

C-E Pam's Place YHA, on the corner of Charlotte St and Boundary St, T4069 5166, www.cooktownhostel.com.au. The main backpackers in town, with dorms, singles and en suite doubles and all the usual facilities including a pool, tour desk and bike hire.

Lizard Island
LL Lizard Island Resort, T9413 6288, www.lizardisland.com.au. With some of the state's best views, the resort's accommodation is in lodges and chalets but the pick of the lot is the superb (and very expensive) Pavilion Suite, with its plunge pool and 4-poster daybed. The resort also boasts a 5-star restaurant and an exciting range of guest complimentary activities from windsurfing to guided nature walks.

🍴 Eating

Cairns *p299, map p300*
There's a huge choice. Many of the mid-range eateries best suited for day or early evening dining are found along the Esplanade. Don't forget the options on offer in the major hotels and in the Pier Complex. Seafood or Australian cuisine is generally recommended. The **International Food Court** on the Esplanade has a number of cheap outlets. See also under Bars and clubs below for cheap pub grub.
🍴🍴🍴 **Red Ochre Restaurant**, 43 Shields St, T4051 0100. Mon-Fri lunch and Mon-Sun

dinner. An award-winning Australian restaurant, offering the best of Australian game fare including kangaroo, crocodile and local seafood favourites.
🍴🍴 **Adelphi's Greek Taverna**, 16 Aplin St, T4041 1500. Good Greek place offering both modern and traditional.
🍴🍴 **Barnacle Bill's**, 103 the Esplanade, T4051 2241. Another well-established seafood favourite.
🍴🍴 **Café China**, Rydges Plaza Hotel, corner of Spence St and Grafton St, T4041 2828. Daily from 1030. Considered the best of all the Chinese restaurants.
🍴🍴 **Dundee's**, Harbour Lights, 1 Marlin Parade, T4051 0399. Daily from 1130 and 0900 Sunday. Well-established favourite offering good value Australian cuisine in a relaxed atmosphere and with views over the harbour. Meat lovers will love the buffalo, roo, croc and barramundi combos. The seafood platters are also excellent.
🍴🍴 **Fish D'Vine Café and Rum Bar**, 17 Abbott St, T4031 6688. Daily from 1700. A new and very relaxed restaurant offering quality affordable seafood, budget cocktails and specifically rums from around the world.
🍴 **Fusion Organics**, corner of Grafton St and Aplin St, T4051 1388. Mon-Fri 0700-1700, Sat 0700-1400. Popular organic café serving up a good healthy breakfast and light lunches for about $15.
🍴 **Gaura Nitai's Vegetarian**, 55 Spence St, T4031 2255. Mon-Fri 1100-1430, 1800-2100, Sat 1800-2100. A lively place that offers great-value vegetarian selections.
🍴 **Mudslide Café**, Shop 5a Aplin St, T4041 6592. Daily 0730-late, Fri-Sat till 0200. Look no further for good coffee and to escape the hype.
🍴 **Willie McBride's**, in Fig Tree Lodge, corner of Sheridan St and Thomas St, T4041 0000. Daily from 1800. For value pub grub in a quieter Irish atmosphere.

Atherton Tablelands *p305, map p308*
Kuranda is awash with affordable cafés and eateries and Yungaburra also has a fair selection. Elsewhere the choice is limited.

¶¶ **Nick's Swiss-Italian**, on Gillies Highway, Yungaburra, T4095 3355, www.nicksrestaurant.com.au. Wed-Sun for lunch and Tue-Sun dinner 1130-2300. Passionately managed with good food, service and live music at the weekends.

¶¶ **Rainforest View**, 28 Coondoo St, Kuranda, T4093 9939. Wide range of dishes and views of the rainforest but it does get packed with tour groups.

¶¶ **Kuranda Hotel**, corner of Coondoo St and Arara St, Kuranda, T4093 7206. Another option with generous pub meals and a pleasant laid-back atmosphere.

¶ **Frogs**, Kuranda, T4093 7405, in the heart of Coondoo St. Daily 0900-1600. The most popular café with the locals.

¶ **Whistlestop Café**, 36 Cedar St, Yungaburra, T4095 3913. Breakfasts from 0700.

Port Douglas and The Daintree
p311, map p312
There are plenty of options in Port Douglas, mostly along Macrossan St.

¶¶ **Rainforest Habitat Wildlife Sanctuary**, 6 km south of Port Douglas centre, T4099 3235, www.rainforesthabitat.com.au. Jul-Oct. For something different consider breakfast or lunch here. It offers both a 'Breakfast with the Birds' or 'Lunch with the Lorikeets, both from $44, which includes park entry. Bookings essential.

¶¶ **2 Fish**, 18 Wharf St, T4099 6350, and ¶¶ **Table 41**, 41 Macrossan St, T4099 4244, are both excellent for atmosphere and seafood.

¶ **Zinc**, in prime location on the corner of Macrossan St and Davidson St, T4099 6260, www.zincportdouglas.com. Given the location it draws the crowds and is a good all-rounder. Relaxed alfresco breakfast or lunch and a lively dinner venue with quality Mod Oz cuisine and a fine cocktail list.

¶ **Beaches Café**, on the Esplanade, overlooking Four Mile Beach, T4099 4998. Daily from 0700. For a good value breakfast and lots of tropical atmosphere.

¶ **Café Ecco**, Shop 1, 43 Macrossan St, T4099 4056. Excellent for healthy lunches and a good breakfast.

¶ **Combined Club**, Wharf St, T4099 5553. This place is unbeatable for the waterfront view and for value.

¶ **Iron Bar**, 5 Macrossan St, T4099 4776. Well known for its imaginatively named and generous Australian dishes.

Cape Tribulation *p313*
See also Sleeping, page 318. Most resorts and backpackers listed have their own restaurants or bistros, for breakfast, lunch and dinner.

¶ **Cassowary Café** in the Ferntree Resort, is licensed and serves tasty breakfast, lunch and dinner with gourmet pizza a speciality.

Bars and clubs

Cairns *p299, map p300*
With so many backpackers descending on the city the nightlife is very much geared to the 'get dressed up (or down), get drunk and fall over' mentality. Finding somewhere to have a few good beers and a good conversation can be more difficult.
There is a wide range of pubs in the town from the traditional Aussie corner hotels to sports bars and, of course, the ubiquitous pseudo-Irish joints.

Cairns Rhino Bar and Bistro, corner of Spence St and Lake St, T4031 5305. Laid-back atmosphere, with live music, a bistro and a good balcony overlooking the main street.

Courthouse Hotel, in the former courthouse on Abbott St, T4031 4166. Daily until late. For something a little classier try the cool (as in temperature) atmosphere here. It is great during the heat of the day or for a little more decorum and offers live jazz on Sun nights and alfresco dining.

Gilligan's, 57 Grafton St, T4041 6566. Arguably the most popular backpacker bar and entertainment venue in Cairns, attached to one of its best backpackers. The poolside beer garden hosts live bands and DJs most nights of the week, with star performers and events staged at the weekends. If it all gets too much the Attic Lounge can provide some solace.

PJ O'Brien's, 87 Lake St, T4031 5333. Daily 1000-0300. The best of the Irish pubs is this popular spot. It has live music most nights and is not too shabby in the food department either.
Toybox, 53 Spence St, T4051 8223. Essentially a gay bar, but it welcomes both straight and gay and has highly entertaining drag shows.
Tropos, corner of Lake and Spence St, T4031 2530. Until 0500. Well established, this venue has regular theme nights.
Woolshed, 24 Shields St, T4031 6304. Very much backpacker-oriented, serving cheap drinks and generally going off well into the wee hours.

O Shopping

Cairns *p299, map p300*
Cairns has excellent shopping. The **Pier** has everything from opals to art works.
Aussie Bush Hats and Oilskins, Bellview Centre, 85 the Esplanade, T4037 0011. Australiana and traditional attire.
Cairns Night Markets, 54-60 Abbott St, T4051 7666. Daily 1630-2300. Over 100 stalls selling a rather predictable array of arts, crafts, clothing, food and souvenirs.
Rays Outdoors, 96 Mulgrave Rd. One of several outlets selling camping equipment.
Rusty's Bazaar, between Grafton St and Sheridan St. Fri evening and Sat-Sun morning. An eclectic conglomerate of colourful consumables.

Atherton Tablelands *p305, map p308*
Yungaburra markets, on the 4th Sat of the month, T4095 2111, www.yungaburra markets.com. 0700-1200. Good reputation for home-made arts, home-grown produce and the odd farm animal.

▲ Activities and tours

Cairns *p299, map p300*
With hundreds of operators in the city vying (sometimes quite aggressively) for your tourist dollar, you are advised to seek unbiased information at the official and accredited VIC. Then shop around before choosing a specific activity, trip, or tour (or combination thereof) to suit your desires, your courage and your wallet. If you are looking to combine activities and save a few dollars try **Raging Thunder**, T4030 7990, www.ragingthunder.com.au.

Aerial tours
Cairns Heli Scenic, T4031 5999, www.cairns-heliscenic.com.au. 10 mins from $150.
Champagne Balloon Flights, T4039 9955, www.champagne balloons.com, **Raging Thunder**, T4030 7990, www.raging thunder.com.au, and **Hot Air**, T4039 2900, www.hotair.com.au, all offer similar hot air balloon trips from $225.
Daintree Air Services, T4034 9300, www.daintreeair.com.au. 60 mins fixed wing flight from $220.
Reefwatch Air Tours, T4035 9808, www.reefwatch.com. Fixed wing tours to Cooktown and the Undara Lava Tubes/outback from $1150.
Sunlover Helicopters, T4035 9669, www.sunloverheli.com.au. 30mins ($295) to reef or rainforest with fly/cruise options from $389.

Bungee jumping
AJ Hackett, McGregor Rd, Smithfield, T4057 7188, www.ajhackett.com.au. Daily 1000-1700. Kiwi bungee jumping guru AJ Hackett has created an attractive jump complex in Smithfield, 15 mins north of Cairns. It offers a 50-m jump and also the popular jungle swing, a sort of half free-fall/half swing that makes what you did when you were a toddler in the park seem awfully tame. Standard bungee $139, swing $89, combo $194. Pick-ups.

Cruises

There are many companies offering half, full or multi-day cruise options that concentrate on sailing, diving or just plain relaxing, with various island stopovers, reef pontoon visits and all manner of water-based activities thrown in. In general, for a basic Inner Reef Island trip without extras, expect to pay anywhere between $85-125. For an Outer Reef Cruise with snorkelling, anything from $125-250. For an Outer Reef Cruise with introductory dive from $135-250 and for a luxury 3-day cruise with accommodation, meals and all activities included, about $500-1200. It all boils down to the type of vessel, its facilities, numbers, optional extras and the actual time allowed on the reef. Generally speaking, the smaller sailing companies do offer the most attractive rates and perhaps more peace and quiet, but lack the speed, convenience and razzmatazz of the fast, modern catamarans.

Big-Cat Green Island Reef Cruises, Reef St Terminal, 1 Spence St, T4051 0444, www.bigcat-cruises.com.au; **Great Adventures**, Reef St Terminal, T4044 9944, www.great adventures.com.au; **Reef Magic**, T4031 1588, www.reefmagic cruises.com.au; and **Sunlover Cruises**, T1800 810512, www.sunlover.com.au, are the main cruise operators in Cairns and like all the main operators are based at the new Reef Fleet Terminal on Spence St. They offer a range of tour options to Green Island, and beyond that, including certified dives, introductory dives, snorkelling, sightseeing and other water-based activities.

Compass, T4031 7217, www.reeftrip.com. An attractive alternative with a good value trip on board a modern vessel to Michaelmas and Hastings Reef, both on the outer reef. Also offered is free snorkelling, boom netting and optional dive extras, from $90. 2-day, 1-night trips are good value at $359.

Ecstasea, T4041 5588, www.divecairns .com.au. A 60-ft luxury yacht that also visits Upolo Cay with free snorkelling, from $115 (introductory dive $180).

Falla, T4041 2001, www.fallacruises.com.au. A charming, former pearl lugger that allows 4 hrs on Upolo Reef 30 km from Cairns, with free snorkelling. Departs 0900, returns 1730, $89, children $59 (introductory dives available).

Great Adventures, based in Cairns, and **Quicksilver**, based in Port Douglas, T4087 2100, www.quick silver-cruises.com.au. Both have huge floating pontoons moored on the outer reef where you can dive, snorkel, view the reef from a glass-bottom boat or with a very fetching-looking goldfish bowl on your head (you had better believe it), or simply sunbathe or watch the underwater world go by, from $199.

Ocean Spirit, T4031 2920, www.oceanspirit.com.au. An even more luxurious trip to Michaelmas Cay on the outer reef is offered on this beautiful vessel. All mod cons at $189, (introductory dive from $75).

Passions of Paradise, T4051 9505, www.passions.com.au. Large, modern catamaran that goes to Upolo Cay and Paradise Reef. From $129 (introductory dive $70). Departs daily 0800, returns 1800.

Diving

Cairns is an internationally renowned base for diving and there are dozens of dive shops, operators and schools. It is also an ideal place to learn, though certainly not the cheapest, costing from $325 for the most basic courses with no accommodation up to $470-1500 for an all-inclusive liveaboard course. Shop around and choose a reputable company with qualified instructors. The best diving is on the outer reef where the water is generally clearer and the fish species bigger. The following are just a sample and are not necessarily recommended above the many other operators. Almost all offer competitive rates and options for certified divers and snorkellers. Also see www.divingcairns.com.au.

Cairns Dive Centre, 121 Abbott St, T4051 0294, www.cairnsdive.com.au. Certification from $440 and a day's snorkel only from $85.

Down Under Dive, 287 Draper St, T4052 8300, www.downunderdive.com.au.

4-day/2-night certification from $480.
ProDive, corner of Abbott St and Shields St, T4031 5255, www.prodive-cairns.com.au. A range of trips including a 3-day/2-night certification with 11 dives from $620.
Reef Encounter, 100 Abbott St, T4031 7217, www.reeftrip.com. A 3-day/2-night certification, twin share, from $699.

Fishing

Cairns has been a world-class big game fishing venue for many years and as a result there are many excellent charters with experienced guides. Black marlin are the biggest species, capable of reaching weights of over 450 kg, which must be a bit like landing a pair of irate sumo wrestlers. Another commonly caught species is the wahoo, whose name is surely derived from the noise you make while catching it.
Cairns Reef Charter Services, T4031 4742, www.ausfish.com.au/crcs. One of the best charter companies, it has a fleet of ocean-going vessels and also offers an exciting range of multi-day ocean and inland trips to catch game fish or the famed barramundi.
Fishing Cairns, T4041 1169, www.fishingcairns. com.au. This place has an informative website listing a wide range of charters.

Horse trekking and mountain biking

Most of these companies offer combination packages with other activities or attractions.
Blazing Saddles, T4085 0197, www.blazing saddles.com.au. Runs a half-day trek suitable for beginners, from $105, children $75. It also offers entertaining half-day ATV safaris from $125.
Dan's Mountain Biking, T4032 0066, www.cairns.aust.com/mtb. Half-day trips to the rainforest in Mulgrave Valley from $85. Full-day Cape Tribulation $125.

Rafting

Fancy tackling a 'Double D-Cup,' opting for the 'Corkscrew,' or going headfirst into the 'Wet and Moisty'? Well, you can with various rafting companies who have christened various rapids with such 'exotic' names. Cairns is the base for some excellent rafting with a wide range of adrenaline-pumping trips down the Barron, North Johnstone and Tully Rivers. It is all mighty fun, but watch out for the 'Doors of Deception'. The minimum age for rafting is usually 13 years.
Foaming Fury, 19-21 Barry St, T4031 3460, www.foamingfury.com.au. Tackles the Barron, half day from $131 and also offers something a bit different with a full-day 2-person sports rafting experience on the Russell River, from $160. It's also recommended for families.
R'n'R, Abbott St, T4035 3555, www.raft.com.au. A similar outfit to **Raging Thunder**, offering full-day trips down the Tully for $195, half day on the Barron for $130.
Raging Thunder, T4030 7990, www.ragingthunder.com.au. Half-, full-, and multi-day trips, as well as heli trips and many other activity combos. Half day on the Barron River from $133, full day on Tully River, $195. Also offers a wide variety of activity combos.

Sightseeing tours

There are numerous trips on offer that combine the Scenic Railway and Skyrail Gondola (see page 302). Others include deductions for the major sights. Ask at the VIC. 1-day 4WD tours to the Daintree and Cape Tribulation generally leave Cairns at about 0700 and return about 1800 and cost $150-175.
Billy Tea Bush Safaris, T4032 0077, www.billytea.com.au. Friendly, entertaining guides, day tours to Cape Tribulation and Chillagoe from $170.
Cairns Discovery Tours, T4053 5259, www.cairnsdiscoverytours.com. Half-day tour of city sights including the Botanical Gardens, Flying Doctor Service Visitor Centre and Northern Beaches, from $65, children $32.
Jungle Tours, T4041 9440, www.jungle tours.com.au. Good value day trips to Cape Tribulation via Mossman Gorge from $145 and overnight trips and combination adventure packages from $185, staying at the Cape's backpacker establishments.

Northern Experience Eco Tours, T4058 0268, www.northernexperience.com.au. Another good company offering a wildlife edge to their day tour, from $137, children $95.

Trek North, T4033 2600, www.treknorth.com.au. Takes small groups to Cape Tribulation via the Daintree and Mossman Gorge, including a cruise on the Daintree River, from $160.

Tropic Wings, 278 Hartley St, T4035 3555, www.tropicwings.com.au. Offers an excellent tour to Kuranda combining the Kuranda Scenic Railway and Skyline Gondola with the addition of many exciting diversions and activities, from $149, children $75.

Tropical Horizons, T4035 6445, www.tropicalhorizonstours.com.au. Very comfortable, quality, small group tours to Port Douglas, Kuranada and the Cape, of up to 11 hrs from $161.

Wooroonooran Rainforest Safaris, T4032 1140, www.wooroonooran-safaris.com.au. Sightseeing and trekking trips in the beautiful Wooroonooran National Park and Mamu Rainforest Canopy Walkway south of Cairns, from $169.

Northern Great Barrier Reef Islands *p304*

Big Cat Green Island Reef Cruises, Reef Fleet Terminal, T4051 0444, www.big cat-cruises.com.au. This is one of the 2 main operators to Green Island. It offers half- and full-day cruises with optional extras from $75, children $40. It includes a choice of glass-bottom boat tour or snorkelling gear ($10 extra for both).

Frankland Islands Cruise and Dive, T4031 6300, www.franklandislands.com. Full-day trip with activities from $129 and camp transfers from $199. Also on offer is certified/introductory diving (full package) from $109 and a range of combo multi sight/tour package deals. The ferry departs daily from Cairns.

Great Adventures, the Wharf, Cairns, T4044 9944, www.greatadventures.com.au. There are 2 main tour operators to Green Island.

This one offers basic transfers from $75, children $38, and a wide range of tour options with activity inclusions and optional extras. Additionally, there is a Green Island and Outer Reef (pontoon) tour from $210, children $105. Added extras include snorkel tour from $36, introductory dive from $138.

Atherton Tablelands *p305, map p308*

On The Wallaby Tablelands Tours, T4050 0650, www.onthewallaby.com. Entertaining guided tours of the Tablelands sights with excellent wildlife canoeing trips as a further option. Their 2-day/1-night accommodation/activity package based at their backpackers hostel in Yungaburra (see page 317) is good value and recommended. It also offers excellent backpacker-oriented wildlife and day/night canoeing.

Port Douglas and The Daintree *p311, map p312*

Cultural tours

Kuku-Yalanji Tours, T4098 2595, www.yalanji.com.au. Just short of the Mossman gorge car park is this operation. It offers excellent 2- to 3-hr Aboriginal cultural awareness walks that will enlighten you on the use of certain plants for medicinal purposes and traditional hunting methods, from $35, children $20. There is also a shop and gallery, open daily 0830-1700.

Diving and snorkelling

All the major reef operators are based at the Marina Mirage Wharf, Wharf St. Almost all of the Cairns-based companies also provide transfers from Port Douglas. The vast majority combine cruising with snorkelling and/or diving, with others being dive specialists. Those listed below are recommended but this does not imply that those not listed are not reputable.

Quicksilver, T4087 2100, www.quicksilver-cruises.com. This is the main operator in Port Douglas. Long established and highly professional, it will shuttle tourists out to their own pontoon on the edge of Agincourt Reef,

where you can spend the day (5 hrs) diving, snorkelling or sunbathing. A basic day cruise with a buffet lunch costs $199, children $100. Diving and snorkelling is an added option.
Tech Dive Academy, 1/18 Macrossan St, Port Douglas, T0422-016517, www.tech-dive-academy.com.

Fishing
There are a posse of charter boats available to take you fishing. The VIC has the most recent charter listings.

Horse trekking
Wonga Beach Equestrian Centre, T4099 1117, www.beachhorserides.com.au. Entertaining rides along Wonga Beach, 20 km north, including Port Douglas transfers from $115, 3 hr.

Spas
Daintree Eco Lodge and Spa , see page 318. Offers massage (1 hr from $130) plus numerous other attractive options. Book ahead.

Wildlife and sightseeing tours
Fine Feather Tours, T4094 1199, www.fine feathertours.com.au. Operated by enthusiastic locals Del and Pat, with full-day birding tours from $235.
Reef and Rainforest Connections, 8/40 Macrossan St, Port Douglas, T4035 5588, www.reefandrainforest.com.au. Offers a wide range to Kuranda, Mossman Gorge, Daintree/Cape Tribulation and Cooktown.
On the Daintree River The search for crocs has become something of a cruise fest and there are dozens of operators. Pick-ups and day tours from Cairns or Port Douglas are available.
Chris Dahlberg's River Tours, T4098 7997, www.daintreerivertours.com.au. Operates an excellent dawn cruise (departs 0600 Nov-Mar and 0630 Apr-Oct), with an emphasis on bird spotting, from $55.
Crocodile Express, T4098 6120. This is the largest and longest serving operator, with 2 cruises. The most popular is their 1½-hr river cruise departing from the village hourly

1030-1600, from $25, children $12. The second is a 2½-hr Estuary Cruise that explores the lower reaches and the mouth of river.

Cape Tribulation *p313*
There are many activities on offer in the region, including crocodile spotting, sea kayaking, horse riding, reef cruising with diving or snorkelling and even candlelit dinners deep in the rainforest. These are best arranged through the main backpackers such as **The Cape Trib Beach House** (see page 318). See also Cairns and Port Douglas-based tour operators. Some do not run in the wet season (Dec-Mar) when access can be severely affected. Also consult the VICs in Cairns or Port Douglas.
Jungle Surfing Canopy Tours, T4098 0043, www.junglesurfingcanopytours.com.au. Offers a spot of 'rainforest canopy surfing', essentially a series of flying fox cables allowing the opportunity to do the inevitable 'Tarzan', from $90. Night wildlife spotting from $40.
Mason's Tours, T4098 0070, www.masonstours.com.au. Its guided rainforest walks are recommended. Their night walk spotting the doe-eyed possums is well worthwhile, from $49. A 4WD day trip exploring the Bloomfield Track to Cooktown with **Mason**'s Tours costs from $240.

Cooktown *p314*
Cooktown offers a number of activities from self-guided local walks and historic town tours to reef fishing, cruising and snorkelling. Many tour operators in Cairns and Port Douglas offer day or multi day trips to Cooktown, some combining road travel with a scenic return flight.

Transport

Trans North, T4095 8644, www.transnorthbus.com services the **Atherton Tablelands** including **Kuranda**, daily.

Car
The wet road conditions around Cairns and far north Queensland can be, in a word, aquatic. For up-to-date conditions and flood warnings, T131111. For RACQ road conditions report T1300 130595.

Campervan rentals and purchase (second hand), **Travellers Auto Barn**, 123-125 Bunda St, T4041 3722, www.travellers-autobarn.com.au. It offers guaranteed buy-backs in Sydney.

Car rental The airport and Abbott St and Lake St in the city have most outlets. **Avis**, 135 Lake St and airport, T4051 5911; **Budget**, 153 Lake St, T4051 9222; **All Day Rentals**, Shop 1/ 62 Abbott St, T4031 3348; **MiniCar Rentals**, 150 Sheridan St, T1300 735577; **4WD Hire**, 440 Sheridan St, T4032 3094. For a standard car and 7-day hire expect to pay from $70 a day. Some of the larger companies like Avis also offer 4WD hire from around $175 per day.

Train
The station is on Bunda St. Travel centre is open Mon-Fri 0900-1700, Sat 0800-1200, T4036 9250. For other long-distance enquiries, T1300 131722, 24 hr, www.traveltrain.qr.com.au. There are 3 coastal train services to/from **Brisbane** and beyond, ranging in standards of luxury and price. The most popular is the fast **Tilt Train** (departs Brisbane Mon and Fri, Cairns Sun and Wed); alternatively there is the **Sunlander** (departs Brisbane 0835, Tue, Sat, Sun and Thu). There is one outback service, the **Gulflander**, that shuttles between **Croydon** and **Normanton**. A local scenic service also operates to **Kuranda**, T4036 9250, www.ksr.com.au, from $45, children $23 ($68 return). Ask about the various holiday and discoverer passes, for price reductions and packages.

Northern Great Barrier Reef Islands
p304
For **Green Island**, ferries leave the Reef Fleet Terminal on waterfront, Cairns, with additional transfers from Palm Beach (Northern Beaches) and Port Douglas.
For **Fitzroy Island**, Fitzroy Island Ferry, T4030 7900, departs from Cairns, day-trip from $68, children $37, www.ragingthunder.com.au.
For **Lizard Island**, see Cooktown page 325.

Atherton Tablelands *p305, map p308*
Most visitors to **Kuranda** make the village part of a day-tour package from Cairns, with the highlight actually accessing it via the Barron Gorge and the Skyline Gondola, the Scenic Railway or both. See page 321 for operators in Cairns. Prices and schedules for the **Skyrail**, T4038 1555, and **Scenic Railway**, T4036 9333, are listed on page 302. **Kuranda Shuttle**, T0418-772953, and **Trans North**, T4095 8644, www.transnorthbus.com share services to Kuranda at the most competitive price. **Trans North** also runs daily services to **Yungaburra**.

Port Douglas *p311, map p312*
Air
Port Douglas is accessed from Cairns International Airport. **Airport Connections**, T4099 5950, www.tnqshuttle.com, offers services at least every hour daily from 0630-1630, $32, children $16.

Bus
Note many accommodation and activity operators offer free or low-cost transfers from Cairns. Ask at the VIC for details.
Coral Reef Coaches, 35 Front St, Mossman, T4098 2800, www.coralreefcoaches.com.au, run regular local bus services to Cairns (and airport) via Mossman from $35.
Sun Palm Coaches, 16 Teamsters Close, Port Douglas, T4087 2900, www.sunpalm transport.com, also connect Cairns with Port Douglas, Cairns Northern Beaches, Daintree, Cow Bay and Cape Tribulation. The main bus stops are on Grant St and at the Marina Mirage (Wharf) Complex.

Cycling/scooter
Holiday Bike and Hire, 6/40 Macrossan St, T4099 6144, hires out bikes.

Cape Tribulation *p313*
Bus
Coral Reef Coaches, 37 Front St, Mossman, T4098 2800, offers daily scheduled services and tour packages from **Cairns** and **Port Douglas**, from $35 one way (Cairns).

Car
Self drive is recommended but all roads in the area can be treacherous in the wet season (Dec-Mar). For road information, T131940, www.131940.qld.gov.au.
Daintree River Ferry, 15 km southeast of Daintree village, runs daily from 0600-2400, pedestrian $2 return, vehicle $20 return. Beyond Cape Tribulation (36 km), the road degenerates into the strictly 4WD Bloomfield Track, which winds its precarious 120 km way to **Cooktown**. Fuel is available 4 km east of Cow Bay village and 6 km north at the Rainforest Village Store. In the event of breakdown contact the RACQ (Cow Bay), T4098 9037.

Cooktown *p314*
Skytrans Airlines, T4046 2462, www.skytrans.com.au, operates regular transfers to **Cairns** from $122 one way (with a 3-day advance purchase). If you are not joining a tour from Cairns or Port Douglas contact Cooktown VIC (see page 314) for the latest information on scheduled bus services. For **Lizard Island**, there are various regional air operators and vessel charter companies but prices and times vary. VIC in Cooktown is

the best place to enquire for the most up-to-date options. Daintree Air Services, T4034 9300, www.daintreeair.com.au, offers a day package from $690, departing from Cairns. Skytrans Airlines, T4040 6700, www.skytrans. com.au, also offers air charters from Cairns or Cooktown.

❶ Directory

Cairns *p299, map p300*
Banks All the major banks have branches in the city centre, especially at the intersection of Shields St and Abbott St. **Internet and library** Cairns City Public Library, 151 Abbott St, T4044 3720. Free internet.
Medical services Cairns Base Hospital, the Esplanade (north), T4050 6333. **Cairns City 24-hr Medical centre**, 120-124 Mulgrave Rd, T4051 2755. **Post** 13 Grafton St, T131318. Mon-Fri 0830-1700. Postcode 4870.
Useful numbers Police, emergency T000, 5 Sheridan St, T4030 7000.

Port Douglas *p311, map p311*
Banks Macrossan St or Port Village Centre.
Internet Port Douglas Video, corner Port Douglas Rd and Barrier St, T4098 5350. Daily 0900-2200. **Medical services** Mossman, T4098 1248. Port Village Medical Centre, Shop 17, shopping centre, Macrossan St, T4099 5043, 24 hrs. **Post** 5 Owen St, T4099 5210. Mon-Fri 0900-1700, Sat 0900-1400. Postcode 4877. **Pharmacy** Macrossan St Pharmacy, 13/14 Port Village Centre, T4099 5223. **Useful numbers** Police, 31 Wharf St, T4087 1999.

Contents

Background

A sprint through history

1606
Spaniard Luis de Torres negotiates his way through the strait between Australia and New Guinea, becoming the first European to glimpse the Australian mainland.

1642
Dutchman Abel Tasman charts the northwest coast of what is now called New Holland. He also finds Tasmania before heading west to 'discover' New Zealand.

1770
Captain James Cook charts the hitherto unexplored east coast of New Holland. He names the 'new territory' New South Wales.

1786
Following the loss of the American colonies, the British government decides to transport felons instead to New South Wales. The following year Arthur Phillip's 'First Fleet' sets out.

1787-1788
Botany Bay is not to Phillip's liking so he explores the harbour just to the north, Port Jackson. Sydney Cove is duly named as the site for the new penal colony.

1801-1803
Matthew Flinders charts the unknown southern coasts and circumnavigates the whole continent in 1801-1803, proving it at last to be one vast island. He also suggests the name Australia for this new continent.

1830s
Numbers of new settlers steadily increase as New South Wales slowly comes to be seen as a land of opportunity. Wool becomes the single most important industry and the Australian sheep population rockets. This is the catalyst for the Murray steamboats, the railways and new non-penal towns.

1850
The Aboriginal population is decimated by various infectious diseases against which the native Australians have little defence. Meanwhile, wool and grain industries are booming and coal and copper are being profitably mined.

1850-1860
Gold is first publicly found in New South Wales and soon after in Victoria, leading to a mass influx of would-be prospectors.

1860
Transportation of convicts ends. Nearly 160,000 had made the enforced trip over the previous 60-odd years, with few returning to their homelands.

1860-1890
Australia's own industrial revolution is in full flow and urbanization of the country continues apace. The indigenous population meanwhile is driven to the margins of society.

1889
NSW prime minister suggests political federation. Two years later a draft constitution is drawn up.

1893
Falling prices lead to an economic crash of unprecedented proportions. Victoria suffers the worst and the state government revives the idea of federation.

1897
Queensland Aborigines Act is introduced. Aboriginal people in the state can be forced to move to a reserve, denied alcohol and the vote, and are paid for work under conditions and wages stipulated by the act.

1898-1900
Colonies vote for federation.

1901
The Commonwealth officially comes into existence on 1 January. Melbourne is the first capital, remaining so until 1927 when Canberra is built.

1902
Women are given the vote.

1914-1918
First World War. Australian (and NZ) troops feature in many campaigns, most famously at Gallipoli, in 1915. Of the 300,000 who go to war, more than 50,000 are killed, a greater number than is lost by the USA.

1927
Canberra's Parliament House opens.

1932
Sydney Harbour Bridge is completed.

1933-1939
Aboriginal Act passed in QLD permits marriage and sexual relations between Aboriginal people and Europeans, with the aim of ultimately 'breeding out' the Aboriginal race.

1939-1945
Second World War. Australia sends troops to Europe. In 1942 Japanese bombers and warships shell Darwin, Sydney and Newcastle. In the same year, Australian troops help prevent occupation of Port Moresby in New Guinea. Out of a population of around seven million in 1939, a little under one million are enlisted or conscripted, of which nearly 40,000 are killed. Over 2000 Aborigines fight in the defence of their country.

1945-

The government pursues a vigorous population programme. Tens of thousands of European economic migrants pour into the country. Many form ghettos in suburbs of Sydney and Melbourne.

1949

Robert Menzies leads his new Liberal party to election victory. A staunch monarchist, he welcomes Queen Elizabeth II to Australia in 1954, the first reigning monarch to make the trip. Immigration policies continue apace. Between 1945 and 1973 about three and a half million people arrive.

1956

Melbourne hosts the Olympic Games.

1960s

Australia sends 8000 troops to fight with the USA in Vietnam, marking a growing shift from British influence. Protest movement against the war is broadened to include Aboriginal people. In the early 1960s new legislation largely removes the paternalistic and restrictive laws relating to Aboriginal people. In 1967 Australians vote in a referendum to allow the federal government to legislate for Aboriginal people.

1972

The Labor Party is elected under charismatic and energetic Gough Whitlam. Within days the troops are recalled from Vietnam and conscription ended, women are legally granted an equal wage structure, 'White Australia' is formally abandoned, a Ministry of Aboriginal Affairs created and 'God Save the Queen' scrapped as the national anthem.

1970s and 80s

Whitlam is sacked in controversial circumstances but he has permanently altered the mood of the nation. The fledgling Green movement begins to make its mark, and 1978 sees Sydney's first Gay and Lesbian march, which will become the Mardi Gras, the biggest event of its kind in the world. The country opens its doors to thousands of Vietnamese boat people.

1988

Australia celebrates the Bicentennial – 200 years of white settlement. Aboriginal people do not join the celebrations.

1992

The High Court rules that native title (or prior indigenous ownership of land) is not extinguished by the Crown's claim of possession in the Murray Islands of Torres Strait. This is enshrined in the Native Title Act of 1993.

1996-1998

The High Court rules that pastoral leases and native title can co-exist but the government of John Howard is opposed. A compromise, the Native Title Amendment Bill, is passed in 1998. In 1997, the Human Rights and Equal Opportunity Commission produces a damning report into the separation of Aboriginal and Torres Strait Islander children from their families and recommends compensation, counselling and an official apology.

1999

'No' vote in a national referendum for an Australian republic, despite polls showing a majority in favour.

2000

The Council for Aboriginal Reconciliation presents a Declaration of Reconciliation to the government. In the same year there are large reconciliation marches all over the country. The Olympics are held in Sydney. The Aboriginal athlete Kathy Freeman wins gold in the women's 400 m track sprint.

2001-2002

Bushfires ravage the surrounding national parks and fringes of Sydney, destroying numerous properties and taking several lives. In 2002, exacerbated by severe drought conditions, Victoria suffers its worst fires for years.

2001

The Liberal-National coalition government of John Howard is returned to power. In the same year, a Norwegian vessel rescues boat people claiming to be refugees from Afghanistan but the Australian government refuses to allow the 'illegal immigrants' to land on the mainland. This not only diminishes Australia's international standing but also polarizes society.

2002

Two nightclubs are bombed in Bali, killing around 200 people, almost half of whom are Australian. Prime Minister Howard continues to support the US invasion of Iraq, despite majority public opposition domestically.

2005

A second terrorist bomb in Bali kills 19.

2006-2007

Australia suffers its worst drought on record. As a result the government slashes economic growth forecasts, reflecting a slump in farm output. Prime Minister John Howard still dismisses the Kyoto Climate Change Protocol and joins the USA in its refusal to sign.

2007

After 11 years at the helm Prime Minister John Howard and his coalition party suffer an unexpected defeat. Kevin Rudd's Labor Party takes the reins, promising a dramatic change of direction in federal climate change policy and a definitive phased withdrawal of the Australian armed forces in Iraq.

2009-2010

On the back of a resources boom fuelled by China and India's rapacious economic development and thanks to sound banking practices Australia survives the worst of the global financial crisis. In 2010 it emerges with the strongest economic growth forecasts of all developed nations. As a result the Australian dollar also becomes one of the strongest world currencies, almost reaching parity with the US dollar and rising by almost 20% against the UK pound. The strength of the Australian dollar impacts tourism, with fewer international arrivals and a rapid rise in Australians holidaying overseas.

Australia today

From the tatters of the Mark Latham-led Labor 2005 election campaign and their dismal failure to prevent John Howard from winning his fourth election as prime minister (making him the second longest-serving prime minister in Australian history), came the Tintin lookalike and political tsunami called Kevin Rudd. Rudd had been the Labor (shadow) minister of foreign affairs between 2001 and 2005 and took over the leadership of the party from Kim Beazley (Latham's replacement and a former leader himself), after a successful leadership ballot in late 2006. This was to be the first change of political circumstance that for Howard would set up the perfect storm for his humiliating downfall. On the wave of Rudd's growing popularity the Labor party built a focused policy campaign in the run-up to the November 2007 election. The opposition tactic was to focus primarily on a combination of old arguments and issues, like matters of trust and war in Iraq, together with the new and highly topical, like climate change. Like George Bush, Howard had a solid reputation as a climate sceptic and was seen to be severely wanting in effective policy on the matter, especially given the fact Australia was in the grip of its worse drought on record. Of course Howard's main campaign drive was to counter with his party's strong economic record and the 'if it ain't broke why fix it' approach, but it had limited effect. In fact, it actually worked in Rudd's favour with too with many voters clearly feeling secure enough economically for a change of the old guard. Beyond specific policies, the other major aspects that undoubtedly contributed to his demise were Howard's own complacency (he had after all been seemingly invincible for 11 years) and his age (in 2007, he was a very dour-looking 68 compared to a youthful-looking Rudd at 50). So on 24 November 2007, as the polls had been predicting for months, Howard lost not only the election but his own constituency seat, and the triumphant Rudd took over.

For the satirists and cartoonists at least it was a dream come true: now they had a country led by the very visual epitome of Tintin minus the dog.

Initially, Rudd, known as a committed workaholic, maintained his popularity, especially given the limited effects on the Australian economy through the global financial crisis. But towards the 2010 election, and despite forecasts that Australia would have the strongest economic growth of any developed nation from 2011, several major back flips in policy replaced its silver linings with clouds. In particular, there was the abandonment of Labor's Emissions Trading Scheme, which left the party and the country clearly wanting with regard to its promised action against climate change. At the time of going to press it seems almost certain that despite the decline and broken promises Labor will enjoy a second term, but clearly for many of the Labor faithful young Tintin and his friends will have to raise their game.

Aboriginal Australia

When the First Fleet arrived with its cargo of convicts in 1788 there were between 300,000 and 750,000 Aboriginal people living in Australia, belonging to about 500 tribes or groups, each of which had its own territory, its own language or dialect and its culture. Naturally, neighbouring groups were more similar to each other, perhaps speaking dialects of the same language and sharing some Dreamtime myths linked to territory borders such as rivers and mountains. However, if a man from Cape York had found himself transported to the Western Desert he would have been unable to communicate with the desert people. He would have found them eating unfamiliar food and using different methods to obtain it. Their art would have been incomprehensible to him and their ceremonies meaningless. If he had been able to speak their language he would have found that they had a different explanation of how they came into existence and his own creation ancestors would have been unknown to them. Each group was almost like a small state or nation.

Dreaming

Every traveller in Australia will encounter the concept of the 'Dreaming' or the 'Dreamtime', a complex idea at the heart of Aboriginal culture. Most Aboriginal groups believe that in the beginning the world was featureless. Ancestral beings emerged from the earth and as they moved about the landscape they began to shape it. They could be in any form – humans, animals, rocks, trees or stars – and could transform from one shape to another. Nor were they limited by their form (kangaroos could talk, fish could swim out of water). Wherever these beings went and whatever they did left its mark on the landscape. A mountain might be the fallen body of an ancestor speared to death, a waterhole the place a spirit emerged from the earth, or yellow ochre the fat of an ancestral kangaroo. In this way the entire continent is mapped with the tracks of the ancestor beings.

Although the time of creation and shaping of the landscape is associated with the temporal notion of 'beginning', it is important to understand that Dreaming is not part of the past. It lies within the present and will determine the future. The ancestral beings have a permanent presence in spiritual or physical form. Ancestor snakes and serpents still live in the waterholes that they created; this is why visitors are sometimes asked not to swim in certain pools, so that these ancestors will not be disturbed. This is also why mining or similar development can cause great distress to Aboriginal people if the area targeted is the home of an ancestral being. The ancestors are also still involved in creation. Sexual intercourse is seen as being part of conception but new life can only be created if a conception spirit enters a woman's body. The place where this happens, near a waterhole, spring or sacred site, will determine the child's identification with a particular totem or ancestor. In this way Aboriginal people are directly connected to their ancestral world.

Ceremonies

Aboriginal people belonged to a territory because they were descended from the ancestors who formed and shaped that territory. The ancestral beings were sources of life and powerful performers of great deeds but were also capable of being capricious, amoral and dangerous. Yet in their actions they laid down the rules for life. They created ceremony, song and designs to commemorate their deeds or journeys, established marriage and kinship rules and explained how to look after the land. In the simple forms related to outsiders, Dreaming stories often sound like moral fables. They were passed on from generation to generation, increasing in complexity or sacredness as an individual aged. With knowledge came the responsibility to look after sacred creation or resting places. Ceremonies were conducted to ensure the continuation of life forces and fertility. Aboriginal people had no concept of land ownership, because they believe that humans, animals and spirits are inseparable from the land; one and the same. Consequently, Aboriginal people of one group had no interest in possessing the land of another group. A different and strange country was meaningless to them. To leave your country was to leave your world.

Ceremony and art were at the very heart of life for these were the ways in which Aboriginal people maintained their connection with the ancestors. During ceremonies the actions and movements of the ancestors would be recalled in songs and dances that the ancestors themselves had performed and handed down to each clan or group. Not only did the ancestral beings leave a physical record of their travels in the form of the landscape but also in paintings, sacred objects and sculptures. Ceremonies maintained the power and life force of the ancestors, thus replenishing the natural environment. Some ceremonies, such as those performed at initiation, brought the individual closer to his or her ancestors. Ceremonies performed at death made sure that a person's spirit would rejoin the spiritual world.

Art

The most immediately obvious feature of Aboriginal art is its symbolic nature. Geometric designs such as circles, lines, dots, squares or abstract designs are used in all art forms and often combine to form what seems to be little more than an attractive pattern. Even when figures are used they are also symbolic representations; an emu may be prey or an ancestral being. The symbols do not have a fixed meaning; a circle may represent a waterhole, a camping place or an event. In Aboriginal art, symbols are put together to form a map of the landscape. This is not a literal map where the 'key' relates to the topography of a piece of countryside, but rather a mythological map. Features of the landscape are depicted but only in their relation to the creation myth that is the subject of the painting. A wavy line terminating in a circle might represent the journey of the Rainbow Serpent to a waterhole. That landscape may also contain a hill behind the waterhole but if it is not relevant to the serpent's journey it will not be represented, although it may feature in other paintings related to different ancestral beings. Unlike a conventional map, scale is not consistent. The size of a feature is more likely to reflect its importance rather than its actual size, or there may be several scales within a painting. Nor is orientation fixed.

To many people Aboriginal art is recognized by its style – dots, X-ray or cross hatching – but what is painted is just as important as how it is painted. Aboriginal people working in traditional forms simply do not paint landscapes, figures or people that they are not spiritually connected to. The idea of painting a landscape just because it is pretty is utterly foreign to Aboriginal art. Also, because of the use of symbols and the fact that Dreaming stories are known only to the ancestral descendants, only the painter and perhaps his or her close relatives will be able to fully understand the meaning of a painting. Those interested should read the excellent *Aboriginal Art* by Howard Morphy.

Wildlife

Wildlife is very much a part of the Australian holiday experience. Living icons like the koala and kangaroo are just as ingrained in our psyche as the famous Opera House or Uluru (Ayers Rock). The list of species reads like a who's who of the marvellous, bizarre and highly unlikely. There are over 750 bird species alone. The following is a very brief description of the species you are most likely to encounter on your travels.

Marsupials

Marsupials (derived from the Latin word *marsupium* meaning 'pouch') can be described as mammals that have substituted the uterus with the teat. Their reproductive system is complex, the females have not one but three vaginas and there is a short gestation and a long lactation. It is a specialist system, developed to meet harsh environmental demands.

The most famous of the marsupials are of course the kangaroos and wallabies. There are over 50 species of kangaroos, wallabies and tree kangaroos in Australia. The most commonly seen are the eastern grey and the red. The eastern grey can be seen almost anywhere in New South Wales, Queensland and Victoria, especially in the wildlife and national parks along the coast. Sadly in the outback most of the red kangaroos you see will be roadkill. Tree kangaroos, meanwhile, live deep in the bush and are notoriously shy and are therefore very seldom seen.

Equally famous is the koala (which is not a bear). Koalas are well adapted to the harsh Australian environment, surviving quite happily on one of the most toxic of leaves – eucalyptus. Koalas are easily encountered in the many wildlife parks throughout the country but, while cuddling one of these impossibly cute bundles of fur is the most seminal Australian experience, do bear in mind that the wild variety may take exception to being manhandled and attempt to rip your arms to shreds. Sadly, koalas are on the decline in most regions of Australia and over 80% of their natural habitat has been destroyed since white settlement began.

There are three species of wombat: the common, northern and southern hairy-nosed variety. Like the koala, they are very well adapted to the Australian environment and spend much of their time asleep. They are also nocturnal. Campsites are the best places to see them, where burrows and small piles of dung will provide testimony to their presence. Sadly, like kangaroos and koalas, they are far more commonly seen as roadkill. Another familiar family member of the marsupials is the possum. There are numerous species, with the most commonly encountered being the doe-eyed brushtail possum and the smaller ring-tailed possum. Both are common in urban areas and regularly show up after dusk in campsites. Another magnificent little possum that may be seen is the squirrel-sized feather-tailed glider, which as the name suggests can glide from tree to tree. All the possum species are nocturnal, hence the huge eyes. The best way to see them is by joining a night spotting tour, especially in Queensland, where in only a hectare or two of bush there may be as many as 18 different species. Other marsupials include the rare and meat-eating tiger quoll, which is about the size of a cat with a brownish coat dotted with attractive white spots, the delightful quokka (like a miniature wallaby), bandicoots, the numbat (endangered) and the bilby.

Star attractions

Many of the following creatures, though widespread, are not always easy to see. With patience sightings are virtually 'guaranteed' in their natural environment at the following places (tours and entry fees sometimes apply):

Dolphins Port Phillip Bay (VIC), Jervis Bay (NSW), Tin Can Bay (QLD) and Tangalooma Dolphin Resort on Moreton Island (QLD).

Dugongs Hinchinbrook Island National Park (QLD).

Eagles and kites NSW Outback especially along the Barrier Highway to Broken Hill.

Echidnas Widespread over the whole country, even Sydney.

Fairy or Little penguins Melbourne and Phillip Island (VIC), even occasionally in Sydney Harbour (NSW).

Flying foxes Botanical Gardens, Sydney, Bellingen (NSW), Cape Tribulation (QLD).

Kangaroos Widespread in the outback – amongst many national parks you're likely to see them in Murramarang national park (NSW South Coast) and Sturt (NSW).

Koalas Great Ocean Road and Raymond Island (VIC), Pilliga State Forest, Coonabarabran and Port Macquarie (NSW), Magnetic Island (QLD).

Platypus Great Ocean Road (VIC), Bomballa (NSW), Eungella National Park and Yungaburra, Atherton Tablelands (QLD).

Saltwater crocodiles Hinchinbrook, Daintree and Cape York (QLD).

Seals and sea lions Cape Bridgewater, Phillip Island and Croajingalong (VIC), Montague Island, Narooma (NSW).

Turtles Mons Repos, Bundaberg and Heron Island, Great Barrier Reef (QLD).

Whales Warrnambool (VIC), Eden (NSW), Hervey Bay (QLD).

Wombats Common throughout, including Wilson's Promontory (VIC), Thredbo River, Snowy Mountains (NSW).

Monotremes

There are only three living species of monotremes in the world: the duck-billed platypus and the short-beaked echidna, both of which are endemic to Australia, and the long-beaked echidna, found only on the islands of New Guinea. Their name meaning 'one hole', refers to their birdlike cloaca, and their most remarkable feature is that they are mammals that lay eggs.

The duck-billed platypus is found only in rivers and freshwater lakes in eastern Australia. They live in burrows, are excellent swimmers and can stay submerged for up to 10 minutes. The duck-like bill is not hard like the beak of a bird, but soft and covered in sensitive nerve endings that help to locate food. The males have sharp spurs on both hind leg ankles that can deliver venom strong enough to cause excruciating pain in humans and even kill a dog. Platypuses are best seen just before dawn.

The echidna is not related to the hedgehog but looks decidedly like one. You will almost certainly encounter the echidna all over Australia, even in urban areas, where they belligerently go about their business and are a delight to watch. They are immensely powerful creatures not dissimilar to small spiny tanks. They are mainly nocturnal and hunt for insects by emitting electrical signals from their long snout, before catching them with a long sticky tongue.

Eutherians

Eutherians are placental mammals. Perhaps the best known is the dingo. Although not strictly endemic to Australia, having being introduced, most probably by Aboriginals over

Park life

Australia's national parks generally constitute natural areas of ecological, cultural or simply aesthetic importance (often a combination of all three) and can claim to encompass almost all of the country's most jaw-dropping and sublime natural attractions. In New South Wales alone there are over 580 national parks and conservation reserves, ranging from a few hectares to the size of small countries, and the degree of public access allowed is as variable. Many have excellent basic camping facilities and the experience is highly recommended.

National parks are generally managed by the state in which they are situated. In New South Wales they are managed by the National Parks and Wildlife Service (NPWS), which is part of the Department of Environment, Climate Change and Water (DECCW), www.environment.nsw.gov.au. In Queensland, national parks are run by the Queensland Parks and Wildlife Service (QPWS), which is part of the Department of Environment and Resource Management (DERM), www.derm.qld.gov.au, and in Victoria by Parks Victoria, www.parkweb.vic.gov.au.

Fees vary from state to state and from park to park. Some parks in NSW, for example, charge $11 a day vehicle entry fee, while other, more high profile, parks such as Kosciuszko cost $16 ($27 from the start of the June long weekend to the end of the October long weekend). In Victoria, a day's pass for Wilson's Promontory costs $10.50 whereas Mornington Peninsula is only $4. Where entry fees are charged it's usually possible to obtain an annual state-wide pass. This costs $65 in NSW and $53.50 in Victoria. If you intend to visit many parks and are here for a while, this is often worth buying, but bear in mind camping fees are usually extra. Passes are sold at park visitor centres and some major VICs. There is no national pass. Full details for each state are given on the websites listed above.

3000-4000 years ago and derived from an Asian wild dog, they are now seen to be as Australian as Fosters lager. Found everywhere on the continent, but absent from Tasmania, they are highly adaptable, opportunist carnivores, which makes them highly unpopular with farmers. The best place to see dingoes is on Fraser Island, off Queensland, where sadly they have come into conflict with humans due to scavenging.

The mighty fruit bat is another placental mammal and a remarkable creature that you will almost certainly see (or smell) on your travels. You can even see them flying around at dusk on the fringes of Sydney's CBD (especially the Botanical Gardens).

Birds

With one of the most impressive bird lists in the world, Australia is a birdwatcher's paradise and even the most indifferent cannot fail to be impressed by their diversity, colours and calls. The most famous of Australian birds is the kookaburra, which is related to the kingfisher. Other than its prevalence, fearlessness and extrovert behaviour, it is its laughing call that marks it out. A much stranger-looking specimen is the tawny frogmouth, a kind of cross between an owl and a frog, with camouflaged plumage, fiery orange eyes and a mouth the size of the Channel Tunnel. Due to its nocturnal lifestyle it is hard to observe in the wild and is best seen in zoos and wildlife parks.

Australia is famous for its psittacines – the parrot family – including parakeets, lorikeets, cockatiels, rosellas and budgerigars, which can be seen at their most impressive

5 best places to spot wildlife

Sydney Harbour (whales, fairy penguins, flying foxes), page 93.
Hervey Bay (whales), page 239.
Mon Repos near Bundaberg (turtles), page 256.
Eungella National Park (platypus), page 274.
Hinchinbrook Island National Park (dugong), page 284.

in the outback, in huge flocks against the vast blue sky. The rainbow lorikeet is a common sight (and sound) in urban areas, while in rural areas and forests the graceful red- white- and yellow-tailed black cockatoos are also a pleasure to behold. Others include the pink galah, the breathtaking king parrot and the evocatively named gang-gang.

Almost as colourful are the bowerbirds. There are several species in Australia, the most notable being the beautiful but endangered regent bowerbird, with its startling gold and black plumage, and the satin bowerbird. Another member of the bowerbird family is the catbird, which, once heard, proves to be very aptly named.

In the bush one of the commonest of birds is the brush turkey, about the size of a chicken, with a bare head and powerful legs and feet. Another well-known bird of the bush is the lyrebird, of which there are two species in Australia. Unremarkable in appearance (rather like a bantam) though truly remarkable in their behaviour, they are expert mimics and often fool other birds into thinking there are others present protecting territory. Their name derives from the shape of their tail (males only) which when spread out looks like the ancient Greek musical instrument.

A far larger, rarer bird of the tropical rainforest is the cassowary, a large flightless relative of the emu with a mantle of black hair-like plumage, colourful wattles and a strange, blunt horn on its head. It is a highly specialist feeder of forest fruits and seeds. Tragically, roadkills are common. Their last remaining stronghold in Australia is in Far North Queensland, especially around Mission Beach, where they are keenly protected. They are well worth seeing but your best chance of doing so remains in wildlife sanctuaries and zoos.

Almost as large, yet flighted, and more often seen around lakes and wetlands, are the brolga and the black-necked stork, or jaribu. The brolga is a distinctly leggy, grey character with a dewlap (flap of skin under the chin) and a lovely splash of red confined to its head. The brolga is equally leggy but has a lovely iridescent purple-green neck set off with a daffodil-yellow eye and rapier-like beak. One of the most impressive birds is the white-breasted sea eagle, which is a glorious sight almost anywhere along the coast or around inland lakes and waterways. They are consummate predators and highly adept at catching fish with their incredibly powerful talons.

The fairy penguin, found all along the southern coastline of Australia, is the smallest penguin in the world. The largest colony is on Phillip Islands near Melbourne, where over 20,000 are known to breed in a vast warren of burrows. The emu, with its long powerful legs, is prevalent yet quite shy, unlike that other giant of the outback, the huge wedge-tailed eagle (or 'wedgie'). Wedgies are most commonly sighted feeding on roadkills, especially kangaroos.

Reptiles, amphibians and insects

The range of reptile, amphibian and insect species is, not surprisingly, as diverse as any other in Australia. First up is the crocodile. There are two species in Australia, the saltwater crocodile (or 'saltie' as they are known) found throughout the Indo-Australian region, and the smaller freshwater crocodile, which is endemic. There is no doubt the mighty saltie is, along with the great white shark, the most feared creature on earth and perhaps deservedly so. Although you will undoubtedly encounter crocodiles in zoos, wildlife parks and farms throughout the country, you may also be lucky (or unlucky) enough to spot one in the wild in the northern regions. Note that in Queensland the many warning signs next to rivers and estuaries are there for a good reason.

The goanna, or monitor, is a common sight, especially in campsites, where their belligerence is legendary. There are actually many species of goanna in Australia. They can reach up to 2 m in length, are carnivores and if threatened, run towards anything upright to escape. Of course, this is usually a tree, but not always, so be warned!

There are many species of frogs and toads in Australia including the commonly seen green tree frog. They are a beautiful lime-green colour. If you find one do not handle them since the grease on our hands can damage their sensitive skin. Another character worth mentioning is the banjo frog. If you are ever in the bush and are convinced you can hear someone plucking the strings of a banjo, it is probably a banjo frog singing to its mate.

Insects are well beyond the scope of this handbook, but there are two that, once encountered, will almost certainly never be forgotten. The first is the huntsman spider, a very common species seen almost anywhere in Australia, especially indoors. Although not the largest spider on the continent, they can grow to a size that would comfortably cover the palm of your hand. Blessed with the propensity to shock, they are an impressive sight, do bite, but only when provoked and are not venomous. Of the huge variety of glorious butterflies and moths in Australia perhaps the most beautiful is the Ulysses blue, found in the tropics, especially in Far North Queensland.

Marine mammals and turtles

Along both the eastern and western seaboards of Australia humpback whales are commonly sighted on their passage to and from the tropics to Antarctica between the months of July and October. Occasionally they are even seen wallowing in Sydney Harbour or breaching the waters off the famous Bondi Beach. The southern right whale is another species regularly seen in Australian waters; likewise the orca, or killer whale. Several species of dolphin are present, including the bottlenose dolphin, which is a common sight off almost any beach surfing the waves with as much skill and delight as any human on a surfboard.

Another less well-known sea mammal, clinging precariously to a few locales around the coast, is the dugong or sea cow. Cardwell and the waters surrounding Hinchinbrook Island, in Queensland, remains one of the best places to see them. Australia is also a very important breeding ground for turtles. The Mon Repos Turtle Rookery, Queensland, is one of the largest and most important loggerhead turtle rookeries in the world. A visit during the nesting season from October to May, when the females haul themselves up at night to lay their eggs, or the hatchlings emerge to make a mad dash for the waves, is a truly unforgettable experience.

Contents

Footnotes

Index → Entries in bold refer to maps.

Notes

Notes

Notes

Credits

Footprint credits
Project Editor: Jo Williams
Layout and production: Davina Rungasamy
Colour section: Rob Lunn
Maps: Kevin Feeney
Proofreader: Beverley Jollands

Managing Director: Andy Riddle
Commercial Director: Patrick Dawson
Publisher: Alan Murphy
Publishing managers: Jo Williams,
Felicity Laughton, Jen Haddington
Digital Editor: Alice Little
Series design: Mytton Williams
Marketing: Liz Harper
Sales: Jeremy Parr
Advertising: Renu Sibal
Finance and administration:
Elizabeth Taylor

Photography credits
All images by Darroch Donald

Printed in India by Nutech

Footprint feedback
We try as hard as we can to make each
Footprint guide as up to date as possible
but, of course, things always change. If you
want to let us know about your experiences –
good, bad or ugly – then don't delay, go to
footprinttravelguides.com and send in
your comments.

Publishing information
Footprint East Coast Australia
4th edition
© Footprint Handbooks Ltd
September 2010

ISBN: 978 1 907263 09 5
CIP DATA: A catalogue record for this book
is available from the British Library

® Footprint Handbooks and the Footprint
mark are a registered trademark of Footprint
Handbooks Ltd

Published by Footprint
6 Riverside Court
Lower Bristol Road
Bath BA2 3DZ, UK
T +44 (0)1225 469141
F +44 (0)1225 469461
footprinttravelguides.com

Distributed in the USA by Globe Pequot Press,
Guilford, Connecticut

Every effort has been made to ensure that
the facts in this guidebook are accurate.
However, travellers should still obtain
advice from consulates, airlines, etc about
travel and visa requirements before travelling.
The authors and publishers cannot accept
responsibility for any loss, injury or
inconvenience however caused.

Map symbols

- ⬚ Capital city
- ○ Other city, town
- ⫶⫶⫶ International border
- ⫶⫶⫶ Regional border
- ⊖ Customs
- ⬯ Contours (approx)
- ▲ Mountain, volcano
- ⇀ Mountain pass
- ᴸᴸᴸ Escarpment
- ⌣ Glacier
- ▦ Salt flat
- ⸚ Rocks
- ▾▾▾ Seasonal marshland
- ▦ Beach, sandbank
- ⋙ Waterfall
- ⌒ Reef
- ═══ Motorway
- ──── Main road
- ──── Minor road
- ‐‐‐‐ Track
- ⁝⁝⁝⁝ Footpath
- ──── Railway
- ⊶▬ Railway with station
- ✈ Airport
- ⛟ Bus station
- Ⓜ Metro station
- ‐ ‐ ‐ Cable car
- ++++ Funicular
- ⛴ Ferry
- ⊐⊐⊐ Pedestrianized street
- ⅀ ⊑ Tunnel
- → One way-street
- ⦀⦀⦀⦀ Steps
- ⌣ Bridge
- ▴▴▴ Fortified wall
- ▦ Park, garden, stadium
- ⊜ Sleeping
- ❷ Eating
- ❶ Bars & clubs

- ▭ Building
- ▫ Sight
- ✝ ✝ Cathedral, church
- ☗ Chinese temple
- ⛩ Hindu temple
- ⚲ Meru
- ◗ Mosque
- △ Stupa
- ✡ Synagogue
- ❶ Tourist office
- ⏛ Museum
- ⊠ Post office
- Ⓟ Police
- Ⓢ Bank
- ◎ Internet
- ♪ Telephone
- ⏲ Market
- ✚ Medical services
- Ⓟ Parking
- ⓐ Petrol
- ⛳ Golf
- ⁛ Archaeological site
- ◆ National park,
  wildlife reserve
- ✺ Viewing point
- ▲ Campsite
- ⌂ Refuge, lodge
- ▥ Castle, fort
- ⤵ Diving
- ♠♣♠ Deciduous, coniferous,
  palm trees
- ✾ Mangrove
- ⌂ Hide
- ♣ Vineyard, winery
- ⚱ Distillery
- ⨲ Shipwreck
- ✕ Historic battlefield
- ⇨ Related map